Real Estate Principles and Practices

Second Edition

Edmund F. Ficek
Illinois State University

Thomas P. Henderson
President, Henderson & Associates
and Illinois State University

Ross H. Johnson
James Madison University

Charles E. Merrill Publishing Company
A Bell & Howell Company
Columbus   Toronto   London   Sydney

Published by
Charles E. Merrill Publishing Company
A Bell & Howell Company
Columbus, Ohio 43216

This book was set in Times Roman and Korinna
Production Editor: Lynn Copley-Graves
Cover Design Coordination: Will Chenoweth

The following state supplements accompany this text:

California: Paul M. Lange (California State University at Fresno)
Illinois: Patricia Carlon, Thomas Henderson (Illinois State University), and
    Ross H. Johnson (James Madison University)
New Jersey: Vincent J. Hubin (Fairleigh Dickinson University)
Ohio: Nicholas Kemock, J.D.
Texas: Harland B. Doak and Thomas B. Taylor (University of Houston,
    Downtown College)
Wisconsin: Garfield R. Stock (University of Wisconsin)

In addition:

Real Estate Examinations Guide: Henderson, Johnson, Kruse, and Ficek

Library of Congress Catalog Card Number: 79–90751

International Standard Book Number: 0–675–08104–1

Printed in the United States of America

1 2 3 4 5 6 7 8 9 10—85 84 83 82 81 80

PREFACE

The real estate business in the 20th century continues its pattern of continual and dynamic change. Although many real estate concepts are built upon English law and early U.S. foundations, recent social, economic, legal, and environmental factors have resulted in an abundance of new federal and state legislation, court decisions, and government regulations. Real estate principles and practices, previously accepted without question, are now being scrutinized, reevaluated, and changed to adapt to these conflicting needs of modern society:

- Environmentalists vs. the industrialist
- Mortgage lenders vs. mortgage borrowers
- Private control vs. public control of land use
- Landlords vs. tenants
- Agriculture vs. urban development
- Private ownership of real estate vs. government control

In recent years, a knowledge of real estate has become an important part of the total business core of knowledge.

This second edition continues our effort to present real estate principles and practices primarily from a business and practical point of view but also with the appropriate legal, economic, mathematical, social, and ethical background. In addition, we emphasize the professionalism of those in the real estate business. To achieve these goals, we have presented the following new or expanded material within existing chapters:

- Time-share ownership, a new concept in condominium ownership (Chapter 3).
- Validity of premarital property settlement contracts (Chapter 4).
- Closing in escrow (Chapter 4, 16, and 17).
- Implied warranties of fitness of real property for occupancy and use (Chapter 5) and Homeowners Warranty (HOW) insurance program (Chapter 11).
- Federal regulations pertaining to residential mortgages (Chapter 7).
- New alternate mortgage arrangements such as the graduated payment mortgage, deferred-interest mortgage, reverse-annuity mortgage, and variable rate mortgage (Chapter 7).
- The mortgage due on sale clause controversy (Chapter 7).

- Transfer of developmental rights to land, a new concept in land-use management (Chapter 10).
- Registration of alien land ownership (Chapter 12).
- Franchising in real estate brokerage, including new state controls (Chapter 13).
- Application of federal and state antitrust laws to real estate brokerage (Chapter 13).
- Recent discrimination developments (Chapter 15).
- A full chapter on ethics and professionalism as related to real estate (Chapter 15).
- Chapters 16 and 17 take a student through a real estate transaction, applying the various concepts discussed in earlier chapters so the student can see how these concepts are integrated together in practice.
- Government forced dedication of subdivision land to public use (Chapter 17).
- Updated addresses and publications of real estate commissions in each state are given in Appendix C.

This book assumes no prior educational or business background in real estate, and the topics are written accordingly. We have presented the concepts and practices in an understandable fashion, while retaining an appropriate depth of coverage needed by real estate professionals. We introduce the basic principles and concepts of real estate initially, and then we explain their application to real estate practices. This text and its supplementary materials are intended for use in all of the following:

1. Basic courses in real estate at the university or community college level;
2. Introductory courses to prepare students for later, more specialized courses;
3. Adult education courses designed primarily for investors, homeowners, and others seeking an understanding of the principles and practices of real estate;
4. Courses directed primarily towards persons desirous of preparing for state real estate licensing examinations; and for
5. Those persons seeking to increase their professional skills as practicing brokers or salespersons, loan officers, mortgage bankers, trust officers, or farm managers.

To facilitate the teaching and learning process, we have developed detailed and comprehensive supplementary materials. Individual supplements for some states provide additional information of real estate principles and practices as applied to those selected states. The *Instructor's Manual* contains in-depth answers to the end-of-chapter problems and provides numerous multiple-choice questions and answers for use by the instructor in preparing examinations. It also gives the answers to the instructor-assigned (Group B) exercises that are in the *Student Workbook*.

A comprehensive, instructionally flexible and functional *Student Workbook* also accompanies the text for use by students and instructors. The *Student Workbook* contains two sets of exercises for each chapter of the book. The first set, the self-study exercises (Group A), provides a means for students to self-test their mastery of the material in each chapter of the text. The answers to the exercises in Group A are included at the back of the workbook. The second set of exercises (Group B) are for instructors to assign to students. Instructors may use these instructor-assigned exercises to prepare students for examinations or as take-home assignments to be graded. As mentioned previously, the answers to this second set appear in the *Instructor's Manual*.

To provide instructors with up-to-date, significant changes in real estate law, practices, and other related topics, each instructor will receive a quarterly newsletter entitled "Real Estate Update" prepared by the authors. This newsletter will contain current legal developments affecting real estate, as well as matters of an economic, financial, social, or ethical nature that are relevant to the real estate business.

A set of *Transparency Masters* is also available to aid instructors in presenting lectures. Finally, a comprehensive glossary appears in the text appendices to provide a convenient and ready access to definitions of important real estate terms and concepts.

Throughout this book, we have alternated the use of he and she and her and his. Also, we have used bold italics to highlight the key terms and concepts where introduced or defined within the text.

For typing and other assistance with the manuscript, the authors are indebted to Thelma Wickenhauser, Nadine Fred, Janet Kuhns, and Sherry McGuire.

Edmund F. Ficek
Thomas P. Henderson
Ross H. Johnson

CONTENTS

1   **The Real Estate Business**   1

Why we study real estate, 1; Property resources, 2; Real estate occupations and careers, 7; The real estate market, 11; Factors related to market demand, 14; Summary, 15; Terms and concepts, 16; Problems, 16; Supplementary readings, 17; Sources of current business data, 17.

2   **Land and Its Description**   19

Physical characteristics, 19; Economic characteristics, 20; Legal descriptions, 22; Rectangular survey, 23; Metes and bounds, 30; Subdivision and lots, 32; Secondary methods used in legal descriptions, 32; State plane coordinate system, 35; Appurtenances, 36; Other physical elements, 36; Airspace, 37; Datum, 37; Water rights, 38; Summary, 39; Terms and concepts, 39; Problems, 40; Supplementary readings, 41.

3   **Rights and Interests in Real Estate**   43

Real estate defined, 43; Nature of land, 43; Concept of private ownership, 46; Estates and other interests in real estate, 46; Concurrent ownership of real estate, 55; Public restrictions on ownership of real estate, 62; Private restrictions on ownership of real estate, 64; Summary, 66; Terms and concepts, 67; Problems, 68; Supplementary readings, 69.

4   **Contract Law and Real Estate Contracts**   71

Characteristics of contracts, 71; Elements of an enforceable real estate contract, 72; Remedies upon a breach of contract, 83; Real estate contracts, 85; Assignments of real estate contracts, 98; Escrow arrangements, 98; Summary, 99; Terms and concepts, 100; Problems, 101; Supplementary readings, 103.

5   **Title Transfer, Deeds, and Recordation**   105

Involuntary transfer of title to real estate, 105; Voluntary transfer of title to real estate, 107; Recording of deeds and other instruments, 119; Summary, 123; Terms and concepts, 125; Problems, 125; Supplementary readings, 127.

6   Leases   129

Leases, 129; Leasehold estates, 129; Requirements of a lease, 131; Rights
and responsibilities of parties, 132; Types of leases, 136; Transfer of interest,
139; Remedies of the landlord, 141; Termination of leases, 141; Changing
nature of the landlord-tenant relationship, 144; Summary, 145; Terms and
concepts, 145; Problems, 146; Supplementary readings, 146.

7   Financing and Mortgages   149

Deed of trust, 149; Mortgages, 150; Minimum requirements of a mortgage
or deed of trust, 152; Classification of mortgages by repayment method, 156;
Other mortgage classifications, 160; FHA, VA, and conventional mortgages,
163; Other financing devices, 166; Remedies of lender upon default, 168;
Mortgage money, 171; The mortgage market, 174; Role of the government,
175; Summary, 178; Terms and concepts, 178; Problems, 179; Supplementary readings, 180.

8   Taxes and Liens   181

Real property taxes, 181; Liens, 187; Summary, 193; Terms and concepts,
193; Problems, 194; Supplementary readings, 194.

9   Home Ownership   197

Trends in home ownership, 197; Advantages of home ownership, 201; Tax
benefits of home ownership, 204; Disadvantages of home ownership, 210;
Rent versus buy, 211; Home ownership considerations, 212; Condominium
ownership, 214; Cooperative ownership, 215; Summary, 216; Terms and
concepts, 216; Problems, 216; Supplementary readings, 217.

10   Land Use Planning and Zoning   219

Urban planning, 220; Zoning, 227; Summary, 223; Terms and concepts,
234; Problems, 234; Supplementary readings, 235.

11   Real Property Insurance   237

Types of insurance, 238; Insurance principles, 241; Types of policies, 245;
Other policy provisions, 247; Summary, 249; Terms and concepts, 249;
Problems, 250; Supplementary readings, 250.

12   Federal Regulations and State Licensing   253

Federal housing, 253; Laws related to fair housing, 254; Consumer protection, 256; Environmental controls, 259; Land ownership by aliens, 261; State
licensing, 262; Summary, 265; Terms and concepts, 265; Problems, 265;
Supplementary readings, 266.

13   **Brokerage Operations**   267

The broker, 267; The broker as an agent, 268; Commissions, 275; Organization of brokerage operations, 277; Franchised brokers, 278; Staffing the
operation, 279; Summary, 282; Terms and concepts, 282; Problems, 283;
Supplementary readings, 284.

14   **Listing, Advertising, and Selling**   285

Listing agreements, 286; Types of listings, 289; Multiple-listing service, 292;
Promotion, 295; Home buyers, 297; The salesperson, 299; Summary, 301;
Terms and concepts, 301; Problems, 301; Supplementary readings, 302.

15   **Ethical and Professional Considerations**   303

Ethics, 303; Ethics in practice, 307; Ethics in advertising, 312; Professional
associations, 313; Summary, 316; Terms and concepts, 316; Problems, 316;
Supplementary readings, 317.

16   **The Transaction—From Offer to Closing**   319

Overview of transaction, 319; The offer and acceptance, 320; A binding
agreement, 323; Clearing contingencies, 326; Escrow, 327; Steps or possible
obstacles to completion of the transaction, 329; Use of computers in
preparation for closing, 337; Summary, 337; Terms and concepts, 337;
Problems, 338; Supplementary readings, 338.

17   **Closing and Conveyancing**   341

The closing, 341; Escrow closing, 342; Documents required at closing, 344;
Closing costs, 346; Proration, 347; The settlement statement, 354; Closing
problem example, 356; Actions subsequent to closing, 360; Summary, 361;
Terms and concepts, 361; Problems, 362; Supplementary readings, 364.

18   **Property Development and Construction**   367

Residential subdivision and development, 367; Commercial and industrial
developments, 379; The building industry, 382; Residential construction,
384; Summary, 394; Terms and concepts, 395; Problems, 395; Supplementary readings, 396.

19   **Appraisal and Value**   397

Appraisal and value concepts, 397; Value concepts, 399; Types of value, 399;
Prerequisites to value, 401; Principles of value, 402; Forces influencing
value, 403; The appraisal process, 404; Cost approach to value, 407; Market
approach to value, 414; Income approach to value—Residential single-
family units, 418; Income approach to value—Income-producing properties,

419; Correlation and final estimate, 429; Summary, 430; Terms and concepts, 431; Problems, 432; Supplementary readings, 434.

20   Property Management   435

Scope of property management, 435; Approaches to property management, 437; The property manager, 437; Organization for property management, 440; Marketing of income property, 442; Operations, 445; Financial control, 447; Consulting services, 449; Summary, 449; Terms and concepts, 450; Problems, 450; Supplementary readings, 451.

21   Real Estate Investments   453

Characteristics of real estate investments, 453; Investment returns, 456; Financial leverage, 456; Equity growth through financial leverage, 458; Depreciation allowances, 458; Methods of calculating depreciation, 460; Capital gains, 467; Analyzing a real estate investment, 470; Alternative investment media, 485; Summary, 485; Terms and concepts, 490; Problems, 490; Supplementary readings, 491.

APPENDICES

A	Glossary	494
B	Residential Construction Nomenclature	510
C	State Commissions and Their Publications	511
D	Present Value Tables	518
E	Amortization Tables: Monthly and Annually	524
F	Remaining Mortgage Balance Tables	529
G	Professional, Trade, and Other Real Estate Associations	536
H	Section of Land Showing Acreage and Distances	540

INDEX   541

Real Estate
Principles and
Practices

The Real Estate Business

A study of real estate involves land and the structures built upon the land. We encounter real estate every day in our home living, our occupations, and our outside activites. Our own homes, a church, an apartment, a retail store, a school, an office building, vacant land, or land used for producing crops or recreational purposes are all real estate. Real estate makes up a substantial portion of the wealth of this or any nation.

WHY WE STUDY REAL ESTATE

Each one of us owns or rents real estate to meet our basic housing needs, and the money we pay for housing represents a significant portion of our personal income. If we purchase a home, we are making a significant investment. Therefore, when we make a decision to rent or buy, or when we select between buying alternatives, we are making an important decision in our life. Although we might first think of real estate as a possible career when we consider the study of real estate, knowledge of real estate is very helpful in our personal lives. Real estate ownership has been a sound investment over the past 50 years. An understanding of real property, what gives it value, and the risks involved are important to each of us.

By recent estimates, the value of taxable real estate in the United States is about $2.9 trillion. This is especially impressive when we compare it in Figure 1–1 to the combined value of stocks on the three major stock exchanges and to the value of savings and currency in circulation.

The differences become more significant when we realize the large amount of nontaxable real estate not included in these figures as owned by the federal

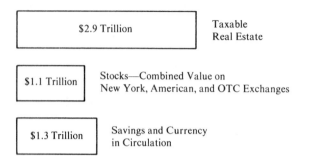

Figure 1–1

Importance of real estate—Shown by comparison

and state governments and by tax-exempt organizations. These figures tend to highlight the importance of real estate in our economy.

A study of real estate also provides an opportunity to consider the many real estate career opportunities. These careers provide rewarding and interesting fields of work. In addition to the careers directly involving real estate sales and brokerage, every business is actually involved with real estate. Each business needs an office or building in which to operate. The selection of location and type of structure on the site can have a serious impact on the success of the business. Real estate also provides opportunities for investment, either personally or from a business standpoint. Knowledge of real estate will help us in evaluating investment opportunities. Thus, we see that the study of real estate provides an opportunity to evaluate a variety of career possibilities, and it also gives us knowledge useful in our personal or business affairs.

PROPERTY RESOURCES

Before proceeding into the legal, economic, and business aspects of real estate, we will discuss some different types of properties and some real estate careers. Property is the basic resource with which real estate professionals work. Real estate professionals are involved with land development, building construction, buying and selling property, financing real estate, property management, and investments in real estate. This text will consider all of these aspects and the ways in which they tie together.

Persons in the real estate business are involved with various types of properties that constitute the resources of the business. Basic land has a wide variety of uses—food production, recreation, development into residential housing, factories, or commercial establishments. Land containing structures is called *improved property* and can be classified as residential, farm, commercial, industrial, or recreational. These categories are based on the use or intended use of the property with its improvements. Urban areas require some of each of these property types. Urban planners usually designate a proper mix of these types to support the industry, commerce, and population of the area.

The United States has become a nation of homeowners. The availability of financing has helped to enable a substantial percentage of families to own their own homes. In addition, inflationary trends and the desire to build up invested interest has given many people the incentive to buy their own homes. Concurrently, many find it necessary to change their place of residence, either to improve their standard of living or to take an occupational opportunity that requires a move to a different locality. These pressures create the need for more residential construction and for a system of marketing new and existing properties.

A recent census of housing shows that, of the approximately 77 million units in the United States, approximately 68 percent were single-family homes, 28 percent were multiunit structures, and the remaining 4 percent were mobile units. About two-thirds of the units are owner occupied, leaving about one-third in rental status. In a typical community, about three to ten percent of the units are vacant or for sale at any time. Over the period of time through 1965–1977, the number of households has increased by about one to two million per year. About 75 percent of the U.S. population lived in urban areas, with 70 percent of the total residing in urban communities with over 50,000 population.

Single and multifamily units

Residential property includes not only the single-family dwelling, but almost any type of structure designed for personal living. These dwellings can be found in urban, suburban, and rural or vacation areas. In addition to the single-family dwelling, other types of residence include the duplex, triplex, and four-family homes. These are forms of housing where owners live in one of the units while renting out the others. Additional forms of residential dwellings are the town house, row house, and garden apartments.

Apartments

Apartments comprise a category of residential real estate defined officially as having five or more living units. Often they have several hundred units. They have become very popular with both older and younger persons. Many in these age groups do not want to be tied to one place, do not have the substantial investment required to own a home, or prefer not to have the considerable responsibilities associated with home care.

Life insurance companies and investment trusts frequently invest in apartments because these investments often produce a relatively high rate of return. Although most apartments in the past have been located in urban centers, there is an increasing trend to construct new apartments in suburban areas. Apartments can be either high, medium, or low-rise or of the garden type. In any case, the success of an apartment as an investment depends to a large extent upon the skill of the property manager, who is responsible for maintaining adequate occupancy rates and for efficiently handling property maintenance. Although some hotels and motels have also been converted into residential housing, they are more suitably classified as commercial properties catering more to transient persons.

Condominiums and cooperatives

Condominiums and cooperatives have become an increasingly important element in the real estate business, and their construction has increased considerably in the past twenty years. Both allow people who prefer an apartment-like environment to enjoy some of the financial advantages of home ownership. Although condominiums and cooperatives both provide a means for a person to invest in his or her own place of residence, there are important differences between the two.

In a *cooperative,* the title to the building and property is held by a corporation. The person who resides in a unit of the cooperative owns stock in the corporation and also has a proprietary lease on his or her apartment. Property taxes are levied against the corporation, and if there is any mortgage, the corporation is the mortgagor.

The *condominium,* in contrast, provides a means whereby each person residing in the building owns his own apartment, just as a home owner owns her own home. The owner of an individual unit in the condominium can sell his unit to someone else, he receives his own individual tax bill, and he can obtain a mortgage on his single unit. The number of condominiums in the U.S. has increased substantially since 1970, with couples over age forty-five whose children have left home representing the dominant buyers. In urban areas, many apartments are being converted to condominiums with the result that those who formerly lived in the apartment are forced to either purchase a unit or move.

Mobile homes

From a legal viewpoint, mobile homes are usually considered personal property and not real property. They are mentioned here, however, because of their impact on the real estate business and because some states have special laws that consider mobile homes that are fixed in position much the same as real property.

Mobile homes consist of movable or portable year-round dwellings constructed without a permanent foundation. They can be towed on their own chassis and connected to utilities. Sometimes a mobile home consists of two or more sections that are towed separately and later combined, or it may be comprised of units that can be telescoped for towing. Mobile homes make up a substantial portion of the housing that can be purchased for under $30,000. Frequently, the units contain many of the conveniences of regular homes. Most mobile homes are situated in mobile home parks where suitable utility connections are available.

Since legally, mobile homes are considered personal property, they are not normally subject to real property taxes. In California, mobile homes without wheels are taxed as homes, however, and similar taxation is under consideration in other states. Mobile homes are subject to annual license fees. By paying rent for the space they occupy, their owners contribute indirectly to the taxing communities. It is often argued, however, that the mobile home owners' share of taxes is not in proportion to their use of schools and other services financed by real estate taxes.

Commercial

Commercial properties include those that offer retail and wholesale services, provide banking or other financial services, provide executive office space, or handle other similar functions. They also include shopping centers and other types of buildings. In general, the category includes most improved property acquired for investment purposes, except apartment houses and similar residential units. The trend to locate commercial property in suburban areas has increased as the population moves out away from urban centers.

Central business districts

Through the 1940s, a central business district included an area's largest department stores, hotels, banks, office buildings, and other retail establishments. These facilities were grouped together for the convenience of pedestrian customers. This central business area also usually served as the center for culture and entertainment. Frequently the state, federal, and municipal government offices were located in this same general area. The central business district served further as the converging point for metropolitan transportation as well as intercity bus and rail transportation and highways. This high concentration of activities resulted in the need for substantial parking facilities in the area, and land in central business areas has tended to have a high per-square-foot value relative to other land.

Shopping centers

The increase in number and size of suburban shopping centers has gone hand-in-hand with the expansion of residential housing in suburban areas. The shopping center has come to be a focal point of suburban living by including not only retail establishments, but also theaters, post offices, churches, and recreational facilities. Its popularity is due primarily to the convenience of having many facilities in one location. Shopping center development provides attractive opportunities for real estate investors because of the high ratio of building-to-land value. Tenants can either rent, buy, or purchase and lease back the store facilities. Developers emphasize the attractiveness of the facility design and the convenience of parking. The placement of a shopping center enhances the expansion of the urban area and the development of residential housing in nearby suburbs.

Cultural centers

In some urban areas, the center of cultural activities is separate from the more congested central business district. The cultural center may group around a university or park. It can include a hospital, stadium, music hall, museum, botanical garden, zoo, and other activities. Secondary urban centers often develop around airports also. There is an increasing trend for these centers to have many facilities formerly found only in a central business district.

Industrial Property

Industrial properties are used for the manufacture and warehousing of industrial and consumer products. This category includes factories, utilities, research laboratories, warehouses, and mining or lumbering operations. Industry has been following the general trend of moving into suburban areas where land is more abundant and parking space is more readily available. The trend has been toward industrial parks, which have one- or two-story buildings rather than the older style multistory structures. Industrial parks provide such advantages as readily available utilities and sewage facilities, maintenance, police protection, fencing, and existing streets. They are also usually situated close to transportation facilities. The trend toward greater use of truck rather than rail transportation has increased the suitability of outlying areas for industrial usage.

Industrial properties can be divided into *light* and *heavy* manufacturing. Heavy manufacturing generally creates more noise, air pollution, and other problems requiring a greater distance from the residential and cultural areas of the community.

Farm and Rural Property

Farm property is used for agricultural purposes such as crops, dairyland, ranches, pasture, orchards, and timber. In the past, farms were often small and were operated by the owner. Today, some farmland near urban areas has been taken over by industrial plants and urban residential expansion. Many other small farms have been consolidated into larger farms to spread costs and permit purchase of mechanized equipment and use of scientific methods to increase yields per acre. Some farmers have sold their property to neighbors, while others act as absentee landlords, with the land being farmed by a tenant. Recently, many farms have been purchased by investors and then leased back to the farmer to operate.

Recreation Property

Land and improvements used principally for entertainment or vacations are classified as recreational property. This category includes lakeside properties, mountain and seaside resort property, golf courses, and amusement parks. As people and the society become more affluent, they seek recreation areas with facilities for boating, fishing, swimming, skiing, hunting, camping, and other leisure activities. Most urban complexes of residential areas and commercial areas have recreation areas set aside.

The government, through its many agencies, owns approximately one-third of all the land in the United States. Much of the land is designated as public areas. Other lands are turned over to public or private agencies for park or recreational use. Still other lands have been sold outright or leased to private citizens or local governments. This policy is in the public interest, since it makes increased use of previously vacant, unused, or unproductive land. It also helps local governments broaden their tax base to support greater services for their citizens.

REAL ESTATE OCCUPATIONS AND CAREERS

There are over 2.5 billion acres of land in the United States and trillions of dollars invested in buildings and other improvements on the land. Persons who select a career in real estate have the opportunity to influence the wise use of this resource. They also have the opportunity to participate in a field where growth is generated by increases in the population and in the gross national product. Residential housing, as well as commercial and industrial needs, provide an ever increasing demand for real estate. As in most challenging and interesting careers, the practitioner must be willing to prepare for a position of responsibility by learning the technical, legal, economic, and business aspects of real estate.

The real estate business includes many, many career opportunities— including entrepreneurial opportunities for a person to run her or his own business, positions in large corporations or institutions, and opportunities for independent professional work. Real estate careers offer personal satisfaction because they offer interesting and challenging work and provide sufficient rewards in terms of prestige and salary for a good standard of living. The careers relate to developing, marketing, financing, and managing real estate. These functional occupations tend to offer more independence than do the functions associated with other types of business.

Land developers and builders may be thought of as performing the *production* function in real estate. They use the land by converting it into improved resources. Real estate brokers can be compared to the *marketing* function, since they provide the services needed for buyers and sellers to transfer ownership of property. The third functional area is *finance,* which is handled by banks, savings and loan associations, and investment companies.

In addition to these three functions, a variety of other professionals are involved in real estate transactions. As legal considerations are very important in every real estate transaction, attorneys become involved. Land planners and architects have the skills needed in development, construction, and urban planning. Property managers, appraisers, and consultants comprise other important professional groups. Each of these performs a highly specialized and important function.

Brokerage

The real estate brokerage operation is similar to the marketing function of other businesses. Brokerage involves buying and selling property by using marketing approaches such as promotion, advertising, and sales. From another viewpoint, the real estate broker is an agent. With professional knowledge and established business as a background, the broker brings together people who wish to buy, sell, lease, or exchange real estate.

Brokerage is the largest branch of the real estate industry, with annual sales in the billions of dollars. Since everyone is a user of real estate, the broker works within a large market and is in a position to help people satisfy their housing needs. As part of this function, the broker also frequently provides the services of securing mortgage money, making appraisals, and managing property.

The broker

The real estate **broker** needs professional as well as managerial capabilities to run a brokerage operation. He or she must have the technical knowledge to carry out the agency function in real estate, as well as the business knowledge to establish a business and manage other people. Many brokers belong to national or local professional real estate associations. The best-known of these is the NATIONAL ASSOCIATION OF REALTORS®, which has established professional and ethnical standards for its members. Most states also require that real estate brokers pass examinations and meet other requirements to obtain a license.

The most important aspect of real estate brokerage is arranging the buying and selling of real estate. Brokers usually are compensated for their services in the form of a fee based on a percentage of the value of the property sold. The brokerage business depends to a large extent on public realization that the broker performs an important service. The success or failure of the individual broker depends to a great extent upon his ability to provide good service to his clients and on his technical knowledge. As a manager, the broker is responsible for operating his business, including setting up an office, hiring people, directing advertising and promotion, and carrying transactions through to completion. The broker is also responsible for office personnel as well as salespeople. Sometimes, too, a broker will manage property for clients, perform appraisals where qualified, and handle other functions. The practice of management has become more scientific during the past two decades, and the broker can often take advantage of newly developed management concepts. He can use computers, market analyses, motivation concepts, studies of consumer behavior, and other techniques to improve his business performance and competitive edge. Many brokers earn very substantial incomes and direct large staffs of people.

The salesperson

The real estate broker hires salespeople to sell real estate under her direction. The salesperson is usually compensated based on the actual sales completed or on listings obtained. Most states require that salespeople be licensed after having passed examinations showing technical competence in the legal, ethical, economic, and business aspects of real estate. Each salesperson must work for a licensed broker; he or she cannot sell independently. As with brokers, much of the success of a salesperson depends on technical competence and the ability to provide services desired by buyers and sellers. Much of this success depends upon the reputation the salesperson builds up in the community. High earnings are available to the salesperson who works hard and is successful.

In any real estate transaction, the salesperson acts for the broker. State regulations require that the broker supervise the salespeople and assume responsibility for their actions. A salesperson can work for only one broker at any one time, usually under a contractual or employment agreement. As in most occupations, the real estate salesperson who enjoys the work and approaches it with a good attitude is often the one who is most successful.

Production

The production aspect of real estate involves two groups of people. One group participates in land subdivision and development—buying land, subdividing, and then reselling lots or constructing buildings. The second group actually builds structures. The builder may be hired by the individual land owners, by property developers, or by corporations that are building as an investment.

Land subdividers and developers

This category of real estate professionals deals in the buying and selling of land, purchasing land for subdividing and development, and managing land development for other owners. Some people are involved in long-term speculation, whereas others are involved in shorter-term improvements. The work may include the purchase of older properties for renovation, alteration, or modernization.

Land can be developed for residential, commercial, industrial, recreational, or other use. The developer is usually required to work closely within applicable urban master plans and local zoning regulations. Compliance with these requirements will also help insure the compatibility and success of the projects. Frequently, the developer will subdivide a piece of land and improve it in steps. This method helps to reduce the initial financing required and allows the value of the land to increase as the development proceeds.

Builders

The construction of buildings represents an important part of the real estate business. The design of the structure by an architect is usually the initial step in the process. Architects consider the contemplated use of the building and the other available land and surroundings in designing a building. From the architect's plans and specifications, the contractor constructs the building. Contractors vary in the size of the operation from one who works alone to build a house to a large contractor who hires many people. Usually the contractor will subcontract out portions of the job such as the electrical work or plumbing. The organized building trades support this specialization. In some cases, the property owner will give the architect the responsibility to oversee the construction and make sure the specifications are met. The owner will normally seek competitive bids from several contractors before selecting one. The contractor will then work for the owner in accordance with a signed contract agreement. Because of potential risks resulting from changes in material or labor costs, bad weather, or the risk of trade union strikes, building contractors often run into financial difficulties. Many, however, make out very well financially.

Financing

Real estate has a long life over which it tends to retain its value. Since it requires substantial initial investment, outside financing is often necessary. Both private and government sources may be involved in financing real estate. These sources provide financing for everything from small residential properties all the way to very large hotels and office buildings to shopping centers and entire housing developments. Banks, saving and loan associations, insurance companies, investment brokers, and the federal government are all involved. All of these institutions employ professionals knowledgeable in real estate to handle their part of the transactions.

Usually the financing institution receives a pledge of the property as security for a loan. In other words, the financial institution holds a mortgage on the property. This system lets the institution obtain an acceptable return on its money and also have good security. At the same time, the real estate developer or individual property owner obtains the funding needed for new construction. Well-paying career positions are available in the real estate financing field.

Investments

Some institutions invest their own funds in real estate with the objective of securing a return on the investment. For example, insurance companies have considerable funds to invest in real estate. In the past, real estate has provided a hedge against inflation, while responding to the needs of expanding population and commerce. Small investors often invest or speculate by purchasing property with a small amount of their own funds. Persons knowledgeable in real estate and investments are sought to fill positions with investment firms or companies such as insurance companies, where investment activity comprises an important part of the company effort.

Consulting and Research

A number of companies, such as the Real Estate Research Corporation in Chicago, have research specialists in the various aspects of real estate. Typical consulting tasks include selecting a location for a company, managing property for a company, disposing of real estate, evaluating investment alternatives, and energy conservation. Independent consultants or counselors offer professional services just as do lawyers or other professionals. Counselors in real estate may belong to the American Society of Real Estate Counselors.

Teaching

Courses in real estate are offered by universities, community colleges, and private organizations. Some universities offer bachelors, masters, or doctoral degree programs in real estate. Most states require at least one course for a license to sell and additional courses for a brokerage license. Some states also require that licensees take courses periodically to maintain their licenses. All of these factors have increased the need for persons to teach real estate. Persons achieving doctorates in real estate fields command high salaries from universities.

Appraisal

Appraisers estimate the value of real estate. Those who estimate for tax purposes are called *assessors.* Financial institutions depend upon appraisers for estimates of value before mortgage loans are made. The appraisers who work independently charge a fee for each appraisal. Other appraisers work for banks, savings and loan institutions, or other companies. Extensive experience and training are required to achieve the professional appraisal designations offered by appraisal societies.

Property Management

Office buildings, hotels, apartments, resorts, and country clubs represent large investments in real estate and require professional property managers. The responsibilities of a property manager include securing and retaining tenants, service, public relations, maintenance, security, and financial management. Frequently property managers specialize in one category of real estate. The property manager carries considerable responsibility and is compensated accordingly.

Legal

The many legal aspects of real estate transactions and ownership are carried out by an attorney at law. Many attorneys, banks, or other institutions have paralegals to assist in the increasingly complex aspects of these real estate transactions. Schools have responded by offering degrees in paralegal and related areas.

THE REAL ESTATE MARKET

All businesses have a function responsible for the *marketing* of their products or services. Marketing any product involves the buying, selling, or exchanging of the product. The concept of a *market,* therefore, includes the buyer and seller and the places or means whereby they get together and transact business. Thus, the real estate market relates to the buying and selling of real estate, the people involved, and the places where the business is conducted. In real estate, however, the terms *buying* and *selling* must be extended to include renting and leasing to a much greater extent than with most other products. Renting and leasing, along with other services, form a large segment of the real estate market.

Real Estate Characteristics

Real estate is different in several ways from other types of products. The main difference is the fixed location. This immobility introduces several factors that affect the market and the way it operates.

Location

The location of a parcel of property strongly influences the property value and price. A new home in one part of a city can vary widely in demand and price from an identical new home in another part of the same city. Location, therefore, is a characteristic of real estate that is of prime importance, whereas with most other products, location has little effect.

Local markets

The second result of this immobility is that the real estate market is made up of a large number of local markets, each isolated to some degree from other local markets. With other commodities, such as automobiles or food, a high demand or short supply in one area can be offset by moving products from other areas where there is an oversupply. This movement is not possible in real estate; therefore, home prices in one city may be considerably higher than they are for similar property in a city only fifty miles away. An oversupply of homes in one area cannot satisfy a shortage in another area. Thus, real estate prices are highly vulnerable to local events such as plant layoffs or declines in local industries.

This immobility and the resulting local markets also mean that brokers and salespeople must be familiar with their local areas. A real estate salesperson who works in an area away from her or his own city will lose some selling advantages due to lack of knowledge of the new locality. The degree of immobility of real estate personnel, although not so constraining as the immobility of the property, results in a large number of brokers and sales personnel. In the United States, there are more than 600,000 real estate salespersons.

Lack of standardization

Another characteristic of real estate is its lack of standardization. No two properties are exactly the same, and few properties are even closely similar. Homes of identical configuration can be different in value because of location, upkeep, paint color, exterior condition, interior decoration or furnishing, and many other factors. Even if the physical features of two homes were almost identical, zoning, deed restrictions, or title encumbrances could make their values considerably different.

Variation in physical makeup and in marketing practices exists between different categories of real property. The methods used to construct, market, and operate office buildings or apartments are much different from the methods used for residences. Industrial property and farm property marketing varies considerably from the first two categories. These widely varying conditions make it logical that real estate professionals specialize. In practice, some brokers handle only industrial property, whereas others restrict their business to residential properties, and still others confine their efforts to farm or rural land.

Long life

Most manufactured products change in style over the years, and real estate does also. Automobiles and electric appliances have a shorter life span, however, and may be discarded after two to ten years. Real property, however, continues as a market factor for fifty to one hundred or even more years. Therefore, the real estate market may contain properties of considerably varying age at any one time. Older properties interact with newer properties, with each influencing the price of the other.

Market Characteristics

The real estate market provides a structure for the transfer of property and associated interests, including leasing, renting, and investing. Although the property characteristics discussed in the previous paragraph constrain the flexibility of the market as a whole, they help balance the supply and demand in the local market. Much of the contribution of real estate professionals is their knowledge and understanding of the local market, since the market differs so much from one locality to the next.

We saw that the immobility of real estate results in local markets. This, in turn, causes the real estate business to be highly decentralized and, to some extent, unorganized. The differences between state laws also add to decentralization. The NATIONAL ASSOCIATION OF REALTORS® advocates standardization of broker and salesperson licensing requirements; today, however, these still differ from one state to another. A broker who lives in one state may have difficulty operating in another state without further education and passing additional examinations. Differences in licensing requirements, therefore, also contribute to the local nature of the real estate market.

The local nature of the market results in an uneven supply and demand in different cities. There may be a strong demand in some cities where economic conditions are good and, at the same time, a weak market in other cities where employment is low or industries are deteriorating. The lack of flexibility to adjust to this shifting demand results in a wide variance in prices, even between towns as close as fifty miles apart. This rigidity makes it difficult to adjust to sudden changes in demand caused by changing economic factors.

Other Factors Affecting the Market

Other factors also affect the strength or weakness of the real estate market. Population trends certainly affect the need for residential housing. The population age grouping in an area also affects the market, since couples with young children will have different housing requirements from older people. Marriage rates, divorce rates, and family size also affect the residential units that are in demand. A shift in any, or all, of these factors has a substantial effect on the demand for each category of residential unit.

The types of employment available in a community also affect the level of income and, thus, the demand and price range of housing available. The rate of unemployment will affect the demand for housing at any particular time. Both of these factors can change within a few months' time and lead to a shift in demand for any category of real estate.

Other important economic factors include inflation, building costs, labor wage rates, and the availability of money for investments and mortgages. A short supply of money for mortgages drives the interest rates up, with resulting buyer resistance to purchasing real estate.

Rental Market

About one-third of the existing housing is in rental units; however, recent trends to convert rental apartments to condominium units in urban centers have caused some changes in this market. The rental housing market satisfies the needs of a segment of the housing market that might be defined by selected groups as follows:

1. Persons with less secure or lower incomes, including mobile or seasonal workers.
2. Newly married couples without sufficient assets or income to meet the down payment, closing cost, or monthly payments needed to buy a home.
3. Single persons.
4. Some professionals or executives who prefer the luxury and convenience of urban centers.

The rental market continues to be a significant proportion of the total real estate market.

FACTORS RELATED TO MARKET DEMAND

The involved nature of the real estate market makes it difficult to predict demand or to correlate it to other factors in the economy. Authorities, however, tend to believe that demand for housing is related to seven factors:

1. *Per capita disposable income.* Lower income families or individuals tend to live with parents or relatives and postpone formation of new households.
2. *Price of housing.* When prices are higher, some families tend to decrease their expenditures for housing.

3. *Formation of new households.* Rates of marriage influence demand.
4. *Construction, demolition, and conversion to condominium units.* Construction of highways and other endeavors cause demolition of units. Conversion to condominiums takes rental units off the market.
5. *Movement of families.* Migration to different areas of the country changes the housing picture.
6. *Liquid assets.* The purchase of real estate requires a substantial down payment.
7. *Living style requirements.* Family size, changes in availability of labor saving appliances, and number of employed persons in the family affect the demand for varied sizes of homes.
8. *Mortgage money availability and cost.*

Measures of Market Conditions

The complex factors involved in the real estate business make it difficult to measure market conditions or predict future market conditions. The following are some of the more frequently used indicators of real estate market conditions.

1. *Vacancy rates.* High vacancy rates indicate a poorer market. Although normal vacancy rates vary from one locality to another, a rate of five percent is often used as a norm.
2. *Deed transfers.* The number of transactions is a good measure of the real estate market and can be tabulated by counting records of deed transfers.
3. *Mortgage foreclosures.* An increase in the rate of mortgage foreclosures tends to correspond to a decline in real estate market activity.
4. *Construction rates.* The number of new units built indicates real estate market activity. Housing starts and building permits are both good sources of this information. Sometimes, however, the demand may shift up or down, but construction does not respond quickly.

Other indexes of economic activity, such as employment and gross national product, correlate with real estate market activity. These indexes are published in business periodicals such as "National Market Letter,"[1] a real estate newsletter that publishes data by region of the U.S.

SUMMARY

Land and improvements on the land provide the resources with which the real estate business works. Improved land can be classified as *residential, commercial, industrial, farm,* or *recreation.*

The development, construction, marketing, and financing of real estate

---

[1]"National Market Letter" (Chicago: Real Estate Research Corporation). Published monthly.

provide a wide variety of interesting and challenging careers. Many of these occupations require a substantial amount of formal education.

The real estate market provides the means for handling the transactions required for all the categories of real property. Although many real estate marketing concepts can be related to the marketing of other products, the real estate market has certain differences that make its transactions unique.

Real estate itself is different from other products: real property is immobile, and each parcel of real estate is different in one way or another from any other parcel. Therefore, the real estate market is local in nature; prices, problems, and demand differ from one place to another.

Although there are a number of published data and indexes purporting to measure the real estate market, in actuality, the large number of contributing factors make it difficult to measure the real estate market accurately.

TERMS AND CONCEPTS

You can check your understanding of these terms against the glossary in Appendix A or by review in this chapter.

Apartment	Finance
Appraiser	Improved property
Assessors	Industrial property
Broker	Marketing
Commercial property	Production
Condominium	Residential property
Cooperative	

PROBLEMS

1–1. What aspects of real estate careers do you personally find most attractive? Which aspects are not attractive to you?

1–2. Review the real estate ads in the classified section of your local newspaper, and identify agents who tend to specialize in certain types of real estate.

1–3. In the area where you are living, how would you describe the geographical limits of the local real estate market?

1–4. What types of real estate would tend *not* to be part of a local market?

1–5. Identify an area of your community where most of the houses are rental units. Identify another area where most are owner-occupied. Explain the differences between the two areas.

1–6. Do you think mobile homes should be considered *real estate* for tax purposes?

1–7. List the factors that cause both a good and a poor real estate market. What other factors are a market influence in your particular area?

1–8. List the factors that authorities feel are correlated to the real estate market. What action by each of these factors would tend to indicate a *good* real estate market?

SUPPLEMENTARY READINGS

Crean, Michael J. *Principles of Real Estate Analysis.* New York: Van Nostrand, 1979. Chapters 1 and 2.

Dasso, Jerome; Ring, Alfred A.; and McFall, Douglas. *Fundamentals of Real Estate.* Englewood Cliffs: Prentice-Hall, 1977. Chapters 1 and 2.

Downs, James C. *Principles of Real Estate Management.* Chicago: Institute of Real Estate Management, 1975. Chapters 1–6.

Goulet, Peter G. *Real Estate.* Encino, Ca.: Glencoe, 1979. Chapters 1 and 10.

Mannheim, Uriel. *How to Do Housing Market Research: A Handbook for Local Home Builders Associations.* Washington, D.C.: National Association of Home Builders, 1973.

Unger, Maurice A., and Karvel, George R. *Real Estate Principles and Practices,* 6th ed. Cincinnati: Southwestern, 1979. Chapters 1 and 2.

Weimer, Arthur M.; Hoyt, Homer; and Bloom, George F. *Real Estate.* New York: Ronald Press, 1978. Chapters 1, 2, and 7.

SOURCES OF CURRENT BUSINESS DATA

"Construction Cost Index." American Appraisal Company, 525 E. Michigan St., Milwaukee, Wisc.

"Dodge Reports." F. W. Dodge Corporation, 119 W. 40th St., New York, N.Y.

"The Housing Letter." The Housing Institute, 350 Fifth Ave., New York, N.Y. (bi-weekly)

"Monthly Construction Report Series." Bureau of the Census, U.S. Department of Commerce, Series C-40 and C-42.

"Monthly Vital Statistics Report." U.S. Department of Health, Education and Welfare.

"National Market Letter." Real Estate Research Corporation, Chicago. (monthly)

"Real Estate Analyst." Roy Wenzlich and Company, 706 Chestnut St., St. Louis. (monthly)

Land and Its Description

The surface of the earth is often referred to as *land,* but a true definition of land includes the earth below the surface and the air space above the land. *Land,* by legal definition, also includes permanent natural things such as trees and water as well as minerals or other elements below the surface of the earth. ***Real estate,*** by definition, includes not only the land as defined above, but also improvements to the land and certain rights to its use. Purchasers of land have the right to assume that they are buying not only the land itself, but also any structures thereon. They also have the right to assume that they are obtaining the right to use and maintain the structures and the land substantially as has been done in the past. Some writers use the term *real estate* to refer to the physical land and structures, whereas they use the term ***real property*** to refer to property rights. These possible differences in definitions should be recognized by the reader; however, this text uses *real estate* and *real property* interchangeably.

PHYSICAL CHARACTERISTICS

Immobility, nonhomogeneity, and *indestructibility* are three distinctive physical characteristics of land. These characteristics have a strong impact on the real estate business and the way in which transactions are handled. They make real property different from other types of property.

Immobility

Buildings, soil, gravel, and other items considered part of real estate might be moved by action of nature or people; however, the piece of land itself is immobile and can never be changed from its geographical location. Because of its fixed position, land has become a primary source of taxation to support local government. The immobility allows the government to use a lien to force the sale of the land in order to collect unpaid taxes. Being immobile, the land is subject to control of the state and local governments in which it exists.

Nonhomogeneity

No two parcels of land, no matter how closely they resemble each other, are ever exactly the same. Even if the size and all physical characteristics were identical, the locations could never be identical. This nonhomogeneity has a significant impact on the buying and selling of real property. A contract to sell a new automobile may be satisfied by providing an identical substitute. In a contract to sell a specific parcel of land, however, there may be no acceptable substitute. With a real estate contract, the buyer can sue for *specific performance,* meaning she can force the sale of the particular parcel of property that was contracted for. The buyer is not obligated to accept another parcel. Under the same line of reasoning, the seller can legally force the buyer to complete a contract of purchase; however, in some cases it may be impractical to enforce.

Indestructibility

Indestructibility, the third physical characteristic of land, causes real estate to be a durable and relatively stable investment. Except for economic factors, land does not depreciate. In fact, it more often appreciates with time. This does not mean that property value cannot be destroyed; for instance, top-soil removal or strip mining might reduce the value or usability of land for agricultural purposes. The value of the property can also be reduced by lack of care or maintenance or other deterioration of improvements on the property or its surroundings.

ECONOMIC CHARACTERISTICS

In addition to the physical characteristics, land also has its peculiar economic characteristics: scarcity, fixed investment, location, and improvements. These economic characteristics also have an impact on the manner in which real estate business is carried out.

Scarcity

Although there is a large amount of land that can be purchased at a low price, land in other, more desirable locations might be *scarce* or very valuable. There is no scarcity of land as such; however, land for specific uses in specific locations is frequently insufficient to meet demand. As population increases, a scarcity of land to produce food might develop; however, in the recent past, the increase in productivity of the land due to fertilizers, better seed, and better crop management has resulted in a decrease in the total demand for land for food production. In many cases however, prices of the best agricul-

Table 2–1

Increases in value of U.S. farmland, 1978–1979, as reported by the U.S. Department of Agriculture

Boom Still On in U.S. Farmland

The boom in farmland prices, a year after showing signs of slowing, is picking up again.

An Agriculture Department report, covering all states but Alaska and Hawaii, puts the value of the average acre of U.S. farmland in November at $528, 12 percent higher than the $471 average for the previous year.

The results, state by state:

	Average Per Acre	Increase in Year
Alabama	$ 492	11%
Arizona	$ 129	7%
Arkansas	$ 635	16%
California	$ 809	16%
Colorado	$ 326	24%
Connecticut*	$2,111	12%
Delaware	$1,694	16%
Florida**	$ 889	10%
Georgia	$ 587	10%
Idaho	$ 496	18%
Illinois	$1,689	12%
Indiana	$1,432	13%
Iowa	$1,375	10%
Kansas	$ 417	9%
Kentucky	$ 708	10%
Louisiana	$ 788	22%
Maine*	$ 475	12%
Maryland	$1,610	7%
Massachusetts*	$1,336	12%
Michigan	$ 896	10%
Minnesota	$ 814	14%
Mississippi	$ 510	18%
Missouri	$ 636	14%
Montana	$ 188	17%
Nebraska	$ 430	10%
Nevada	$ 103	7%
New Hampshire*	$ 785	12%
New Jersey	$2,126	5%
New Mexico	$ 100	7%
New York	$ 629	6%
North Carolina	$ 728	4%
North Dakota	$ 285	7%
Ohio	$1,411	17%
Oklahoma	$ 417	10%
Oregon	$ 326	11%
Pennsylvania	$1,131	12%
Rhode Island*	$2,087	12%
South Carolina	$ 554	3%
South Dakota	$ 235	10%
Tennessee	$ 645	13%
Texas	$ 332	13%
Utah	$ 264	7%
Vermont*	$ 642	12%
Virginia	$ 838	17%
Washington	$ 541	8%
West Virginia	$ 474	15%
Wisconsin	$ 753	13%
Wyoming	$ 114	13%

*Projected dollar values based on average rate of change in six New England states.

**Florida values based on changes in Alabama and Georgia.

Source: Reprinted from U.S. News & World Report. Copyright 1979 U.S. News & World Report, Inc., Jan. 8, 1979.

tural land have increased substantially as shown in Table 2–1, which also shows the considerable price variations from state to state.

In urban areas, the ability to construct higher buildings, combined with expressway construction, which gives greater access to more land, has also reduced the scarcity of land. Further expected improvements in land use may reduce this scarcity in the future; concurrently, however, new uses for land drive values up. Feelings that all land is scarce have caused land booms in the past that are sometimes followed by price collapses when it becomes evident that there is not a real demand for the land.

Fixed Investment

A second economic characteristic of land is the fixed nature of the investment, or *fixity.* Most modifications or improvements to the land cannot be moved, and it may take twenty or thirty years to repay the investment; thus, the investment is long lasting. Buildings and associated facilities, once installed, become part of the real estate. This characteristic makes the value of a land investment highly dependent on the economic changes in a specific location or on changes in people's preferences. The property improvements are tied to the neighborhood in which the land is located. Therefore, the expenditure to purchase or improve land must consider how long the land's usefulness will last.

Location

Location, or *situs,* is the third economic characteristic of land. Similar pieces of real property may have extremely different values just because of the difference in location. This difference can be caused by people's preference for natural attributes, such as weather, good soil, scenery, or for human-made factors, such as schools, cultural attractions, or places of employment. Both affect the quality of the land, and, thus, the value. Changing conditions such as population shifts or industrial build-up or decline frequently cause some land to increase substantially in value and other land to deteriorate in value.

Improvements

The fourth economic characteristic of land is its ability *to be modified* or improved, with the associated impact upon value. Improvement *on* the land includes buildings, fences, or other things that then become part of the real estate. In contrast, improvements *to* the land include access roads, nearby schools, construction of recreational facilities and industries, and other factors that make the real estate more valuable, often without modifying the site itself.

LEGAL DESCRIPTIONS

The process of conveying real property from one party to another requires a positive method of property identification and description. These legal descriptions are used in contracts and deeds that convey real property from one person to another. It is necessary that any piece of real property can be unquestionably differentiated from any other piece and the exact boundaries determined. In some instances, an estate has been adequately described and conveyed by a name such as "The Highmark Estate"; however, the instances where property can be so identified are rare and sometimes open to question. Any lapse of time must not interfere with this ability to be able to clearly define the property and any improvements on it. If one person owns a parcel of property for thirty or forty years, many things can change. In the intervening period, street and road names may be changed, or neighboring properties might change ownership. If raw land, it may be subdivided or pieces sold from the main parcel. Houses can be torn down and replaced by apartments, or other factors may make the simple street address insufficient to identify the property clearly.

The legal description for real property provides this positive legal identification and the means to identify the exact same parcel clearly at a later date. Several methods are available to assure the identification of land such that there is no question as to the property involved or of its exact boundaries. The technical capabilities of land surveyors and the accuracy of their instruments are necessary to provide these exacting methods.

The three primary means for legally describing real estate are (a) *rectangular survey,* sometimes called *government survey,* (b) *metes and bounds,* and (c) *subdivision and lot,* sometimes called *plat map.* Two secondary methods are (d) monuments and (e) street and number. These secondary methods are often used to supplement the primary methods. Legal descriptions use one or more of these methods, and it is not unusual for a parcel of real property to be described by a combination of all five methods. These legal descriptions are used in deeds and in contracts.

RECTANGULAR SURVEY

The rectangular survey system, or government survey system, was adopted by Congress in 1785. At that time the United States was expanding rapidly to the west, and it became evident that a simple and accurate method for identifying land was needed. Vast new land areas were being opened, and the government wanted to encourage settlement by assuring ownership rights to settlers. The rectangular survey system is based upon lines running north and south called *meridians,* which intersect with *baselines* running east and west. Certain of these meridians are called *principal meridians* or *prime meridians.* The map in Figure 2–1 shows the principal meridians in the United States and the baseline associated with each principal meridian. As shown on the map, the rectangular system applies to most of the U.S., except for the white areas (the original thirteen states and Texas). In the area covered by the rectangular survey system, any piece of property is officially located relative to one particular meridian and its baseline. A piece of land is not

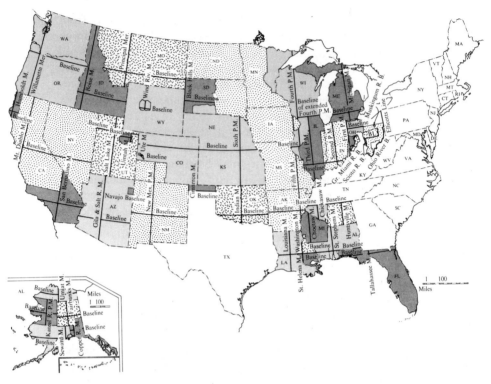

Figure 2–1
Principal meridians of the government rectangular survey system

Source: U.S. Department of the Interior, Bureau of Land Management. "Public Land Statistics, 1970."

necessarily identified from the closest principal meridian; however, the location of any one parcel of land is never described from more than one principal meridian and the single baseline associated with that principal meridian.

The portion of the United States to which the rectangular grid system applies is divided into areas such that each area relates to a single principal meridian. As an example, Figure 2–2 shows a group of midwestern states and the specific areas associated with each meridian. These areas do not necessarily follow state lines. There are two principal meridians actually in Illinois, the third and fourth principal meridians; however, an eastern piece of Illinois is related to the second principal meridian, which is located in Indiana. Each piece of land in Illinois is associated with one of these three meridians. These principal meridians are numbered, where others have names, such as the Tallahassee Meridian or Michigan Meridian (shown in Figures 2–1 and 2–2).

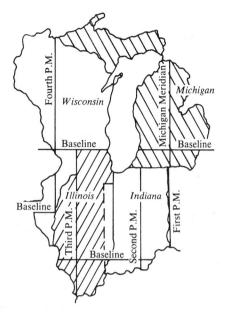

Figure 2–2
Some principal meridians and associated base lines

Township

The rectangular grid system subdivides land into smaller and smaller squares as necessary to describe precise locations of real property. The basic unit is the township, which is a square six miles on each side. Starting at the baseline in Figure 2–3, township lines run parallel to the baseline at each six-mile interval both north and south of the baseline. Those townships in the first tier are identified as T1N, or "township-one-north." The second tier is T2N, and so on. This system extends as far as necessary to cover the area related to the principal meridian and baseline. Townships numbered T30N or T40N are not unusual, since there is no limit on the numbers. Every fourth *township line* is also called a *parallel* or *standard parallel* or is sometimes called a *correction line.*

Range lines run every six miles east and west of the principal meridian to form the east and west boundaries of the township. Every fourth *range line* is called a *guide meridian* or just a *meridian.* Guide meridians run true north, but they are not exactly parallel to each other since they meet at the poles. This results in the need for a correction as shown in Figure 2–3a. The term *check* or *quadrangle* is used to describe a block of sixteen townships bounded by a parallel and a meridian, but it is seldom used in a legal description.

A particular township is designated, for example, as T9N, meaning the ninth tier of townships above the baseline, and as R3E to designate the third tier of townships east of the principal meridian (Figure 2–3).

Figure 2–3a

Detail of intersection of parallel and guide meridian

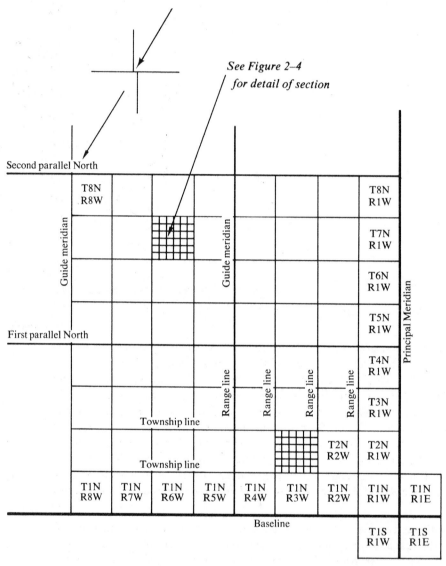

Figure 2–3

A grid of four checks (or quadrangles).

Each check is 24 miles by 24 miles and contains 16 townships.

Section

The next smaller unit in the rectangular system is the **section,** which is one mile square or one square mile. Two of the townships in Figure 2–3 are divided into sections, and Figure 2–4 shows the numbering of sections within

6	5	4	3	2	1
7	8	9	10	11	12
18	17	16 s	15	14	13
19	20	21	22	23	24
30	29	28	27	26	25
31	32	33	34	35	36

Figure 2–4

A township of 36 square miles contains 36 sections each one mile square

a township, beginning with one at the upper right corner and sweeping left and right back and forth towards the bottom. Section 16 in any township was designated as a *school section* in the original survey to assure adequate land for schools within each township.

To locate smaller tracts of land within a section adequately, the section is subdivided into halves, quarters, or other fractions until a small enough part is defined to identify the parcel of land involved clearly. Figure 2–5 shows examples of portions of sections and the identifying description. A parcel of land might be defined as the NW ¼ of the SE ¼ of the SW ¼ of Section 10. In

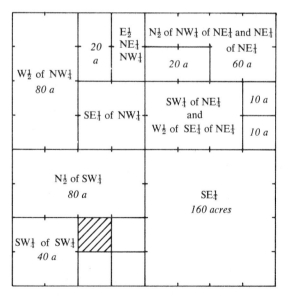

Figure 2–5

The section divided into various size parcels of land.
The section contains 640 acres.

relating a verbal description to the corresponding diagram, it is easier to start with the last item (i.e., SW ¼) and work backwards. This approach breaks the section into smaller and smaller parts.

Try to locate NW ¼ of SE ¼ of SW ¼ in Figure 2–5. Working backwards, the SW ¼ is the lower left quarter of Figure 2–5. This verbal description then defines the cross-hatched area. A whole section is 640 acres, so the SW ¼ would be 160 acres. The SE ¼ of that would be forty acres, and the cross-hatched area would then be ten acres. Notice that the odd sized pieces can be described by using *and* to replace *of* in the description, as illustrated by N ½ of NW ¼ of NE ¼ and NE ¼ of NE ¼, giving the sixty-acre tract in the upper right corner. The "and" indicates there are two pieces making up the total parcel.

The concepts around which the rectangular (or governmental) survey system is laid out permit their use in describing a piece of property very clearly. A complete legal description for a piece of land could then be the NW ¼ of the SE ¼ of the SW ¼ of Section 10 in T9N R3E of the third principal meridian.

Land Measures

The following land measures are important in the use of the rectangular system and other legal description methods:

      1 mile = 5,280 feet = 1.61 kilometers
      1 acre = 43,560 square feet = 160 square rods = 4,050 square meters
      1 rod = 16½ feet = 5.03 meters
      1 section = 1 square mile = 640 acres = 259 hectares
      1 circle = 360 degrees (360°)
      1 degree = 60 minutes (60′)
      1 minute = 60 seconds (60″)
      1 hectare = 100 ares = 10,000 square meters
      1 yard = 3 feet = 0.91 meters

Corrections

Theoretically, each township is exactly six miles square and contains thirty-six square miles. Due to the shape of the earth, however, meridians eventually converge at the poles, so that in the northern hemisphere the north side of a township will be about fifty feet shorter than the south side. The rectangular survey system tries to compensate by establishing every fourth township line as a correction line, while leaving intervening townships a full six miles wide at top and bottom.

The detail would then appear as in Figure 2–3a, where a guide meridian is drawn by starting 24 miles from the principal meridian and drawing a line parallel to the principal meridian. Thus the square of sixteen townships is slightly narrower at the north than at the south. In practice, all townships are made square except those with their left side along a guide meridian or their north boundary along a parallel. In Figure 2–3, all townships with a R4W, R8W, T4N, or T8N would have a correction and would not be absolutely square. Inaccuracies in survey, however, can also result in a township being unintentionally different from the exact six mile by six mile size. Since many townships contain less than the thirty-six square miles, rules have been established for making the adjustments. The rules provide that any shortage is taken from sections on the north and west boundary of a township, so that all other sections are surveyed to exactly one mile square.

The physical layout of the land may also cause sections not to be complete squares. Part of a section being under a lake could cause this situation. Other irregular shaped sections occur where gaps were left in the original survey, which was carried out by survey teams. Gaps often occurred at junctions of areas surveyed by different teams. When the original government survey was completed, the survey results were recorded in U.S. district land offices. This recorded survey is the basis for describing land in that area.

Government Lots

In the original survey, lakes, streams, or other land features were sometimes encountered that created fractional pieces of land less than a quarter section in size. These pieces were designated in the original survey as *government lots.* These government lots were identified by number, and the lot number given to a piece of land in the original survey is the legal description for that piece for land.

A typical use of government lot numbers is illustrated in Figure 2–6, where

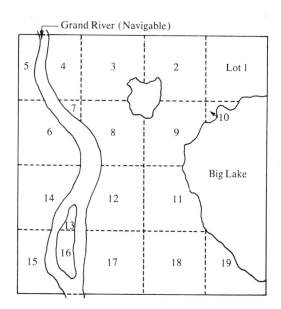

Figure 2–6
Designation of government lots

the dotted lines represent one sixteenth of a section. A piece of land might then be completely described as Government Lot 4 in Section 22, T3N R4W of the fourth principal meridian.

METES AND BOUNDS

The oldest method of describing land is by "metes and bounds." The method of metes and bounds can be likened to a walk around the edges of the property. *Metes* refers to distance measures using feet, inches, rods, meters, or other measure. *Bounds* refers to directions or landmarks used to locate the boundaries of the property. Bounds can refer to natural monuments such as trees or rocks, or to artificial monuments such as stakes, walls, or posts, or to boundaries such as roads or streams on which the method may rely. The system can also use distances and directions only as computed from a survey.

In the states equivalent to the original thirteen colonies and a few others, the method of metes and bounds is very significant since the states were not surveyed in the rectangular system. Maine, New Hampshire, Vermont, Massachusetts, Connecticut, Rhode Island, New York, New Jersey, Pennsylvania, Virginia, West Virginia, Delaware, Maryland, Kentucky, Tennessee, North Carolina, South Carolina, Georgia, Texas, and parts of Ohio are not covered by the rectangular survey system.

Each "metes and bounds" description must have a starting point or *point of beginning* (*p.o.b.*). This point is usually identified relative to a road, stream, or some natural or artificial monument. Care must be taken in selecting the point of beginning since destruction of the item used can invalidate a property description. Starting at the p.o.b., the description proceeds clockwise around the property. It returns to the p.o.b. to form the enclosed parcel of land. As an example, the following is a metes and bounds description of the property shown in Figure 2–7.

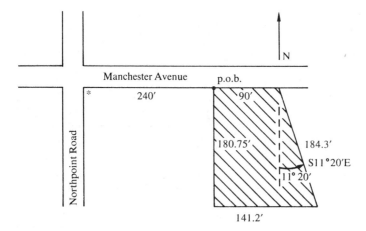

Figure 2–7
Property with metes and bounds description

Commencing at a monument set at the SE point of the intersection of Manchester Avenue and Northpoint Road, proceed 240 ft directly East along Manchester Avenue to the point of beginning (p.o.b.); then 90 ft further directly East along Manchester Avenue; then S11°20′E for 184.3 ft; then directly West 141.2 ft; then 180.75 ft directly North to the point of beginning.

Note that once the p.o.b. is located, the complete parcel can be identified by only distance measurements and directions, which can be readily accomplished by a surveyor with a transit and tape.

Sometimes a metes and bounds description includes reference to natural monuments such as a tree or large rock. It could also refer to artificial monuments such as a concrete post, edge of a concrete road, or corner of a building. In Figure 2–7, assume that the description reads "then S11°20′E for 184.3 ft, more or less, to the center of a concrete fence post." The only difference from the first description is that the concrete post has been introduced as an additional artificial monument. Frequently a long pipe is driven into the ground at the corner of a lot to serve as this monument. It is against the law to remove stakes inserted for property identification purposes. What if a later survey found the distance to be different from that in a property description? Distances and directions in a deed always give way to monuments if there is any discrepancy. The words "more or less" in the description allow for clarification of any apparent discrepancy and, therefore, actually strengthen the description. If the property were in a rural area with no street or other clearly recognizable bounds, it could be important to carry measures to the hundredths of a foot and express direction in degrees, minutes, and seconds. For a parcel of land, the distance along the road or along a lake is often used to determine value or to assess taxes. In Figure 2–7, this *front footage* is ninety feet.

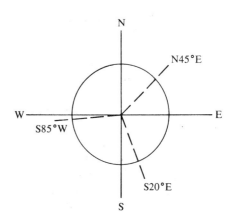

Figure 2–8

Direction measurements used in surveys

Directions or bearings can be measured from magnetic north and south, usually called *magnetic bearings,* or from a meridian, usually called *true bearings.* Figure 2–8 shows magnetic bearings along with some examples of directional bearings. The bearing is the direction in which the surveyor is heading as she leaves a corner while walking around the property clockwise. Figure 2–8 shows that a bearing can deviate not more than ninety degrees from either north or south. A direction such as N95°E would more properly be expressed as S85°E.

SUBDIVISION AND LOTS

The construction of new homes in an urban area usually involves the breaking up of a tract of land into lots as sites for building houses. Most municipalities require a careful survey of the subdivision tract showing blocks, lots, and streets, and each lot is assigned a lot number. Most local governments apply stringent regulations over the subdivision of land both for residential and industrial development. Prior to proceeding with any work, the developer must have the land surveyed and laid out in a *plat map,* showing lots, their exact sizes, streets, utility easements, and any areas dedicated to park area. Frequently, portions of the subdivision are set aside for parks or shopping centers. The process of setting aside a parcel of land for public use is called *dedication.* If Figure 2–7 were expanded to include other lots, it would look much like a plat map. The plat map is part of the material submitted to the government department with responsibility to review and approve the plan. Sometimes the review may involve a public hearing. When approved, the survey is recorded in the office of the Recorder of Deeds; the plat map is maintained in the county Deed Registry Office. In any later conveyance of these lots from the developer to a buyer, or from the original purchaser to a new buyer, the lot number and plat map reference form a legal description.

SECONDARY METHODS USED IN LEGAL DESCRIPTIONS

The three primary methods used in legal descriptions are rectangular survey, metes and bounds, and subdivision and lots. Other methods are monuments, tracts, and street address. Most legal descriptions use more than one of these methods. The objective is to use as much description as necessary to establish an unquestionable identity for the land. There are many natural and artificial features of land that affect the ease or difficulty of property description and identification. The impact of natural features such as lakes and streams or of artificial features such as fences become important in legal descriptions. They can serve as easily observable boundaries; however, a body of water may interfere with the ability to survey accurately, or the route of a stream or shoreline may change. A statement of quantity (i.e., 5.4 acres) is usually considered supplementary information. If inconsistencies occur in a legal description, the usual order of precedence is (a) natural monuments or landmarks, (b) artificial monuments, (c) adjacent boundaries or adjoining tracts, (d) courses (directions) and distances, and (e) quantity.

Monuments

Monuments provide a means of land description, usually used in conjunction with metes and bounds, rectangular survey, or subdivision; however in a few situations, they might be used alone. *Monuments* are points on the surface of the earth that serve as relatively permanent reference points from which to identify land. They can be either tangible or intangible. Tangible monuments such as trees, rocks, streams, posts, and streets, can be seen visibly. An example of an intangible monument would be the corner of a section in the rectangular survey system. It can be accurately located by survey, but is not visibly identifiable unless a stake has been placed there.

In a remote area where land is relatively cheap, a parcel of property might be described solely by monuments. A forested plot used for hunting or camping would be an example. In these situations, possible small errors in the property line would not be of such significance to justify the expense of a survey. The familiarity of the land to both buyer and seller could be sufficient to assure that each has the same tract in mind, and actual acreage or distances are of less importance. A metes and bounds description for the property illustrated in Figure 2–9, using recognizable features only, would read in this way:

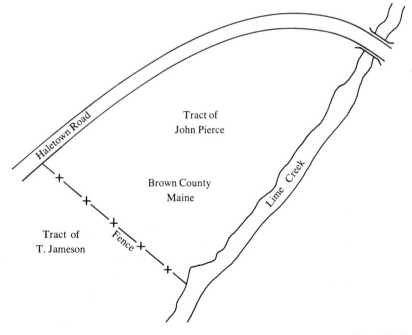

Figure 2–9
Property described by features of the land

Commencing at the bridge where Haletown Road crosses Lime Creek, proceed in a general southwest direction along Lime Creek about one-half mile to the fence separating the seller's property from the property of Jameson. Then follow this fence to where it intersects Haletown Road, and along Haletown Road to the point of beginning.

Street and Number

The property identification familiar to almost everyone is the street address. Over a period of years, however, street names sometimes change and new subdivisions or streets are constructed. The construction of houses or apartments on previously vacant lots, or the destruction of older buildings and new construction may result in the renumbering of property. Sometimes streets are permanently closed and the signs removed. These and other factors make the use of street name and house number an unreliable means for permanent and unquestionable identification of real estate. In a deed or contract, however, a legal description will usually be followed by a phrase such as this:

known as 815 Manchester Road, Jonesville, Illinois

This statement assures the parties of the transaction that both have the same property in mind.

Tracts

Well-known names of tracts of land have been held to be sufficient legal description in some cases. A deed might convey "The Mt. Pleasant Estate" and be held a valid conveyance. A parcel of property might also be described by reference to neighboring tracts, sometimes showing the name of the owner of the adjacent tract.

In addition to one or more of the formal methods of description, deeds sometimes contain a so-called *"being" clause.* For example, the clause might state,

"Being the same property as conveyed to the grantor by Jack and Martha Jones by deed dated June 24, 1971."

Roads and Fences

When land is conveyed from a seller (grantor) to a buyer (grantee) using reference to a road, the grantee secures title to the middle of the road, providing of course that the grantor held such title. This established precedent is valid unless the contract clearly states otherwise. The public right prevails, however, for use of the road. If a public road is abandoned at some time, the property owner again assumes ownership of land to the center of the old road.

Fences can be built either on a property line or entirely on either of the adjacent properties. If the fence is completely on one property, over a number of years the fence often becomes recognized by both parties as the boundary. In this case, the fence can become the actual legal boundary whether or not it is on the original property line, if it is used as a boundary for a set number of years.

Streams and Lakes

Streams frequently form the natural boundary for real property. Where these bodies of water form the property boundary, the grantee takes title to property to the center of nonnavigable streams. For *navigable* waterways, the high water mark is the common law boundary; however, in some states the low water mark is the boundary by statute. A natural question is the definition of a navigable stream, since a raft can be used on almost any depth water. Navigable streams are those identified as navigable on a federal survey map. The land between the high and low water marks of navigable streams or rivers is known as *flat land,* and the rights of the property owner are subservient to the public use of the river or stream for navigation purposes.

Owners of land edging on navigable lakes are considered to own to the high or low water mark (depending on the state law) of the lake, and the submerged portion of the navigable body of the water is considered to be held in title by the state.

The owner of a piece of property has the right of uninterrupted flow of that stream as well as the right to nonpollution of the water. Obviously, the value of a piece of land can depend upon the availability of usable water for humans, livestock, or irrigation. Artificial changes in the flow of natural bodies of water are not permitted if they injure the rights of another owner. Gradual changes in the bed of a nonnavigable stream due to deposit of soil (*accretion*) will change a boundary, but a sudden change (such as that following a torrential rain) does not affect the boundary if the original course of the stream can be located and the stream is restored to its previous course.

Water identified as a *meandered* lake or stream (as in Figure 2–6) means that the land owner of the adjacent pieces of land pays taxes on the land only. Meandered water is identified on an original government survey map maintained in the county courthouse.

STATE PLANE COORDINATE SYSTEM

Since the methods described so far depend heavily on physical landmarks, those methods are sometimes supplemented by reference to points in the state plane coordinate system. Points have been specified in each state that were located in latitude and longitude in a project initiated by the U.S. Coast and Geodetic Survey in 1933. Although not readily understood by lay persons, the coordinates are often used, particularly in laying out highways and utility lines.

APPURTENANCES

Certain rights or easements pass from the grantor to the grantee along with the real property. These are called *appurtenances.* A right of way through property is a common type of easement. Following the legal description in any deed, the following clause will usually appear:

"together with the appurtenances and all the estate and rights of the party of the first part in and to said premises."

OTHER PHYSICAL ELEMENTS

The ancient doctrine of common law held that ownership of land extends from the depths of the earth to the reaches of heavens. Ownership of land includes rights not only on the surface of the earth, but also to an indefinite distance upwards and downwards, subject of course to limitations by law, such as the rights of air travel.

Unless specified otherwise in the deed, an owner of land obtains rights to the minerals below the surface of the land and usage of the space above the surface of land.

Minerals

Solid minerals such as coal and metal ore are real property and remain as such until removed from their natural position in the earth. Once mined, however, the minerals become personal property. When real property is transferred, the rights to minerals beneath the ground go with the land, unless specified otherwise; a pile of coal, however, would not go with the land unless specified otherwise. A property owner could, however, retain the surface land and sell the mineral rights alone; or she could sell the surface land to one party and separately sell the mineral rights to a different buyer. In other cases, an owner might sell the surface land and withhold the mineral rights for himself.

When the mineral rights to a property are sold, however, they would be useless without a means of extraction. If the document of conveyance is silent as to the right of access, the person receiving the mineral rights acquires the right of extraction by implication. It is important for the document to describe the surface rights, since the manner of entrance to the subsurface can affect the appearance and value of the land. In an alternative kind of agreement, a party may be sold the *right to extract* minerals for a set period of time, such as two years. If the right of surface entry were expressly denied in the deed, the person owning the mineral rights would need access from an adjacent property. In any case, only a limited amount of minerals can be extracted without injury to the surface or adjacent property support. In most states, sand, gravel, and limestone are not considered to be minerals.

Oil and gas are different from solid minerals since a well drilled on one piece of property can extract oil or gas from a surrounding area. Many states, therefore, say that a property owner has the *right to drill* on his or her land for oil or gas. This right passes with the conveyance of real property and can be sold separately, just as mineral rights. This right to drill can also be leased to another party. A number of the petroleum producing states apply the ownership in place theory to gas and oil; however they also apply the *rule of capture,* which states that a landowner takes ownership to gas and oil from wells on her or his land even though part of it could have migrated from adjoining land.

AIRSPACE

In common law it was understood that the landowner owned the airspace above her or his land to the heavens. Following a series of court challenges to this concept, the U.S. Supreme Court in 1946 decided that the landowner owns as much space above the ground as can be occupied or used. It is not necessary that the space be occupied in a physical sense, so a person does not own a fixed distance into the air. Federal and state law have declared sovereignty over the navigable airspace. Many court cases still arise involving litigation related to take-off and landing in places where aircraft fly at low altitude, causing noise that can disturb the landowner. Sometimes these rights are purchased by the airport authority.

A landowner may sell or lease the airspace over his or her land. The Prudential tower in Boston was built over the Massachusetts Turnpike, and many buildings have been constructed in the airspace over railroad tracks in Chicago and New York. In the condominium form of ownership, the airspace is theoretically subdivided into blocks that are owned by the individual condominium owners.

DATUM

Air rights and condominium interests create the need for a method to identify property clearly in terms of its height. Systems for measuring property elevation have been in effect for over a hundred years. The mean sea level at New York harbor is defined as U.S.G.S. (United States Geological Survey) *datum* and serves as a base point from which to determine elevations. Most cities also have their own official "datum" so that the elevation of any local point can be readily measured and specified. In a larger city, however, it is not practical to start a survey from the official datum; therefore, benchmarks are established at many points throughout a city. Each benchmark has its recognized official elevation with respect to the official datum. A surveyor can begin at any benchmark to perform a property survey where elevation needs to be measured.

There are also many U.S.G.S. benchmarks throughout the United States, so that elevations can be established by a surveyor with respect to datum at New York harbor. Condominium property laws enacted by most states rely upon datum for the determination of elevation of floor and ceiling surfaces. These are important boundaries between condominium properties, since they define the boundaries of ownership.

WATER RIGHTS

Water is considered by common law to be part of real property, whether above or below the surface. Underground waters, except those flowing in underground streams, are called *percolating waters.* Different states specify either ownership of underground water or the right to use subsurface or ground waters. In some ways, these rights to use water below the surface are similar to the rights to extract oil or gas. In some localities, restrictions have been placed on use of water to that which is "reasonable and necessary." These restrictions are brought about by scarcity of water or the need to avoid pollution. The right to use underground water is sometimes referred to as an *overlying right,* which gives the right to extract and use these waters for the benefit of land owners.

The owner of land adjacent to a stream, lake, or ocean acquires certain rights and obligations. If the body of water is in movement (such as a stream or river), the rights are called *riparian rights* and the owner is referred to as a *riparian owner.* The term *littoral rights* is used where the property is adjacent to a lake, pond, or ocean where the water is not flowing, and the owner is called a *littoral owner.* These rights include swimming, boating, fishing, and the right to take water from the body. The owner of property that is not riparian can acquire rights to use water from a source that is neither riparian nor underlying her or his own land. If a person uses water from a source continuously for a period of time set by statute without permission from the owner, *prescriptive rights* to the water can be legally acquired. The doctrine of *correlative rights* in some states provides that during periods when water is short and insufficient to meet the demands of all regular users, each user can use only a reasonable share.

In some of the western states where water is scarce, the doctrine of *prior appropriation* applies. In order to secure rights to use water, a person applies for a permit. As long as there is plenty of water in the stream or river, all persons with permits can use water from it. When the supply of water becomes insufficient, such as in a drought period, the persons with the permits issued earlier would have priority in using the water. When the water right becomes perfected, it becomes attached to the land of the permit holder.

A property owner has the right to collect and use or to protect his or her property against surface waters such as those caused by storms or the flooding of a stream. *Surface water* is defined as water that does not flow in a well-defined channel and is not confined to a well-defined basin. Surface waters are governed by two rules: (a) the ***common enemy*** rule applies in most states and means that surface water can be warded off by a landowner as long as it is not done maliciously or through negligence; (b) the ***natural flow rule*** says that water should be allowed to flow in its natural path, and a landowner can be liable for damages caused by her or his altering of the natural conditions. Many recent decisions apply the ***reasonable conduct rule*** stating that a landowner cannot be held liable if the change resulted from reasonable use of the land.

SUMMARY

Land has certain physical characteristics that make it different from other property. These are immobility, nonhomogeneity, and indestructibility. It also has the economic characteristics of scarcity, fixity, and situs.

Legal descriptions are important in the preparation of contracts and deeds when conveying real property from one party to another. The three primary types of legal description are rectangular survey, metes and bounds, and subdivision and lot (plat map). The rectangular survey system is used in all states except the original colonies and Texas.

The ownership of land includes not only the surface of the land itself, but also rights to minerals beneath the ground, air rights above the ground, and rights to surface and underground water. These rights ordinarily go along with the land, but they can be sold or leased separately from the land surface area.

TERMS AND CONCEPTS

You can check your understanding of these terms against the glossary in Appendix A or by review of this chapter.

Accretion	Metes
Appurtenances	Monuments
Baseline	Navigable
Being clause	Overlying right
Bounds	Parallel
Check	Plat map
Correction line	Point of beginning (p.o.b.)
Datum	Quadrangle
Dedication	Reasonable conduct rule
Erosion	Rectangular survey
Fixity	Right to extract
Flat land	Riparian rights
Front footage	Rule of capture
Government lots	School section
Guide meridian	Section
Littoral owner	Situs
Meandered	Subdivision and lot
Meridian	Township

What are the differences or relationships, if any, between the following? Check your responses from the chapter text or from the glossary.

Artificial monument and Natural monument

Common enemy rule and Natural flow rule

Correlative rights and Prior appropriation

Magnetic bearings and True bearings

Mineral rights and Oil rights

Mineral rights and Right to extract minerals

Parallel and Baseline

Prime meridian and Guide meridian

Principal meridian and Prime meridian

Range line and Township line

Real estate and Real property

Right to extract and Right to drill

Riparian rights and Littoral rights

Riparian rights and Water rights in general

Surface water and Percolating water

PROBLEMS

2–1. List the physical and economic characteristics of land. Why are they separated into two groups of characteristics?

2–2. What limitations are placed on a person's rights to the airspace over her or his land?

2–3. On the grid of Figure 2–3, locate the following townships:

    (a)   T3N–R3W

    (b)   T5N–R1E

    (c)   T1S–R7W

    (d)   Township 5 north–Range 5 west

    (e)   Section 14 T2N–R3W

    (f)   Section 23 T7N–R6W

    (g)   The school section of T2N–R3W.

2–4. Draw a sketch similar to Figure 2–5. Then draw in and identify the following parcels of land. Determine the acreage of each:

    (a)   NW¼ of NW¼

    (b)   N½ of NE¼ of NE¼

    (c)   S½ of SW¼ of SE¼

    (d)   N½ and SW¼ of SW¼

2–5. Describe each of the following parcels of land by the rectangular system and determine the acreage:

2–6. Sketch the property in accordance with the following metes and bounds description:

> Commencing at a monument at the corner of Arce Street and Barnes Avenue, proceed 600 ft North along Arce Street to the point of beginning where a stake is placed; then 186 ft further along Arce Street; then 214 ft 7 in. more or less N87°6″W to a concrete fence post; then 190 ft S8°14″W; then 219 ft more or less to the point of beginning.

2–7. Sketch a check bounded on the south by a baseline and on the west by a principal meridian. Indicate the following:

   (a) T3N–R3E
   (b) T1N–R4E
   (c) T5N–R4E

2–8. Sketch a township and identify sections 8, 19, and 32.

2–9. A parcel of land along the seashore is 80 ft on the shoreline by 260 ft deep. Land sells for $150 per front foot. What is the price of the property?

2–10. Land sells for $1,200 per acre. What is the price of the N½ of the NE¼ of the SW¼?

2–11. Rental of warehouse space was specified as $1.20 per sq ft per yr. What would be the monthly rental for a space 8 ft by 12 ft?

2–12. Storage space rents for $0.20 per cu ft per yr. What is the yearly rental for a space 10 ft by 20 ft by 8 ft high?

2–13. Due to drought, a stream provides only sufficient needs for half of the regular users. What are the differences in rights of riparian owners and owners of prior appropriation?

2–14. Discuss whether you think that a town could take air space by eminent domain.

2–15. Assume that you are leasing mineral rights to your property. What provisions should you place in the agreement?

2–16. During a heavy rainstorm, a stream changed its course and left about 100 sq ft of your former land on the opposite side of the stream. What should you do?

SUPPLEMENTARY READINGS

Bergfield, Philip B. *Real Estate Law*. New York: McGraw-Hill, 1979. Chapters 2 and 3.

Burby, William E. *Real Property*. St. Paul, Minn.: West, 1965. Chapter 6.

Davis, Raymond E., and Foote, Francis S. *Surveying—Theory and Practice*. New York: McGraw-Hill, 1953. Chapters 22 and 23.

Ellis, John T. *Guide to Real Estate License Examinations*. Englewood Cliffs, N.J.: Prentice-Hall, 1974. Chapter 8.

Galaty, Fillmore W.; Allway, Wellington J.; and Kyle, Robert C. *Modern Real Estate Practice*. Chicago: Real Estate Education Corporation, 1978. Chapters 2 and 9.

Harwood, Bruce. *Real Estate Principles*. Reston, Va.: Reston Publishing Company, 1977. Chapter 2.

Herubin, Charles A. *Principles of Surveying*. Reston, Va.: Reston Publishing Company, 1974.

Henszey, Benjamin N., and Friedman, Ronald M. *Real Estate Law.* New York: Warren, Gorham and Lamont, 1979. Chapter 3.

Kratovil, Robert, and Werner, Raymond J. *Real Estate Law,* 7th ed. Englewood Cliffs, N.J.: Prentice-Hall, 1979. Chapter 5.

Murray, William G. *Farm Appraisal and Valuation.* Ames, Ia.: Iowa State University Press, 1967. Chapter 4.

U.S. Department of the Interior. "Public Land Statistics, 1970." Washington, D.C.: Bureau of Land Management, 1970.

Rights and Interests In Real Estate

REAL ESTATE DEFINED

The term *real estate* in its broader and perhaps most accurate definition includes land, every interest or estate in land, and the permanent improvements thereon. As mentioned earlier, in the real estate business the terms *real property* and *real estate* are frequently used synonymously. However, these terms are also used to mean either the land itself or an interest or estate in the land. Either meaning is technically correct, in that *real estate* is composed of a physical element as well as an ownership element. The physical element is the land and things of a permanent nature contained therein or affixed thereto. The ownership element refers to the nature, duration, quantity, and quality of rights that one or more persons may possess in land.

NATURE OF LAND

As we have seen, *land* includes the earth, the area above the surface, the area beneath the surface, and anything permanently added thereto or formed therein by nature or human beings.

The physical extent of land includes all things that are of a permanent nature, whether they be found on or affixed to the land or embedded beneath its surface. The term, therefore, includes growing things such as trees, natural ponds, and lakes found upon the earth's surface, and minerals and other matter found within the earth.

Air Rights

Before airplanes, spaceships, and orbiting satellites, it was almost universally accepted that not only did the boundaries of a parcel of land extend downward to the center of the earth, but also they extended upward to infinity. Now the space above the land may be entered for legitimate travel; however, the owner is entitled to recover for any actual damages suffered. Rights to the space over the surface of the land are commonly referred to as *air rights*. As the population density in our urban areas increases, air rights become even more important and valuable. In several large cities, the railroads have sold their air rights, together with small physical portions of their land, to buyers who have subsequently constructed multiple story commercial and office buildings in the air space above the railroad tracks. The buildings are attached to and rest upon foundations embedded in small sections of land along the railroad tracks.

Fixtures

Land also includes permanent *improvements* made by people. Objects of personal property may be so attached to or used with land that they are legally considered part of the land. The personal property is said to become a *fixture.* Once personal property becomes a fixture, it becomes the property of the owner of the land to which it is attached.

Whether an article of personal property can be considered a fixture is governed by the intention of the person who attaches or uses the personal property with the land. This intention is rarely expressed. Consequently, the courts must look to all the facts and circumstances surrounding the attachment or usage to determine whether or not it was intended to become a fixture.

Where parties expressly agree as to whether or not an item of personal property is to be a fixture, the courts are generally willing to enforce their expressed intention. For example, a landlord and tenant agree that the tenant may build an automobile garage on the land and remove it prior to the expiration of the lease. The garage, even though attached to the land, is considered personal property and may be removed by the tenant. A well-established exception to this rule is when the article of personal property is permanently added into a building and its removal would substantially destroy the structure or the fixture itself (e.g., plumbing, electrical wiring, beams, or bricks). Regardless of the expressed agreement of the parties, such articles of personal property are fixtures.

If the parties have not expressly indicated their intention, the courts use the following guidelines:

1. *The method by which the personal property is attached to the land.* Attachment may be by gravity, by physical connection, or by incorporation. The personal property becomes a fixture if it is so attached to the land or building that it cannot be removed without materially

damaging the land or building or destroying the personal property itself (e.g., masonry blocks in a wall, a heating system consisting of pipes and coils, structural steel or wood girders, railroad tracks, or a house trailer bolted on a concrete foundation).

2. *How the personal property relates to the existing use of the land.* Personal property designed for and used in the "normal use" of a specific parcel of land may be classified as a fixture. As a general rule, personal property that is reasonably necessary to the use of the land or building thereon need not be physically attached to the land or buildings to be classified as a fixture. As an example, window screens, storm windows and doors, industrial machinery placed upon the land by its owner, and hog sheds located on a hog farm are fixtures.

3. *The nature of the annexor's interest in the land.* In some cases, the legal interest of the annexor of personal property will be considered by a court in determining his or her intention. An owner of land who attaches personal property that relates to the existing use of the land clearly intends to install a fixture. However, personal property may be attached to land by persons having no legal interest in the land whatsoever, such as an intentional or mistaken trespasser or a person having only a temporary legal interest, such as a lessee or a licensee.

4. *Wrongful or mistaken annexation.* As a general rule, the owner of the land is entitled to all fixtures attached to his land by a trespasser, whether intentionally or by mistake. Some courts offer relief to the mistaken improver either in the form of a lien to the extent of the value of the improvement or permission to remove the fixture on the condition that he reimburse the owner for any damage caused by the removal.

Trade Fixtures

Personal property that is attached to leased land or buildings by a lessee for use in his or her trade or business is generally held to be a *trade fixture.* The trade fixture principle has been interpreted to apply to fixtures for trade, business, agriculture, or domestic use. Examples include: (a) *trade and business* (bowling alleys, overhead crane, restaurant equipment); (b) *agriculture* (tool sheds and chicken houses); (c) *domestic* (bookshelves, carpeting, and mirrors). A lessee is entitled to remove trade fixtures at any time prior to the expiration of the lease, unless the fixture has become an integral part of the land or building and its removal would materially damage the land, building, or the fixture itself. If they are not removed before the lease expires, the property becomes a fixture and legally belongs to the owner of the land or building to which it was attached.

Regardless of the method of *annexation,* if *expressly* agreed upon by the lessor and lessee, the lessee has the right to remove fixtures. The lessee's obligation is to reimburse the owner of the land for any physical damage caused by the removal.

CONCEPT OF PRIVATE OWNERSHIP

Ownership is a creature of law. It cannot exist unless recognized and enforced by a sovereign power. When a sovereign power does recognize and enforce certain rights in property, the person who possesses them is said to be its *owner* and possess *title* to it. *Ownership* is thus defined as the *right* to control, possess, enjoy, and dispose of property in such manner as is not contrary to law. These rights are further broken down into the right to use, to sell, to make a gift of, to destroy, to improve, to profit from, to remove objects from, and to pass title by a will upon the owner's death. It includes rights over contiguous and surrounding areas affecting the use of land, such as the right to lateral support of soil, to light and air, to ingress to and egress from the property, and to be free of nuisances on adjoining properties. One or more persons may possess some or all rights in land recognized by law. When two or more persons own rights in land, they are said to be **concurrent owners.**

Rights to land are not absolute and unrestricted. They are limited by rights possessed by other persons and by powers of government, as shown in Figure 3–1. An owner of land may not exercise personal rights thereon so as to cause wrongful injury to the person or property of another. In addition, rights are subject to the powers of government, such as (a) **eminent domain** (power to acquire title to private real estate for a public purpose in exchange for just compensation), (b) **police power** (power to regulate the use of land for the public welfare), (c) **power of taxation** (to raise revenue), and (d) **escheat** (the power to take title to land owned by a person who died intestate without heirs).

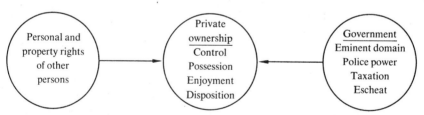

Figure 3–1
Rights to land and restrictions on private ownership

ESTATES AND OTHER INTERESTS IN REAL ESTATE

The law recognizes certain rights in land and refers to them as **estates;** however, not all rights in land constitute estates. Estates are classified according to the quality, quantity, and extent of the rights held by one or more persons. Each estate is identified by the types of rights and privileges a person possesses and may exercise toward his or her land and adjacent land owned by others.

In order for a right that relates to land to be an estate, it must be presently possessory or become possessory in the future (nonpossessory). Possessory and nonpossessory rights may be owned simultaneously by two or more different persons in the same parcel of land. The nonpossessory estate is known as a *future interest.* A future interest does not become possessory until a preceding possessory estate terminates and any existing condition precedents have been fulfilled. Examples of future interests are the vested and contingent remainders discussed later in this chapter. Figure 3–2 identifies the various estates in land.

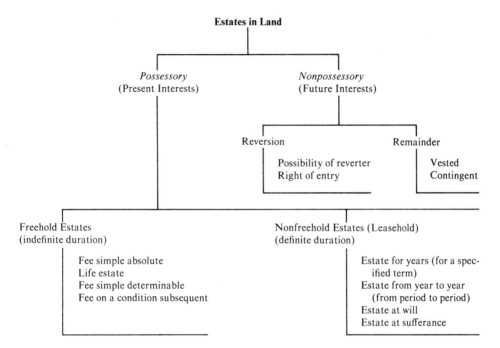

Figure 3–2
Estates in land

Possessory Estates

Possessory estates are classified on the basis of their duration, that is *freehold estates* and *nonfreehold estates* (leasehold estates). Freehold estates exist for an indefinite length of time. Nonfreehold estates (leasehold estates) exist for a determinable length of time. Figure 3–2 identifies the various freehold and nonfreehold estates.

Freehold estates

Fee Simple Absolute   The owner of a *fee simple absolute estate* possesses all of the rights an individual can have in land. It is restricted only by the rights of other individuals and the powers of government. The fee simple absolute estate has the following characteristics:

1. It is freely transferable during the lifetime of the owner, by either gift or sale;

2. It is inheritable either by a will executed by the owner or by intestate succession (by state statute) if the owner dies without a will;
3. It has no time limit on its existence;
4. As qualified above, the owner possesses unrestricted possession, use, and enjoyment of the land.

FEE SIMPLE ABSOLUTE

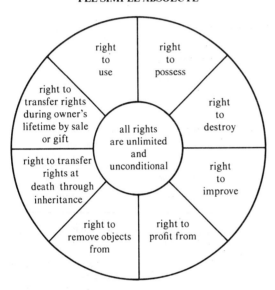

Figure 3–3
Fee simple absolute

Life Estate   The **life tenant** is entitled to possession and use of the land and the income from it. He may mortgage, lease, sell, or give away the estate, but the duration of the estate remains governed by the life of the person or persons originally designated.

The life tenant's possession and use of the land is restricted by his or her duty not to commit waste. **Waste** occurs whenever the life tenant acts or fails to act in relationship to the land, causing the interests of the reversioner or remainderman to be injured. Examples would be failure to pay taxes or mortgage payments or material change of the original use of the property, such as converting it from farming to industrial.

Life estates are created either by a conveyance by an owner of the estate or by operation of law. A life estate created by conveyance is known as a *conventional life estate*. A *legal life estate* is one created by law without the consent of the owner.

Conventional life estates are usually created through the use of deeds, wills, and trusts. Legal life estates are created by state law. **Dower, curtesy,** and **homestead** are examples of legal life estates. These estates do not exist in all states; and where they do exist, the quantity and quality of rights created in the life tenant vary widely from state to state. Curtesy, dower, and homestead laws apply only to land located within the state.

The duration of a life estate is measured by the life or lives of one or more persons. Its duration can be measured by the life of its owner (life tenant), for example, "to A for his life." It can also be measured by the life of a person other than the life tenant, for example, "to A for the life of Z." Where the duration of the life estate is measured by the life of someone other than the life tenant, it is called a life estate *pur autre vie* (for the life of another). An ordinary life estate (whose duration is measured by the life of the life tenant) is not inheritable, and it terminates upon the death of the life tenant. However, a life estate *pur autre vie* does not terminate upon the death of the life tenant, and the life tenant's ownership interest continues until the death of the person by whose life the estate is measured. If the life tenant should die before the person by whose life the estate is measured dies, the ownership interest of the life tenant will pass to the life tenant's heirs. The ownership interest received by the heirs will remain in existence until the death of the person by whose life the interest is measured.

Upon termination of any life estate, the estate either reverts back to its original owner or the owner's heirs (*reversion*), or it is vested in any person (*remainderman*) who is designated to receive it upon termination. Reversionary and remainder interests will be discussed later in this chapter.

Fee Simple Determinable (Qualified Fee) (Base Fee)   A *fee simple determinable* is a fee simple subject to a condition. For example, A, by deed, conveys fee simple to B "so long as" the premises are used for residential purposes only. When the condition no longer holds, ownership *automatically* reverts back (reversion) to the person (reversioner) who created the estate or the heirs in fee simple. The interest retained by a grantor of a fee simple determinable is referred to as a *possibility of reverter.*

Fee Simple on a Condition Subsequent   A fee simple subject to a condition subsequent is a fee simple that may be ended by the person who created the estate or that person's heirs upon the happening of a contingency. For example, A, by deed, conveys a fee simple in a parcel of farmland to B and provides that A retains the right to terminate the estate if it ceases to be used for farming purposes by exercising the *right of entry* (to sue for possession). The feature that distinguishes this estate from the fee simple determinable discussed above is that the *fee simple on a condition subsequent* does not terminate and revert back automatically upon the happening of the stated event. The right of entry must be exercised to terminate the estate and cause its reversion.

Nonfreehold estates (Leasehold estates)

A *lease* is both a contract and a conveyance of an interest in land. It is a transfer by one person named the *lessor* (landlord) of the right of exclusive possession of land for a limited period of time to a second party named the *lessee* (tenant) in consideration of the payment of rent. The lessor retains a reversionary right; that is, the lessor is entitled to a return of the legal interest upon the expiration of the lease.

Leasehold estates are classified and identified according to their duration. The four common leasehold estates are:

1. Estate for years (for a specified term);
2. Estate from year to year (from period to period);
3. Estate at will;
4. Estate at sufferance.

A detailed discussion of leases is provided in Chapter 6.

Nonpossessory Estates (Future Interests)

A *future interest* is a presently existing estate, but it does not entitle its owner to immediate use and possession of land in which the estate is held. Use and possession are postponed until the termination of a preceding estate or the occurrence of a condition, or both. The estate can take the form of a reversion or a remainder.

Reversion

Reversion is an estate remaining with a person or that person's heirs after the conveyance of a lesser estate to another. A *lesser estate* is conveyed whenever a person conveys one or more but not all rights in the property. The interest or estate remaining with the grantor is a *reversion*. The following estates are accompanied by a reversion:

1. A life estate where the estate returns to the grantor after the death of the person by whose life the estate is measured.
2. Leasehold estates.
3. A life estate with a contingent remainder. If the contingency does not occur, the estate will automatically revert back to the grantor or the grantor's heirs upon the death of the life tenant.
4. Fee simple determinable (qualified fee). The reversionary interest created by the conveyance of this estate is called a *possibility of reverter*.
5. Fee simple on a condition subsequent. Upon such a conveyance, the grantor retains a *right of entry,* exercisable only upon the happening of the condition.

As a general rule, reversions are inheritable and freely transferable during the life of the person who owns the reversionary estate. However, some state statutes prohibit the creation of the possibility of reverter and right of entry and also do not allow transfer or inheritance of any of such existing estates.

Remainder

A **remainder** is a presently existing estate in land where the actual use and possession of the land is postponed until the occurrence of an event that may or may not occur. Remainders are classified as being either *vested* or *contingent*.

A *vested remainder* is an estate in land whereby the right to immediate use and possession of land depends *only* upon the termination of a preceding estate (e.g., A deeds a parcel of land to B for life with remainder to C and C's heirs). In this case, C is called the *remainderman.* A vested remainder is an inheritable estate. Therefore, upon the remainderman's death prior to the death of the life tenant, the remainder will pass to the heirs. It is also transferable either by sale or gift, and it may be mortgaged as security for a debt or other obligation.

A *contingent remainder* is an estate in land whereby a person's right to use and possession of the land depends *not only* upon the termination of a preceding estate *but also* upon the happening of some event that may or may not take place. As an example, A deeds a parcel of land to B for life with remainder to C and her heirs, if C retains her maiden name. As a general rule, contingent remainders are transferable either by will, intestate succession, or by a conveyance during the remainderman's lifetime.

Easements

Legal nature of an easement

An *easement* is not an estate in land. It is a nonpossessory *right to use* or enjoy the land owned by another person for a specific purpose and in a specific manner. It does not include the right to possess or remove any part of the land, below or on its surface.

Easements may be *appurtenant* or *in gross.* An easement appurtenant cannot be created without two parcels of land. The parcels of land need not be adjacent. Land that is subjected to use and enjoyment is referred to as the *servient estate.* The *dominant estate* is the land for whose benefit the easement was created. If the easement is created for use in connection with another specific parcel of land, it is said to be an *easement appurtenant.* If a dominant estate does not exist, it is an *easement in gross.* As a general rule, an easement in gross is personal to the person to whom it was granted and, therefore, is not transferable. It terminates upon its owner's death. However, some states have provided that easements in gross are freely transferable. This is especially true if the easement is commercial in nature. However, an easement in gross can always be made freely transferable by agreement of the parties in the contract who originally created the easement. Easements appurtenant are said to "run with the land"; that is, the benefits to the dominant estate and the burdens of the servient estate continue regardless of any change of the ownership of either estate. Both easements appurtenant and easements in gross are irrevocable. The following exemplify easements appurtenant:

1. A common driveway on a boundary line between two lots, each lot owned by a different person;

2. A right of one owner of a tract of land to use water from an adjoining tract for irrigation purposes;

3. A right to cross another person's adjoining tract at a specified place for the purpose of ingress or egress.

The following exemplify easements in gross:

1. Utility easements for electric power lines, water mains, or sewers;

2. Easements for railroads;

3. Right to use a lake owned by another for swimming purposes;

4. Cable television (CATV).

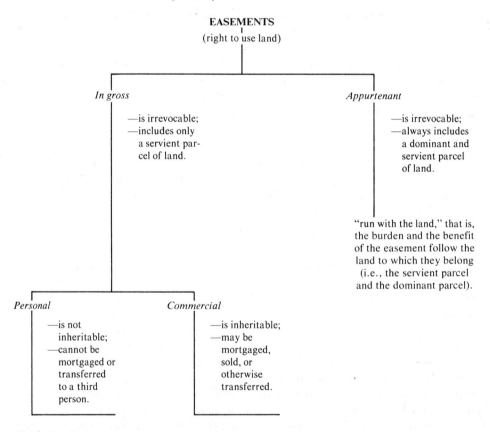

EASEMENTS
(right to use land)

In gross
—is irrevocable;
—includes only a servient parcel of land.

Appurtenant
—is irrevocable;
—always includes a dominant and servient parcel of land.

"run with the land," that is, the burden and the benefit of the easement follow the land to which they belong (i.e., the servient parcel and the dominant parcel).

Personal
—is not inheritable;
—cannot be mortgaged or transferred to a third person.

Commercial
—is inheritable;
—may be mortgaged, sold, or otherwise transferred.

Figure 3–4
Types and characteristics of easements

Creation of easements

An easement is a legal interest in real estate and, therefore, a contract, grant, or reservation creating an easement must be in writing to satisfy the Statute of Frauds. Easements are created in a number of different ways:

1. By agreement;

2. By grant or reservation;

3. By implication;
4. By reference to plat;
5. By prescription;
6. By necessity.

Easement by Agreement Easements may be created *by agreement* wherein the parties make clear their intention to create the interest. A party wall, party driveway, and water rights are possible easements by agreement.

Easement by Grant or Reservation An owner of land may create an easement by executing and delivering a deed wherein title to the land is transferred to another party and either an easement is *granted* in favor of the tract conveyed or an easement is *reserved* for the benefit of the land retained.

Easement by Implication An easement that is created by operation of law rather than the express intention of the parties is called an *easement by implication.* The requisite elements for creation of an easement by implication follow:

1. One person owns two tracts of land;
2. He or she subjects the use of one tract for the benefit of the other tract;
3. The use is apparent and obvious;
4. The use is continuous;
5. The use is necessary; and
6. At some time thereafter, the owner transfers title to one of the tracts of land to another person without mentioning easements.

Some easements by implication are described:

1. Jones owns Lots A and B. Sewage from his house on Lot B drains through an underground pipe running across Lot A. There is a visible catch basin on the surface of Lot A. If Peters buys Lot A, she will own it subject to an implied easement for sewage drainage across her lot.
2. Amos owns two adjacent parcels of land. Both parcels are improved with homes. Amos resides in the home on Lot A and leases Lot B with its improvements to Hendricks. A driveway runs down the boundary line of the adjacent lots and is used for ingress and egress purposes for both lots. Amos subsequently conveys Lot B to James. A party driveway easement was created by implication.

Easement by Reference to Subdivision Plat In this, each person who purchases a lot in a subdivision automatically acquires an easement for use of the streets, alleys, picnic areas, or swimming beach shown on the recorded plat as public areas.

Easement by Prescription An *easement by prescription* (or by adverse use) arises when an unauthorized person uses another's property adversely to the owner's interest, visibly, openly, notoriously, and continuously for a period of time established by state statutes. The time period varies in different states up to a period of twenty years. Some states have passed laws that enable a landowner to prevent the creation of an easement by prescription by posting signs prohibiting use of the land (i.e., no trespassing).

Easement by Necessity   An *easement by necessity* arises when an owner of land conveys a parcel of the land to another under such circumstances that the buyer has no access to the land except through the land of strangers or that of the seller. The buyer is entitled to a reasonable right of way over the seller's land.

Use of the easement

The owner of the easement has the right to use the servient estate only for the purpose for which the easement exists. For example, if X has right of way easement across the land of Y, X has no right to lay water pipes in the servient estate or to use the right of way to benefit a parcel of land other than the dominant estate.

Maintenance and repair of the easement

Unless otherwise agreed, the owner of the servient estate has no duty to make the easement parcel ready for use, to repair it, or to do any other act for the benefit of the easement owner. On the other hand, the easement owner has the right to take any measures necessary to make her or his easement reasonably usable. For example, an owner of an easement for ingress and egress by a railroad would have the right to improve the existing track and track bed, lay down new track, and rebuild bridges. In the case of a shared driveway, however, each party would share equally the obligation to repair and maintain the driveway.

Termination of easements

An easement is terminated under any of the following circumstances:

1. *By the fulfillment of the purpose for which it was created.*   For example, a grant of right of way is made for so long as the dominant estate is used as a stable. Thereafter, the dominant estate was used for the purposes of a laundry and ceased to be used as a stable. The easement terminated. As another example, a right of way easement is granted in order to construct a nuclear power plant. The easement will end at the time the plant is completed.

2. *By written release by the owner of the dominant estate.*

3. *By an intentional abandonment of the easement.*   For example, a manufacturing corporation owned a railroad right of way as a means to transport ore to its processing plant. The corporation removed the rails and ties and tore down its processing plant. The easement was extinguished.

4. *By destruction of the servient estate.*   For example, a party wall is totally destroyed by fire.

5. *By prescription.*   For example, the owner of the servient estate prevents the use of an easement for a statutory period of time. The period of time

is usually the same as that necessary to acquire an easement by prescription.

6. *By merger.* The dominant and servient estates become owned by one person.

A *license* is the permission to use land that is in the possession of someone other than the licensee. It is not an estate in land. It does not entitle the licensee to the exclusive possession or enjoyment of the land. A license differs from an easement in that it can be created orally and be terminated at the will of either party. It is personal in nature and consequently is not transferable or inheritable (e.g., permission to swim in a private lake or to harvest strawberries).

A *profit à prendre* (or profit) is a nonpossessory interest in land that carries with it the right to remove the soil or the produce of soil belonging to another. Examples are the right to take minerals, to dig coal, or to cut timber. It may be created by agreement, grant, or prescription and can be classified as either a profit appurtenant or a profit in gross. If the right to remove may be exercised only for the benefit of a dominant estate, the right is a *profit appurtenant.* Where the right to remove is not restricted for the benefit of a dominant estate, it is a *profit in gross.* A profit appurtenant automatically is attached and belongs to any subsequent owner of the dominant estate, even though it was not mentioned in the conveyance. A profit in gross does not automatically follow ownership of the dominant estate; however, it is freely transferable. Profits are terminated in much the same manner as are easements: by fulfillment of purpose, by release, by abandonment, by merger, by destruction of the servient estate, or by prescription.

CONCURRENT OWNERSHIP OF REAL ESTATE

Rights to a specific parcel of land may be owned by one individual or simultaneously by two or more persons. Each co-owner simultaneously possesses an undivided interest in the entire estate and does not have an unrestricted claim against any specific portion of the physical property itself. The interests of the co-owners need not be identical or equal to each other.

One or more persons may possess *different simultaneous estates* in the same parcel of land. Each person is said to be a co-owner; however, the respective rights of each in the land are not identical. For example, A has a life estate and B and C have a remainder interest in the same parcel of land. As a second example, A has a fee on a condition subsequent and B has a right of entry. They each own a separate and distinct estate.

Frequently, one or more persons possess *identical and simultaneously existing* legal interests in the same freehold or nonfreehold estate. For example, A and B are granted the same interest in a remainder, or C and D receive a life estate in a farm. Persons may possess identical legal interests in the same property even though each person's fractional share may differ.

Concurrent ownership as discussed here is synonymous with cotenancy. The parties who are co-owners are called *cotenants*.

Joint Tenancy

A *joint tenancy* exists whenever two or more persons own an entire estate and also an undivided part thereto. Their ownership consists of the unities of time, title, interest, and possession and carries with it the *right of survivorship*. Upon the death of one joint tenant, the surviving joint tenant or tenants continue as co-owners of the estate in joint tenancy until the last survivor. The last survivor acquires sole ownership in fee simple. Joint tenancy is not an inheritable interest.

At common law a joint tenancy could not be created unless the unities of time, title, interest, and possession were conveyed to the co-owners simultaneously. Therefore, an owner of fee simple could not create a joint tenancy by a conveyance to himself and another person. To avoid the common law rule, owners can utilize a "straw man." The fee simple owner conveys title to a distinterested party under an agreement that he reconvey the estate to the original owner and others as joint tenants. Many states have made this procedure unnecessary by statute which provides that the unities need not be acquired simultaneously. They allow a joint tenancy to be created by a conveyance from the owner of the estate to himself (the owner) and others as joint tenants.

A joint tenancy cannot be created by operation of law. The law will not imply a joint tenancy. When the intent to create a joint tenancy is not clearly expressed, the courts hold that the conveyance created is a *tenancy in common.* A grantor who wishes to create a joint tenancy must make the intention clear by indicating that the co-ownership created carries with it the right of survivorship. For example, "to A and B as joint tenants, not as tenants in common, with the right of survivorship" or "to A and B as joint tenants, with right of survivorship."

A joint tenant may arbitrarily sever his undivided legal interest by conveying or mortgaging the interest. Upon doing so, the conveyed or mortgaged interest becomes an interest held in tenancy in common. Where two or more joint tenants remain after severance, they own the remaining undivided interest in joint tenancy as between each other. For example, A, B, and C own in joint tenancy. A conveys her interest to D. D owns one-third in tenancy in common; B and C own two-thirds in joint tenancy.

Tenancy in Common

A *tenancy in common* exists whenever two or more persons own only an undivided fractional interest in an estate. It is created by a grant or devise to two or more persons where it is clearly indicated that a tenancy in common was intended or where the character of the estate conveyed cannot be established with certainty.

Tenants in common need not own equal undivided interests. Their estates are freely transferable during each tenant's lifetime and are inheritable by will or intestate succession.

Tenancy by the Entirety

A *tenancy by the entirety* is essentially a joint tenancy. However, it differs from a joint tenancy in the following three ways:

1. The tenants by entireties must be husband and wife;
2. Neither tenant by the entirety can sever his or her legal interest without the consent of the other; and
3. The legal interest of either tenant cannot be reached by his or her creditors.

A tenancy by the entirety can only be created when allowed by state law.

Tenancy in Partnership

Under the Uniform Partnership Act, which has been adopted in most states, partners may own partnership real estate in their own names or in the name of the partnership itself. This act creates a special type of ownership called *tenancy in partnership.* It differs from both joint tenancy and tenancy in common as follows:

1. One partner alone cannot sell, assign, or mortgage any legal interest in the property without the consent of the other partners;
2. A partner's personal creditors cannot attach his or her legal interest in the partnership property;
3. A partner's legal interest in partnership property is not subject to dower or homestead and is not inheritable.

It is similar to joint tenancy in that, upon a partner's death, that partner's legal interest goes to the surviving partners; however, it vests in the surviving partners only for partnership purposes.

Community Property

The *community property* concept of ownership exists in conjunction with marital property rights and is followed in Arizona, California, Idaho, Louisiana, Nevada, New Mexico, Texas, and the state of Washington. The underlying theory is that a husband and wife should share equally any property acquired during their marriage and through their joint efforts. Each spouse owns one-half of the community property regardless of in which spouse's name the legal title is held.

The laws in the community property states vary widely. However, each state does recognize two types of property that may be owned by the spouses: "separate property" and "community property." Separate property is solely owned by one spouse. It is owned by the spouse prior to marriage or subsequently acquired by one spouse alone during marriage by inheritance or by *inter vivos* (during the recipient's lifetime) gift. As a general rule, all other property acquired by one spouse during marriage by a joint effort with the other spouse is community property.

Condominium Ownership

Most states have enacted statutes providing for creation and protection of condominium ownership, which has become very popular in the United States.

For a *condominium* to come into existence legally, and before any individual units may be sold, the owner-developer must file both a condominium declaration and a three-dimensional subdivision plat that comply with the state condominium law, as well as any other applicable state law. In a condominium, each owner obtains a fee simple interest in the unit that he exclusively occupies and a tenancy in common interest in all other parts of the land and buildings shared and used in common with other owners. The condominium laws prohibit a unit owner from bringing an action to partition or otherwise dividing the common elements. The property made subject to condominium law may be an apartment or an office building. The areas shared by the owners are referred to as the *common elements.* Common elements include the foundation, roof, basement, stairway, elevators, swimming pools, parks, auto parking areas, and so forth.

The owner of an individual condominium unit possesses the following rights and duties:

Rights:
1. To own the fee simple in the unit concurrently with others,
2. To mortgage the unit,
3. To sell, lease, or make a gift of the unit,
4. To use the common elements,
5. To insure the unit.

.   *Duties:*
1. To pay real estate taxes assessed against the unit,
2. To pay the proportionate share of any assessments for taxes and maintenance attributable to the common elements,
3. To make repairs and improvements to the unit at his or her own expense,
4. To observe the rules and regulations governing the use of the units as well as the common elements.

Not all condominium laws provide for methods of termination of condominiums. Unless the condominium statute or the condominium declaration provides for a method of termination, termination could not occur except by unanimous consent of the owners.

Time-share ownership is a unique method of obtaining the benefits of condominium ownership and at the same time sharing the use of residential units with other owners of the same condominium. This type of ownership is especially desirable in a recreational setting where the purchaser desires a vacation home for only that part of a year during which she plans to occupy the home (e.g., high-rise buildings at an oceanside resort are declared into a condominium). The individual units are then sold to multiple buyers, granting each buyer the right to use the unit during a specified part of each year.

There are three types of time-share ownership.

1. *Tenancy in common (time-span ownership).* The purchasers of each unit are owners as tenants in common. Each owner's undivided legal interest is equal to the fraction of the year that she is to occupy the unit. The exclusive right to occupy the unit during a specified time period each year is acquired by virtue of an occupancy agreement signed by each tenant in common.

2. *Interval ownership.* In this situation, the purchasers receive a deed whereby they simultaneously receive title and the right to occupy. The deed to each owner creates a recurring estate for years (for a term) for the agreed-upon period of each year of the term and a remainder to all owners as tenants in common. The number of years designated as the term of the estate for years is an estimate of the useful life of the building.

3. *Vacation license.* Under a vacation license, the developer retains the fee simple ownership and transfers the right to occupy the units to the time-share purchasers for a specified period of time of each year for a stated number of years.

Cooperatives

In the *cooperative* form of ownership, all of the land and its improvements are owned and developed by a corporation. To finance its operation, the corporation relies on debt and equity capital. The corporation usually finances a portion of its acquisition costs by mortgaging the land and its improvements. It acquires the balance by selling stock to prospective tenants. Upon becoming a shareholder, each person is entitled to receive a long-term lease of an individual unit (apartment or office). The rent to be paid takes the form of an annual assessment by the board of directors of the corporation. The amount assessed each tenant is equal to that tenant's pro rata share of the total cash needed by the corporation to pay its obligations for taxes, mortgages, and operating expenses. Unlike condominium ownership, the tenant's interest in a cooperative is personal property. The cooperative owner may transfer ownership by an assignment of his or her stock, but the owner of a condominium interest must use the formalities of a deed in order to transfer the estate. (See Table 3–1.)

Syndicates

A *syndicate* is an association of a group of persons or entities or both under a contract for the express purpose of dealing in real estate and real estate transactions for profit.

Table 3–1
Characteristics of condominiums and cooperatives

	Condominium	Cooperative
Owners of the real estate	Unit owners	Corporation
Funding of purchase of the real estate	a. Construction mortgage loan b. Conversion of existing apartment house into condominium	a. Sale of stock (equity capital) b. Mortgage loan
Legal status of residents	Owners	Owners of stock in the corporation and lessees of the units
Nature of the legal interest possessed by the owners	Real property	Personal property
Type of ownership	a. Fee simple absolute of each apartment unit b. Tenants in common in the common elements	a. Corporation is owner of the real estate in fee simple absolute b. Tenants own their stock and lease the units
Transfer of ownership interests	Unrestricted right to transfer title by deed	Stock and leases cannot be transferred without consent of the board of directors
Management of the complex	Board of managers	Board of directors
Funding of operational expenses	By assessments	Rent
Enforcement of assessments or rents	Foreclosable lien	Foreclosable lien
Termination of form of ownership	a. By unanimous consent of unit owners b. Destruction of the condominium without sufficient insurance proceeds to rebuild	Dissolution of the corporation

Land Trusts

The land trust was developed in Illinois. In recent years, Virginia, North Dakota, Indiana, and Florida have authorized its use. A *land trust* by statute (a statutory trust) is that type of trust where, by deed, a trustee receives complete record title to real estate restricted by a concurrent agreement whereby the beneficiary retains full management and control (power of direction) over the real estate. The interest of the beneficiary is personal property. The beneficiary has the right of possession, the right of income, and the right to proceeds from a sale of the trust property. The trustee's duty is to execute deeds and mortgages and to deal otherwise with the real estate only at the written discretion of the beneficiaries. (See Figure 3–5.)

DEED IN TRUST

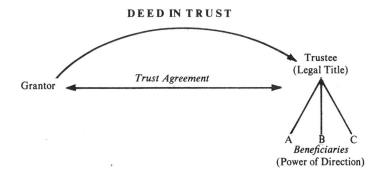

Figure 3–5
Land trust

The important advantages of a land trust are as follows:

1. The shares of the beneficiaries may be easily transferred by assignment of their interest.
2. The complexity and lack of flexibility of co-ownership of land is eliminated. A third party knows that he can deal safely with the trustee alone.
3. Identity of the beneficial owners is not disclosed in public records.
4. Mortgage loan financing is easily obtainable using the trust real estate as security and without providing for the personal credit of the beneficial owner.
5. Probate can be avoided by providing for succession of ownership upon the death of a beneficiary.
6. Dower, curtesy, and homestead do not attach to the trust real estate.
7. A lien of judgment against a land trust beneficiary does not attach to the trust real estate.
8. Beneficiaries do not have the right of partition.

These are the primary disadvantages of this type of trust:

1. The beneficiaries are liable for injuries caused by negligence in their possession, maintenance, and operation of the trust real estate.

2. Where there is more than one beneficiary and they are deadlocked in that they are unable to agree with respect to operation, lease, or sale of the trust real estate, upon petition the trust may be terminated, thereby frustrating the purpose of the trust.

PUBLIC RESTRICTIONS ON OWNERSHIP OF REAL ESTATE

Public limitations on ownership exist for the purpose of protecting the rights of the community as a whole as well as providing for the common welfare. To fulfill these purposes, the courts have consistently upheld and enforced the inherent power of government to regulate the use of property and to deprive a private person of personal ownership of property for the public welfare. Public limitations and restrictions on private ownership are imposed by the right of eminent domain, police power, the right of taxation, and the escheat of land.

Eminent Domain

The right of *eminent domain* is the inherent power of the federal and state governments to acquire title to private property for public use without the owner's consent. This power can be and has been delegated to governmental subdivisions and quasipublic corporations, such as public utilities and railroads, but due process of law must be followed. A government's obligation is to pay *just compensation* for the value of the estate acquired. Examples of clearly public use are public parks, roads, and public buildings.

The only exception to the public use requirement is in the area of condemnation and acquisition of title to real estate for urban renewal purposes. In such cases, the courts have held that the taking need only be for a public purpose. The real estate need not be subjected to a public use after the exercise of eminent domain. Under these holdings, the government may condemn a slum area and sell it to a private developer to be used for private purposes.

Police Power

Police power is the inherent power of government to regulate the use of real estate to provide for the public health, safety, morals, and the general welfare of the community. State legislatures frequently delegate police power through enabling acts to political subdivisions, such as counties, cities, and villages. The most common types of exercise of police power are subdivision regulations, zoning, and building ordinances.

Subdivision regulations

A *subdivision* is a tract of land divided into lots suitable for residential purposes. Before a subdivider can legally begin selling lots in a subdivision, the sale must first be approved by the appropriate city or county. Approval will not be granted unless the subdivision complies with the criteria set forth in the subdivision regulations, which typically require (a) compliance with zoning ordinances, (b) posting of security by the developer to assure proper completion of improvements shown on the subdivision plat, such as roads, utilities, street signs, and recreation areas, (c) compliance with building codes when the subdivider is to construct buildings, and (d) dedication of land for public streets, schools, parks, and other recreational areas. (Subdivisions are covered in detail in Chapter 18.)

Zoning

Zoning ordinances are laws passed by local political units such as municipalities and counties to regulate and control the use of land. Land is usually zoned into classifications such as residential, agricultural, commercial, industrial, or special use (schools, churches, and hospitals). Most zoning ordinances provide regulation of more specific types of use, such as designated minimum lot size, building areas, square feet of living area, and building set-back lines. As long as the use imposed by the zoning ordinance is not discriminatory, unreasonable, or arbitrary, it is a valid and enforceable restriction on the use of private property. (Zoning is covered in detail in Chapter 10.)

Building codes

A *building code* is an ordinance enacted by a local political unit (county or city) specifying detailed standards and requirements for remodeling existing structures and constructing new buildings. A typical building code may designate the types and quality of construction materials allowed to be used and provide a set of standards for electrical, heating, and plumbing installations. Most building codes prohibit remodeling, construction, or occupancy without a building or occupancy permit from the political unit having jurisdiction.

Local ordinances provide for a city or county officer to make periodic as well as annual inspections to ensure that the land owner has complied with both the zoning ordinances and the provisions of any building code. Where a violation is found, the land owner is required to take appropriate action to comply with the law. Appropriate action may be as drastic as the complete removal and relocation of a part of a building to comply with set-back lines. Most ordinances also require a fine and, in some instances, imprisonment for flagrant violations. (Building codes are covered in detail in Chapter 10.)

Taxation and Tax Liens

Taxes are levied by various state and local political units to raise the revenue necessary to provide for the community welfare. One of the most controversial and important taxes is that imposed upon real estate. Most tax laws consider real estate taxes as a *lien* upon land effective a specified date. A tax lien is an encumbrance that renders title to land unmarketable until the lien is discharged. The failure to discharge a real estate tax lien is legal cause for a land owner's title to be divested in legal proceedings initiated by the taxing unit. Such proceedings usually take the form of a court-ordered tax sale. (Taxation and tax liens are covered in detail in Chapter 8.)

Environmental Protection Laws

Both Congress and state legislatures have enacted statutes restricting the use of land for the purpose of protecting people and their environment. These laws deal primarily with air, water, and noise pollution. In most instances, the provisions of these statutes are enforced by governmental regulatory agencies. However, some statutes allow a private individual to bring a lawsuit for damages or to obtain an injunction against any person in violation of air, water, or noise pollution standards.

Some state antipollution statutes make it a crime to cause pollution wrongfully and provide for the payment of a fine for so doing.

PRIVATE RESTRICTIONS ON OWNERSHIP OF REAL ESTATE

Private restrictions on ownership exist for the purpose of protecting the rights of other persons. The following are examples:

Nuisance

An owner of real estate may not use her property so as to create a *nuisance* by interfering substantially with the use and enjoyment of real estate owned by another. For example, acid from a nearby zinc-processing plant drifts onto and damages the fruit trees of a land owner; noise from incoming and outgoing airplanes at an airport causes a nearby land owner to be deprived of his peace of mind. Some courts have awarded damages or granted injunctions to land owners injured in their person or property by the nuisance.

Waste

Where one or more persons have rights in the same parcel of land, the person rightfully in possession has a duty to all co-owners not to commit any act that may impair the value of the land. Examples of this are where a life tenant fails to pay real estate taxes on the land, a joint tenant in possession fails to discharge a mortgage, a tenant removes minerals, or a life tenant changes the contemplated use of the land or fails to make necessary repairs.

Restrictive Covenants

Restrictive covenants are limitations on the use of land imposed by private individuals on the land of others by provisions in a contract or deed. Restrictions may be of any type so long as they do not violate public policy. They may be imposed by any grantor, whether the land being sold is a single lot or multiple lots in a subdivision development. Since the purposes of restrictive covenants are basically the same as those for zoning laws, the uses restricted are generally similar. These restrictions include set-back lines, minimum living areas, residential use, style of architecture of buildings to be constructed, maximum height of buildings, prohibition on number of structures on a particular lot, and prohibition of mobile or prefabricated homes.

Restrictive covenants are enforceable by injunction issued by a court. Courts generally will not grant an injunction under the following circumstances:

1. A substantial or complete change in the characteristics of the neighborhood (e.g., area is restricted to residential, but over the years it has become predominantly commercial);
2. Abandonment, which results whenever the restrictions are voluntarily violated by owners throughout the neighborhood so as to indicate intent to disregard the original neighborhood plan;
3. Where a property owner has personally violated the restriction;
4. Where a state statute has provided a time limit on a restriction and the time limit has expired;
5. Where the deed or agreement itself established a time limit on the restriction and the time limit has expired.

Conditions

A *condition* is a restriction on use of land provided for in a deed that is accompanied by a possibility of reverter or a right of entry. The possibility of reverter provides for automatic reversion of title, if the condition is violated, to the grantor who created the condition or to the heirs. A right of entry allows the grantor who created the condition or the heirs to enter the land and take possession. Upon taking possession, title reverts to the owner of the right of entry.

A properly recorded condition is enforceable against all subsequent grantees or others who may acquire an interest in the land subject to the condition.

Conditions are not generally looked upon favorably by the courts. Consequently, many states have enacted laws prohibiting the creation of conditions, voiding any attempted transfer of conditions, and placing a time limit on the enforceability of already existing conditions.

Easements and Profits

As previously defined, easements and profits are interests in land owned by someone other than the owner of the land they burden. They are restrictions upon the use of land to which they attach because the owner of the land may not use the land so as to interfere with existing easements and profit rights. If properly recorded, all subsequent owners take the land subject to these restrictions.

Liens

A *lien* is the right of a creditor to subject property owned by his or her debtor to a forced sale and to use the proceeds for repayment of the debt. Examples of private liens are real estate mortgages, mechanic's liens, and judgment liens. The lien theory of mortgages is defined and discussed in Chapter 7.

Mechanic's liens are statutory liens granted to persons who provide labor or materials in the construction or improvement of land and buildings. Most state mechanic's lien statutes contain the following provisions:

1. Identification of those parties that may acquire the lien;
2. Indication as to when the lien was attached to the land;
3. Identification of the extent of the lien;
4. Method of perfecting the lien against third parties who have or may acquire an interest in the land;
5. Duration of the lien;
6. Method of enforcement of the lien;
7. Priority, if any, over existing liens;
8. Identification of lienable labor and materials.

In most states, a judgment rendered by a court of competent jurisdiction creates a **judgment lien** that attaches to all of the real estate owned by the judgment debtor and located within the state.

A lien causes title to be "unmarketable" and is a deterrent to the debtor attempting to sell, mortgage, or convey his property. Until released, compromised, or satisfied, a lien remains an encumbrance upon title to real estate. (See Chapter 8.)

Tort Liability Arising Out of Use of Land

As a general rule, a landowner is under a duty to use, possess, and maintain property so as not to injure the person or property of others intentionally or negligently. A violation of this duty is a private wrong called a *tort*. Some state statutes impose additional liability for damages upon a landowner for injuries caused while using the property *even* in a lawful, rightful, and nonnegligent manner. Examples are keeping dangerous animals on the land or carrying on blasting.

SUMMARY

Real estate includes land, every interest or estate in land, and any improvements to it. Personal property may become a part of the land by being permanently affixed to the land with the intent that its character change. Once personal property is attached, it is said to be a *fixture* and becomes the property of the owner of the land. The exception to this rule is trade fixtures, which remain the property of the annexor. A *trade fixture* is personal property that is attached to leased premises by a lessee for use in business, agricultural, or domestic activities conducted by the lessee on the premises.

Ownership is a creature of law. It cannot exist without being recognized and enforced by a sovereign power. Ownership consists of various rights a person possesses in a parcel of land. These rights have been identified as the right to control, possess, enjoy, and dispose of land. Ownership is not absolute and unrestricted. Rights in land are limited by the rights possessed by other persons and by the powers of political institutions.

Rights in land may be classified as estates or as other interests that are something less than an estate. In order to be classified as an estate, a person's rights must be presently possessory or become possessory in the future. A nonpossessory estate is known as a *future interest.*

Possessory estates are classified as *freehold* and *nonfreehold estates.* Freehold estates exist for an indefinite period of time, while nonfreehold estates exist for a determinable length of time. The following estates are freehold: fee simple absolute, life estate, fee simple determinable (qualified fee) (base fee), and a fee on a condition subsequent. Nonfreehold estates are also known as *leasehold estates* and include an estate for a term, an estate from period to period, an estate at will, and an estate by sufferance.

A future interest (nonpossessory estate) does not entitle its owner to immediate use and possession of the land in which the estate is held. Use and possession are postponed until the termination of a preceding estate or the occurrence of a condition or both. Reversions and remainders are future interests.

Other interests, although not estates, consist of rights in real estate. These interests include *easements, licenses,* and *profits à prendre.* Easements are created by agreement, grant or reservation, implication, reference to plat, prescription, or necessity.

Rights to a specific parcel of land may be owned concurrently by two or more persons. These persons are called *cotenants.* They possess simultaneously undivided, equal or unequal, and similar or dissimilar interests in an estate. Types of concurrent ownership are joint tenancy, tenancy in common, tenancy by the entirety, tenancy in partnership, community property, condominium ownership, cooperative, syndicate, and land trust.

All private ownership is limited and restricted by the powers of government and private rights of other persons. Public limitations and restrictions on private ownership are imposed by the right of eminent domain, police power, the right of taxation, and escheat. Private restrictions on private ownership include the law of nuisance and waste, restrictive covenants, conditions, easements and profits, liens, and the law of negligence torts (private wrongs).

TERMS AND CONCEPTS

You can check your understanding of these terms against the glossary or by review in this chapter.

Annexation	Curtesy
Building code	Dominant estate
Community property	Dower
Concurrent ownership	Easement
Condition	Easement appurtenant
Condominium	Easement by agreement
Contingent remainder	Easement by grant or reservation
Cooperative	Easement by implication

Easement by necessity	Nuisance
Easement by prescription	Ownership
Easement in gross	Police power
Eminent domain	Possibility of reverter
Escheat	Power of taxation
Estate	*Profit à prendre*
Fee simple absolute	*Pur autre vie*
Fee simple determinable	Real estate
Fee simple on a condition subsequent	Remainder
Fixtures	Restrictive covenant
Freehold estate	Reversion
Future interest	Right of entry
Homestead	Right of survivorship
Improvements	Servient estate
Joint tenancy	Subdivision
Judgment lien	Syndicate
Land	Tenancy by the entirety
Land trust	Tenancy in common
Lease	Tenancy in partnership
License	Time-share ownership
Lien	Tort
Life estate	Trade fixtures
Life tenant	Vested remainder
Mechanic's lien	Waste
Nonfreehold estate	Zoning

PROBLEMS

3–1. T leased a factory building from L to be used in manufacturing machinery. To transport steel from one place in the factory to another, T installed an overhead moving crane weighing four tons. Installation of the crane required steel I-beams to be welded in place and to be set in concrete foundations. Prior to the expiration of the lease, T attempted to remove the crane but was prevented from doing so by L. L claimed that he was the owner of the crane. Is he correct? Explain.

3–2. L and T entered into a lease which provided that the lessee could remove all structures placed on the premises by her. T constructed a cabin on the leased premises. It rested on the land by means of posts and footings. Wiring and plumbing were installed. Prior to the expiration of the lease, T sought to remove the cabin but was prevented from doing so by L. L claimed that the cabin was a fixture and therefore could not be removed. Is he correct? Explain.

3–3. Discuss and explain the concept of ownership.

3–4. Determine and explain the estate or estates existing after the following conveyances:
  (a) To A for life.
  (b) To A for the life of B.
  (c) To A for life, and after A's death to A's children.

(d) To A for life, remainder to B and C, if B and C have attained age 25 at the time of A's death.

(e) To A and her heirs.

(f) To the city of Chicago in fee simple so long as the land is used as a park.

(g) To A in fee simple on the condition that liquor is never sold on the land.

(h) To A the use and possession of an apartment house until the completion of A's home which is presently under construction.

3–5. L orally gave X permission to graze his cattle upon L's land. X grazed his cattle on L's land for four years. During the four years, L sold his land to Y. A personal dispute arose between Y and X, and Y refused to allow X to graze his cattle any longer. X sued Y, claiming that he possessed an irrecoverable right to graze his cattle on Y's land. Is he correct? Explain.

3–6. L, in writing, granted XYZ corporation the right to use water from a well upon her land and to lay a pipeline across the land to adjacent land owned by the XYZ corporation. XYZ corporation sold its land to T. L, who personally disliked T, ordered him to cease drawing water from the well and to remove the pipeline immediately. T sued L. Who wins? Explain.

3–7. L owned two adjoining lots. He constructed a driveway on the boundary line between the lots. L then sold one of the lots to T. Ten years later L asked T to share in the cost of providing a new surface for the driveway. T refused. L then sued T, asking the court for an order stopping T from using the driveway in as much as it involved a trespass on L's portion of the lot occupied by the driveway. What was the decision? Explain.

3–8. L and T owned land as "joint tenants with right of survivorship." L died, leaving a will wherein she devised all of her real estate to Z. Who is the owner of the land? Explain.

3–9. L, T, and Z owned land in joint tenancy with right of survivorship. L wanted to sell the land but T and Z refused to join in any conveyance. L executed and delivered a deed to the land to Y. Y died, leaving a will wherein he devised all his real estate to his son, S. What legal interests, if any, do L, T, Z, and S have in the land? Explain.

3–10. What are the advantages and disadvantages of condominium ownership?

3–11. L and T, a married couple, lived in a community property state. During their marriage, L inherited a farm from his grandfather which was valued at $500,000. Shortly thereafter, T received a lifetime gift of 2,000 shares of General Motors stock from her father. L and T each claim community property interests in the property acquired by the other. Are their claims valid? Explain.

3–12. Contrast the characteristics of the condominium and cooperative types of ownership.

SUPPLEMENTARY READINGS

Atteberry, William L.; Pearson, Karl G.; and Litka, Michael P. *Real Estate Law,* 2nd ed. Columbus, Oh: Grid, 1978. Chapters 2, 3, 5, and 6.

Bergfield, Philip B. *Principles of Real Estate Law.* New York: McGraw-Hill, 1979. Chapters 1–3 and 5–8.

Burby, William E. *Real Property,* 3rd ed. St. Paul: West, 1965.

Kratovil, Robert, and Werner, Raymond J. *Real Estate Law,* 7th ed. Englewood Cliffs, N.J.: Prentice-Hall, 1979. Chapters 2–4, 6, 16, 17, 26, and 28–30.

Ring, Alfred A., and Dasso, Jerome. *Real Estate Principles and Practices,* 8th ed. Englewood Cliffs, N.J.: Prentice-Hall, 1977. Chapters 5, 6, and 22.

Siedel, George J., III. *Real Estate Law.* St. Paul: West, 1979. Chapters 1, 2, and 4.

Contract Law and Real Estate Contracts

The process of transferring a title to real estate from a seller to a buyer involves a number of stages over a considerable period of time. In the purchase of property other than real estate, the buyer usually assumes that the seller has good title, pays for the item, and takes possession of it immediately or has it delivered within a relatively short time. In contrast, in the sale or exchange of real estate, it is common to ascertain that the seller is the true owner and that no other person has adverse interests in the property prior to full payment of the purchase price and transfer of title.

To facilitate and to assure transfer of a title free of adverse interests, contracts are extensively used by brokers, sellers, and buyers. Two important and widely-used contracts are the listing agreement between the broker and his client and the contract for sale of real estate entered into between the seller and buyer. Other important contracts are options, mortgages, leases, escrow agreements, and installment land contracts. A thorough understanding of the laws of contracts is important to the real estate broker. This chapter will cover basic elements of contract law, as it applies to real estate transactions.

CHARACTERISTICS OF CONTRACTS

A contract can be express or implied in fact. An *express contract* is one in which the terms are stated in words, either orally or in writing. An *implied in fact* contract is one that is evidenced by the acts or other conduct of the parties.

A contract can also have the characteristic of being bilateral or unilateral. A *bilateral contract* consists of a promise in exchange for a promise. For example, A promises to pay $100,000 if B promises to give A title to a farm. A *unilateral contract* is made up of a promise in exchange for an act or a forbearance. For example, Jill promises to give Jack title to her apartment complex if Jack marries her.

For any agreement between two or more parties to be enforceable in a court of law, it must contain the necessary elements of a contract. If all of these elements are present, the contract is said to be *valid.* Where one or more elements is missing, the agreement is either void or voidable by one or more of the parties to it. A *void contract* is an agreement whose subject matter or performance is against public policy. It is not a contract at all in the eyes of the law. An example is a contract for the purchase of an illegal distillery. A *voidable contract* remains in existence until the person who has the power to rescind it takes affirmative action to do so. As an example, a building contractor, while negotiating a contract for the sale of a newly constructed home, intentionally and falsely represented to the buyer that the home was not constructed on top of previously existing refuse land fill. This contract is voidable by the buyer on the grounds of fraud. The buyer may affirm or disaffirm the contract within a reasonable time after discovering the truth.

An *unenforceable contract* is neither void nor voidable, but is unenforceable because of the existence of a condition. For example, an oral contract for the sale of real estate is unenforceable because it is not in writing as required by the Statute of Frauds; likewise, a contract cannot be enforced because of the running of the Statute of Limitations which requires a lawsuit to be filed within prescribed time limits after a breach of contract occurs.

ELEMENTS OF AN ENFORCEABLE REAL ESTATE CONTRACT

An enforceable real estate contract has six necessary elements: agreement (mutual assent), consideration, reality of assent, legally competent parties, a legal objective and subject matter, and the contract must be in writing as required by state statutes.

The Agreement (Mutual Assent)

An agreement can never be reached without an offer and acceptance of the terms of the offer.

Offer

An *offer* is a promise made by one person called the *offeror* to another person known as the *offeree* that the offeror will act or refrain from acting on the condition that the offeree in turn will act or refrain from acting. As shown in

Figure 4–1, to be a legal offer, the promise must meet the following three requirements. First, it must exhibit **contractual intent,** that is, the offeror, through words or conduct, must appear to intend to enter into a legal obligation with the intended offeree. *Test:*   Under all of the circumstances, was the offeree justified in interpreting the promise as an offer? The test is objective rather than subjective. Therefore, promises obviously made in jest, rage, or extreme excitement; invitations to negotiate (such as circulars or advertisements); quotations of prices sent on request; and invitations to bid at auctions are not legal offers. In each of these situations, the offeree, as a reasonable person, should understand that the offeror did not intend the promise to have contractual intent.

Second, an offer must be **communicated** to the intended offeree. No person can accept an offer unless that person knew of its existence prior to her purported acceptance. Only the person or persons intended to be offerees can accept an offer. An offer made to John Javonsky cannot be accepted by Phillis Marcos.

Third, the promise must contain **complete and definite terms.** The offeror need not state the terms of the offer with absolute certainty. However, he must make them sufficiently definite to allow a court to determine the intention of the parties and thereupon assign their respective legal obligations. Most courts agree that the terms required to be included in a valid real estate contract are the identity of the parties, the time of performance, a description of the subject matter, (the quantity), and the price to be paid. Absence of any one of the essential terms will prevent a promise from being a legal offer.

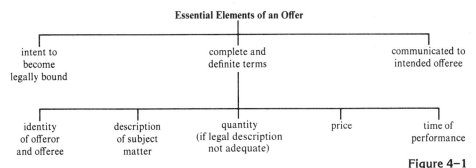

Figure 4–1

Essential elements of an offer

Termination of offers

Once made, an offer does not last for an indefinite period. Figure 4–2 indicates that an offer terminates when, prior to acceptance, it lapses, either by its own terms or after a reasonable time if its duration is not stated, by revocation by the offeror, by a rejection of the offer by the offeree, or by the death or insanity of the offeror or offeree. An attempted acceptance after an offer is terminated is, in legal effect, a new offer to contract according to the terms of the original offer. If accepted, a contract is formed.

An offeror may state that the offer must be accepted within a specified period of time. The offeree does not have the right to accept after the expiration of the specified time. The offer is said to have *lapsed.*

If no definite period of time is specified in the offer, the offer *lapses* after the expiration of a reasonable time. What is a "reasonable" length of time depends on the circumstances surrounding the transaction and the custom in the community wherein the real estate is located.

The offeror may either expressly or impliedly *revoke* the offer prior to its acceptance. An offeror's revocation is effective at the time it is communicated to the offeree or the offeree's agent. An example of an express revocation is when an offeror telephones or writes to the offeree and states that the offer is revoked. An implied revocation occurs when the offeree receives information indicating that the offeror has taken such action as to make it impossible to perform the promise in the offer. For example, an offeror offered to sell a certain parcel of land to X. Thereafter, the offeror sold the same parcel to Y. Y informed X of the sale. The offer has been impliedly revoked.

An express or implied manifestation by the offeree that he is not willing to be bound by the terms of the offer constitutes a *rejection.* It is effective when it is communicated to the offeror or the offeror's agent. An offer may be rejected expressly, by a counteroffer, or by a conditional acceptance. A *counteroffer* results whenever the offeree's acceptance modifies one or more of the terms of the offer, (e.g., X offers to sell to Y with possession and delivery of deed to be on July 1, 1981). Y accepts the offer but states that he must have possession and delivery of deed on June 1, 1981. However, a mere inquiry as to whether the offeror would be willing to change the terms of an offer is not a rejection or a counteroffer. A conditional acceptance is a statement by the offeree that he will accept the offer only if a specified event occurs. (X offers to sell land to Y. Y accepts but states that his acceptance is subject to his successful negotiation of a loan and mortgage for part of the purchase price.) If conditional acceptance or counteroffer is accepted by the original offeror, a contract is formed composed of the original terms modified by the new terms and conditions.

Offers can also terminate by *operation of law,* regardless of the intention of the parties. If the specified subject matter of the offer is destroyed, the offer is terminated automatically. Death or insanity of either the offeror or offeree will also terminate an offer. No notice of death, insanity, or destruction of the subject matter is necessary for termination of an offer by operation of law. (See Figure 4–2.)

Acceptance

An *acceptance* is an offeree's express or implied indication of willingness to be bound by all terms of an existing offer. It must comply exactly with the terms of the offer and any requests made by the offeror. It must be absolute and unconditional. As was the case in determining whether or not a valid offer

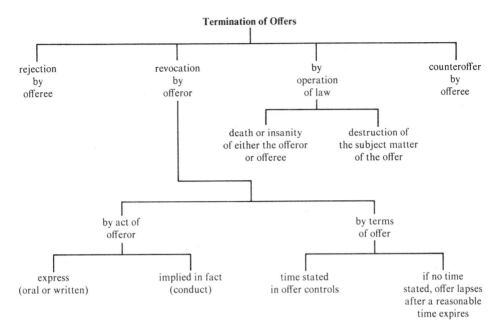

Figure 4–2
Termination of offers

exists, the objective test is used in determining the intention of the offeree, that is, what a reasonable person would be justified in believing as to the intentions of the offeree under the circumstances surrounding the transaction. The acceptance may be by words or conduct. For example, X writes a letter to Y offering to sell real estate to Y on specified terms. Y replies by letter, stating that he accepts the offer. A contract is formed. X writes a letter to Y offering to sell her farm on specified terms and states that the unoccupied farm is available for possession at any time. Y takes possession and plants corn. A contract is again formed. Silence (as a general rule) does not result in an acceptance, even though the offer so indicates.

As with the rejection, an acceptance is effective when it is communicated to the offeror or his agent, according to the express and implied stipulations of the offeror. Where the offeror specifies the time, place, or method of communication, the offeree must comply. If she does not, her purported acceptance is not effective and no contract is formed. Communication of an acceptance may be actual or constructive. *Actual communication* occurs when the offeror or his agent receives an oral or written notification of the acceptance. *Constructive communication* is effective at the time it is sent. It is communication by operation of law, and the offeror need not ever receive actual communication of the acceptance in order for him to be bound. Constructive communication occurs whenever the offeror expressly or impliedly specifies the manner in which the acceptance is to be communicated (i.e., by mail, by telephone, by telegraph, by messenger, etc.), and the offeree forwards her acceptance by the method specified. Where no means of communication is specified in the offer, the offeror is held to have impliedly authorized a reply by the customary, usual, or reasonable means of communication. For example, X sends Y an offer to sell his home by mail. Y accepts the offer by mail. A valid contract exists at the time Y properly posted his letter of acceptance. As another example, X writes to Y and offers to sell her farm. In the offer she requests Y to reply by telegraph. Y sends his telegram of acceptance; however, it is lost and never received by X. A contract exists at the time the telegraph message was given to the telegraph office.

The elements of a valid acceptance are illustrated in Figure 4–3.

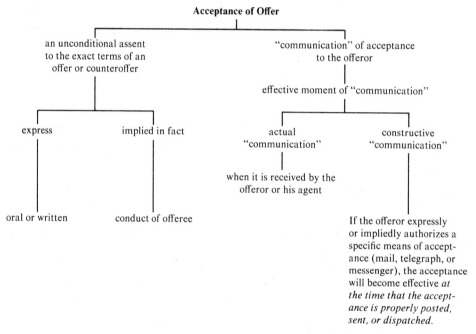

Figure 4–3
Acceptance of offer

Consideration

In order for a promise to be binding, it must be supported by legally sufficient consideration. *Legally sufficient consideration* consists of two elements: a presently bargained-for exchange and a legal detriment to the promisee. A promisee incurs a legal detriment when, in exchange for a promise, he does or promises to do something he is not legally obligated to do or he refrains or promises to refrain from doing something he has a legal right to do. As an example, X promises to sell her home to Y, and Y in exchange promises to transfer ownership of 500 shares of General Motors stock to X. Consideration is present. Since neither X nor Y was under a preexisting legal duty to make these promises, by doing so, they each incurred a legal detriment. As a second example, X promises to convey a parcel of land to Y in exchange for Y's promise not to construct a hog-feeding complex on Y's property that adjoins X's property. Consideration is present. X incurred a legal detriment by promising to do something he had no previous legal duty to do. Y incurred a legal detriment by promising to refrain from doing something she had a legal right to do.

The consideration must be presently bargained for as the exchange for the promise. For example, X saves Y from drowning. Y thereafter promises to convey title to his farm to X as a reward to X for saving Y's life. Y's promise is *not* supported by consideration because X did not save Y's life in exchange for Y's promise.

The value of the consideration exchanged need not be equal or adequate. A promise to sell one's home in exchange for an amount $5,000 below its market value would be supported by legally sufficient consideration.

A few state statutes remove the requirement of consideration where the promise is made under seal. A promise is made under seal when a promisor's signature is accompanied by the word "Seal," or the letters "LS" (*locus sigilli,* Latin, meaning the place of the seal), or the phrase "Witness my hand and seal."

Reality of Assent

Mutual assent by parties is essential to every contract; that is, each must have agreed with the other under his own free will. If a party has become a party to a contract against his free will, the contract is voidable at his election. A party's will may be overcome by deception (innocent misrepresentation or fraud), by fear (duress), by trust and confidence (undue influence), or by mistake (mutual mistake). In order to avoid the contract (*rescission*), the injured party must return any consideration he received under the contract. He, in turn, is entitled to the return of any consideration (*restitution*) he gave to the other party.

Fraud is the intentional misrepresentation or concealment (intentional nondisclosure) of a material fact upon which another contracting party justifiably relied to his detriment. For example, a seller of a house who painted over its basement walls to cover water marks left by flooding is guilty of fraud. As another example, a seller of a house was guilty of fraud when he intentionally failed to disclose to the buyer that the septic system backed up in wet weather.

Innocent misrepresentation is identical to fraud except that misrepresentation is not made intentionally.

Duress is any wrongful action or threat of action made by one contracting party against the other party to the contract or to his family under such circumstances as to force the latter to enter into the contract against his free will.

Undue influence occurs when one party places all of her trust and confidence in another so that the dominant party's will is in effect imposed upon that of the dominated party.

Mutual mistake requires that both parties contracted under a mistaken belief that certain material facts regarding the contract were true, such as the terms of the contract, the identity of the parties, and the existence, nature, quantity, or identity of the subject matter. The mistake must be mutual. If one party only is mistaken, the contract is valid and enforceable against him.

Legally Competent Parties

Certain parties by operation of law do not have the legal capacity to enter into binding contracts. Parties *lacking legal capacity* include infants, minors, mentally ill persons, and drunkards. Contracts entered into by parties lacking legal capacity are voidable, that is, they are valid until disaffirmed. Only the party who lacks legal capacity has the right to disaffirm the contract. To *disaffirm,* a party having a legal incapacity need only tender return of any consideration he has received and indicate that he no longer desires to be bound. Upon doing so, the disaffirming party is entitled to have returned to him any consideration previously transferred to the other party to the contract. After a party acquires legal capacity, he may become bound to his previously voidable contract by inaction or action on his part that indicates a willingness to be bound. When this occurs, he is said to have *ratified* the contract and thereby caused it to be enforceable against him.

Infants (Minors)

To have legal capacity, a party must be of legal age. Many state laws provide that a person is an *infant* (minor) and does not become of legal age until he reaches age twenty-one, although the legal age ranges as low as eighteen in some states. All infants' contracts are voidable even though the subject matter of the contract is a necessity to the infant, and the infant has the right of disaffirmance prior to attaining his majority and within a reasonable time thereafter. The extent of the reasonable time depends on the circumstances. As an example, X, age nineteen, purchases a hardware store from Y for $50,000. Three days after X attained age twenty-one, she decided to quit the hardware business and tendered back a deed to the hardware store to Y. Y refused to accept the deed or to pay back the $50,000. The contract is voidable by X. X may disaffirm the contract within a reasonable time after she attains age twenty-one. Three days would be a reasonable time. X is entitled to the return of $50,000, and Y must accept the deed. As a general rule, the infant's right of disaffirmance is not destroyed by fraudulent misrepresentation of her age; however, such action may subject her to damages for fraud.

Mentally ill persons

If a contract is entered into by a party after he was declared insane or mentally *incompetent* by a court, the contract is void from its inception. Adjudication (court declaration) of insanity or mental incompetency removes all capacity to contract from a mentally incompetent person and usually transfers it to a legal representative named a *guardian* or *conservator.* As a general rule, where there has been no adjudication of insanity or mental incompetency, the test is whether or not a party's mental condition was such that she did not understand the nature and consequences of the transaction. If the contract is made by the incompetent prior to his or her court adjudication of insanity, the contract is merely voidable.

Drunkards

A contract made by a party who is intoxicated to a degree that he did not understand the nature and consequences of the transaction is voidable by him within a reasonable time after he becomes sober and acquires knowledge of the contract.

Corporations

A *corporation* is a legal entity created by and owing its continued existence to the law of the state of its incorporation. Its power to enter into valid contracts is governed by the law of the state of its incorporation and the express and implied powers granted to it in its articles of incorporation. Most corporations, through their agents, have the power to enter into contracts for the purchase, sale, mortgage, and lease of real estate.

A Legal Objective and Subject Matter

A contract is void from its inception if its objective or its subject matter is *illegal.* Neither party can enforce the contract by court action or recover any consideration given in completion of an illegal contract. Ignorance of the law is *not* a valid defense by any party. A contract will be *illegal* if it is in violation of the common law, is prohibited by statute, or is contrary to public policy.

Violation of common law

The *common law* is a body of legal rules and principles developed by the courts. A contract in violation of the common law is illegal and void. As an example, X sells her furniture store and business to Y. In the sales contract, X agrees not to compete with Y in the furniture business in the entire state of Illinois for a period of 100 years. This agreement not to compete is illegal and void because it imposes an unreasonable restraint of trade; therefore, it is in violation of the common law. A reasonable restraint of trade is valid under the common law.

Prohibited by statute

Legislatures, in exercising a government's inherent police power, regulate the making of contracts. For instance, consider a state statute that renders invalid any oral listing agreement with a real estate broker. Another example is a state statute that voids any *exculpatory clause* in a lease, that is, any provision exonerating a landlord from liability for injuries caused to the tenant by the landlord's *own* negligence.

Contrary to public policy

The public policy of a state is reflected in its constitution, statutes, and judicial decisions. The public policy of one state may differ from that of another. A court will decide each case dealing with an alleged violation of public policy on its own facts. The following circumstances are generally held to be against public policy: (a) an agreement to pay a member of a zoning board a specified amount in return for her favorable vote on a zoning matter, or (b) an agreement with a trustee of a land trust which, if carried out, would cause the trustee to breach his fiduciary duty to his beneficiary.

In some instances, an agreement is illegal in part only. In such cases, the court will enforce the legal part if it can be separated from the illegal part.

In Writing

All states have a statute that requires certain contracts to be in writing. This law is commonly referred to as a *Statute of Frauds.* A contract that is not in writing, as required by the Statute of Frauds, is not enforceable by the courts. However, if one or both of the parties has performed his obligations, the courts usually hold the agreement to be enforceable. For *a writing* to be sufficient, it may take the form of a formal contract or consist of a series of letters, a check, telegrams, receipts, or any combination thereof. It is only necessary that all of the writings incorporate each other by reference, so that the court recognizes them as the intended contract.

Most Statutes of Frauds also provide that the only parties bound to the contract are those who sign. Therefore, if one party signs, she is bound. If both sign, both parties are totally bound. If neither party signs, the contract is totally unenforceable. The *signature* may appear anywhere on any of the writings representing the contract.

In addition to the requirements previously mentioned, a writing to satisfy a Statute of Frauds must contain a sufficiently detailed description of the subject matter, identification of the parties, and a statement of the essential terms of the contract.

An understanding of the following provisions of a typical Statute of Frauds is important to any study of real estate and real estate transactions.

Contract to answer for the debt or default
of another person (Guaranty)

A contractual promise to pay the debt owed by another person must be in writing to be enforceable. This statute only applies to *collateral* (secondary) promises. It does not apply to *original* (primary) promises. For example, a father tells a landowner that, if the latter will give title to his land to the son, he, the father will pay for it. The father's promise is original (primary) and need not be in writing. As a contrasting example, X owns a ranch that is encumbered by a $250,000 mortgage debt. X sold the ranch to B under a contract of sale wherein B agreed to make a down payment of $200,000 and assumed and agreed to pay X's mortgage debt. B's promise to pay X's mortgage debt is collateral (secondary) and is not enforceable unless in writing.

Contract in consideration of marriage
(Antenuptial agreement)

A contract in consideration of marriage occurs whenever an engagement (contract) to marry contains any promise that is additional to the mutual promises to marry; for example, the parties to an engagement agree to a property settlement (a division of real and personal property) should they legally separate after marriage.

Contracts not to be performed within one year

Any contract that, by its terms, cannot be fully performed within one year of its date is unenforceable unless in writing. As an example, X and Y entered into an oral lease in which X agreed to lease a certain parcel of real estate to Y for a period of two years. The contract is unenforceable at its inception. *Exception:* Where one party to the contract has totally performed his or her promise, the entire contract is enforceable even though it is oral. For example, L and T entered into an eighteen-month oral lease. L insisted on and received the total amount of rent in advance. The oral lease is binding.

Contracts for the sale of an interest in real
estate

Any contract that affects any private ownership rights in real estate must be in writing. For example, contracts to sell real property (real estate), a mortgage, a grant of a right to remove minerals or gravel, and grants or reservations of easements must be in writing. *Exception:* If a buyer under an oral contract to sell real estate takes possession and makes either valuable improvements *or* a payment (partial or total) of the purchase price, the contract is binding.

The distinction between real estate and personal property is important for the purposes of the Statute of Frauds. This distinction is a part of the law of property (discussed in Chapter 3).

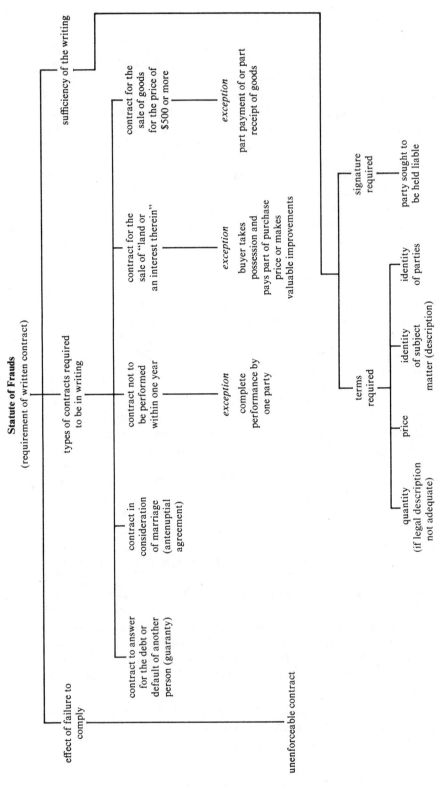

Figure 4-4
Statute of Frauds

Contracts for the sale of personal property
for the price of $500 or more

Many buyers of real estate also simultaneously negotiate for the purchase of personal property found on the premises. The purchase price of the personal property frequently exceeds $500. In order to satisfy the provisions of the Statute of Frauds, the parties must either list the items of personal property in the real estate contract itself or execute a separate written contract, commonly referred to as a *bill of sale. Exception:* If a buyer pays for or receives possession of some or all of the agreed-upon items of personal property, the contract is binding as to the items paid for or received even though the contract was oral.

Where the purchase price of the personal property is below $500, an oral contract is binding on the parties. Because of the difficulty of proving oral contracts, it would be advisable to list all items of personal property in the real estate contract, regardless of the agreed-upon price.

REMEDIES UPON A BREACH OF CONTRACT

Contracting parties are allowed by law to state a sum to be received by one party as damages in case of breach by the other. This type of provision is called a *liquidated damages* clause. It is valid and enforceable as the sole remedy of the injured party, if the sum agreed upon was reasonably related to the probable damages that the parties forecasted as resulting from a future breach. As an example, X enters into a contract for the sale of an apartment building to Y. X and Y agree that if possession of the apartment house is not delivered to Y on July 1, 1982, X is to pay Y $2,000 each month until the possession is delivered. The monthly rental revenue from the apartment house has been $1,800 each month for the last two years. This is a valid and enforceable liquidated damages clause. If the damages agreed upon in the contract are excessive, the liquidated damages provision will be void. If either an existing liquidated damages clause is void or the parties neglected to include any liquidated damages provision and a breach occurs, the injured party has the right to assert the common law remedies against the party in default explained below and summarized in Table 4–1.

Table 4–1

Remedies upon breach of real estate sales contract

Remedies	Buyer	Seller
1. Sue for damages (actual monetary loss)	×	×
2. Specific performance	×	×*
3. Rescission	×	×
4. Restitution of earnest money	×	
5. Retention of earnest money		×
6. Liquidated damages if agreed upon in the contract of sale	×	×

*In most states.

Remedies of the Buyer

If the seller defaults, the buyer can choose a remedy from among the following:

1. *Specific performance.*   Under the remedy of **specific performance,** the buyer can obtain a decree by a court ordering the seller to perform her agreement. An example would be a court order requiring a defaulting seller of real estate to deliver a deed to the buyer conveying title to the property as agreed upon.

2. *Sue for damages.*   The buyer can seek a judgment by a court ordering the seller to pay **damages** suffered by the buyer as a result of the seller's default. For example, X contracted to sell his factory building to Y. Upon X's default, Y purchased a substantially equivalent factory building from Z. However, six weeks elapsed before he was able to locate and purchase Z's building, and Y was required to pay $4,000 more to Z than the purchase price under his previous contract with X. Y is entitled to his actual damages, consisting of $4,000 plus a reasonable rental value of the factory building for the period of time that elapsed between X's default and Y's purchase of the factory building from Z.

3. *Rescission of the contract and restitution.*   Upon a seller's default, the buyer is entitled to notify the seller that she considers the contract terminated (**rescission**) and can recover (obtain **restitution** of) any consideration (earnest money) previously paid to the seller.

Remedies of the Seller

Upon the buyer's breach of contract, the seller can choose a remedy from among the following:

1. *Sue for damages.*   The seller is entitled to file a lawsuit and recover from the buyer his actual monetary loss (**damages**) suffered as a result of the buyer's breach.

2. *Rescission of the contract.*   The seller has the right to notify the buyer that the contract is terminated. As a condition precedent to an effective **rescission,** the seller must return all payments (earnest money) previously received from the buyer.

3. *Specific performance.*   As a general rule, **specific performance** is available to a seller of real estate. However, a few states do not allow this remedy.

4. *Retention of earnest money as damages.*   Unless otherwise agreed in the contract, the seller has the right to rescind the contract and **retain the earnest money** as damages. *Earnest money* is a cash deposit paid by a prospective buyer as evidence of her good faith intention to perform her contractual obligation. If the amount is not unreasonably large (usually ten percent or less), the courts will allow the seller to retain the earnest money as damages in case of the buyer's breach. Technically, a down

payment is not intended to be earnest money; therefore, unless provided for in the contract, a seller does not have the right to retain a down payment as damages as a result of the buyer's breach.

REAL ESTATE CONTRACTS

No specific form of contract is necessary to bind parties to a real estate transaction. As previously discussed, the contractual agreement may be in the form of a letter, check, receipt, telegram, memorandum, or a combination of such writings. It is only necessary that the writing or group of writings contain all the essential elements of a contract and be signed by the parties. Persons engaged in all aspects of real estate transactions must be familiar with the numerous types of contracts to carry out their legal and ethical responsibilities successfully.

In actual practice today, most real estate transactions are begun and completed using local standard printed forms. Only in the more complicated transactions is there a tendency for the parties to require a contract whose provisions are tailor-made to their needs by an attorney. Printed forms used in the real estate business are not standardized throughout the United States or even in counties within a state. However, there is an increasing use of standardized forms prepared by state real estate boards. Where standardized forms have not been adopted, the forms in use differ in name, language, and scope of their coverage of subject matter. Therefore, it is important to the real estate broker and salesperson to be aware of the real estate form contracts commonly used in their market area and to understand the legal implications of the provisions in each. The provisions of a form contract entered into by the parties will determine their rights and obligations even though the parties may have misunderstood when they signed. When choosing the appropriate form contract and aiding in its completion, the broker must be careful to see that the contractual provisions will legally fulfill the desires of the parties involved and protect their individual interests.

The contracts most commonly used in the real estate business are these:

1. Listing agreement;
2. Deposit receipt and offer to purchase;
3. Contract for the sale of real estate;
4. Installment land contract;
5. Option to buy or sell;
6. Contract for the exchange of real estate;
7. Lease.

It is impossible to list and describe the multitude of form contracts currently used throughout the United States. The following discussion will explain the nature of the transaction involved (regardless of the form used) and describe the most common provisions found in representative real estate contracts.

The Listing Agreement

A *listing agreement* is a contract of employment whereby a broker is appointed as a special agent with limited authority to act for his principal in exchange for a commission. It is important that the agreement set forth the authority granted to the broker and the conditions upon which the principal is willing to dispose of her property. If the broker exceeds his authority or does not find a buyer ready, willing, and able to comply with the principal's conditions, the principal need not bargain with the buyer and she is not obligated to pay a commission to the broker.

The formation and enforceability of a listing agreement is governed by general common law pertaining to contracts and by specific state statutes. Under the common law, the agreement need not be in writing. However, at least seventeen state statutes now require a written agreement for the broker to be entitled to his commission. Other states require a written agreement only for exclusive listing agreements.

The typical completed form listing agreement will usually contain the following information:

1. Names of broker and seller;
2. Listing price;
3. Agreed-upon amount of commission and time of payment;
4. Description of the property involved;
5. Seller's terms and conditions;
6. Duration of the listing;
7. Authority of the broker;
8. Personal property to be included as part of the transaction;
9. Type of listing, (e.g., net listing, open listing, exclusive listing, or exclusive right to sell).

Many state laws or real estate commission regulations require inclusion as well as exclusion of certain provisions in listing agreements. It is the responsibility of the broker to ensure that the listing agreement he uses, whether it be in a form contract or otherwise, is binding and enforceable between himself and his principal and that it complies in every way with the laws in the state in which he is licensed and does business.

Mandatory provisions

The following statements are often required in listing agreements: (a) That it is illegal for either the principal or the broker to discriminate on the basis of race, color, religion, sex, or physical disability; (b) No amendment or alteration of the listing agreement shall be valid unless in writing and signed by the parties; (c) If the listing is exclusive, a statement of the exact duration of the contract must be included.

Prohibited provisions

In addition to requiring minimum provisions, some state statutes also prohibit the inclusion of certain clauses, such as (a) a clause automatically extending the listing period, (b) a clause providing for a net listing agreement, or (c) a clause prohibiting recordation of the contract.

A more in-depth discussion of listing contracts and practices is found in Chapter 14.

Deposit Receipts and Offers to Purchase

During the process of negotiating a real estate contract, the original offer may have been made by either the seller or the buyer. Many *oral* offers and counteroffers may take place between the parties prior to a written finalization of their agreement. If oral negotiations are concluded with a definite offer and an unconditional acceptance, an oral contract is formed. However, as previously discussed in this chapter, oral contracts for the sale of an interest in real estate are not enforceable, under the provisions of the Statute of Frauds, by either the seller or the buyer. Consequently, it is essential that the parties state their agreement in some form of writing.

In some real estate market areas, a printed form designated a "Deposit Receipt" or an "Offer to Purchase" is used by brokers to set out the terms and conditions of the real estate sales contract. Although titled a ***Deposit Receipt*** or an ***Offer to Purchase,*** these forms contain all of the essential elements of a contract. These forms may be signed and initiated by either the seller or the buyer. The most common procedure is for the broker to have the buyer sign the form and forward it to the seller for his signature.

Regardless of which party initiates negotiation, a completed and signed deposit receipt or offer to purchase constitutes a legal offer to enter a contract pursuant to its terms and conditions. Upon its acceptance, a contract is formed. An acceptance may be made orally or in writing, either by a separate, signed correspondence or by a signature on the deposit receipt or offer to purchase. Some type of written and signed acceptance is essential to bind the offeree under the Statute of Frauds which provides that, for both parties to be bound, both parties must have signed the required writing. If one party (offeror) signs, he will be bound to the contract upon oral acceptance by the other party (offeree). The nonsigning party is not bound. She may choose to either become bound by signing the form or reject the contract as being unenforceable against her. For example, when a deposit (earnest money) is paid to the broker and the deposit receipt is signed by the prospective purchaser (offeror), the seller (offeree) is not bound until she signs the form itself or some other writing that indicates her acceptance.

Therefore, under the Statute of Frauds, the signatures of both parties are not necessary to enforce a printed form agreement that contains the necessary elements of a contract. A seller can enforce a written contract signed only by the buyer, and a buyer can enforce a written contract signed only by the seller.

The broker must be certain that the form contract contains only those terms and conditions of sale his principal had authorized in the listing agreement. Failure to do so will legally justify a refusal to accept the offer as well as a refusal to pay the broker's commission. However, if the seller accepts and signs the form contract containing materially different terms and conditions than she previously authorized, she is obligated to pay the broker the agreed-upon commission.

A deposit receipt usually contains a receipt for the required deposit, a description of the property involved, the terms and conditions of the sale, and a statement of the exact amount of the commission to be paid the broker. It may or may not require the formalization of a more detailed contract in the future. The offer to purchase differs from the deposit receipt in that it generally does not contain a receipt for "earnest money" or any statement of the amount of broker's commission.

Many buyers fail to realize that, under contract law and the Statute of Frauds, their signature on the deposit receipt or offer to purchase may bind them to its terms without a signature of the seller. Others believe that the receipt is a preliminary agreement prior to the completion of a subsequent detailed contract. In an attempt to reduce misunderstanding by the buyer who signs deposit receipts, at least one state, Illinois, prohibits the use of a form designated as *offer to purchase* when it is intended to be a *binding contract*. Illinois requires that all other forms used by brokers that are also intended to be binding must clearly so state in the heading of the form in enlarged bold type.

The Contract for the Sale of Real Estate

A contract for the sale of real estate does not convey legal title to the property. Only a deed properly executed and delivered to the buyer will convey legal title. However, after execution of the sales contract and prior to delivery of the deed, the buyer has an interest in the real estate known as *equitable title.* Having equitable title, the buyer may effectively record his contract. He also acquires an insurable interest in the property. The buyer and the seller are legally co-owners of the real estate until absolute title is transferred to the buyer by delivery and acceptance of a deed from the seller.

This contract is one of the most important and frequently used instruments in the real estate business. As we have said, a real estate contract may be legally sufficient in that it meets the minimum requirements of the law, yet it may be totally inadequate to protect the interests and fulfill the expectations and desires of both the seller and buyer. It is therefore important to use an adequate contract form.

The parties

Every real estate sales contract must ***name the seller and buyer*** in order to be enforceable. The seller must agree to sell and the buyer to buy; otherwise the remedy of specific performance would not be available in case of default by either party.

Seller   The seller must have clear legal title or be authorized to convey the property on behalf of the holder of title. A careful buyer will require up-to-date evidence of title or authority to convey title. To ensure title in the seller or her authority to convey title, the following must be considered by the buyer:

1. If title is held by a trustee, executor, administrator, conservator, or guardian, the buyer (or her representative) should examine the trust agreement under which the trustee acts or the court order granting power to convey to the executor, administrator, conservator, or guardian.

2. If title is in a corporation, the buyer must be certain that the corporate officers who sign the contract have the power to do so under the corporate charter and bylaws.

3. If title is held by co-owners, all must be named as sellers and each must sign the contract.

4. If title is held in severalty by a married person, the spouse of that person should sign the contract to release and extinguish any homestead or inchoate dower rights or rights in community property.

5. Where the contract is to be signed by an agent, the agent's authority to do so must be evidenced by a written power of attorney signed by the title holder and the spouse, if any.

6. If title is in a partnership, the partnership agreement should clearly indicate that the person who signs the contract has full authority to act.

7. If title is held by an infant, a legal guardian must be appointed and authorized by a court to convey title in the infant's behalf.

Buyer   The seller's primary concern for proper identification of the person who signs the contract as buyer is that he have legal capacity to do so as well as the financial ability to pay the purchase price. If there are two or more buyers, the contract should indicate the type of ownership by which they wish to acquire title (tenancy in common, joint tenancy, etc.).

Quality of title

The contract should identify the ***quality of title*** to be conveyed to the buyer. Almost all real estate sales contracts are intended to convey fee simple title. Many form contracts do not expressly provide that fee simple is to be conveyed. However, most courts hold that a conveyance of a fee simple is intended when there is no indication otherwise. To avoid legal difficulties, the parties should specifically provide in the contract that the seller agrees to convey fee simple to the real estate.

Legal description

A contract must contain a description of the property that is sufficient to provide a reasonably certain identification of the property. Whenever possible, a **legal description** of the property should be used; it should be the same as that appearing on the abstract of title, the seller's title policy, or the Torrens Certificate. If the property cannot be identified from the provisions in the contract itself, the courts hold the contract to be void. It is legally hazardous and not good practice to use only the street address to describe the property. The various types of legal descriptions were fully explained in Chapter 2.

In sales of residences and commercial properties, disputes may arise as to whether a certain item of property is or is not included in a sale. A contract for the sale of real estate does not include items of personal property unless the items are specifically listed. Whenever a sale includes items such as wall-to-wall carpeting, window air conditioners, drapes, or stoves that might legally be personal property, the interests of the parties should be protected in one of two ways: first, by providing a contract provision that lists the items in question and states that it is the intention of the parties that these items are to be considered as part of the transaction; second, by having a bill of sale convey title to such items. Many form contracts provide a space for the parties to list any personal property that is to be included as part of the sale.

Price

The purchase price and the method and time of its payment must be stated in such detail that there can be no ambiguity. No price terms should be left to be established by future negotiation, or else the contract is incomplete and unenforceable. The **purchase price** may be payable in cash or property. Where a cash payment is required, it is customary for the contract to require a partial payment at the time the contract is signed, with the balance to be paid upon delivery of the deed at closing. Where the property is to be sold encumbered with an existing mortgage, the contract should specify when and how much cash is to be paid and whether the buyer shall take "subject to" or "assume and agree to pay" the outstanding mortgage. In other situations, the contract may require that the seller receive a "purchase money mortgage" as part of the purchase price. In such case, it is important that the contract specify in detail the terms and conditions of the mortgage. Mortgages are discussed in detail in Chapter 7.

Form of deed

The contract should specify the **type of deed** to be delivered to the buyer. The usual deeds provided for in contracts are general warranty, special warranty, grant, bargain and sale, and quitclaim. Where the conveyance is to be by a trustee or executor, the type of deed to be given is usually provided for in the applicable state statutes. Most trustee or executor deeds take the form of special warranty deed or quitclaim deed.

If the contract is silent as to the type of deed to be given the buyer, most states allow the seller to give a deed without covenants, such as a quitclaim deed. Deeds are discussed in detail in the next chapter.

Title exceptions

This provision of the contract sets forth the seller's intention to convey title subject to specified encumbrances and restrictions commonly referred to as *title exceptions.* A provision for specific exceptions implies an agreement that the title will be free from all others. Unless the contract provides otherwise, the seller must convey **marketable title** and the buyer is obligated to accept nothing less. A title is not marketable unless it is free from all liens, encumbrances, and restrictions not excepted in the contract. The exceptions commonly provided for in form contracts are as follows:

1. *Existing leases of a specified duration.*   A lease is a conveyance of an estate in land and creates an encumbrance upon it. A buyer should investigate the rights of lessees by examining the lease prior to signing the contract.

2. *Special assessments.*   Special assessments are imposed by a political unit, such as a city, for local improvements (e.g., streets, sidewalks, and drainage improvements).

3. *General taxes.*   Real estate taxes become a lien during the year in which they are levied; however, they may not be due until the following year. Because the buyer must pay these taxes to release the lien, it is customary to provide that he receive a pro rata credit on the purchase price.

4. *Private restrictions on the use or enjoyment of the premises.*   The use of land may be restricted by private restrictions created by a previous deed or subdivision plat. Contract forms usually provide that the seller will convey in fee simple and clear of encumbrances. Unless the contract is expressly made subject to existing private restrictions, the buyer may reject the title if it is subject to restrictions as to its use and enjoyment.

5. *Zoning and building codes or ordinances.*   Although commonly found in form contracts, this exception is unnecessary and ineffective because zoning and building codes do not affect title. They merely regulate the use of the property. The buyer is held to have knowledge of the existence of these laws. Before signing the contract, a prudent buyer should examine all pertinent zoning, building, and fire and health regulations to determine whether these laws would prohibit his intended use of the property and whether the seller's current use of the property is in violation of these laws. This may be particularly important because of recent changes in land use controls and the enactment of new land conservation laws.

6. *Existing indebtedness.*   For example, "Said real estate is subject to the following encumbrance: Mortgage to Savings and Loan Association in

the amount of $50,000 which will be assumed by Buyer, if so provided herein, but if not so provided then it may be satisfied out of purchase price and released when deed is delivered." A seller's title is not considered marketable if encumbered by a mortgage. If the mortgage is not excepted, the buyer is not obligated to accept title. The contract clause quoted above is for the seller's benefit, because it allows the seller to use the proceeds from the sale to discharge an existing mortgage. It obligates the buyer to accept a deed upon release of the mortgage.

7. *Easements.* Unless excepted, easements of record render the title unmarketable.

8. *Encroachments.* Encroachments are improvements on land that extend over and upon neighboring land or on adjoining streets or alleys or improvements on neighboring land that extend over and upon the land to be sold. Encroachments render title unmarketable unless excepted in the contract. Where there may be any question as to the existence of encroachments, the buyer should insist that the contract require that the seller provide a survey.

Earnest money requirement

It is customary for form contracts to require the buyer to pay a cash deposit to the broker, his principal, or in escrow. This down payment or deposit is commonly known as **earnest money.** The contract usually provides that, if the buyer performs, the earnest money applies to the purchase price. To provide for the case of a buyer's default, the following provision is included in form contracts: "Then at the option of the seller, the earnest money shall be forfeited as liquidated damages and the contract shall be null and void." Courts have consistently upheld these provisions as long as the amount to be retained by the seller upon the buyer's default was not so large as to constitute a penalty.

Provision for prorating

Form contracts generally provide for adjusting or **prorating** one or more of the following items as of the date of possession or delivery of deed. Where the parties desire a different date, such as in the case where the transaction is to be closed in escrow, the contract should specify such date. The mathematical calculations involved in prorating are covered in detail in Chapter 17.

General Real Estate Taxes   The contract usually provides for prorating based on the most recently ascertainable taxes, which usually consist of the latest amount paid.

Rents   Unless otherwise agreed in the sales contract, the title holder on the date rent is due is entitled to the rent. The contract should, therefore, provide for prorating of rent as of the closing date.

Insurance Premiums   If the buyer is going to receive an assignment of the seller's fire insurance policy, the prepaid premium should be prorated.

Sewer and Water and Other Utility Charges These charges should be handled by instructing the municipality to read the meter at the date of closing and thereafter bill the buyer for water subsequently used. If utility charges have been prepaid according to some sort of "easy payment plan" or "level payment plan," they should be prorated.

Miscellaneous

1. Fuel or supplies on hand; for example, LP gas (liquid propane gas), firewood, coal, and fuel oil.
2. Interest on mortgages to be taken subject to or assumed.

The contract should specify all items to be adjusted or prorated.

Furnishing evidence of title

Unless agreed upon in the sales contract, the seller is not obligated to furnish the buyer evidence that her title is good. Without such a provision, the buyer would be legally obligated to make his own title search at his own expense. Form contracts usually provide that the seller furnish one of the following forms of evidence of title:

1. *Abstract of Title.* An **abstract of title** is a chronological history of publicly recorded instruments and legal proceedings that have affected title to the property, commencing with government ownership of the real estate and brought up to the current date. Deeds, mortgages, other instruments affecting title, and legal proceedings are all included in the abstract. For the most part, abstracts are prepared by lawyers and abstract companies. Each abstract includes an abstractor's certificate that discloses what records the abstractor *did and did not* examine and the last date covered by his search of the records. The buyer's attorney should examine the abstract and prepare her opinion as to the status of title.

2. *Title Insurance Policy.* A **title insurance policy** is a contract of indemnity. The title insurance company agrees to indemnify the owner (buyer) and/or his mortgagee against loss incurred by reason of those defects in the title not expressly excepted in the policy. The insurance company also agrees to defend, at its own expense, any lawsuit filed against the insured based on a defect in title.

3. *Torrens Certificate.* A few cities and counties use the **Torrens system** of registration of title to land. Under this system, title is initially registered by written application to the county court in the county wherein it is located. A court hearing establishes ownership in the applicant, and the court issues an order for the registration of the real estate in the name of the owner. The title is registered with the Registrar of Titles. No lien or judgment is valid unless it is entered on the original title certificate by the Registrar. Once registered, a certificate of title is appropriate evidence of title.

4. *Attorney's Certificate of Title.*   When an ***attorney's certificate of title*** is required, no formal abstract of title is prepared. The attorney conducts her own search of the public records. Based on what is revealed by her examination, she will issue the written opinion *(certificate of title)* of the current status of the title.

Fire clause

Under common law, the ***risk of loss*** from fire or other casualty to the premises falls upon the purchaser during the pendency of the sale regardless of which party is in possession of the premises. Some courts have stated that the risk of loss remains on the seller until a deed is delivered to the buyer. Some states have resolved the conflict by enacting statutes (***Uniform Vendor and Purchaser Risk Act***) which provide that the seller retains the risk of loss until legal title is transferred to the buyer or the buyer is given possession of the premises.

A buyer may protect himself by including the following clause in the contract:

> If the premises are totally or substantially destroyed by fire or other casualty before this transaction is completed, the buyer may, at his option, accept the insurance proceeds or other settlement and complete the transaction or declare this contract void, and the amount of earnest money paid by the buyer is to be refunded. Seller at her own expense shall maintain insurance on the premises against fire with extended coverage for their full insurable value until this transaction is completed.

Provision for escrow

The parties to a sales contract may choose to provide that the transaction be closed in escrow. An escrow arrangement protects the buyer against the death or incapacity of the seller and assures the seller that the money is available to close the transaction. Escrow arrangements are discussed in detail subsequently in this chapter and in Chapter 17.

Provision for possession

The parties may agree to any ***possession date;*** however, without a contract provision to the contrary, the right of possession passes to the buyer at the time he receives the deed from the seller.

Time of the essence clause

Where the contract does not provide ***that time is of the essence,*** courts usually allow the buyer or seller a reasonable time after the agreed upon closing date to comply with the terms of the sales contract. If the contract provides that time is of the essence, failure of the buyer or seller to close on the agreed-upon date places him immediately in default.

Installment Land Contract

The installment land contract is known by various names throughout the United States, such as "contract for deed," "land contract," or "installment contract." It is most correctly called an ***installment land contract,*** and the real estate is commonly referred to as being *sold under contract.* These real estate contracts are generally used when the buyer is unable to pay the entire purchase price himself and cannot obtain sufficient mortgage financing. For example, lenders often will not take a mortgage on unimproved land (i.e., land without a building). Another use is to spread taxable income from the sale of real estate over several years.

Under an installment land contract, the seller retains legal title as security for the payment of agreed-upon installments made up of principal and interest. The buyer becomes the "beneficial owner" immediately upon signing the contract and making a nominal down payment. However, the buyer is not entitled to delivery of deed until the full purchase price has been paid and all of his other obligations under the contract have been fully performed.

Unless the contract provides the contrary, the buyer is not entitled to possession until the entire purchase price has been paid and the deed is delivered to the buyer. Once the buyer rightfully does take possession, he has absolute and exclusive control over the property. There is, however, one qualification to the buyer's complete control. He may not commit "waste." If the buyer commits any act toward the land that substantially impairs the security value (***waste***) of the real estate, the seller may get a court order refraining the buyer from such acts. Examples are a buyer who refuses to pay real estate taxes, allows buildings on the land to deteriorate, or materially changes the use of the property.

The interests of the seller and buyer are freely assignable during their lifetimes and pass by inheritance upon their deaths. The buyer is entitled to all profits from the land and must meet only his installment obligations to the seller.

To protect his interest against subsequent purchasers or mortgages from the seller, the buyer must record the installment land contract.

A common installment land contract form contains the following provisions:

Description of premises

Here the parties mutually agree to sell and buy property designated by its legal description.

Price and terms

This clause sets forth the total purchase price. It indicates the required down payment together with the amount of principal and accrued interest to be paid in installments. The time and place for payment of installments is stated in detail.

Possession of the premises
The seller agrees to give exclusive possession of the property to the buyer on or before a specified date, for the entire life of the contract subject only to the buyer's default in any terms of the contract.

Escrow
An escrow agent is named and appointed for the seller and the buyer. This provision requires that the original signed copy of the installment land contract be deposited with the escrow agent. The seller is required to turn over to the escrow agent an executed general warranty deed to the buyer, together with either an abstract of title, a title insurance policy, or a Torrens certificate. Under the escrow agreement, which can be incorporated into the contract, the escrow agent binds herself not to deliver the seller's deed to the buyer until the buyer pays all installments of principal and interest and other charges provided for under the contract. Escrow arrangements are discussed in detail subsequently in this chapter and in Chapter 17.

Right to prepayment
This provision usually grants the buyer the right to prepay installments of principal and apply the prepayments against future installments.

Grace period
The buyer is granted a period of time, usually thirty to sixty days after his default, to make overdue payments. During the grace period, the seller is unable to declare a forfeiture. This also provides for an acceleration clause that authorizes the seller to declare the entire purchase price due and payable upon the buyer's failure to pay any one installment of principal and interest as required in the contract.

Right to assign and to mortgage
Here the seller retains the first option to repurchase the property from the buyer when the buyer wishes to sell or assign (transfer) his interest during the life of the contract. The provision usually requires that the buyer also secure written consent from the seller prior to mortgaging his interest.

Taxes and assessments
This clause usually provides that the seller and buyer pay a pro rata share of ther property taxes levied during the year the buyer takes possession. Prorating is done as of the date buyer is given the right of possession. All subsequent taxes and assessments are required to be paid by the buyer.

Insurance
The buyer agrees to pay the seller the unearned portion of prepaid insurance currently in force on improvements on the premises and assigned to the buyer. The buyer also agrees to maintain insurance, from date of possession, on all improvements in a sufficient amount to cover the full insurable value of the improvements, payable to both the seller and buyer as their interest may appear.

Oil, gas, and mineral rights

Unless oil, gas, or minerals are currently being removed from the premises, neither the seller nor the buyer alone has the right to remove oil, gas, or mineral deposits or lease rights to third parties. This provision should be included if the property is located in areas of oil and gas development. The parties should specify their respective mineral rights.

Default and forfeiture

This provision requires buyer to *forfeit* to the seller all payments made by him prior to his *default* on the terms of the contract. In most states, the seller is entitled to the payments as **liquidated damages** and is granted the right of immediate reentry and possession of the premises. In some states, such as California, statutory and common law restrictions are imposed to prevent a forfeiture of monies by a defaulting buyer. A few states allow the buyer a grace period after his default, when he can reinstate the contract by payment of monies in default.

When a buyer records the installment land contract and subsequently defaults, there is a cloud on the seller's title even though she has exercised her right of reentry and taken possession from the buyer. To clear her title, a seller may attempt to obtain a quitclaim deed from the defaulting buyer, file a strict foreclosure suit against the buyer, or file a bill to quiet title.

Options to Buy or Lease Real Estate

An *option* is a contract containing a continuing offer that grants the optionee the legal right to buy or lease real estate owned by the optionor at a stated, fixed price during a specified period of time. Because it is a contract, it cannot be revoked by the optionor. The optionee is not usually obligated to purchase the property or lease the premises; however, he can become bound if he expressly or impliedly accepts the offer within the time allowed in the option. To be enforceable, the option must be in writing under the Statute of Frauds. As an example, X, in exchange for $500, promises Y that if Y wants to purchase within thirty days of current date, X will sell an identified apartment house to Y for a price of $150,000. The option may or may not provide that the consideration paid for the option be applied to the purchase price after acceptance of the option.

Options to buy or lease commercial property are sometimes made conditional upon changes in zoning, obtaining licenses or building permits, securing options on adjacent land, or other events. If the conditional event does not occur, the optionee is not legally obligated to purchase or lease.

Contracts for the Exchange of Real Estate

Contracts for the exchange of real estate are essentially the same as contracts for the sale of real estate already discussed. The only important difference is that, in an exchange contract, both parties transfer title to real estate to each other, whereas in the sales contract the seller is required to transfer title to real estate in exchange for actual cash received or a promise to pay cash in the future. Where the market values of the exchanged properties are not equal, the contract will provide for a cash adjustment ("boot").

In other respects, exchange contracts are governed by the same common law and statutory rules and contain essentially the same provisions as sales contracts.

Leases

A lease is a contract whereby the owner (lessor) of real estate binds herself to give exclusive possession and control of all or a part of the premises to another person (lessee) in exchange for consideration (rent). Leases are discussed in detail in Chapter 6.

ASSIGNMENTS OF REAL ESTATE CONTRACTS

As a general rule, unless otherwise stated in the contract or prohibited by common law or statute, real estate contracts such as options, leases, and contracts for the sale or lease of real estate are freely assignable. An *assignment* is a legal transfer of rights a party possesses under a contract with another. For example, X enters into a contract for sale of real estate to Y. Y, finding himself unable to raise the purchase price, discovers Z, who agrees to pay Y $300 for Y's rights to purchase the property from X. A valid assignment was made, and X is legally bound to carry out the terms of the contract as if Z had been the original party.

ESCROW ARRANGEMENTS

Many real estate transactions are closed "in escrow." An *escrow arrangement* consists of an oral or written contract under which a deed or other instrument, property, money, or any combination of these items is deposited with a third party (*escrow agent, escrowee,* or *escrow trustee*) to be held and delivered upon the performance of one or more specified conditions. The contract that specifies the conditions to be performed by the parties to the escrow is called the *escrow agreement* or *escrow instructions.*

A valid real estate closing in escrow is dependent upon the existence of an enforceable written contract for the sale of real estate. The contract for the sale of real estate may be found in a separate writing or in the escrow agreement. Once a valid escrow has been executed, the required instruments, property, or money have been delivered to the escrow agent, and all conditions in the contract for the sale of real estate and the escrow agreement are performed, the escrow is irrevocable as long as all conditions in the contract are met.

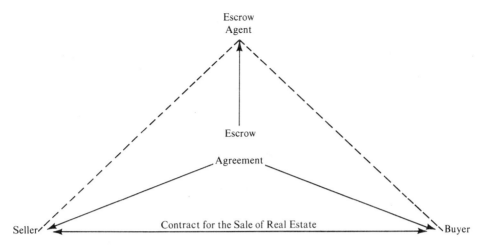

Figure 4–5
Escrow arrangement

Doctrine of Relation Back

Usually there is a length of time between the date the seller and buyer execute the contract of sale and the closing date (i.e., the date title is conveyed by deed and the purchase price paid). During this period of time, the seller or buyer may die or otherwise become legally incompetent. Without the *doctrine of relation back,* the decedent's estate would have to be probated or a conservator appointed as a result of the incompetency, thus causing expense and delay in closing the transaction. If, before the death or incompetency of the seller or buyer, a properly executed deed is deposited in escrow (under a valid contract of sale and escrow agreement) and is later delivered by the escrow agent in compliance with the escrow conditions, its delivery (transfer of title) *relates back* to (is effective on) the date that the deed was deposited with the escrow agent.

SUMMARY

Contracts are used extensively in the real estate business to assure transfer of title free of adverse interests. Several kinds of contracts are widely used for real estate transactions. These are the listing agreement, deposit receipt and offer to purchase, contract for sale of real estate, options, contract for the exchange of real estate, leases, and installment land contracts.

A legally enforceable contract must contain the following elements: an agreement (offer and acceptance), consideration, reality of assent, legally competent parties, and a legal objective and subject matter. It must also be in writing as required by state statutes.

The parties to a contract are allowed by law to agree upon the remedies available in case of a breach (e.g., liquidated damages and forfeiture by the seller). In the absence of an agreement to the contrary, the law grants several remedies to the parties. Upon the buyer's breach, the seller may sue for damages, rescind the contract, or sue in equity for specific performance. If the seller defaults, the buyer may sue in equity for specific performance, sue for damages, or rescind the contract and obtain restitution. Generally, real estate contracts are freely assignable to third parties by either gift or sale.

The most common form contracts are the listing agreement, deposit receipt, offer to purchase, contract for the sale of real estate, installment land contract, option, contract for the exchange of real estate, and lease. It is important to be aware of the legal implications of the provisions found in the form contracts being used in a market area.

Many real estate transactions are closed in escrow. An escrow is the deposit of a deed or other instrument, property, or money with a third person to be delivered by that person to the parties upon the performance of one or more agreed-upon conditions.

TERMS AND CONCEPTS

You can check your understanding of these terms against the glossary or by review in this chapter.

A writing	Escrow arrangement
Abstract of title	Evidence of title
Acceptance	Exculpatory clause
Actual communication	Express contract
Assignment	Forfeiture
Attorney's certificate of title	Fraud
Bilateral contract	Guardian
Common law	Illegal
Communicate	Implied in fact contract
Complete and definite terms	Incompetent
Conservator	Infant
Consideration	Innocent misrepresentation
Constructive communication	Installment land contract
Contractual intent	Lapse
Corporation	Legal capacity
Counteroffer	Legal description
Damages	Legally sufficient consideration
Default	Liquidated damages
Deposit receipt	Listing agreement
Disaffirm	Marketable title
Doctrine of relation back	Mutual mistake
Duress	Name the seller and buyer
Earnest money	Offer
Equitable title	Offer to purchase

Operation of law	Statute of Frauds
Option	Time is of the essence
Possession date	Title exceptions
Prorate	Title insurance policy
Purchase price	Torrens system
Quality of title	Type of deed
Ratify	Undue influence
Rejection	Unenforceable contract
Rescission	Uniform Vendor and Purchaser
Restitution	Risk Act
Retain the earnest money	Unilateral contract
Revoke	Valid
Risk of loss	Voidable contract
Signature	Void contract
Specific performance	Waste

PROBLEMS

4–1. On June 1, B wrote S, "I'll buy your farm in McLean County for $150,000." S waited two weeks and then wrote B, "I accept your offer of June 1 to buy my farm." B received S's letter the next day and immediately wrote S, "Your acceptance is too late, I have already purchased a farm." S sues B for breach of contract. B defends on the following grounds: (a) no contract existed, and (b) even if a contract existed, the Statute of Frauds was not complied with. Are any of B's defenses valid? Explain.

4–2. B sent to S an offer to buy S's farm for $50,000; S wired B, "Will you pay $69,500?" B wired back, "No." Thereupon S mailed an acceptance at the $50,000 price. Is there a contract? Explain.

4–3. B, in writing, offered to buy a tract of land for $75,000 from S and expressed a willingness to pay S $200 should S agree to allow B to purchase the land during the period of time between July 15 and August 31, 1982. S accepted B's offer and received payment of $200. On August 5, 1982, S tendered to B $200 and renounced any liability. On August 30, 1982, B advised S in writing that she wanted to buy S's land. S refused to sell. Was any contract formed? Explain.

4–4. S and B entered into a written contract for the sale of land for $200,000. During negotiations, S induced B to sign the contract by telling him that he had paid $225,000 for the land 10 years ago, but that the land was currently worth $205,000. B later discovered the land to have a value of $150,000. B sued for rescission. What was the result? Explain.

4–5. On January 1, 1981, S sold and delivered to B a properly executed deed to a parcel of land. B paid a purchase price of $35,000. It was later discovered by both S and B that the land had a market value of $75,000 at the time of the sale to B. S sued to void the sale and deed on the grounds that she did not receive adequate consideration. Is she correct? Explain.

4–6. S had been declared incompetent by a court, and X had been appointed her conservator. Subsequently, S sold and delivered an executed deed to B for

$100,000 cash. B did not know of S's incompetency. X learned of the transaction between S and B and sued to declare the deed a nullity. What was the result? Explain.

4–7.   S owned a retail store in the city of Oz. Oz has a population of 50,000. There are other retail stores handling the same merchandise as is sold in S's store located in Oz. S sold his store to B and agreed not to open a competing retail store in Oz for at least 2 years. Two months later S opened a competing store approximately six blocks away. B sued S and requested a court order refraining S from conducting a retail business in the city of Oz. S defended on the basis that the contract was illegal. What was the result? Explain.

4–8.   On September 5, 1980, S orally contracted to sell B ten acres of timberland for $50,000, deed to be delivered and purchase price paid on October 4, 1980. On October 4, 1980, B tendered the purchase price to S. S informed B that she did not wish to go ahead with the deal and refused B's money. B sued for specific performance. The court held in favor of S. Why? Explain.

4–9.   On March 1, 1981, S and B entered in a written contract for the sale of a twenty-unit apartment house. The contract called for S to deliver possession and deed to B on April 1, 1981. The contract did not contain a "fire clause." On March 15, 1981, the apartment house was totally destroyed by fire. On April 1, 1981, S tendered possession and deed and demanded the purchase price from B. B refused to pay. S sued for the purchase price. What was the result? Explain. How could B have avoided the problem presented here?

4–10. Evans decided to purchase a ten-acre tract of land from Expando, Incorporated, the developer. The customary form contract of sale was prepared and signed by Evans and an authorized agent of Expando. The contract was silent in respect to marketable title and the type of deed to be delivered to the buyer. At the closing, Expando, Incorporated offered to Evans a quitclaim deed without covenants (warranties) of title and revealed that there was an existing mortgage on the land in the amount of $500,000.

(a)   What effect does the omission of mentioned items have upon the validity of the contract?

(b)   Assume that Evans refused to accept the quitclaim deed and pay the purchase price. Is her refusal legally justified?

(c)   If her refusal is legally justified, what are her legal remedies against Expando, Incorporated?

4–11. S and B entered into a written contract for the sale of real estate which provided that the deed was to be delivered by S and the purchase price paid by B on May 1, 1980. The contract provided that "time is of the essence." S failed to deliver the deed on May 1, 1980, but was ready and willing to do so on the next day. B refused the deed and informed S he no longer considered the contract binding. S sued B for the purchase price. What was the result? Explain.

4–12. Tom Larson entered into a contract to sell a 4,000 acre farm to his son Scott for a sales price of $16,000,000. Tom Larson executed a deed to the farm naming Scott as grantee and delivered it to the Bank of Tarlock as escrow agent. Scott also deposited the purchase price with the Bank of Tarlock. Before the bank could deliver the deed to Scott, Tom was afflicted by a rare disease and died leaving a will disposing of all his property to his wife,

Lorraine, and his sons, Jeff, Eric, and Steve. In probate, Lorraine, Scott, Jeff, Eric, and Steve each claim to be owners of the 4,000 acre farm. Whose claim is correct? Explain.

SUPPLEMENTARY READINGS

Bergfield, Philip B. *Principles of Real Estate Law.* New York: McGraw-Hill, 1979. Chapters 9, 13, and 16.

Corley, Robert N., and Robert, William J. *Principles of Business Law,* 11th ed. Englewood Cliffs, N.J.: Prentice-Hall, 1979. Chapters 7–15.

Kratovil, Robert, and Werner, Raymond J. *Real Estate Law,* 7th ed. Englewood Cliffs, N. J.: Prentice-Hall, 1979. Chapters 11, 13, and 14.

Ring, Alfred A., and Dasso, Jerome. *Real Estate Principles and Practices*, 8th ed. Englewood Cliffs, N. J.: Prentice-Hall, 1977. Chapters 8, 9, and 12.

Smith, Len Y., and Roberson, Gale G. *Business Law—Uniform Commercial Code,* 4th ed. St. Paul: West, 1977. Chapters 3–12.

Title Transfer, Deeds, and Recordation

As we know, land has several special physical characteristics—most importantly, immobility—that distinguish it from other kinds of property. Because of its immobility, the estates and rights in land and the methods required to transfer these estates and rights are prescribed by state laws of the state in which the land is located. As discussed in Chapter 3, title to land is in reality both the quantity and quality of rights a person possesses in a specific parcel of land. A person's title may be in fee simple or consist of some other interest in land. Unless otherwise stated, *title,* as used in this chapter, is defined as any ownership interest in land regardless of its quantity, quality, or duration.

Private title to land in the United States was originally acquired in two ways, by either a grant from the federal government or a grant from a foreign government. Thereafter, a recorded history of a title to a given parcel of land may reveal a series of voluntary and involuntary transfers, involving private individuals as well as political and quasipublic units. This history of title is called a *chain of title.* The chain of title, when compiled in a written form together with a statement of all liens or liabilities to which the title may be subject, is referred to as an *abstract of title.*

INVOLUNTARY TRANSFER OF TITLE TO REAL ESTATE

There are several ways title to real estate can be transferred without the consent of its owner.

Condemnation

Condemnation is a legal proceeding whereby title to land, in exchange for just compensation, is taken by a governmental unit, permanently or temporarily, for a public purpose. The taking is pursuant to the government's power of eminent domain.

Adverse Possession

A private individual who has no interest in a parcel of land may acquire title to it by *adversely possessing* it for a statutory period of time. The required time of possession varies from state to state, with maximum durations ranging upwards to twenty years. Some state laws provide shorter periods of possession when the possession is under *"color of title"* (possessor named as grantee in a void or otherwise ineffective deed) and/or accompanied with payment of real estate taxes assessed on the land.

For possession to result in ownership, it must be hostile (without permission) to the owner's title, actual, open, exclusive, notorious, and continuous during the statutory period.

Continuous adverse possession by different persons will result in title being acquired by the person in possession at the end of the statutory period. This process of obtaining the benefit of another's adverse possession is called *tacking.*

Even though a person has satisfied all the requirements to vest title in himself by adverse possession, the title of record will still be in the previous owner who recorded his deed. To obtain record title in himself, an adverse possessor must file a *bill to quiet title* with a court where the land is located. Upon finding title to be in the adverse possessor, the court will enter a judgment to that effect. The judgment is then recorded, showing title of record to be in the adverse possessor.

Foreclosure Sale

A *foreclosure* sale is an involuntary sale of a debtor's title to land pursuant to either an agreement between a debtor and creditor or by a decree of a court. The proceeds of the forced sale are used to satisfy the debtor's unpaid obligation. Foreclosure sales may arise out of the following circumstances.

1. A landowner defaults in payment of assessments or real estate taxes.
2. A mortgagor defaults in payment of her real estate mortgage debt.
3. A landowner fails to discharge a perfected mechanic's lien on his land.
4. A debtor fails to discharge a judgment lien attached to her land.

Partition Sale

A *partition* sale is a court-ordered sale for purposes of severing undivided interests in land such as joint tenancies and tenancies in common. Any co-owner may, without the consent of other owners, petition a court for an order of partition sale. Where the land cannot be physically divided without materially impairing the value of the land, the court will order the land sold and the proceeds divided according to the respective joint owners' undivided interests in the land.

Accretion

Accretion is an act by which one owner of land acquires title to a portion of land owned by another through the gradual and imperceptible deposit of quantities of sand or soil by natural causes, such as water or wind. Accretion of land may be the result of two processes, alluvion and dereliction. *Alluvion* is the process by which sand or soil is washed up on land by water or blown upon the land by wind to form firm ground. *Dereliction* occurs when a sea or stream shrinks and remains below its original water mark. *Erosion* is the sudden or gradual wearing away of land by the action of water, wind, or ice.

Escheat

Escheat is the legal process where title to land reverts to a county or state upon the death of a landowner who dies without a valid will and without leaving any heirs.

Community Property

If property qualifies as community property, title to one-half is automatically vested in each spouse. It is unimportant in whose name legal record title is held. Title to one-half of the real estate in a community property state vests in each spouse regardless of the intent. In that sense, transfer of title is involuntary.

VOLUNTARY TRANSFER OF TITLE TO REAL ESTATE

Where the owner of property initiates the transfer of title of his own accord, the transfer is considered voluntary.

Public Grant or Patent

A private person may obtain title to public lands either by a statutory *grant* or by *patent* from a state or federal government. A *patent* is a document that transfers title to land from a government to a private individual. A person may automatically receive title to public lands without a patent if legislation is passed granting title to her or to a class of persons to which she belongs (*grant*).

Will (Testate Succession)

Title to real estate may be acquired by will. A *will* is a written instrument executed by an owner of property that disposes of title to his property, to take effect at the time of his death (*testate succession*). The person executing a will is known as a *testator*. Upon his death he is said to have died *testate*. A gift of real estate by will is called a *devise,* and the person to receive the gift is known as the *devisee.*

Each state has enacted laws providing for the kinds of interests in property that may be disposed of by will. Any estate that an owner may transfer during his lifetime may usually be disposed of by will.

For a will to be valid, a testator must have **testamentary capacity,** that is, he or she be a minimum age specified by law and have sufficient mental capacity at the time the will is executed. Most states have established age eighteen as the minimum age necessary to execute a will. Even though a testator may have been of legal age at the time she executed her will, the will may be voidable on the basis that she lacked sufficient mental capacity. A testator lacks mental capacity when she executes a will while "insane," or if she is induced to do so by undue influence, duress, fraud, or mistake.

In addition to the requirement of testamentary capacity, a will must usually be in writing and be executed with certain formalities. Oral wills are permitted only in a few states. As a general rule, the following requirements must be met in order to have a validly executed will.

1. *Writing.* The writing can be in any form (e.g., typewritten, handwritten, or printed).
2. *Signature.* Any mark that is intended to be the signature of the testator is valid. The signature may be located anywhere in the will. However, the most common and safest location of the signature is at the bottom of each page and at the end of the will.
3. *Publication.* The testator is required to declare to witnesses that the instrument is his last will and testament before or at the time of affixing his signature. He need not reveal the contents of the will.
4. *Attestation.* Formal wills are required to be witnessed and signed by two or more persons. The *attestation* clause says that the will was signed by the testator, that he declared it to be his last will and testament, and that the witnesses at the request of the testator and in his presence and in the presence of each other signed their names as attesting witnesses.

Specific provisions in a will or an entire will may be modified or revoked by a subsequent will or codicil of the testator, by a testator's deliberate and intentional destruction of the will, or by operation of law caused by certain changes in the testator's family relationships (marriage, divorce, birth of a child). A *codicil* is an instrument, executed with the formalities required of a will, that modifies or revokes an existing will.

Where a will has been revoked by the testator or is declared void by a court, the title to all property owned at the time of a person's death will pass according to intestate laws of descent and distribution.

Descent (Intestate Succession)

If a landowner dies without leaving a will, or if her will fails to dispose of all of her property, she is said to have died totally or partially *intestate.* By not choosing to execute a will, she has in a sense voluntarily allowed state law to designate those persons who are to receive title to her land upon her death.

The title to land is transferred to the heirs according to the statute of descent and distribution in the state in which the land is located. These statutes not only prescribe the persons to inherit the property, but also designate the proportionate share each is to receive.

The purpose of these statutes is to provide for an orderly transfer of title and also to carry out the probable intentions of an intestate decedent. Under these statutes, heirs who are blood relatives are most favored. The order of priority of inheritance and the amount inherited are usually determined by the closeness of an heir's relationship to the decedent. The following statements for descent and distribution of intestate property are typical of several state laws. We provide them as an illustration.

1. If there is a surviving spouse and also a descendant, spouse takes one-third of all property, surviving children share equally in two-thirds, and any descendants of deceased children share equally in the share that their parent would have taken if living (i.e., *per stirpes*).

2. If there is no surviving spouse but one or more surviving descendants, children share equally in the entire estate and any descendants of deceased children share equally in the share that their parent would have taken, if living (i.e., *per stirpes*).

3. If there is a surviving spouse but no surviving descendants, the surviving spouse takes the entire estate.

4. If there is no surviving spouse or surviving descendants, but a brother, sister, parent, or descendant of a deceased brother or sister is living, then parents, brothers, and sisters share equally in all the property (allowing a sole surviving parent a double share). Descendants of a deceased brother or sister share equally the portion their deceased parent would have taken, if living (i.e., *per stirpes*).

5. The order of distribution continues through the surviving maternal and paternal grandparents and their descendants; if none survive, then to the maternal and paternal greatgrandparents and their descendants; and if none survive, then to collateral (nephews, nieces, brothers, sisters) heirs.

6. Finally, if no spouse survives or known relative of the decedent is living, the real estate escheats to the county or state in which it is located.

Administration of decedent's estate

Whether a person dies testate or intestate, his estate must usually be submitted to a court for administration. If the decedent died testate, his will must be filed with the court and be probated to pass record title to the devisees. The court will appoint an *executor* who becomes the personal representative of the estate. The personal representative appointed by a court to administer an intestate estate is named an *administrator.* The personal representative's duties are to collect, preserve, and distribute all of the decedent's property, to pay all debts and taxes owed by the decedent and the estate, and to make final distribution of the decedent's property according to the will if the decedent died testate and, if not, according to law. The personal representative must file a final report with the court. Upon court approval of the report, he is legally discharged from his duties and the estate is ordered closed.

Transfer of Title by Sale

One of the most valuable rights of ownership is the right to sell. This right is legally protected, and any agreement or restriction depriving a landowner of her right to sell her land is null and void. The right to sell is limited only by the power of each state to regulate the methods and formal requirements for transfer of ownership to lands within its jurisdiction.

Transfer of Title by Gift

Title to real estate may be transferred without an exchange of value. It is a landowner's right to give away his land if he wants; however, he may not do so with the intent to defraud his existing or subsequent creditors. Creditors may have a deed set aside if it was executed and delivered by the grantor to a grantee without receipt of adequate value in exchange. This is true even though the deed recites that value was received. On the other hand, a deed properly executed and delivered in exchange for a reasonable value will not ordinarily be set aside by the courts on the basis that it is in fraud of creditors. Even though a conveyance is not in fraud of creditors, it may be set aside if it violates a provision of the Federal Bankruptcy Reform Act of 1978. For example, a conveyance is in violation of the act where it gives preference to one of the grantor's creditors as against another, if the conveyance was made within 90 days of the date a petition in bankruptcy was filed against the grantor.

The most common method of transferring title to real estate by *gift* is by an unconditional delivery of a deed to the intended grantee by the owner during her lifetime. The grantee may be a private person, a charitable organization, a religious institution, or a governmental entity. Where the grantee of a gift deed is a governmental entity, the transfer of title is said to be by *dedication.* Dedication may also occur by a subdivider's designation in a subdivision plat for certain streets and other areas to be for public use. The designated public areas become owned by the government unit upon its acceptance of the subdivision plat.

Conveyance by Deed

A *deed* is a written instrument properly executed and delivered by an owner of real estate to convey title to another person. For a deed to be operative, it must transfer a present legal interest. The person who executes the deed is called the *grantor,* and the recipient is the *grantee.*

The essential difference between a deed and a will is that the deed passes a present legal interest in the real estate, while a will does not become operative until the death of the testator. An instrument that attempts to transfer title at the death of its owner is void unless it is executed with the formalities required of a will. By their legal nature, deeds take effect upon delivery and are irrevocable, while wills are always revocable during the testator's lifetime and take effect only upon his death.

Unlike a contract, consideration is not necessary for a deed to be effective when it is properly executed and delivered to the intended grantee. A deed is further distinguished from a contract in that a contract for the sale of real estate transfers no legal title but binds the seller to execute and deliver a deed transferring legal title to real estate to the buyer. Where a deed contains covenants and is delivered in exchange for valuable consideration, however, the courts consider the covenants to be binding promises and award legal relief for their breach.

Requirements for a valid conveyance by deed

There are a number of requirements which must be met before a conveyance by deed is valid. These requirements are described here, although all of them may not be required in each state.

A Writing   Statutes in most states require a conveyance of a freehold estate to be *in writing.* The document must be signed by the grantor or her duly authorized agent.

Names and Addresses of Parties   Every deed must have *a grantor and a grantee.* If a grantor or grantee or both are not named in the deed, it is void. Even though not generally required by state law, the addresses of the grantor and grantee should be given for identification. Where the real estate is owned jointly, the deed should name all co-owners as grantors.

If the real estate is located in a state that provides for curtesy, dower, or homestead rights, the grantor's spouse must also be named as a grantor in order to release these rights. This is true even if the real estate is not jointly owned by the spouses.

Where property is to be conveyed jointly to two or more persons, each grantee must be named and the type of joint ownership identified. For example, "Maria Cisneros and Juan Cisneros, as joint tenants, with right of survivorship, not as tenants in common."

A grantor who acquired title to real estate prior to marriage must be identified in the deed by her maiden name and her married name. It is also important to set forth the marital status of the grantor in the deed to facilitate title search and help prevent ambiguities in the chain of title.

Signature of Grantor   A deed must be *signed by the grantor* or his duly authorized agent. When a grantor is unable to write, his mark, properly witnessed, is a valid signature. A grantor who himself is unable to be physically present to sign a deed may appoint another person, called his *attorney in fact,* to sign in his behalf. The appointment of an attorney in fact must be contained in a written instrument, signed by the landowner, and delivered to the appointed agent. This instrument is commonly referred to as a *power of attorney.* It includes authority to accomplish all acts necessary to sell and convey the landowner's real estate.

Where the grantor is to be a corporation, the deed must be signed by a duly authorized officer of the corporation. A corporate officer's authority to execute a deed and transfer title to corporate real estate must be granted by formal action by the board of directors. In some instances, formal action of the shareholders may be required in addition to formal action by the board of directors. As a general rule, the corporate seal must also be affixed to the deed.

Without the signature of the grantor, or that of his duly authorized agent, the deed is void and conveys no title. A signature of the intended grantee is not required for a valid deed.

Legal Capacity of Grantor   A grantor must have **legal capacity** to convey title by deed. Legal capacity is established by state laws. State laws generally classify deeds as being void or voidable depending on the type and degree of incapacity of the grantor. A deed will be declared void whenever it has been executed by a person who has been judged incompetent by a court. In such cases, the *incompetent* is totally without legal capacity. Her court-appointed guardian is the only person legally able to act in her behalf. Incompetency may be based upon mental illness, habitual drunkenness, drug addiction, or an inability to conduct business for any physical or mental reason.

A person who has not been adjudicated an incompetent may nevertheless not have sufficient legal capacity in certain circumstances. In such cases, her deed is voidable by herself or her legal representative, within a reasonable time after she obtains legal capacity. A deed will be held to be voidable when it is executed by a minor or by any person who is under duress, undue influence, or insane.

Description of the Land   The Statute of Frauds requires that the property being conveyed by a deed *be sufficiently described* so that it is clearly identifiable and distinguished from other parcels of land. A description in a deed is adequate if the land intended to be conveyed can be identified by reference to some other writing such as a plat, another deed, a contract, map, or survey. However, for the extrinsic writing to be incorporated by reference, it must be specifically referred to in the deed as containing the description of the land.

Granting Clause   The **granting clause** identifies as well as transfers title to the grantee. Where there is no clear indication in a deed that a lesser estate was intended to be transferred, the law assumes that the grantor intended to convey a fee simple. For example, a deed to "John Jones" as grantee is sufficient to convey a fee simple absolute.

To be effective as a deed, the writing must contain *words of conveyance.* In warranty deeds, the phrases "convey and warrant" or "grant, bargain, and sell" are commonly used as words of conveyance. In quitclaim deeds, the phrases are usually "convey and quitclaim," "remise, release, and quitclaim," or "quitclaim all interest." Words of conveyance indicate the grantor's intention to make a present conveyance. They also determine the grantor's warranties and obligations to the grantee, should the grantor's title prove nonexistent or defective. Not all words of conveyance create warranties or impose obligations upon the grantor. Later in this chapter we will discuss types of deeds and warranties created.

Delivery and Acceptance   A properly executed deed does not transfer title to real estate until it is delivered during the lifetime of the grantor. *Delivery* is the intent of the grantor that the deed shall presently transfer title to the grantee. The intent of the grantor can be shown by his words or conduct. The best evidence of delivery is the physical transfer of the deed from the grantor to the grantee or his agent without any reservation of right of control over the deed or any conditions attached.

An effective delivery may result even though there is no actual physical transfer of the deed to the grantee prior to the death or legal incapacity of the grantor. For delivery to occur this way, the words and conduct of the grantor must clearly show that he intended that the deed immediately convey title to the grantee. Consider the following examples: (a) The grantor, at the grantee's request, sends the deed to the grantee's agent, an attorney. Before the grantee receives the deed from her attorney, the grantor dies. (b) The grantor executes a deed and mails it to the grantee, but before the grantee receives the deed, the grantor dies. (c) A grantor transfers a deed to an escrow agent to be delivered upon the payment of the purchase price, but before the purchase price is paid and the escrow agent releases the deed to the grantee, the grantor dies. In each of these cases, the court held that an effective delivery had taken place.

A deed, even though physically transferred to the grantee, will not be held to have been delivered unless the grantor really intended to divest himself of possession of the deed and the title it represents. Such intention is not present where a grantor is under fraud, duress, undue influence, or mistake. Any deed obtained under any of these circumstances may be set aside by a court. As a general rule, a grantee must accept the deed from the grantor for a valid delivery to take place. *Acceptance of a deed* means that the grantee intended to obtain ownership of the real estate. His intention may be indicated expressly by his oral or written words or impliedly by his acts or other conduct.

Common provisions found in deeds

Due to variations in state laws governing the transfer of title to real estate, deeds may vary in form and content. Nevertheless, almost all deeds have similar basic provisions. In addition to the previously discussed provisions required in a valid deed, the following provisions are usually included in deeds utilized throughout the United States:

Seal   In most states, a seal is not essential to the validity of a deed. In states where a *seal* is required, it is sufficient for the deed to contain a phrase stating that it is sealed or to use the written or printed word "Seal" or the phrase "Witness my hand and seal." The importance of the seal in those states where it is required is that it raises a presumption that consideration was given in exchange for the deed. To rebut the presumption, actual proof must be presented that no consideration was in fact paid in exchange for the deed.

Attestation   *Attestation* is the act of witnessing a grantor's signature on a deed at his request and subscribing it as a witness. In most states, attestation is not required for the validity of a deed, unless the signature on the deed is by mark. Even though not required, attestation is important for proof of a grantor's signature after her death or if she becomes otherwise unable to verify her own signature.

Acknowledgment   An *acknowledgment* is a formal declaration in a deed, by the grantor and before an authorized official, that the instrument was executed freely and voluntarily. The acknowledgment can be made before a notary public, a military officer, a judge, or a justice of peace. An acknowledgment is usually unnecessary for the validity of the deed. However, in most states a deed cannot be recorded unless it is acknowledged. The inability to record a deed is serious. An unrecorded deed is not legally protected against innocent "purchasers" who acquire a lien or an interest in the real estate subsequent to the delivery of the unrecorded deed.

As a practical matter, all deeds should be acknowledged. Where a grantor is not available to testify in court, the acknowledgment itself may be introduced as evidence of the genuineness of the grantor's signature and of the instrument itself.

Recitation of Consideration   Although not necessary for the validity of a deed, consideration is usually stated as having been received by the grantor. The consideration recited can be *nominal,* that is, the amount stated bears no relationship to the value of the real estate. An example would be, "$20.00 and other good and valuable consideration." Some state statutes require trustee and court-ordered deeds to recite the actual consideration received.

Exceptions or Reservations   Following the description of the land, the deed may provide any *exceptions* or *reservations* to the grantor in the granting clause. An example of an exception would be a deed conveying "the West one-half of the Southwest Quarter of Section 25, . . . excepting therefrom one acre in the Southwest Quarter of said Southwest Quarter." An illustration of a reservation would be a deed conveying "Lots 36, 37, 38, and 39 of Pleasant Hills Subdivision in Section 1, . . . reserving, however, to the grantor, her heirs, and assigns forever, the minerals upon and underneath said land."

Habendum   The **habendum** establishes the quantity of the estate conveyed to the grantee. It usually begins with the words, "To have and hold the premises. . . ." Where there is a conflict between the granting clause and the *habendum,* the courts consistently hold that the estate described in the granting clause takes precedence over that described in the *habendum.* It is important that both clauses have an identical description of the estate conveyed to the grantee.

Any limitation, encumbrance, or restriction on the estate to be conveyed should be stated in the *habendum.* If not stated, the grantor is assumed to be making a conveyance that is free and clear of all such limitations, encumbrances, or restrictions.

Any intended limitation of the estate conveyed by the reservation of a life estate or by declaration of trust should be clearly set forth in the *habendum.*

When the grantee has agreed to take subject to or to assume and agree to pay an existing mortgage, the intent of the grantor and the grantee should be made clear. This is usually accomplished by the use of the words "subject to" or "the grantee hereby assumes and agrees to pay," followed by a detailed description and identification of the mortgage.

A subdivider often wants to control the future use of unimproved lots in a subdivision. His purpose is to create restrictions that can be enforced by and against the landowners in the restricted subdivision. These restrictions are called **restrictive covenants.** Restrictive covenants are listed in the *habendum* or in a separate instrument called a "declaration of restrictions" incorporated by reference in the deed.

Covenants of Title   **Covenants** (warranties) *of title* may be expressly stated in a deed or implied from words of conveyance used by a grantor. The following are five important covenants (warranties) that may be expressed or implied in a deed:

1. *Covenant of seizin.*   A promise by the grantor that she possesses title and has the right to convey it.
2. *Covenant of quiet enjoyment.*   A promise by the grantor that the grantee shall not be disturbed in his possession of the property by the grantor or others having a better title to the property.
3. *Covenant against encumbrances.*   A promise by the grantor that there are no existing encumbrances on the property.
4. *Covenant of further assurance.*   A promise by the grantor that he will execute or obtain any additional document necessary to perfect title in the grantee.
5. *Covenant of warranty forever.*   A promise by a grantor that he will forever warrant title to the property.

In many states, the five covenants (warranties) of title are implied by law when the grantor uses such words as "convey and warrant" or "warrant generally." Words of conveyance such as "grant, bargain, and sell," "convey and quitclaim" or "quitclaim all interest" do not imply covenants of title as a matter of law. For covenants to be made in a quitclaim deed, they must be expressly stated.

Covenants do not guarantee a marketable title or even any title to the grantee. However, a breach of covenant entitles a grantee to recover his actual damages against the grantor. The first three covenants bind the grantor only to her immediate grantee, while the last two may be enforced by subsequent grantees of the property in question.

Nontitle Covenants or Warranties   Unless expressly stated in the deed, a grantor is generally held not to have made any **nontitle covenants** or warranties. A grantee is said to take the property at his own risk. However, when a builder or real estate developer sells and delivers a deed to a newly constructed home to a grantee, many courts have modified the common law. They have established a common law warranty of *fitness for occupancy or use*. If the home purchased from the builder or developer is not reasonably fit for occupancy or use, the buyer can recover damages. This warranty is not implied in a sale of a home by a homeowner other than a builder or developer.

Waiver of Dower, Curtesy, and Homestead   In some states, the signature of a grantor's spouse on the deed is not enough to release dower, curtesy, and homestead rights. These states require that the deed contain a clause specifically releasing and relinquishing these rights.

Date   A date is not essential to the validity of a deed.

Common types of deeds

Quitclaim Deed   A **quitclaim deed** contains no covenants or warranties, express or implied. It merely purports to transfer any title presently possessed by the grantor. A quitclaim deed usually contains words of conveyance such as "remise, release, and quitclaim," "convey and quitclaim," or "quitclaims all interest." The quitclaim deed is commonly used to remove a cloud on title or by a grantor who is not certain that he actually has title or that it is free from encumbrances and other adverse interests.

General Warranty Deed   A warranty deed contains the covenants (warranties) of seizin, quiet enjoyment, encumbrance, further assurance, and warranty forever. A **general warranty deed** usually contains words of conveyance such as "convey and warrant" or "warrant generally." The covenants of general warranty apply to defects coming into existence while the grantor possessed title but also to those which occurred before. If a grantor does not have any title to the real estate at the time she delivers the deed to the grantee, but she subsequently acquires title, the grantee is said to have good title. The grantor is stopped, by virtue of her covenants (warranties), from stating that she did not have title at the time she executed and delivered her warranty deed to the grantee. The grantee is held to possess title by virtue of the ***doctrine of after acquired title.***

Special Warranty Deed   A ***special warranty deed*** contains the same covenants (warranties), express or implied, as the general warranty deed, except that the grantor covenants only against claims or defects of title arising during the time he possessed title. A special warranty deed usually contains words of conveyance such as "warrant specially." In some states, the use of the word "grant" alone will create a special warranty deed. The *doctrine of after acquired title* also applies to special warranty deeds. The special warranty deed is commonly used by guardians, trustees, executors, administrators, or by grantors who have acquired title at a foreclosure sale.

Grant, Bargain, and Sale Deed   Most states provide that a ***grant, bargain, and sale deed*** usually carries with it two or three covenants (warranties). These covenants pertain only to claims asserted by, through, or under the grantor. The covenants commonly implied by law are these:

1. That the grantor has not divested herself of any interest in the property prior to delivery of the deed.
2. That the title is free from any encumbrances brought about or allowed by the grantor.
3. That the grantee shall not be disturbed in his possession (quiet enjoyment) of the property by the grantor or others having better title to the property.

Specialty deeds

Deeds used for special situations are called ***specialty deeds.*** Specialty deeds usually take the form of either a special warranty deed or a quitclaim deed. They derive their names either from the fiduciary status held by the grantor or from the special purpose they fulfill. Specialty deeds are generally used in circumstances where a grantor wishes to pass whatever title he may possess, but he does not wish to acquire the burden of all or any of the covenants (warranties) of title. The following are specialty deeds:

Deed of Trust   The ***deed of trust*** is also referred to as the *trust deed*. It is a form of mortgage in that a debtor (trustor) conveys her land to a disinterested person (trustee) in trust for the benefit of a creditor (beneficiary) as security for the repayment of the debt. This deed usually contains a power of sale clause that empowers the trustee to foreclose and sell the property upon the debtor's default and turn over the proceeds to the creditor in satisfaction of the outstanding debt.

Deed in Trust   A ***deed in trust*** is ordinarily used to create a land trust or to transfer title to real estate to a trustee of an existing trust.

Tax Deed   A *tax deed* is given to a purchaser of real estate after a tax foreclosure sale and, if required by state law, the expiration of the redemption period. It usually is in the form of a special warranty or quitclaim deed.

Trustee's Deed   A *trustee's deed* is simply a deed, executed by a trustee, for the purpose of transferring title to real estate held in trust. A trustee's deed usually takes the form of a special warranty deed.

Cession Deed   A *cession deed* is a statutory form of quitclaim deed used to convey the road, street, highway, or alley rights of an owner to a legally incorporated governmental unit, such as a city or county.

Executor's Deed   An *executor's deed* is a deed executed by a court-appointed representative of a decedent who died leaving a will, transferring title to the decedent's real estate. The executor's authority to execute deeds and transfer title to a decedent's real estate is found either in the decedent's will, which may grant the executor power to sell, or in a court order authorizing the executor to sell the decedent's real estate.

Deed of Gift   A *deed of gift* is merely a deed that transfers title to real estate without consideration being received in exchange.

Deed of Surrender   A *deed of surrender* is a deed that brings about a merger of two lesser estates into a fee simple. Some examples are (a) A reversion is conveyed to a life tenant; (b) A life estate is conveyed to the owner of the reversion; (c) A life estate is conveyed to the owner or owners of the remainder interest. A deed of surrender usually takes the form of a warranty deed.

Administrator's Deed   An *administrator's deed* is a deed executed by a court-appointed representative of a decedent who died without leaving a will (intestate). An administrator must receive authority from the court to transfer title to the decedent's real estate.

Guardian's deed   A guardian is a court-appointed representative of a living person who lacks legal capacity to contract or convey in his own behalf. Such persons include infants, insane persons, habitual drunkards, the mentally retarded, or the aged. A *guardian's deed* is a deed executed by the legal representative of the incapacitated person in his behalf and pursuant to court order. The deed customarily used is a special warranty deed which recites that court authority has been granted to convey.

Deed in Partition   A *deed in partition* is a deed executed by a court-appointed person conveying title to real estate sold at a court-ordered partition sale. The grantor is usually the officer making the sale or some person specially appointed by the court.

Deed of Release   A *deed of release* is used to clear title to real estate. It is executed by a grantor who has or may have a legal interest in real estate owned by another. Such interests may be a mortgage lien, a dower or curtesy interest, a remainder interest, or a reversionary interest that has ripened because of the happening of a condition subsequent. Once the deed of release is recorded, the cloud on the title is removed.

Deed of Confirmation   A *deed of confirmation* is commonly referred to as a *correction deed*. It is usually a quitclaim deed used to correct an error in a prior recorded deed such as in the description of the real estate, names of the parties, or the estate conveyed.

Deed in Foreclosure   A *deed in foreclosure* is a court-ordered deed conveying title to a grantee who was a purchaser of real estate at a prior foreclosure sale. It is delivered after a redemption period has passed. The grantor is an officer appointed by a court. A foreclosure sale may result from a debtor's failure to satisfy a mortgage lien, a tax lien, a judgment lien, or any other lien created by law or the parties.

RECORDING OF DEEDS AND OTHER INSTRUMENTS

All states have statutes allowing *recordation* (recording) of certain instruments that affect title to real estate. Although these laws vary from state to state, their provisions are substantially similar. The effect of a properly recorded instrument is to give *constructive notice* (public notice) to any person who subsequently acquires an interest in the real estate that a prior adverse interest exists. The process of recordation establishes priorities between adverse legal interests. As a general rule, the *recording statutes* provide that the first party to record his interest has first priority in law, if, at the time of recordation, he was without actual notice of an unrecorded adverse interest.

The purpose of recordation is two-fold: first, it provides a means of protecting existing estates or other legal interests in real estate; and second, it protects the interests of subsequent purchasers against secret, unrecorded interests. The owner of an existing interest is assured protection only if she properly records her interest. A subsequent "purchaser" is assured of a superior interest in the real estate when he relies on the public record and acts in good faith, without *actual notice* of any unrecorded adverse interest.

As a general rule, any writing that affects title to real estate may be recorded. Most state laws allow the following instruments to be recorded: deeds, contracts for the sale of real estate, installment land contracts, leases, mortgages, deeds in trust, powers of attorney, releases of mortgages, assignments of mortgages, and *profits à prendre*. In addition, deeds in a foreign language are recorded *only if* accompanied by a written English translation.

Each state law establishes the place where instruments must be recorded. As a general rule, a public office in the county in which the real estate is located is the designated office for recordation. The public officer who is required by statute to maintain these public records may be a county clerk, recorder, or registrar.

Recording Systems

Deeds and other instruments that have been recorded must be indexed by the county clerk, recorder, or registrar. Most states authorize two types of indexing systems, the *grantor-grantee index system* and the *tract index system.*

Grantor-grantee index

In the **grantor-grantee index** system, separate index books are maintained for "grantors" and "grantees." As each deed or other instrument is recorded, it is indexed by year and in alphabetical order both under the name of the "grantor" in the grantor's index and under the name of the "grantee" in the grantee's index. The *grantor's index* includes not only the names of grantors in deeds but also the names of lessors, mortgagors, trustors in deeds of trust (trust deeds), and other transferors of any legal interest in real estate. The *grantee's index* includes all grantees named in deeds, lessees, mortgagees, and others who received legal interests in real estate. Each index contains the following information: type of instrument; name of grantor and grantee; date of the instrument; description and index book; page and date of recordation.

Tract index

A few states maintain a tract system of recordation. It differs from the grantor-grantee index system in that the **tract index system** is compiled according to parcels of land rather than by names of parties to a deed or other instrument. In each county, the recorder maintains a map that contains all parcels of land within a tract and their assigned reference (identification) numbers. The tract index contains a separate page for each parcel of land identifying each parcel by its reference number and description. Each index page contains a list of all recorded deeds or other instruments affecting title to the identified parcel. To research the title to a parcel of land, the researcher need only locate the parcel on the recorder's map, obtain its reference number, and use the reference number to find the appropriate page in the tract index.

Requirements for Recordation

In order to be recorded, an estate or other interest in real estate must be evidenced by a writing. In most states, a deed or mortgage is not effectively recorded unless it is executed properly and contains an acknowledgment. A few states require an attestation in addition to the acknowledgment. An improperly executed deed, mortgage, or other instrument is not operative to give constructive notice to subsequent purchasers.

In at least one state, Illinois, no deed will be accepted for recordation by any Recorder of Deeds or Registrar of Titles unless revenue stamps, evidencing the payment of the state transfer of title tax, have been purchased from the appropriate public official and affixed to the deed. In addition, a written transfer declaration, signed by at least one buyer and one seller or their attorneys, must accompany the deed. The declaration must recite the full consideration paid for the property together with other details pertaining to the transaction. The effect of recording the declaration is to make public the actual purchase price of all real estate.

Chain of title

Properly dated and recorded instruments reveal a continuous chain of title dating from an original grant from the government or from a foreign government up to present date. The *chain of title,* when compiled in a written chronological form together with a statement of all liens, court judgments, or other liabilities to which title may be subject, is referred to as an *abstract of title.*

Bona fide purchaser

A *bona fide purchaser* is a party who has paid value for an estate or other legal interest in real estate without actual or constructive notice of an already existing estate or legal interest in the same parcel. A purchaser has *actual notice* when he has knowledge of a prior unrecorded estate or other legal interest. He has *constructive notice* of recorded estates or legal interests. In addition, the law accords constructive notice of any adverse legal interests of the parties in possession of the real estate. This is true even though the subsequent purchaser does not inspect the premises and investigate the possible rights of those in possession. For example, A owns a home. She leases the basement of her home to students from the local university. The leases are unrecorded. B purchases A's home. B does not inspect the home and is unaware of the leases. B is held to have constructive notice of the existing leases.

Effect of Unrecorded Instruments

An unrecorded instrument is valid between the parties to it; however, a subsequent bona fide purchaser acquiring an interest in the property will take priority over a prior unrecorded interest. For example, A deeds land to B; however, B does not take possession and also fails to record his deed. A deeds the same parcel of land to C, who pays value in good faith without actual notice of B's interest. C records her deed. One day later B records his deed. In this case, C is the exclusive owner of the parcel of land.

Not all existing liens need to be recorded to have priority over even a bona fide purchaser for value. These liens are statutory in nature and are either direct liens on specific parcels of real estate, such as real estate taxes, special assessments, and mechanic's liens, or general liens on all real estate owned by the debtor in the state. Examples of the latter liens are inheritance tax, judgments, and franchise taxes.

The Torrens System of Title Registration

A few states have laws enabling cities and counties to adopt the *Torrens system* of land title registration voluntarily. Even where a county or city has established the Torrens system, registration of titles is not compulsory upon the landowner. Consequently, in any given city or county under the system, a landowner need not register her title. The title would then remain under the system prescribed by state recording statutes. Once title to property has been registered, the property cannot be removed from the Torrens system except by court order.

Registration procedure
The purpose of the registration procedure is to confirm and establish registered title in a present owner of real estate together with any outstanding adverse legal interests and encumbrances. Once title is registered, irrevocable ownership is established in the registrant, subject only to any adverse legal interests, liens, or encumbrances established by the court in the registration proceedings. Although the procedures for registering title vary, the following series of required steps appears to be common to all the states.

1. A written application to register title is filed by the owner of real estate in a court in the county in which the real estate is located. The application is required to list all information regarding the owner's title, including any existing adverse legal interests, liens, or encumbrances. Registration is usually limited to fee simple estates.

2. The application is referred by the court to a title examiner whose duty is to conduct an extensive title search and submit to the court a report on the status of the title as revealed by the records.

3. Actual notice of the title proceeding is sent by the court to all parties who appear to have an adverse legal interest in the owner's title. Constructive notice (notice by publication in a newspaper) is given to all other parties who may have a legal interest in the property.

4. A court hearing is held, and the court orders the recording officer to register the title in the owner in fee simple or otherwise, together with any adverse legal interests, liens, or encumbrances, and to issue a *Certificate of Title* to that effect.

5. The Registrar of Titles prepares an original and a duplicate copy of the Certificate of Title. The original is recorded in the registration book, and the duplicate is delivered to the owner.

After the title is registered, any adverse legal interest, lien (other than tax liens), or encumbrance acquired against the registered property is not valid unless it is filed with the Registrar of Titles and entered upon the original title certificate. Priority between registered interests, liens, or encumbrances is on a first-to-register, first-in-priority basis. The originals of all documents evidencing an adverse interest, lien, or encumbrance are usually retained by the Registrar of Titles until discharged or released.

Certain defects in title, such as tax liens and rights of a party in possession under a lease, may not be covered by a Torrens certificate. For his protection, the buyer should require a tax search and make an inspection of the land.

Transfer of ownership

Under the Torrens system, title to real estate does not pass upon the delivery of a deed to the grantee. The transfer of title occurs at the time a new certificate is registered and issued in the name of the grantee.

Where title to registered real estate passes by will, intestate succession, or judicial sale, the Registrar of Titles will make the appropriate change pursuant to court order.

Duty to defend title and reimbursement for loss

An owner of registered title is required to defend her title at her own expense if it is challenged. The Registrar of Titles is not required to defend the owner of registered title. Should the owner's title be defective due to an error made by the Registrar of Titles, the owner is entitled to recover her actual losses by filing proof of her claim with the county. State laws require an indemnity fund, made up of a portion of registration fees, to be established to indemnify owners for their losses.

SUMMARY

Because of the immobility of land, the estates and rights in land, together with the methods required to transfer these estates and rights, are prescribed by law in each state. Private title to land in the United States originates in grants from either the federal government or a foreign country. Each subsequent transfer of title to a specific parcel of land is revealed in a recorded history of a series of voluntary and involuntary conveyances.

Title to real estate may be involuntarily divested from its owner by condemnation, adverse possession, foreclosure sale, partition sale, accretion, escheat, and community property.

An owner may accomplish a voluntary transfer of title to his land by will (testate succession), public grant or patent, descent (intestate succession), sale, and gift.

The most common legal device used to transfer title to real estate is the deed. For valid conveyance to be made by deed, the following legal requirements must be met: (a) a writing, (b) signature of the grantor, (c) sufficient description of the land, (d) legal capacity of the grantor, (e) identification of the grantor and grantee with reasonable certainty, and (f) delivery by the grantor and acceptance by the grantee.

In some, but not all, states, the following additional requirements are necessary for the validity of a deed: (a) a seal, (b) attestation, and (c) an acknowledgment.

Due to variations in state laws governing the transfer of title to real estate, deeds vary in form and content. However, almost all deeds contain similar basic provisions, such as the names and addresses of the parties, a recitation of consideration, words of conveyance, a granting clause, a description of the real estate, exceptions and reservations, *habendum,* covenants of title, waiver of dower, curtesy and homestead, date, signature, seal, attestation, and acknowledgment.

General warranty, special warranty, quitclaim, and grant, bargain, and sale deeds are the most common types. In addition, there are numerous specialty deeds that are designed and used to accomplish a specific purpose. These include deed of trust, deed in trust, trustee's deed, cession deed, executor's deed, deed of gift, deed of surrender, administrator's deed, guardian's deed, deed in partition, deed of release, deed of confirmation, and deed in foreclosure.

For a grantee or other person to protect her estate or legal interest in real estate against parties who may subsequently acquire rights in the same property, she must properly record the instrument, which serves as constructive notice to all persons who may subsequently deal with the property. Failure to record may result in an owner's complete loss of her legal interest or, at the very best, a subordination of her legal interest to that of a third party. All states have statutes allowing recordation of certain instruments that affect title to real estate. Recordation is made with the public officer who is in charge of the public records in the county where the real estate is located. For an instrument to be recorded effectively, it must be properly executed and (in some states) attested or acknowledged. The most common system of recordation is the grantor-grantee index. A few states use a tract index system for recordation.

A few states have passed laws providing for the Torrens system of title registration. Under this system, an owner of real estate may voluntarily initiate legal proceedings to confirm and establish registered title in his name. After a judicial hearing is held, title is registered in the owner with the county Registrar of Titles. Thereafter, transfer of title does not pass upon the delivery of a deed to the grantee, but rather it occurs at the time a new certificate is registered and issued in the name of the grantee. Registration of title passed by will, intestate succession, or judicial sale is accomplished pursuant to court order.

TERMS AND CONCEPTS

You can check your understanding of these terms against the glossary or by review in this chapter.

Abstract of title

Acceptance of a deed

Accretion

Acknowledgment

Actual notice

Administrator

Administrator's deed

Adverse possession

Attestation

Attorney in fact

Bill to quiet title

Bona fide purchaser

Certificate of Title

Cession deed

Chain of title

Codicil

"Color of title"

Condemnation

Constructive notice

Covenants of title

Dedication

Deed

Deed in foreclosure

Deed in partition

Deed in trust

Deed of confirmation

Deed of gift

Deed of release

Deed of surrender

Deed of trust

Delivery

Devise

Doctrine of after acquired title

Escheat

Exception

Executor

Executor's deed

Foreclosure

General warranty deed

Gift

Grant

Grant, bargain, and sale deed

Grantee

Granting clause

Grantor

Grantor-grantee index

Guardian's deed

Habendum

Incompetent

Intestate succession

In writing

Legal capacity

Nontitle covenants

Patent

Partition

Per stirpes

Power of attorney

Quitclaim deed

Recordation

Recording statute

Reservation

Restrictive covenants

Seal

Specialty deed

Special warranty deed

Tacking

Tax deed

Testamentary capacity

Testate succession

Torrens system

Tract index system

Trustee's deed

Will

Words of conveyance

PROBLEMS

5–1. The city of Philadelphia passed an urban redevelopment law providing for the creation of a Redevelopment Authority. The purpose of the law was to accomplish the clearance, reconstruction, and rehabilitation of blighted areas within the city. The Authority was given the power to acquire property by purchase or eminent domain and to sell or lease the property acquired to private developers. A lawsuit was filed, alleging that the law was invalid because it authorized the taking of property for private use. What was the result?

5–2. A, B, and C own a thousand acres of land in joint tenancy. B and C farm the land and share income from their operations with A. A became dissatisfied with merely receiving income from the farm and filed a lawsuit asking the court to sell the farm and divide the proceeds equally between A, B, and C. What was the result?

5–3. What effect, if any, do each of the following facts have upon the validity of a will?

(a) The signature of the testator is only on the first page of a will consisting of three pages.

(b) The instrument was handwritten by the testator.

(c) The instrument contained the signature of one attesting witness.

(d) The instrument did not purport to give away all of the testator's property.

(e) The will was not delivered to the sole designated beneficiary before the testator died.

(f) The testator, at the time he signed the will, thought that he was signing a contract for the purchase of cattle.

(g) The testator, at the time he signed the will, was mentally ill.

5–4. T wanted to make a gift of a farm to each of her three sons. She properly executed three deeds conveying a parcel of farmland to each son. The deeds contained a proper attestation and acknowledgment. T placed the deeds in her safety deposit box and informed her sons of what she had done. She died, leaving a will disposing of all her property to her daughter. The sons and the daughter each claim title to the farms. Who has title to the land? Explain.

5–5. G sold land to B and delivered to B a general warranty deed. B later discovered that G never had title to the land. Nevertheless, he filed a lawsuit to quiet title on the basis that the warranties of title in the deed "guaranteed" title to him. During the lawsuit, X appeared and proved that she owned title to the land at the time G delivered his deed to B. Who presently had title to the land? Explain.

5–6. G, while insolvent, delivered a properly executed, attested, and acknowledged deed to E, the named grantee. The deed recited that it was given to E in exchange "for $20 and other good and valuable consideration." In a lawsuit to set aside the deed, G testified that she never intended to receive nor did she receive any consideration from E.

(a) Will the deed be set aside? Explain.

(b) Could X and Y, who were G's creditors at the time G delivered the deed to E, set aside the deed? Explain.

5–7. X subdivided his land into thirty-six residential lots. He recorded the subdivision plat together with a declaration of restrictions. One of the restrictions prohibited the construction of any "building" on any lot "other than one detached single-family dwelling." All deeds subsequently delivered were made subject to the restrictions. Y purchased a lot and constructed a large ranch-style home. Some years later he erected a 12 ft × 12 ft structure used as a playhouse by his children. Y's neighbor Z, who disliked Y intensely, filed a lawsuit asking the court to order the removal of the playhouse. What was the result? Explain.

5–8.   S sold a parcel of land to B, delivering to B a general warranty deed. B did not take possession of the land or record her deed. S subsequently sold the same parcel of land to X, delivering to X a general warranty deed. X recorded his deed. X did not have knowledge of S's deed to B.

   (a)   As between S and B, is B's unrecorded deed valid? Explain.
   (b)   As between B and X, who owns title to the land? Explain.

5–9.   Carson properly executed a quitclaim deed conveying his land, Redacre, to Dennis in exchange for a price of $150,000. Carson delivered the deed to Dennis, who promptly had it recorded. Several weeks later, Carson, being desperate for money, sold Redacre to Scott for $100,000. Carson properly executed and delivered a deed to Scott that contained the following words of conveyance, "convey and warrant generally." Scott also recorded his deed. Both Dennis and Scott claimed ownership of Redacre. Dennis filed a bill to quiet title against Carson and Scott. This lawsuit resulted in a judgment in favor of Dennis. A short time later Scott sued Carson for damages.

   (a)   What was the legal rationale for the court to declare Dennis to be the owner of Redacre?
   (b)   Will Scott be successful in his lawsuit against Carson? Explain.

5–10.   List and explain the five types of covenants (warranties) made by a grantor who executes and delivers a general warranty deed to the grantee.

5–11.   G executed and delivered a deed to B. The deed was not acknowledged. Is the deed valid? Explain. Will B have difficulty recording her deed? Explain.

SUPPLEMENTARY READINGS

Burby, William E. *Real Property,* 3rd ed. St. Paul: West, 1965.

Bergfield, Philip B. *Principles of Real Estate Law.* New York: McGraw-Hill, 1979. Chapters 10–12 and 14.

Henszey, Benjamin N., and Friedman, Ronald M. *Real Estate Law.* Boston: Warren, Gorham, and Lamont, 1979. Chapter 6.

Institute for Paralegal Training. *Introduction to Real Estate Law.* St. Paul: West, 1978. Chapters 3, 4, and 10.

Kratovil, Robert, and Werner, Raymond J. *Real Estate Law,* 7th ed. Englewood Cliffs, N.J.: Prentice-Hall, 1979. Chapters 6–9.

Ring, Alfred A., and Dasso, Jerome. *Real Estate Principles and Practices,* 8th ed. Englewood Cliffs, N.J.: Prentice-Hall, 1977. Chapters 9 and 11.

Leases

The possessory rights to real estate may be temporarily transferred from one individual (the landlord) to another (the tenant) by a formal, written lease or by oral agreement. In either situation, a landlord-tenant relationship arises; however, there are important differences between the landlord-tenant relationship created by a formal, written lease and that created by periodic tenancy without a lease. In the first instance, the rights and duties of the parties to the lease are spelled out in the contract and are governed by rules of law. In the second instance, where no written lease exists, the duties and responsibilities of each party are implied by law.

LEASES

A lease is both a *contract* and a *conveyance* of an interest in real estate. The contract element specifies the rights and duties of the parties to the lease. The lease also conveys the landlord's right to occupy the land to the tenant for the term of the lease. The parties to a lease are called the **lessor** or *landlord* and the **lessee** or *tenant*. The lessor's interest is called the *leased fee estate,* which consists of the right to receive the contract rent stipulated in the lease plus the *reversion* or the return of the property at the expiration of the lease. The lessee's interest is known as the *leasehold estate,* which consists of the use and occupancy of the property.

LEASEHOLD ESTATES

There are four types of leasehold estates: (a) *Estate for Years;* (b) *Estate from Year to Year;* (c) *Estate at Will;* (d) *Estate by Sufferance.* Each of these has different stipulations as to the rights of the lessee, period of time they cover, and manner in which they terminate.

Estate for Years (Estate for a Stated Term)

The term, *Estate for Years,* is misleading because the period of time (or term) of the lease may be any fixed period, whether it's for two months, six months, one year, or two years. Thus, the more descriptive term, *Estate for a Stated Term,* is often used. The Estate for Years (Estate for a Stated Term) has a fixed beginning and a fixed end. The estate may be terminated by agreement of the parties at any time, by the expiration date stipulated in the lease without the need for prior notice by either party, or by merger of the leasehold and leased fee interests. An Estate for a Stated Term is not terminated by the death of the landlord or tenant.

Estate from Year to Year (Estate from Period to Period)

An *estate from period to period* may be from week to week, month to month, year to year, or for several years. Such an estate is automatically renewed for succeeding periods unless proper notice of termination is given by the landlord or tenant. It differs from an estate for a stated term in that it does not have a definite termination date. The length of time for which the estate is renewed is dictated by the period for which the rent is paid.

An estate from period to period is generally created in one of two ways. First, the landlord and tenant may contract to rent by the month or by the year, without specifying the number of months or years the lease is to run. The rental arrangement then continues indefinitely for successive periods of time until one of the parties gives proper notice.

The estate from period to period may also be created through the actions of a holdover tenant and the landlord. When a tenant continues to occupy the leased premises after the expiration of the lease, he is called a *holdover tenant.* If the tenant continues to pay rent that is accepted by the landlord, and in the absence of an agreement to the contrary, an estate from period to period is created. (The landlord may, at her option, hold over the tenant by accepting the rent, or have him evicted). The successive period of the new estate cannot exceed one year. For example, if the original lease term was for six months, the newly established estate from period to period is six months. If the original lease term was five years, the newly established estate from period to period is limited to one year. Before an estate from period to period can be terminated, the landlord or tenant must give proper notice. Although the amount of notice varies from state to state, a notice of one week is generally required to terminate an estate from week to week; one month's notice is generally required to terminate an estate from month to month. The notice required to terminate an estate from year to year ranges from three to six months. In most states, notice must be in writing and delivered to the tenant or landlord or to a resident in the landlord's or tenant's residence, if above a certain age, or delivered by certified or registered mail with return receipt, or by posting on the premises. This type of lease may be oral or written, depending on the term of the lease and the Statute of Frauds in the various states.

Estate at Will

Estate at will is an estate of indefinite duration that can be terminated at the "will" of either the landlord or tenant. It may arise by implication or by express agreement. Although common law rule does not require advance notice of termination by either party, statutory laws and judicial decisions in most states now require notice. An estate at will terminates upon the death of either the landlord or tenant.

Estate by Sufferance

An *estate by sufferance* occurs when a tenant comes into possession of the property lawfully and then, after her rights have expired, continues to hold possession of the property without the consent of the owner. Under common law, she is not entitled to any notice. Many states, however, have statutory provisions that require the landlord to give the same notice as that required under an estate at will. In at least one state, Illinois, recovery of double the annual rate of rent is allowed if the tenant fails to vacate after a proper written demand by the landlord. The nature of the estate by sufferance makes it the lowest estate in law.

REQUIREMENTS OF A LEASE

Leases may be written, oral, or implied, depending on the term of the lease and various state statutes. The Statute of Frauds requires any lease with a term in excess of one year to be in writing. Some states, however, consider oral leases longer than one year to be valid. No particular form or wording is necessary to create a valid lease. If the intent to convey possession of property from one party to another for a specific period of time is clearly expressed in the lease and the lease meets all other requirements, a valid lease exists. A valid lease is a contract and must meet the requirements of a contract as specified in Chapter 3. These requirements include the following:

1. *A Mutual Agreement* (offer and acceptance).
2. *Consideration.*
3. *Reality of Assent.*
4. *Legally Competent Parties.*
5. *Legal Objective.*
6. *Description of the Premises.*   The leased property should be described with certainty to assure a "meeting of the minds." A street address should not be used exclusively because it does not specify what land or common property is included. The legal description of the property, combined with a statement of the lessee's right to light and air, use of

hallways, staircases, elevators, sidewalks, drives, alleys, and so forth should be used, especially if the property has several tenants.

7. *Term of the Lease.*   The term of the lease should specifically indicate a date of beginning, a date of ending, and the duration of the lease. Some states have statutory laws that limit the term of the lease. In the absence of such laws, leases may be of any duration.

8. *Signatures.*   The lease must be signed by the landlord because the courts construe the lease as a conveyance of real estate. The tenant need not sign the lease. The taking of possession and paying rent constitutes acceptance of the lease by the tenant. As a practical matter, however, it is good business to get signatures from both the landlord and the tenant.

Joint and Several Liability   When two or more tenants sign the same lease, they are generally held to be *jointly and severally liable* for the rent. In other words, if three tenants share a building, all three tenants sign on the same lease, and two of the tenants fail to pay their share of the rent, the landlord can hold the third tenant liable for all the rent. The tenants would be able to avoid joint and several liability by signing separate leases that stipulate their separate obligations.

RIGHTS AND RESPONSIBILITIES OF PARTIES

In the absence of express provisions regarding the rights and responsibilities of the parties to the lease arising from the landlord-tenant relationship, those rights and responsibilities are implied and created by operation of the law. The nature of the implied rights and responsibilities of the landlord and tenant dictated by the operation of the law varies from state to state because of varying state statutes and court decisions.

The Uniform Residential Landlord and Tenant Act (URLTA) has been proposed by the National Conference of Commissioners on Uniform State Laws and has been submitted to all states for consideration and adoption. The purpose of URLTA is to (a) "simplify, clarify, modernize and revise the law governing the rental of dwelling units and the rights and obligations of landlords and tenants; and (b) to encourage landlords and tenants to maintain and improve the quality of housing." To date, over a dozen states have adopted modified versions of URLTA.

When the landlord and tenant expressly state *covenants* (promises) in a lease, they can bypass the operation of rules of law that would otherwise govern their relationship. A *covenant* is a promise to do something or refrain from doing something in regards to the leased property. Express covenants sometimes stipulate the remedy for the breach of a particular covenant. In the absence of an expressed remedy, the usual remedy is to sue for damages.

Some of the common covenants and conditions in a lease (whether implied or expressed) are described in the following sections.

Possession

The landlord implicitly covenants to give possession of the leased property to the tenant at the agreed time. The tenant's right to use and occupy the premises gives him complete control of the property for the term of the lease. In the absence of lease provisions to the contrary, the tenant may refuse to allow the landlord to enter the leased property for almost any reason.

The landlord does have the right to enter premises that have been abandoned by the tenant, in order to care for the property. In this situation, however, the landlord should exercise care so that her reentering the property is not misconstrued as an acceptance, without protest, of the tenant's surrendering of the property, thereby terminating the lease without tenant liability.

Once the current tenant gives notice to the landlord of his intention not to renew the lease, the landlord also has the right to enter the premises at reasonable times to show the rental property to prospective tenants. Most leases expressly provide that the landlord has the right to reenter the property, but they usually state the reasons for which she may enter. It would not be reasonable to let the landlord enter at will.

Use of the Property

In the absence of lease provisions to the contrary, the tenant has the implied right to use the property for any legal purpose. If he uses it for an illegal purpose, the landlord has grounds for eviction. In practice, leases may express that the property can be used only for certain purposes or may specifically prohibit other uses. The tenant may negotiate a provision in the lease that prevents the landlord from leasing other parts of the same building to a competitor. Such provisions are valid. When a tenant leases an entire building, he has the implied right to erect and maintain signs on the exterior of the building, so long as zoning codes do not prohibit such signs. As always, lease provisions to the contrary will overrule the implied right.

Rent

Most leases specify that the rent is to be paid in advance. In the absence of such a provision, in most states, the rent is due at the end of the term. When a tenant *assigns* his leasehold interest to a third party *(assignee),* the assignee becomes liable for the rent. This, however, does not release the original tenant from liability. If the assignee defaults on the rent, the landlord can bring action against the original tenant as well as the assignee. A *sublessee,* on the other hand, is usually not liable to the landlord for rent unless he specifically assumes such liability. Subleasing versus assigning the leasehold interest is more fully explained later in the chapter.

The amount of rent is usually stipulated in the lease. On long-term leases, *escalation clauses* are commonly inserted to allow for automatic rent increases to protect against inflation. In the unusual situation where the rent is not specified in the lease, the landlord is entitled to a reasonable rental value based on current market rent.

Repairs and Maintenance

By common law, the tenant had an implied duty to make the repairs that are necessary to prevent *waste* of the building and return it to the landlord at the expiration of the lease in the same condition he found it, normal wear and tear excepted. Until recently, the rule of *caveat emptor* (let the buyer beware) prevailed in the relationship of landlord and tenant, and the landlord was under no obligation to repair the leased premises. Today, however, many states have statutory laws requiring the landlord to keep any building leased for dwelling purposes in condition fit for habitation. Some states have granted the tenant of a dwelling unit the right to deduct minor repair bills from the rent to maintain habitability. The limitations of the right are many and they vary from state to state. The tenant may vacate the premises, if they become uninhabitable, on the grounds of *constructive eviction.* In multiple-tenant properties, the landlord has an implied duty to repair and maintain common areas such as hallways, elevators, stairways, entrances, and sidewalks. The lease should spell out the respective duties and responsibilities of the landlord and tenant to make repairs. If such provisions are stated, they should be worded very carefully. Generally, a lease provision to make repairs does not carry with it the duty to make any structural changes. If the tenant agrees to make repairs, he is generally obligated to keep the premises in reasonable repair. If the landlord agrees to make specific repairs, she has the implied assent to enter the building for such repairs. However, she is not obligated to make repairs not specified.

Improvements

Unless otherwise specified in the lease, neither the landlord nor the tenant has a duty to make improvements. Due to the tenant's implied duty to return the property in the same condition he found it, he is precluded from making any alterations or improvements unless the lease specifically allows it or the landlord agrees. Most long-term leases have provisions for making alterations and improvements to keep the building from becoming functionally obsolete. All improvements (fixtures) become the landlord's property unless otherwise specified. Occasionally, provisions may be made to allow the tenant to remove some improvements prior to the expiration of the lease. Certain items that are installed to aid the tenant in his trade are considered *trade fixtures* and, being classified as personal property, are removable before expiration of the lease.

Where the lease provides the tenant with the right to make improvements, the landlord should insure that she is protected from a mechanic's lien should the tenant fail to pay the subcontractors who did the work. The lease may stipulate that the tenant be required to obtain lien waivers from those performing the work, or the landlord may be given the right to pay off any mechanic's lien and add it to the amount of rent payable by the tenant.

Waste

As mentioned earlier, the tenant has an implied obligation not to commit waste. *Waste* is the neglect, alteration, destruction, or misuse of property committed by the party lawfully in possession to the detriment of the estate or interest of another party. Waste is generally classified as either voluntary or permissive. *Voluntary waste* is caused by any unreasonable or improper use of the leased property resulting in damage. *Permissive waste* is caused by an omission or failure to act to protect or preserve the leased property. A tenant who commits waste is liable to the landlord for damages.

Taxes, Assessments, and Insurance

Unless there are lease provisions to the contrary, the tenant is under no implied obligation to pay real estate taxes, special assessments, or insurance on the leased property. On long-term commercial leases, however, the lease may stipulate that the tenant is to pay such expenses. This type of lease is sometimes referred to as a *net lease.*

Security Deposits

Unless the lease states otherwise, the tenant is under no obligation to pay a security deposit to the landlord. Most leases, however, do provide for a security deposit. Where a security deposit is used, the courts usually allow the landlord to retain all or a part of it if the tenant breaches the lease. The amount retained by the landlord is usually determined by the amount of actual damages. Several states have passed legislation requiring the landlord to keep the security deposits in a separate escrow account or to pay interest to the tenant on the security deposit.

Exculpatory Clauses

Many standard leases contain *exculpatory clauses* that attempt to absolve the landlord from any liability to the tenant arising from negligence on the part of the landlord. The validity of such clauses is questionable under the common law. Several states have passed legislation outlawing them.

Option to Renew

There are several variations of an *option to renew* clause. Many standard lease forms contain automatic renewal clauses that bind the tenant to a new lease term equal to the original term if he does not provide sufficient notice in writing to the landlord stating his intent not to renew. In this instance, the careless tenant may find himself bound to an unwanted renewed lease.

To avoid this situation, some states require the landlord to notify the tenant of the automatic renewal clause prior to the date the lease is to terminate. Other states require that the automatic renewal clause stand out from the other lease provisions to prevent such an important clause from going unnoticed by the tenant.

Other common option to renew clauses provide that the tenant, at his option, is entitled to renew the lease at any time prior to the expiration of the lease.

Option to Purchase

An *option to purchase* is a unilateral contract in which the optionor agrees to keep an offer open and irrevocable for a stated period of time in return for the optionee's payment of money. In a lease containing an option to purchase, the rent provisions in the lease are considered sufficient consideration to support the option. In many instances, the terms of the option may provide that the lease payments can be applied to the purchase price. The option to purchase terminates upon termination of the lease. Death of the optionor or optionee does not affect an option.

Right of First Refusal Option

The *right of first refusal* option clause provides the lessee with a prior right to purchase the property in the event the lessor receives an offer to purchase. It differs from the standard option to purchase in that the lessee has the right to meet any offer that the lessor receives.

Subordination Clause

A *subordination clause* is sometimes included in a lease to enable the lessor to place a first mortgage on the property after a lease has been executed. Without the subordination clause, leases signed before the mortgage have priority over the mortgage. The subordination clause acts to subordinate the senior position of the lease to the later recorded mortgage.

TYPES OF LEASES

Leases are contracts entered into for the mutual benefit of all parties. The varying needs of landlords and tenants require flexibility in the lease document. Leases are generally classified as long-term or short-term. This classification is rather arbitrary and has no legal significance, except that statutory provisions generally require leases with terms exceeding one year to be in writing. Leases are further subdivided according to how the amount of rental payment is derived. The most common types of leases are described on the following pages.

Fixed Rental Lease

A *fixed rental lease,* sometimes called a *flat lease,* stipulates a fixed rental that is to be paid over the duration of the lease. Fixed rental leases may be further classified as either gross leases or net leases.

Gross lease
A *gross* rental *lease* requires that the landlord pay the taxes, insurance, and all other expenses out of the fixed rental amount received from the tenant.

Net lease

The *net lease* requires that the tenant pay a net fixed rental to the landlord in addition to some or all of the fixed and operating expenses of the leased property. The net lease enables the landlord to receive a net rental return from the property over the years and assures that the amount will not diminish with increasing operating expenses.

Index Lease

Even with net leases, however, the corrosive effect of inflation diminishes the purchasing power of the landlord's fixed return. Consequently, an *escalation clause* may be inserted in the lease to guard against inflation. This is called an *index lease.* The escalation clause provides for an annual increase in rental payment based on a defined rule, formula, or index. One index commonly used is the ***Consumer Price Index.***

Reappraisal Lease

In lieu of an escalation clause tied to an index, the lease may provide that the rental rate escalates in the same proportion as the market value of the property increases. Such a provision generally stipulates that the property be reappraised at certain intervals and the rental rate adjusted accordingly. The reappraisal lease is subject to attack, however, because of the uncertain nature of market value estimates. As a result, reappraisal leases are seldom used.

Percentage Lease

Percentage leases are very common in the retail trade business. The rental amount generally includes a base or minimum monthly rental plus a percentage of the gross sales over and above a specified amount. The tenant will usually demand that a maximum rental be stipulated in the lease.

Although the percentage rental is sometimes based on net income or gross profits rather than gross sales, such practice is generally not recommended because of the inability of the landlord (and sometimes the tenant) to determine either net income or gross profits. Since the landlord's rental is extremely dependent on the tenant's business operation, the landlord should enter into such leases only after careful analysis of the tenant's credit and past performance. Lease provisions should clearly define what is included in gross sales, when and what type of report the tenant is to submit to the landlord, and whether or not the landlord had the right to inspect or audit the tenant's books.

Agricultural Lease

Agricultural leases are as many and varied as residential or commercial leases. They may be long-term or short-term. Some may give the tenant full managerial responsibility, while others provide for considerable landlord supervision. Some leases are filled with elaborate covenants and conditions, while others include only the minimum requirements. Some common agricultural leases are discussed in the next sections.

Cash rental lease

The *cash rental lease* stipulates that the farm tenant is to pay the landlord a fixed amount per acre for the right to farm the land. The rent may vary from two or three dollars per acre to over one hundred dollars, depending on the region of the United States and the productivity of the land. The tenant buys his equipment, seed, fertilizer, and pays all other expenses associated with the farming operation. The landlord pays the real estate taxes only. All profits from the farming operation accrue to the tenant. Cash rental leases are very common for pasture and grazing land.

Crop/livestock share lease

Crop or livestock share leases are the most common agricultural leases in the United States. The lease stipulates the exact sharing of crops, livestock, and expenses between the landlord and tenant. In this type of lease, the landlord shares the risk involved in production and usually receives from twenty-five to fifty percent of the crops or livestock produced.

Share-cash lease

Occasionally, cash-rent provisions are spelled out for a part of the farming operation, with crop-share provisions applied to the balance. This arrangement is called a *share-cash lease*.

Sale-Leaseback

The *sale-leaseback* is a financing device that involves just what the name implies: An owner of real estate sells her property and simultaneously agrees to lease it back from the buyer, usually on a long-term, net lease basis. The parties to the lease are called the *seller-lessee* and the *buyer-lessor*.

Buy-build-sale-leaseback

In some instances, a firm may purchase a site in a location of its preference, build a structure to suit its needs, and then search for an investor who is willing to execute a sale-leaseback. In such cases, the firm gets the location and building it wants, and the subsequent sale-leaseback frees up fixed capital the firm had tied up in real estate and enables it to use all its funds in the day-to-day operation of the business.

Sale-leaseback–buyback

Occasionally, the sale-leaseback includes an option, called *sale-leaseback-buyback,* for the seller-lessee to repurchase the property at the end of the lease term. This financing device, in effect, allows the seller-lessee to obtain one hundred percent financing on his building. Such leases must be carefully drawn to avoid Internal Revenue Service scrutiny. If the buyback price stated in the lease is a nominal value rather than fair market value at the time of sale, the Internal Revenue Service will probably rule that it was not a lease at all, but rather a long-term mortgage, and any tax benefits enjoyed during the lease term will be disallowed.

Advantages to seller-lessee

In summary, the major advantages of a sale-leaseback to the seller-lessee are these:

1. The sale frees up fixed capital that can be used more effectively as working capital or business expansion capital for an ongoing business.
2. The sale frees the seller-lessee of management problems associated with real estate ownership.
3. The seller-lessee retains use of the property.
4. The seller-lessee can deduct the total lease payments from his income when computing income taxes.
5. It enables the seller-lessee to obtain maximum financing without experiencing the many restrictive covenants that would be associated with bonds or other long-term financing devices.

Advantages to buyer-lessor

The buyer-lessor is usually a life insurance company, a pension fund, a church organization, or occasionally, an individual investor seeking a long-term, relatively secure investment. The major advantages of a sale-leaseback to the buyer-lessor are these:

1. The rate of return on long-term leases is generally higher than that offered on first mortgages and other long-term investments of similar risk.
2. The buyer-lessor can commit large amounts of investment funds for a long period of time, thereby avoiding the recurring problem of reinvesting in shorter-term investments.
3. The buyer-lessor has more control over the real estate she owns than she would have if she merely held the first mortgage.
4. The buyer-lessor may take advantage of financial leverage by mortgaging her property.
5. The buyer-lessor can depreciate the building portion of her investment and deduct it from her taxable income.
6. The buyer-lessor benefits from any equity growth through property appreciation.

TRANSFER OF INTEREST

Landlord's Interest

The landlord may freely sell, assign, or mortgage his *fee interest* in real estate. If he sells his interest, the grantee takes title subject to the lease and becomes liable for all the covenants in the lease. Such transfer, however, does not relieve the original landlord of his liability for the covenants unless the lease specifically releases him. Cancellation clauses are sometimes inserted in a lease to allow the landlord to cancel the lease upon proper notice if the property is sold. Possession of the property by a lessee is constructive notice to a purchaser that a lease exists.

Finally, the landlord may mortgage his interest in the leased fee. If the landlord defaults on the mortgage, the tenant's interest may or may not be affected, depending on whether the mortgage was recorded prior to the lease or after the lease. If the lease was made prior to the mortgage, the mortgagee must honor the lease unless a provision in the lease makes it subject to all the mortgages on the land. If the lease is made subsequent to the mortgage, the mortgagee can, upon foreclosure, terminate the rights of the tenant. To avoid eviction, the tenant may enter into a new lease arrangement with the mortgagee.

Tenant's Interest

The *leasehold interest* (tenant's interest) in real estate is considered personal property and may be freely assigned, sublet, or mortgaged unless provisions to the contrary are specified in the lease.

Assignment

When a tenant (assignor) assigns a lease, she transfers the entire remaining term of the lease to the assignee. In an *assignment* of the leasehold interest, the assignee becomes liable to the original landlord for rent. This, however, does not relieve the assignor from liability. The landlord may sue either the original tenant (assignor), or the assignee, or both for breach of the lease. If the original tenant is sued by the landlord for rent payments, the tenant has cause of action against the assignee.

Sublet

When a tenant transfers only part of the remaining term of the lease or only a part of the leased premises to the sublessee, she is subleasing. In a *sublease,* the sublessee is liable to the sublessor (original lessee) only, and not to the original landlord. The original tenant remains liable to the landlord unless she is expressly relieved of such liability by the landlord.

Mortgage

When the tenant decides to mortgage her leasehold interest, she is confronted with *leasehold mortgage* payments in addition to lease payments. The double payments of the tenant greatly increase the risk of default and, upon foreclosure, the mortgagee is faced with the necessity of taking over the lease. As a result, leasehold mortgages are generally available only to tenants with excellent credit ratings. Many states have statutory laws to regulate which leasehold interests may be mortgaged. In Arizona, for example, for a life insurance company to place a leasehold mortgage, the unexpired term of the lease must be at least twenty-one years.

Many leases provide that the lease cannot be assigned, sublet, or mortgaged without the written consent of the landlord. Such provisions are valid. However, it is generally held to be against public policy for the landlord to unreasonably withhold consent.

REMEDIES OF THE LANDLORD

There are several remedies open to the landlord if the tenant defaults in the lease agreement.

Distress for Rent Due

Common law provides the landlord with the right of *distress for rent due,* which is to seize any property owned by the tenant for rent due. The property is usually seized without notice and is held by the landlord until the rent is paid or until a court order allows the landlord to sell it. Many leases specifically provide for the landlord's rights to distress. Many state statutes, however, have abolished or modified this questionable procedure because of constant misuse and abuse on the part of landlords.

Confession of Judgment (Cognovit)

The *confession of judgment* lease provision allows the landlord's attorney to appear in court without the tenant's knowledge or consent and plead guilty in the tenant's behalf to any breach of the lease so charged by the landlord. Although such a provision is of questionable efficacy, it is still legal in several states.

Sue for Rent Due

The landlord may sue on the lease to collect rent as stipulated in the agreement. Such rights are available to the landlord whether or not specified in the lease.

Eviction

Eviction is a legal process used to remove a tenant from the premises for breach of the lease. The landlord can have the tenant evicted if she breaches the lease contract in any material way. He may then reenter the property and take possession. Generally, once the tenant is evicted, she has no further liability to pay rent unless the lease contained a survival clause. The *survival clause* provides that the tenant's liability survives the eviction.

TERMINATION OF LEASES

Leases may be terminated in a variety of ways. The most common methods are by (a) notice, (b) expiration of term, (c) breach of condition, (d) surrender and acceptance, (e) destruction of property, (f) condemnation, (g) merger, (h) constructive eviction, (i) actual eviction, and (j) foreclosure.

Notice

With estates from period to period, estates at will, and estates by sufferance, the lease may be terminated upon giving proper notice. If the period is from year to year, common law requires a notice of six months. Many states have shortened the notice requirement by statute. If the period is less than a year, the notice is usually equal to the period of the lease.

Expiration of Term

Estates for years (estates for a stated term) are terminated on the last day of the term without need of notification.

Breach of Condition

The lease usually gives the landlord the right to terminate the lease and to take possession of the leased property upon default of the tenant. Some states have statutes outlining the landlord's right to reenter upon default. In either case, the tenant should ensure that the landlord is required to give notice of default and allow the tenant a reasonable time to cure it.

Surrender and Acceptance

Surrender and acceptance involves the surrender of the unexpired portion of the lease by the tenant and the voluntary acceptance of the lease by the landlord. Upon surrender and acceptance, the landlord reacquires possession and relieves the tenant of future liability for rent. The Statutes of Frauds in many states require the surrender and acceptance to be in writing.

Surrender and acceptance should not be confused with *abandonment.* If a tenant abandons leased property, she does so without permission from the landlord and thereby remains liable for rent. The lease usually provides that the landlord may, upon the abandonment, reenter the property to protect it without having the courts construe it as a voluntary acceptance. In this way, the landlord may continue to hold the tenant liable for rent.

Destruction of Property

By common law, when agriculture was the predominant industry, the tenant was held liable for the rent even after the destruction of the improvements. It was felt that the tenant derived the majority of his utility by farming the ground, not by using the buildings. Today, however, the majority of the tenants are concerned primarily with the use value of the buildings. As a result, many states have passed statutes relieving the tenant from the liability of paying rent if the improvements have been substantially damaged and terminating the lease if the property has been destroyed. Many lease forms have similar provisions.

Condemnation

Unless otherwise specified in the lease, when all of the leased property is taken by condemnation, the lease is terminated and the tenant is reimbursed for the unexpired portion of the leasehold interest. The value of the leasehold interest is the present value of the difference between the rent stipulated in the lease (contract rent) and economic rent (market rent) at the time the property was condemned. The tenant's claim to the award is superior to that of the landlord. The proceeds in a condemnation suit must first go to the tenant to satisfy her claim before the landlord acquires his share. Consequently, most landlords insert a *condemnation clause* in the lease which provides that the lease will be terminated upon condemnation, with all the proceeds going to the landlord.

Merger

When the tenant's interest in real estate (leasehold interest) is merged with the landlord's interest (leased fee interest), the lease is terminated. A *merger* occurs when the tenant purchases or inherits the leased premises from the landlord. The leased fee interest merges with the leasehold interest to form fee simple ownership, and all property rights are vested in the new owner of the fee.

Eviction

An *eviction* is the dispossession or deprivation of the tenant from all or part of the leased premises at the instigation of the landlord. Evictions may be classified as actual eviction by law, constructive eviction, or partial eviction.

Actual eviction by law is a statutory right of the landlord if the tenant breaches the lease provisions. It involves a judicial proceeding to dispossess (evict) a tenant legally. If the judgment is in favor of the landlord and the tenant is dispossessed, the lease is terminated. Most state statutes list which conditions in the lease are grounds for legal eviction if breached.

Constructive eviction occurs when the leased premises become uninhabitable or untenantable for the use specified in the lease as a result of acts or omissions of the landlord that force the tenant to remove himself. The tenant is then no longer liable for rent. Failure of the landlord to make repairs or to provide heat and electricity or other provisions agreed to in the lease may result in constructive eviction.

Partial eviction may be constructive or actual. *Partial constructive eviction* occurs when the landlord, due to her acts or omissions, makes a part of the leased premises untenantable. The tenant may move out of the entire leased premises and is no longer liable for rent. *Partial actual eviction,* on the other hand, occurs when the landlord actually evicts the tenant from only a part of the leased premises. In this situation, the tenant can continue to occupy the remainder of the premises without paying rent. Such a situation may arise when the landlord, whose business occupies a portion of the building, decides to expand and, in doing so, unlawfully evicts a tenant from an area previously occupied and leased by him.

Foreclosure

As mentioned earlier, the landlord has the right to mortgage his leased fee interest. If the mortgage is foreclosed, however, and the mortgage is senior to the lease, the lease rights of the tenant are automatically cut off. This situation is not always attractive to the mortgagee since he becomes the owner of a newly unleased property with no income stream. Consequently, the mortgagor may insert a *nondisturbance clause* in the mortgage which provides that, in case of foreclosure, the tenant's right will not be disturbed. If, on the other hand, the *lease antedates the mortgage,* the tenant's rights are not cut off by foreclosure. The mortgagee merely becomes the new landlord of the tenant, and both parties must adhere to the lease provisions.

Death of Parties

In an estate at will, the death of either the landlord or the tenant will terminate the lease.

CHANGING NATURE OF THE LANDLORD-TENANT RELATIONSHIP

The legal relationship between landlord and tenant was derived from the common law or custom established during the late fifteenth century and refined by centuries of judicial interpretation to satisfy the needs of an agrarian and feudal society. Land law was the first area of law to become established because the majority of wealth and, consequently, litigation stemmed from land and its ownership. It seems that those subjects of law that were settled earliest have become the most difficult to change.

The scales on the balance of justice have been tipped in favor of the landlord for centuries, because of his superior bargaining position. Now, however, consumer protection organizations have focused in on the inequitable landlord-tenant relationship and have encouraged tenants to organize and fight against the archaic one-sided law. Many state legislatures have responded to the demands of tenant unions by passing legislation to protect the tenant. As mentioned earlier, the Uniform Residential Landlord and Tenant Act (URL-TA) has been adopted or is being considered in many states. In addition the courts are handing down decisions in favor of the tenant by declaring certain provisions in the lease to be against public policy. The following list includes some of the recent laws or decisions affecting the landlord-tenant relationship.

1. Distress has been outlawed in some states.
2. Exculpatory clauses releasing the landlord from all liability arising from his negligence have been found void in many cases.
3. Some statutes allow the tenant to make necessary repairs and deduct it from rent.
4. Some city ordinances require the landlord to deposit money in an escrow account to be released for repair work.
5. Evictions are legal only by court order in some states.

6. Some states require the landlord to pay interest on any security deposit held by him.

7. Certain contracts of adhesion where the landlord, with his superior bargaining position, dictates lease provisions on a "take it or leave it basis" have been held to be unconscionable and void.

SUMMARY

One of the many rights inherent in the total bundle of rights associated with ownership is the owner's right to occupy and use the premises. If the fee owner does not use the property himself, he may temporarily transfer the possession and use rights to a tenant by means of a lease, thereby providing the tenant with a leasehold estate or interest in the property for the duration of the lease. Various types of leasehold estates may be created, depending on the nature of the lease and the various state statutes. The lease, whether oral or written, creates a landlord-tenant relationship between the lessor and lessee. In the absence of lease provisions to the contrary, the relationship is determined by common law and state statute. Historically, common law has put the landlord in a superior bargaining position. Recently, however, the scales of justice have been moving in the direction of the tenant.

TERMS AND CONCEPTS

You can check your understanding of these terms against the glossary or by review in this chapter.

Condemnation clause	Lease antedating the mortage
Confession of judgment	Leasehold mortgage
Consumer Price Index	Lessee
Covenants	Lessor
Distress for rent due	Merger
Escalation clause	Option to renew
Eviction	Partial eviction
Exculpatory clause	Sale-leaseback
Fixed rental lease	Subordination clause
Holdover tenant	Surrender and acceptance
Joint and several liability	Waste

What are the differences, if any, between the following?

Assignment and Sublease	Partial constructive eviction and
Constructive eviction and Actual	Partial actual eviction
eviction	Percentage lease and Index lease
Gross lease and Net lease	Right of first refusal and Option
Estate by sufferance and Estate	to purchase
at will	Sale-leaseback and Sale-leaseback-
Estate for years and Estate from	buyback
period to period	Sublessee and Assignee
Leasehold interest and Leased	Surrender and acceptance and
fee interest	Abandonment
Nondisturbance clause and	
Survival clause	

PROBLEMS

6–1. What is the main difference between a reappraisal lease and an index lease? Which of the two is most commonly used? Why?

6–2. How is an estate from year to year created? How is it terminated?

6–3. Comment on some of the remedies of the landlord that you feel are unfair to the tenant.

6–4. What is a nondisturbance clause in a lease? Whom does it protect?

6–5. What are the main advantages of a sale-leaseback to the seller-lessee?

6–6. What are the legal requirements for a valid lease?

6–7. Assume you own a building in a retail area and have a prospective tenant who is starting up an ice cream parlor. Her initial investment in equipment is high and her cash position is poor. What provisions in the lease would you suggest to entice the prospect into renting your building and allow you to make a satisfactory return on your investment?

6–8. Assume that, as lessee, you sign a lease on a building on January 1, 19X0. In March of 19X0 the lessor mortgages the leased premises. The lessor then defaults and the mortgagee forecloses. What are your rights, if any?

6–9. Give some examples to illustrate the difference between voluntary waste and permissive waste.

6–10. Under what circumstances will a court enforce an agreement that a security deposit shall serve as liquidated damages for a tenant's breach of a lease provision?

6–11. Give two examples of situations where a tenant might have the right to repair and deduct the repair costs by state statute or court decision.

6–12. Give two examples of landlords' liability with respect to common areas in a leased premises.

6–13. What are the tenant rights when the landlord sells the property? What if the landlord died?

6–14. Distinguish between a sublease and an assignment of a lease.

6–15. What are some of the risks of a landlord retaking possession of a leased premise without first resorting to legal action?

SUPPLEMENTARY READINGS

Anderson, Ronald A. *Business Law: Principles and Cases,* 7th ed. Cincinnati: Southwestern, 1979.

Barlowe, Raleigh. *Land Resource Economics.* Englewood Cliffs, N.J.: Prentice-Hall, 1958. Chapter 14.

Bellavance, Russell C. *Real Estate Law.* St. Paul: West, 1978. Chapter 9.

Bergfield, Philip B. *Real Estate Law.* New York: McGraw-Hill, 1979. Chapters 23 and 24.

Burby, William E. *Real Property.* St. Paul: West, 1965. Chapters 10–15.

French, William B., and Lusk, Harold F. *Law of the Real Estate Business,* 4th ed. Homewood, Ill.: Irwin, 1979. Chapter 17.

Hoagland, Henry E., and Stone, Leo D. *Real Estate Finance.* Homewood, Ill.: Irwin, 1973. Chapters 9 and 10.

Kratovil, Robert. *Modern Mortgage Law and Practice.* Englewood Cliffs, N.J.: Prentice-Hall, 1972. Chapter 7 and 26–32.

Kratovil, Robert, and Werner, Raymond J. *Real Estate Law,* 7th ed. Englewood Cliffs, N.J.: Prentice-Hall, 1979. Chapter 37.

O'Donnell, Paul T., and Maleady, Eugene L. *Real Estate Fundamentals.* Philadelphia: Saunders, 1975. Chapter 7.

Ring, Alfred A., and Dasso, Jerome. *Real Estate Principles and Practices,* 8th ed. Englewood Cliffs, N.J.: Prentice-Hall, 1977. Chapter 24.

Tosh, Dennis S., and Ordway, Nicholas. *Real Estate Principles for License Preparation.* Reston, Va.: Reston Publishing, 1979. Chapter 13.

Unger, Maurice A., and Karvel, George R. *Real Estate Principles and Practices,* 6th ed. Englewood Cliffs, N.J.: Prentice-Hall, 1979. Chapter 24.

Financing and Mortgages

The vast majority of all real estate purchases are financed through the use of credit. Most buyers provide a down payment and rely on debt financing to furnish the balance. The primary source of debt financing in real estate is the mortgage. Generally a mortgage loan involves two instruments, the *mortgage* and a *note;* however, a bond is used in some states rather than a note. In some instances the seller is willing to sell on a contract for deed with no money down, thereby providing the buyer with 100 percent financing. On occasion, the buyer may have sufficient savings to purchase real estate on an all-cash basis, thereby bypassing any financing problems. However, the 100 percent financed transaction and the all-cash transaction represent the two extreme positions; most transactions involve the use of either a mortgage or a deed of trust coupled with the note.

DEED OF TRUST

In several states, the **deed of trust** (or **trust deed**) is used frequently instead of the mortgage. The deed of trust serves the same purpose as the mortgage; however, the deed of trust involves three parties instead of two, as illustrated in Figure 7–1. The borrower (trustor) executes the deed of trust, which conveys the property to a third party (the trustee). A note is held by the lender as evidence of the debt, the same as with a mortgage. If the borrower defaults, the property is transferred to the lender or is sold through legal proceedings.

The remainder of this chapter discusses mortgage requirements, clauses, covenants, classifications of mortgages, remedies, and sources of funds. These same requirements, clauses, and so forth apply to deeds of trust.

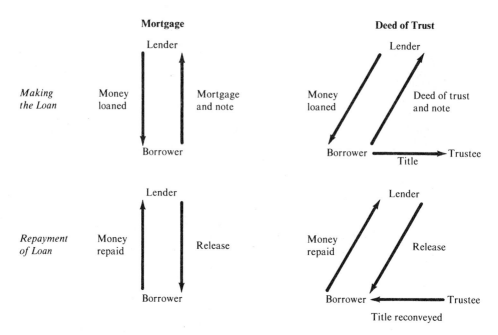

Figure 7–1
Mortgage compared to a deed of trust

MORTGAGES

The *mortgage* is a contract between the *mortgagor* (borrower) and the *mortgagee* (lender), that pledges a specific parcel of property as security for a debt. The mortgage contract is not fully standardized, but rather can be adapted to fit the needs of a variety of lender and borrower situations. The mortgage contract refers to the note (or bond) and the debt. It also lists the rights of the mortgagee and the responsibilities of the mortgagor arising from the debt. Both a debt and a pledge of property must be present for a mortgage to exist. The mortgage follows the debt and exists for the life of the debt. If the debt is paid or becomes unenforceable, the mortgage is *defeated* and the borrower obtains a title unencumbered by the mortgage.

The Note

The *note* is a contract that gives evidence of the debt. The person who mortgages property incurs a personal liability to repay the debt. Essentially, a general lien against all the debtor's property exists until the note is paid off. As a result, upon the default of the debtor, the creditor may obtain a deficiency judgment against other assets of the debtor if the foreclosure sale does not bring sufficient proceeds to cover the debt. Occasionally, however, the debtor and creditor may agree that the specific property pledged in the mortgage is the sole security for the debt, in which case deficiency judgments could not be obtained.

The Pledged Property

In general, any interest in real estate that can be sold or assigned can also be mortgaged. Personal property also may be mortgaged by means of a *chattel mortgage.* A relatively new concept in real estate financing is the use of a *package mortgage,* which combines a loan on real estate with a loan on personal property such as furniture and appliances. Whatever the type of mortgage used, the pledged property should be adequately identified by a legal description, if real estate, and by serial number if personal property.

History of the Mortgage

Real estate has been used as security for loans for centuries. The concept of mortgages originated in England around the fourteenth century. The earliest mortgage was actually a deed of the property to the lender with a provision for return of the property to the borrower upon payment of the debt. If the borrower defaulted on the debt, the pledged security was lost to the lender without need of a foreclosure sale. In addition, the borrower still remained liable for the debt. Although by law the lender was entitled to take possession of the property at the time the mortgage was signed, he usually allowed the borrower to keep possession. This early interpretation of mortgage law fostered many abuses among lenders. It was common for lenders actually to encourage default, thereby obtaining absolute ownership of the mortgaged property. Many borrowers who felt they were unjustly deprived of their property petitioned the king for relief. In cases of extreme hardship, the king would give the borrowers a chance to redeem their property upon payment of the delinquent obligation. Thus, the *equity of redemption* was born around 1625.

With the equity of redemption operating in favor of the borrower, the lender found himself in an untenable position. There was no time limit within which the borrower had to exercise his right of redemption. The lender was forced to reconvey the property to the borrower whenever he paid the delinquent debt. This obvious inequity was eventually eliminated when the courts began allowing the lender to bring suit against the borrower to cut off or foreclose his equity of redemption after a stated period of time, usually from six months to two years. This action is known as *strict foreclosure* and is still used today to some extent. The more common practice today is *foreclosure by sale.* The pledged property is sold at public auction, and the proceeds are used to pay off the debt. Any sale proceeds in excess of the debt are turned over to the borrower. The foreclosure by sale also acts to foreclose or cut off the equity of redemption. Some states have passed a *statutory right of redemption,* which allows the borrower to redeem her property within a period of time after the foreclosure sale. The time within which an individual is able to exercise her statutory right of redemption varies from state to state, but it is usually one to two years.

Title Theory and Lien Theory

As the mortgage law evolved in England over the years, two different schools of thought developed and have given rise to two different mortgage theories in the United States today.

States that recognize and practice the *title theory* of mortgage law require that title and possession of the mortgaged property transfer to the lender upon execution of the mortgage. In title theory states, a *defeasance clause* is included in the mortgage contract. This double-edged provision allows the borrower to defeat the mortgage and reacquire possession and ownership upon full payment of the debt. On the other hand, if the borrower defaults, her rights are automatically terminated and the defeasance clause allows the lender to retain title to the property. In some states the title theory has been modified to allow the borrower to remain in possession of the mortgaged property as long as she abides by the terms of the mortgage contract.

States that recognize and practice the *lien theory* of mortgage law hold that the mortgage, when executed, merely creates a lien in favor of the lender, and the borrower retains both possession and title. Again, the equity of redemption allows the delinquent borrower the right to redeem the property at any time prior to foreclosure by paying off the debt. The borrower also has the opportunity to redeem her property after foreclosure in those states having a statutory right of redemption.

MINIMUM REQUIREMENTS OF A MORTGAGE OR DEED OF TRUST

Although many organizations are encouraging the adoption of a standardized mortgage document, to date none exists. However, every mortgage contract must meet certain minimum requirements in order to be valid. The requirements for a valid mortgage contract are these:

1. The mortgage contract must be in writing.
2. Parties to the mortgage contract must be competent and must have the capacity to enter into a contract.
3. A mortgaging or granting clause must be included in the contract. This clause *pledges* or *grants* the property as security for the debt depending upon whether the state subscribes to lien theory or title theory.
4. A legal description of the pledged property is necessary. Also, if any personal property is covered by the mortgage, it must be identified.
5. A description of the debt and the terms of the debt should be stated with sufficient accuracy to prevent the parties from substituting other debts in its place. In practice, the note is usually made a part of the mortgage by referring to it in the mortgage. The *note* is generally not recorded,

because the mortgagor is reluctant to tell the world about her debts. The *mortgage,* on the other hand, should be recorded to protect the mortgagee's priority. A mortgage must be acknowledged before it can be recorded; however, an unrecorded mortgage is valid between the mortgagor and the mortgagee.

6. The specific promises or covenants agreed to by the mortgagor must be included. These are the *do's* and *don'ts* the mortgagor agrees to in exchange for the loan.

7. The mortgage must be executed (signed) by the mortgagor and the mortgagor's spouse (if married) to waive dower and homestead rights. These rights have been modified or eliminated in some states.

Common Mortgage Covenants and Clauses

There is no single, standardized mortgage contract today. The provisions in each mortgage and/ or note will differ somewhat because of the varying needs of the borrowers, the varying degrees of security offered by the pledged properties, changing conditions in the mortgage market, localized lending policies, and state laws. However, certain clauses are common to most residential mortgages and to deeds of trust. They are as follows:

1. *Covenant or promise to pay indebtedness.*

2. *Covenant to pay taxes and insurance.*   The mortgagor agrees to pay the taxes and insurance on the mortgaged property. The mortgagee is very concerned that the mortgagor pay the taxes because unpaid taxes become a first lien on the property. The insurance clause insures the pledged property against loss by fire, wind, and rain. The mortgagee is usually provided with the right to pay any unpaid taxes, assessments, or insurance premiums and add such payments to the amount owed on the mortgage. Many lenders ensure that taxes and insurance are paid by providing the mortgagor with a budget mortgage, whereby the monthly payment includes not only principal and interest but also taxes and insurance.

3. *Covenant against removal.*   This clause prohibits the mortgagor from removing or demolishing any of the buildings or fixtures from the pledged property because such removal could cause a loss in the value of the pledged property.

4. *Estoppel certificate or certificate of no defense.*   This clause obligates the mortgagor to furnish the mortgagee, upon request, a written statement acknowledging the current loan balance and whether or not any defenses exist against the debt. The rule of estoppel means that the mortgagor cannot later assert that the balance due was different from that stated on the certificate.

   The mortgagee uses the *estoppel certificate* if and when he decides to sell the mortgage. Since neither the mortgage contract nor the note specifies the exact loan balance at a given time, the certificate is given to the mortgage purchaser to assure him of the existing balance of the loan and to certify that the mortgagor has no defenses against the claim.

A number of other clauses are found in mortgages. The acceleration clause, interest escalation clause, and prepayment clauses are in most mortgages. These and other special clauses are described in the following sections.

Acceleration Clause

The mortgage contract and the associated note often stipulate that any default in payments or in any of the other covenants agreed-to will cause the remaining loan balance to become immediately due and payable. This provision is called the *acceleration clause.* In the absence of this provision, the mortgagee's only recourse in case of default is to sue on the note or to foreclose. In either of these actions, the mortgagee can only collect the amount presently due rather than the entire debt. This would create the need for a series of actions rather than a single, final action.

Foreclosure proceedings are expensive and cumbersome and generally create bad public relations. As a result, most lenders provide a grace period before they exercise the acceleration option. They are willing to accept late payments or restructure the terms of the loan to facilitate payment. These practices, however, do not constitute a waiver of the mortgagee's right to accelerate the debt if she deems it necessary.

Interest Escalation

The rate of interest to be paid on the debt is stated in the note and sometimes, although not necessarily, in the mortgage. Some states now have *usury* laws that limit the interest rate that can be charged on residential loans. Such laws, however, do not usually apply to commercial or business loans. Three types of interest *escalation clauses* are common. The first generally provides that the rate of interest on the mortgage loan will automatically escalate to the highest legal rate upon default.

A second clause often used provides that the interest rates will increase if the property is not used by the mortgagor as his primary residence. The reasoning here is that rental property does not receive the same care as owner-occupied property.

The third provides that the rate of interest charged on the debt will vary according to some standard index, generally the prime interest rate. This clause is more common in commercial or business loans and is extremely popular in periods of rapidly rising interest rates. Recently there has been agreement among many institutional lenders that such a practice should be adopted for residential loans. This *variable rate mortgage* concept will most likely be a common practice in residential mortgages within a few years.

Prepayment Clause

The *prepayment clause* allows the mortgagor to prepay the debt before it becomes due. Without this provision, the lender is not required to accept advance payments. The repayment clause may allow full or partial prepayment and may, at the discretion of the lender, include a penalty for prepayment. Some lenders place provisions in contracts allowing up to 20 percent of the unpaid balance to be paid in any one year. Many lenders use a clause requiring a prepayment penalty only if the mortgagor is refinancing with another lender.

The mortgagor exercises her prepayment option when she sells the property and pays off the loan before its maturity. It also allows the mortgagor to refinance during periods of falling interest rates. Occasionally, the prepayment penalty on commercial loans is too severe to make refinancing a feasible alternative.

Covenant to Pay Attorney's Fees

This provision stipulates that, if it becomes necessary for the mortgagee to hire legal counsel to collect the debt or to foreclose the mortgage, the legal fees will be paid by the mortgagor.

Receiver Clause

The *receiver clause* is common in mortgages on income-producing property. It provides that, in case of default, a court-appointed receiver steps in and collects the rents and pays the necessary bills between the commencement of foreclosure action and the actual sale. Such a provision prevents the mortgagor from "milking" the property during the interim period and ensures that proper maintenance will be performed to protect the property value.

Owner's Rent Clause

The *owner's rent clause* provides that, in case of default, the mortgagor agrees to pay rent to a court-appointed receiver during the interim between the commencement of foreclosure action and the actual sale. This provision is a necessary supplement to the *receiver clause* when the mortgagor occupies the pledged premises, because the receiver is entitled to enforce only those contracts that the owner had. The owner obviously did not have a contract with himself. As a result, the owner's rent clause becomes necessary if rent is to be collected from the owner himself.

Subordination Clause

Generally, the priority of mortgages as to lien rights is determined by the date of recording of each lien. The mortgage that is recorded first establishes the earliest lien right. In case of foreclosure, the holder of the earliest lien is paid from the sales proceeds first. Junior lien right holders are then paid off in ascending order. The established order or priority can be altered through the use of a subordination clause. Simply stated, the *subordination clause* provides that the holder of a prior lien right agrees to subordinate his priority to a subsequent lienholder. The question arises as to why anyone would subordinate his priority on a voluntary basis. This example illustrates the use of a subordination clause:

The seller of a vacant parcel of land may take back a "purchase money mortgage" from the buyer as part of the selling price. In such a case, the seller becomes the mortgagee rather than a financial institution. When he records the purchase money mortgage (PM mortgage), the priority of his lien right is established. If the buyer plans to obtain a construction loan later in order to build on the vacant land, he must ensure that the purchase money mortgage contains a subordination clause where the seller subordinates his prior lien to that of the lending institution furnishing the construction loan. This is necessary because lending institutions are not allowed to make loans on anything other than first mortgages. By agreeing to a subordination clause, a land developer may facilitate the sale of his land and may be able to command a somewhat higher selling price. Also, even though the seller has taken a junior lien holder position, the construction of the improvement on the mortgaged land increases the value of the pledged property and thereby provides additional security to the original seller in case of foreclosure.

Default in Prior Mortgage Clause

This *default* clause is commonly used in junior mortgages to protect the junior mortgage lender. It provides that, in the event the mortgagor defaults on the first mortgage, the junior mortgage holder may pay the delinquent amount and add it to the balance of the second mortgage loan. This right is exercised by the junior mortgage lender upon default of a prior mortgage when the real estate market is temporarily depressed, and the possibility exists that the proceeds from a foreclosure sale would not be sufficient to cover the junior lienholder.

Alienation Clause (Due on Sale)

Many mortgages contain an *alienation clause* that gives the lender the right to call the entire balance due if the property is sold. It is used by lenders to eliminate old loans in times of rising interest rates. Upon sale, the lender may increase the interest to the current rate.

CLASSIFICATION OF MORTGAGES BY REPAYMENT METHOD

The varying needs of borrowers and lenders give rise to many variations in the way in which mortgages are repaid. The note and mortgage will define the repayment method to be used based on the needs of the lender and the borrower. Some currently used repayment methods are described under the following categories:

Straight-Term Mortgage

The *straight-term mortgage* loan provides for repayment of the principal amount of the loan at maturity. No provision is made to reduce the principal during the term of the loan. The borrower pays interest only at stated intervals, usually monthly, quarterly, semiannually, or annually. The term of the loan usually varies from one to five years. Term mortgages were very common on residential loans before the depression; however, the financial crisis of the 1930s precipitated large numbers of foreclosures because of the inability of borrowers to pay the lump sum upon maturity. For this reason, this type of loan has become less common.

Fully Amortized Mortgages

The *fully amortized mortgage* provides for gradual repayment of the total principal amount over the term of the loan. The borrower makes periodic payments, usually monthly, quarterly, semiannually, or annually, which include both principal and interest. At maturity, the outstanding loan balance is reduced to zero. The term of fully amortized-residential mortgages generally varies from twenty to thirty-five years.

Partially Amortized Mortgages

The *partially amortized mortgage* provides for gradual repayment of a part of the principal over the term of the loan. The borrower makes periodic payments (e.g., monthly, quarterly, semiannually, or annually) which include both principal and interest, so that at maturity, only part of the principal is paid off. The balance of the principal (the *balloon payment*) is due at maturity. The periodic payments on the partially amortized mortgage are less than those of a fully amortized mortgage of the same amount with the same terms. These reduced payments toward the principal will necessarily leave a loan balance at maturity. Newly formed businesses with large start-up costs and cash flow problems are likely candidates for partially amortized mortgages. The lender logically assumes that the cash flow crisis experienced by the new firm is short-term and that within a few years, when the loan has matured, the more experienced firm will be in a position to either pay off or refinance the balance.

Graduated Payment Mortgages (GPM)

The primary purpose of a *graduated payment mortgage,* sometimes called a *flexible payment mortgage,* is to reduce the monthly payments in the early years of the loan. A family may be just getting settled or require funds to fix up the home initially. With this type of mortgage, the monthly payments increase gradually each year for a stated period, usually five or ten years. The payments then remain fixed for the balance of the mortgage term, which is typically twenty-five to thirty-five years. The interest rate remains fixed for the term of the mortgage loan, just as with the traditional fully amortized mortgage. The lower payments during the early years often do not cover all of the interest actually due during those years. In Figure 7–2, it can be seen that, during the early years, the outstanding balance actually is greater than the original amount of the mortgage loan. The disadvantages of this type of loan

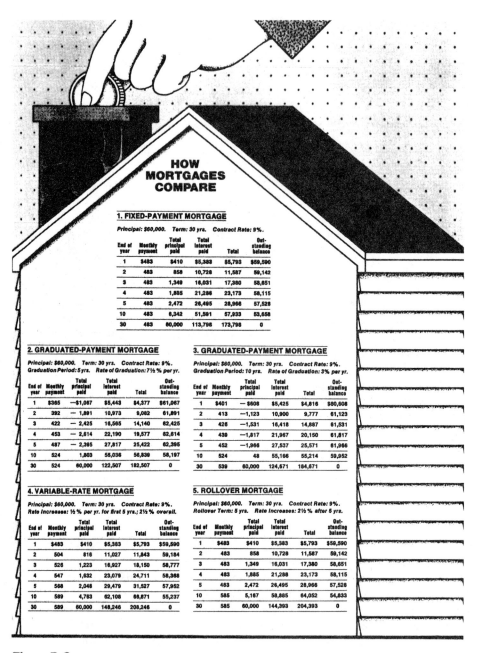

HOW MORTGAGES COMPARE

1. FIXED-PAYMENT MORTGAGE

Principal: $60,000.   Term: 30 yrs.   Contract Rate: 9%.

End of year	Monthly payment	Total principal paid	Total interest paid	Total	Out-standing balance
1	$483	$410	$5,383	$5,793	$59,590
2	483	858	10,728	11,587	59,142
3	483	1,349	16,031	17,380	58,651
4	483	1,885	21,288	23,173	58,115
5	483	2,472	26,495	28,966	57,528
10	483	8,342	51,591	57,933	53,658
30	483	60,000	113,798	173,798	0

2. GRADUATED-PAYMENT MORTGAGE

Principal: $60,000.   Term: 30 yrs.   Contract Rate: 9%.
Graduation Period: 5 yrs.   Rate of Graduation: 7½% per yr.

End of year	Monthly payment	Total principal paid	Total interest paid	Total	Out-standing balance
1	$365	−$1,067	$5,443	$4,377	$61,067
2	392	− 1,891	10,973	9,082	61,891
3	422	− 2,425	16,565	14,140	62,425
4	453	− 2,614	22,190	19,577	62,614
5	487	− 2,395	27,817	25,422	62,395
10	524	1,803	55,036	56,839	58,197
30	524	60,000	122,507	182,507	0

3. GRADUATED-PAYMENT MORTGAGE

Principal: $60,000.   Term: 30 yrs.   Contract Rate: 9%.
Graduation Period: 10 yrs.   Rate of Graduation: 3% per yr.

End of year	Monthly payment	Total principal paid	Total interest paid	Total	Out-standing balance
1	$401	− $608	$5,425	$4,816	$60,608
2	413	−1,123	10,900	9,777	61,123
3	426	−1,531	16,418	14,887	61,531
4	439	−1,817	21,967	20,150	61,817
5	452	−1,966	27,537	25,571	61,966
10	524	48	55,166	55,214	59,952
30	539	60,000	124,671	184,671	0

4. VARIABLE-RATE MORTGAGE

Principal: $60,000.   Term: 30 yrs.   Contract Rate: 9%.
Rate Increases: ½% per yr. for first 5 yrs.; 2½% overall.

End of year	Monthly payment	Total principal paid	Total interest paid	Total	Out-standing balance
1	$483	$410	$5,383	$5,793	$59,590
2	504	816	11,027	11,843	59,184
3	526	1,223	16,927	18,150	58,777
4	547	1,632	23,079	24,711	58,368
5	568	2,048	29,479	31,527	57,952
10	589	4,763	62,108	66,871	55,237
30	589	60,000	148,246	208,246	0

5. ROLLOVER MORTGAGE

Principal: $60,000.   Term: 30 yrs.   Contract Rate: 9%.
Rollover Term: 5 yrs.   Rate Increases: 2½% after 5 yrs.

End of year	Monthly payment	Total principal paid	Total interest paid	Total	Out-standing balance
1	$483	$410	$5,383	$5,793	$59,590
2	483	858	10,728	11,587	59,142
3	483	1,349	16,031	17,380	58,651
4	483	1,885	21,288	23,173	58,115
5	483	2,472	26,495	28,966	57,528
10	585	5,167	58,885	64,052	54,833
30	585	60,000	144,393	204,393	0

Figure 7–2
How mortgages compare

are the negative equity early in the loan period and the greater total cost over the life of the loan (see Figure 7–2).

Economists estimate that this type of loan would bring home ownership within the means of 2.5 million additional families per year. At present, HUD, FHA, and many federally chartered savings and loan associates offer these plans.

The Flexible-Loan Insurance Program (FLIP) is a variation in which a portion of the down payment is placed in a savings account, drawing interest. Money is automatically withdrawn from the savings account during the first five years (until depleted) to go toward the monthly mortgage payment.

Variable Rate Mortgages (VRM)

As the name implies, the *variable rate mortgage* is a contract under which the interest rate charged varies or fluctuates over the life of the loan. The rate charged is generally tied to the prevailing interest rates in the bond and money markets. This mortgage contract is designed to alleviate the problems of lending institutions during periods of inflation when they are holding low-yielding fixed rate mortgages (FRM) but must pay increasing rates of interest for money, thereby reducing the spread and ending up with lower profits. The variable rate mortgage avoids the problem of committing mortgage funds for long periods of time at fixed rates of interest, and it ensures an acceptable spread between interest costs paid and mortgage rates charged by the lender.

There are two other variations to the variable rate mortgage. With a *rollover mortgage,* the rate is fixed for a set period (usually three to seven years). At the end of the period, the loan is renegotiated. With an *escalator mortgage,* the lender can change the rate based on his evaluation of economic conditions. In the first two methods above, any revised rate is based on an index, whereas in the last method it is based on an opinion.

Reverse Annuity Mortgages (RAM)

In many instances, older people on fixed incomes require additional money to cover the rising costs of living. Rather than sell their home to raise the additional money needed to cover their expenses, they may enter into a *reverse annuity mortgage* contract to satisfy their income needs. Once they sign the reverse annuity mortgage (RAM), the monthly payments they were making stop and a reverse procedure begins. The elderly couple begin to receive monthly annuity payments from the lending institution. Essentially, the couple are borrowing the equity that they have built up in the house over their lifetime. They are charged the going rate of interest for the loan. The loan is paid off whenever the property is ultimately sold or upon the death of the mortgagor.

One variation of the RAM mortgage provides that the lending institution will loan up to 80 percent of the equity in one lump sum. The mortgagor will then purchase a single-premium life annuity insurance contract with the proceeds. Again, the RAM mortgage is paid off when the property is sold or upon the death of the mortgagor.

Budget Mortgage

When a property is financed with a high loan to value mortgage, the lending institution may require that, in addition to monthly principal and interest payments, the borrower also pay monthly installments on the real estate taxes and insurance for the pledged property. This *budget mortgage* assures the mortgagee that these expenses will be paid when due and allows the mortgagor to budget the expenses over twelve months rather than in one lump sum payment.

OTHER MORTGAGE CLASSIFICATIONS

Previously, we classified mortgages by repayment method. Mortgages can also be grouped according to what is included in the mortgage or by other special provisions. Some of the often-used types of mortgages are discussed in the following sections:

Package Mortgages

The *package mortgage* is a recent concept in which the mortgage loan covers not only the real property itself, but also the fixtures and equipment that are customarily sold with the property. Types of items that may be covered include dishwashers, dryers, garbage disposals, air conditioners, refrigerators, and stoves. Package mortgages provide several advantages to the borrower:

1. He need obtain only one loan instead of several.
2. He deals with only one lender and makes only one payment.
3. He spreads the cost of the equipment over a much longer period of time.
4. He pays a much lower rate of interest than would be allowed on an installment plan.

The borrower also has a uniform payment throughout the life of the mortgage rather than much larger payments in the early years. He needs much less "front" money. These mortgages will probably grow in popularity as more and more builders offer a packaged product.

Blanket Mortgage

A *blanket mortgage* covers or blankets several pieces of real estate as security for a loan. Such mortgages are common in financing a new subdivision. As the individual lots are sold to various customers, the subdivider/mortgagor must free the lots from the mortgage to convey title. This is accomplished by the insertion of a *partial release clause* in the mortgage. It stipulates that, upon payment of a certain release price, each lot will be individually released from the mortgage. Since, as a rule, the best lots in a subdivision are sold first, the release price for individual lots will usually be considerably higher than the average mortgage value of the individual lots, thereby assuring adequate security for the remaining loan balance.

As an example, assume a blanket mortgage covers 10 lots as security for a $100,000 loan. The average mortgage value of the individual lots is $10,000 ($100,000 ÷ 10). However, the individual release price for each lot may be as high as $17,500 to compensate for the earlier sale of the best lots.

Open-End Mortgage

A borrower may require additional funds to repair and/or improve her mortgaged property in the years following the original mortgage loan. An *open-end mortgage* allows the borrower to obtain such funds under the original terms of the mortgage or under other terms stipulated in the mortgage. The total loan can go up to, but it cannot exceed the original loan amount. Such advances are available at very little extra cost and may be repaid over the term of the loan. As a result, open-end advances are considerably more favorable than the standard home improvement loan, which provides for a much higher interest rate and must be repaid in a few short years.

Questions of priority arise when intervening liens are created between the time of the original mortgage and the subsequent reopening of the mortgage for the additional loan. The majority of the states subscribe to the theory that the priority of the additional debt depends upon whether or not such advances were obligatory. If the lender was obligated to make such additional advances to the borrower as a result of a written or verbal commitment, the priority of the additional advance coincides with the priority of the original mortgage. On the other hand, if the lender was not obligated (discretionary) to make the additional advance of funds, the intervening lien has priority over the additional advance of funds.

Purchase Money Mortgage (PM)

A *purchase money mortgage* is given by the purchaser of real estate to the seller as part payment of the purchase price. PM mortgages, when properly executed, give special protection to the mortgagee. Although the seller is usually the mortgagee, a third party who furnished part of the purchase price may hold the PM mortgage. The seller is generally willing to take back a PM mortgage to facilitate a sale during periods of "tight" money or when he sells on an installment contract in order to spread his gain over several years. The purchase money mortgage may be a junior or senior lien.

Wrap-Around Mortgages

A *wrap-around mortgage* is actually a second mortgage that engulfs or wraps around an existing first mortgage. It is used primarily to obtain additional funds when it is impossible or impractical to refinance the existing loan. The wrap-around loan is based on the property's current market value. The funds advanced to the borrower represent the difference between the principal amount of the wrap-around loan and the current loan balance on the first mortgage loan. The borrower and the original lender or first mortgagee have no future dealings. The borrower makes her payments to the wrap-around lender who, in turn, funnels a portion of the payment to the first mortgagee to cover the debt service on the first mortgage.

As an example, assume that an investor purchased an apartment building ten years ago for $125,000 with 80 percent financing at 8 percent interest for twenty-five years, fully amortized. Today her property is worth $200,000, and she would like to obtain some extra funds by refinancing, but her first mortgage has a heavy prepayment penalty. She decides to use a wrap-around second mortgage. Table 7–1 shows the results.

Table 7–1

Wrap-around mortgage

		Debt Service
First mortgage loan (80% of $125,000)	$100,000, 8%, 25 yrs	$ 9,368
Remaining loan balance today	$80,000	
Present market value of property	$200,000	
Wrap-around second mortgage (80% of 200,000)	$160,000, 10%, 25 yrs	$17,627
Funds advanced to borrowers	$80,000 ($160,000–$80,000)	

The borrower receives an additional $80,000 in funds. She pays $17,627 to the wrap-around lender who, in turn, funnels $9,368 to the original lender for debt-service payments on the original $100,000 loan. The balance of the payment is retained by the wrap-around lender and is used to reduce the $80,000 loan he advanced.

Construction Loans (Interim Financing)

Construction loans are used to provide the funds necessary to pay for material and labor during the construction process. These are called *interim loans.* Since high risks are involved in completing the building on time and within the projected budget, the interest rate charged on such loans is higher than on conventional financing. In most instances, before a lending institution will commit to a construction loan, it will require a "standby" or "takeout" commitment from a permanent lender, whereby that institution agrees to provide the permanent financing upon completion of the project. The "takeout" commitment assures the construction lender that the construction loan will be paid off once the building project is completed. Although the construction loan may finance the entire cost of construction, most lending institutions place the funds in an escrow account from which the funds are released at various stages of construction after the contractor provides the necessary lien waivers.

The order of priority of *mortgages* or deeds of trust is generally determined by the date they are recorded. A *senior mortgage* is a first mortgage that was recorded prior to any junior mortgage. A *junior mortgage* may be a second, third, or fourth mortgage, depending on how many mortgages were recorded ahead of it. Priority of a mortgage determines the degree of risk exposure to the lender. Senior mortgages create the least risk and result in lower interest rates charged to the borrower than what would be charged on junior mortgages. In the event of default and foreclosure of a mortgage, the proceeds from the foreclosure sale are distributed to the various mortgagees in order of their priority.

Junior or secondary financing is used when the buyer either (a) does not have sufficient funds to pay the difference between the first mortgage loan and the purchase price of the property or (b) wants to maximize his financial leverage.

FHA, VA, AND CONVENTIONAL MORTGAGES

There are three types of mortgages, classified as to whether or not a government agency insures or guarantees the loan.

The Federal Housing Act of 1934 created the Federal Housing Administration whose primary objective was to stimulate the depressed housing industry by providing more and better means of financing mortgage loans. The FHA is essentially an insuring agency. It generally does not make loans itself, but rather insures approved FHA lenders against loss on mortgages placed by them. Both the property and the borrower must meet certain standards and requirements to qualify for an *FHA insured mortgage* loan. An approved FHA appraiser must appraise the property before a loan is made. The borrower pays one-half of one percent of the loan amount as premium for the FHA insurance. The interest rate on FHA mortgages is set from time to time by the Secretary of Housing and Urban Development. As a result of the insurance, most lenders are willing to make loans on terms not otherwise possible. Section 203 loans (loans on single-family, owner-occupied residences) enable the borrower to obtain a thirty-year loan at a loan-to-value ratio of approximately 97 percent. The maximum loan amount on a single family house is $60,000. The borrower may pay more for the property than the appraised value; however, she must make up the difference (in cash) between the loan amount and the selling price. The borrower cannot use a second mortgage to cover the down payment, nor can she pay discount points.

Presently, FHA also administers dozens of subsidized, unsubsidized, and public housing programs.

FHA discount points

As mentioned above, the interest rate charged on FHA mortgages is set from time to time by the secretary of HUD. When this rate is not competitive with conventional mortgage rates, prudent lenders normally would bypass FHA mortgage loans and invest in the higher yielding conventional loans. FHA mortgage rates are made competitive with conventional mortgage rates through a process known as *discounting* that uses **discount points.** To *discount* means to take away. Generally, one (1) point of the mortgage principal is discounted for each ⅛ percent difference between the FHA interest rate and the conventional interest rate. For example, in a $10,000, thirty-year mortgage, if the FHA rate were at 9 percent and the conventional rate was 9½ percent, the one-half percent difference is equivalent to four-eighths; thus, the face amount of the mortgage would be discounted four points (see Table 7–2). The seller must pay the discount points for FHA mortgages. Buyers are not allowed to pay FHA discount points.

Table 7–2
Computing discount points

FHA		*Conventional*
9%- - - - - - - - ½% Difference - - - - - - - 9½%		
equals		
(⁴⁄₈'s or 4 points)		
Face amount of note:	$10,000	
discounted by 4%	− 400	
Lender's cash advance	$ 9,600	
points paid by seller	400	
(4 points)		

The investor who pays $9600 for a $10,000, 9 percent mortgage will receive $900 interest (9 percent) the first year plus $400 (4 percent) discount. In other words, if the mortgage were paid off in the first year, the lender would yield 13 percent. However, if the loan ran the full thirty years, the lender's yield would be 9 percent interest plus one-thirtieth of 4 percent per year since the total discount must be divided by the life of the loan. Historically, lenders have found that the average life of a single-family mortgage is eight years; consequently, most lenders compute one percent of discount as equal to ⅛ percent interest. In the above example, the effective FHA yield would be 9 percent per annum interest plus ⁴⁄₈'s or ½ of 1 percent interest, or an effective yield of 9½ percent on the loan.

VA Guaranteed Loans

The Servicemen's Readjustment Act of 1944 (the GI Bill) was passed to provide benefits for World War II veterans. It has since been amended to include veterans of Korea and Vietnam. Veterans who served 180 days or more active duty after January, 1955, are eligible. Vietnam veterans need to have served only 90 days active duty. Section 503 enables the veteran to obtain a partially guaranteed, first mortgage real estate loan. Both the borrower and the property must meet certain requirements. To qualify for VA financing, the veteran applies for a "Certificate of Eligibility." If the property is approved, a "Certificate of Reasonable Value" is issued. The Veterans' Administration guarantees lenders against loss in the event that the veteran defaults and the foreclosure sale does not bring sufficient money to cover the mortgage debt. The guarantee is limited to $25,000 or 60 percent of the loan, whichever is less.

Before the VA will commit to a *VA guaranteed loan,* the property must be appraised by an approved VA appraiser. The lending institution, not the VA, determines the maximum loan amount. No down payment is required on a VA loan, and terms of thirty years are available on single-family residences. The maximum allowable interest rate that can be charged is about the same as for an FHA guaranteed mortgage. This rate is set by the VA administrator. VA loans can be assumed by purchasers who do not qualify as veterans; however, the veteran remains liable unless he receives a release of liability from the lender. No prepayment penalty can exist in a VA mortgage. Presently, FHA and VA loans combined account for about 30 percent of all outstanding single-family property mortgages.

Conventional Mortgages

A *conventional mortgage* is one that is neither government insured nor guaranteed. Since the conventional lender is not provided with either government insurance or a guarantee against loss, his risk is higher. The higher risk of conventional loans is reflected in both a higher interest rate and a larger down payment requirement. The specific terms and provisions of the loan are established by the individual lenders and vary according to local market conditions, consumer needs, and state regulations. The interest rate is not set, but is determined by the market, although many states have *usury* laws to set the maximum rate that can be charged on residential mortgages.

In 1957, a private mortgage insurance corporation (Mortgage Guaranty Insurance Corporation) made mortgage insurance available to conventional lenders so that they could compete with the high loan-to-value mortgages offered by FHA and VA loans. The insuring company charges a one-time premium of one-half of one percent of the loan amount payable at closing plus an annual premium of one-fourth of one percent of the loan payable as part of the monthly payment. Upon default, the insuring company does one of two things:

1. Takes possession of the foreclosed property and pays the insured mortgagee the remaining debt balance, or
2. Pays 20 percent of the outstanding debt.

Recently, there has been a very rapid increase in the number of private mortgage insurance companies as well as a concurrent increase in the use of insured conventional mortgages.

OTHER FINANCING DEVICES

Installment Land Contract

The *installment land contract* (or as described in Chapter 4, *contract for deed*) is a common method of financing the purchase of real estate when money is tight. The buyer and seller enter into a contract which provides that the buyer is to furnish a nominal down payment to the seller and pay the balance of the selling price to the seller on an installment basis over a period of years. The buyer takes possession at the signing of the contract and pays the taxes and insurance on the property. The seller contractually agrees to deliver the deed to the buyer upon final payment of the selling price. Meanwhile, the deed is usually held in escrow. In the case of default, the contract seller generally retains the down payment and all other payments as liquidated damages. Installment land contract sales generally command a higher selling price than ordinary sales because of the low down payment and the lack of loan closing costs.

Participation Agreements

Participation agreements in a mortgage, sometimes called *kickers,* enable the lending institution to participate in the earnings or equity growth of the property that it is financing. The use of kickers or sweeteners is prevalent during periods of tight money to induce the reluctant lender into making the loan.

Assuming or Taking Subject to Existing Financing

Another method of financing real estate is to take over the existing financing on the property being sold. Such a strategy may be very advantageous in periods of tight money or when the interest rate on the seller's property is considerably lower than prevailing rates. The buyer may either *assume and agree to pay* the existing mortgage debt, or she may purchase *subject to* the existing mortgage. Under either alternative, the buyer must make the mortgage payments and abide by all other provisions stipulated in the mortgage contract, or she may lose the property through foreclosure.

When the buyer purchases *subject to* an existing mortgage, she is not personally liable to pay the debt. The worst that can happen to her upon default and foreclosure is that she will lose her property and any equity she had in it. If the foreclosure sale does not bring sufficient proceeds to cover the debt, the lender has recourse against only the original mortgage holder and may sue him for a deficiency judgment.

On the other hand, if the purchaser *assumes* the existing mortgage, she assumes personal liability and becomes coguarantor on the debt. In the event of default and foreclosure, the lender has recourse against both the buyer and the original mortgagor (or the seller) for any deficiency. The buyer is primarily liable; but if she does not have sufficient assets to pay the deficiency judgment, the lender will sue the seller. The seller, in turn, will take legal action against the buyer to collect on the deficient monies owed him.

Upon occasion, when the financial standing of the buyer is strong or the pledged property itself is sufficient protection, the lending institution will give the seller under an assumed mortgage a *release of liability*. However, institutions are not usually inclined to do so.

Sale-and-Leasebacks

The *sale-and-leaseback* is a financing device whereby an investor either purchases or builds a building, sells it, and simultaneously leases it back for a long-term period of time. Many different variations to a sale-leaseback exist, and they are covered in depth in Chapter 6.

Municipal Bonds (Tax Exempt)

Recently, cities have raised single-family mortgage money by selling tax-exempt *municipal bonds*. The bond proceeds are loaned through local savings and loans who earn a fee for processing the loan and collecting the monthly payments. The municipalities determine who qualifies for the bond money. Most cities reserve the money for low- and moderate-income families. Since the interest on such bonds is not taxable to the purchaser of the bonds, the mortgage money can be offered at rates of anywhere from $1\frac{1}{2}$ to 3 percent below the going rate on conventional mortgage loans. The concept is not without its critics. Some complain that pouring low interest mortgage money on the housing market will only increase the inflation of home prices. Others are concerned that the large influx of bond offerings will hinder the sale of municipal bonds for the more traditional public building programs. Savings and loan associations that do not participate in the program complain that those who do, engage in unfair competition. The Internal Revenue Service, which could lose millions of tax dollars, has complained sufficiently to cause the President to call for legislation limiting the use of such bonds.

Refinancing

Refinancing occurs when an investor obtains a new loan to pay off an old one. Properties are generally refinanced for one of the following reasons:

1. To take advantage of falling interest rates or longer mortgage terms, thereby reducing debt service payments and increasing the cash flow to the equity investor.

2. To generate more investment capital for the investor by borrowing against the increased equity created primarily through property appreciation. This creates "tax free" cash that may be reinvested in other properties, thereby increasing investment holdings. This refinancing process is known as "pyramiding."

3. To pay off the seller in a contract for deed sale that contains a refinancing clause requiring the contract buyer to pay off the contract in a stipulated period of time.

4. To generate cash to meet any other financial obligations.

Assume a property was purchased ten years ago for $125,000. The investor purchased it with an 80 percent, twenty-five year, 9 percent interest fully amortized mortgage, and the property has been appreciating 5 percent per year since the purchase. By refinancing, the investor can generate $68,000 tax free cash as follows:

Beginning of investment

Purchase price $125,000	$100,000 First mortgage
5 percent appreciation/year or 50 percent appreciation	Loan balance is being reduced annually through amortization of the loan.

Ten years later

$187,500 Current market value <u>×.80</u> $150,000 New 1st mortgage −82,000 Pay off old first mortgage $ 68,000 "Tax free" cash generated	$82,000 Approximate current loan balance

REMEDIES OF THE LENDER UPON DEFAULT

The purpose of the mortgage is to provide security for the lender in case of default by the mortgagor. Because of this security, the lender is more willing to lend the money. If there is a default, there are several remedies available to the mortgagee to recover the money due.

Strict Foreclosure

Under *strict foreclosure* or foreclosures by writ of entry, the lender petitions the court and asks that the mortgagor's equity of redemption be cut off or foreclosed. The court then establishes a period of time within which the mortgagor must pay the debt or forfeit all interest in the property forever to the lender. There is no judicial foreclosure sale. If the value of the property exceeds the amount of the debt, the lender has profited. If the value of the property is less than the debt, the borrower may still be held liable for the deficiency. Very few states permit strict foreclosure today. Its two main advantages are that it eliminates both the expensive and time consuming judicial sale and the statutory redemption period.

Judicial Foreclosure

Judicial foreclosure is the most commonly accepted remedy in most states today. Although the procedures vary from state to state, the action involves a court proceeding to foreclose or cut off the mortgagor's equity of redemption and to sell the pledged property at a public auction to pay off the debt. If the sale proceeds are not sufficient to cover the debt, the lender may sue for a deficiency judgment; however, deficiency judgments have been eliminated in several states. If the proceeds from the foreclosure sale are in excess of the senior lienor's claims, the excess is distributed according to the property rights of junior lien holders or the mortgagor. If there is no excess, the junior lienors may seek a judgment for full payment of their claims. In those states not having a statutory right of redemption, the successful bidder at the foreclosure sale receives a chancellor's or sheriff's deed. Some states provide the mortgagor one last chance to redeem his property after foreclosure for a set period of time. This statutory period of redemption varies from state to state and may be as long as two years. In these states, the successful bidder is given a *certificate of sale* and receives the deed after the statutory period of redemption has expired.

Steps in a Foreclosure

The following procedures are included in a *foreclosure:*

1. The title is searched or an abstract is prepared to identify all parties who have an interest in the property to be foreclosed. The search may reveal junior lienors who will be summoned to the foreclosure proceedings so that they may protect whatever interest in the property they have.
2. Summons and complaint are served on the mortgagor and any junior lienors revealed in the title search.
3. If the mortgagor has a defense against the foreclosure, he files an answer to the complaint, resulting in a trial by jury.
4. If the mortgagor does not answer the complaint, foreclosure proceeds to a conclusion and a judgment degree is obtained by the mortgagee on the amount to be collected. This decree is filed with the court, and a court order directs the property to be sold at a public auction.
5. Notice of the foreclosure sale is given to all known defendants and published in a local newspaper.
6. Bids are made on the property. The mortgagee can, and usually does, bid on the property up to the amount of the mortgage to protect his interest in it. The successful bidder receives a certificate of sale in those states having *statutory rights of redemption.* (A deed would be given to the

successful bidder in those states not having a statutory right of redemption.)

7. If surplus money remains after the first mortgage is paid off, junior mortgagees who have filed a *surplus money action* will be paid off in order of their priority. If the sale proceeds are not sufficient to pay off the first mortgage, the mortgagee may file for a *deficiency judgment* on the note. (Some states do not allow deficiency judgments.)

8. After all periods of redemption expire, the successful bidder receives a deed.

Foreclosure by Exercise of Power of Sale (Foreclosure by Advertisement)

In several states, nonjudicial foreclosure by exercise of power of sale (foreclosure by advertisement) is permitted. This type of foreclosure requires that the mortgage contain a *power of sale* clause which stipulates that the mortgagee may advertise, sell, and disperse the proceeds of the pledged property without the need of judicial action. Although this method of foreclosure is speedier and less expensive than judicial foreclosure, in many states the mortgagee relinquishes her right to deficiency judgments and the mortgagor relinquishes his redemption rights. Since foreclosure by exercise of power of sale is not confirmed by a judicial proceeding, it is subject to attack. However, the mortgagee can request a judicial foreclosure rather than foreclosure by exercise of power of sale if she prefers to do so.

Other Less Common Remedies

Foreclosure by management
Lenders may stipulate in the mortgage agreement that, upon default by the borrower, the lender can take over the property and manage it until the delinquent amounts have been paid. This places the mortgagee in a position of property manager.

Foreclosure by entry
Foreclosure by entry is allowed in Massachusetts, Rhode Island, Maine, and New Hampshire. There the mortgagee may peaceably enter the property (unopposed by the mortgagor) in the presence of witnesses. She can then place the property for sale. If the mortgaged property has a market value that is higher than the debt, the mortgagor is entitled to the difference. He is also given a statutory right of redemption that varies from one to three years.

Foreclosure by voluntary deed
The mortgagor may voluntarily quitclaim deed his interest in the mortgaged property to the lending institution to avoid the embarrassment of a foreclosure. If the *voluntary deed* procedure is followed, the mortgagor may later claim that he was pressured into signing the quitclaim deed and seek to have it invalidated. Junior liens are not satisfied or eliminated by a voluntary deed, which leaves it as a less satisfactory method.

MORTGAGE MONEY

Supply of Mortgage Money

The principal supply of mortgage money comes from the savings of individuals, businesses, and governments. Repayment of outstanding loans also funnels more money back into the mortgage market. Finally, the Federal Reserve System, guardian of our money supply, may influence the supply of money in the mortgage market. The supply of funds increases when individuals, corporations, and governments save more, when borrowers increase the rate of payment on existing loans, and when the Federal Reserve increases the money supply.

In an unregulated economy, interest rates are determined by the free interplay of the supply of and demand for money. As the money supply increases relative to demand, interest rates will fall. As the money supply decreases relative to demand, interest rates will rise. An oversupply of credit (money) relative to the availability of goods and services for sale in our economy creates inflation and forces prices up. An undersupply of credit (money) relative to the availability of goods and services available for sale creates a deflationary effect and forces prices down. Since the availability of credit is fundamentally tied to our economy, the U.S. government keeps a watchful eye on the money supply and attempts to regulate it when necessary through the Federal Reserve, so that the money supply increases at a rate commensurate with the growth of our economy. Three major steps can be taken by the Federal Reserve to influence the availability and cost (interest rate) of money:

1. The Federal Reserve may change the discount rate it charges its member banks for loans made to them. If the Federal Reserve raises the discount rate, member banks are discouraged from borrowing funds. If the discount rate is lowered, member banks are encouraged to borrow and make available more loanable funds.

2. By selling government securities in the open market, the Federal Reserve can absorb money and thereby tighten credit. By buying government securities in the market, the Federal Reserve puts money in the hands of lenders and thus increases bank deposits and loanable funds.

3. Every major bank in the country is a member of the Federal Reserve. As such, banks are required to maintain a certain percentage of their assets in reserve, thereby making them unavailable for loans. The Federal Reserve has the authority to raise or lower the reserve requirements, thereby increasing or decreasing the availability of loanable funds.

Unlike the stock market, there is no single, organized market for money. Hundreds of users of money compete with one another. As a result, the money market is composed of a series of submarkets throughout the country. The mortgage market is competing for funds along with the bond market, notes, bills, commodities, and other submarkets. Investors with funds compare alternative investments in terms of risk and yield. As the risk and yield changes between the various alternative investments, investors seek those investments with the highest yield commensurate with risk.

When the return offered by financial institutions is greater relative to stocks and bonds, funds flow into the financial intermediaries, which in turn provide money for mortgage loans. This phenomenon has been called *intermediation.* When the return offered by stocks and bonds is more attractive than that offered by financial intermediaries, investors withdraw their savings from the financial institutions and reinvest in stocks and bonds. This phenomenon is called *disintermediation.* During periods of rising interest rates, short-term open-market securities become more attractive to investors than long-term savings accounts in financial intermediaries because they respond more quickly to investments offering higher yields.

Sources of Mortgage Money

Persons wanting mortgages have a variety of sources to which they can apply. The major sources of mortgage money are savings and loan associations, mutual savings banks, commercial banks, life insurance agencies, mortgage companies, and pension funds, as well as individual lenders. Each of these organizations plays an important part as a source of mortgage money.

Savings and loan associations

Savings and loan associations are private institutions that operate under state and federal regulations. There are over 3,300 stated chartered associations and over 2,000 federally chartered associations with combined assets of over $300 billion. The purpose of organizing savings and loan associations is to encourage savings for home ownership. Savings and loan associations are the second largest financial intermediary in the country. State and federal laws prescribe the standards for chartering new institutions, determine operating procedures, and control the kinds of loans and investments that can be made. Savings and loan associations are specialized lending institutions and are, to a large extent, limited to making loans on improved real estate. Business loans and consumer loans are outside the scope of the lending authority of savings and loan associations. The majority of their funds are invested in residential mortgages. Over 48 percent of all outstanding one- to four-family residence loans are placed by savings and loan associations. Although savings and loans are capable of making FHA and VA loans, most of their loan portfolio was made up of conventional loans. Federally chartered savings and loans have a 100-mile limitation placed on most of their lending activity. Also, their maximum loan-to-value ratio is 95 percent. State associations generally have similar limitations.

Mutual savings banks

Mutual savings banks were started over 150 years ago in the industrialized northeastern part of the U.S. Their purpose was to encourage savings by low- and moderate-income factory workers. Today, all mutual savings banks are located in the northeastern eighteen states and Puerto Rico. Approximately three-fourths of the total assets of all savings banks are in the two states of Massachusetts and New York. Savings banks have fewer restrictions placed on their loans than do savings and loan associations. As a result, they can make personal loans as well as real estate loans. Nonetheless, in 1973 over 75 percent of their total loans were in the form of mortgages. Before 1950, savings banks were regulated in their conventional mortgage lending by a lending radius similar to that for savings and loans. As a result, they tended to invest more heavily in FHA and VA loans because, unlike conventional mortgage loans, FHA and VA were not subject to the normal lending radius limitations and restrictions. Approximately 40 percent of savings banks' assets are in FHA or VA loans. Nonetheless, with the geographic concentration of savings banks in the northeast, the area soon had an oversupply of funds. In 1950, laws were passed allowing out-of-state lending, thereby enabling lenders to move money from capital surplus areas to capital deficit areas across the country.

Commercial banks

Commercial banks are the largest of all lenders. They can be either state or federally chartered. State chartered banks are regulated by a state bank board and generally are given greater leeway on their lending practices than are federally chartered banks. The latter are regulated by the Comptroller of Currency and the Federal Reserve Board.

The deposits received by commercial banks are classified as either *time* or *demand* deposits. Only time deposits may be used to finance real estate. Although both savings and loans and commercial banks are regulated in the maximum rates they can pay depositors on different types of savings accounts, thrift institutions historically have been permitted to pay more on time deposits than have commercial banks. As a result, commercial banks were unable to compete for the long-term savings money. Thus, they concentrated their efforts on making short-term loans with their demand deposits. Today, less than 15 percent of the total assets of all commercial banks are invested in mortgage loans; they hold approximately 30 percent of the total outstanding mortgage loans. (See Figure 7–3.)

Table 7–3
Total assets of financial intermediaries (Billions of dollars)

Financial Intermediary	1978
Commercial Banks	1190
Savings & Loans	510
Life Insurance Companies	380
Mutual Savings Banks	158

Source: Federal Reserve Board.

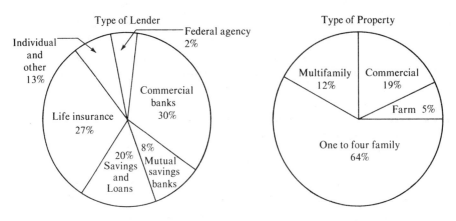

Figure 7–3
Sources of financing (Mortgage loans outstanding, 1978)

Life insurance companies
All life insurance companies are chartered under state laws and are regulated by the charter state as well as other states in which they operate. Their broad investment powers coupled with their huge money resources make them a principal source of financing for nonresidential mortgage financing. As of 1978, life insurance companies held 27 percent of all mortgage loans outstanding. About 20 percent of the mortgages are VA guaranteed or FHA insured. The inflow of premium dollars for life insurance companies is not subject to the same fluctuations as is money to most lenders. Consequently they have a more consistent availability of loanable funds. Only a few states restrict life insurance companies to a geographical lending radius, thus allowing them to make loans throughout the country. The trend is for most life insurance companies to deal through mortgage companies and mortgage bankers when placing a mortgage loan rather than to operate their own lending offices. Some small life insurance companies originate loans out of their home offices. The usual loan-to-value ratio for conventional loans placed by life insurance companies on residential property is 66⅔ percent.

Other sources of mortgages
Savings and loan associations, commercial banks, mutual savings banks, and life insurance companies provide the bulk of funds for real estate mortgages. Pension funds, endowed institutions, direct government lending, real estate investment trusts, and individuals are other sources that borrowers may use.

THE MORTGAGE MARKET

The mortgage market is a part of the overall capital market and, as such, competes with all other forms of long-term investments for the savings dollar. Money is highly sought; it tends to move toward those investments offering the highest yield commensurate with the risk. If yields are higher for corporate bonds than they are for mortgages of equivalent risk, money will flow out of the mortgage market and into the bond market.

Unlike stocks, bonds, and other major instruments in the capital market, a mortgage is a nonhomogeneous, personalized, and localized investment. The risk and return of a mortgage varies with local loan-to-value ratios, local interest rates, real estate values and economic trends in the area, and the credit worthiness of the mortgagor. These factors, coupled with the facts that (a) there is no standardized mortgage contract, and (b) savings and loan institutions have a limited lending radius, cause the mortgage market to be subject to extreme geographic localization. It is also much less fluid than most of the other investment markets. As a result, the *primary mortgage market,* which is the market where the loans are originated between borrower and lender, is essentially made up of local submarkets throughout the country. Mortgage funds in one submarket may be dried up at the same time other submarkets have a surplus of mortgage funds.

Secondary Mortgage Market

The factors that cause the primary mortgage market to be subject to extreme localization have prevented the development of a national mortgage market. For mortgage funds to move more freely between the various submarkets across the country, it was necessary to provide some standardization and a method to protect the "secondary" lender. The *secondary mortgage market* is comprised of various investors who purchase preexisting mortgages, that is, mortgages that were originated by other lenders. Some lending institutions may operate in both the primary market and the secondary market. For example, mutual savings banks not only originate new mortgages in their localized area, but also purchase existing mortgages from other institutions across the nation. Pension funds, on the other hand, are not set up to originate mortgages, but they purchase preexisting mortgages in the secondary mortgage market. Mortgage companies operate almost exclusively in the primary mortgage market through direct lending to home buyers.

When the secondary mortgage market experiences a decrease in demand, the original lenders in the primary market are unable to liquefy (sell) their existing mortgages to obtain more loanable funds. The secondary mortgage market must be active to provide the original lenders with a source to liquefy their mortgage portfolio, thereby assuring a future supply of loanable funds.

ROLE OF THE GOVERNMENT

There is a need for a national mortgage market and a smooth flow of mortgage funds across the various submarkets. The government has supported the secondary mortgage market through several federal agencies to accomplish this need.

Federal National Mortgage Association
(FNMA, "Fannie Mae")

FNMA (Fannie Mae) is a quasigovernmental institution that was authorized by Congress in 1938. Its purpose then and now is to purchase FHA insured mortgages from approved mortgagees so that these primary lenders can obtain more funds and make new loans. Every week, Fannie Mae announces the money it has available to buy mortgages, and mortgage lenders bid for the money. The bid is below par (100) if money is tight and above par if money is plentiful. For example, lender A desires to sell FNMA $100,000 in FHA mortgages at a bid price of 97. This means lender A would receive $97,000, or 97 percent of par value. If lender B bids 96, he is willing to receive $96,000 in return for $100,000 of mortgages, and he would be the successful bidder if the terms and risks of the two mortgage packages are similar. The mortgages purchased by Fannie Mae are continually being resold to investors. In 1948, Fannie Mae was authorized to purchase VA-guaranteed mortgages also. In 1968, the National Housing Act provided for the splitting of the Federal National Mortgage Association into two bodies: (a) the Government National Mortgage Association *(GNMA),* which is a government corporation operating out of the Department of Housing and Urban Development (HUD), and (b) Fannie Mae, a government sponsored but now privately owned corporation.

Today Fannie Mae is a private corporation operating with a public purpose. It sells and purchases conventional, FHA insured, and VA guaranteed mortgages with its private capital to provide a consistent flow of capital funds to the mortgage market. In addition, it is seeking to standardize mortgage documents such as the mortgage contract itself, the note, and property appraisal forms.

Government National Mortgage Association
(GNMA, "Ginnie Mae")

With the splitting of the Federal National Mortgage Association into two entities in 1968, Fannie Mae was allowed to concentrate on its primary function of maintaining an active secondary market for mortgages and was relieved of its two secondary responsibilities by the newly formed Government National Mortgage Association within the Department of Housing and Urban Development. The two functions that were transferred from Fannie Mae to Ginnie Mae were:

1. Management and liquidation of previously acquired mortgages;

2. Provision for special assistance for government lending programs as determined by the President. These programs are designed to meet two specific needs: (a) to make financing available for housing in underdeveloped areas where conventional financing is unavailable; and (b) to stimulate the mortgage market when a severe decline causes construction of housing to stagnate and threaten the national economy.

In addition to the two functions adopted from Fannie Mae, Ginnie Mae is also involved in Congressional programs of financial assistance for cooperative housing, housing for the armed forces, and low- and moderate-priced FHA/VA housing.

Ginnie Mae accomplishes its special assistance mission by purchasing mortgage loans from private lenders that would not otherwise be purchased because of the large risks involved. Presently, Ginnie Mae has over twenty special assistance programs. The Government National Mortgage Association's operations are financed through the sale of securities backed by a pool of mortgages and the U.S. Treasury.

The Federal Home Loan Bank System (FHLB)

The Federal Home Loan Bank System was created by Congress in the midst of the financial crisis of 1932. The *FHLB System* is similar to the Federal Reserve System. It is composed of a federal home loan bank board, twelve regional banks, and member institutions. All federally chartered savings and loan associations are required by law to belong to the system. Qualified state chartered savings and loan associations, mutual savings banks, and life insurance companies may join voluntarily. At present, there are over 4,154 member institutions. The primary purpose of the FHLB is to provide its member institutions with a line of credit to meet the changing demands for mortgage money in their local areas and to supplement the lending resources of institutions in capital-deficit areas by helping to shift funds from capital surplus areas.

Lastly, and most important, the system ties the mortgage-lending institutions to the capital markets through the efforts of its subsidiary, the Federal Home Loan Mortgage Corporation ("Freddie Mac"). The FHLB System regulates and oversees its members. It does not originate loans to home buyers, but rather acts as a conduit to provide loanable funds to member institutions.

Federal Home Loan Mortgage Corporation ("Freddie Mac")

Freddie Mac, a subsidiary of the Federal Home Loan Bank System, was created in 1970. Its primary purpose was to create a secondary mortgage market for conventional mortgages. Freddie Mac buys conventional mortgages, pools them, and sells bonds in the capital market with the pooled mortgages as security. It may also purchase FHA and VA mortgages. This action links the mortgage market with the overall capital market, thereby increasing the market's fluidity. Freddie Mac can also buy and sell conventional mortgages, pool them, and sell bonds with the pooled mortgages as security. These conventional mortgages, however, are not guaranteed by FNMA.

SUMMARY

The varying risks involved in financing different types of real estate in localized markets across the United States has hampered the development of a national mortgage market. However, the federal government has been instrumental in creating new and better means of mortgage financing and making mortgage funds more available to purchasers through governmentally guaranteed, insured, or subsidized programs. Two of the most important of these are FHA and VA programs. Dozens of different types of mortgage contracts are available to meet the individual needs of the borrower.

The purchaser of real estate is able to obtain a mortgage loan from any one of several institutions across the country. The primary sources are savings and loan associations, mutual savings banks, commercial banks, and life insurance companies.

The mortgage instrument will continue to be one of the primary means of financing real estate purchases in the future. It provides security to the lender and a resulting lower rate of interest to the borrower.

TERMS AND CONCEPTS FOR REVIEW

You can check your understanding of these terms against the glossary or by review in this chapter.

Alienation clause	Municipal bonds
Balloon payment	Note
Budget mortgage	Open-end mortgage
Certificate of sale	Owner's rent clause
Conventional mortgage	Partial release clause
Default	Partially amortized mortgage
Deficiency judgment	Power of sale
Discount points	Prepayment clause
Disintermediation	Primary mortgage market
Escalator mortgage	Receiver clause
Estoppel certificate	Refinancing
FHA insured mortgage	Reverse annuity mortgage
FHLB System	Rollover mortgage
Foreclosure	Sale-and-leaseback
Foreclosure by sale	Secondary mortgage market
Freddie Mac	Senior mortgage
Fully amortized mortgage	Straight-term mortgage
Graduated payment mortgage	Subordination clause
Installment land contract	Surplus money action
Interim loan	Trust deed or deed of trust
Intermediation	Usury
Junior mortgage	VA guaranteed loan
Mortgage	Variable rate mortgage
Mortgagee	Voluntary deed
Mortgagor	

What are the differences or relationships, if any, between the following?

Acceleration clause and Escalation
clause
Equitable redemption and Statutory
redemption
Lien theory and Title theory
Package mortgage and Blanket
mortgage

FNMA and GNMA
Savings and loan associations and
Mutual savings banks
Strict foreclosure and Judicial
foreclosure
Wrap-around mortgage and Purchase
money mortgage

PROBLEMS

7–1. In your opinion, should deficiency judgments be outlawed?

7–2. Differentiate between taking title *subject to* and *assuming* a mortgage.

7–3. Why is an owner's rent clause inserted in a mortgage contract? How does it differ from a receiver clause?

7–4. When is a wrap-around mortgage used?

7–5. Explain the purpose of an estoppel certificate.

7–6. Explain, in general, how the secondary mortgage market functions.

7–7. What is the relationship between the primary and secondary mortgage markets?

7–8. Differentiate between an FHA insured and a VA guaranteed loan.

7–9. How can the Federal Reserve influence the availability and cost of credit?

7–10. Assume that you are originating a second mortgage loan. Why do you charge a higher interest rate than on a first mortgage loan? What can you do to reduce the risk of loss?

7–11. Assume that landowner A is selling his farm to developer B on contract for deed. Why might the developer insist on a subordination clause in the sales contract? What might the landowner request if he agrees to subordinate?

7–12. From Figure 7–12, estimate how much less a person would pay the first year for a graduated payment mortgage over a fixed payment mortgage. (Use both the five- and ten-year graduation periods.) What would the difference be for the total payments over the thirty years?

7–13. What are the alternatives available to the mortgagee in case of default of the mortgagor?

7–14. Consider a professional person, such as a dentist. Under what circumstances over her lifetime would the different types of mortgages (classified by payment) be to her advantage? Why?

7–15. Why might a person who is eligible for a VA mortgage still select a conventional mortgage?

7–16. If you had a chance to "assume" a VA mortgage or take it "subject to," which would be the better deal? Answer the same question for a conventional mortgage compared with a VA mortgage.

7–17. What is the advantage of a debt-equity combination?

7–18. Under what circumstances would a construction loan be used?

7–19. What factors caused interest rates to go up as high as 12 percent during 1979?

SUPPLEMENTARY READINGS

Atteberry, William. *Modern Real Estate Finance*. Columbus, Oh.: Grid, 1972.

Beaton, William R. *Real Estate Finance*. Englewood Cliffs, N.J.: Prentice-Hall, 1975.

Bellavance, Russell C. *Real Estate Law*. St. Paul: West, 1979. Chapter 8.

Davey, Homer C., and Mercer, H. Glenn. *Real Estate Principles in California*. Englewood Cliffs, N.J.: Prentice-Hall, 1972. Chapters 8 and 9. ·

Hoagland, Henry E., and Stone, Leo D. *Real Estate Finance*. Homewood, Ill.: Irwin, 1973.

Kratovil, Robert, and Werner, Raymond J. *Real Estate Law,* 7th ed. Englewood Cliffs, N.J.: Prentice-Hall, 1979. Chapters 20 and 21.

Maisel, Sherman J., and Roulac, Stephen E. *Real Estate Investment and Finance*. New York: McGraw-Hill, 1976.

Pearson, Karl G. *Real Estate Principles and Practices*. Columbus, Oh.: Grid, 1973. Chapter 9.

Ring, Alfred A. *Real Estate Principles and Practices*. Englewood Cliffs, N.J.: Prentice-Hall, 1972. Chapters 8, 11, 13, and 15.

Sirota, David. *Essentials of Real Estate Finance*. Chicago: Real Estate Education Company, 1976.

Smith, Halbert C.; Tschappat, Carl J.; and Racster, Ronald L. *Real Estate and Urban Development*. Homewood, Ill.: Irwin, 1973. Chapter 14.

Unger, Maurice A., and Karvel, George, R. *Real Estate Principles and Practices,* 6th ed. Cincinnati: Southwestern, 1979. Chapters 15 and 16.

Unger, Maurice A., and Melichee, Ronald W. *Real Estate Finance*. Cincinnati: Southwestern, 1974.

Weidemer, John P. *Real Estate Finance*. Reston, Va.: Reston Publishing, 1977.

Taxes and Liens

The rights and interests of people who own real estate have been discussed. These rights, however, are subject to the rights and needs of others, including the public and the government. Taxes and liens are two means of exercising these external rights.

REAL PROPERTY TAXES

Funds obtained from real estate taxes are used to support public schools, street improvements, parks, police and fire protection, and other governmental operations. The power to tax is vested in the legislative branch of the government and is limited by the Constitution. The taxes are levied on real property by cities, counties, or other local governing agencies. The amount of taxes and the method of levy and assessment vary considerably from state to state and from town to town within a state; however, the procedures involved are usually very similar.

An understanding of taxes and the taxing system is important when handling real estate transactions for two reasons. First, the taxes on property entail such a substantial amount of money that they act as a constraining influence on buyers in purchase decisions. A real property tax is a charge or burden that must be paid each year; thus, it affects the value of the property. Second, at the closing of a real estate transaction, the taxes are prorated such that the seller and buyer pay their correct portions. This *proration,* or allocation, affects the amount of money needed by the buyer at the closing.

Two basic types of taxes are related to real property. The first is the *general tax,* which is based on the value of the property. The second consists of *special assessments.* A special assessment is a levy to cover costs of improvements, such as sidewalks or street lights, which primarily benefit certain properties.

General Taxes

General taxes are levied by local governing agencies such as cities, towns, counties, and school districts. Taxes levied on real estate provide a substantial portion of the funds required for the general operations of local government, including schools, fire and police protection, parks, and salaries. These taxes, being based on the value of the property, are called *ad valorem* (from the Latin, *at value*) taxes. General taxes are levied based on the ability to pay concept, since owners of more expensive property pay higher taxes than owners of lower priced property.

The taxation process consists of several steps. These steps occur in sequence as follows:

1. Determination and appropriation of the amounts of money needed to operate the government;
2. Assessment of property and allocation of the levy to each property;
3. Collection of the taxes.

Budget and levies

Budgeting is the first step in the taxing process. At the beginning of the budgetary period, which is usually every year, the legislative body determines how much money is needed by each segment of the local government, such as the schools or street maintenance. These needs are then compared to an estimate of the money available from taxes. If the projected funds available do not meet the expected expenses, either the expenditures must be reduced or the sources of money must be expanded. This budgeting step is then followed by an *appropriation,* which is a formal enactment or law defining exactly how all of the money is to be spent and indicating the sources of the funds, including the real property tax. Following the appropriation, the legislative body of the town, county, or other taxing unit votes to decide the method used to impose this tax on persons or property. This process is called *tax levy.* Frequently, the taxing bodies are limited by law or local referendum as to the maximum amount or rate of tax that can be levied on real estate.

Assessed value

Each parcel of real property in a locality is assigned an assessed value in order to determine the amount of taxes to be paid by the property owner. The property value is estimated by a tax assessor employed by the city, county, or other governing organization. The total property value is generally estimated separately for the land and building and then combined on the tax bill. The methods and procedures for appraisal will be covered later in Chapter 19. However, the value for tax assessment purposes is usually quite different from the market value or expected selling price. Frequently, state laws or local rules establish the assessed value as a certain percentage of market value.

These percentages vary from 25 to 100 percent. Farm property is an exception, for farms are often assessed at market value even though other property is assessed at a lower percentage. The town, county, or tax district making the tax levy maintains a tax list (usually called an ***assessment roll***) that defines each piece of property under its jurisdiction, together with its latest assessed value.

When estimating property value, the assessor considers factors such as recent selling prices of similar property, estimated cost of reproducing the structure, the location, depreciation, and income from the property. The typical assessor is experienced in the profession and uses systematic procedures to arrive at property values. The assessor tries to assess all property in a locality at a fixed percentage of its market value, so that the tax will be equitable. Constitutional provisions require that property taxation be uniform in a locality to ensure that owners of similarly valued property pay the same amount of taxes; however, this uniformity is not always easy to achieve because of the many variables affecting value.

Since there is considerable room for difference of opinion as to the value of a specified parcel of property, property owners who do not agree with their assessed value or who feel that an error was made can *appeal* their assessment to the established local review agency. This agency may be called the *board of review, board of organization, town tribunal,* or *board of appeal,* depending on the taxing unit. Property owners who still do not agree with the rulings of those agencies can appeal further to the courts.

Tax calculations

The general tax is based upon the assessed value and the tax rate. Assume that a house has an estimated market value of $30,000 and that the local policy is to assess property at 60 percent of market value. The assessed value can be calculated as follows:

Assessed value = 0.60 × $30,000 = $18,000

The tax rate is determined by dividing the amount of money needed by the city (assume $4,000,000) by the assessed value of all property (assume $200,000,000). In this case, the city would need to collect two cents for each dollar of assessed valuation or, in other words, $2.00 per $100 of assessed valuation.

$$\text{Tax rate} = \frac{\$4,000,000}{\$200,000,000} = .020$$

Tax rates are usually expressed as dollars per $100 of assessed value, or mills per dollar. Assume that the tax rate was $2.00 per $100 of assessed value, which is the same as $.020 per dollar or 20 mills per dollar. The tax in our example would be figured in this way

Tax = .020 × $18,000 = $360

or by the other method of calculation,

$$\text{Tax} = 2.00 \times \frac{\$18,000}{100} = \$360$$

The tax of $360 would then be billed to the taxpayer.

Tax collection
States and localities differ in billing methods and the date when a tax is due. In most cases, the taxpayer is allowed to pay the taxes in installments. For example, half of the year's taxes could be due in May and the remaining half in September. Often a city, county, school district, or other unit will set its own tax rate. In order to avoid duplication in the tax bill mailings, however, it is usual practice for the county to collect the total taxes on a combined bill.

Enforcement
Taxes and special assessments must be valid and enforceable, however. This means the tax must be for a legal purpose, must be levied properly, and must be applied uniformly to the affected properties. General taxes, if not paid, become a tax lien against the property. Tax liens take priority over any other existing liens (as discussed later in this chapter), and the property can be sold, within the constraints of the law, to satisfy the lien.

If a property is sold at a tax sale, the original owner of the real estate, who lost the property due to nonpayment of taxes, has a right to redeem the property within a specific period of time, usually defined by individual state statute. This is known as the *right of redemption.* If an owner should redeem her property by later payment of the tax, she will be required to pay an additional interest penalty, often as much as two percent per month, depending upon state law.

Equalization
Sometimes taxes are levied by the state government based upon property values. To avoid duplication of the assessing functions, the state will base the taxes upon the assessments made by local assessors under local rules. To assure that all property owners in the state pay a fair and uniform share of the state tax, an *equalization factor* is established by the state. For example, property in a county that assesses property at 60 percent of market value would be adjusted relative to other counties in the same state that assess their property at 50 percent of market value. To illustrate, assume there are similar houses in each of two counties, with a market value of $40,000 each. The assessed value in the first county would be 0.60 × $40,000, or $24,000. In the second county, the assessed value would be 0.50 × $40,000, or $20,000. If the state equalization factor were based on 50 percent of market value, the assessed value in the first county would be equalized by multiplying the assessed value of $24,000 by 5/6, resulting in $20,000, the same as the other county. The objective is to levy a state tax on assessed values already on the books (so that a separate state assessment is not needed), but adjust the tax so that all state residents pay a tax in the same proportion to market value.

These equalization factors are established by a body, usually called the state *board of equalization.*

Most states have laws that exempt certain types of property from real estate taxes, provided the property is used for tax-exempt purposes. Typical properties not taxed are hospitals, educational institutions, and real estate owned by religious organizations. Also, governments or their agencies do not tax themselves or each other. This includes property owned by the state or federal government and properties used for parks, schools, or recreation. It is important that taxing bodies use great care to determine the tax-exempt status of a given property because, when any property is exempt from taxes, other properties must bear a higher tax burden.

Many states have a provision whereby the property taxes of senior citizens are reduced. Usually, a formula is specified by state law to reduce the tax that is based on income and ability to pay. This provision has been adopted because older persons often purchased their homes in the 1930s or 1940s. They are now retired and have lower incomes. It is not uncommon for a house to have appreciated from $5,000 to $30,000 since the 1930s. This would bring about a proportional increase in taxes. The objective of the special law is to prevent loss of property by these senior citizens due to their inability to pay the property tax. Some states also have special veterans' exemptions.

Local governments sometimes grant tax *exemptions* or reductions in tax in order to attract new industries. The rationale is that the economic advantage provided by the new industry outweighs the tax loss.

Property taxes vary considerably throughout the United States. Tax rates are usually lower in small towns, but they also vary widely from city to city. Property taxes on a $60,000 house may be less than $200 in one place and up to $3000 in other locations. This wide variation can be due to types of property in the community, level of services offered, government efficiency, and other sources of revenue available. Some cities in the southwest obtain income from oil wells on city property. Northern cities may have considerable expenses for snow removal. Some towns collect separate trash collection fees and add sewer fees to water bills. In other cities, higher taxes result from such things as larger welfare payments, subsidized public transportation, more parks, libraries, or other services.

Large amounts of exempt property also cause rates to be higher; however, the federal government will reimburse local governments in areas where federal installations exist. Areas with high-priced homes usually generate more taxes than they consume in services. Many local areas benefit from more taxes than they consume in services; many also benefit from federal government revenue sharing. Higher wage rates in some large cities result in higher tax rates.

Last, but not least, some cities are managed more efficiently than others, either due to the layout of the city or because of better management.

Variations may also exist within a city, even though it is the objective to have equal taxes for properties of equal value. Sometimes properties sold are automatically reassessed based on the sale price, whereas other properties may not be reassessed until the regular periodic schedule. All of these factors affect the amount of taxes in a locality.

Special Assessments

Certain municipal improvements benefit the community as a whole, whereas other improvements benefit owners of specific parcels of real estate or limited areas. Installation of sidewalks in a residential area would typically fall into the second category. *Special assessments* are taxes levied upon specific parcels of real estate that will be solely benefited by a proposed improvement. Where the primary purpose of an improvement is to benefit the public in general, such as the widening of a street to facilitate through traffic, the improvement is normally not financed by special assessments, even though incidental benefits may also accrue to the properties in the immediate neighborhood.

Originating an assessment

Procedures for originating and implementing a special assessment will vary from state to state; however, certain steps are usually involved. The idea for improvement may originate in either of two ways. First, the legislative authority in the locality, such as the city council, may originate the proposed improvement. The second method is for the property owners who want the improvement to petition for it. In either case, notices would be given to property owners affected, and hearings would be held to hear their views and to ascertain the pros and cons of the proposal. Following the hearings, the authorized legislative authority, such as the city council, may pass an ordinance approving the action and setting forth the costs and the properties to receive the special assessment.

Assessment roll spread

A method is needed to allocate the total improvement cost among the benefited property owners fairly and equitably. The amount of assessment allocated to each parcel of real estate is determined by either (a) front footage or (b) estimated benefit from the improvement. Thus, each piece of property will not necessarily be assessed the same amount. This allocation is often called the *assessment roll spread.* Following any hearing, if the assessment is approved, it becomes a lien on the properties involved and bills are issued to property owners for payment. Property owners usually have the option to pay the full amount at one time or to pay yearly installments with interest on the unpaid balance. Special assessments are enforced by the same means as general property taxes.

LIENS

A *lien* is a claim by one person against property belonging to someone else in which the property is security for payment of a debt. It is a legal right that permits a creditor to have the debt satisfied out of the property of the debtor. The lien may entitle the creditor to have the property of the debtor sold to satisfy the debt, whether or not the debtor agrees. The enforcement of the lien is normally carried out through a court action. Liens can be categorized in different ways. The first category groups liens as either equitable liens or statutory liens. An **equitable lien** is sometimes called a *voluntary lien* and is placed with the consent of the owner. For example, consider this case: an owner requests a mortgage and signs the note to obtain the loan. In the process, the mortgagee acquires a lien on the property. **Statutory liens** are different and exist where the law allows a creditor to file a lien without owner concurrence; for this reason, these liens are also called *involuntary liens.*

Liens are also classified as either specific liens or general liens. A **specific lien** is placed against a specific parcel of real estate. These include mechanic's liens, mortgages, tax liens, and other liens against a single parcel of property. A **general lien,** in contrast, affects all real and personal property of a debtor and might result from state or federal inheritance taxes, judgments, or debts of a deceased person.

Each state has its own law or statutory provision covering requirements for liens. An understanding of liens is important in the real estate business because a lien affects the value or marketability of a parcel of property. When a piece of property is forceably sold to satisfy one or more creditors, liens are paid off in the sequence in which they are recorded, except in the case of tax liens, which have priority. The buyer in a real estate transaction must make sure as part of the title examination that the property being purchased is not encumbered by liens. If there were liens on the property, the liens would remain as a liability for whoever owns the property. The lien holder could foreclose and force sale of the property to satisfy the lien. Therefore, liens must be paid off or otherwise settled prior to or during the closing of the transaction.

A pending lawsuit relating directly to the land can be recorded as a *lis pendens.* The purchaser of a property would then take the title subject to the rights of parties as finally determined by the judgment or decree.

Types of Specific Liens

Specific liens are against one parcel of real estate and do not affect other property of the debtor. There are several different types of specific liens, including mechanic's liens, mortgage liens, vendor's liens, vendee's liens, and attachments.

Mechanic's liens

Mechanics are persons such as carpenters or electricians who provide the labor or services used in the construction or improvement of real property.

Material suppliers provide the lumber or other supplies used in the construction. Laws in all states give these mechanics (whether they be contractors, subcontractors, or laborers) and material suppliers some security that they will be compensated for their work and material by granting them the right to place a *mechanic's lien* against the property on which the labor or materials were used. Some states include services of surveyors, truckers, and architects. This right is derived from the theory that the value of the property has been enhanced, and therefore the parties contributing to the increased value should have a right of security for the work or materials furnished. The mechanic's lien is a specific lien because only the property on which the work was performed and improved in value is subject to the lien.

The fact that work was carried out is not always sufficient to allow a lien to exist. In some states, the lien claimant must show proof of being hired by the property owner. In other states, it is sufficient if the lien claimant can show that the property owner had knowledge of the work, even though the work was ordered by someone else. Laws governing these latter cases are known as *consent statutes.* The owner is said to give implied consent because he had knowledge of the work and did not object to it. Thus, the agreement to perform the work can be *express* or *implied,* but need not be in writing.

A mechanic's lien is usually established when the claimant files a notice of the claim under oath with the county clerk. Some states require that a copy of the notice also be mailed to the owner of the property against which the lien is being filed. The lien must contain a description of the property, the name of the owner, the name and address of the lien claimant, the name of the person who originally ordered the work, and dates when work was ordered, started, and completed. These dates are very important since some states allow liens to take precedence based on the date when the work was ordered, whereas others use the date on which the work was started. The contract price, amount paid to date, and balance due must also be given on the notice of claim. The balance due then becomes the amount of the lien.

Since property owners are sometimes subjected to false claims, there are also statutory provisions to protect them. Frequently, the owner will hire a *contractor,* and the contractor in turn may hire one or more *subcontractors.* When a contractor has completed his work, the property owner has the right to hold back a portion of the amount due until the contractor has furnished an affidavit or proof that all subcontractors and material suppliers have been paid. This procedure is important, since in many states subcontractors, as well as the general contractor, have the right to file a lien against the property on which they performed their work.

The law in these states imposes upon the property owner the obligation to assure that subcontractors as well as the contractor are paid. What happens when an owner pays the contractor, but the contractor fails to pay the workers or the material supplier? Sometimes a contractor may run short of cash and use the money for other projects he is working on. The fact that the contractor had been paid by the owner does not remove the right of a subcontractor to file a lien. This means that the property owner must be careful to require the contractor to have signed releases from all workers and suppliers before the owner pays the contractor. An alternative is to assure that the contractor is bonded. Other states require a subcontractor to give the property owner advance notice of amounts due to them so that the owner can know how much to withhold. Sometimes a tenant will order work on the property she rents. An owner is not, however, liable for payment for work ordered by a tenant without the owner's knowledge and consent. If a person holding less than a fee simple estate authorizes work to be done, only his interest can be attached.

Mechanics and material suppliers are allowed a set period of time in which to record a lien; therefore, a lien might exist but not appear on the record in the recorder's office. The lien must, however, be filed while the work is still in progress or within a period established by law (typically three months) after completion of the work to maintain its priority. When filed, it is effective retroactively in priority to the date the work was completed or the supplies were furnished. In cases where a mechanic fails to file within the set period and pretends to perform additional work, the courts have not allowed this pretense to preserve the priority beyond the allowed period of elapsed time.

A lien does not continue for an indefinite period of time, nor does it automatically assure the lien claimant of his money. The lien expires in a time set by state law, usually one or two years, unless the lien claimant takes action to enforce the lien. Enforcement consists of taking action to foreclose the lien by initiating a court action resulting in a sale of the property and paying off the lien from the sale proceeds. Since there is often a considerable amount of time from the filing of a lawsuit until the judgment is rendered, a creditor can give notice of his claim against a parcel of real estate by recording the notice in the county where the real estate is located as a *lis pendens*. Its filing prevents the expiration of the lien and takes priority among liens at the time the notice is recorded. The right to a mechanic's lien is coupled with the right of the mechanic or material supplier to take legal action against the persons who ordered the work on the basis of contractual liability.

Discharge of a Mechanic's Lien   There are several ways to remove or make ineffective a mechanic's lien:

1. The property owner can pay the amount of the claimed debt to the lien claimant. A **certificate of execution** or **satisfaction of lien** would then be signed by the lien claimant, acknowledged, and filed with the county clerk's office.

2. A lien expires after a set period of time unless an action has been taken by the lien claimant to enforce it. A court order can then be obtained to remove the lien from the record.

3. The owner can deposit money into court or post a bond equal to the amount of the lien. The property is then freed and the lien claimant has recourse to the bond or money deposited.

4. The property owner may disagree with the lien and have the lien claimant served with notice to commence action to foreclose within a period of 30 days. The objective is to bring the claim into court for trial. If the lien claimant should fail to prosecute or should lose the court action, the lien is discharged by order of the court.

Mortgage lien

A mortgage is executed by the property owner to borrow money, using the property as security. The property owner signs a mortgage note that becomes a lien against the property. (Mortgages were discussed fully in Chapter 7.) When the mortgage is paid off, the lien is discharged. If the mortgage payments are not paid when due, the mortgagee can foreclose on the property. A mortgage lien is a voluntary lien, since the owner requests the mortgage and agrees to the lien upon execution of the mortgage instrument. It is also a specific lien, since the lien is against only the specific parcel(s) of real estate. Most mortgage institutions will accept only a first mortgage; thus, there will be no other liens with higher priority. Any second or further mortgages would have a lower priority, just as would any liens filed at a later time. A mortgage lien can be transferred by the mortgagee to another party by assignment of the mortgage and mortgage note.

Tax lien

If taxes or special assessments are not paid, they become a specific lien against the property on which they were levied. Property tax liens take priority over other liens, even though other liens may have been recorded earlier. The property can be sold to enforce the tax lien. Mortgage institutions, in order to preclude the possibility of having tax liens take priority over their mortgage liens, often require that the mortgagor pay amounts each month in addition to interest and payment on principal. The lending institution will then accumulate these monies and pay the tax when due. These monies are called *impounds,* and some institutions pay interest on these impounds, whereas others do not.

Vendor's lien

A *vendor's lien* (or *seller's lien*) arises when a seller conveys real estate and receives a mortgage from the purchaser for the balance of the purchase price. The seller receives a *purchase money mortgage* that becomes a lien on the property for the balance due. The lien can be enforced by foreclosure if the buyer does not make payments in accordance with the contract agreement.

Vendee's lien

A *vendee's lien* (or *buyer's lien*) arises when a contract is drawn up for a real estate transaction, the buyer gives the seller a deposit, and then the seller defaults. Since the seller defaults and refuses to go through with the transaction, the buyer then has a lien against the property. This lien would be for monies paid as deposits under contract plus any other money expended by the buyer as part of examining the title for the property. This type of lien can also be enforced by foreclosure, just as any other lien.

Attachments

Suppose that one person A is suing another person B for monetary damages. Under certain circumstances, the plaintiff A is allowed by statute to file a lien or ***attachment*** against real property of the defendant B, pending the outcome of the court action. The objective of the plaintiff's action is to assure that, when the court action is completed and a judgment is rendered, there will be property of the defendant available to pay the amount awarded by the court. The plaintiff must file a bond to pay any costs and damages that the defendant may suffer if the defendant wins the suit. This condition tends to protect against malicious, nuisance, and other unjustified suits.

Bail bond lien

A bail bond is used to release a person from jail where he is being held on a criminal charge. Real property can be used as bail in lieu of cash, and a bail bond lien is then filed against the property to secure the bond. When the person is released, the bail bond lien is discharged by a certificate obtained from the state's attorney or a court.

Conditional bills of sale

Certain articles of personal property, such as stoves, furnaces, air conditioners, elevators, or other items, can be installed in real estate as a property improvement. The articles can be purchased under agreement, called a ***conditional bill of sale.*** The title does not pass until the goods have been paid for completely. The seller can file the conditional sales agreement in the county recorder's office in the same way that any real estate document is recorded. It then takes priority in the same manner as a lien.

Types of General Liens

General liens normally affect all of the debtor's property, both real and personal. General liens can come about from judgments, decedent's debts, state inheritance taxes, federal estate taxes, corporation franchise taxes, and conditional bills of sale. Each of these can constitute a claim or lien against real property.

Judgments

A ***judgment*** is a court order that may result in an award of money to the plaintiff. A judgment for an award of money becomes a lien against real and personal property of the debtor. The court order is accompanied by a ***writ of execution*** that may direct the sheriff to seize and sell the debtor's property in sufficient amount to pay the judgment and any expenses involved in the sale. The judgment can take priority over other liens based on the date the judgment was entered in court, the date the writ of execution was issued, or the date the judgment was filed. The priority depends on the individual state law. A judgment lien is attached to all real property held by the debtor and under the jurisdiction of the court. It remains in effect for a period of time governed by state statute, usually ten years.

When any judgment is paid or otherwise satisfied, the debtor should obtain a formal receipt from the lien claimant or court to be recorded so that there is no later question that the judgment has been satisfied and no longer exists as an encumbrance on the property.

Decedent's debts

Upon someone's death, title to his real property passes to his devisees by will or to his heirs by law if there is no will. The property is subject to liens existing at the time of the debtor's death. In addition, debts of the deceased person can become liens against the property. In the process of settling the estate, the debts are paid first out of personal property in the estate; but if debts still remain, the real property can be sold to pay the debts. Until these debts are paid, they are a lien against the decedent's real property. A buyer of property from an estate should obtain proof that all debts of the decedent have been paid; if not, the property can be taken to satisfy the debt, and the buyer could lose the money paid for the property.

Federal estate tax

Transfer of the net estate of a decedent is subject to a federal estate tax. The tax is progressive, so that larger estates are taxed at a higher percentage. A resident of the United States is allowed a certain exemption. A general lien can be filed by the federal government. for this tax that attaches to all property in the estate.

State inheritance tax

In most states, a tax is levied against an inheritance. By statute, the state acquires a lien upon the real property of the estate, and a clear title cannot be given until the tax is paid. Persons purchasing property from an estate should make sure that any inheritance taxes have been paid or that the title has been cleared.

Corporation franchise tax

Corporations are assessed a franchise tax in accordance with the state law. The tax is based upon either capital stock or income and becomes a lien on the property of the corporation until paid.

Priority of Liens

As mentioned earlier, liens usually take on priority in the order in which they are filed or recorded. If there is a foreclosure on the property and it is sold for less than the value of all liens and mortgages, the liens of highest priority would be paid first and other lien holders are paid in the order of their priority. A holder of a lien may wilfully make it subservient to another lien. For example, the holder of a lien on a parcel of land in a development may agree to make her lien subordinate to a construction mortgage for a house.

Taxes and special assessments, if not paid, become the highest priority liens without regard to dates. Mortgage institutions will usually require the home owner to deposit monthy installments on the tax, called **impounds,** to assure that the tax is paid when due so that no tax lien takes priority over the mortgage lien.

SUMMARY

Real property taxes are an important means of obtaining funds for schools, street construction and repair, and other aspects of the local government. Taxes fall into the two primary groupings of general taxes and special assessments. General taxes are levied throughout the community based on estimated property values as related to the funds needed by the local government. Special assessments are levied on properties that benefit from special work being done, and the amount is based on the cost apportioned as to the benefit each property owner receives from the improvement.

A lien is a claim against a property owner causing the property to become security for payment of a debt. Of the many types of liens, two primary groups are the most important. Statutory liens are allowed by law, whereas equitable liens are those in which the property owner requests or agrees to the lien. An example of an equitable lien is a mortgage. Liens can also be classified as specific or general. Specific liens attach to one parcel of property, whereas general liens attach to all a person's property. With some exceptions, liens take priority by date of recordation, so that any foreclosure and sale of a property will result in higher priority liens being paid first. This could mean that some lien holders would not be paid.

TERMS AND CONCEPTS

You can check your understanding of these terms against the glossary or by review in this chapter.

Ad valorem	Judgment
Appropriation	*Lis pendens*
Assessment roll	Mechanic's lien
Attachment	Proration
Certificate of execution	Purchase money mortgage
Conditional bill of sale	Right of redemption
Consent statutes	Satisfaction of lien
Equalization factor	Tax levy
Exemption	Writ of execution
Impound	

What are the differences or relationship, if any, between the following?

Contractor and Subcontractor	Specific liens and General
Equitable liens and Statutory	liens
liens	Vendor's lien and Vendee's lien
General taxes and Special	
assessments	

PROBLEMS

8–1. The objective in a community is to have the assessment be 40 percent of market value. If the assessment is $24,000, what would you expect the house to sell for in the open market?

8–2. The assessed value on property A is $21,000. The general tax rate is $1.85 per $100 of assessed value. What is the tax?

8–3. The tax rate in Jarvis township is 24 mills per dollar of assessed value. The assessed value of house B is $19,400. What is the yearly tax?

8–4. The general tax on property C is $684 per year. The lending institution wants the mortgagor to make monthly deposits with the lending institution. How much should be paid each month in addition to interest and payment on principal to have sufficient funds to pay taxes when due?

8–5. What is the order or priority among a number of liens on the same property?

8–6. If you were building a house, or having a substantial improvement made, list precautions you could take against mechanic's liens.

8–7. Describe what a mechanic must do to enforce a mechanic's lien.

8–8. List the types of government services that a property owner helps finance by paying property taxes.

8–9. If a property is foreclosed, and the proceeds are more than sufficient to pay a tax lien or mechanic's lien, what happens to the surplus? What if the proceeds are not sufficient?

8–10. If a property owner disagrees with her property tax assessment, describe the steps she might take to contest the assessment.

8–11. Outline the steps a local taxing body would take in arriving at a tax rate.

8–12. A city has a budget of $740,000 to be paid out of property taxes. Total taxable property in the city is $100,000,000, and the assessment ratio is 40 percent. Determine the total assessed value of all property and the tax rate needed to support the budget.

8–13. Mr. D'Angelo owns a house with a 188 ft. frontage. His property is valued at $97,000, with a city assessment ratio of 55 percent. His yearly tax bill was $1997.00. Calculate the millage rate (mills per dollar) in the city. Also determine his bill if the city were to assess owners $45 per front foot for paving the street.

8–14. D'Angelo is considering buying another property with a market value of $76,550. The current assessment rate is 70 percent, and the tax rate is 31 mills. What is the property tax?

8–15. Mr. Jones sold his house to Mr. and Mrs. Axon. The Axons' attorney later found a mechanic's lien on the property. What options are available to the buyer and seller?

8–16. Six counties in a state assess property at 50 percent of market value. County K assesses at 65 percent of market. Property A in County K is assessed at $13,000. If a state tax were imposed based on assessed property values, to what value should property A be revalued, based on an equalization factor?

SUPPLEMENTARY READINGS

Beeman, William J. *The Property Tax and the Spatial Pattern of Growth Within Urban Areas.* Washington D.C.: Urban Land Institute, 1969.

Bergfield, Philip B. *Principles of Real Estate Law.* New York, McGraw-Hill, 1979. Chapters 17 and 22.

Case, Karl E. *Property Taxation: The Need for Reform.* Cambridge, Mass.: Ballinger, 1978.

French, William B., and Lusk, Harold F. *Law of the Real Estate Business.* Homewood, Ill.: Irwin, 1979. Chapter 20.

Harwood, Bruce. *Real Estate Principles.* Reston, Va.: Reston Publishing, 1977. Chapter 13.

King, Alvin T. *Property Taxes, Amenities and Residential Land Values.* Cambridge, Mass.: Ballinger, 1973.

Kratovil, Robert, and Werner, Raymond J. *Real Estate Law*, 7th ed. Englewood Cliffs, N.J.: Prentice-Hall, 1979. Chapter 39.

Peterson, George E. *Property Taxes, Housing, and the Cities.* Lexington, Mass.: Lexington Books, 1973.

Rawson, Mary. *Property Taxation and Urban Development: Effects of the Property Tax on City Growth and Change.* Washington: Urban Land Institute, 1961.

Ring, Alfred A., and Dasso, Jerome. *Real Estate Principles and Practices.* Englewood Cliffs, N.J.: Prentice-Hall, 1977. Chapter 25.

Home Ownership

In 1890, approximately half the families in the United States owned their own homes. The U.S. was primarily rural then, and each family worked together as a productive unit using its home as a place of work as well as a residence. Later the industrial revolution pulled much of the population away from the farm and into urban areas to take advantage of employment opportunities. Urbanization of the young work force led to a decrease in home ownership and a corresponding increase in renters. By 1920, home ownership had dropped to 46 percent. In the early 1920s the downward trend reversed, and home ownership increased to about 48 percent. Then the crash of the stock market in 1929 signalled the beginning of the Depression, which resulted in thousands of mortgage foreclosures. Home ownership decreased every year for the next ten years. By 1940, only 44 percent of families in the United States owned their own homes. The Depression spawned dozens of federal statutes designed to cure the ills of our economy. The Federal Housing Act of 1934 created the Federal Housing Agency and was one of the more successful programs. The FHA introduced long-term amortized loans with high loan-to-value ratios. It provided FHA-insured loans to many qualified borrowers who would otherwise have been unable to finance a home purchase. Also, the Federal National Mortgage Association ("Fannie Mae") created a secondary market for mortgages to encourage the flow of mortgage funds from areas of cash surplus to cash deficit areas. The federal government's commitment to better housing and more favorable mortgage financing provided the impetus for an unprecedented increase in home ownership between 1940 and 1960, when the percentage jumped from 44 percent to 62 percent. Between 1960 and 1970, home ownership increased at a very slow pace. The slow increase was attributable to rising land and construction costs, the tight money market, and a dramatic shift in the composition of our population. This population shift resulted in a very large number of very old and very young heads of households who typically rent rather than buy. Today, over 65 percent of all homes are owner-occupied, and 45 percent of the home buyers have working spouses to help with the high monthly mortgage payments.

Changing Nature of Home Ownership

Home ownership in the United States has, for years, been looked upon as a "way of life." Thus at one time, the majority of Americans subscribed to Max Weber's concept of the *Puritan ethic,* which emphasized serving God through hard work and thrift. The Puritan ethic denied the value of leisure and preferred that people use all their time to perform God's work. Over the years, the Puritan ethic gradually gave way, and leisure time lost its sinful overtones. In the 1970s, the hippie subculture epitomized the "life of leisure"—a new way of life that is permeating our entire culture. Status is derived not by work, but by freedom from work. Young and old alike attach a high value to leisure time. The desire for more leisure time to experience new things and develop new relationships has altered the individual's attitude toward home ownership. Traditional, single-family home ownership carries with it certain time-consuming chores and tends to immobilize the family. As a result, new concepts in home ownership are evolving to satisfy the needs of a young, mobile, leisure-seeking culture.

Planned unit developments (PUDS) and condominiums are now being offered with features that include care-free maintenance, on-site rental managers, time-sharing, and a package of amenities to satisfy the most leisure-minded occupant.

Low cost, low maintenance mobile homes are rapidly increasing in sales. Today they account for a full third of all new single-family dwellings. The demand for secondary homes is continuing to increase. Approximately 5 percent of the families in the United States own vacation homes. More than one out of every ten new homes now under construction is a vacation home. A continuing increase in the mobility of the population, coupled with increasing leisure time and rising incomes, will undoubtedly generate a concurrent increase in the demand for low maintenance, low cost primary residences, whether rented or owned, coupled with an increase in the demand for secondary homes, whether purchased outright, bought on a time-sharing basis, or rented.

Changing Physical Characteristics of
New Single-Family Housing

A recent survey conducted by the NATIONAL ASSOCIATION OF REALTORS® reveals that newly constructed detached homes are larger and contain more amenities than homes built in the past. New homes built in 1977 contain an average 1,715 sq ft of living space, or 10 percent more space than homes built five years earlier.

The number of new homes with fireplaces doubled in the same five year period, and by 1977, two out of three homes included at least one fireplace. Over one-half of the new homes built in 1977 were equipped with central air conditioning. Three out of four new homes built in 1977 included at least two bathrooms, compared to 57 percent in 1972. Of the new homes built in 1977, 82 percent had dishwashers, compared with only 53 percent in 1972; 92 percent of these homes contained stoves, and 11 percent contained refrigerators, reflecting little or no change over 1972.

The following features of new homes have not changed significantly over the last 5 years. Of the homes built in 1977, 59 percent were one-story, 29 percent had two or more stories, and 12 percent were split-level design. Two out of three homes had two-car garages, 15 percent had a one-car garage, 5 percent had carports and 13 percent had no parking facilities. Two out of three homes built in 1977 had three bedrooms.

The number of new homes built in 1977 containing basements varied considerably from one region to another. In 1977, over 80 percent of the new homes built in the north and north-central regions had basements, compared to only 20 percent in the south and 28 percent in the west.

Financial Characteristics of Single-Family Homes

Figures 9–1 and 9–2 show the total number of existing and new single-family home sales in the United States from 1977 to 1979. As can be seen, existing

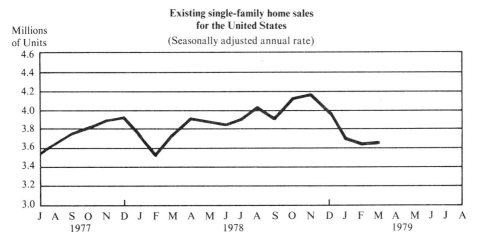

Figure 9–1

Existing single-family home sales (last half 1977 through March, 1979)

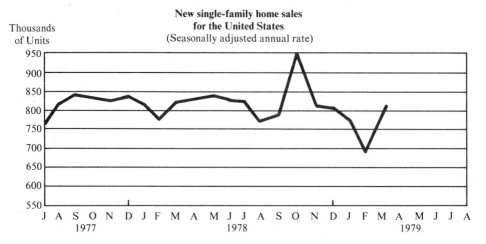

Figure 9–2
New single-family home sales (last half 1977 through March, 1979)

single-family home sales peaked at just under 4.2 million units in 1978, and new single-family home sales peaked at 900 thousand units. The drop in sales of both new and existing single-family homes in 1979 is attributed primarily to rising interest rates.

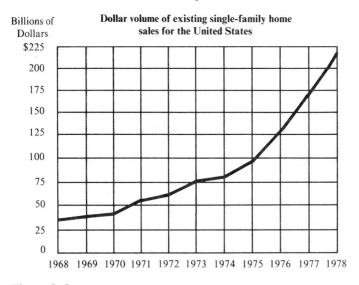

Figure 9–3
Dollar volume of existing single-family home sales (1968–1978)

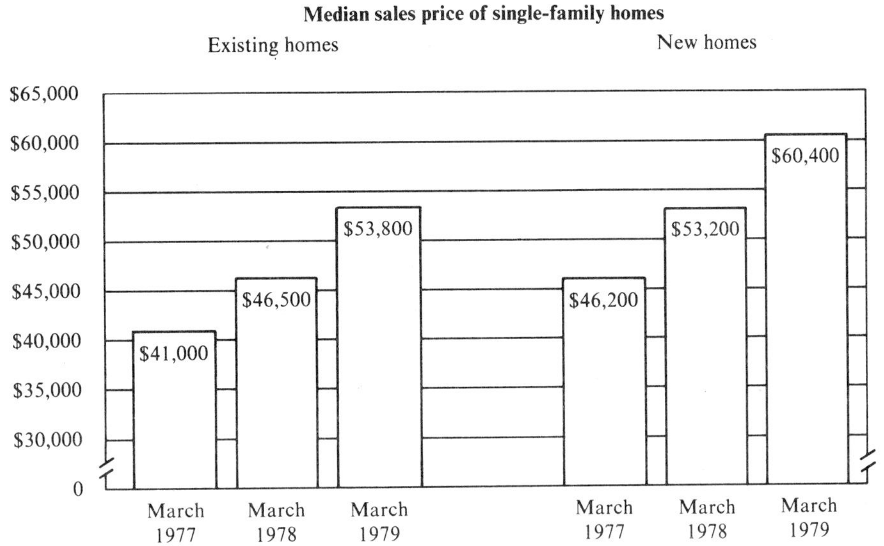

Median sales price of single-family homes

Existing homes   New homes

Figure 9–4

Median sales price of existing and new single-family homes (March, 1977 through March, 1979)

Figure 9–3 shows the dollar volume of existing single-family home sales in the United States for a ten-year period ending in 1978. As can be seen, the dollar sales volume has been increasing constantly over the ten-year period.

Figure 9–4 shows the median sales price of existing and new single-family homes from 1977 through March, 1979. The median resale price of existing single-family homes in March, 1979, was $53,800, up 15.7 percent from the previous year. The median sales price of new single-family homes in March 1979, was $60,400, up 13.5 percent over the previous year.

Figure 9–5 shows the relationship between single-family home price increases and the Consumer Price Index. The figure depicts the fact that, in eight out of ten years, real estate prices have kept pace with or exceeded the Consumer Price Index, thereby establishing real estate ownership as an effective hedge against inflation.

ADVANTAGES OF HOME OWNERSHIP

The advantages of home ownership are many and complex, and their importance varies with each home owner. The many advantages can be broadly classified into two areas: (a) social or psychological and (b) economic. Legislation has also been favorable toward home owners.

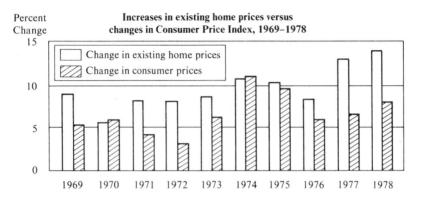

Figure 9–5

Increases in existing home prices versus changes in Consumer Price Index (1969–1978)

Social or Psychological Advantages

The sociopsychological advantages may be further subdivided into four areas.

Security

Home ownership provides the family with a sense of security and belongingness that is not available to the renter. The home owner is not under the constant threat of increasing rents or eviction. He is able to remodel or repair his home as he pleases and when he pleases, without having to obtain the consent of a recalcitrant landlord. The home owner thereby acquires a certain "peace of mind."

Civic responsibility

Through ownership, the individual becomes keenly aware of real estate taxes, special assessments, zoning restrictions, and other police powers that are unfamiliar to most renters. The home owner can determine where her tax dollar goes and whether or not it is being utilized efficiently and effectively. Special assessments are levied against her to finance certain improvements that accrue to specific properties. The home owner again has an opportunity to determine the need for such improvements and may voice her opinion at a public hearing. Also, the home owner is faced with zoning restrictions that are implemented by local municipalities to control land use and growth. The objectives of zoning ordinances are honorable, but political favoritism can sometimes make them a farce. The home owner becomes sensitive to any zoning changes that may adversely affect her property value. She soon learns that 50 to 70 percent of the real estate tax dollar goes toward financing local schools and roads. As a result, she is interested in efficiently run public

schools and road construction programs and acts to guard against misman-
agement or misappropriation of the tax dollar. These political, economic, and
social implications of home ownership provide the basis of an understanding
of local government and help develop a sense of civic responsibility.

Pride

Most home owners are exceptionally proud of their homes, and this pride is
manifested in the care given their investment. A neighborhood with a high
percentage of owner-occupied homes will typically be better cared for than a
neighborhood that has a substantial portion of rental units. The typical
renter, having no vested interest in the property, usually does not exercise the
same care in maintaining the property as an owner does.

Enhances self-image

Although certain segments of our society claim to dismiss materialism as a
reflection of success, most people still perceive a strong relationship. Also, for
many people, a home enables them to extend their personality and express
themselves creatively and tangibly through interior decorating, landscaping,
and architecture.

Economic Advantages

There are several economic advantages of home ownership.

Investment

Nearly all home purchases are financed by mortgage loans. The loans are
amortized so that a portion of each monthly payment goes toward principal
and a portion toward interest. The principal portion of the payment reduces
the loan balance and produces a corresponding increase in the owner's equity,
provided property values remain constant. If property values increase, the
total increase accrues to the equity owner even though he has only a small
down payment invested in the property. The monthly loan payment therefore
acts as a "forced savings" program to the home buyer.

Hedge against inflation

In an inflationary economy, wise investors place their money in investments
that keep pace with or exceed the rate of inflation. Otherwise, the investor's
purchasing power diminishes. Real estate is one of the few investments that
has historically kept pace with or exceeded the general rate of inflation, and
thus is considered a *hedge against inflation.*

Credit

Merchants and financial institutions are particularly interested in an individual's home ownership status when extending credit. Home ownership implies
stability, responsibility, and civic pride, all of which are personal traits that
tend to reduce the risk to the creditor and increase the possibility of credit
being extended to the home owner.

Favorable Legislation

Homestead Act
Many states recognize a real property right known as *homestead.* Such rights vary from state to state, but they generally exempt a homestead from forced sale or foreclosure. Also, a homestead cannot be mortgaged or sold during the lifetime of the husband or wife without the consent of both parties. Upon the death of a spouse, the remaining spouse and/or children can continue to live on the homestead until the children reach majority age, without regard to the provisions in the deceased spouse's will or creditor's claims.

Some states provide the taxpayer relief by exempting the first $500 to $5,000 of assessed property value from taxation. If the living spouse remarries, homestead rights for both the spouse and the children are usually relinquished.

Statutory rights of redemption
Many states have passed legislation enabling a delinquent borrower to redeem his foreclosed property up to two years after the foreclosure sale. This "right" was discussed more fully in Chapters 7 and 8.

TAX BENEFITS OF HOME OWNERSHIP

Home ownership also accrues many tax benefits. These are described on the following pages.

Interest Expense

The vast majority of all home purchases are financed through first mortgage loans. These loans are fully amortized so that the borrower pays off the principal during the term of the loan. In the early years, the major portion of the monthly payment goes toward interest expense. The interest expense is deductible against personal income taxes.

Real Estate Taxes

Real estate taxes on the home are also tax deductible. The combined deductions of interest expense and real estate taxes can add up to several thousand dollars in the early years of the loan.

Depreciation

Although a single-family, owner-occupied home cannot be depreciated for tax purposes, if the home is a duplex and the extra unit is rented out, the rental unit can be depreciated. Depreciation is a tax deductible, noncash flow expense. Chapter 19 provides a detailed explanation of various available depreciation techniques.

1975 Investment Tax Credit

Although the tax credit legislation was temporary, it shows that the government may, from time to time, increase the advantages of home ownership through favorable tax legislation. Early in 1975, the economy was experiencing a severe recession. The housing and construction industries were almost at a standstill in many parts of the country. The federal government attempted to provide some relief to the industry by passing a tax bill for an unprecedented tax credit equal to 5 percent of the purchase price—up to $2,000—on any new home purchase provided the following guidelines were met:

1. The homes had to be under construction or completed before March 26, 1975.
2. The home purchased had to be the principal place of residence. Single-family structures, residential units in new condominiums or cooperatives, and mobile homes qualified.

The *investment tax credit* reduces the amount of income taxes payable by the amount of credit. A $2,000 tax credit reduces the taxes payable by $2,000.

Residential Energy Credit

The 1978 Tax Reform Act includes a provision for a tax credit on energy saving devices installed in the home. The tax credit is allowed on all homes, whether rented or owned, as long as it is the taxpayer's principal residence. The tax credit has the effect of reducing the taxpayer's tax liability by the amount of the credit. The tax credit is 15 percent of the cost of any items that qualified as energy saving devices, up to a maximum tax credit of $300. The credit is available from 1977 to 1986.

Favorable Capital Gain Treatment

A house is considered a capital asset. If it is held over one year, any gain on sale is classified as a long-term capital gain and taxed at the favorable capital gain rates. The long-term capital gain tax liability is determined by excluding 60 percent of the gain and adding the balance to the taxpayer's taxable income. If the house were held for less than one year before being sold, any gain on sale would be considered a short-term capital gain and taxed as ordinary income. Losses are not recognized on the sale of primary residences.

Deferred Gain on the Sale of a Principal Residence

Any taxes on the profits resulting from the sale of a principal residence that has been held for over one year may be deferred if, within eighteen months before or after the sale of the old residence, the taxpayer purchases a new principal residence that is equal to or exceeds the *adjusted selling price* of the old residence. If a new principal residence is built, the construction must start either before the sale of the residence or within eighteen months after the sale. The taxpayer has two years within which to occupy the new construction as his principal residence, as shown in Figure 9–6.

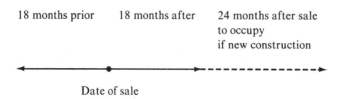

Figure 9–6
Sale of principal residence

The gain, if any, is computed by subtracting the *adjusted basis* of the old residence from the *amount realized on sale*. The **adjusted basis** is the original cost of the property plus the value of any capital improvements and expenses incurred in the purchase of the property. The **amount realized on sale** is the selling price less selling expenses.

The **adjusted selling price** is the net amount realized on the sale minus any *fixing-up expenses* incurred to increase the salability of the house. The fixing-up expenses must be incurred within ninety days before the sale and paid for within thirty-days after the sale.

Fixing-up expenses are considered only when computing the **recognized gain** on the sale of a residence that is replaced by a new one. They are not deductions from the selling price to be taken in computing **realized gain.** As a result, they do not affect the gain that will be taxed when the seller ultimately sells the property and does not replace it.

If the adjusted selling price of the old residence exceeds the purchase price of the new residence, the excess is recognized as gain and taxed in the year of sale.

Any **deferred gain** (gain not taxed in the year of sale) is subtracted from the purchase price of the new residence, thereby reducing its basis.

The home owner may buy and sell as many homes as she likes during her lifetime and continue to defer taxes provided that,

1. The house is a primary residence.
2. The home owner makes no more than one transaction per 12 months.
3. The new residence is not purchased and resold before the old residence is sold.

General formulas

Computation of Realized (total) Gain

Amount realized on sale (selling price less selling expense)
Less: Adjusted basis of old residence (original cost of the property plus the value of any capital improvements and expenses incurred in the purchase of the property)

Realized Gain

Computation of Recognized Gain

Adjusted selling price (the amount realized on sale minus any fixing-up expenses)
Less: Cost of new residence

Recognized gain

Example #1

Taxpayer A buys a home in 1960 for $20,000 and sells it in 1975 for $30,000. Within a year, A buys a new home for $35,000. The $10,000 profit that was made on the sale is not taxable at the time of sale because the cost of the new home purchased ($35,000) exceeded the selling price of the old residence ($30,000).

The $10,000 gain is subtracted from the cost of the new residence.

Cost of new home	$35,000
Less: Deferred gain	−$10,000
Adjusted basis of new residence	$25,000

Ten years later, the taxpayer sells the new house for $40,000 and does not replace it. His total gain is realized at this time.

Selling price of home	$40,000
Less: Adjusted basis	−$25,000
Recognized gain	$15,000

Note: The $15,000 gain is composed of the $10,000 deferred gain from the sale of the first home plus the $5,000 gain realized on the sale of the second house.

Example #2

Mr. and Mrs. Janski sold their primary residence and incurred a capital gain of $2,330 ($32,655–$30,325). They deferred payment on the total gain, however, by purchasing a new residence within eighteen months for $38,000, which exceeded the adjusted sale price of $32,355. The calculations follow:

Basis of the Old Residence

Jan., 1970	Purchase price	$25,000
Jan., 1970	Legal fees	$ 125

July, 1971	Added one room	$ 1,500
Sept., 1972	Bought new furnace	$ 1,200
April, 1973	Built two-car garage	$ 2,500
Adjusted basis		$30,325

Adjusted Sales Price

Selling price		$35,000
Less: Selling expenses		
Broker's sales commission	$2,100	
Title search	30	
Title insurance	50	
Revenue stamps	40	
Legal fees	125	
		−$ 2,345
Amount realized on sale		$32,655
Less: Fixing-up expenses		−$ 300
Adjusted selling price		$32,355

Realized (total) Gain

Amount realized on sale	$32,655
Less: Adjusted basis of old residence	$30,325
Realized gain	$ 2,330

Computation of Recognized Gain

Adjusted selling price	$32,355
Less: Cost of new residence	−$38,000
No recognized gain	

Note: Since the purchase price of the new residence ($38,000) exceeds the adjusted selling price of the old residence ($32,355), the total realized gain of $2,330 ($32,655 − $30,325) is deferred. The deferred gain is subtracted from the purchase price of the new residence so that, if and when it is eventually sold and not replaced, the deferred gain will finally be recognized and taxed.

Basis of New Residence

Purchase price		$38,000
Less: Unrecognized gain		
Amount realized on sale	$32,655	
Basis of old residence	−$30,325	
		−$ 2,330
Adjusted basis of new residence		35,670

Homeowner Over Age 55

The Revenue Act of 1978 gives taxpayers who are 55 years old or older a *once-in-a-lifetime* exclusion of up to $100,000 ($50,000 for married taxpayers filing separately) of the gain realized on the sale of their primary residence. To qualify for an **over 55 exemption,** the taxpayer must

1. Be at least 55 years of age (if spouses own their home jointly, only one spouse need be over 55).

2. Have owned and used the home as their primary residence three out of the last five years (the three years need not be consecutive).

For purposes of the exclusion, a *primary residence* includes not only a single-family residence, but also a condominium or cooperative.

The exclusion does not apply separately for each spouse. If married taxpayers use their once-in-a-lifetime exclusion and later divorce and remarry, neither spouse is entitled to a second exclusion.

Taxpayers over 65 years of age who had previously excluded portions of their gain on sales made prior to July 26, 1978, may still avail themselves of the $100,000 exclusion. The exclusion is *once-in-a-lifetime,* and if a taxpayer elects to use the exclusion by excluding less than the maximum $100,000, the balance *is not* available for exclusion in later years.

Example

On December 1, 1979, John and Mary Henderson, both age 55, sold their primary residence for $175,000. They had purchased the home in 1959 and lived in it until the time of sale. The basis of the property at the time of sale (cost plus any capital improvements) was $60,000. The Hendersons incurred selling expenses of $10,000. They elect to take their *once-in-a-lifetime exclusion.* The taxable gain is computed as follows:

Sales price	$175,000
Less: Selling expenses	−$ 10,000
Amount realized on sale	$165,000
Less: Adjusted basis of old residence	−$ 60,000
Realized gain	$105,000
Less: Exclusion	−$100,000
Gain recognized	$ 5,000

The $5,000 recognized gain is considered a long-term capital gain; thus, the Hendersons will add 40 percent of the long-term gain to their ordinary income and be taxed accordingly.

Installment Sales (Contract for Deed)

If a home owner elects to sell her home on the installment basis and payments in the year of sale do not exceed 30 percent of the selling price, she may report the gain over the period in which she receives the principal payments rather than in the year of sale.

Example

If the selling price of the home was $50,000, the profit was $20,000, and the principal payments were $5,000 annually, the seller reports a gain of $2,000 each year.

$$\frac{\$20,000}{\$50,000} \times \$5,000 = \$2,000$$

Expenses of Selling and Purchasing
a New Residence

When an employee or self-employed individual is required to move to a new location that is at least thirty-five miles further from his former residence than was the former job site, certain nonreimbursed moving expenses can be used to offset ordinary income, subject to limitations.

DISADVANTAGES OF HOME OWNERSHIP

Although the list of ownership advantages is lengthy, the prospective home owner would be remiss if he or she did not consider the many disadvantages, any one of which may be important enough to dissuade a person from purchasing.

Down Payment Required

First, the down payment requirement may be sufficiently burdensome to keep many prospects from purchasing their home. If the family nest egg is used as a down payment for the purchase of a house, the family may be unable to meet other financial emergencies and may be forced to curtail other activities requiring money. The nonliquid nature of the real estate investment precludes the home owner from rapidly converting ownership equity into emergency cash.

Property Taxes

The increasing real estate taxes create an additional burden. Even though the taxes are deductible from ordinary income, they nevertheless require a cash outflow from savings. On an annual basis, real estate taxes range from 1 to 2 percent of the property's value. Special assessments are constantly being levied against specific properties to improve streets, sidewalks, and sewage facilities. Such assessments, although payable over several years, can amount to several thousand dollars.

Maintenance

Wide fluctuations in repair and maintenance costs can be incurred, depending on the age of the building, the quality of the construction, and the extent to which the home owner can do the maintenance himself. The prospective home owner should allow for annual repair and maintenance expenses of from $1\frac{1}{2}$ to $2\frac{1}{2}$ percent of the value of the structure. If the prospective home owner does much of the maintenance and repair work himself, he necessarily curtails his leisure activities. The maintenance, repair, and yard work necessary in owning a home may create an undesirable hardship.

Commuting

The suburban location of many single-family homes requires expensive and time-consuming commuting. It also decreases the opportunity for the cultural activities located in central business districts.

Illiquid Investment

Finally, the home owner may be forced to sell at a time when the real estate market is in a slump. If so, he must be willing to either accept a low offer for his home or retain ownership until the market recovers. In the meantime, he may need to purchase another home in a new location. The traumatic experience of double house payments, even if for just a short time, may be enough to turn the most ardent home owner into a lifelong tenant.

Expenses of Sale

When the home owner does sell, he incurs the expense of the broker's sales commission and legal fees. These expenses range from 8 to 10 percent of the value of the property and can negate the paper profit on many homes that have been held for under three years. Obviously, then, a fundamental factor in the prospective home owner's decision whether or not to buy is the length of time he expects to occupy the home. If it appears that the holding period will be less than three years, it may be economically unsound to buy.

RENT VERSUS BUY

The topic of rent versus buy is popular on radio, television, and in the press. The proponents of renting state their case or the columnist dutifully lists the advantages of renting, and the proponents of buying counter by advancing their theories. Occasionally, impressive looking rent-versus-buy analysis forms are used to quantify and compare the two alternatives. Who wins usually depends upon the vested interests of the designer of the forms. The apartment owner convincingly uses the forms to demonstrate that renting is definitely the best alternative. Conversely, the broker who sells homes is just as convincing in arriving at the other alternative. Unfortunately, many people try to compare the high cost of owning a twelve-room house with the low cost of renting a six room apartment. Obviously, comparing apples to oranges is seldom very enlightening.

In addition, any attempt to quantify or measure the value of pride, independence, civic responsibility, and the other nonquantifiable advantages of home ownership or the nonquantifiable advantages of renting would be a gross oversimplification. Indeed, a recent survey conducted by the United States League of Savings Associations found that the majority of reasons for home ownership were noneconomic and nonquantifiable. Of the reasons given for purchasing a home, 62 percent were related to social and personal needs. Prominent noneconomic reasons for purchasing homes included a better environment for children, privacy, freedom and independence to improve the property, and the desire for more space. Only 38 percent of the reasons given were classified as economic. We submit that similar noneconomic reasons would prevail if a survey of renters were to be conducted.

How, then, can we attach any credence to such oversimplified comparisons? A more realistic approach would require the individual to compare the satisfaction (or utility) gained from tenancy in relation to its cost against the satisfaction derived from home ownership against its cost. The satisfaction derived from renting or owning may be monetary or nonmonetary, just as the costs may be.

The satisfaction derived and costs incurred will vary from individual to individual. As a result, there will be a continuing demand for rentable units from those people who conduct their own analysis and determine for themselves that renting is more advantageous than buying. There will also be more and more demand for owner-occupied homes by those people who analyze their needs and conclude they will be best satisfied by purchasing a home. Family circumstances, family composition, changing cultural beliefs, income, age, and increasing mobility of the work force will strongly influence the relative merits of these two ways of life.

HOME OWNERSHIP CONSIDERATIONS

For families, the decision to purchase a home is the largest financial undertaking of a lifetime. The average selling price of a new home in the United States is now over $60,000. With 90 percent financing at 10 percent interest over thirty years, the monthly principal and interest payments alone are $472. Although high interest rates and increasing construction costs had a dampening effect on single-family home sales in 1979, many people were buying rather than waiting for interest rates to go down. The rationale behind "buying now" is that interest rates will probably remain high for the next year or so, and concurrently, home prices were expected to increase 10 to 14 percent in 1980. The net result is that it would have cost even more in initial investment and monthly payments if the prospective purchaser delayed purchasing. Thus, the purchaser who buys now will benefit from property appreciation which, as shown in Figure 9–5, has generally kept pace with or exceeded the general rate of inflation over the last several years.

It is not uncommon for the typical family to own and occupy four to five homes in a lifetime. Nonetheless, many pitfalls await the unwary purchaser. When shopping for a home, the purchaser may want to seek the help of a realtor. Realtors are professionally trained in all phases of real estate marketing, and they subscribe to a strict code of professional ethics.

Figure 9–7, a convenient checklist, can be used by the prospective home purchaser to ensure that all the important features of each home considered are carefully analyzed.

HOUSING REQUIREMENTS

(Insert property addresses at top of columns)

NEIGHBORHOOD

	1	2	3	4	5
Stable residential neighborhood?					
Close to employment?					
Close to schools?					
Close to public transportation?					
Close to recreational facilities?					
How is the area zoned?					
Is there fire & police protection?					
Are the streets paved, well lighted & marked?					
Are there fire hydrants?					
Are there storm sewers?					
If new construction, builder reputation?					

SITE

	1	2	3	4	5
Lawn condition?					
Does lot drain away from house?					
Is Driveway concrete, blacktop or gravel, what condition is same?					
Are there sidewalks? If so, condition?					
Is lot size adequate?					
Is there city sewage or septic tank? If septic, how big & how much drainfield & is it adequate?					
Is there city water or well? If well, how deep & condition of same?					
How are taxes?					

HOUSE DETAIL

	1	2	3	4	5
What style of home . . . ranch, bi-level, tri-level, quad-level, two-story. What is the condition of same?					
If ranch style, is there a basement, crawlspace or slab?					
Is there an entry closet?					
Does it conform to easy furniture arrangement?					
Are bath(s) conveniently located?					
Is kitchen storage adequate?					
Is there a laundry area? If so, what floor?..........					
Is there adequate dining area?					
Is there a familyroom? If so, what floor?..........					
If no familyroom, is there enough space to add one?					
Is there a fireplace?					
Is there adequate play area?					

GARAGE

	1	2	3	4	5
Is there a garage or carport?					
If so, is it attached or freestanding?					
What size? One car, two car, three car?					
Does the garage have a floor drain?					
Is the garage heated?					

EXTRAS

	1	2	3	4	5
Is there a patio or deck?					
Is there a grill?					
Is there a utility shed or outbuilding?					
Is there a swimming pool?					

CONSTRUCTION OF HOME

	1	2	3	4	5
What kind of roof? (Average is 210 Lb. asphalt strip shingles with life span of 10-15 years. A slate, aluminum or copper roof is more expensive but requires little maintenance and will last a lifetime.)					
Are gutters in good condition & adequate?					
For exterior siding, homes will usually have wood siding, aluminum, hardboard, brick, stucco, asbestos or concrete block. What is the condition of the exterior walls on this home?					
Foundations are either block or poured. How are the following?					
a) Is foundation in good repair?					
b) Are there water marks along the basement walls?					
c) Is there a floor drain in basement?					
Is water heater adequate? Also what condition?					
Are pipes cast iron, plastic, steel or copper?					
How is wiring? Old, new, partially old & new?					
Sufficient outlets?					
Electrical service . . . 110 only, 220 only, both?					
Are there storms & screens? If so, what are their conditions?					
How is home insulated & how much in roof & side walls?					
What type of heat? Gas, electric, hot water? How old is furnace? ...... What condition is it in?					
Is home air conditioned? If so, what condition is the unit in & how old?					

OTHER

	1	2	3	4	5
Does home have dishwasher?					
Does home have built-in range?					
Does home have refrigerator?					
Does home have a disposal?					
Does home have a trash compactor?					
Do the washer & dryer remain?					
Is there a sump pump?					
Is there adequate garbage pickup?					
Are there any monthly assessments? If so, what are they?					
How much do the utility bills run per month?					
Heat					
Water					
Electric					

Figure 9–7

House hunting checklist

Source: Reprinted with permission of J. C. Ebach Realty, Bloomington, Illinois.

CONDOMINIUM OWNERSHIP

The many advantages and disadvantages of home ownership described in this chapter also apply to the condominium, with some exceptions. *Condominium ownership* consists of an individual interest (just like a single-family dwelling) in an apartment, plus an undivided common interest in the common areas such as elevators, halls, lawn, parking area, heating plant, and so forth. The condominium owner can sell, mortgage, lease, or otherwise transfer her unit just as she would a regular residence. In addition to residential condominiums, professional buildings, office buildings, medical clinics, or recreational developments can use the condominium form of ownership.

Formation

State condominium laws provide that a developer or property owner must execute and record a master deed to the condominium. The deed must be accompanied by a declaration, bylaws, detailed layout (*condominium map*), floor plans, and elevations of all sides. An *elevation* is a pictorial drawing as seen from one side of a building. Once filed, the condominium status of the property can be removed only with the consent of *all* owners. Provisions are made for transfer of the developer's rights to the owners association when all units have been sold. It is important that the maintenance of the common units be conveyed free of any liens or encumbrances.

Advantages

The condominium concept has a number of advantages, with the result that the increase in the number of units built and sold since 1970 has been phenomenal.

1. The cost to own a condominium is generally lower than the cost of ownership of a single family dwelling of similar size.
2. The owner can enjoy the use of common facilities, such as a swimming pool, for a fraction of the cost of owning a pool individually.
3. The owner does not need to do the actual work of maintaining the yard, the exterior of the building, or the heating and air conditioning systems, although he does share in these maintenance costs. He still maintains the interior of his own unit, however. In response to public acceptance of condominiums, many apartments are being converted to condominium ownership.

Disadvantages

The main cause of dissatisfaction among condominium owners derives from their lack of control of how things are to be done. Since the majority rules, the association may spend more money than some tenants desire, or there may be a difference of opinion as to how the association money should be spent. Frequently, the monthly payments for maintenance and operation turn out to be well above the original estimate. Inefficiency or excessive management fees can contribute to this. Friction can also arise between the developer and the tenants as to who has certain maintenance responsibilities during the period of time when some of the units are yet unsold. The transition period up until the time there is full control by the association can result in problems or litigation. Sometimes items thought to be commonly-owned elements, such as the recreational facilities, are actually, by terms in the agreement, leased facilities, and the leasing cost continues over a longer period. In other cases, the recreational facilities described to the unit buyer turn out not to be part of the original purchase, but rather to be added later at extra cost. In other cases, bankruptcy of the developer creates problems for the owners. In some condominiums, parking spaces may cost extra or be leased. Although many of these problems can be avoided by careful scrutiny of the purchase agreement, the possibility of friction among unit owners still exists. Other disadvantages often voiced are similar to the disadvantages of renting, such as lack of privacy, noise, and being too close to the neighbors.

Time-Sharing

Some condominiums in recreational areas are sold on a time-sharing basis. For example, the Massanutten Development Company in Virginia sells fee simple interest in units for two weeks out of each year. In other words, a person can own the unit for the first two weeks in June of every year. This interest can be sold or transferred just as any other property.

Condominium Conversion

Many apartment owners are converting their apartment buildings to condominiums. Often, the current renters in an apartment to be converted would prefer to rent rather than purchase a condominium and therefore oppose the conversion. In 1979, the city of Chicago implemented a moratorium on condominium conversions, thereby preventing existing apartment building owners from converting them to condominiums. Later, however, a federal judge struck down the moratorium.

COOPERATIVE OWNERSHIP

A cooperative is different from a condominium in many ways. In *cooperative ownerships* a person purchases shares in a corporation that owns the entire building. In return for ownership of stock in the corporation, the owner receives a lease for occupancy of a unit. This legal interest is considered personal property. Each unit owner pays a share of the total expenses, but the corporation pays property taxes and maintenance and holds the mortgage. Usually, there are restrictions on a person's ability to assign the lease, and approval of the board of directors is usually needed to sell an interest in a cooperative. A typical sales contract for a co-op interest might read, "Fifteen shares of stock in Alton Apartments, Inc., entitling owners to proprietary use of Apartment #29 and parking area #29, along with use of all common elements." All decisions are made by a board of directors elected by the shareholders.

In the cooperative, if one tenant-owner fails to pay her share of the taxes or mortgage debt, the others may have to make up the difference or run the risk of foreclosure. Also, if a person leaves the cooperative, she receives only her original investment, and the property appreciation accrues to the remaining owners.

SUMMARY

Home ownership has, and will continue to be, a primary consideration of most families in the United States at some point in their lifetimes. Government-insured, guaranteed or subsidized loan programs, increased long-term credit availability, favorable housing legislation, rising incomes, and tax considerations are all factors that help to make home ownership an economically attractive alternative. These economic factors, coupled with the nonmeasurable social and physical advantages, will continue to influence many people into home ownership, whether it be of the single-family, detached variety or the increasingly popular condominium or cooperative.

The movement toward home ownership will be tempered by the demand for more leisure time and mobility, population age distribution, increasing land and construction costs, and mortgage money availability.

Whatever the type of ownership chosen, the prospective buyer should be careful to scrutinize all the physical aspects of the dwelling, as well as the details of the contract before signing.

TERMS AND CONCEPTS

You can check your understanding of these terms against the glossary or by review in this chapter.

Adjusted basis	Hedge against inflation
Adjusted selling price	Investment tax credit
Deferred gain	Over 55 exemption
Fixing-up expenses	Puritan ethic

What are the differences or relationships, if any, between the following?

Adjusted selling price and	Recognized gain and
Amount realized on sale	Realized gain
Condominium ownership and	
Cooperative ownership	

PROBLEMS

9–1.   Mr. Taxpayer purchased a residence in 1965 for $20,000. He spent $5,000 on capital improvements and sold the property in 1980 for $40,000. He incurred selling expenses of $2,500. What is the amount of the gain?

9–2.   Referring to question no. 1, assume Mr. Taxpayer purchased a new home within six months after he sold his old residence. He paid $35,000 for his new home. How much of the gain is taxed? How much is deferred?

9–3.   What is the rule behind fixing-up expenses? Are they used in calculating realized gain?

9–4.   At age 57, taxpayer Smith sells his home for $75,000 and retires to Florida. He paid $25,000 for the home seven years ago. Assuming that he is entitled to the over 55 exemption, how much of the gain is taxable? Assume he sold the house for $150,000. How much would be taxable?

9–5.   In your opinion, why did the legislature pass the investment tax credit for new housing? Is it available on other purchases?

9–6.   Should and can the conversion of apartments to condominiums be restricted?

9–7.   List the main advantages and disadvantages of condominium ownership.

9–8.   If you owned a cooperative, would it be easier or more difficult to sell than a condominium? Why?

9–9.   If a senior citizen, age 57, sold her house for $95,000, she would have a recognized gain of $55,000. Under what circumstances might you recommend that she go ahead and sell? Delay sale?

9–10.   Explain the difference between a tax credit (as for energy credit) and a tax deduction.

SUPPLEMENTARY READINGS

Pearson, Karl G. *Real Estate Principles and Practices.* Columbus, Oh.: Grid, 1978. Chapters 15–18.

Ratcliff, Richard U. *Real Estate Analysis.* New York: McGraw-Hill, 1961. Chapter 8.

Ring, Alfred A., and Dasso, Jerome. *Real Estate Principles and Practices.* Englewood Cliffs, N.J.: Prentice-Hall, 1977. Chapter 22.

Shenkel, William M. *Modern Real Estate Principles.* Dallas: Business Publications, 1977. Chapter 21.

Unger, Maurice A., and Karvel, George R. *Real Estate Principles and Practices,* 6th ed. Cincinnati: Southwestern, 1979. Chapter 10.

Wendt, Paul F., and Cerf, Alan. *Real Estate Investment Analysis and Taxation.* New York: McGraw-Hill, 1979. Chapters 1 and 4.

Land Use Planning And Zoning

Land use *planning* can originate from either public or private sources. Public agencies plan for the orderly and logical development of a community. The objective of private planning is to maximize the efficiency and utility of a site or parcel of land.

To be effective, land use plans must provide a means to assure that the objectives are achieved. A variety of legal measures are available, both public and private, to restrict uses and assure conformance to the plan. Public planning can be enforced by zoning. Private plans can be implemented by restrictions or covenants placed in deeds, plat maps, or related documents.

Most public land use planning takes place in urban areas or land surrounding the urban area. Substantial changes in urban areas are brought by economic, social, and political forces. The resulting expansion of urban areas is often rapid and accompanied by the creation of blight areas and slum areas as well as problems in transportation, water pollution, and sewage. Many cities or urban areas have commissions to deal with urban expansion and its related problems. These commissions have been established in order to bring about orderly and planned change. Their primary approach is to establish a *master plan* for the urban area. The master plan attempts to balance the residential, industrial, commercial, and recreational areas. It is then necessary to enforce the plan through restrictions on land use that are implemented by (a) zoning regulations and building codes (as discussed in this chapter) and (b) requirements for starting subdivisions of residential or industrial construction (as discussed in Chapter 18).

URBAN PLANNING

The transition from horse-and-buggy to heavy automobile and truck traffic has caused the cities to undergo substantial changes. In the past, many cities expanded without controls or plans. In fact, in the 1920s, cities frequently developed in a manner that blocked further orderly growth. Areas were developed without provision for utilities, transportation, or parking, although the future needs for off-street parking could not have been foreseen at that time. Since 1950, however, most urban areas have set up commissions to establish a plan and enforce it. In some cases, the commissions have been established as advisory, and consequently enforcement has been difficult, if not impossible.

In the 1950s and 1960s, urban planning progressed to the stage of a profession in itself. Today, some universities offer undergraduate and graduate degrees in urban planning to prepare people to assume responsible positions in city government. City planning has become as much an art as a science, involving ecological considerations, human relations, and economic knowledge, in addition to the ability to solve the technical problems of urban areas.

Although there was a heavy trend of population movement to urban areas in the years from 1940 to 1960, there has also been a concurrent trend for urban areas to decentralize. The growth of the total urban area is often accompanied by the establishment of suburban communities. Some of these communities resist being formally incorporated into the nearby city because of the higher tax burden imposed.

In a sense, urban planning results from competition between urban areas as well as from pressures from within the area. New industries locate in urban areas where there are social advantages and pleasant living, as well as in areas having lower costs and other economic advantages. Carefully planned industrial parks attract industries, whether they be companies just starting or older companies moving from a site that is too small or in an area that has become blighted.

Levels of Planning

Urban area planning takes place at the federal, regional, state, and local levels. Federal planning may deal with overall national needs, whereas a regional plan may deal with a problem in a particular area. As examples of regional planning, urban areas around the Great Lakes work together on water conservation problems. Communities around New York City work together on transportation and traffic, and communities around Los Angeles cooperate on smog control.

Cities and urban areas derive their planning powers from state laws. State laws authorize municipalities to incorporate under a charter from the state and to operate within these delegated powers. State legislatures have also given these municipalities the right to establish planning commissions under legislation referred to as *enabling acts.*

A local area will then establish a planning commission to set objectives and to set up the means for control. This planning body may be either elective or appointed. It may be either advisory or have executive responsibility, although experience has shown that a planning commission, in order to be effective, needs the authority to enforce its decisions.

The development and implementation of the master plan require funds. Initial funds can be secured from bond issues because the plan usually results in building projects that increase taxable values. Thus, they provide for a return through future taxes of amounts substantially higher than the original costs of the master plan.

Planning Procedure

The planning commission will usually begin by reviewing the present community layout. Meeting with local civic and business organizations is an important step in learning their needs and gaining support for plans as they are formulated. The commission will normally require a staff to carry out much of the work, usually under the guidance of a director. An initial step is to make a land survey or prepare a map showing all the physical aspects of the area, including streets, land elevation, existing buildings, utilities available, and other important factors.

Along with the physical layout, the urban area economics must be extensively analyzed. Many questions must be answered. What is the past and future economic character of the area? What types of industry are prevalent and what other industries might be attracted to the area? Is industry in the area sufficiently diversified to avoid economic downturns or situations where certain industries become depressed or obsolete?

The primary technique for analyzing community income and economic prospects is *economic base analysis.* This process is carried out by determining planned increases in employment for the various types of industry in the area. Part of the analysis will include a study of the effects of industrial employment upon service employment in the area. Sources of service employment are barber shops, restaurants, retail stores, and other businesses where the customers are primarily local. Other measures of economic activity should also be measured and projected. These factors would include the number of households, commercial structures, bank deposits, and motor vehicles. The past and present population should be studied along with future projections. This study should include racial makeup, occupations, employment, and any apparent long-term trends.

The result of this initial effort is the master plan for the area. It designates areas for residential, commercial, recreational, and industrial use. It may also break areas down into lower classifications, such as the type of residences permitted. Figure 10–1 shows a typical allocation for various uses. The

single family residential	RA-8, RA-20
multi-family residential	RB-5
high rise residential	RH-3
light commercial	CL-10
general commercial	CG-20
commercial recreation	CR-20
light industrial	IL-40

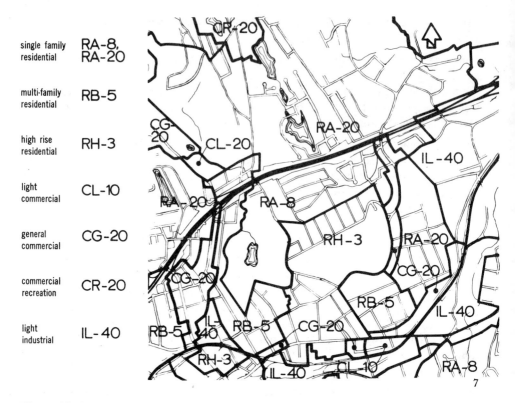

Figure 10–1
Land allocation map

Source: New Hampshire, Office of State Planning. *Handbook of Subdivision Practice.* 1972, p. 7.

planners will then determine what public facilities are needed to support the master plan. These facilities include utilities, transportation, schools, and recreational areas.

Those responsible for planning also have to consider how the master plan will influence the tax structure, so that an excessive burden is not placed on some individuals or organizations. Excessive tax burdens could force companies or individuals to avoid or move out of the urban center or community to a more favorable tax area.

The plan should also include requirements and procedures for developers of subdivisions to submit plans for approval. Those responsible for reviewing the plans will see whether the proposed development conforms to the master plan and whether it provides adequate utilities, open area, parking facilities, or school areas needed to support and meet the master plan objectives. These would include water supply, sewage disposal, and utility needs. Subdivision plans must be approved before any work can start. The procedures of submitting a plan and having it approved apply to industrial site developments as well as to commercial and residential area developments. See Chapter 18 for the procedures involved.

Planned Unit Development (PUD)

Residential developments of ten acres or more that incorporate areas for public, commercial, or industrial use are often defined as *planned unit developments* (PUD). The original plan will set aside areas for single family residences, apartments, retail store areas, parking, schools, parks, golf courses, and sometimes industrial use.

The objective of the PUD is to provide for commercial, recreational, and educational facilities located conveniently to the housing. The plan may provide for a variety of residential uses such as single-family dwellings, apartments, townhouses, or condominiums. Typically, each type of area would have a specified limit of the allowable density (persons per acre). For example, the planned community of Columbia, Maryland specified average residential area limits of 3.8 persons per acre. See Figure 10–2, the Wilde Lake development in Columbia.

A PUD requires extensive planning and a large initial investment. It is frequently necessary to work out arrangements with local governments to obtain approval for different concepts in zoning and taxing. The PUD would then replace the existing land use provisions. Usually, a considerable number of years would be needed to complete the planned unit development.

Traffic Design

Quite often urban plans will suggest street layouts such that certain streets carry through traffic whereas other streets are curved or laid out so as to be free from heavy traffic. Buffer zones are often prescribed to separate industrial areas from residential areas. Many downtown areas or residential areas have traffic routed around them. The important criterion is to make sure that people and material can be moved readily throughout the area. Public transportation must also be considered as part of the total traffic design.

Much of the rest of urban planning revolves around the traffic plan. It is better to establish streets, beltways, and freeways that meet the overall urban area requirements than to improve existing transportation to meet needs as congestion develops. It is also important to separate the through traffic from the local traffic. In large urban areas, the through traffic includes vehicles going from one part of the urban area to another.

Urban Renewal

As part of the overall urban master plan, certain areas are often selected for complete renovation or renewal. Areas of severe deterioration, frequently near city centers, are good candidates for renewal. The most drastic proce-

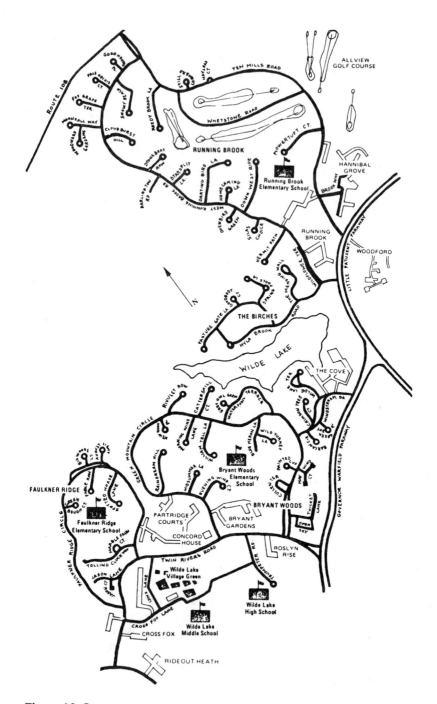

Figure 10–2
*In the Wilde Lake community of Columbia,
elementary schools help to define the neighborhoods*

Source: National Association of Home Builders. *Land Development Manual.* Washington, D.C.: 1974, p. 59.

dure is to level all structures in an area and completely rebuild. This step can be initiated and financed either by public bonds, federal assistance, or private financing. In other areas where deterioration is less severe, some properties are renovated, often to retain aesthetic advantages, whereas other buildings are demolished and rebuilt. Areas near downtown Philadelphia, St. Louis, and Baltimore are good examples of some areas being completely demolished and rebuilt, while other areas are largely renovated.

Federal, state, and local authorities also provide public housing in areas to be rehabilitated or provide subsidies for such projects. Some of these projects have been successful; others have not. Those projects that allow the occupants to own or eventually own their homes tend to be more successful in maintaining a desirable environment than those that rent or lease units. The same incentives to home ownership discussed in Chapter 9 would apply here.

GROWTH CONTROLS

Local and state governments sometimes find it desirable to limit growth in order to curtail congestion, to preserve aesthetic factors, or to avoid overloading existing utilities.

Building Moratoriums

Sometimes a community decides it needs more time to study growth problems. It has the right to withhold building permits and approval of new subdivisions and to delay permits to connect with municipal sewer or water supplies. A temporary suppression is called a *building moratorium,* or sometimes, *zoning freeze.* In shoreline developments, this moratorium may be imposed while an environmental impact study is being made.

Density Controls

Overcrowding in certain areas and planning for a balance in the community can be achieved through zoning regulations to limit population growth. Some ordinances designed to achieve this, however, have been declared invalid by the courts. Examples of ordinances declared invalid were those that (a) restricted apartments to a certain number of units, (b) prohibited multifamily unit constructions, (c) specified minimum lot sizes, (d) specified minimum floor areas, or (e) specified minimum cubic feet in the building. Courts have held these to be invalid in certain cases where the primary result was to restrict an area to more affluent families or exclude newcomers to the area in order to avoid burdens on public utilities, or where discrimination exists against the poor or certain racial groups.

Land Reutilization Authorities

Several cities have established a *land reutilization authority* (LRA) to acquire and manage tax delinquent and foreclosed land. Parcels can be set aside until larger tracts are accumulated for possible reuse. The parcels are then marketed for development.

Ground Leases

Considering that the cost of land is 20 to 25 per cent of the cost of a development project, ground leasing becomes one of the major incentives (along with a tax abatement) that a local government can offer to developers. Vacant or underutilized land owned by educational or religious organizations, railroads, or pension funds can be leased to developers. This provides profits for the lessee and savings in initial investment for the developer.

Transfer Development Rights

The process of land use planning and zoning tends to be unfair to landowners who are prevented from developing their land. At the same time, those owners whose property is authorized for development often obtain windfall gains. Since some land is needed for the more valuable uses and other land must be reserved for open areas, the property owners have been placed in a position of conflict and fairer solutions have been sought.

Transfer development rights (TDR) is a new concept in the direction of alleviating this conflict. Under the TDR concept, all land in a community carries transfer development rights. These rights are considered much like one of the bundle of rights going with land ownership. The owner whose land has been designated as open space can sell her TDR to another landowner. This other landowner can then develop his land with a greater *land-use intensity* (LUI). Figure 10–3 shows (a) how a developer can develop a quarter acre parcel with regular rights, (b) how it could be developed if he owned TDR from an additional quarter acre, and (c) how it could be developed if he owned TDR for an additional three quarters of an acre. Under this concept, TDR's could be sold on the open market just like common stock.

The TDR concept can also be used to save historical sites. Developer D owns a landmark building that he plans to demolish to build an apartment. D also

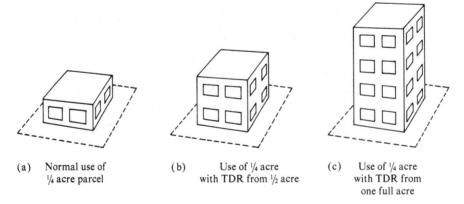

(a) Normal use of ¼ acre parcel

(b) Use of ¼ acre with TDR from ½ acre

(c) Use of ¼ acre with TDR from one full acre

Figure 10–3
Implementation of transfer development rights (TDR)

owns other land nearby. The city can transfer the development rights to the landmark site so that D can build a more extensive building on his other land than would normally be permitted. A similar approach can be taken to preserve farmland or open land. Farmland can be preserved by the farmer selling the development rights. The taxable value (and taxes) of the land without development rights would then be much less than land on the edge of a city that could be developed.

ZONING

Implementing the plan for an urban area depends heavily upon the power to zone. *Zoning* is a means for regulating and controlling land and its use even though property is privately owned.

The right to regulate land usage derives from the ***police power of government.*** Usually, municipalities acquire the rights to establish and enforce zoning requirements from state laws.

Although there have been court challenges to zoning on the grounds that they interfere with a person's rights guaranteed by the constitution, courts have upheld the rights of municipalities to exercise and enforce zoning powers. The basis has been that the rights of the majority cannot be infringed by rights of particular individuals.

Some zoning ordinances have been challenged in the courts as discriminatory. The basis is that restrictions for minimum lot size and for single-family dwellings discriminate against lower income persons. In some cases, the courts have struck down those ordinances as having been created to exclude certain people rather than to protect the general public or to plan the urban area.

Purpose of Zoning

The first real zoning ordinance was passed by New York City in 1916. The objective was to control land use to keep undesirable activities out of residential areas, hold down population densities, and provide for more homogeneous use of land. More recent laws have cited additional reasons, such as promoting health and morals, reducing traffic congestion, providing safety from fire, panic, vandalism, and crime, and providing adequate air and light. To accomplish this, zoning must be consistent with an overall urban master plan.

Restrictions on construction in a community or area are called ***building codes.*** Many requirements are based on national standards, such as for electrical wiring, fireproof materials, or structural safety. Their primary objective is safety. Others vary by locality or from area to area within a city, such as restrictions to brick construction for conformity. Codes affecting use and occupancy of residential property are called ***housing codes.*** These also vary from locality to locality, such as requirements for occupancy per unit area or window area per room.

The following exemplify typical types of *protective zoning:*

1. Limits on height or width of construction.
2. Maximum or minimum setback from street or minimum distance of structure from property lines.
3. Type of materials or procedures used in construction, wiring, or plumbing.
4. Restrictions on display of signs or billboards.
5. Limitation on type of business allowed or usage of property.
6. Limit on number of occupants per apartment.
7. Limit on number of families per residence.
8. Specific way to position garages or other structures on the lot.
9. Minimum lot sizes.

Zoning is often used as a planning tool to encourage land usage for its most necessary or best use. This is called *directive zoning.* Zoning ordinances must be integrated into overall urban planning, however, since experience has shown that highly restrictive zoning tends to cause the area to remain underdeveloped.

Bulk zoning is used where the primary purpose of the requirement is to control density and avoid overcrowding. Restrictions on setbacks, side or court areas, building height and size, and percentage of open areas are examples of bulk zoning. Figure 10–4 shows a method by which the allowable height of a structure varies with the area or distance from the lot line. *FAR* (floor area ratio) is the index of building bulk and height used to assess the intensity of land use. It is the total floor area in the building divided by the lot area:

$$\frac{\text{Total floor area}}{\text{Lot area}} = \text{Floor area ratio (FAR)}$$

Some ordinances also specify a required amount of off-street parking area, or they may require off-street loading areas for trucks to unload in shopping areas. Some zoning ordinances go beyond these limits. Certain cities, such as Williamsburg, Virginia, require that new buildings conform to a certain type of architecture. This is known as *aesthetic zoning* and sometimes applies to shopping or other areas. *Incentive zoning* specifies that the street floors of office buildings be used for retail establishments. This has been used effectively to provide retail areas where investors are primarily interested in constructing office space.

When authorities are studying an area for original zoning or changes in zoning, *hold zoning* or *interim zoning* can be applied. This prevents developers from initiating usage of the land in a way that would negate the study results.

Zoning Categories

Zoning regulations generally restrict the use of land to one of several overall classifications: residential, commercial, industrial, agricultural, and recrea-

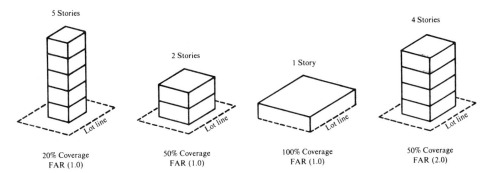

5 Stories

2 Stories

1 Story

4 Stories

20% Coverage
FAR (1.0)

50% Coverage
FAR (1.0)

100% Coverage
FAR (1.0)

50% Coverage
FAR (2.0)

Figure 10–4

Configurations illustrating FAR (floor area ratio)

Source: National Association of Home Builders. *Land Development Manual.* Washington, D.C.: 1974, p. 12.

tional. These are called *land use districts.* A district limited to single-family residential units is typically designated R–1. Other designations might be R–2, R–3, B–1 (business), C–1 (commercial), and so forth. The objective is to provide a degree of use that is homogeneous within an area and to avoid mixtures among the categories.

Restrictions to *residential use* are the best known to most people. These restrictions prevent commercial or industrial buildings in an area, or they restrict signs. Usually the residential restriction would allow only a particular type of use. The highest classification (R–1 for example) would be for single-family residences. Sometimes, a higher classification would also specify minimum lot sizes for each home. The next category (R–2) typically permits structures designed for from two to four families, or it permits row houses, a series of houses having common walls. The third level (R–3) or category of residential use allows apartments, schools, and churches. Normally, zoning is *cumulative* such that R–3 would permit all uses from R–1 and R–2.

Commercial zoning is also subdivided where the highest group (i.e., C–1) would include shops, restaurants, or office buildings. Usages considered less desirable, such as service stations or garages, would have a lower classification (i.e., C–2).

Industrial zoning is the third category, which may also be broken down further into groupings such as light, medium, and heavy manufacturing. The classification of industries by group would also take into consideration noise, smoke, and other factors that particular industries might introduce into the area. Some communities use *industrial performance standards* rather than listing prohibited industries. Standards are established for noise, air pollution, fire, and explosives. Industries are then permitted in the area as long as the standards are met.

Agricultural zoning permits farming, dairying, and raising of animals or poultry. It often excludes commercial or industrial uses.

Recreational zoning includes parks and similar uses.

Spot zoning sets aside certain areas for purposes different from the general area requirements. A certain area within a residential area may be spot zoned as a shopping center, the justification being that a shopping center is needed within a reasonable distance of any community.

Some urban areas have also restricted the construction of residences or apartments in industrial or commercial areas. These regulations protect industrial users against possible future lawsuits. Without these restrictions, the owner of the residential properties could claim that the industrial use adversely affects his health or welfare because of noise, odors, or traffic. At that point, the fact that the industries were there first could lose its impact, and a company could be forced to move or to install expensive abatement equipment. Sometimes, C–1 or R properties are not permitted in C–2 areas; this is called **noncumulative zoning.** If specific purposes are prohibited (e.g., drive-in theaters or mobile home parks), the zoning is called **exclusionary zoning.**

A new concept, inclusionary zoning, was first used in California in 1979. *Inclusionary zoning* laws require that new housing developments contain a certain percentage of low- or moderate-income properties.

Enforcement

All zoning laws, housing codes, and building codes contain provisions that allow the local authorities to enforce the regulations. Without these provisions, the regulations would be meaningless. Before initiating new construction or making a change in existing construction, the property owner or her agent must obtain a permit. At that time, she must submit evidence to show that the contemplated project complies with zoning requirements. If a private party initiates construction or takes action to change existing construction without having approval, any citizen or official can ask for an **abatement** or court order to halt the action.

If any unauthorized change is made without approval, a court order can be requested to require the building to be restored to its original status. In a situation where a building is occupied by more than the allowable number of persons or families, a court order can be obtained to end the violation. In addition to these methods of enforcement, the municipality can levy fines either in place of or in addition to the other remedies. Frequently, a fine will be levied on a time basis, such as a fine of $20.00 per day until the violation is remedied. This counteracts intentional stalling.

A written permit must be obtained from the local authorities before starting new construction or remodeling. It must be displayed at the scene of construction. As construction proceeds, an inspector will check the work to make sure it complies with building codes. Before the new or remodeled structure can be used, a notice of completion must be filed and a certificate of occupancy obtained. This certificate can be applied for when the building permit is requested; however, the certificate must be signed by the authorized inspector prior to actual occupancy of the building. If this certificate is not obtained or approved, use of the building or release of mortgage funds may be held up. It is important to understand these procedures and requirements, since a delay in occupancy may result in substantial financial loss to the owner and builder.

Changes in Zoning

Action to change zoning can be initiated by a property owner, either to tighten restrictions or to make the restriction more lax. For example, a property developer may request a zoning status change from farm area to single-family residential to protect his investment and assure potential home buyers that future construction or use will not deteriorate the area and reduce their property value. On the other hand, an owner of property in a deteriorating neighborhood or changing area may request rezoning to commercial or apartment usage to increase the value and possible uses of the property.

The first step in requesting a zoning change is to submit a petition to the local board or body having zoning authority. Usually, this petition must be published in a local newspaper by either the petitioner or the authorities. A sign describing the pending action must also be displayed at the property for a specified period of time. The notifications should specify a time and place for a public hearing on the proposed change. A typical procedure (California) is shown in Figure 10–5. This public hearing provides a place for all interested parties to be present and heard before any decision is made. The decision of the board is not always final, however, since any person who feels that he has been aggrieved may appeal to higher authority or eventually to the courts. If other remedies are prescribed, such as appeal to other boards or officials, these appeals must be carried out before an appeal is made to the courts. Judicial relief from burdensome zoning must usually be based on constitutional grounds. Courts usually have upheld zoning ordinances; however, the courts in many cases have granted relief from arbitrary, unreasonable, or discriminatory zoning provisions.

Nonconforming Use

Whenever any zoning regulation is enacted, existing structures or uses that do not comply with the new requirements must be protected. Provisions allow this *nonconforming use* since it would not be fair to a property owner to have retroactive zoning requirements. If there already was a service station in an area designated residential, the service station could continue to operate. This condition may prevail only as long as the use is continuous. If, however, the facility was not used as a service station for a set period of time designated by law (such as three years), then the service station could not be reactivated. If the service station were destroyed by a fire, the regulations would not usually allow it to be rebuilt on the same site. Usually a zoning ordinance will also prohibit any enlarging or modification of the structure that is intended to continue it in a nonconforming use.

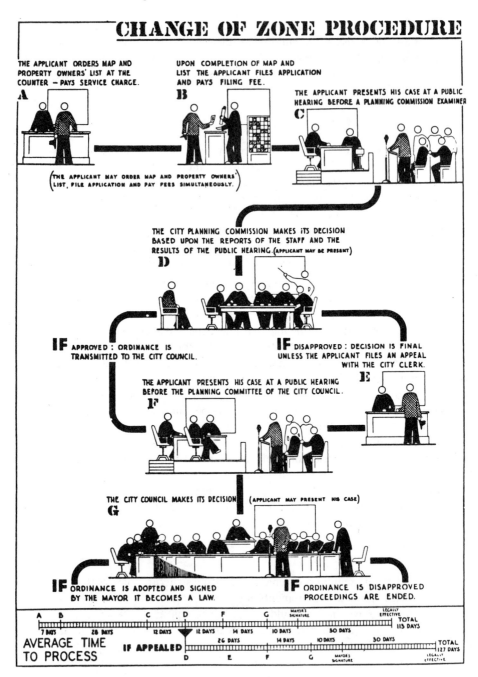

Figure 10–5

Zoning change procedure in California

From Fred E. Case, *Real Estate Economics*, p. 254. Reprinted with permission of the California Association of Realtors.

Some ordinances contain *amortization* provisions to establish the time by when nonconforming uses must be phased out. The theory is that the purpose of the zoning change cannot be fully realized as long as nonconforming uses exist. Courts have held this to be a reasonable exercise of police power.

Relief by Administrative Action

Instead of going through the zoning change procedure, a property owner may seek relief from strict compliance with a zoning ordinance or building codes through zoning authorities. Generally, authorities can grant either variances or conditional use permits. These actions are allowed to permit sufficient flexibility to meet hardship cases, situations where the relief would not disrupt the general zoning scheme, or special needs.

Conditional use permit

A *conditional use permit* allows a special use if deemed desirable for public convenience. A service station may be built in an area zoned for industrial use where the service to people in the area is necessary.

Variances

A nonconforming use relates to a use that existed prior to the enactment of the ordinance. A *variance,* on the other hand, permits doing something that an existing zoning ordinance forbids. Variances or exceptions are granted where the ordinance brings about a harsh or unique hardship for an individual. As an example, a lot may be of such size or shape that it would be unreasonable to build a structure that conforms to the setback requirements. In another instance, a lot may be too narrow to allow construction conforming to side area restrictions. A variance may then be allowed to permit a structure that violates the side area requirement. In any decision to grant a variance, the approving body must still consider the broad intent of the zoning ordinance, however, and would not permit just any usage.

The procedure for obtaining a variance is similar to that for requesting a change in zoning. The zoning board will hear petitions for changes in zoning or variances from the zoning requirements. The board must, however, act within any area master plan in its decisions. The burden of proof lies with the person making the petition. Usually the board will make an on-site inspection of the property involved to establish the validity of the request. A variance will usually be turned down if it is felt that the primary intent is to increase the value of the property to the owner. Petitions to obtain a variance that extends a present nonconforming use will usually be rejected.

SUMMARY

Land use planning is a necessary prerequisite to achieving balanced city or suburban growth. Although the primary responsibility for land use planning rests with the municipal government, it can receive substantial assistance from state and federal agencies. While orderly growth takes financial backing, the funds generated often more than compensate for the initial costs.

Zoning is a key factor in implementing and enforcing any land use plan. One objective of zoning is to allocate areas for residential, commercial, industrial, and recreational use so that the well-being of the public as a whole is enhanced. Building codes and other restrictions also are aimed at the health, welfare, and safety of the area population. Means are available to change zoning or to obtain exceptions where hardship has resulted.

TERMS AND CONCEPTS

You can check your understanding of these terms against the glossary or by review in this chapter.

Abatement	Inclusionary zoning
Amortization	Land-use intensity
Bulk zoning	Land use district
Conditional use permit	Master plan
Economic base analysis	Planned unit development (PUD)
Enabling acts	Police power of government
FAR	Transfer development rights (TDR)

What are the differences or relationships, if any, between the following?

Aesthetic zoning and Incentive zoning
Building codes and Housing codes
Cumulative and Noncumulative zoning
Directive zoning and Protective zoning
Hold zoning and Interim zoning

Industrial performance standards and Exclusionary zoning
Nonconforming use and Variance
Planning and Zoning
Residential, Commercial, Industrial, Agricultural, and Recreational zoning
Variance and Spot zoning

PROBLEMS

10–1. List the steps necessary to secure a change in zoning.

10–2. Make a rough sketch of your community and label land allocations as in Figure 10–1.

10–3. Identify streets in your community that are designed to carry through traffic.

10–4. List the elements of a good land use master plan.

10–5. Look for examples of two of the following in your community:

(a) Nonconforming use.

(b) Variance.

(c) Spot zoning.

(d) Conditional use permit.

10–6. Discuss how a planned unit development (PUD) is different from a normal development in zoning requirements, degree of planning, and amount of investment needed.

10–7. An acre of land is allowed development rights sufficient for six townhouses. If transfer development rights are allowed, from how much land must the developer obtain rights in order to construct fifteen townhouses on the acre plot?

10–8. Do you think amortization provisions are fair as applied to nonconforming use?

10–9. If you wanted to construct a garage closer to the lot line than allowed by zoning or the building code, what technique would you use?

10–10. In what cases do you feel a court of law might set aside zoning restrictions?

10–11. How is interim zoning of benefit to the community planning board?

10–12. Why might a community want to limit growth? What are some means of accomplishing this?

SUPPLEMENTARY READINGS

Berman, Daniel S. *Urban Renewal.* Englewood Cliffs, N.J.: Prentice-Hall, 1969.

Bergfield, Philip B. *Real Estate Law.* New York, McGraw-Hill, 1979. Chapters 19 and 20.

Beuscher, Jacob H.; Wright, Robert W.; and Gilelman, Morton. *Land Use—Urban Planning.* St. Paul: West, 1976.

Clawson, Marion, ed. *Modernizing Urban Land Policy.* Baltimore: Johns Hopkins University Press, 1973.

Crawford, Clair. *Handbook of Zoning and Land Use Ordinances—With Forms.* Englewood Cliffs, N.J.: Prentice-Hall, 1974.

Crawford, Clair. *Strategy on Tactics in Municipal Zoning.* Englewood Cliffs, N.J.: Prentice-Hall, 1969.

David, Philip. *Urban Land Development.* Homewood, Ill.: Irwin, 1970.

Gold, Seymour M. *Urban Recreation Planning.* Philadelphia: Lea & Febiger, 1973.

Goodman, William I., and Freund, Eric C. *Principle and Practice of Urban Planning.* Washington, D.C.: International City Managers Association, 1968.

Grieson, Ronald E. *Urban Economics: Readings and Analysis.* Boston: Little, Brown, 1973.

Hagman, Donald G. *Urban Planning and Land Development Control Laws.* St. Paul: West, 1971.

Harrison, Bennett. *Urban Economic Development.* Washington, D.C.: Urban Institute, 1974.

Hinds, D. S. *Winning at Zoning.* New York: McGraw-Hill, 1979.

Krueckeberg, Donald A. *Urban Planning Analysis.* New York: Wiley, 1974.

National Association of Home Builders. *Land Development Manual.* Washington, D.C.: 1974.

Rasmussen, David W. *Urban Economics.* New York: Harper, 1973.

Sayalyn, Lynne B. *Zoning and Housing Costs*. New Brunswick, N.J.: Center for Urban Policy Research, Rutgers University, 1973.

Siedel, George J., III. *Real Estate Law*. St. Paul: West, 1979. Chapter 13.

Smith, Halbert C., Tschappat, Carl J., and Racster, Ronald. *Real Estate and Urban Development*. Homewood, Ill.: Irwin, 1977. Chapter 14.

Witheford, David K. *Zoning, Parking, and Traffic*. Saugatuck, Conn.: Eno Foundation for Transportation, 1972.

Real Property Insurance

Although insurance is a specialized professional field of its own, it relates to real estate, or real property, in a number of ways. Knowledge of real property insurance is important to the owner for his own protection, to the property manager so that she can properly manage the property, and to the real estate broker, who often is asked to advise his clients as to their insurance needs.

Insurance is a contract arrangement between two parties whereby one party, called the *insurer*, agrees to indemnify the other party, called the *insured*, against losses the insured may incur. The insurance company is taking the risk that a particular event will not occur. The insurance contract, called the *insurance policy*, describes the risks covered. Usually, the policy is on a standard printed form and must conform to state requirements. In exchange for the coverage against loss, the insured pays a *premium* to the insurer. Premiums paid to the insurance company are used to finance overhead expenses and to build up reserves to pay losses due under the policies. Optional coverage to the basic insurance policy can be added by an *endorsement* or *rider*.

A property owner does not have to take out insurance because the person can assume all risks. Actually, a home owner does take certain risks, but the wise property owner will at least insure against those risks for which he could not stand the loss, such as complete or substantial destruction of his property. The home owner can, of course, try to eliminate or reduce the risk. Some businesses or individuals become *self-insurers* by setting aside certain funds to cover risks. They feel that it is more economical to save the premium and take the risk; however, they must make sure that there are actually sufficient funds available to handle potential risks. Usually, a lending institution will require sufficient insurance to cover its interest if there is a mortgage on the property.

When a property owner takes out insurance on her property, considerable confidence is placed in the insurance company. Often, home owners have a substantial part of their life savings invested in the home. They would undergo a substantial loss if the insurance company could not make good on the policy. States have responded to this problem by closely regulating insurance companies through requirements for incorporation or operation, as well as for audits and reporting.

Insurance companies are in a position of great responsibility and large potential risk. To avoid the possibility of incurring losses simultaneously on a substantial portion of their policies, companies try to diversify their risks. They diversify in two ways. First, they seek policyholders over a wide geographical area. The other method is to handle a variety of different types of insurance, such as life, fire, and automobile insurance. Some insurance companies reinsure some of their policies with other insurance carriers.

Many large insurance companies have salespeople in many different cities and towns. Because of the need to cover widespread areas, some smaller companies use independent brokers to handle their policy sales. These independent brokers will usually handle policies for a number of different insurance companies. Sometimes the real estate broker is also a licensed insurance agent or broker.

Insurance provides many social and economic benefits. Many businesses could not operate without this protection. It provides a means whereby a major financial loss does not fall upon one or a few individuals; but rather many pay a small share of the total loss.

TYPES OF INSURANCE

A number of different types of insurance are related to real property. They are listed by perils as follows:

1. Loss due to fire, windstorm, or other natural elements.
2. Loss due to breakdown of artificial elements, such as water pipes or sprinkler systems.
3. Liability for injury of other persons due to the condition of the property, or damage to another person's property due to conditions on the insured property.
4. Theft, vandalism, or other crime.
5. Loss of property due to defects in the title or loss in value of the property due to defects or problems related to the title.
6. Construction defects in a home.

Insurance Against the Elements

Property damage can be caused by the elements of fire, air, water, and earth. This can result from windstorm, flood, and earthquake, although a basic real property insurance policy may cover only fire, or fire and windstorm, excluding water and earthquake damage. In some locations, these additional coverages can be obtained by paying extra premiums and obtaining *endorsements* to the policy. Flood insurance is discussed separately.

Liability Insurance

Liability insurance protects the property owner against claims for injury to others or damage to the property of others. Legal principles hold a property owner liable for compensating payments where it can be shown that another person suffered loss or injury due to the property owner's negligence. These claims can arise due to a condition of the property or activities that take place on the property. A property owner is required to take ordinary care of the property and to use ordinary skill in managing it. When a third party is injured because of owner negligence, the property owner may be held liable. For instance, a fall on a sidewalk not cleared of ice could be a result of inadequate care. Sometimes a property owner's liability will depend on whether or not the third party had a valid right to be on the property. A trespasser will have less chance of recovery than would a repairperson or friend who had a legitimate reason to be on the property. The owner of land is required to exercise a greater degree of care toward his invitee than toward a trespasser on his land.

Loss from Crime

Insurance can be purchased against losses from burglary, theft, or other criminal acts. Insurance policies may provide coverage primarily related to personal property within the real property. The loss could be perpetrated either by trespassers or by a person allowed on the premises. If a policy only covers burglary, the insurer will probably require some evidence of forceable entry, such as visible marks of tools or other means of entry. Sometimes it is difficult to tell whether an item such as a wristwatch was stolen or lost or just misplaced. Some companies use a "mysterious disappearance" clause which, for an extra premium, reimburses for a loss without evidence of burglary.

Flood Insurance

Up until 1968, flood insurance was not offered by most insurance companies. It was felt that only those in high-risk areas would be interested, and that would cause the rates to be very high. A joint effort of the insurance industry and the federal government resulted in the National Flood Insurance Program. As an encouragement to purchase flood insurance, the federal government subsidizes rates and reinsures companies against catastrophic losses. At the same time, the federal government desires to discourage further construction in flood-prone sites. Therefore, before flood insurance can be sold in an area, the community must enact and enforce restrictions against further construction in locations subject to flooding.

Insurance Against Structural Defects

New home buyers can purchase a warranty against structural defects under the Home Owners Warranty (*HOW*) Program. The Home Owners Warranty Corporation (a private company) offers policies that cover single-family homes as well as high-rise or low-rise condominiums. If a builder has been approved by the company, a new home buyer can purchase a policy at a cost of $2.00 per $1,000 of sale price. During the first two years, the builder agrees to repair all structural defects, and the insurer warrants the next eight years of the ten-year warranty period.

Buyers of homes already covered by one of a variety of home protection insurance policies are provided coverage against mechanical equipment failure and, in some cases, structural defects.

Title Insurance

When a piece of real property is purchased, it may be difficult to completely prove that the title is clear and that there will be no future claims on the title. Sometimes claims or other defects in the title unexpectedly show up later to cast a cloud on the title or otherwise reduce its value or make it difficult to sell. As an example, a woman may claim to be the wife of a deceased owner, whereas the records showed the deceased owner to be single. A title insurance policy, as illustrated in Figure 11–1, protects the property owner against loss of value or marketability. The property owner pays a one-time premium when purchasing a title policy. It provides insurance for as long as that person holds title to the property. Title insurance companies almost always have an established staff to investigate records and examine titles before the company accepts the risk of insuring a particular piece of property.

In addition to standard coverages, title insurance companies offer special endorsements at additional cost to cover risks that are less likely to occur, are not a part of public records, or are otherwise hard to ascertain. Figure 11–1a shows some typical items that may be excluded from a regular title insurance policy. Title insurance differs from other kinds of insurance that cover risks against future happenings, since title insurance is against risks that may have occurred in the past but are not yet known or apparent.

The cost of a title insurance policy is based upon the value of the property at the time of acquisition or the face amount on the policy. There will usually be a minimum cost of $50.00 to $75.00 even if the value is only $1,000. A typical rate structure scale graduates to $125 for $10,000, $200 for $30,000, and $300 for $60,000.

INSURANCE PRINCIPLES

Although land itself is considered to be indestructible, any structures on the land are subject to damage from fire, wind, other natural elements, or human causes. Insurance protects against loss from these risks.

Coverage

Usually, a person will pay a premium sufficient to cover damage to a certain percentage of the market value of the property. This is reasonable, since the land itself is not destroyed. If a property owner does not insure his property to the full extent of its value, the insured is a *coinsurer*. The insurance company would only pay a portion of the total amount of loss. Usually, a company will agree that insurance covering 80 percent of property value is sufficient to allow full reimbursement for any damage resulting in partial loss. Sometimes an individual may have sufficient resources to repair any damage or cover losses and will not purchase insurance. This person is a *self-insurer;* however, most people are not willing or able to assume the risk of a large loss.

If there is a mortgage on the property, the mortgagee or lender will require the property owner to carry sufficient insurance to cover the interest the mortgagee has in the property.

Indemnity

It is not intended that a person be able to profit from insurance; nor is insurance intended as a gambling or speculative proposition. The principle of **indemnity** states that the purpose of insurance is to reimburse the insured for any loss, and the objective is to restore her to the place she was before the loss occurred. To collect the insurance, the applicant must have an **insurable interest** in the property at the time of the loss. This means that, in the event of property destruction, the person would suffer a financial loss. As an example, X could not take out insurance on the property of a friend, Y, unless X was in a situation to suffer financial loss if damage occurred to Y's property.

Insurance Rates

The insured pays a premium for a certain amount of coverage. This relationship of premium to coverage is called a *rate*. If a person pays $120 a year for $40,000 fire insurance coverage, the yearly rate would be computed as follows:

$$\text{Rate} = \frac{\$120}{40,000} = 0.003,$$

or $3.00 per $1,000 of coverage. The rate will depend on the amount of risk involved according to the type of construction, location of the property, or other factors that affect the likelihood of the event insured against. It will also vary with the quality of and distance from fire protection. Typically, brick

POLICY OF TITLE INSURANCE

issued by

The Title Guarantee Company

BALTIMORE, MARYLAND 21202

SUBJECT TO THE EXCLUSIONS FROM COVERAGE, THE EXCEPTIONS CONTAINED IN SCHEDULE B AND THE PRO-VISIONS OF THE CONDITIONS AND STIPULATIONS HEREOF, THE TITLE GUARANTEE COMPANY, a Maryland corporation, herein called the Company, insures, as of Date of Policy shown in Schedule A, against loss or damage, not exceeding the amount of insurance stated in Schedule A, and costs, attorneys' fees and expenses which the Company may become obligated to pay hereunder, sustained or incurred by the insured by reason of:

1. Title to the estate or interest described in Schedule A being vested otherwise than as stated therein;

2. Any defect in or lien or encumbrance on such title;

3. Lack of a right of access to and from the land; or

4. Unmarketability of such title.

EXCLUSIONS FROM COVERAGE

The following matters are expressly excluded from the coverage of this policy:

1. Any law, ordinance or governmental regulation (including but not limited to building and zoning ordinances) restricting or regulating or prohibiting the occupancy, use or enjoyment of the land, or regulating the character, dimensions or location of any improvement now or hereafter erected on the land, or prohibiting a separation in ownership or a reduction in the dimensions or area of the land, or the effect of any violation of any such law, ordinance or governmental regulation.

2. Rights of eminent domain or governmental rights of police power unless notice of the exercise of such rights appears in the public records at Date of Policy.

3. Defects, liens, encumbrances, adverse claims, or other matters (a) created, suffered, assumed or agreed to by the insured claim-ant; (b) not known to the Company and not shown by the public records but known to the insured claimant either at Date of Policy or at the date such claimant acquired an estate or interest insured by this policy and not disclosed in writing by the in-sured claimant to the Company prior to the date such insured claimant became an insured hereunder; (c) resulting in no loss or damage to the insured claimant; (d) attaching or created subsequent to Date of Policy; or (e) resulting in loss or damage which would not have been sustained if the insured claimant had paid value for the estate or interest insured by this policy.

IN WITNESS WHEREOF, the Company has caused this policy to be signed and sealed, to become valid when countersigned by a validating officer or agent of the Company, all in accordance with its By-Laws.

SPECIMEN

The Title Guarantee Company

By _John W. Brown Jr._
                              President

ATTEST: _Harwood D. Jackson_
                              Secretary

This policy valid only if Schedules A and B are attached.

Figure 11–1
Title insurance policy

POLICY NUMBER:
HO-00001

DATE OF POLICY:
January 5th, 1975

VALID ONLY IF ATTACHED TO
A.L.T.A. 1970 OWNER'S POLICY

SCHEDULE A

NAME OF INSURED

AMOUNT:
$50,000.00

JOHN DOE and
MARY DOE, his wife

1. The estate or interest in the land described or identified herein and which is covered by this policy is:
Fee Simple.

2. The estate or interest referred to herein is at Date of Policy vested in:
The Insured.

3. The land referred to in this policy is described or identified as follows:
All 10.618 acres of land, more or less, on the Southeast side of Black Acres
Road in the Tenth Election District of Baltimore County, in the State of Maryland,
as described in a Deed dated January 3rd, 1975 and recorded on January 5th, 1975
in the Land Records of Baltimore County in Liber E.H.K.Jr. No. 0000, folio 01,
from John Doe, Jr., to the Insured.

SCHEDULE B

This policy does not insure against loss or damage by reason of the following:

1. Rights or claims of parties other than the Insured in actual possession of any or
all of the property.
2. Unrecorded easements, if any, on, above or below the surface; and any discrepancies
or conflicts in boundary lines or shortage in area or encroachments, which a correct
survey or an inspection of the premises would disclose.
3. Possible unfiled mechanics' and materialmen's liens.
xxxThexdomanxxxxxkexyxxhomexkeadyxxommmnityxxpxxperkyyxxxxxkhexxxxxxxxxxxxxxxxxx
xxxxxxxxxxxxxxxxxxxxxxxxxxxxxxxxxxxxxxxxxxxxx

4. Subject to a right of way from James Smith, et al, to the Baltimore Gas and
Electric Company dated May 16th, 1921 and recorded among the Land Records of Baltimore
County in Liber W.P.C. No. 000, folio 03, as to a right of way 30 feet wide.

5. Subject to covenants, conditions, etc., in a Declaration dated March 11th, 1953
from the XYZ Corporation and recorded among the Land Records of Baltimore County
in Liber G.L.B. No. 0000, folio 05.

6. That portion of the property which lies within the bed of Black Acres Road is
subject to the use in common with others entitled thereto.

7. Subject to the rights of others to the use of the waters of Black Acre Run or
any other streams, runs, or branches which may traverse or bind the property hereby
insured.

8. Taxes and other public charges (including assessments by any County, Municipality,
Metropolitan District or Commission) payable on an annual basis have been paid through
the fiscal year ending June 30th, 1975. This Policy does not insure against the balance
of any public charges (including assessments by any County, Municipality, Metropolitan
District or Commission) payable on an annual basis subsequent to the fiscal year ending
June 30th, 1975. Nor does this Policy insure against possible future tax levies nor
against possible public charges as defined above that have not been levied or assessed.

Figure 11-1a

homes would have lower rates than frame homes; tile roofs would have a lower rate than wood shingle roofs. An area with a past history of tornadoes or a place near a forest fire area would have higher rates than locations where the threat was less likely. Rural properties distant from a water hydrant would have a higher rate than city properties. This type of rate system provides an incentive to construct safer structures and select better locations. In some cases, policies may allow special deductions for safety devices—fire extinguishers, special locks, alarm systems, or anything that tends to prevent or reduce the loss potential. Usually, the insurance company will set up standard rates for classes of property in order to avoid an involved analysis of each property to be insured.

Cancellation of Policy

The insured can cancel a policy and receive a rebate of unearned premium; however, this rebate will not usually be a proportional part of the total paid. Frequently, the insurance rates for a three-year period will be less than three times the one-year rate. If an insured cancelled his three-year policy within the first year, he would then be charged at the one-year rate or *short rate,* so that the refund would be less than two-thirds of the total paid. This provision could apply even though the company allowed the insured to pay the three-year premium in installments of thirds. The insured should also remember to notify the company at the time he desires a cancellation. If a person sold his home but failed to notify the insurance company, he might receive a rebate only from the date of notification rather than from the date of title transfer.

If the company cancels the policy, it must give notice for the period required by state law and refund a proportionate amount rather than the short rate. Concealment or misrepresentation of facts by the insured can void the policy. For example, the insured may fraudulently conceal from the company that he rents out rooms in order to obtain a lower rate, making the policy voidable. Policy coverage can also be denied if, in violation of a policy provision, a person allows a risk to increase, such as leaving the home vacant for 60 days without notifying the insurance company.

Deductible Amounts

The primary purpose of insurance is to protect a person against a risk she cannot afford. Where full coverage is provided against any amount of risk, the insurance company must handle a large number of small claims. Often, the paperwork for a small claim takes as much time as that for a large claim. To encourage policyholders to be self-insurers on small losses, insurers provide *deductible amount* clauses in policies. For a $50.00 deductible policy, the property owner would pay the first $50.00 of any loss. This option also tends to encourage policyholders to take greater care to prevent losses. Deductible often cost considerably less than full coverage policies. Because property owners can absorb these smaller losses, and because some state laws permit

permit only deductible policies, they are frequently used in real property insurance policies.

TYPES OF POLICIES

Fire Insurance

The basic protection against property loss has been the standard fire insurance policy. Most companies use a standard form. The policy indemnifies the property owner against losses incurred due to what courts term "unfriendly fires." If the insured person deliberately sets a fire, the insurance could not be collected.

The basic policy insures against direct loss from fire or lightning. In case of fire, the insured is reimbursed for the actual loss up to the face value of the property and no more. This includes the costs to remove personal property from a home endangered by fire. Damage from smoke would also be included, but not from smoke resulting from a defective chimney or situation where the fire was not classified as "unfriendly." The policy also excludes damage from fire caused by war, rebellion, or civil disturbance; however, these coverages are available as an extended coverage endorsement.

The insured value is usually interpreted to be the maximum amount to reproduce the lost property. If there is a partial loss, the insurer will pay the amount required to reproduce the original property less depreciation. Usually when a loss occurs, the insured obtains estimates of repair or replacement. Sometimes it is necessary to call in an appraiser to establish the original property value and the value remaining after the loss. If the insured and the insurer cannot agree on the loss, an arbitrator may be selected. Once in a while, the dispute will go to the courts for settlement.

The policy will describe the property insured. It may or may not include structures such as garages, barns, or other outbuildings.

Extended Coverage

Endorsements can be added to a basic fire insurance policy to extend the coverage either to additional structures on the property or even off the property, or to additional perils such as windstorm, hail, riot, civil disturbance, falling trees, or bursting water pipes. Other policies also have *extended coverage* for theft, losses associated with personal property, and liability, either by separate endorsement or by use of a broad form that includes coverage of other risks. Some mortgage companies will insist that the owner carry extended coverage as a condition to making a mortgage loan.

Homeowner's Policy

The *homeowner's policy* is a single package policy designed to give the property owner protection against a wide variety of risks. These include losses from fire, windstorm, and other natural elements plus other possible risks. The additional risks might include liability to third parties, theft, water damage, explosion, vandalism, riot and commotion, fall of aircraft, smoke, earthquake, and glass breakage. The home owner is able to secure all of these coverages in one policy at a lower cost than by purchasing them under separate endorsements.

Homeowner policies provide various types of coverage and cover different uses. For example, HO-2 (Homeowner Two) is for owner-occupied dwellings, and HO-4 is for tenants. Other forms provide various exclusions or supplemental coverages.

Rent and Leasehold Insurance

An owner of an apartment or other income-producing property is subject to the same risks as the home owner and other additional risks. If rental property is damaged, the owner can lose the rent from the property as well as incur expenses related to repairs or restoration. *Rent insurance* can be purchased to give the owner continued income in case of loss of rent due to fire or other covered provisions. *Rental insurance* provides reimbursement for potential, rather than actual, rent loss.

In some instances, a tenant on a long-term lease may be paying considerably less than economic (market) rent. This situation creates a positive leasehold interest that may have considerable value to the tenant. Destruction of the leased property could wipe out the tenant's leasehold interest. He can protect himself against this loss by purchasing a *leasehold* insurance policy.

Business Property Insurance

The various types of businesses and differences in types of properties associated with each business necessitate a variety of insurance coverage. The risks due to fire, windstorm, and other elements are similar to residential risks. In addition, many businesses also have considerable merchandise or inventories that also need to be insured. A business is also subject to loss of earnings if the damage causes the business to be interrupted or closed. This is often referred to as a *consequential loss* since it is not directly due to the peril insured against. Insurance for these risks can be obtained either by individual policies, as extensions to a basic policy, or in a package policy similar to a home owner's policy. Public liability is also an important factor in a business, since the premises are frequented by customers. Businesses face possible lawsuits resulting from bodily injury or property damage through negligence or alleged negligence of the business owner. The insurance ordinarily covers not only the actual damages paid, but also the legal costs associated with the lawsuit.

OTHER POLICY PROVISIONS

A person purchasing real property insurance should be aware of a variety of clauses that may appear in policies and restrict coverage. Home owners are often not aware of the meaning of these provisions until a loss occurs and coverage is denied.

Pro Rata and Coinsurance

Since it is not the intent of insurance to provide a recovery greater than the actual loss, the policy will usually contain *pro rata liability* and *coinsurance* clauses. The following pro rata liability clause or one similar will appear in most policies.

> This insurer shall not be liable for a greater portion of any loss than the amount insured against bears to the total insurance carried on the property against the peril involved, whether collectible or not.

This pro rata clause prevents a property owner from collecting an amount greater than the actual loss through policies with different insurance companies. For example, assume an owner has $10,000 insurance with Company X and $30,000 with Company Y. Loss was determined to be $20,000. Each company would be liable in the same proportion as the insurance carried. Then Company X would be liable for ¼ × $20,000, or $5,000, and Company Y would pay ¾ × $20,000, or $15,000, giving the insured the exact amount of the loss. She could not collect more than the actual loss.

A coinsurance clause is different. In the past, property owners often reasoned that most losses are less than the entire value, and therefore they would carry insurance less than the total value. This was unfair to the insurance company and their insured who carry full coverage. Therefore, the owner who takes $20,000 insurance on a property valued at $50,000 is interpreted as carrying the $30,000 balance as his own risk. If there were a loss of $5,000, the company would only pay ⅖ of $5,000, or $2,000. The owner would be responsible for the $3,000 balance.

The typical fire insurance policy will provide that coverage to 80 percent of the property value is required in order to warrant the reimbursement of 100 percent of losses. Therefore, on a property valued at $40,000, the owner must carry 80 percent, or $32,000 insurance coverage to collect 100 percent of the losses.

If, for example, the owner only carried $24,000 insurance, the company would say that the home owner carried the balance of $8,000 at his own risk. If there were a loss of $10,000, the insurance company would calculate its portion of liability in this way:

$$24/32 \times \$10,000 = \$7,500$$

The owner would have to make up the $2,500 balance on his own. Thus, a home owner should increase his insurance as the property value grows.

Otherwise, he may find himself in the position of being a coinsurer without intending to do so.

Insurance companies now have available automatic increases in coverage based on an inflation index.

Diminution by Loss

When an insurance company pays a loss on a policy, the insurance remaining in force often becomes less than the original policy value. (Some home owner's policies may state different provisions.) If an insured had a $30,000 policy and then a $5,000 loss was paid, the remaining coverage would be only $25,000, even after the repair was made. This is called *diminution by loss* of the policy value. It is necessary to apply for a new policy in the original amount and pay an additional premium in order to reinstate the full coverage.

Subrogation

Assume that party A had fire insurance on her property. Due to the negligence of B, the property was damaged by fire. Party A can collect from her insurance company; however, the principle of *subrogation* provides that the insurance company can attempt to collect from B. In this process, the insurer can go to court as a representative of A, and a provision to this extent will usually appear in the policy.

Actual Cash Value

Many homes are old and have lost value due to deterioration. If an *actual cash value* clause appeared in the policy and the home were destroyed, the company would pay the reproduction cost minus depreciation. This means that the home owner would not be able to replace the home without adding some of his own money. If the words "replacement cost" were substituted in the policy for "actual cash value," the insurance company would not deduct for depreciation. Premiums are substantially higher when the policy provides for payment of loss at replacement cost.

Loss Payable Endorsement

A *loss payable endorsement* clause is always required by mortgage companies to protect their interest. If there is a loss, the proceeds check is made payable to the owner and mortgagee jointly.

Named on Policy Clause

Only the person whose name appears on a policy (or the heirs if the person named dies) can collect on the policy restricted by a *named on policy clause*. If the property is sold, the former owner no longer has an insurable interest in the property. The policy does not cover the new owner unless the insurance company accepts her as the insured. In another application, if two owners own a property on a fifty-fifty basis, but only one person's name appears on the policy, only half of the loss can be recovered.

Claim Procedures and Establishing Amount of Loss

If a loss occurs, it will be necessary to determine the amount of reimbursement due. After suffering a loss, the policyholder will usually file a claim with the insurance company as an initial step. There are several approaches to determining loss. One way to establish the amount is to determine the property value just prior to the loss and then try to establish how much the value is reduced by the loss. Estimating the cost of replacement is another approach; however, other factors such as depreciation or obsolescence may have reduced the value such that a restoration would actually leave the owner with a property of greater value than originally. To avoid a profit by the property owner, the usual procedure is to determine the restoration cost and subtract for depreciation. Thus, the owner would pay part of the restoration cost. In cases when the value or loss cannot be so easily measured, such as in personal injury cases, the matter usually must be resolved by negotiation or court appeal.

SUMMARY

Insurance is a means of shifting and distributing the burden of loss so that one or a few individuals do not suffer a very large loss. The insured pays a premium to the insurance company, and the insurer in turn takes the risk of loss from fire, windstorm, theft, liability, or other perils defined in the policy.

There are a variety of perils that can be insured against, and the insured can select those he desires and then pay the rate for that coverage. He can also select deductible amounts and thereby assume a portion of the risk. Sometimes, this proportionate risk may be assumed unintentionally by the insured by not maintaining adequate coverage.

TERMS AND CONCEPTS

You can check your understanding of these terms against the glossary or by review in this chapter.

Consequential loss	Insurable interest
Diminution by loss	Liability insurance
Endorsement	Premium
Extended coverage	Self-insurer
Homeowner's policy	Short rate
HOW	Subrogation
Indemnity	Title insurance

What are the differences, or relationship if any, between the following?

Deductible amount and Pro rata	Rent insurance and Leasehold
Insured and Insurer	insurance
Pro rata liability and Coinsurance	Rent insurance and Rental insurance

PROBLEMS

11–1.   Your fire insurance policy on your home is to be renewed. It covers protection against fire and lightning. What additional coverage might you consider?

11–2.   Your homeowner's policy has not been changed for four years. Explain how to evaluate your present coverage and determine if it is sufficient.

11–3.   A fire insurance policy contains an 80 percent coinsurance clause. The original cost of the property was $24,000, and the present value is $32,000. The insurance carried at present is $22,000. If there is a fire loss of $8,000, what portion will the insurance company pay, assuming no reduction for depreciation?

11–4.   Describe the effect of each of the following clauses on an insurance policy.
   (a)   Actual cash value,
   (b)   Replacement cost,
   (c)   Subrogation,
   (d)   Diminution by loss,
   (e)   Named on policy.

11–5.   Calculate the annual fire insurance premium for a $64,000 policy at a rate of $.365 per $100 of coverage.

11–6.   The rate for a homeowner's policy is $.39 per $100. The insurance company will offer a two-year policy at 1.85 times the annual rate and a three-year policy at 2.7 times the annual rate. On a $50,000 house, determine the saving for a two-year policy or a three-year policy over a six-year period.

11–7.   In problem 11–6, assume that Mr. Roth took out a three-year policy. If he cancelled after one year, what would be his refund at the short rate?

11–8.   A property owner had a fire loss of $20,000. He had carried a $30,000 policy with company A, and a $40,000 policy with company B, on a property valued at $35,000. What would the owner collect from each company?

11–9.   Kurt and Karla Schmidt carried $40,000 insurance on a residence valued at $70,000. They suffer a loss of $15,000. The company would have paid the entire loss if they had carried 80 percent coverage. What can the owners recover on the loss?

11–10.   Ms. Alton pays $4.20 per $1000 on her homeowner's policy with a face value of $60,000. Her home was recently appraised at $84,000. If she wants to be insured 100 percent against losses, how much additional premium would she have to pay?

SUPPLEMENTARY READINGS

Bickelhoupt, David L. *General Insurance.* Homewood, Ill.: Irwin, 1974. Chapters 4, 5, 8, 18, 19, and 21.

Elliott, Curtis M., and Vaughn, Emmett J. *Fundamentals of Risk and Insurance.* New York: Wiley, 1972. Section III.

Huebner, S. S. *Property and Liability Insurance.* Englewood Cliffs, N.J.: Prentice-Hall, 1976.

Keeton, Robert E. *Insurance Law.* St. Paul: West, 1971.

Long, J. D., and Gregg, D. W. *Property and Liability Insurance Handbook.* Homewood, Ill.: Irwin, 1965. Chapters 5–10, 19, 23–27, 31, 32, 41, and 49.

Mehr, Robert I., and Commock, Emerson. *Principles of Insurance.* Homewood, Ill.: Irwin, 1976. Chapters 13, 15, 16, 22, 29, and 32.

Nelson, David Robert. "Why Builders Should Know HOW." *Real Estate Review,* vol. 8, no. 1 (Spring 1978), pp. 46–53.

Federal Regulations and State Licensing

Federal, state and local laws directly affect the demand and supply of real estate, as well as practices in the real estate profession. Particular areas where federal laws apply include low-income housing, urban renewal, insured or guaranteed mortgages, fair housing, and laws designed to protect the consumer. State laws, on the other hand, primarily control the licensing and practice of real estate brokers, salespersons, and others in related activities.

State licensing requirements vary considerably from state to state. Many of the provisions, however, seem to be consistent. The NATIONAL ASSOCIATION OF REALTORS® has worked toward consistency in licensing regulations from state to state. The License Law Committee of NAR, in cooperation with the National Association of Real Estate License Law Officials (NARELLO), has published a suggested pattern for real estate license law.[1]

Federal regulations concerning real estate financing and mortgages were discussed in Chapter 7; legislation covering urban renewal, land use, and low-income housing was discussed in Chapter 10. Other aspects of federal and state law are discussed in other chapters as they relate to specific topics.

FEDERAL HOUSING

Since the formation of the Public Housing Administration in 1937, the federal government has become increasingly involved in providing housing

---

[1]NATIONAL ASSOCIATION OF REALTORS®, *Real Estate License Law—Suggested Pattern*, 4th ed. Chicago: 1975.

within the financial means of more families. The original program was supplemented by the Housing Acts of 1949, 1954, and 1961. In 1965, another law provided a rent supplement program that subsidized payments to the landlord so that low-income families would pay no more than 25 percent of their income for rent. There have been several extensions of the law since then.

The first government endeavors in housing resulted in public housing projects owned by a local housing authority. Initial projects were concentrated in inner city areas; however, later projects have spread to the suburban areas. Although the local government authority has the primary responsibility for starting and administering the current projects, the Department of Housing and Urban Development (HUD) is available to provide technical assistance when requested. Projects are begun only after a local housing authority studies the community and the available housing. The study determines existing low-income family housing standards, extent of blighted areas, vacancies available, and overcrowding. Based on the findings, HUD may approve a proposed program and allocate certain units to a community. Assistance from HUD is available in the form of grants, annual subsidy contributions, loans, and government guarantees of bond issues. The grants and loan guarantees are used to initiate projects, whereas the annual federal contributions help maintain the availability of housing for the lowest income groups.

LAWS RELATED TO FAIR HOUSING

A basis for protection against discrimination was begun with the Civil Rights Act of 1866 and was supplemented 102 years later by the Fair Housing Act of 1968. These laws make it illegal to interfere with the rights of individuals and provide penalties for enforcement. It is illegal to coerce, interfere, intimidate, or threaten a person in the process of buying, selling, or renting real estate.

Civil Rights Act of 1866

Congress passed the *Civil Rights Act* of 1866 following the Civil War. This act provided that "all citizens of the United States shall have the same right, in every State and Territory, as is enjoyed by white citizens thereof to inherit, purchase, lease, sell, hold and convey real and personal property." The intent of the act was to prohibit discrimination based on race.

The law provides means to enforce the provisions. Where there is an instance of racial discrimination, the complainant can take the case to a federal court. The Supreme Court decision in 1883 effectively limited the act's application to federal housing. An executive order in 1962 required the elimination of discrimination on (a) federal government owned or leased real estate, (b) property affected by federal grants or funds, or (c) government insured mortgages. Title VI of the Civil Rights Act of 1964 broadened the scope of antidiscrimination into any areas where the federal government provided assistance. In a situation where a real estate broker or salesperson is found to have discriminated because of race, the court could force the sale or rental of the property or could award damages.

Fair Housing Act of 1968

The *Fair Housing Act* of 1968 expands the Civil Rights Act by making it illegal to discriminate based on race, color, religion, or national origin in connection with the rental or sale of most housing as well as land designated for residential use. The act clearly covers both single-family housing and multifamily housing as follows:

1. Single-family housing

   (a) Houses not privately owned;

   (b) Houses privately owned by an individual person who owns three or more houses, or one who, in any two-year period, sells more than one of which she was not the most recent occupant;

   (c) Privately owned housing when a broker or other person involved in the business of selling or renting houses is used and/or when discriminatory advertising is used.

2. Multifamily housing

   (a) Housing of five or more units;

   (b) Housing of four or fewer units, if none of the units is occupied by the owner.

The 1968 Fair Housing Act prohibits certain acts if based on race, color, religion, or national origin:

1. Refusal to sell, rent to, negotiate with, or deal with a person;

2. Stating different terms or conditions for buying or renting to different people;

3. Advertising housing as available only to certain persons;

4. Making false statements concerning the availability of housing for sale or rent;

5. Calling attention to the possibility that minority groups may move into an area in order to persuade an owner to sell or rent;

6. Any practices by banks, savings and loan associations, insurance companies, or other commercial lenders that deny loans or specify different terms or conditions to different persons;

7. Refusing to admit anyone into a brokers' organization, multiple listing service, or other service.

Where there is an apparent violation of the Fair Housing Law of 1968, the complainant can report it to Fair Housing, HUD, Washington, D.C. 20410, or to the nearest regional office. The complainant may write a personal letter or form provided by any post office or HUD office to report a complaint. When the complaint is received, HUD will send a copy to the person charged, who then can file a written answer. After an investigation, HUD may take a number of actions. HUD can (a) attempt informal conciliation to end any discriminatory practice, (b) inform the complainant of his right to court action, or (c) refer the complaint to the Attorney General or to an equivalent state or local agency. The individual may, as an alternative, seek remedy by local, state, or federal court action.

Supreme Court Ruling on Balanced Neighborhoods, 1979

A racially mixed group of residents of Bellwood, Illinois brought suit under the Fair Housing Act in 1979 to stop real estate agents from attempting to illegally tip the racial balance in a neighborhood. The suit charged two real estate agencies with steering black home buyers to the integrated Bellwood neighborhood while guiding whites into other predominantly white areas. The U.S. Supreme Court, in ruling against the real estate agents, stated that everyone in Bellwood could suffer economic losses if the area's stability were undermined.

State Antidiscrimination and Fair Housing Laws

Most of the states have adopted fair housing laws paralleling the federal laws. The provisions are very similar to those defined above for the federal laws. Some states have recently expanded the provisions to prohibit discrimination based on sex, marital status, age, physical handicap, or other factors. The provisions for each state are covered in booklets available from sources listed in Appendix C.

CONSUMER PROTECTION

A number of federal laws and regulations were designed to protect the consumer against unscrupulous persons involved in real estate. These laws have been promoted by both consumer interest groups and legitimate business interests.

Consumers may be involved with real estate transactions only a few times in their lives, and the amount of money they allocate toward a real estate transaction is usually substantial. Many of the provisions—the "fine print" in the documents—are difficult for the consumer to comprehend. Much legislation is designed to help the consumer in this respect.

Truth-in-Lending Law

The federal *Truth-in-Lending Law* is part of the Consumer Credit Protection Act of 1968. The Board of Governors of the Federal Reserve System was given responsibility to implement the law and subsequently issued Regulation Z, which went into effect on July 1, 1969. Its objective is to let consumers know exactly what they will be paying in credit charges for a transaction so that they can compare costs to other sources of credit for possible savings. The law does not regulate interest rates on loans, since legal limits on interest that can be charged for specific purposes are governed by state usury laws. The law and Regulation Z require that the interest rate be clearly specified and that it include any charges listed under other names that are legally defined as interest.

Compliance with Truth-in-Lending

The act requires that anyone who offers, extends, or arranges credit must make certain disclosures to the consumer. The most important disclosures are (a) the total finance charge; (b) the annual percentage rate (APR); (c) date finance charge begins; (d) number of payments; (e) due dates of payments; (f) prepayment penalties; and (g) total of all payments. However, the total of all payments need not be stated in cases involving a first mortgage or contract for deed on a dwelling. The *annual percentage rate* is the total annual cost of credit and must include not only the interest, but also the "points" and any other fees. The following fees must be included in the calculation: application fees, inspection fees, finders' fees, termite inspection costs, disclosure statement fees, closing fees, points, loan discount fees, prepaid interest, VA funding fees, or prepaid mortgage insurance premium (MIP) on FHA loans. The objective is to provide the borrower with the means to compare financing costs.

Truth-in-Lending and advertising

When the Truth-in-Lending Law became effective on July 1, 1969, the advertising of real estate credit was placed under the jurisdiction of the Federal Trade Commission (FTC). The intent of this law is to make bait advertising of credit terms a federal offense. For example, if an advertisement offers homes at $1,000 down, the ad is in violation if the seller will not usually accept this amount as a full down payment. Or if an advertisement mentions credit terms, the annual percentage rate must be spelled out and stated as such in those words. The words "Buyer can assume 9% mortgage" would be improper in an advertisement if other charges will be made that fall into the definition of finance charges. The act provides both criminal and civil penalties for violations.

Consumer Credit Protection Act

The **Consumer Credit Protection Act** of 1968 and Regulation Z apply to consumer credit transactions where the security for the loan is real property used as the principal residence of the borrower. The act provides that the customer receive a notice of his right to rescind certain transactions up through the third business day following receipt of the disclosure and rescission notice. If the customer decides to rescind the transaction, he must notify the creditor in writing and is then not liable for any charge. The lender must return any deposits or property given as a down payment.

Equal Credit Opportunity Act of 1975

The *Equal Credit Opportunity Act* prohibits discrimination in obtaining credit because of race, color, national origin, religion, age, sex, or marital status. Prior to this time, these factors were often taken into account when a lender evaluated the loan application of a potential borrower. For example, single or divorced women often had difficulty in obtaining mortgage loans. Mortgage lenders must also observe Regulation B of the Federal Reserve Board, which outlines procedures to follow in determining the eligibility of mortgage loan applicants.

Real Estate Settlement Procedures Act (RESPA)

The Real Estate Settlement Procedures Act, administered by HUD, has the objective of providing potential home buyers who are arranging financing with information on the total costs involved. The lender must advise the buyer, seller, and any others involved of all charges to be levied. Each person who applies for a home mortgage loan must be furnished with a booklet entitled *Settlement Costs* published by HUD. The lender usually provides an estimate of total closing costs. The purposes are to (a) allow a buyer to shop around and compare costs and (b) to let the buyer know how much cash will be needed at settlement. RESPA applies to all first mortgage loans of one- to four-family residential properties where the lender is under federal regulations. The law bans referral fees and bars sellers from requiring buyers to purchase title insurance from any particular company. The law does not apply to commercial property. Procedures in the law are discussed in greater detail in Chapter 16.

Magnuson-Moss Consumer Product Warranty Act

The Magnuson-Moss Consumer Product Warranty Act is designed to protect the consumer in the sale of good where warranties are specified, including protection when builders offer such warranties in respect to home appliances. A warranty must be designated as "full' or "limited," and the rights of the buyer must be defined in case defects should occur. Warranties must also be written in simple, easily-understood language. A builder who offers a warranty that does not meet the requirements of the act could be subject to a $10,000 per day fine. The act does not, however, require that warranties be given. The Home Owners Warranty (HOW) program discussed in Chapter 10 meets the provisions of the Magnuson-Moss Act.

Interstate Land Sales Full Disclosure Act (ILSFDA or ILSA)

During the early 1960s, it came to the attention of the U. S. Senate Special Committee on Aging that elderly persons were being persuaded to purchase retirement or other property that often turned out to be useless or undesirable. Sometimes land that was represented as a vacation retreat or retirement property turned out to be a swamp or desert. The *Interstate Land Sales Full*

Disclosure Act, passed by Congress in 1968, has been successful in limiting fraudulent schemes or other activities involving misrepresentation, sight unseen selling, and overdevelopment of available water resources.

Jurisdiction of ILSFDA

ILSFDA provides that anyone selling or leasing fifty or more (or potentially fifty or more) lots of unimproved land as part of a common plan in interstate commerce must comply with provisions of the act. HUD has taken the position that a condominium of fifty or more units may fall within the act's jurisdiction. The law does not apply to situations where all lots are five acres or more, to cemetery land, to certain commercial or industrial developments, or to cases where 100 percent of the sales are intrastate.

Statement of record and property report

The developer under the ILSFDA must file a **statement of record** to HUD containing information on the nature of the development, including title condition, encumbrances, location of roads, improvements, utilities, schools, recreational areas, and other services available to the property owners. It must also include copies of the legal instruments used in selling, such as contracts, deeds, bills of sale, and so forth. A second document, called a **property report,** is also required. It has less detail than the statement of record. A copy of the property report must be given to purchasers prior to purchase of any property. Its purpose is to make purchasers aware of planned improvements, possible problems such as wet property in low areas, planned utilities and their cost, availability of roads and their condition and maintenance, and many other items that potential purchasers should know about. HUD, however, does not approve the project nor endorse the development in any way. The main purpose of these two documents is to make the information available. The buyer of a property in a subdivision under ILSFDA has three working days to rescind the purchase.

State Regulations

Some states have regulations that apply to intrastate land sales, whereas some supplement the federal ILSFDA. Arkansas and Pennsylvania, for example, require that any developer proposing sale within the state of land located outside the state shall submit particulars to the State Real Estate Commission for approval.

Many states have laws related to the purchase or lease of subdivided land within the state. New York, for example, requires the filing of an *offering statement* with the Department of State. In one of its provisions, the statement prohibits the conveyance of land if it is encumbered by a mortgage or lien such as to affect clear title.

ENVIRONMENTAL CONTROLS

A broad interpretation of the word **environment** would include physical, social, cultural, and aesthetic factors. As related to real estate, environmental concerns can be limited to actions that will affect land, air, water, minerals, and objects of aesthetic or historic significance.

In this chapter, we shall briefly define the government environmental legislation that impacts upon real estate transactions. Prior to the 1960s, the laws of police power, trespass, and nuisance served to protect owners' enjoyment of their property and the health of the public in general. Due to population growth, new industries, and increased awareness of problems, the government has enacted legislation intended to protect the environment.

National Environmental Policy Act (NEPA), 1969

The stated purposes of NEPA are (a) to declare a national policy to encourage harmony between humans and their environment; (b) to promote efforts to reduce damage to the environment; (c) to increase understanding of the environment; and (d) to establish a Council on Environmental Quality. The act refers to federal actions, but the agency guidelines extend to private activities. Proposed actions affecting real estate shall include an *environmental impact statement* (EIS) that considers the impact of proposed major projects on the quality of the environment, including indirect as well as direct effects. Although the act does not prescribe sanctions for failure to comply, complaining parties have generally sought injunctions that have frequently been granted. The Environmental Protection Agency (EPA) was established by executive order in 1970 to establish and enforce standards. Many of the states have followed up with similar legislation.

Air Pollution Controls

The Air Quality Act of 1967, as amended in 1970, requires the Environmental Protection Agency to establish air quality standards to protect the public health and welfare. The individual states are given primary responsibility for control within their boundaries. Air pollution is related to land use since the location and design of industrial buildings and transportation facilities have an influence on the climate and air in the cities.

Water Quality

Although owners of riparian land have always had the right to take actions in cases where watercourses were polluted, the problem has become too general to be resolved by individual lawsuits. Two types of water pollution exist. *Chemical pollution* results from the release of toxic chemicals into rivers and lakes (e.g., the damage caused by the release of Kepone into the James River). The discharge of sewage or other wastes results in *biological pollution.* The objectives of the Federal Water Pollution Control Act, as amended in 1972, are to restore and maintain the chemical, physical, and biological integrity of the nation's waters. The legislation deals with (a) elimination of the discharge of pollutants into navigable waters by 1985; (b) protection of fish and wildlife; (c) prohibition of the discharge of toxic pollutants; (d) financial assistance for publicly-owned waste treatment works; and (e) encouragement for research and development.

The Safe Drinking Water Act of 1974 has as its purpose the assurance of minimum standards for water supply systems. The EPA was entrusted with formulating the regulations and administrating the program.

Coastal Zones

In 1972, Congress passed the Marine Protection, Research and Sanctuaries Act (sometimes called the Federal Ocean Dumping Act), which regulates the discharge and dumping of waste into the offshore areas of the ocean. In the same year, the Coastal Zone Management Act was passed to encourage states to preserve, protect, develop, and restore coastal areas. This act has made a broad impact on real estate activities, since coastal waters are defined to include the Great Lakes area and their connecting waters, harbors, bays, marshes, and other areas that have a measurable quantity of seawater. The federal government provides grants to share in the administration costs of programs. It also requires permits for new developments or other projects, in addition to the environmental impact statements.

Noise Control

The Noise Control Act of 1972 impacts upon real estate values and uses including, but not limited to, aircraft noise. Although noise control responsibility rests primarily with the states, federal legislation extends to vehicles that move about in interstate commerce. Noise from aircraft can substantially affect land values near airports.

Solid Waste

The Resource and Recovery Act of 1976 replaced the federal Solid Waste Disposal Act. The term *solid waste* might be more appropriately referred to as *discarded materials*. Dumps for discarded materials can pose a threat to health and the environment as well as to property values. The new act deals with recoverable materials, hazardous wastes, waste as a potential source of energy, and guidelines for waste disposal.

LAND OWNERSHIP BY ALIENS

In the years before 1979, citizens and corporations in other countries acquired real estate in the U.S. at a record rate. Many U.S. citizens are concerned that rich agricultural land is being bought up and converted to other uses, thereby threatening future food sources.

Legislation on alien ownership of land dates back to the past century when laws were enacted to prevent foreign investors from acquiring large tracts for tenant farming. Currently, seven states (Connecticut, Indiana, Kentucky, Mississippi, Nebraska, New Hampshire, and Oklahoma) prohibit land ownership by nonresident aliens. Other states have major restrictions on alien ownership.

On the federal level, there is no restriction on land purchased by aliens; however, Congress has approved legislation requiring foreign citizens and corporations to disclose their U.S. farm and timberland holdings. Federal restrictions also exist that limit how alien land can be used.

STATE LICENSING

All states and the District of Columbia have laws regulating the licensing of real estate brokers and salespeople. The primary purpose of these laws is to protect the public against incompetency or dishonesty in real estate transactions. The laws are also intended to enhance standards by which brokers and salespeople perform their functions and to protect licensed brokers and salespeople from improper or unfair competition. These laws control the issuance of licenses to practice, as well as their suspension or revocation when violated. In most states, the law establishes a state board or real estate commission that has the responsibility to implement the laws and the right to issue and enforce regulations. The commission has the power to issue, suspend, or revoke licenses of real estate brokers or salespersons. In some states, other people involved in real estate, such as appraisers (state of Nebraska) or escrow agents (state of Washington), require licenses. The commission can also turn over evidence of violations to the state's attorney general for prosecution or request a court to issue an injunction.

The Right to License

The legal basis for a state's right to license derives from the police power of the state. The exercise of this control is especially important in real estate because the average person transacts real estate business very infrequently. In addition, the amount of money involved is relatively large, usually including much of a person's total life savings or potential future earnings.

Courts have upheld the constitutionality of real estate licensing laws when tested as violating the Fourteenth Amendment. The tests charged that the laws deprive a person of a means of making a livelihood in selling real estate. The courts have responded that the restrictive requirements are not unreasonable in that the real estate business requires skill, competence, and trust to protect the interest of the public. This licensing authority is not unusual. States also regulate the practice of law, medicine, nursing, teaching, pharmacy, and other areas where a degree of competency is required.

Educational Requirements

Real estate professionals recognize that experience alone is not adequate to meet competition and provide the proper service to clients. Activities carried out by real estate professionals depend heavily upon an academic base. The increased need for educational depth and background in these and other subjects has been recognized by both professional associations and state legislative bodies. State statutes include educational prerequisites for taking licensing examinations. Professional associations also have educational or classroom prerequisites for professional designations. Concurrently, there has been an increasing trend for universities and community colleges to either expand the number of real estate courses offered or provide degrees or majors in real estate.

Typical Licensing Regulations

Although the regulations for obtaining and maintaining a license vary from state to state, similarities do exist:

1. *License.* A broker or salesperson must be licensed before participating in a real estate transaction for a fee.
2. *Education.* Frequently, a high school diploma and/or a specified number of hours of classroom study are required for either a salesperson or a broker. In some states (e.g., Oregon), continuing periodic courses are required. In Indiana, a B.S. degree is required for a broker's license.
3. *Experience.* Experience in real estate prior to application for a broker's license is needed in some states.
4. *Examination.* Sales candidates and broker candidates take different examinations. More than twenty states use the standard ETS (Educational Testing Service) examination. Other states use ACT (American College Test) services, tests, or the multistate examination.
5. *Fees.* Fees are required for both the original license and the periodic renewals. Fees are used to administer and enforce the law and to provide education.
6. *Reputation.* Applicants must submit evidence of good reputation and competency. Written references from real estate professionals or others are usually needed.
7. *Sponsor.* State laws often require that a salesperson be sponsored by a licensed broker for whom he will work after obtaining the license.
8. *Reciprocity.* Most states have reciprocal agreements allowing credit for experience or a license from another state.
9. *Minimum age.* The minimum age is usually eighteen for a salesperson and twenty-one for a broker.
10. *Recovery fund.* Some states require licensees to furnish a surety bond or contribute to a recovery fund. Persons who sustain losses due to negligence or fraud by a licensee and cannot make recovery from the licensee may obtain reimbursement from the fund.
11. *Individual licenses.* Licenses are issued to individuals and not to associations or corporations.
12. *Display.* Display of the license in the broker's place of business is

required. Pocket cards are also carried by each licensed sales representative and broker.

13. *Employment severance.*   Salespersons' licenses are usually returned to the state when employment with a particular broker ends.

14. *Administration.*   The license law is handled by an appointed body, different in name from state to state (see Appendix C), but made up of paid officials and employees.

15. *Suspension.*   Fraudulent activities or violations of state regulations or laws can result in suspension of licenses.

16. *Exemptions.*   It is common practice to exempt certain persons from the need to have a license as follows:

    (a)   A public officer in duties related to real estate.
    (b)   Attorneys at law acting in their capacity related to real estate.
    (c)   Court-appointed administrators or executors.
    (d)   Any person selling or buying real estate for her- or himself or through a power of attorney.

17. *Brokerage.*   Operations must be physically separated from other types of business.

18. *Advertising.*   Advertising must include the name under which the broker is registered.

19. *Prizes.*   Prizes, lotteries, and so on cannot be used to induce business.

20. *Housing.*   Regulations exist to support fair housing laws.

Typical Violations

Although a person should be familiar with the laws and regulations in his or her individual state, a number of violations are clearly defined as part of many state laws. These include the following:

1. Placing a "For Sale" or "For Rent" sign on a property without written consent of the owner.

2. Failure of a broker to keep a client's funds (i.e., deposit on a purchase) separate from the broker's business account.

3. Untruthful or misleading advertising.

4. Misrepresentation, whether intentional or innocent.

5. Acting for more than one party in a transaction without both parties' knowledge.

6. Accepting compensation or other items of value from anyone other than an employing broker for real estate-related activity.

7. Payment of fees, gifts, or other consideration by a broker to other than the broker's employees or other licensed brokers.

8. Conviction of a felony.

9. Using blind ads, that is, ads without the registered broker's name.

10. Performing services ordinarily performed only by licensed attorneys at law.

11. Failure to give a client a copy of the listing agreement.

SUMMARY

Federal legislation in the areas of civil rights, fair housing, consumer protection, and environmental protection affects the activities of all persons engaged in the real estate business. All people involved in any area of real estate should fully understand these laws and how they affect their occupations. State legislation follows, implements, or supplements the federal regulations but differs from state to state.

All states have statutes requiring the licensing of real estate brokers and salespeople. Some states also license others in the real estate business. The laws provide a state commission to implement the law and define penalties for violations.

TERMS AND CONCEPTS

Annual percentage rate
Biological pollution
Chemical pollution
Civil Rights Act
Consumer Credit Protection Act
Environment
Environmental impact statement
Equal Credit Opportunity

Fair Housing Act
Interstate Land Sales Full
    Disclosure Act
Property report
Recovery fund
Statement of record
Truth-in-Lending Law

PROBLEMS

12-1. List the legislative acts that are designed to protect the consumer, and state the intended purpose of each law.

12-2. What arguments can be made for and against consumer protection laws?

12-3. What types of situations are covered by environmental protection laws?

12-4. What factors do you think might be covered in an environmental impact statement?

12-5. List six examples of actions with respect to real estate that would require an environmental impact statement.

12-6. Why do you think that commercial real estate transactions are exempt from RESPA?

12-7. What does *disclosure* mean? List three laws and what they require to be disclosed.

12-8. Why do some federal laws encourage states to establish laws rather than impose federal requirements? Give two examples of laws that do this.

12–9.   *Redlining* is defined as a practice whereby lenders refuse to lend money for purchase of homes in certain neighborhoods. Give arguments for and against this practice.

12–10.   Give an example of a type of improper activity that may have induced RESPA, Truth-in-Lending, and the Interstate Land Sales Full Disclosure Act.

12–11.   What actions can a state Real Estate Commission take to enforce the state law? Can the commission impose fines or imprisonment for violations?

12–12.   Can a person recover from a state recovery fund for each of the following? Must other steps be taken first in each case?

(a)   The contract price was $5000 higher than appraised value.

(b)   A broker represented a septic system as being in good order when it was defective.

(c)   A real estate salesperson stated that a client must purchase title insurance from company A. The client later discovered that she paid $200 more than another company charges.

12–13.   If a person sells real estate for others but charges no fee or commission, does he need a license? Discuss.

12–14.   List some persons from whom a real estate salesperson cannot receive compensation or gifts of value.

12–15.   How does the Bellwood ruling by the U.S. Supreme Court affect real estate brokers?

SUPPLEMENTARY READINGS

Bergfield, Philip B. *Real Estate Law*. New York: McGraw-Hill, 1979. Chapter 21.

Galaty, Fillmore W.; Allaway, Wellington J.; and Kyle, Robert C. *Modern Real Estate Practice*. Chicago: Real Estate Education Corporation, 1978. Chapter 21.

Harwood, Bruce. *Real Estate Principles*. Reston, Va.: Reston Publishing Company, 1977. Chapters 19 and 23.

Henderson, Thomas P.; Johnson, Ross H.; Kruse, Dennis; and Ficek, Edmund F. *Real Estate Examinations Guide*. Columbus, Oh: Charles E. Merrill, 1977. Chapter 12 and Appendices.

Henszey, Benjamin N., and Friedman, Ronald M. *Real Estate Law*. Boston: Warren, Gorham, and Lamont, 1979. Chapter 14.

Levine, Mark Lee. *Real Estate Fundamentals*. St. Paul: West, 1976. Chapters 39–41.

Rose, Daniel. "Landmarks Preservation and the Law." *Real Estate Issues* (Summer 1979).

Semenow, Robert W. *Questions and Answers on Real Estate*. Englewood Cliffs, N.J.: Prentice-Hall, 1978. Chapter 9.

Shenkel, William M. *Modern Real Estate Principles*. Dallas: Business Publications, 1977. Chapters 3, 4, 16, and 22.

Smith, Halbert C.; Tschappat, Carl J.; and Racster, Ronald L. *Real Estate and Urban Development*. Homewood, Ill.: Irwin, 1977. Chapter 15, 17, and 18.

State laws governing licensing of brokers and salespeople can be obtained from the office of the real estate commissioner (or equivalent) in each state. (See Appendix C for the addresses of state agencies.)

Brokerage Operations

Real estate brokerage can include one or more of the following functions: listing, selling, buying, leasing, renting, exchanging, appraising, or managing real property. License laws usually define a real estate *broker* as a person or firm who, *for compensation,* engages in buying, selling, renting, leasing, or exchanging real estate *for others.* In all states it is unlawful to engage in real estate brokerage without a valid broker's license.

THE BROKER

A real estate broker's primary asset is expertise or know-how. A broker does not sell a product, but rather provides a service. Consequently, success depends upon skill in bringing interested and willing parties together in order to complete transactions successfully. To be effective, brokers must have the necessary background, including knowledge of the law, the locality, property values, ownership, and sources of financing. They also need managerial and sales ability.

Proper representation of a seller and adequate service to a buyer require that brokers possess specialized knowledge and qualifications. They need to be aware of local property values. They must be able to correlate the needs of a buyer with the various available properties. They must be aware of building activities, the local real estate market, and the availability of financing. They must also know the state and local statutes and regulations and have enough knowledge of the law to handle the interests of the seller and buyer properly and to avoid jeopardy to all persons involved. A willingness for hard work and long hours and the ability to get along with people are also important attributes. Since real estate can be bought and sold without a broker's services, brokers must be able to convince a prospective client that it is worthwhile to pay the fee or commission, rather than try to handle it alone. In all of its facets, brokerage requires extensive knowledge.

A Broker is Not

Some aspects of real estate should not or cannot be performed by the broker. Brokers must recognize those activities that are beyond their legal and practical limitations—those that require the services of an attorney, surveyor, or other professional. The continued success of a brokerage depends upon the ability to acquire clients, to integrate all facets of the business, and to complete transactions both quickly and to the satisfaction of the client's needs and interests.

Specializing Brokers

The brokerage business can be segmented into two groupings based on either the type of property or the type of service. Residential brokers deal primarily with single-family units or those with two to four families. Others might deal mainly with apartments, whereas commercial brokers work with income-producing properties and industrial brokers handle transactions involving industrial properties.

Some brokers handle transactions other than sales, such as negotiating leases, securing mortgages, or handling exchanges of property. Exchanges of property often provide tax advantages to the parties involved. In selling real estate, the broker who is also willing to take property in trade on a sale can sometimes encourage transactions that otherwise might not be within the financial capability of a buyer. In most exchanges, both parties pay a commission based upon the value of their property sold or exchanged. These commission rates may differ from rates customarily charged in sales of property. As in regular sales transactions, the contract agreements must make each party aware that both are paying a commission to the broker. Failure to do so would result in a breach of the broker's duty to her or his principal.

When brokers negotiate leases, they are usually paid a percentage of the rent to be collected.

THE BROKER AS AN AGENT

Any person or entity who acts at the request and in behalf of another in dealing with third persons is an *agent,* and the person for whom the agent acts is known as the *principal.* The status of agent does not automatically carry with it the authority to enter into contracts in behalf of the principal. That authority must be either expressly or impliedly granted to the agent, or the principal must in some way hold the agent out to a *third party* as having authority.

By law, an *agent* is defined as one employed by and under the control of another (principal) to represent the principal in dealings with others. The *agency* creates a *fiduciary* relationship, meaning that each must place trust and confidence in the other, and each must also exercise a certain degree of fairness and good faith.

Types of Agents

Agents can be classified either by how the agency arises or by the extent of authorization. If the authorization has been delegated by the principal, the relationship is an *actual agency.* When a third person has relied upon the principal's express or implied representations that the agency existed, the agency is called an *ostensible agency.*

Classification as to extent of authorization creates either a universal agent, a general agent, or a special agent. A *universal agent* has the authorization to perform all lawful acts for the principal. A *general agent* has the authorization to transact all business in either a certain place or of a specific type, such as all real estate affairs. Finally, the *special agent* is authorized by the principal only to perform a certain action or to handle a particular affair. The most common type is the special agency, where the broker is authorized by a seller to find a buyer for a particular parcel of property.

Agency Relationship

A principal/agent relationship arises whenever a person or entity is given authority to negotiate for or to buy, sell, exchange, or lease real property or any interest therein. However, the typical real estate broker usually does not have the authority to contract with third persons in behalf of her principal.

Most brokers are usually hired to produce a specified result, that is, to obtain a buyer or lessee who is ready, willing, and able to comply with the principal's terms. Once the principal/agent relationship is established, it is subject to common law and applicable state statutes.

While conducting her brokerage business, the broker may hire sales representatives to perform some or all of the necessary activities. It is the salesperson who is usually in active personal contact with prospective buyers or lessees and negotiates the transaction according to the terms requested by the principal. The broker, however, remains responsible to the principal for the performance of their agreement.

In most states, the contract of employment between the principal and the broker must be in writing in order to be binding. In some states, however, verbal listing agreements are fully enforceable. A written agreement should always be executed to establish proof of employment and to leave no doubt as to the rights and duties of the parties. A written agreement typically contains the (a) property identification or address, (b) seller's name, (c) broker's name, (d) listing price, (e) commission and share between listing and selling broker, (f) duration of agreement, and (g) type of listing (as described in Chapter 14).

Any person who is legally competent to enter into a contract (see Chapter 3) can be legally bound to a listing agreement. A person who is able to contract for himself is not only legally capable of appointing an agent but also of acting as an agent himself. The authority of a real estate broker to act as an agent for a buyer or a seller is based on the provisions of the applicable state licensing law and of the terms of the listing agreement. A broker's authority to act cannot be unlimited or unrestricted. Any action by the broker against public policy or in violation of state licensing laws may cause the broker to be fined or lose her license.

Duties

The broker has a number of responsibilities not only to his principal, but also to the third party involved in a transaction. If the seller were the principal, a potential buyer would be a third party and the broker would have certain responsibilities toward her. For instance, the broker is responsible to represent a property to the buyer properly. If the broker is hired by a seller and makes a willful misrepresentation to the buyer, the broker can be held liable. For example, if the broker stated that a basement was dry and it turned out to have water problems, the buyer could hold the broker responsible. The buyer would also have recourse against the seller, since the broker was his agent; however, the seller can then sue the broker for fraudulent misrepresentation. This assumes, of course, that the seller did not misrepresent the situation to the broker in the first place. In any case, the broker would have only second-hand knowledge of the basement condition. The broker should, however, ask the seller significant questions about the condition of the property at the time the listing agreement is made. When a broker employs a salesperson to deal directly with the buyer, the broker is responsible for the salesperson's actions.

The broker is also required to exercise care and skill in carrying out his duties. If he drew up an offer and acceptance that was signed by both parties, and the buyer decided later not to be obligated because the document was poorly worded, the seller could hold the broker responsible for damages. It is the responsibility of the broker to understand his business and to know when it is necessary to obtain legal advice. The broker can also be held accountable for misconduct by secretly buying property from his principal, making secret profits, not disclosing material facts to the principal, or not accounting for deposits he holds.

The broker has the duty to be loyal to his principal. For instance, he cannot act for both parties in the transaction without the knowledge of both. Obviously the seller, who is looking for the highest price, and the buyer, who is looking for the lowest price, have conflicting interests. Even though the broker's task involves bringing buyers and sellers together, he is still responsible as an agent to his principal. The fact that he thought he was acting in the interest of both parties does not help. This situation might occur where a broker is hired by a buyer to find a certain type of property. He happens to have a listing on a similar piece of property. If a contract is made with only the broker and buyer knowing about the dual representation and the broker collects a commission from the seller, the seller may sue the broker if she finds out. In addition, the buyer may refuse to pay a commission. The broker would be guilty of fraud and could lose either or both commissions as well as his license.

The broker cannot have any other conflict of interest. For example, he cannot receive a fee from a lending institution for placing a mortgage, since he would not then be acting in the client's best interest to obtain the best available mortgage rate.

All significant information that comes to the attention of the broker must be disclosed to his principal. Conversely, in dealing with the buyer, the broker violates his duty to the principal (seller) if he indicates that the seller will accept less than the listed price. The broker must also give his client notice of information or conditions, such as changes in the mortgage market, changes in zoning, or information on other offers. In summary, the broker has his primary responsibility to sellers from whom he holds listings, but he still has certain responsibilities to prospective buyers. In the case of a multiple-listing broker who himself does not have the listing, he is still an agent of the seller since any commission would come from the seller.

Agency—Further Ramifications

Usually an agent is authorized by the principal to perform certain acts on his behalf. The agent is bound within these constraints in any action she takes. The principal need not accept acts performed outside of the agent's authority; however, the principal may ratify acts performed by the agent outside of those authorized. The principal then, in effect, has authorized the act. The principal can ratify by direct or express confirmation of the act or by implication. If the agent performs an unauthorized act in the presence of the principal and the third party, by not interfering or countermanding a statement, the principal implies ratification. The third party has been led to believe that the agent was acting within her authorization. The principal cannot in any case, however, ratify a portion of the act and not the whole act.

A broker can be held responsible for any negligence in performing her duties as an agent; however, the agent cannot be held liable for an honest mistake. Suppose a broker has a letter from authorities stating that a residence is now in school district A, and she tells this to the prospective buyer. If, in the meantime, the district has been changed back to B, she has made an honest mistake and would not be held liable. If she told a prospective buyer that a developer would pave the streets without having knowledge that it was certain, she could be held liable for misrepresentation. In such a case, the broker's license is subject to revocation for misrepresentation and she is open to lawsuit by the parties to the transaction.

Although the broker or sales representative can be held responsible for statements misrepresenting the property, she cannot be held responsible for exaggerations that are clearly not true. For example, the statement by a salesperson that "the owner is the best housekeeper in town" would not normally be construed by a prudent buyer to be factual.

Frequently, a broker is employed by a principal to negotiate, but is not to reveal the identity of the principal. In this case, the broker can either state that she is representing a principal who wants to be kept unknown or proceed as if she is buying for herself. If conditions later place the seller in a position to sue, he can sue the broker in either of these situations. If a true principal is later revealed, the seller can also sue that principal if there is cause. If, however, the broker states that she is acting for an undisclosed principal, she can state in the contract agreement that she does not assume any liability under the agreement. This clause is binding if the third party agrees to the provision by signing the contract.

Duration of Agency

Listing agreements usually specify the broker's period of employment. This period is required by law in some states. The broker is entitled to the commission only if he procures, within the specified time period, a prospect who is ready, willing, and able to purchase. If, after the agreement expires, the seller advertises on her own and a prospect appears and enters into a contract, no commission is due, even though the buyer may have previously negotiated with the broker. In other cases, the broker has been awarded the commission if the owner shows bad faith, if she deliberately delays the negotiations, or if the negotiations had begun during the listing agreement period and were concluded beyond the listing expiration time. The broker will usually protect himself by a listing agreement clause extending for 60, 90, or 120 days the right to a commission from a sale where he had negotiated with that buyer during the listing agreement period.

When no specific listing time period is agreed upon, the seller may, without liability, terminate the listing after a reasonable time. This is true even if the broker is in the process of negotiating, unless the negotiation is essentially complete. In this case, the broker's expenditure of money and time does not prevent revocation, since his taking of a listing is expected to result in his spending time and money. The definition of reasonable time will vary with the task, since it might be expected that a typical single-family residence would sell more quickly than a tract of land or a special purpose building.

If the agreement provides for extraordinary expenditures by the broker, however, the seller might be responsible for damages, if the seller terminates the listing agreement. As an example, a listing agreement which provided that the broker spend money to improve the property to make it more salable could not be arbitrarily terminated by the seller. Provisions like this make the listing agreement more like a *bilateral contract,* or *agency coupled with an interest.* A listing agreement providing that the broker advertise at least twice a week in the local newspapers identifies a legal obligation of the broker. In these cases, revocation of the agreement by the seller has not been sustained by court decisions.

The agency, of course, terminates when the real estate has been sold. After a broker has performed by providing a buyer, the owner cannot terminate the agreement. With an open listing where more than one broker can sell, it is understood that the agreement with all brokers ends when any one broker or the owner herself locates a buyer. The owner is not responsible for notifying each broker, since the brokers recognize that the property might be sold and the agency terminated at any time. In good practice, however, the owner is expected to notify the brokers within a reasonable time if the property is sold, and a prudent owner will do this as promptly as possible. In the case where a broker finds a buyer but does not notify the owner, and the owner in the meantime signs a contract with another buyer, the first broker loses his commission. It is the duty of the broker to promptly notify the owner when he finds a buyer.

Deposits and Accountability

The broker, as an agent of the principal, is responsible for monies or property entrusted to her. In some ways, the broker is acting in the position of a trustee and can be held responsible under laws pertaining to trustees as well as those regulating brokers. She must not mix funds held for the client with her own funds. A broker normally maintains a special account for holding funds of clients. State laws make mixing (*commingling*) of clients' funds with the broker's own funds a basis for revocation of license.

Without authority in the listing agreement, the broker does not have the right to accept an *earnest money deposit* from the buyer on behalf of the seller. If the contract has not been signed and the broker embezzles a deposit, the buyer must bear the loss if it cannot be recovered. The broker is, however, liable to the seller if she refunds a buyer's deposit without the seller's consent.

Agency Termination

There are several ways for an agency to terminate:

1. An agency is terminated upon completion of the desired act. If a buyer is found who is ready, willing, and able to purchase the property, the agency is completed.

2. The agency terminates when the stated period ends. The principal *may* terminate an agency at any time; however, compensation may be due to the agent for services performed, such as for advertising or time spent on the property. If the broker has provided a buyer ready, willing, and able to buy, termination of the agency will not preclude the recovery of the commission. Nor can the principal terminate a contract without commission if the agent is in the process of negotiating with a third party. If an agency is wrongfully terminated by the principal before the act is completed and the duration of the agency expires, the agent could collect damages.

3. Death or insanity of either party terminates an agency.
4. An agency *may* be terminated by bankruptcy of the principal.
5. In the case of an agency to handle real estate, the agency will be terminated if the property is destroyed.
6. An agency is terminated if the agent's license is revoked or suspended.

More Than One Broker

There are some situations that involve more than one broker in a listing or transaction. Due to the frequency of cobrokering and the use of multiple listing services, it is important to examine the relationships between the persons involved.

More than one broker employed by seller
The seller can employ more than one broker by using an open listing (whereby the owner can also sell it herself without paying a commission). The law is clear in this case that if one of the brokers, or the owner herself, sells the property, the sale terminates the agencies of the others by removing the subject property from the market. If more than one broker was involved with the same client, it may be difficult to resolve who was actually the *procuring cause.* A generally accepted rule is that, if a broker sets in motion a sequence of events without break in continuity, and a sale results, he is entitled to a commission even though he may not have conducted all of the negotiations. The mere fact that a broker showed a property first does not assure that he becomes the procuring cause. If he abandons a prospect, another broker who later shows the property and completes the sale may be considered the procuring cause. If more than one contract is offered, the seller has the right to accept any one or none of them.

Cobrokering
The practice of cobrokerage is recognized as a valuable marketing procedure for seller, buyer, and brokers. Figure 13–1 shows the fiduciary relationships between the persons involved, whether they be part of a multiple listing service or not.

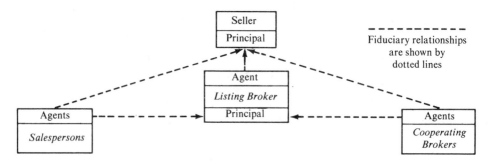

Figure 13–1
Fiduciary relationships in cobrokerage

The *cobrokers* are subagents of the listing broker as well as agents of the principal. Thus, cobrokers, their salespersons, as well as the salespersons of the listing broker owe a fiduciary duty to both the seller and the listing broker. This, however, does not remove the listing broker's responsibility if there is a problem. A fiduciary relationship requires all involved to exercise good faith, professional skill, and diligence in accordance with the instructions of either principal. Failure to discharge a duty by any of these would result in a breach of the fiduciary relationship that could make the agent (or agents) liable. Generally, it is assumed that the agents will share the commission in the event that a subagent procures a sale.

COMMISSIONS

The broker is compensated for handling transactions in the form of a *commission* or percentage of the price. The broker is entitled to the commission when he has obtained a buyer ready, willing, and able to purchase. Once this purchaser is found, even if the seller reconsiders and decides not to sell before the contract is signed, the commission is still due. Thus, the seller can decline a contract and not sell her house, but she still owes a commission to the broker. The seller has no responsibility to the buyer until the contract is signed. Even if the buyer, after the contract is signed, refuses to go through with the contract, the broker has still done his job and is owed the commission.

In conducting a brokerage operation, it is important to define the terms *ready, willing, and able* to determine when commissions are due. *Able* means to have the necessary funds to make the payments required and to close the deal within the specified time. The buyer need not actually have the funds, but she should be able to borrow them or secure a mortgage. A *willing* buyer is one who is willing to enter into a valid contract to purchase the property. The broker has produced a *ready* buyer when she is identified by name to the seller.

If the sale is not completed because of some fault of the seller, the broker is still entitled to his commission. This could occur if either the owner or spouse refuses to sign the contract or deed, if there are defects in the title, if the owner is guilty of fraud, if the buyer and seller agree to cancel the sale, or if the seller is unable or unwilling to give possession within a reasonable time.

Some agreements between the seller and broker include a clause to the effect that, if the deal is not completed, there is no commission. An equivalent provision may specify that the commission will be paid out of the sale price. In either case, the broker receives no commission if the buyer defaults or if the title cannot be cleared; however, courts have held that the arbitrary refusal by the seller to complete the contract does not mean that the commission is not due.

Other factors affect whether or not a commission is due. If the broker does not have the exclusive right to sell, the broker who has been the procuring cause in the sale is due a commission. When the owner and several brokers have been active in the process, the broker must prove that he was the procuring cause and that the commission is due him. Where more than one broker was involved, the courts have held that the broker whose efforts predominated is entitled to the commission. If a broker finds a prospect and introduces her to the owner, but the owner alone carries out the negotiations, courts have held the broker to be the procuring cause. To avoid these potential problems, brokers prefer a listing where they have the exclusive right to sell.

When an owner has hired a broker as her agent and then later, without knowing that the agent dealt with the buyer, sells the property herself to a buyer procured by the agent, the broker might be entitled to a commission. Courts have held that the seller might reasonably suspect that the buyer was procured by her agent and should check the broker regarding each prospect. It could not be reasonably expected that a buyer, trying to get a good price, would reveal this fact. In some states, however, courts would not award a commission, holding that the broker should have advised the seller of each prospect encountered. The broker can protect himself by being careful in the listing agreement and in his operations. The listing agreement should specify that the commission is due if the property is sold within a specified time to a person with whom the broker had negotiated. The broker might also advise the seller of each prospect with whom he negotiates.

Failure to Pay Commission Due

If the seller fails to pay the commission due, the broker's only remedy is to sue and obtain a judgment against the seller. The broker cannot block the sale of the property, nor can he file a lien against the property unless the listing contract provides this right. In order to enforce payment in litigation, the broker would need to (a) show that he was employed by the client, (b) show that he was the procuring cause of the sale, and (c) show that the buyer was ready, willing, and able, as defined above. In most cases, these factors are subject to various interpretations. If the listing agreement were silent as to the rate of commission, the agent would be allowed a reasonable rate. Some states require that the commission be specified in the listing agreement.

Restraint of Trade

Certain activities have been held to be a violation of antitrust laws. In Baltimore, Maryland, several real estate brokerage firms were convicted by jury of a conspiracy to raise commissions on residential properties from six to seven percent. The U.S. Department of Justice has instituted suits where real estate boards were accused of fixing commission rates in the area. Tie-in arrangements have also been declared illegal. In real estate, a *tie-in* arrangement exists, for example, when a condition of the sale of a lot is that the purchaser will not resell the lot unless she lists the property with a specific broker.

ORGANIZATION OF BROKERAGE OPERATIONS

A real estate brokerage operation, like any other business, may be organized as an individual proprietorship, a partnership, or a corporation. The individual proprietorship is the most common, especially where the enterprise is small and can be readily managed by one person. In this case, the individual proprietor owns the entire business and directs its operation. He may operate the business under his own name, a trade name, or an alias. If he operates under the alias, he must register the assumed name in the office of the local recorder and usually must have his state registration under the alias so that any person can readily determine his true identity. The objective is to prevent any broker from using an alias for fraudulent purposes.

Two or more persons can enter into a legal agreement to go into business jointly in the form of a partnership. State regulations and the partnership agreement define their responsibilities to each other and to the public. In most cases, a written agreement between the partners is required by law. It must be registered in the local recorder's office. A partnership can be either a general partnership or a special partnership. A *special partnership* is formed for a specific purpose, such as the sale of lots in a subdivision. In contrast, a partnership entered into for the purpose of carrying on a business, such as a real estate business, is called a *general partnership*. Real estate brokerage operations are often general partnerships. State laws require that all partners doing real estate business be licensed as brokers.

Incorporation is the third form of business organization. A corporation is an enterprise that has the status of an individual in many ways but is separate from the individuals operating the company. The owners of the business have a limited financial liability in its operation. A person can invest a sum in the business and be financially liable only for the amount invested. State laws regulate organizing and operating corporations. Typically, the owners invest money in exchange for shares of stock in the business. The distribution of the shares of stock represents the degree of ownership by each.

Advantages and Disadvantages

Each form of organization has advantages and disadvantages. Some of these are outlined below.

Proprietorship
Advantages:
  Ease of formation
  Personal satisfaction in running business
  Ability of owner to do as he desires
  All profits to owner
Disadvantages:
  Personal liability for business losses
  Limited capital available

Partnership
Advantages:
Greater capital available
More skills and experience
Not subject to corporation taxes
Disadvantages:
Personal liability for financial losses
Disagreements (unanimity is usually required for major decisions)
Limited sources of new capital (loans, increase in number of partners, or new contribution of existing partners)

Corporation
Advantages:
Limited liability of stockholders
Greater capital available (through sale of stock)
Life extends beyond death of any owners
Greater ease of business growth
Disadvantages:
Close state or federal regulation
Double taxation (taxes on the corporation's earnings in addition to income taxes for individual stockholders)
Greater costs in initial organization

The Broker as a Manager

In addition to fulfilling her duties as an agent, a broker has the responsibility of running a profitable business. These management responsibilities include a number of activities to various degrees depending on the size of the operation. The securing of listings is, of course, one of the important functions. The implementation of programs in advertising, publicity, and sales promotion are also important elements, just as they are in any business. Staffing and managing the sales force becomes a greater task as the size of the sales force grows. Finally, the broker has the responsibility of selecting the location for the office, defining the type of business or the type of clients to be served, financing the operation, and assuring that the operation continues on a profitable basis.

FRANCHISED BROKERS

There has been a tremendous growth in franchised brokerage operations. These franchisors do not own the individual franchises directly, but rather they lease their trade names, service marks, operating procedures, reputations, and national referral services to the individual broker. In return for this, the *franchisee*-broker is expected to follow certain prescribed methods of operation, to pay a one time fee for the franchise, and to pay a percentage of gross sales or net profits. The franchisor usually also offers training for salespeople. National advertising is another advantage of franchise operations.

Many states have enacted special laws or regulations to alleviate some problems that have occurred with franchises. Some clients have expected that, if a problem occurs with the franchisee-broker, the client can hold the franchisor responsible. This is not the case. Also, in some instances, there are two or more franchisees of the same franchisor in one metropolitan area. A client who has dealt with one of them may remember the broker only by the *service mark* and have difficulty identifying the particular broker contacted. To prevent this confusion, it is usually required that, in advertising, the broker's name be at least as prominent as the franchisor's name or service mark. The public interest is served by the efficiency of a large-scale operation, licensee training, the national referral service, and the requirement of the Lanham Act that the owner of a service mark police those it licenses.

STAFFING THE OPERATION

In expanding his business, the broker will be involved in hiring two kinds of employees. One group consists of salespeople who perform the actual showing and selling of property. These persons may be full or part-time employees. State license laws usually define a *real estate salesperson* as one employed by a licensed real estate broker to negotiate the sale, purchase, lease, or exchange of real estate for others and for compensation under the broker's direction and guidance. The salesperson, in her actions with the public, acts for her employing broker and not in her own capacity as an individual. Agreements are drawn up by a salesperson in the name of her broker and usually must be signed by the broker. Thus, the broker is responsible for the dealings of his sales force. Any litigation would be with the broker rather than with individual salespeople. Each person is, however, bound by the same rules and regulations as the broker and must exercise good faith to all parties and faithfulness to the principal.

The second category of employees, the office personnel, run the office and handle the other business functions. Both groups support the broker in his operations; the broker is responsible for the actions of each salesperson and each employee.

Staffing the brokerage office with qualified and competent personnel involves problems similar to staffing any business operation. Employees usually appreciate certain considerations from their employer, including fair wages, continuing employment in exchange for competent performance, fair working hours, pleasant working conditions, a feeling of contribution to the firm, respect, and the ability to improve earnings and status. The broker also wants employees who will contribute to his goals of growth, reputation, and profit. The broker can work towards achieving these objectives through guidelines such as these:

1. Provide a worthy firm image, as well as self-image.
2. Seek qualified job applicants through advertisements or placement offices.

3. Carefully screen applicants, as to both their physical and mental capabilities. It is better not to have the reputation of hiring frequently and letting people go who do not perform. Physical exams before employment are important. Job applications should be used to collect data on the applicants. The broker should check the references and the validity of data supplied, particularly from any prior employers. State licensing requirements also help to screen candidates for technical competence.

4. Carefully interview each applicant. Determine career objectives, reasons for entering the real estate business, previous employment and reasons for changing, family status, outside interests, education, and expected earnings.

5. After hiring, introduce the new employee to others in the office. Provide training and help during the early weeks of employement. Regular follow-up discussions with employees are important to their continuing satisfactory performance.

6. Define a specified trial period for new employees.

7. Give periodic performance appraisals to review performance, suggest improvements, and provide opportunity for increases in compensation. Keep aware of what competitors are paying to stay competitive and to retain the best salespeople.

Employee Versus Independent Contractor

Whether a real estate salesperson is an employee or an independent contractor is significant. If legally an *employee,* the broker would have to pay FICA taxes, withhold for income tax purposes, carry Workmen's Compensation Insurance, and incur liability for on-the-job accidents. In determining the form of relationship between a broker and his sales force, the Internal Revenue Service looks more at the details of the operation rather than the terminology used by a particular broker. In either case, the broker can provide office space, telephone service, and secretarial services. The following characteristics define the concept of the *independent contractor.*

1. No set office or working hours;
2. Licensee pays own license fee and professional association dues;
3. Salesperson pays own automobile and insurance costs;
4. Salesperson has freedom in selling and operating procedures;
5. There are no sales quotas;
6. Salespeople set their own vacation times;
7. There is no minimum salary, and fringe benefits and sick pay do not exist;
8. Salesperson pays own FICA tax;
9. Sales reports to the broker are not required;
10. Either party may terminate the relationship, but accrued fees earned prior to the termination are still due;
11. A contract exists between the broker and each salesperson.

Compensation

The most common method used to compensate real estate salespeople is *commission.* The employment agreement between each sales representative and the broker should specify how commissions are shared between the broker and salesperson. If a broker held a listing and one of his salespeople made the sale, the salesperson could receive from 30 to 70 percent of the commission received, depending on the employment agreement. Brokers allow experienced salespeople or broker-salespeople a greater share since they are able to handle most aspects of a transaction on their own. An inexperienced salesperson would require more guidance and assistance in carrying out a transaction.

In a typical case, the commission is paid by the seller upon selling the property and completing the transaction. If the selling price were $40,000, a typical six-percent commission would be $2,400. It is common for the salesperson who procured the listing to receive from 10 to 25 percent of the total commission upon sale of the listed property. This is also a usual practice if the property is multiple-listed. The sharing of the commission between the listing broker and the selling broker is based on individual agreements or local practice. In the example, if the listing broker's share was 50 percent, the brokerage would receive 50 percent of $2,400, or $1,200. This compensates for time and effort spent on promotion and advertising of the property. It also includes the listing salesperson's share of 10 percent of $2,400, or $240. In the example, the selling broker would receive 50 percent, since the selling effort is normally considered greater than the promotion effort, and that would give the selling broker $1,200. Suppose that the employment agreement between the selling salesperson and his broker provided 60 percent to the salesperson, then the selling salesperson would receive $0.6 \times \$1,200$, or $720; the broker gets $0.4 \times \$1,200$, or $480. The complete breakdown is as follows:

Listing salesperson	$ 240
Listing broker	960
Selling salesperson	720
Selling broker	480
Total	$2,400

Again, the breakdown varies with local custom and agreements between particular brokers. The salesperson should fully understand his employment agreement so that there will be no misunderstanding when a sale is completed.

Normally, the salesperson is expected to furnish his own automobile for business use and to pay the associated expenses such as gas and maintenance. The salesperson is entitled to take these expenses as deductions on his federal income tax return. To support the tax deduction, there should be a written agreement between the broker and salesperson. The salesperson should also keep records of mileage and expenses.

Some brokers have adopted a system whereby the salesperson gets 100 percent of the commission. In return, the salesperson pays "rent" to the broker for use of the office space, the broker's name, and other services.

SUMMARY

Real estate brokerage usually includes the function of bringing real estate buyers and sellers together. The functions of managing or leasing real property, renting, and handling property exchanges are also included. State laws regulate the operations of real estate brokers.

The success of the real estate broker depends upon his technical and managerial skills. His source of income primarily derives from commissions or fees for performing services for clients. There is an agency relationship between the broker and the client, who are the agent and principal respectively, and the authority of the broker depends upon their mutual agreement. The broker must understand his responsibilities as an agent and act accordingly with respect to the principal, cobrokers, his salespeople, and third parties. The agreement between the broker and the client should specify the duration of the agreement. It can be terminated after a reasonable time or by other means.

One of the important functions of a broker is to hold deposits belonging to others. Therefore, he is obligated to set up a special account separate from his own funds.

In addition to his responsibilities as an agent, the broker has the responsibility of managing a business. This includes financing, marketing, organizing, staffing, and controlling the organization. It is important for the broker to understand the ramifications of the employee versus independent contractor concepts, since they affect his dealings with IRS.

Recently, there has been increased franchising of real estate brokerages by national franchisors. This has resulted in advantages to clients; however, the public has often been confused by the responsibilities and obligations of the franchisor. Consequently, special regulations have been issued by state real estate commissions that apply to franchising.

TERMS AND CONCEPTS

You can check your understanding of these terms against the glossary or by review in this chapter.

Agency	Earnest money deposit
Bilateral contract	Fiduciary
Broker	Franchise
Cobroker	Principal
Commingle	Procuring cause
Commission	Ready, willing, and able

Service mark   Tie-in
Special agent   Third party

What are the differences or relationship, if any, between the following?

Actual agency and Ostensible agency   Franchisee and Broker
Agent and Agency   Listing agreement and Agency
Agent and Procuring cause   coupled with an interest
Employee and Independent contractor   Universal agent and General agent

PROBLEMS

13–1. List the three methods of organizing a real estate brokerage office. State two advantages and two disadvantages of each method.

13–2. List some things that a broker can do to achieve better broker-salesperson relationships.

13–3. Broker A had an agreement with his salesperson E that the salesperson would receive 10 percent of the total commission for each listing obtained, plus 40 percent of all monies coming to the brokerage from property sold. The multiple-listing service of which brokers A, B, and C were members provided that the listing salespeople got 10 percent of the commission, the selling broker got 50 percent, and the listing broker got 40 percent. Salesperson E listed a house for $42,000, and later sold it to a client for $40,000. The commission was six percent. Determine the commission earned by each.

13–4. In 13–3, salesperson F, working for broker B, listed a house at $54,000. Salesperson E sold the property at the list price. Determine the allocation of commission.

13–5. In 13–3, E listed a property at $64,000. Salesperson F, working for broker B, presented A with a signed offer for $64,000 and a check for $2,000 earnest money. B presented the offer to Kaiser, the owner of the house, who said he had changed his mind. Who is entitled to how much commission, if any?

13–6. What are the three types of agents? Give an example where a real estate broker could be each type of agent.

13–7. What are some functions of a broker in marketing real estate for clients?

13–8. What are some of the responsibilities of a broker from a business/finance point of view?

13–9. If you were a broker, would you prefer to have your salespeople be *employees* or *independent contractors*? What are some things to do to convince the IRS that your salespeople are what you say they are?

13–10. What actions should an agent in a fiduciary relationship be careful of, whereas an independent contractor would have less concern?

13–11. List some provisions in a listing agreement that may cause it to be considered noncancellable by the principal.

13–12. How can a franchisee-broker advertisement cause possible confusion to a client?

13–13. What actions by a broker or group of brokers might be considered restraint of trade?

SUPPLEMENTARY READINGS

Case, Frederic E. *Real Estate Brokerage.* Englewood Cliffs, N.J.: Prentice-Hall, 1965. Chapters 3 and 4.

Cyr, J. *Training and Supervising Real Estate Salesmen.* Englewood Cliffs, N.J.: Prentice-Hall, 1973.

French, William B., and Lusk, Harold F. *Law of the Real Estate Business.* Homewood, Ill.: Irwin, 1975. Chapter 11.

Hines, Mary Alice. *Principles and Practices of Real Estate.* Homewood, Ill.: Irwin, 1976. Chapter 11.

NATIONAL ASSOCIATION OF REALTORS®. *Handbook on Multiple Listing Policy.* Chicago, 1975.

O'Donnell, Paul T., and Maleady, Eugene L. *Principles of Real Estate.* Philadelphia: Saunders, 1975. Chapters 2 and 3.

Pearson, Karl G. *Real Estate Principles and Practices.* Columbus, Oh: Grid, 1978. Chapters 5–11.

Realtors National Marketing Institute. *Real Estate Office Management–People, Functions, Systems.* Chicago, 1975. Chapters 7–19.

Ring, Alfred A., and Dasso, Jerome. *Real Estate Principles and Practices.* Englewood Cliffs, N.J.: Prentice-Hall, 1977. Chapters 13 and 16.

Semenow, Robert W. *Questions and Answers in Real Estate.* Englewood Cliffs, N.J.: Prentice-Hall, 1978. Chapter 1.

Semenow, Robert W. *Selected Cases in Real Estate.* Englewood Cliffs, N.J.: Prentice-Hall, 1973, pp. 90–265.

Shenkel, William M. *Modern Real Estate Principles.* Dallas: Business Publications, 1977. Chapter 16.

Weimer, Arthur M.; Hoyt, Homer; and Bloom, George. *Real Estate.* New York: Ronald Press, 1978. Chapter 16.

Listing, Advertising, And Selling

The real estate broker deals both with sellers and prospective buyers of real estate. The broker's relationship with the seller involves obtaining properties to list. The dominating reasons that home sellers turn to real estate brokers rather than trying to sell their property on their own are because they need technical assistance and are hesitant to take risks. Many have difficulty making a decision as to the price to ask and want advice in preparing their homes for showing. The seller also needs assistance in obtaining mortgages for prospective buyers and in making contact with potential buyers.

Statistics indicate that home owners who try to sell for themselves are usually not successful. They also show that sales completed by the owners themselves often are at a lower price than with an agent, possibly due to the seller's lack of bargaining or appraisal skills. Since a prospective buyer may hesitate to tell a homeowner her reasons for rejecting the property, the owner may not get the feedback that an agent could obtain for him. Sometimes these comments can be used effectively to improve the property for future showings. Minor paint damage, pets in the house, or other factors can often be easily corrected and may make a significant difference. The agent is trained to screen prospective buyers, whereas the the home owner selling on his own would be subject to visits of people who are just looking or possibly even persons evaluating the house for future burglary. Finally, when a buyer is found, the inexperienced seller may execute an invalid contract or a contract that does not protect him against potential problems. Research indicates that about five out of six home buyers come into contact with a broker in the buying process.

LISTING AGREEMENTS

The broker can be either the agent of the seller or the agent of the buyer. When the broker is the seller's agent, the listing agreement, usually called the *listing,* serves as the contract between the seller and the broker. Listings are important since they form a reservoir of properties for future sales.

Sources of Listings

There are many ways a broker or salesperson can secure listings. The following are important sources:

1. Company reputation and previous client referrals.
2. Sold signs (another home may now be needed by sellers).
3. Classified advertising (a nice ad attracts other sellers).
4. Calling on owners who have homes for sale.
5. Expired listings of other firms.
6. Building contractors.
7. Referrals from out-of-town brokers.
8. Company personnel departments (new employees).
9. Recent promotions (desiring upgrading of home).
10. Recent marriages, deaths, or births (a different home is needed).
11. Vacant rental properties.
12. Door-to-door canvassing (some might decide to sell later).

Working With the Seller

As mentioned, the needs for technical assistance and for avoiding risks dominate sellers' reasons to use brokers to handle their property. Therefore, in his attempt to obtain a listing, the broker can concentrate his attention on providing this assistance and on building confidence in his ability as a broker to bring about a sale. Salespeople can increase their chances of obtaining a signed listing agreement in the following ways:

1. Determine recent sale prices of comparable properties.
2. Be aware of other properties for sale in the area and the degree of buyer interest.
3. Present to the seller a route to approach the property which, for example, would pass by other nice properties, and avoid those with less eye appeal.
4. Check the county offices to determine plat or other information about the property.
5. Bring measuring equipment or other materials necessary to obtain data to complete a listing form.
6. Be able to describe arrangements with sources of mortgages for potential buyers.
7. Check out school districts.

The broker or salesperson can gain the seller's confidence by any of a number of approaches:

1. Present data showing his selling record.
2. Make constructive suggestions for increasing the property's marketability.
3. Discuss the agent's methods for screening and qualifying buyers.
4. Show how contacts with brokers can increase the number of prospective buyers.
5. Describe his resources, such as number of salespeople or advertising budget.
6. Present a schedule outlining when advertising will start and other factors related to getting the project underway.
7. Explain benefits of a multiple-listing service, referral system, home protection plan, or other services.

Once a property owner selects a broker to list the property, the broker must establish the price and other terms and complete the necessary forms and documents.

Establishing Price

Establishing the price is often the broker's most difficult task. The owner naturally wants to secure the highest price for her property. She may have an unrealistic opinion about its value. Some unscrupulous brokers inflate the value of a prospective lister's property to obtain the listing; the intent is often to induce the owner to reduce the price later when early sales efforts fail. This practice is not considered ethical, especially since the broker is the seller's agent. In doing this, the broker is not acting in the best interest of his principal. This practice not only delays the sale, but also causes the broker to spend extra money, time, and effort during the time when the property is listed at an unrealistic price. Prudent brokers will refuse to list property where the owner insists upon an unrealistically high price. These brokers, in turn, often develop a reputation for rapid turnover of properties and this works to their long-term benefit. Before accepting a listing, it is the duty of the broker to advise the owner of his estimate of the property value.

A careful inspection of the property by the broker or salesperson is very important. It is necessary not only to help estimate the value but also to aid the broker to show the property favorably. In the inspection process, the broker can also make suggestions that may improve the salability of the property. He should recommend improvements that may cost little or nothing (such as rearranging the furniture to make a room appear larger) or other changes where the increased sale value would considerably exceed the cost of improvement. He should not recommend expensive changes or those that may delay sale of the property.

Residential Property Listing Contract
Exclusive Right to Sell

In consideration of your efforts to sell I/we hereby grant the exclusive right to sell, advertise and place a sign on the property described in this listing for the gross selling price of _____
$ _____

This exclusive right to sell is in force until 12:00 o'clock midnight the _____ day of _____, 19 ____.

I/we further agree to furnish a complete Abstract showing good and merchantable title to the premise, or, to furnish a Title Guaranty Policy and to convey said premises by Warranty Deed clear of all encumbrances, except the·following: _____
_____

I/we further agree that if the said property is sold or exchanged by any person during the term of this listing, or within sixty (60) days thereafter to any person with whom any negotiations were held during the term of the listing, to pay to said broker _____ % commission on whatever sale price or exchange value the deal is consummated.

OWNER _____ Date _____ 19____
OWNER _____ Date _____ 19____

In consideration of the foregoing listing and authorization the undersigned agrees to use diligence in procuring a purchaser.

_____ By _____
        Broker   Agent for Broker

Area		Address		City		$	
Listing No.		No. Rms.		Bedrooms		Baths	
Owner		Ph.		Tenant		Ph.	
Lot Size		Zoning		Taxes	Style		Age
Basement/Crawl/Slab			Garage	AC			Fireplace

Rooms	Size		Floor	Brms.	Size		Floor	Elementary	
LR				1				Jr. High	
DR				2				Private	
Fam.				3				High School	
Kit.				4				Possession	

Lender		Special Assessments: $	
Mortgage Bal.	Int. Rate	Sewer	Heat
Payment (Principal & Interest)		Water	Roof
Reason For Selling		Water Heater	
		Windows	Septic Tank
Remarks:			

Showing Instructions		Commission	
Listing Broker		Key	
This information is believed to be accurate but is not warranted	Phone		Sales Rep.

Figure 14–1

Listing form for a residential property

Figure 14–1 shows a typical listing form for a residence. A photograph of the house and an accurately completed listing form provide the basic essential data to promote the property. In a multiple-listing system, the photos and listing forms are either published in a bound book or distributed on individual pages to all brokers and salespeople for insertion in a loose-leaf notebook.

Whether bound or loose, the listings are usually grouped first as residential, then commercial, and finally lots and acreage. Within each grouping, properties are placed in price sequence. In larger cities, the listings may also be grouped by location. In some cases, there will be a separate section for suburban or farm properties. A map of the metropolitan area is always included in the booklet to assist agents in locating homes in a specific area. As brokers complete the listing form, they can also use it as a checklist for points to inspect and questions to ask of the property owner. Different types of listings are available to suit the particular needs of sellers and brokers. Figure 14–2 illustrates a typical listing form for commercial, farm, lots, and acreage properties.

TYPES OF LISTINGS

There are three basic types of listings: the open listing, the exclusive agency, and the exclusive right to sell. These differ mainly in restrictions as to who can sell and when a commission is due. The net listing is an additional category, but it overlaps the three basic categories.

Open Listing

Unless specified otherwise, a listing agreement creates an open listing. Open listings are often handled informally without a written agreement; however, some states require that all listing agreements be written. An owner who declares, "I'm ready to pay a commission to anyone who finds a buyer for my house" would, in effect, be creating an open listing. With an *open listing,* either the property owner, the broker, or other hired brokers can sell the property; however, only the broker who is actually the *procuring cause* is entitled to a commission. If the property owner sells the property herself, no commission would be paid the broker. A broker is the procuring cause, however, if he is the primary cause of the buyer and seller getting together and completing a transaction, even though the owner actually handles the sale herself.

There are several disadvantages to an open listing. One is the possibility of disagreement as to who was the procuring cause in a particular transaction. Disagreement can occur when more than one offer is made at about the same time. Brokers holding open listings will seldom do any advertising and will hesitate to exert much effort because of the uncertainty of receiving any commission. Open listings are used frequently, however, because an owner

Commercial, Farm, Lots, or Acreage
Listing Contract
Exclusive Right to Sell

In consideration of your efforts to sell I/we hereby grant the exclusive right to sell, advertise and place a sign on the property described in this listing for the gross selling price of _____
$ _____ .

I/we further agree to furnish a complete Abstract showing good and merchantable title to the premise, or, to furnish a Title Guaranty Policy and to convey said premises by Warranty Deed clear of all encumbrances, except the following: _____
_____

I/we further agree that if the said property is sold or exchanged by any person during the term of this listing, or within sixty (60) days thereafter to any person with whom any negotiations were held during the term of the listing, to pay to said broker _____% commission on whatever sale price or exchange value the deal is consummated.

OWNER _____ Date _____ 19____
OWNER _____ Date _____ 19____

In consideration of the foregoing listing and authorization the undersigned agrees to use diligence in procuring a purchaser.
By _____ By _____
        Broker   Agent or Broker

Area	Address		Town		$	
Listing No.			Lot Size			
Owner		Phone		Zoning		
Construction		Roof	Gas	Taxes		Year
Age	Floors	Water	Heat	Electricity		Basement
Parking	AC	Sewer	Rest Roms	Possession		
Schools						
Terms:				Possession		
Gross Income	$					
Less Operating Expense	$					
Net Yield	$					
Present Lease:						
Remarks						
Showing instructions:			Key:			
Listing Broker			Phone			
Salesperson			Phone			
This information is believed to be accurate but is not warranted			Commission			

Figure 14-2
Listing form for a farm or commercial property.

may not be willing to give up the right to sell her property herself in order to avoid paying a commission.

Exclusive Agency Listing

An *exclusive agency listing* bars the property owner from hiring more than one broker, but it still allows her to sell the property on her own without payment of a commission. If the property owner sells the property through her own efforts, the listing agreement comes to an end. There is then no liability on the owner's part to pay a commission. The broker will usually prefer an exclusive agency listing over an open listing since it is more likely that his efforts will result in a commission. He may be willing to advertise the property, since other brokers cannot compete. The property owner, in turn, can expect a greater effort from a particular single broker than if other brokers were also involved.

A controversy can arise from the exclusive agency agreement, however, if the seller sells directly to a person who had also dealt with the broker. Usually, the listing agreement will specify a period of time when a commission is still due if a person who has dealt with the broker buys the property directly from the seller. In some localities a *coexclusive agency* can be used whereby either of two brokers or the owner can sell.

Exclusive Right to Sell

An *exclusive right to sell* provides that the broker will receive a commission if the property is sold within the time limit prescribed in the listing agreement, regardless of who sells it. The owner can still sell the property herself; however, she would still owe a commission to the broker. Usually, the exclusive right to sell names a time after the listing agreement ends wherein the broker is still entitled to a commission if the property is sold to a party who inspected the property during the listing agreement period. A broker preparing a listing contract should clearly state in the agreement that a commission will be due if the property owner sells the property herself, since courts have held that the words "exclusive right to sell" might not be sufficiently clear to the average property seller. If both parties do not fully understand the agreement, the courts might hold that there was no meeting of the minds and that, therefore, the contract is not valid.

Net Listing

A *net listing* provides that the seller will receive a predetermined or net amount of money for the property. A net listing agreement may be any one of the three types already discussed. The broker is then considered free to set any selling price he chooses and retain all money received above the seller's specified amount. The theory is that the broker is able to receive a fee based on his selling ability and the seller is guaranteed a net amount. The net listing is illegal in some states. Its concept is basically questionable, both ethically and legally. To illustrate the problems that may arise, consider an example where the property owner wants $40,000 for her property. The broker may advertise the property at $44,000. Assume that he showed the property to a customer, and the customer made an offer of $40,200. This would place the broker in an unfair position, especially if he had spent considerable funds in promotion of the property. The broker must present each offer to the property owner. If the offer of $40,200 was accepted by the owner, the broker would receive only $200 for his efforts. On the other hand, a broker may get an unsuspecting client to set a "net" amount far below market value and pocket an exorbitant fee.

To avoid this conflict of interest, a broker, if offered a net listing by the seller, normally should calculate a fair commission and offer to list the property at a list price calculated as follows:

$$\text{Owner wants} \qquad\qquad \$40,000$$
$$\text{Commission desired} \qquad\qquad 6\% \text{ of price}$$

$$\text{Price} = \$40,000 + 0.06 \times \text{Price}$$
$$\text{Price} - .06 \text{ Price} = \$40,000$$
$$\text{Price} = \frac{\$40,000}{1 - 0.06} = \frac{\$40,000}{0.94} = \$42,553$$

If sold at $42,553, the commission is $0.06 \times \$42,553 = \$2,553$, and the owner gets the balance of $40,000. Establishing a listing price this way reduces the possible conflict of interest or other problems that may arise.

MULTIPLE-LISTING SERVICE

A *multiple-listing service* (MLS) consists of a formal arrangement between real estate brokers in an area where any member broker has the opportunity to sell listings held by other members. Listing agreements entered into between member brokers and property owners provide that the listing will be distributed to other member brokers. The advantage to the seller is that she receives greater coverage, since many brokers can show the property. The advantage to the potential buyer is that one agent can show all of the multiple-listed properties. The buyer need not spend time telling several agents about his needs and desires. The broker, too, will be more likely to find a suitable property for a particular customer.

Commissions

The commission rate is a matter for negotiation between the seller and the broker at the time the listing agreement is made. Multiple-listing services recommend a listing contract period (usually about 90 days) for residential properties. The listing period for commercial, industrial, or agricultural properties usually ranges from 90 to 180 days. These periods allow the broker a reasonable time to advertise and sell the property. Any indications of rate fixing by local real estate boards are coming under the scrutiny of the Federal Trade Commission as violations of antitrust laws.

Typical commission ranges are as follows:

1. Single-family residence—four to seven percent;
2. Commercial—six to ten percent;
3. Farmland—two to five percent.

There is a growing tendency to use flat rates, however, such as $2,000 for a residential property of any price.

In the usual multiple-listing arrangement, the commission is divided between the listing broker and the selling broker in accordance with rules agreed upon by the member brokers. The salesperson obtaining the listing gets a portion of his broker's share. The salesperson's listing and selling commission may vary from area to area or in accordance with the agreement between him and his broker.

Procedures

Brokers and salespeople pay an initiation fee for joining the multiple-listing bureau in their locality. They also pay a monthly membership fee for which they receive copies of the listings or weekly books showing all multiple-listed properties for sale in the area. Multiple-listing services normally require that all multiple-listed properties be taken as an exclusive right to sell listing. Some boards allow the seller one or two "named exceptions" in the exclusive right to sell contract. In other words, if a seller had been trying to sell the property herself prior to signing an exclusive right to sell listing contract, she may specifically name one or two potential buyers with whom she had been dealing. If either of those two potential buyers buys the property during the term of the listing, the seller need not pay the listing broker the sales commission. Boards in some areas permit a broker to hold a listing agreement for a specified number of days before it is given to the multiple-listing service. During this period, the listing broker can attempt to sell the property on his own. The prudent seller, however, may object to this lapse and may specify in the agreement that the listing be provided to the multiple-listing service within a specified number of days or immediately.

MLS Policy

Multiple-listing services subscribe to certain policies dealing with what the service does and does not do. The following state some of the important provisions:

1. An MLS does not fix or recommend commission rates, nor does it suggest sharing arrangements.
2. An MLS has neither dealings with nor responsibilities to buyers or sellers.

3. There are no restrictions on cooperation with nonmembers nor on sharing arrangements between members.

4. An MLS does not regulate advertising or the use of "For Sale" or "Sold" signs.

5. An MLS does not restrict political activities of members.

6. An MLS does not reject listings based on price, quality of property, or rate of commission.

7. It is open to any REALTOR® who wants to join.

8. The preferred method of financial support is a monthly fee per member plus a fee per listing.

9. Net listings are not accepted, and all contingencies must be noted on the listing agreement.

10. Listed properties can be withdrawn at any time.

11. Negotiations are to be handled through the listing broker.

12. Statistical marketing data is compiled by MLS.

Local Market Data

The United States is actually a set of markets or regions whose activities or production are summed up to create a Gross National Product (GNP). Although the GNP may continually grow from year to year, some local markets grow faster and others may actually decline. Real estate markets are local. The distance from one market to another may be as close as 50 or 100 miles. The following economic factors have a strong bearing on a local real estate market:

1. Percentage of persons unemployed;
2. Sales;
3. Total personal income;
4. Industries moving in or out of area.

Local sales data is often available to brokers through the local multiple-listing service that publishes weekly and quarterly summaries of sales data for the area. Table 14–1 shows a typical report. This type of information can be used by a real estate broker to

1. Compare quantity and dollar figures to earlier years;
2. Show weekly trends;
3. Compute the firm's share of the market.

A broker can use the following ratios to judge her performance, as well as the local market performance:

1. Percent of homes in area for sale;
2. Sales volume compared to prior years;
3. Her share of property sales;
4. Her share of listings.

Table 14-1

Weekly data compiled by a typical multiple-listing service

Weekly Market Analysis

Total number of active listings	621
$ Amount of all active listings	38,248,121.00
Total number of new listings	68
$ Amount of all new listings	3,959,831.00
Total number of sold listings	31
$ Amount of all sold listings	1,463,857.00
Total number of co-op sales	17
$ Amount of all co-op sales	684,200.00
Average listed prices:	
All active units	59,841.40
Expireds and withdrawns	50,160.24
All sold units	46,291.18
Actual sold price average	47,221.20
Average list-to-sale price difference	1,118.04
% of sale price to list price	96.42%
Average days on market (actives)	61 days
Average days on market (solds)	48 days

PROMOTION

Selling is aided by promotion, which includes activities such as advertising, public relations, holding open houses, and distributing brochures or publications. These activities help present the broker's products or professional abilities to prospective purchasers or sellers and to the public in general. Brokers who concentrate on residential properties will have different promotion strategies from brokers who emphasize commercial or farm real estate.

Promotion is an important part of the real estate broker's effort, just as marketing is part of any business effort. As such, it requires a strategy, a budget, planning, and controls, all as an integral part of the brokerage operation. Strategy considers what the broker has to sell and who the potential customers will be. It also considers the constraints of the resources available, such as number of salespeople and financial resources, as well as the resources of competitors. Thus, strategy involves factors external to the operation as well as internal aspects.

Sometimes promotion is used as a device to mislead by providing improper or insufficient information; however, research has shown that misleading promotion usually does more harm than good. Promotion should be better utilized as a method of providing information to prospective buyers to help them make good purchases.

Advertising

Real estate advertising can be classified in several ways—according to its objective, the medium used, and the form of message presentation. Understanding each of these factors is necessary to select a good advertising strategy and implement it successfully.

Kinds of advertising and their objectives

Advertising can be classified as specific advertising, name advertising, and institutional advertising. *Specific advertising* promotes individual parcels of real estate or particular related services. The objective is to sell or rent a specific property described in the ad or to secure customers for the broker's services. Specific advertising usually appears in newspapers, brochures, or flyers.

The second category is *name advertising.* The purpose of name advertising is to display the name of the firm before the public. This advertising aims to enhance the firm's reputation and image in the eyes of potential home buyers or sellers. Newspaper advertising can accomplish this goal, as can radio or television announcements, billboards, office signs, or activity news items in newspapers.

Institutional advertising has as its objective the creation of a favorable public opinion toward the real estate brokerage business. It is intended to influence public opinion so that potential sellers or buyers will select a broker rather than sell or buy on their own. Membership or other fees provide the funds to support much of the institutional advertising.

Advertising media

Newspapers are the most widely used medium for advertising by real estate brokers. They are used to implement specific, name, and institutional advertising. Classified advertising in newspapers is used primarily for specific advertising of property, but the ads also are designed for name advertising. Brokers group their specific listings into attractive arrangements not only to exhibit their available listings, but also to place their names attractively before the public. A seller in the process of selecting a broker often looks in the classified section of the local newspaper to choose a broker who uses attractive advertising. Thus, the specific ads also act as name advertising.

Since potential buyers are interested in up-to-the-minute information on available property, the daily newspaper serves the broker well. Sunday newspapers tend to carry a greater number of listings, since the local potential buyers often have more leisure time to carry out their search on Sundays. In addition, out of town buyers often look for real estate on weekends.

Other advertising media suitable for real estate brokers' ads are magazines, radio, television, outdoor signs, booklets, home shows, and other displays. Industrial properties, rural estates, farms, or unusual properties are often advertised in nationally distributed specialty or trade magazines that reach particular groups of readers. Whereas newspapers have a short life, magazines often lie around and are read over periods of months in libraries, waiting rooms, and so forth. Signs, booklets, and displays are primarily intended to bring the broker's name before the public.

Real estate advertising is often positioned to provide notice to people who visit specific places such as motels, restaurants, or personnel departments of local industries. Some brokers maintain connections with a referral network of brokers in other cities to get contacts with potential buyers before their families actually visit the community.

Billboards, bus signs, and signs on real estate offices are common ways to reach the public. "For Sale" and "Sold" signs on listed properties are one of the best means of providing name advertising. These signs provide name advertising for the broker, as well as specific advertising for the individual house. The billboard in Fig. 14–3 meets the criteria: (a) the copy is simple enough for drivers to read; (b) the elements catch the eye; and (c) the name of company is large enough to easily read.

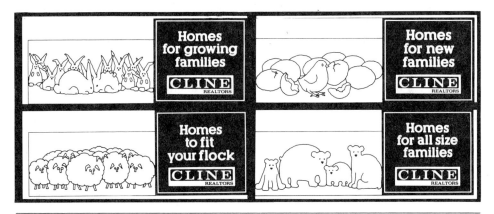

Source: Cline REALTORS®, Cincinnati, Ohio. Material is protected by international copyright. Billboard advertising is being marketed through Identity Campaigns, Inc., 565 East 4500 South, Suite A210, Salt Lake City, Utah 84107. Permission granted limits reprint use to textbook publication only.

Figure 14–3
Example of billboard advertising

HOME BUYERS

Motivations

Studies show that lack of knowledge of real estate and perceived high risks in selling are the primary motivators for potential home buyers to select the services of real estate brokers. About 80 percent of home buyers come into contact with one or more real estate brokers during the search process, usually to help them with difficult decisions. The problems that buyers must resolve relate to determining the price that they can actually afford to pay, the right time to purchase, where to buy, and the means to obtain financing. The decisions are easier for people who have previously purchased a home than for first-time buyers, so that a higher percentage of first-time buyers rely on brokers. Buyers new to an area also have more need for technical information. In addition, they often have only a short time in which to look and decide, which forces them to place greater reliance upon a broker. (However, sometimes potential buyers suspect brokers of bias and therefore turn to friends or relatives or rely on their own intuition in the home buying process.)

Brokers and salespeople should try to understand why people buy rather than rent homes. Several significant advantages of home ownership were discussed in greater detail in Chapter 9. The salesperson can use these to convince a potential buyer of the advantages of home ownership.

Sources of Buyers

Real estate brokers seek potential buyers from a number of sources. People moving to the area from other places, usually as a result of a change in job, provide an important source. Although advertising in local newspapers and listings in the yellow pages provides some contact with these people, many brokers count upon referrals through company personnel departments, banks, and others. Some brokers also have arrangements with brokers in other cities. People selling their homes in one city provide early contacts when they let their broker know of their plans to move to another particular city.

Prospective Buyer Analysis

Prospective buyers for real estate can be grouped into three categories: (a) those who need a place to live; (b) those who prefer a place different from their present residence; and (c) those who are primarily looking but not yet seriously interested. The constraints and motivations of buyers from each group will be different. A large portion of those in the first group are moving from another area. The home selection process is affected by time requirements, since the family does not want to be divided for a lengthy period. A frequent problem of these buyers is the inability to sell their currently owned property. These people need to find a satisfactory place to live within cost and time constraints.

The second group of potential buyers simply wants to move to a different property, whether bigger, smaller, better located, or otherwise different. In this case, the prospective buyer can afford to inspect a number of alternative properties carefully over a period of time while searching for a bargain or a property that meets all desires. In this case, the broker or salesperson can expect to spend more time and effort to conclude a transaction.

The broker in either case should spend time to evaluate and qualify each prospective buyer carefully to serve the client better and to make the most efficient use of his own time. It does not serve the best interests of either the client, the seller, or the broker to show properties not within the buyer's price and need constraints. This does not, however, preclude the possibility that prospective buyers will change their constraints. This possibility should always be kept in mind. In almost all cases, one or more of their desires will have to be set aside as the available alternatives are considered. Frequently, buyers will learn early that their monetary limits were too low for the quality of home desired. Also, their specifications may change as they are further exposed to properties. The broker should determine each client's resources and the type of property that will meet the client's needs by asking questions. The following information is needed to evaluate a prospective client's needs and qualifications:

1. Name, address, and telephone number;
2. Business address and telephone number;
3. Desired price range for property;
4. Address of present property owned and whether it is presently for sale or will need to be sold before buying another home;
5. Money available for a down payment; family income, and desired monthly payment;
6. Marital status and family size;
7. Type home desired (size, style, and location);
8. Why client came to this brokerage office;
9. Reasons for moving;
10. How long they have been looking;
11. Are they working with other brokers;
12. What homes they have looked at;
13. Any special needs (i.e., basement, fireplace, garage, etc.);
14. If right home is found, is there anything to prevent them from purchasing immediately.

Once this analysis of the buyer has been completed, the salesperson can make his plans and formulate a strategy to serve the buyer's interest and also to plan the most efficient use of his own time.

THE SALESPERSON

Making a living as a real estate salesperson involves two primary tasks: (a) obtaining property to list and (b) securing buyers for property. Success depends upon many facets, such as understanding the motivations of sellers and buyers, knowing advertising and selling techniques, and having the ability to close a sale by bringing the parties into an agreement.

Attributes of Salespeople

Surveys have shown that people in the process of buying homes prefer certain characteristics displayed by salespeople, including the following:

1. Friendly, cooperative, and unpressuring;
2. Willingness to help and give time to the customer;
3. Sincerity, honesty, and straightforward approach;

4. Providing a source of helpful information;
5. Efficient planning, showing properties of interest, and following through on buyer's requests for more information;

In contrast, certain practices used by some salespeople have been identified as the most negative:

1. Showing homes that did not fit needs;
2. Misrepresentation or attempt to mislead;
3. Using pressure techniques or being too aggressive;
4. Not taking adequate time;
5. Lack of knowledge about homes, locations, financing, or other pertinent information.

Selling Ability

The art of "salesmanship" is sometimes considered to be dependent upon personality and persistence. In the real estate business, possibly more than in other sales occupations, the technical capabilities and approaches used by the broker and salesperson are usually more significant. A systematic sales approach will include an analysis and frequent reanalysis of the needs of the potential buyer, a systematic evaluation of the available properties listed, a careful plan to show the properties efficiently so that the buyer's time is not wasted, and providing factual information that the buyer needs to make the proper decisions.

As the seller's agent, the broker must help the seller list the property at a realistic price, and he must also provide advice on preparing the property for showing. This coordinated approach, working with both the seller and buyer, and particularly considering responsibility to the seller, can result in success-ful selling and satisfied buyers and sellers. Satisfied buyers and sellers make future prospective clients themselves who also recommend other potential clients.

Providing proper information to prospective buyers begins with adequate knowledge of the community. Basic knowledge of transportation, schools, shopping facilities, churches, and other important facilities is required. The second necessary element is a broad knowledge of the real estate market in general, including proper pricing and sources of financing. The third element is understanding the buyer and his needs, financial abilities, and personal desires. Keeping current on available properties is the fourth requirement. Knowledge of location, lot size, home size, age, and construction, and existing mortgage money availability are all necessary to respond to the queries of the buyer as the property is shown. Successful salespeople are able to guide the prospective buyer to a decision, without pressing the prospect into uncomfort-able situations or beyond his desired constraints.

Some salespeople have successfully used the *locational farm concept.* This means that the salesperson concentrates efforts in a specific geographic area within the local community.

SUMMARY

The degree of success of a broker or salesperson depends primarily upon his ability to secure listings from sellers and then to consummate sales to prospective buyers. This ability depends heavily upon technical knowledge of real estate. It also depends upon understanding the motivations of sellers and buyers and being able to satisfy their needs and provide the services they expect.

The open listing, exclusive agency listing, and exclusive right to sell are the three basic types of listing contracts. Most real estate brokers, as well as multiple-listing services, prefer the exclusive right to sell, which provides that the broker earns a commission regardless of who sells the property, as long as a ready, willing, and able buyer is found within the period specified in the listing agreement.

The success of the broker also depends upon promotion. The real estate broker has several advertising media open to him, but the newspaper is the most heavily used. Well-designed advertising not only helps the broker to sell the advertised properties, but also attracts potential buyers and other sellers to the broker.

TERMS AND CONCEPTS

You can check your understanding of these terms against the glossary or by review in this chapter.

Locational farm concept	Open listing
Multiple listing service	Procuring cause
Net listing	

What are the differences or relationships, if any, between the following?

Exclusive agency listing and Exclusive right to sell
Name advertising and Institutional advertising and Specific advertising

PROBLEMS

14–1.   Joanne Cushing, a salesperson for C & R Realty, has talked with Bob Axel, who has been trying to sell his home on his own. It is a three-bedroom home, and Bob has priced it at $43,000. Bob has asked Joanne to come over and discuss the possibility of having an open listing of the property with C & R Realty. Make a list of materials and information that Joanne should bring to the meeting with Bob.

14–2.   What type of listing should Joanne recommend? Make a list of information to present to Bob to justify this recommendation.

14–3.   If Bob desires a net listing at $42,000, what listing price would you suggest to obtain a commission of six percent?

14–4.   After listing Bob's property, Joanne receives a long distance call from Julio Marcos who is coming to town on Saturday to look for a home. Prepare a list of questions to ask Mr. Marcos.

14–5.   What are the different types of advertising and their objectives?

14–6.   What are some quantitative measures of local market activity that the broker could compile from MLS data?

14–7.   What are some quantitative measures that a broker could use to determine the performance of his business?

14–8.   What are some quantitative measures that a salesperson could use to compare her performance with that of other salespersons?

14–9.   Discuss whether a real estate salesperson is selling a product or a service.

14–10. Visit a broker's office or a model home. Make a list of the promotional devices used. Which do you think are most effective? Least effective? What other devices should have been used?

14–11. How might a real estate firm evaluate which of its advertising methods are most effective?

14–12. Cut out the classified ad section from a local newspaper and select what you judge to be the five most effective ads. What were your criteria for the selections?

SUPPLEMENTARY READINGS

Conover, Joseph A. *Thirty Days to Great New Success in Real Estate Sales.* Englewood Cliffs, N.J.: Executive Reports Corporation, 1973.

McMichael, Stanley A. *How to Operate a Real Estate Business.* Englewood Cliffs, N.J.: Prentice-Hall, 1967.

McMichael, Stanley A. *The Real Estate Salesman's Handbook.* Chicago: NATIONAL ASSOCIATION OF REALTORS®, 1969.

O'Donnell, Paul T., and Maleady, Eugene L. *The Practice of Real Estate.* Philadelphia: Saunders, 1978. Chapters 1–12.

Ring, Alfred A., and Dasso, Jerome. *Real Estate Principles and Practices.* Englewood Cliffs, N.J.: Prentice-Hall, 1977. Chapter 14.

Weimer, Arthur M.; Hoyt, Homer; and Bloom, George F. *Real Estate.* New York: Ronald Press, 1978. Chapter 16.

Wigginton, F. Peter. *The Complete Guide to Profitable Real Estate Listings.* Homewood, Ill.: Dow Jones-Irwin, 1977.

Ethical and Professional Considerations

Most professional business people—whether lawyers, bankers, or engineers—although competitive with each other in their day-to-day dealings, work together to implement the ethical and professional aspects of their professions. In a specific city or town, real estate brokers compete to list property and to make sales. At the same time, these brokers work together to maintain ethical standards in their dealings with the public, their clients, and with fellow brokers. In most states, statutes also govern certain ethical considerations. These standards are more important in real estate brokerage than they are in some other businesses where the clients and the public are more familiar with the service performed or the product provided. As we know, over a lifetime, a person may only use a broker's services once or twice and, therefore, may not comprehend all of the numerous and involved details. The typical real estate transaction may include appraisal, financing, and other elements with which most clients are unfamiliar. Furthermore, the transaction is important because of the large amount of money involved. The sale or purchase of a home may affect the life earnings and savings of a family.

ETHICS

Ethics means different things to different people and the rules are not as rigid as those described in the chapters on real estate law. Often, ethics deals with subjective factors, but these factors do not reduce the importance of ethics in the real estate business. Most communities have a large number of indepen-

Figure 15-1

NATIONAL ASSOCIATION OF REALTORS®

Code of Ethics[1]

PREAMBLE...

Under all is the land. Upon its wise utilization and widely allocated ownership depend the survival and growth of free institutions and of our civilization. The REALTOR® should recognize that the interests of the nation and its citizens require the highest and best use of the land and the widest distribution of land ownership. They require the creation of adequate housing, the building of functioning cities, the development of productive industries and farms, and the preservation of a healthful environment.

Such interests impose obligations beyond those of ordinary commerce. They impose grave social responsibility and a patriotic duty to which the REALTOR® should dedicate himself, and for which he should be diligent in preparing himself. The REALTOR®, therefore, is zealous to maintain and improve the standards of his calling and shares with his fellow-REALTORS® a common responsibility for its integrity and honor. The term REALTOR® has come to connote competency, fairness, and high integrity resulting from adherence to a lofty ideal of moral conduct in business relations. No inducement of profit and no instruction from clients ever can justify departure from this ideal.

In the interpretation of his obligation, a REALTOR® can take no safer guide than that which has been handed down through the centuries, embodied in the Golden Rule, "Whatsoever ye would that men should do to you, do ye even so to them."

Accepting this standard as his own, every REALTOR® pledges himself to observe its spirit in all of his activities and to conduct his business in accordance with the tenets set forth below.

ARTICLE 1

The REALTOR® should keep himself informed on matters affecting real estate in his community, the state, and nation so that he may be able to contribute responsibly to public thinking on such matters.

ARTICLE 2

In justice to those who place their interests in his care, the REALTOR® should endeavor always to be informed regarding laws, proposed legislation, governmental regulations, public policies and current market conditions in order to be in a position to advise his clients properly.

ARTICLE 3

It is the duty of the REALTOR® to protect the public against fraud, misrepresentation, and unethical practices in real estate transactions. He should endeavor to eliminate in his community any practices which could be damaging to the public or bring discredit to the real estate profession. The REALTOR® should assist the government agency charged with regulating the practices of brokers and salesmen in his state.

ARTICLE 4

The REALTOR® should seek no unfair advantage over other REALTORS® and should conduct his business so as to avoid controversies with other REALTORS®.

ARTICLE 5

In the best interests of society, of his associates, and his own business, the REALTOR® should willingly share with other REALTORS® the lessons of his experience and study for the benefit of the public, and should be loyal to the Board of REALTORS® of his community and active in its work.

ARTICLE 6

To prevent dissension and misunderstanding and to assure better service to the owner, the REALTOR® should urge the exclusive listing of property unless contrary to the best interest of the owner.

---

[1]The code was adopted in 1913 and was amended or revised in 1924, 1928, 1950, 1951, 1952, 1956, 1961, 1962, and 1974.

Figure 15-1, continued

ARTICLE 7

In accepting employment as an agent, the REALTOR® pledges himself to protect and promote the interests of the client. This obligation of absolute fidelity to the client's interest is primary, but it does not relieve the REALTOR® of the obligation to treat fairly all parties to the transaction.

ARTICLE 8

The REALTOR® shall not accept compensation from more than one party, even if permitted by law, without the full knowledge of all parties to the transaction.

ARTICLE 9

The REALTOR® shall avoid exaggeration, misrepresentation, or concealment of pertinent facts. He has an affirmative obligation to discover adverse factors that a reasonably competent and diligent investigation would disclose.

ARTICLE 10

The REALTOR® shall not deny equal professional services to any person for reasons of race, creed, sex, or country of national origin. The REALTOR® shall not be a party to any plan or agreement to discriminate against a person or persons on the basis of race, creed, sex, or country of national origin.

ARTICLE 11

A REALTOR® is expected to provide a level of competent service in keeping with the Standards of Practice in those fields in which the REALTOR® customarily engages.

The REALTOR® shall not undertake to provide specialized professional services concerning a type of property or service that is outside his field of competence unless he engages the assistance of one who is competent on such types of property or service, or unless the facts are fully disclosed to the client. Any person engaged to provide such assistance shall be so identified to the client and his contribution to the assignment should be set forth.

The REALTOR® shall refer to the Standards of Practice of the National Association as to the degree of competence that a client has a right to expect the REALTOR® to possess, taking into consideration the complexity of the problem, the availability of expert assistance, and the opportunities for experience available to the REALTOR.®

ARTICLE 12

The REALTOR® shall not undertake to provide professional services concerning a property or its value where he has a present or contemplated interest unless such interest is specifically disclosed to all affected parties.

ARTICLE 13

The REALTOR® shall not acquire an interest in or buy for himself, any member of his immediate family, his firm or any member thereof, or any entity in which he has a substantial ownership interest, property listed with him, without making the true position known to the listing owner. In selling property owned by himself, or in which he has any interest, the REALTOR® shall reveal the facts of his ownership or interest to the purchaser.

ARTICLE 14

In the event of a controversy between REALTORS® associated with different firms, arising out of their relationship as REALTORS®, the REALTORS® shall submit the dispute to arbitration in accordance with the regulations of their board or boards rather than litigate the matter.

ARTICLE 15

If a REALTOR® is charged with unethical practice or is asked to present evidence in any disciplinary proceeding or investigation, he shall place all pertinent facts before the proper tribunal of the member board or affiliated institute, society, or council of which he is a member.

ARTICLE 16

When acting as agent, the REALTOR® shall not accept any commission, rebate, or profit on expenditures made for his principal-owner, without the principal's knowledge and consent.

ARTICLE 17

The REALTOR® shall not engage in activities that constitute the unauthorized practice of law and shall recommend that legal counsel be obtained when the interest of any party to the transaction requires it.

Figure 15–1, continued

ARTICLE 18

The REALTOR® shall keep in a special account in an appropriate financial institution, separated from his own funds, monies coming into his possession in trust for other persons, such as escrows, trust funds, clients' monies and other like items.

ARTICLE 19

The REALTOR® shall be careful at all times to present a true picture in his advertising and representations to the public. He shall neither advertise without disclosing his name nor permit any person associated with him to use individual names or telephone numbers, unless such person's connection with the REALTOR® is obvious in the advertisement.

ARTICLE 20

The REALTOR®, for the protection of all parties, shall see that financial obligations and commitments regarding real estate transactions are in writing, expressing the exact agreement of the parties. A copy of each agreement shall be furnished to each party upon his signing such agreement.

ARTICLE 21

The REALTOR® shall not engage in any practice or take any action inconsistent with the agency of another REALTOR®.

ARTICLE 22

In the sale of property which is exclusively listed with a REALTOR®, the REALTOR® shall utilize the services of other brokers upon mutually agreed upon terms when it is in the best interests of the client.

Negotiations concerning property which is listed exclusively shall be carried on with the listing broker, not with the owner, except with the consent of the listing broker.

ARTICLE 23

The REALTOR® shall not publicly disparage the business practice of a competitor nor volunteer an opinion of a competitor's transaction. If his opinion is sought and if the REALTOR® deems it appropriate to respond, such opinion shall be rendered with strict professional integrity and courtesy.

ARTICLE 24

The REALTOR® shall not directly or indirectly solicit the services or affiliation of an employee or independent contractor in the organization of another REALTOR® without prior notice to said REAL-TOR.®

Note: Where the word REALTOR® is used in this Code and Preamble, it shall be deemed to include REALTOR-ASSOCIATE®. Pronouns shall be considered to include REALTORS® and REALTOR-ASSOCIATES® of both genders.

dent brokers, and each broker has considerable freedom of action in carrying out business. The ethical or unethical practices of a few brokers or salespeople can reflect on the profession as a whole within a certain community. These examples illustrate some practices that might occur.

Example 1:   Ms. Adams, a broker, knew that two other brokers had offered to list the Bayes' home at $55,000. Ms. Adams told the owners that she would list it at $65,000, and she did not mention that this was much higher than a recent sale price for a similar home. Is this ethical?

Example 2:   Mr. Broker held an exclusive listing on the Karls' home, and Mr. and Mrs. Prospect had just given him an offer at the listed price. Mr. Broker knew that Mr. Karl had become very ill two days before and that the Karls would probably not be able to afford the new home they were planning to build. Mr. Broker knew, however, that by law the Karls would be bound to sell and he would earn a commission. Should he take the offer?

In some cases, a broker will be faced with decisions of ethics versus immediate returns. As with any business, however, the ethical way may preserve the good company image and do the business the most good in the long run.

How can we judge what is ethical and what is not? The Code of Ethics of the NATIONAL ASSOCIATION OF REALTORS® (Figure 15–1) establishes a set of guidelines. State laws and/or regulations define certain actions that are not permitted. If a situation arises that is not defined by either of these, a broker or salesperson might ask, "What if the public knew I did this?"

ETHICS IN PRACTICE

State laws, professional association codes, and tradition have resulted in a substantial number of practices that are generally considered ethical and others considered unethical. Most persons engaged in the real estate business try to be completely ethical in all aspects of their work. There are always a few, however, who may not act ethically. In some cases, the novice may act unethically without realizing the implications. It is with these thoughts that we explore ethics in practice.

Much of the remainder of this chapter will center around illustrative examples. Because state statutes and regulations differ, some actions cited as unethical may also be unlawful in some states. Even in these cases, however, there are always borderline cases requiring interpretation.

Ethics in Listing a Client's Property

In the example cited earlier, a broker offered to list a property at $65,000 even though she knew that comparable properties had sold closer to the $55,000 price suggested by other brokers. Her reasoning may have been that, once she got the listing, she could later recommend a drop in the listed price.

It is the responsibility of a real estate broker to advise a prospective client of the fair market value of a property. She should suggest that a property appraiser be consulted if the appraisal is beyond her own capabilities. It is unethical to list a property either too high or too low without advising the owner of the reasonable market value. To do this would violate the broker's duty as an agent of the seller. It is clearly unethical to suggest a high list price to a client as a strategy to obtain a listing.

Consider Brooks Realty. They have acquired a reputation of fast turnover of the properties they list. Ms. Ames, in hearing of this reputation, offered to list her house with Brooks at $69,500. Mr. Brooks, on examination of the property, stated he could take the listing only if the price were $66,000. He cited recent comparable sales. In this case, Mr. Brooks had built his reputation on selling his clients' property within a reasonable time, and he felt that his reputation was more important that just another listing. He might also have considered that the time he spent showing a home priced too high could be better spent elsewhere.

Some brokers think in terms of never turning down any listing on the basis that they might sell the property. This is clearly unethical. If a broker lacks the expertise needed to handle a certain type of industrial property, for example, the listing should not be accepted. If a broker becomes ill and cannot serve his principal in a diligent manner, the listing should be given up. If a property is in an area of the city distant from the broker's office where he cannot properly handle it, he should refuse to list it.

A broker who is a member of a multiple-listing service should distribute the listing information to other brokers immediately. It is unethical to delay distribution and try to sell it himself.

As another example illustrating ethics, a broker should not take listings that compete with his own operations. If the broker owns lots for sale, he could not usually be expected to adequately serve a seller of similar lots.

A listing whereby the broker will buy the property at a lower price if it is not sold in 60 days also presents ethical conflicts. If the purchase and resale prospects look good, the broker might not give the principal diligent service as his agent.

Relationships with Buyers

Although the broker has primary responsibilities as agent of the seller, the broker also has duties and obligations to the buyer. The stated primary purpose of real estate broker and salesperson licensing is to protect the public. One way to do this is to educate licensees so that they are aware of the legal and professional aspects of the job of broker or salesperson. Many buyers have never owned or purchased a home and depend upon the licensee for guidance.

In some cases, the broker will be the agent of the buyer. If a prospect came to town and asked of a broker, "Can you find me a home with about five to ten acres," the broker would then act for the buyer in this search. If it turned out that the broker could match up one of his listed properties with the buyer's needs, the broker would be obligated to inform both parties if he expects to collect a commission from each.

Buyer qualification

The process whereby the broker obtains informaton about the buyer's needs, family size, income, available down payment, and so on is called **buyer qualification**. Both ethically and from the standpoint of efficient use of everyone's time, the broker should restrict showings to properties that the buyer can reasonably be expected to purchase. Also it would not be ethical to lead the buyer into a contract where the monthly payments would be beyond her abilities.

Misrepresentation

The term **misrepresentation** relates to false statements. A victim of misrepresentation can recover in a court of law; however, certain elements must be proved:

1. That a representation regarding a material fact was made as a statement of fact, which was untrue and known to be untrue by the party making it, or else recklessly or innocently made;
2. That it was made for the purpose of inducing the other party to act upon it;
3. That the other party did, in fact, rely on the representation; and
4. The other party was damaged by his reliance upon the statement.

A recent case can be cited—*Ford vs. Cournale 36 C.A. 3d 172* (Ca. 1977). This was an action for misrepresentation against a real estate broker and his sales representative. In this case, the court found that the broker had misrepresented facts about the income of an apartment house by assuring the purchaser that the apartment house would give her a net income of between $700 and $900 per month. Neither the broker nor the salesperson made any check on the expenses in connection with the operation of the apartment house. The salesperson admitted that the statement was based on 100 per cent occupancy and that he knew the vacancy figures were not and could not be totally accurate. The broker also admitted that he did not expect the purchaser to conduct an independent investigation or check any other information, and he was aware that she was depending on his representations. The court allowed the plaintiff a judgment against the broker.

There are other possible serious consequences of misrepresentation:

1. The buyer may be able to cancel the contract for sale of the property.
2. The buyer may be able to collect damages, as above.
3. The principal, if damaged, may refuse to pay a commission or collect damages.
4. The broker or salesperson may lose his or her license.

No longer entirely valid is the old law of *caveat emptor* (let the buyer beware) which held that, if the buyer failed to discover defects, that was his bad luck. Courts are getting away from this concept.

We will now discuss the different types of misrepresentation.

Intentional misrepresentation—fraud

A seller (or salesperson) states that a basement is dry even though he knows that water comes in when it rains. In this case, the person making the statement knows that it is false; hence, this is called *intentional misrepresentation*. Reckless or careless statements are usually taken by courts to be intentional also.

Negligent, without due diligence

A broker may be careless or negligent in his statements and, as a result, someone is damaged; for example, a broker advertises a three-family apartment with potential income of $480 per month. After the sale, the buyer learns that the neighborhood was zoned for a limit of two families per building. In this case, the broker could have determined the limitation. (The court might have ruled that the buyer could also have determined this and was thus partly to blame.)

Innocent misrepresentation

A salesperson may make a statement, believing it to be true. As an example of *innocent misrepresentation,* the seller might indicate to the salesperson that the basement is dry, and the salesperson repeats it to the buyer, who relies on it. In this case, the buyer could probably either sue the seller for damages or cancel the contract. The broker may still be due a commission.

Nondisclosure—concealment

Is mere silence a misrepresentation? In our previous example, assume that the salesperson knew that water came into the basement during heavy rains; however, the buyer never asked anything, and the salesperson remained silent about the matter. Courts have held that it is the responsibility of the principal or agent to disclose *latent defects,* that is, those not observable by reasonable inspection of the property. The salesperson's silence can be considered as misrepresentation though *nondisclosure* (fraud). As another example, a broker's silence on a known pending change in zoning or a flaw in the title could also be considered misrepresentation by concealment. If the salesperson had not known about the leaky basement or the broker had not known about the pending change in zoning, the misrepresentation would have been innocent. Suppose that, in the leaky basement example, the seller had recently repainted the basement walls so that evidence of water would not be noticed. A court decision, *Batey vs. Stone 192 SE2d 528* (Ga. 1972), held this to be fraud, even though no statement was made; thus, intentional misrepresentation (or fraud) can take place by acts as well as words.

Some suggestions

What can brokers or salespeople do to protect themselves against these possible situations? The following are some positive actions they might take:

1. Ask the seller outright about the roof, basement, septic system, and other potentially problematic aspects of the property. Make a list of facts detailing everything.

2. Guard against making statements regarding unknowns such as the condition of the furnace, presence of termites, or property value. If the buyer asks about them, an expert can be called in.

3. Any stated defects to be taken "as is," such as a damaged swimming pool, should be stated in the contract agreement.

4. The contract should state that the appliances, the furnace, and so on are to be in good working order on the date of closing.

5. Where work is still being done on a house, the down payment should be held in a trust account until the work is completed.

Thus, we see that misrepresentation is not always within the control of brokers or salespeople; however, they can take certain actions to protect themselves, as well as the buyers and sellers.

Legal Matters

Although a real estate broker or salesperson needs knowledge of laws as they apply to real estate, he must take care not to engage in activities considered to be the practice of law. One of these borderline areas is the drawing up of a contract. As a general practice, attorneys and real estate professionals have agreed that the broker can fill in printed contract forms for the parties to sign. If the contract is more complicated, it should be drawn up by an attorney.

It is unethical for a real estate broker to give legal advice or to engage in activities considered to be the practice of law. Instead, he should recommend that a buyer or seller obtain legal counsel for legal matters. If asked by a client to perform a legal task, the broker should refuse and suggest that the client consult her attorney. Even if a form contract is used, the broker or salesperson should suggest that the client is free to consult an attorney before signing. If the client asks the broker to recommend an attorney, the broker should suggest three or more alternative names of attorneys.

In some localities, the tax assessor reviews current real estate transaction documents for use in updating the assessments. The broker should not be a party to showing misleading figures on legal documents. If a house sold for $50,000, it is improper to show $40,000 on the deed to mislead the tax assessor. It would be proper to state a nominal value such as "$5.00 and other consideration," however. Anyone should know this is not the real sale price and would not be misled.

Frequently, a buyer might need a larger mortgage so that she will have more funds to make improvements on a house she desires to purchase. It would be unethical for the salesperson to suggest actions to mislead the lending institution or others, such as using extra tax stamps on the deed to make it appear that a higher purchase price was paid, since the tax is proportional to the sale price.

Ethics in Selling

When a broker tries to close a particular sale, it is sometimes tempting to use statements or actions that are misleading, untrue, or otherwise unethical. A statement to the buyer that the owners will probably take less because "they have to be moved by June 1," "the husband is very ill," or "they are getting divorced" is unethical unless the seller has authorized use of the information. Lack of diligence by the broker in representing her principal or in making factually unsupported statements about the property are not ethical. For this reason, a broker should never accept a listing that she does not intend to pursue diligently.

Courts, in deciding cases involving misrepresentation, take into account the seller's ability to comprehend or evaluate facts about the property. The broker or salesperson (and perhaps the seller) often has or should have superior knowledge about such factors as the community, zoning, soil conditions or problems, and services available. A broker who purchases from a client a parcel of property, when only the broker knows the land is going to be rezoned as commercial, would be acting unethically. A salesperson who knows the land is not suitable for a septic system would be acting improperly to show the land to a prospective builder.

Buyers will frequently ask questions about the condition of the property. Questions about the condition of an appliance, for example, usually cannot be answered by the salesperson without further checking. Any statements made without consulting the owner would be improper. Representing that a home is well-insulated would not usually be based on expert knowledge. Stating that "The view from the property is beautiful" would, however, fall into the acceptable category of "*puffing.*" The salesperson must be able to determine the line between puffing (mere opinion) and misrepresentation of fact.

Responsibilities to the General Public

A broker or salesperson has responsibilities to third parties. Consider a buyer who wants to purchase a lot on the edge of a residential area and have it rezoned as a liquor store. Should the broker lend assistance in obtaining the zoning change? The broker could expect to place himself in the position of opposing the residents who would resist the change. If he were successful, he could earn a commission, but he could also tarnish his public image. From a purely ethical point of view, is he doing the right thing? If he lived in the area, he would probably not like the change.

Real estate brokers have considerable influence over the formation and character of a community. They can promote premature speculative subdivision development or conversion of open areas to use. They can also lend opposition or support to tax increases to provide schools or parks or to set aside historical sites.

Sometimes a broker publicizes the sale of a property to a minority family in the hopes that it will induce others in the neighborhood to list and sell with him; this is called *blockbusting,* a practice that is both unethical and illegal in all states. The broker can go even further and try to purchase adjacent property at distressed prices. A broker has ethical duties to others beyond those with whom he deals directly.

ETHICS IN ADVERTISING

We sometimes hear of cases of blatant misrepresentation in advertising. If there is a likelihood or intention that an ad may deceive the intended reader, it probably falls into the unethical category. The following are some examples of advertising that will likely deceive the intended reader:

1. Stating "Sale by Owner" and listing the licensee's telephone number (illegal by many state laws).
2. Using the word "institute" or some word implying nonprofit in the agency name.
3. Advertising an attractive home when there is really no intent to sell in

order to draw prospective buyers to look at less attractive homes. This is sometimes called the *bait and switch* tactic.

4. Allowing an ad to run after the property has been sold.

5. Advertising a low price that does not mention incomplete construction (e.g., appliances, furnace) or that calls them "extras" in small print.

6. Using altered photographs, such as adding trees, grass, or a lake where none exists, or touching up the photos to add a sidewalk or paved street.

7. Including a garage, porch, or patio in the advertised square foot area.

8. Using the phrases "sacrifice price" or "below market value" without ascertaining the true appraised price.

9. For investment property, showing income based on unrealistic expenses or full occupancy.

10. Stating "four bedrooms" when one room is 6 × 7 feet, or "two baths," when one lacks a shower or tub.

It is also unethical (and sometimes illegal) for a broker to advertise a property before obtaining a clear intent to sell from the owner.

Relations with Other Real Estate Professionals

A broker should conduct her business so as to be fair to her fellow brokers. Legitimate disagreements between brokers should be settled by the local board whenever possible. Brokers should also be fair to other brokers in referrals or other instances where there is a dual contribution. Advertisements derogatory to other brokers or implying better deals or commission rates would be improper. The following are some examples of unethical actions:

1. A broker rejecting an offer submitted by another broker without submitting the offer to the principal or owner.

2. Leaving a sign on a property after the expiration of a listing or along with the sign of the new exclusive listing broker.

3. Soliciting a listing from a home owner listed with another broker or asking when an exclusive listing will expire.

4. Criticizing other brokers based on untrue or unproven information.

5. Delaying a sale due to a dispute with another broker.

6. Collaborating with another broker to set commission rates.

7. Starting litigation against another broker before attempting to negotiate the dispute.

Local chapters of professional associations provide a means whereby real estate licensees can resolve differences.

PROFESSIONAL ASSOCIATIONS

Real estate brokers have organized both nationally and locally to promote high professional standards. The goals and objectives of professional real estate associations follow:

1. Promote high standards.
2. Protect the public.
3. Exchange ideas and information.
4. Support legislation in the interest of the public and of real estate professionals.
5. Cooperate in the growth of urban and rural areas with respect to real estate.

Other types of real estate specialists can belong to independent professional groups in their special area, or they can join institutes that are part of the NATIONAL ASSOCIATION OF REALTORS®.

National Association of Realtors

The National Association of Real Estate Boards (*NAREB*) was organized in 1908. It changed its name to the NATIONAL ASSOCIATION OF REALTORS® (*NAR*) in 1974. It acts as a parent organization for local real estate groups. Members of local real estate boards who are affiliated with the national organization are called REALTORS®. Thus, the word REALTOR® is a registered trade name and is not correctly used to identify any real estate broker unless a member of the NATIONAL ASSOCIATION OF REALTORS®:

To promote ethical practices, the NATIONAL ASSOCIATION OF REALTORS® developed and adopted a code of ethics in 1913. All members of the NATIONAL ASSOCIATION OF REALTORS® and local affiliated boards subscribe to this code. The code has been significant in elevating the real estate business to a position of public respect. It also provides a helpful guide to all engaged in the real estate business. The code is broken down into articles dealing with relations to the public, relations to the client, and relations to the fellow REALTOR®. It has frequently been amended to reflect necessary changes in the business as it relates to society.

The professional organization functions at three levels—national, state, and local. Real estate brokers who belong to the local board also belong to the state and national organizations.

Policy objectives
NATIONAL ASSOCIATION OF REALTORS® lists the following policy objectives:

1. To encourage rehabilitation and construction with emphasis on private housing, through the use of tax incentives, subsidies for low-income families, code enforcement, and expanded mortgage financing.
2. To discourage restrictive practices that increase costs of construction and inhibit employment.
3. To exempt government-backed loans from state usury laws.

4. To allow accelerated depreciation and capital gains credits.
5. To replace public housing with interest-subsidized home ownership for low-income families.
6. To eliminate slums.
7. To encourage mass transportation systems.
8. To limit property taxes to reasonable rates.
9. To promote free-market and free-enterprise farms.
10. To discourage banking industry expansion into real estate operations.

The *GRI* (Graduate Realtors Institute) designation is awarded to persons who have completed a specified GRI course study in aspects of real estate such as appraisal, law, finance, property management, or related topics.

Membership categories

Full membership in the NATIONAL ASSOCIATION OF REALTORS® is open to licensed real estate brokers, whereas others can obtain membership in other categories.

1. *Active Members* are licensed real estate brokers actively engaged in the real estate business in the territory covered by the local board. They often control activities of their associates or employees and are called *REALTORS®.*
2. *Associate Members* are licensed real estate salespeople holding either a broker's or a salesperson's license and are associated with a REALTOR®.
3. *Affiliate Members* are individuals in the community or members of local firms interested in the affairs of the local board. They do not vote or hold office on the board.
4. *Honorary Members* are retired former active members who meet local eligibility requirements.

Special institutes

The main function of the NATIONAL ASSOCIATION OF REALTORS® is to raise professional standards. The association sponsors special institutes to disseminate published information and promote professional education. These special institutes and their member designations are listed in Appendix G.

Other Professional Organizations

Several other professional or nonprofit organizations operate in the various specialized areas of real estate. Some of these serve groups such as appraisers, property managers, home builders, or others. These are also listed in Appendix G.

SUMMARY

Ethics is an important consideration in all aspects of real estate transactions. Ethical standards appear in codes of professional organizations or state laws and regulations; however, all aspects of ethics are not specifically defined. Therefore, brokers and salespeople should have an understanding of a wide variety of actions that could have unfavorable consequences or tarnish their public image.

Real estate brokers are professionals who compete with one another for business, yet work together as members of professional associations to maintain standards of ethics and exchange ideas.

TERMS AND CONCEPTS

You can check your understanding of these terms against the glossary or by review of this chapter or Appendix G.

Blockbusting	Latent defect
Buyer qualifications	Misrepresentation
Caveat emptor	Nondisclosure
GRI	

What are the differences or relationships, if any, between the following?

Intentional misrepresentation and	NAR and NAREB
Innocent misrepresentation	REALTOR® and Broker

PROBLEMS

After reading each case, review the text and the appropriate article of the Code of Ethics that applies and give your opinion as to whether or not a violation took place:

15–1. Broker A, as the agent of Seller B, sold a house to Buyer C, filling in a standard form contract of purchase drafted by legal counsel. At the time Broker A presented the contract for Buyer C's signature, she explained that the contract was a standard form generally used in the area. She suggested that the buyer have his own attorney review it. Buyer C said he would read it over carefully, and if there was any lack of clarity in it he would consult an attorney about it. He later returned with a signed contract, saying it was clear and satisfactory to him.

At the closing, Buyer C said he misunderstood the date of possession of the property.

15–2. Broker A was approached by Client B to appraise a house for rental purposes. Client B explained he had recently inherited the property, recognized that it had been neglected, and wanted the appraisal to have some definite idea of the property's value before discussing it with negotiators for the local urban renewal agency.

Several months later, Client B complained to the broker, specifying that he had been overcharged for the appraisal. Client B explained that the appraisal fee he had agreed upon with Broker A was one-tenth of one percent of the valuation shown in his appraisal report.

15–3.   As she had done in the past, Broker A mailed to her fellow brokers descriptions of properties listed with her. Her objective was to invite the cooperation of the other brokers. As indicated in her mailing, some of the properties described were listed exclusively with Broker A, and some were listed on an open or nonexclusive basis. Broker B received a copy of Broker A's mailing, became interested in one property described, noted that it was not exclusively listed with Broker A, contacted the owner directly, and obtained his own nonexclusive listing of the property. When this action came to the attention of Broker A, she filed a complaint with the Board of Realtors charging Broker B with unethical conduct.

15–4.   Broker A used a classified advertisement including a description of a property with the words, "Call Ms. J, 429-8406."

15–5.   Property Manager A, acting as management agent for Owner B, offered a house for rent to a tenant, stating to the prospect that the house was in good condition. Shortly after, the tenant entered into a lease and moved into the house. He later filed a complaint against the property manager charging misrepresentation because he found a clogged sewer line and a defective oven.

15–6.   Broker J usually sent out letters to each of the neighbors after he sold a house and the buyers moved in. The letter suggested that the residents should stop by and visit the new neighbor. What do you think of this practice?

15–7.   Seller K, in accepting an offer from Buyer B through Broker X, insisted that the contract contain a clause stating that the house is purchased "as is." What should the broker do? What should he say to the clients?

15–8.   List some statements that could be considered "puffing."

15–9.   List some defects in a home where nondisclosure could be considered as misrepresentation. What do these defects have in common?

15–10. The Beyers moved into a home they had just purchased through Broker B. One week later it rained hard and about an inch of water came into the basement. The possibility of this defect was never mentioned during the negotiations. The broker claimed that he knew nothing about the problem before the Beyers mentioned it. What can the Beyers do?

15–11. Mr. James, a broker, has the policy that the seller should always set the purchase price of his or her property. James has never suggested to a seller that the price was too low or too high, nor has he ever turned down a listing. What are the business, ethical, and legal considerations of his policy?

SUPPLEMENTARY READINGS

Individual state statutes and regulations (see Appendix C for addresses of state agencies).

NATIONAL ASSOCIATION OF REALTORS®. *Interpretation of the Code of Ethics.* Chicago: 1978.

Pivar, William H. *Real Estate Ethics.* Chicago: Real Estate Education Company, 1979.

State of Wisconsin. Real Estate Examining Board. *Wisconsin Real Estate Law.* Milwaukee: 1976. Chapters 2 and 4.

The Transaction–
From Offer to Closing

Prior chapters have dealt with the many facets of real estate. This chapter will integrate this material as it applies to a residential property transaction from offer to closing (settlement). Chapter 17 will then cover the completion of the transaction with the closing.

OVERVIEW OF TRANSACTION

Once a client has decided to purchase a parcel of real estate, the broker or salesperson plays a key part in bringing about a valid agreement between the two parties. The agent should also assure to the extent possible that the necessary steps take place to prepare for the closing and final conveyance of the property from seller to buyer. The broker has an ethical responsibility to assist both the seller and the buyer, who may lack knowledge or experience in the steps that must take place prior to the closing. The salesperson and broker are also fulfilling their own interests, since in most cases the seller, as principal, plans to pay the broker from the proceeds of the sale. This chapter will detail the events from the time the buyer decides to make an offer on a parcel of real estate up through the point where all the contingencies are settled and questions of title validity are resolved.

As discussed in Chapter 4, the transfer of title to real estate from one party to another is usually initiated by a written contractual agreement. The primary reason is to protect the interests of both parties. When an item of personal property is purchased, such as an automobile or refrigerator, the item purchased is quickly turned over to the buyer. Real estate is different because, at the time of agreement to buy, the purchaser has no assurance that the title is without defects or even that the seller is in fact the sole or true owner. A contract is necessary to bind the purchaser and seller while the necessary investigations and steps are carried out to bring about a valid conveyance of the property from the seller to the buyer.

The lay person may consider the documents and procedures cumbersome; however, shortcuts can lead to problems. The omission of provisions or failure to use precise terminology can lead to disagreements or misunderstandings, and possibly even lawsuits.

Flow Chart

The flow chart in Figure 16–1 shows the steps involved in a typical residential transaction from the offer until the closing (or settlement). The chart also shows who usually has the primary responsibility for each step.

THE OFFER AND ACCEPTANCE

Prior to the sale, the property had been listed with a real estate broker at an agreed-upon list price. The listing agreement between the broker and seller provides that a commission will be paid to the broker when he has produced a buyer who is ready, willing, and able to purchase the property. Several steps are necessary to bring about this contractual agreement between the buyer and seller. Assume a broker or one of his salespeople locates a prospective purchaser who has inspected a house and wants to make an offer. If the prospective purchaser is very anxious to buy the property and believes that the price is firm (i.e., the seller will not reduce the price), she may offer to pay the list price. The purchaser might also offer to pay the list price if the property is newly listed or she otherwise feels that someone else may stop her from getting the property by coming in with another offer at the list price. The salesperson/broker first prepares the offer. The salesperson/broker secures the purchaser's signature and presents the written offer along with the buyer's deposit check, or *earnest money,* as it is usually called, to the seller for his acceptance. If there are no contingencies or exceptions to the seller's listing conditions and no other offers have been previously accepted, then the broker has provided a ready, willing, and able buyer and has earned his commission.

In some states, it is customary to use a *deposit receipt* when the broker is accepting earnest money from a prospective buyer where the intent is to meet all terms of the listing. When the broker plans to use a deposit receipt, it becomes more important that the listing agreement define all terms carefully. The well-designed deposit receipt will contain the provisions of a lawful binding agreement.

Listing is Not an Offer to Sell

If a broker presented an offer from a buyer at the full listing price without contingencies, does the seller have to sell? The answer is NO! An *offer* and an

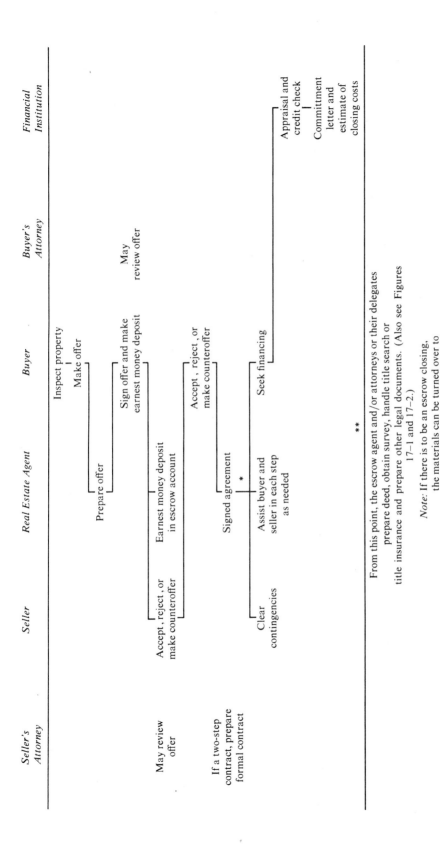

Figure 16-1
Flow chart of steps involved in a typical transaction to purchase residential real estate

acceptance are required to have a binding contract. If a listing could be construed to be an offer to sell, then acceptance at full price would be the contract. If the listing is not an offer, then the buyer is merely making an offer to purchase.

Courts have held that the listing agreement is only a private contract between the broker and the property owner and does not concern the buyer. It is an agency agreement that binds a seller to pay a commission if the broker finds a buyer. If the buyer's offer meets all the terms specified in the listing agreement, the seller may owe a commission. However, the buyer cannot force the consummation of the sale unless the buyer's offer is accepted by the seller or his duly authorized agent (i.e., attorney in fact under a written power of attorney from the seller).

Inspection of the Property

In any transaction, the buyer or his representative should inspect the property for any noticeable defects or problems. A prudent buyer will also question the seller about defects not readily observable (*latent defects*) such as roof leaks or basement seepage, which could only be noticed in wet weather. The seller and the broker have a legal responsibility to disclose any known latent defects to the buyer, and the lack of disclosure or falsification is possible cause for rescinding the contract later or for recovery of damages from either the seller or the broker. The principle of *caveat emptor* (let the buyer beware) does, however, apply to defects that can be observed by a reasonable inspection. Most agreements contain a clause that the buyer has inspected the property and finds it acceptable.

Negotiation and Contingencies

The case where the prospective buyer offers at full list price and in accord with all of the seller's conditions is not common. In most instances, the buyer makes an offer to purchase either at an amount below the listed price or with certain contingencies, exceptions, or provisions. Some common differences between the listing and offer follow:

1. Offer a price lower than the list price.
2. Offer contingent upon buyer being able to obtain a mortgage at a specified interest rate or other terms.
3. Offer contingent upon occupancy by the buyer at a date different from that in the listing agreement.
4. Offer contingent upon certain additional items to be included with the sale, such as carpeting, TV antenna, or draperies.
5. Offer contingent upon the seller giving the buyer a *purchase-money mortgage.* This is essentially a loan made by the seller to the prospective buyer. The buyer may not have a sufficient down payment and asks the seller to accept a mortgage on the property as part of the price.
6. Offer contingent upon evidence of freedom from termites.

7. Offer contingent upon sale of other property presently owned by the buyer.

All of these contingencies except the last one can usually be resolved or negotiated within a few days. The last contingency depends upon an event that is highly uncertain and, therefore, should be unacceptable to the seller. Acceptance of condition number 7 might tie up the property for an indefinite period of time.

After the broker or the salesperson has prepared the offer, including the contingencies desired by the potential buyer, the offer is presented to the seller with an earnest money deposit. The judicious buyer will specify in the offer the time limit within which the seller must accept the offer. If the offer is not accepted by the specified date, the buyer can then proceed to make another offer without the risk of being under contract to purchase two properties. The buyer can, however, revoke the offer at any time *prior* to acceptance.

If the seller accepts the buyer's offer, he will sign it. If the offer is made up correctly, as discussed in Chapter 4 on contract law, a binding agreement exists. Frequently, however, the seller may agree to some of the proposed conditions in the written offer but not to others. He may make a *counteroffer,* whereby he agrees to some of the conditions and proposes a compromise on the price. Typical compromise conditions might include:

1. A change in price.
2. A requirement that the buyer apply for a mortgage within three days and obtain a commitment within two weeks, or some other specified number of days. This statement assures the seller that the property will not be off the market for a long period in case the buyer has difficulty obtaining a mortgage commitment from a financial institution.

If a counteroffer is to be made, the salesperson/broker will make the changes in the offer form and have the seller initial them and sign the form; then she will present the counteroffer to the prospective buyer. Legally, this means the seller has rejected the original offer. He cannot later change his mind and accept it and require the buyer to abide by the original offer. Upon being advised of the counteroffer, the buyer can now either accept it or reject it or make a further counteroffer. This process continues either until an agreement is reached or one party discontinues the process.

A BINDING AGREEMENT

In the selling process, the real estate broker needs to bring about a binding agreement between the seller and buyer such that any differences between them are resolved. A more formal contract can be drawn up later by legal counsel, who may add other suggested provisions. In some cases, the buyer and seller might go directly to legal counsel to have the contract drawn up without going through the offer and acceptance process. In other cases, the buyer and seller can draw up a valid contract themselves without the aid of a broker or a lawyer; however, legal advice is recommended to make sure a binding agreement is formed (Chapter 4). If the initial document drawn up is the final contract, it is called a *one-step* process.

The offer and acceptance form, if used, sometimes provides that a more formal contract will be drawn up within a specified time (two-step process); however, the buyer and seller should always assume that the form being signed is a valid contract.

Forms

Printed offer and acceptance forms for transfer of real estate can be purchased in most stationery stores, and state or local Boards of REAL-TORS® have their own recommended forms. However, there is actually no set required form or format. The offer to purchase agreement form used by the Educational Testing Service in their examinations is shown in Figure 16–2. In our discussions in this chapter, other clauses will be discussed in addition to those shown in Figure 16-2.

Provisions in the Agreement

It is sometimes said that the usual offer and acceptance is not a binding agreement; however, its validity as a contract depends on its provisions. It is not necessary to have a lawyer prepare a binding contract. Both parties should assume that they are entering an enforceable agreement. In Chapter 4 the following elements necessary to form a binding contract were discussed:

1. Competent parties to the contract—seller and purchaser;
2. Offer and acceptance—a meeting of the minds;
3. Consideration—each party must obligate him or herself;
4. Adequate property description;
5. In writing and for a legal purpose.

In the case of married persons, it is frequently said that it takes two to sell and one to buy. Either of the married partners can become obligated to purchase; however, both parties must agree to sell property that is owned jointly.

The agreement should also contain the following facts:

1. Date agreement is prepared.
2. Names and addresses of purchaser and seller.
3. Name of broker (not necessary for a binding agreement between purchaser and seller).
4. Location of property.
5. Description of property (usually the legal description; it must be sufficient to assure there is a meeting of the minds concerning the property involved). The street address is usually included.

OFFER TO PURCHASE AGREEMENT

This AGREEMENT made as of _____ , 19_____ ,

among. _____ (herein called "Purchaser"),

and _____ (herein called "Seller"),

and _____ (herein called "Broker"),
provides that Purchaser agrees to buy through Broker as agent for Seller, and Seller agrees to sell the following described real estate, and all improvements
thereon, located in the jurisdiction of _____ ,
(all herein called "the property"): _____
_____ , and more commonly known as _____
_____ (street address).

    1. The purchase price of the property is _____

Dollars ($_____), and such purchase price shall be paid as follows:

_____

    2. Purchaser has made a deposit of _____ Dollars ($ _____)
with Broker, receipt of which is hereby acknowledged, and such deposit shall be held by Broker in escrow until the date of settlement and then applied
to the purchase price, or returned to Purchaser if the title to the property is not marketable.

    3. Seller agrees to convey the property to Purchaser by Deed with the usual covenants of title and free and clear from all monetary encumbrances,
tenancies, liens (for taxes or otherwise), except as may be otherwise provided above, but subject to applicable restrictive covenants of record. Seller further
agrees to deliver possession of the property to Purchaser on the date of settlement and to pay the expense of preparing the deed of conveyance.

    4. Settlement shall be made at _____ on or before
_____ , 19_____ , or as soon thereafter as title can be examined and necessary documents prepared, with allowance of
a reasonable time for Seller to correct any defects reported by the title examiner.

    5. All taxes, interest, rent, and impound escrow deposits, if any, shall be prorated as of the date of settlement.

    6. All risk of loss or damage to the property by fire, windstorm, casualty, or other cause is assumed by Seller until the date of settlement.

    7. Purchaser and Seller agree that Broker was the sole procuring cause of this Contract of Purchase, and Seller agrees to pay Broker for services
rendered a cash fee of _____ per cent of the purchase price. If either Purchaser or Seller defaults under such Contract, such defaulting party shall
be liable for the cash fee of Broker and any expenses incurred by the non-defaulting party in connection with this transaction.

Subject to: _____
_____
_____
_____

    8. Purchaser represents that an inspection satisfactory to Purchaser has been made of the property, and Purchaser agrees to accept the property in
its present condition except as may be otherwise provided in the description of the property above.

    9. This Contract of Purchase constitutes the entire agreement among the parties and may not be modified or changed except by written instrument
executed by all of the parties, including Broker.

    10. This Contract of Purchase shall be construed, interpreted, and applied according to the law of the jurisdiction of   and shall
be binding upon and shall inure to the benefit of the heirs, personal representatives, successors, and assigns of the parties.

All parties to this agreement acknowledge receipt of a certified copy.

WITNESS the following signatures:

_____   _____
                  Seller   Purchaser

_____   _____
                  Seller   Purchaser

_____
                  Broker

Deposit Rec'd $ _____

Personal Check   Cash

Cashier's Check   Company Check

Sales Agent:

Figure 16–2

A sample offer to purchase agreement form

6. The price to be paid for the property, defining the earnest money deposit made at the time of the acceptance of the offer and exactly how and when the balance of the purchase price is to be paid. Any elements left to later negotiation may make the contract unenforceable. Provisions may include the following:

   (a) Additional deposit to be paid upon signing a formal contract, usually bringing the total deposit up to about 10 percent of the purchase price (if a two-step agreement).
   (b) Assumption of the seller's existing mortgage by the buyer.
   (c) Seller to take a purchase-money mortgage from the buyer.
   (d) Balance due at closing. It will often specify payment in cash or certified check, since ownership of the property will be transferred at the closing and the seller will not want to risk being involved with a bad check.

7. Type of deed to be furnished. The buyer should normally require a warranty deed (or a deed with English covenants). This is the most desirable deed from the buyer's viewpoint. In some states the **grant deed,** backed up by title insurance, is common. In a **warranty deed,** the seller assumes full responsibility for a valid title without limit of time and, at any time in the future, the buyer has recourse for damages against the seller if the title is defective.

8. Place and date of settlement (closing).

9. Provision for proration of taxes, interest (if an assumption), and rent or expenses if an income property.

10. Responsibility if damage occurs to property before settlement. The most fair provision is to have seller responsible as long as he has possession of the property.

11. Statement establishing broker's fee (may be covered in a separate agreement between the broker and client).

12. Contingencies (discussed in next section):

    (a) Provision for termite inspection.
    (b) Ability of buyer to obtain an adequate mortgage at a specified percentage of purchase price and specified interest rate.
    (c) Provisions related to tenants, easements, or other factors.

13. Statement that purchaser has inspected property and finds it acceptable (does not waive latent or hidden defects).

14. Signature of purchaser and seller (broker's signature is optional).

CLEARING CONTINGENCIES

Conditions in the agreement stating actions that must take place before the agreement becomes binding are called *contingencies.* The buyer may insert a clause that the contract is contingent "upon her obtaining an 80 percent mortgage at no greater than 9.5 percent interest for 30 years." The buyer should specify that a certificate will be provided showing no termite infestation or structural damage, or that if termites are found, the seller will pay for treatment. If the buyer plans a commercial venture, for example, she may insert a clause, that the sale is contingent on getting the zoning changed. As another example, the buyer may specify that the sale is contingent on being able to obtain the seller's existing liquor license. In the case of a building lot, the contingency may specify favorable soil tests for drainage or the ability to support footings for a eight-story building.

If a conditional clause is put in the contract by the buyer for her own benefit, she may later waive it and still have a valid contract. If the buyer inserts a condition that requires her own action, such as securing a mortgage, but if she makes no effort to secure the mortgage, the clause is no longer in effect. The buyer is still bound to the remaining terms of the contract. The seller should protect himself against unreasonable delay to fullfill a condition by specifying a time allowed for the buyer to apply for a mortgage. The seller takes the risk that, if the buyer changes her mind on the purchase, she may make only a token effort to obtain the mortgage. The contingency should also specify the terms of the mortgage required, or the buyer may judge the terms unacceptable. If no terms were specified, a court will determine whether or not the terms obtained by the buyer are reasonable. If found to be reasonable, the court will enforce the contract.

It is in the broker's interest to see that these conditions are cleared as soon as possible. For instance, he could order the termite inspection, with concurrence of the seller. He could use his contacts to find a mortgage lender, help the buyer apply for the mortgage, and then follow up with the financial institution to obtain a response. A letter of commitment furnished by the financial lending institution to make a mortgage loan at the specified rate will satisfy this condition, but the lending institution will want an appraisal and credit report first. If for any reason the buyer will not be able to obtain a mortgage, prompt determination of that fact will permit the seller to place the property back on the market. Sometimes a *back-up offer* is written if another client is also interested in the property. If done, the second offer should be an unconditional offer to become binding if the first offer fails, or to become inoperative if all contingencies in the first offer are fulfilled.

ESCROW

When the agreement is completed and the contingencies are cleared, the buyer and seller will need to decide if they will have a regular *closing (settlement)* with a meeting or if they will want an escrow closing. This chapter will discuss the advantages and disadvantages of the escrow closing and Chapter 17 will explain the closing steps by means of flow charts.

If the buyer and seller agree on an escrow closing, they will jointly select a third person, called an *escrow agent, escrow holder, escrowee, or escrow officer,* to carry out the remaining steps to complete the real estate transaction. The escrow procedure is used widely on the west coast. It is used in other areas when one or more of the parties cannot be present at the closing or for other reasons. The escrow holder is the agent of both the buyer and the seller. The buyer gives sufficient funds to the escrow holder to complete the transaction, along with precise written instructions. The seller gives the escrow holder the deed and other documents, along with his instructions. The instructions are usually contained in an *escrow agreement* between the buyer, seller, and escrow agent. After all instructions have been complied with, the escrow agent will convey the property.

The escrow agent can be a bank, a title insurance company, or an independent escrow company. One dictionary defines *escrow* as "a deed, bond, or other written engagement, given to a third person, and delivered to the grantee when specified conditions have been fulfilled." The escrow holder is a trustee who holds the money and documents. He usually does not perform the functions of an attorney. In California, escrow holders are licensed and bonded corporations. They are permitted to prepare legal forms for buyer and seller signature that in other parts of the United States only attorneys at law can prepare. In some cases, the escrow agreement gives the escrow agent the responsibility to clear all contingencies.

Why Escrows are Used

The use of escrow in real property transactions dates back to England in the fifteenth century. Some advantages of the escrow method of closing are as follows.

Conditional and irrevocable agreement

When the documents are turned over to the escrow agent, the money from the buyer is turned over also. This deposit is *conditional* and *irrevocable* in that the buyer will get the money back if all the conditions of the contract agreement (such as clear title) cannot be met; however, the buyer cannot revoke the agreement if all conditions are met. This is also true without an escrow closing; however, the nonescrow closing may require court action to reach a settlement of differences. Therefore, we can say that the escrow closing is less likely to "fall through."

Death of seller or buyer

In an escrow closing, the title to the property actually passes to the buyer when the materials are turned over to the escrow agent. When the escrow is not used, death of the seller before the closing often raises complications in executing the deed, sometimes resulting in a judicial proceeding. If the deed was properly executed by the grantor, the principle of *relation back* would cause title to be passed at the time the deed was delivered to the escrow agent.

Several parties

Sometimes real estate transactions involve several parties, especially if a tract is being split up or if property exchanges are involved. A formal meeting for all parties at a regular closing may become burdensome, so an escrow closing is used.

Broker tasks

In a regular closing, the listing broker may have responsibility for preparing some of the closing papers. She also is accountable for the earnest money deposit up until the closing. With an escrow closing, the broker is relieved of this responsibility. Also, the death of the broker could not interfere with an escrow closing.

STEPS OR POSSIBLE OBSTACLES TO COMPLETION OF THE TRANSACTION

The parties to the transaction and the broker should understand the types of problems that can be encountered and their consequences. Two categories of obstacles could prevent the completion of the transaction. The first type is the failure of one party to carry out his obligations either intentionally or unintentionally. The second includes defects in title or the inability of the seller or buyer to conform to a contingency clause in the contract. This second category prevents the fulfillment of the agreement and would usually make the contract null and void, unless both parties were willing to change the contract and accept the conditions. Some other steps are also necessary prior to closing the transaction.

Failure to Perform

Either the buyer or the seller might fail to carry out one or more of the provisions stated in the contractual agreement. This failure to perform usually does not affect the right of the broker to his commission; however, it will interfere with the completion or closing of the contract and thus delay the availability of the commission or result in litigation. If one party fails to perform in accordance with the contractual agreement, there are various remedies available to the other party. (These are discussed in Chapter 3 and reviewed here.) They are similar whether it be the buyer or seller; however, it is not as easy for the seller to enforce some remedies as it is for the buyer.

Sometimes the seller changes her mind or is unwilling to go through with the agreement. She may receive a better offer or decide not to sell. In this case, the buyer may agree that the contract be rescinded and ask for return of his earnest money together with any costs he may have endured. A second alternative would be to sue for breach of contract, with the intent of securing damages for the breach of agreement. The third alternative is to sue for specific performance. A court can force either party to carry out the contract agreement and complete the transaction. This forced compliance to the contract is called *specific performance.*

A buyer may also change his mind. For example, if he had intended to move to the town for a new job and the job offer was cancelled, he would not buy the house. If the buyer refused to carry out his contractual obligation to purchase the property, the seller may sue for damages, sue for specific performance, or declare the contract void and keep the earnest money or deposit. If the buyer who refuses to carry out the contract was from out of state or did not own real estate himself, the cost of enforcing the contract may not be worth the effort. Forfeiture of the earnest money is often the most practical course of action. In this case, the broker may settle for part of the earnest money in lieu of his full commission, especially if he regains the listing and the chance to sell the property again.

In either of these cases, the party who refuses to comply with the contract should be advised of the potential results of her or his failure to perform. In the case of the buyer with the cancelled job offer, the broker could suggest that the buyer confirm his obligation to buy and then have the broker resell the property.

Marketability of Title

A *marketable title* is a title free from all liens and encumbrances. Conversely, an unmarketable title either has a serious defect or is encumbered. Normally, the encumbrances are to be removed by settlement or suit. Before settlement and transfer of title, the purchaser or mortgage lending institution should require an examination of the title to see if there are any defects or encumbrances. Four types of title examination procedures are used to determine the marketability of the title: (a) abstract and opinion; (b) attorney direct search and opinion; (c) title insurance; and (d) the Torrens System.

Abstract and opinion
When an abstract is used, an abstractor searches the records and prepares an *abstract* (chain of title) showing all recorded legal instruments affecting the property. The abstractor certifies that the abstract is complete and turns it over to the purchaser's attorney who renders an opinion on the marketability of the title.

Attorney direct search and opinion
The attorney makes a direct examination of the records in the recorder's office, compiles a *brief of title,* and renders an opinion as to the marketability of the title. The purchaser and the lending institution rely on the opinion of the attorney. If the attorney has made a mistake and the title later turns out to be defective, the purchaser can sue the lawyer for damages. A lawyer will usually carry insurance against this risk.

Title insurance
Title insurance companies are authorized to do business in the various states in which they operate. They issue policies insuring the title to property based upon the abstract or the company's own records. As in any title examination, the records must be updated to the closing date of the transaction. If a subsequent defect in title becomes evident, the insurance company must pay the costs or losses of the insured owner. (See Chapter 11.)

The buyer should find out if a recent survey of the property exists. If not, he should require that a survey be performed. The *survey* will identify the exact boundaries of the property and determine if all structures are completely within property boundaries. It will establish whether the improvements are in complete compliance with municipal ordinances, such as being set back a minimum distance from the lot line of any structures. It also will show if any structures on the property encroach upon property belonging to someone else. A garage extending onto the neighboring property is an example of an *encroachment.* Encroachments onto the property would also be identified.

Surveys are performed by licensed land surveyors. They are an essential step prior to any contemplated purchase of real estate, new property construction, modification to existing structures, or fence construction. The survey assures that the structure would comply with all existing setback requirements. It would also establish if a fence is within the property line. The survey is especially important if any new construction is part of the purchased property. The drawing showing the results of the survey should then be turned over for examination as part of the title search. Since many mortgage institutions require a survey by a licensed surveyor, the buyer should coordinate with the mortgage company to avoid duplication of effort and cost.

Destruction of the Property

What happens if structures on the property are destroyed by fire or windstorm after the contract agreement? The common law rule is that the property has been sold upon signing of the contract, and the buyer is obligated to go through with the purchase transaction. The other view states that the seller has agreed to provide the property in the condition existing at the time of agreement and, therefore, further risk is the *seller's.* Laws or court decisions in California, Connecticut, Illinois, Kentucky, Maine, Massachusetts, Michigan, New Hampshire, New York, Oregon, Rhode Island, South Carolina, South Dakota, and Wisconsin have put the risk on the seller who, having possession, is in the best position to protect the property. In all states, the risk is placed on the seller where loss is due to seller negligence or where a delay in closing is the fault of the seller and a good marketable title could not be furnished. In the absence of any specific provision in the contract, a court may set an equitable settlement.

The party in possession is in the better position to prevent fire damage. Thus, possession is an important factor in determining liability. Some states have adopted the Uniform Vendor and Purchaser Risk Act which provides that, in the absence of specific provisions in the contract, the party in possession is liable for destruction of the property between the time of contract signing and the closing.

A well-written contract will specify exactly what is to happen if the property is damaged or destroyed so that litigation will not be necessary. A commonly used clause provides that, in case the property is damaged, the buyer will accept the insurance and the remainder of the damaged property as settlement. With this clause, the purchaser needs to make sure that the insurance coverage is adequate not only to restore or replace the property, but also to compensate for the lack of ability to use the property as a place to live or source of income while being rebuilt. If the contract does not contain a specific provision to cover damage or destruction of the property, it is best for both parties to assume that they would have the responsibility and protect their respective interests by seeing that there is adequate insurance.

Time is of the Essence

If an agreement specifies that *time is of the essence,* it means that the parties have agreed that time is a critical factor and that failure to conform to dates specified will cause a breach of contract that can terminate the deal. If this clause is not in the contract, either party has a reasonable amount of time to perform after the date specified for closing. Since it is easy for delays to come about in the transaction, this clause should not be used unless dates are critical.

Death of One Party

A contract will normally state that the agreement is binding on heirs. If either the buyer or seller dies, the other can enforce the contract against the decedent's estate. If the sellers are joint tenants and one dies, the survivor then has legal title and is bound to complete the contract. If husband and wife have contracted to purchase real property, and one dies, the survivor and the estate of the deceased would be liable to the seller if there were default on the contract.

Warranties or Representations by Seller

Sometimes the seller makes warranties or representations in the contract regarding such factors as zoning, condition of septic system, or nonreceipt of violation notices. The best procedure for the buyer is to state in the contract that the representation or warranty survives the closing. Another procedure is to place the warranty in the deed also. If either of these is not done or the representation is stated in the contract as a condition, and the buyer goes ahead and closes without making sure the warranty is met, the buyer, by closing, will be held to have either agreed the condition was met or to have waived the warranty. This is called a *merger* of the contract into the deed.

Real Estate Settlement Procedures Act

The Real Estate Settlement Procedures Act *(RESPA)* was first enacted by Congress in 1974 and amended in 1975. The primary objective of the act was to assist home buyers in understanding the settlement process and the related costs. By requiring the lending institution to provide a "good faith" estimate of all of these costs for the home buyer, it was reasoned that home buyers could shop around and perhaps obtain better terms. The act requires the use of a standard form when a lending institution finances the sale of a one-family residence. A prospective buyer who applies to a lending institution is furnished with the booklet, *Settlement Costs and You—A HUD Guide for Home Buyers.*[1] This booklet describes the many aspects of a settlement under the following categories:

1. *What happens and when.*   This describes the sequence of events from the time a home is selected until the settlement. Chapters 16 and 17 of this book cover these same events.

2. *Shopping for services.*   This portion deals with the role of the real estate broker, selecting an attorney, selecting a mortgage lender, and securing title services.

3. *Home buyers' rights.*   This section describes the estimates the borrower is entitled to receive, including effective interest rates. It also describes certain unfair practices and the rights of the home buyer to file complaints to HUD.

4. *Home buyers' obligations.*   This section describes the objectives of the home buyer to repay the loan and to maintain the property in a proper state of repair.

Part Two of the booklet provides an item-by-item discussion of possible settlement services home buyers may require and for which they may be charged. The booklet contains the Uniform Settlement Statement form along with worksheets for use in comparing costs.

Other objectives of RESPA

In addition to providing assistance to home buyers, the act provides for certain other safeguards to the home buyer. It prohibits the acceptance of fees or *kickbacks* for referrals where no service is performed. For example, a title insurance company could not pay a fee to an attorney for referral of business. RESPA also prohibits a seller of real property from requiring that the buyer purchase title insurance from a particular company. Escrow deposits or *impounds* are payments collected along with the mortgage payments that are placed in a special account to pay property taxes or insurance when due. Some lenders do not pay interest to the borrower on these deposits. RESPA prohibits the lending institution from collecting amounts greater than those needed to make the tax and insurance payments.

Itemized disclosure

The act provides that an itemized disclosure (settlement statement) be provided to both the buyer and the seller. This is to be prepared on a standard form as shown in Figure 16–3. The following items or costs must be specified. The numbers refer to the circled numbers in the figure.

---

[1]*Settlement Costs and You—A HUD Guide for Home Buyers.* Available from savings and loan institutions or others handling mortgages. Washington, D.C.: Department of Housing and Urban Development, 1976.

A. U.S. DEPARTMENT OF HOUSING AND URBAN DEVELOPMENT	B. TYPE OF LOAN:
DISCLOSURE/SETTLEMENT STATEMENT	1. ☐ FHA 2. ☐ FMHA 3. ☐ CONV. UNINS.
	4. ☐ VA 5. ☐ CONV. INS.
	6. FILE NUMBER 7. LOAN NUMBER

If the Truth-in-Lending Act applies to this transaction, a Truth-in-Lending statement is attached as page 3 of this form. | B. MORTG. INS. CASE NO.

C. NOTE: This form is furnished to you prior to settlement to give you information about your settlement costs, and again after settlement to show the actual costs you have paid. The present copy of the form is:

☐ ADVANCE DISCLOSURE OF COSTS. Some items are estimated, and are marked "(e)". Some amounts may change if the settlement is held on a date other than the date estimated below. The preparer of this form is not responsible for errors or changes in amounts furnished by others.

☐ STATEMENT OF ACTUAL COSTS. Amounts paid to and by the settlement agent are shown. Items marked "(p.o.c.)" were paid outside the closing, they are shown here for informational purposes and are not included in totals.

D. NAME OF BORROWER	E. SELLER	F. LENDER

G. PROPERTY LOCATION	H. SETTLEMENT AGENT	I. DATES
		LOAN COMMITMENT / ADVANCE DISCLOSURE
	PLACE OF SETTLEMENT	SETTLEMENT / DATE OF PRORATIONS IF DIFFERENT FROM SETTLEMENT

J. SUMMARY OF BORROWER'S TRANSACTION		K. SUMMARY OF SELLER'S TRANSACTION	
100. GROSS AMOUNT DUE FROM BORROWER:		**400. GROSS AMOUNT DUE TO SELLER:**	
101. Contract sales price ①		401. Contract sales price	
102. Personal property ②		402. Personal property	
103. Settlement charges to borrower ③		403.	
104.		404.	
105.		Adjustments for items paid by seller in advance:	
Adjustments for items paid by seller in advance:		405. City/town taxes to	
106. City/town taxes to		406. County taxes to	
107. County taxes to		407. Assessments to	
108. Assessments ④ to		408. to	
109. to		409. to	
110. to		410. to	
111. to		411. to	
112. to		**420. GROSS AMOUNT DUE TO SELLER**	
120. GROSS AMOUNT DUE FROM BORROWER: ⑤		*NOTE: The following 500 and 600 series sections are not required to be completed when this form is used for advance disclosure of settlement costs prior to settlement.*	
200. AMOUNTS PAID BY OR IN BEHALF OF BORROWER:		**500. REDUCTIONS IN AMOUNT DUE TO SELLER**	
201. Deposit or earnest money ⑥		501. Payoff of first mortgage loan	
202. Principal amount of new loan(s) ⑦		502. Payoff of second mortgage loan	
203. Existing loan(s) taken subject to		503. Settlement charges to seller	
204. ⑧			
205.		504. Existing loan(s) taken subject to	
Credits to borrower for items unpaid by seller		505.	
		506.	
206. City/town taxes to		507.	
207. County taxes to		508.	
208. Assessments to		509.	
209. ⑨ to		Credits to borrower for items unpaid by seller:	
210. to		510. City/town taxes to	
211. to		511. County taxes to	
212. to		512. Assessments to	
220. TOTAL AMOUNTS PAID BY OR IN BEHALF OF BORROWER ⑩		513. to	
		514. to	
300. CASH AT SETTLEMENT REQUIRED FROM OR PAYABLE TO BORROWER		515. to	
		520. TOTAL REDUCTIONS IN AMOUNT DUE TO SELLER	
301. Gross amount due from borrower		**600. CASH TO SELLER FROM SETTLEMENT:**	
		601. Gross amount due to seller	
302. Less amounts paid by or in behalf of borrower ( )		602. Less total reductions in amount due to seller ( )	
303. CASH ☐ REQUIRED FROM OR ☐ PAYABLE TO BORROWER: ⑪		603. CASH TO SELLER FROM SETTLEMENT	

Figure 16–3
Disclosure/Settlement Statement form

Page 2

L. SETTLEMENT CHARGES	PAID FROM BORROWER'S FUNDS	PAID FROM SELLER'S FUNDS
700. SALES/BROKER'S COMMISSION based on price $ @ %		
701. Total commission paid by seller ⑫		
Division of commission as follows:		
702. $ to		
703. $ to		
704.		
800. ITEMS PAYABLE IN CONNECTION WITH LOAN.		
801. Loan Origination fee % ⑬		
802. Loan Discount % ⑭		
803. Appraisal Fee to ⑮		
804. Credit Report to ⑯		
805. Lender's inspection fee ⑰		
806. Mortgage Insurance application fee to ⑱		
807. Assumption/refinancing fee ⑲		
808.		
809.		
810.		
811.		
900. ITEMS REQUIRED BY LENDER TO BE PAID IN ADVANCE.		
901. Interest from to @ $ /day ⑳		
902. Mortgage insurance premium for mo. to ㉑		
903. Hazard insurance premium for yrs. to ㉒		
904. yrs. to		
905.		
1000. RESERVES DEPOSITED WITH LENDER FOR: ㉓		
1001. Hazard insurance mo. @$ / mo.		
1002. Mortgage insurance mo. @$ / mo.		
1003. City property taxes mo. @$ / mo.		
1004. County property taxes mo. @$ / mo.		
1005. Annual assessments mo. @$ / mo.		
1006. mo. @$ / mo.		
1007. mo. @$ / mo.		
1008. mo. @$ / mo.		
1100. TITLE CHARGES:		
1101. Settlement or closing fee to ㉔		
1102. Abstract or title search to		
1103. Title examination to ㉕		
1104. Title insurance binder to		
1105. Document preparation to		
1106. Notary fees to ㉖		
1107. Attorney's Fees to ㉗		
1108. Title insurance to ㉘		
1109. Lender's coverage $		
1110. Owner's coverage $		
1111.		
1112.		
1113.		
1200. GOVERNMENT RECORDING AND TRANSFER CHARGES ㉙		
1201. Recording fees: Deed $, Mortgage $ Releases $		
1202. City/county tax/stamps: Deed $, Mortgage $		
1203. State tax/stamps: Deed $, Mortgage $		
1204.		
1300. ADDITIONAL SETTLEMENT CHARGES		
1301. Survey to ㉚		
1302. Pest inspection to ㉛		
1303.		
1304.		
1305.		
1400. TOTAL SETTLEMENT CHARGES		

NOTE: Under certain circumstances the borrower and seller may be permitted to waive the 12-day period which must normally occur between advance disclosure and settlement. In the event such a waiver is made, copies of the statements of waiver, executed as provided in the regulations of the Department of Housing and Urban Development, shall be attached to and made a part of this form when the form is used as a settlement statement.

1. Contract sales price
2. Personal property
3. Settlement charges
4. Prorated adjustments paid by seller
5. Gross amount due from borrower
6. Deposit or earnest money
7. Principal amount of loan(s)
8. Existing loan(s) taken subject to
9. Prorations credited to borrower
10. Total amounts paid by or in behalf of borrower
11. Cash required from borrower
12. Real estate brokers' sales compensation
13. Loan origination fees (expenses of lender to originate loan, usually a percentage of the loan)
14. Loan discount points (where a point is one percent of the loaned amount)
15. Appraisal fee
16. Charge for credit report
17. Lender's inspection fee
18. Mortgage insurance application fee (for FHA or VA loans)
19. Assumption/refinancing fee
20. Prepaid interest (from settlement date to first monthly payment)
21. Prepaid mortgage insurance premiums (required for FHA loans)
22. Prepaid hazard insurance premium (fire or home owner's insurance policy)
23. Reserves deposited with lender (for lender to make future tax and insurance payments)
24. Settlement, closing, or escrow fee
25. Title charges
26. Notary fees
27. Attorney's fees
28. Title insurance
29. Government transfer taxes and charges
30. Survey
31. Inspections (presale inspections for buyer's benefit, including termites or pest inspections to be paid by seller).

A completed form is to be provided to seller and buyer at settlement date. If the exact charges are not yet known, the lender must provide a good faith estimate. The booklet also provides other information useful to the buyer.

USE OF COMPUTERS IN PREPARATION FOR CLOSING

Mortgage departments in banks and saving and loan associations are making increased use of computers in the closing preparation. The need for computer use has grown due to a large volume of closings, increased government forms required, and the many calculations that must be performed.

As the steps are completed for a mortgage loan transaction, the information is placed into the computer. At any time, the status of the transaction can be checked to determine what incompleted steps remain. When all the steps have been completed, the calculations are made by the computer, and the parties can proceed with the closing.

SUMMARY

A residential property transaction begins when a potential buyer decides to make an offer on a parcel of property. When an agreement is reached, a contract will result between the buyer and the seller. If the agreement includes any contingencies, each must be cleared before an enforceable binding agreement exists.

An agreement will specify either the date of closing when the parties will complete the transaction or, in the case of an escrow closing, the name of the escrow agent who will handle the transaction for the two parties.

A number of obstacles could interfere with the completion of the property transaction. These may occur either because one of the parties fails to perform his or her responsibilities or because of something not controllable by either party. The broker and the parties to the transaction should take steps to help assure that the transaction will be completed.

TERMS AND CONCEPTS

You can check your understanding of these terms against the glossary or by review in this chapter.

Abstract	Escrow agreement
Acceptance	Impounds
Caveat emptor	Marketable title
Closing	Offer
Contingency	Purchase-money mortgage
Counteroffer	Relation back
Default	RESPA
Earnest money	Settlement
Encroachment	Specific performance
Escrow	Survey
Escrow agent	Time is of the essence

What are the differences or relationship, if any, between the following? Check your responses from the chapter text or from the glossary.

Conditional and Irrevocable	Grant deed and Warranty deed
Defects and Latent defects	One-step transaction and Two-step
Escrow closing and Regular closing	transaction

PROBLEMS

16–1. Seller A and buyer B sign a contract for sale of a house. Prior to closing, some defects in the title are discovered. What options does the buyer have? What options are open to the seller?

16–2. Seller A and buyer B have signed a contract for sale of a house. Prior to the closing, seller A tells buyer B and the broker that she will not go through with the sale and offers to return the earnest money to B. What options are open to the buyer? What options does the broker have?

16–3. Broker X has just obtained the necessary signatures to complete the contract for sale of a house. Make a checklist of things he should do prior to closing.

16–4. Prepare a checklist for a broker to use when drawing up a binding agreement.

16–5. Seller A and buyer B have signed a contract for sale of a house; X was the listing and selling broker. B later advises the broker that the job offer he had was rescinded, and he will not be moving to town. What options are open to broker X?

16–6. A broker holds an exclusive right to sell listing. She brings a signed offer to the seller at the list price with no conditions. Is the seller obligated to sell? To pay the commission?

16–7. A clause in a contract states that the sale is contingent upon the seller replacing the furnace. If this is not completed by the time of closing, what can the buyer do? What if the buyer wants to obtain possession, but the seller refuses to replace the furnace?

16–8. A buyer submits an offer contingent upon obtaining a mortgage. Does the seller need to insert any clause to protect himself before signing?

16–9. You have signed a contract to purchase a property. When the survey is completed, it shows the garage one foot over on the neighboring lot. What are your possible options?

16–10. If a contract to purchase real estate is both conditional and irrevocable whether there is an escrow closing or not, how does the escrow closing give greater protection to the seller?

16–11. A house under contract was two-thirds destroyed by fire prior to the closing. What would happen if the contract stated the property was held at risk of the seller? Of the buyer?

SUPPLEMENTARY READINGS

Bergfield, Philip B. *Real Estate Law*. New York: McGraw-Hill, 1979. Chapter 13.

Friedman, Milton R. *Contracts and Conveyances of Real Property*. New York: Practicing Law Institute, 1972.

Gray, Charles D., and Steinberg, Joseph C. *Real Estate Contracts: From Preparation Through Closing.* Englewood Cliffs, N.J.: Prentice-Hall, 1970.

Harvey, David C.B. *Harvey Law of Real Property Title and Closing.* New York: Clark Boardman Company, 1972. 3 vols.

Mann, John. *Escrows—Their Use and Value.* Chicago: Chicago Title and Trust Company, 1975.

O'Donnell, Paul T., and Maleady, Eugene L. *Principles of Real Estate.* Philadelphia: Saunders, 1975.

Reilly, John W. *The Language of Real Estate.* Chicago: Real Estate Education Company, 1977.

Semenow, Robert W. *Questions and Answers on Real Estate.* Englewood Cliffs, N.J.: Prentice-Hall, 1979. Chapter 2.

Semenow, Robert W. *Selected Cases in Real Estate.* Englewood Cliffs, N.J.: Prentice-Hall, 1973.

U.S. Department of Housing and Urban Development. *Settlement Costs and You—A HUD Guide for Home Buyers.* Washington, D.C.: 1976.

Wisconsin Real Estate Examining Board. *Wisconsin Real Estate Law.* Milwaukee: 1976. Chapters 5 and 6.

Closing and Conveyancing

The legal title to a parcel of real property passes from the seller to the buyer when the instrument of *conveyance* (deed) is delivered to the buyer. Completion of the transaction (closing or settlement) takes place at a meeting of the parties except when an escrow closing has been selected.

THE CLOSING

Usually, a meeting is held during which all of the pertinent documents are available and the transaction is concluded. If the buyer is obtaining a mortgage, the buyer's loan will be closed at the same meeting, and the mortgage funds will be disbursed by the lender. Figure 17–1 illustrates the main elements of the transaction. At this meeting, the financial aspects will be settled, the deed will be signed and delivered, and the key or token of possession will be transferred from the seller to the buyer. Sometimes, however, the actual date of property possession may be later or earlier than the title transfer date. This meeting—called a *closing* or *settlement*—includes the buyer and seller, their attorneys, representatives of any lending institution involved, and the real estate broker. The alternative to the meeting is to appoint an escrow agent to handle the closing as illustrated in Figure 17–2.

The contract of sale should specify that the closing take place by a certain date and at a specified place. The contract terms should provide enough time from contract execution to the closing to permit completion of the title search, survey, inspections, removal of encumbrances, and any other matters that must be completed before the conveyance of the property. If the time of closing is not specified in the contract, the courts will usually require it to take

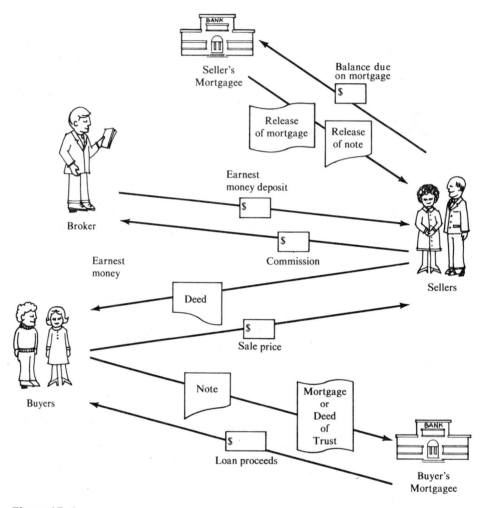

Figure 17-1
Actions at settlement (meeting)

place within a reasonable time. If it does not take place by the time specified in the contract, usually a monetary adjustment will be worked out to compensate for the delay. If the seller is unable to deliver on the required date, usually the buyer will receive a per diem payment. If the contract specifies that "time is of the essence," the conveyance must take place on the date specified.

ESCROW CLOSING

In some states, most residential real estate transactions are closed in *escrow.* In any state, however, it is sometimes not convenient for either the buyer or the seller to be present at the closing. This might happen if the seller were

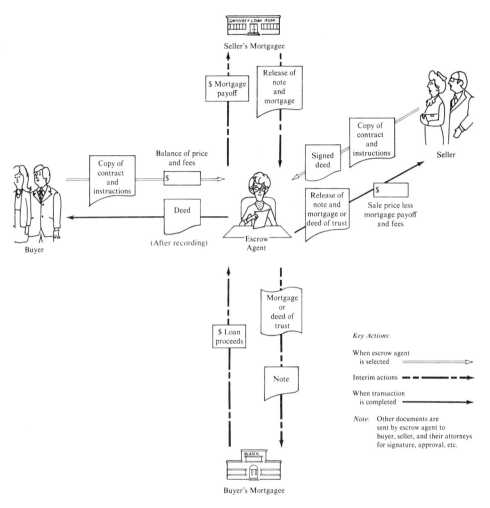

Figure 17-2
Actions for escrow closing

moving to a distant city before the date of closing. In this case (as discussed in more detail in Chapter 16), the buyer and the seller may select a third party to carry out the closing and complete the transaction. This procedure is called *closing in escrow,* and the person or institution who handles the transaction is called an *escrow agent.* The escrow agent serves both the buyer and the seller. In some states, such as California, escrow agents are licensed and bonded. The seller delivers the deed to the escrow agent, and the buyer gives the necessary money to the escrow agent. The escrow agent is instructed to have the title examined. If the title is shown to be valid, the escrow agent pays the proceeds of the sale to the seller. In an escrow closing, the title officially passes on the date of delivery of the deed to the escrow agent; therefore, even if the grantor or grantee dies, marries, or goes bankrupt in the interim between delivery of the deed to the escrow agent and completion of the proceedings, the transaction is still carried through, as shown in Figure 17–2.

DOCUMENTS REQUIRED AT CLOSING

Certain documents are needed at the closing, whether regular or escrow, to verify that the contract requirements have been met and to provide the necessary information and documentation to complete the transaction. The following documents should be available at closing.

Deed

The deed should be properly executed and ready for delivery to the buyer. It must be the type specified in the contract (e.g., a warranty deed) and must comply with all provisions of the contract. It must (a) be in a form acceptable for recording, (b) show the marital status of grantor(s) and grantee(s), and (c) meet all specified elements for a valid deed, including words of conveyance, specified consideration, and property description.

Lien Discharges

The seller must provide a certificate showing discharge of each lien and mortgage, if there are any.

Insurance Policies

If insurance policies are to be transferred from seller to buyer, the seller must secure insurance company approval, have the policy assigned to the buyer, and bring these documents to the closing. If the buyer is obtaining a new policy, a copy must be available to assure the mortgagee that adequate protection exists.

Cashier's Check

It may be required that the balance due from the buyer be paid by a cashier's check, especially if the buyer uses an out-of-town bank.

Receipts

The seller should bring current receipts for taxes paid, assessment receipts, and receipts for sewage or water service payments.

Title Insurance

If the seller is required to supply title insurance or an abstract, these should be brought to the closing along with any attorney's opinions needed.

Affidavit of Title

The seller must furnish an *affidavit of title* covering the period between completion of the title search and the actual closing. The affidavit should be signed by the seller and state that, during this interim period, there have been no divorce proceedings, judgments, bankruptcy proceedings, or other events that have affected title. The affadavit also states that no repairs or improvements have been made or that any made have been paid for in full. This action protects the buyer against possible liens or claims that originated during this period. The affidavit may also state that fixtures or any personal belongings in the property are paid for, that there are no existing violations or defects in title, and that the seller is the sole current owner.

Certificate of Occupancy

If the property is newly constructed or improved, the seller is required to furnish a *certificate of occupancy,* signed by the proper government official, stating the property is fit for occupancy and that plumbing and electrical requirements and other building code requirements are met.

Survey

The seller must provide a *survey* if so specified in the contract. The survey is used to provide evidence of the existence or nonexistence of encroachments.

Leases

If the property is leased, the seller must assign and deliver the leases to the purchaser. The seller should also furnish an affidavit stating the amounts of rent collected to date and the exact amount of security deposits held by the seller. The security deposits are turned over to the buyer. The seller should send a letter to each tenant advising the tenant of the change in ownership, and copies of the letters should be brought to the closing.

Termite Certificates

Termite certificates should be supplied by the seller if required by the contract.

Fees and Commissions

The attorney's fees and broker's commission are usually paid at the settlement.

Employee Records

If the property (e.g., an apartment building) should involve paid employees, the seller should bring their employment records and data, along with copies of letters notifying each employee, the property manager, or any other involved persons of the change in ownership.

Bill of Sale

A bill of sale is prepared if any personal property is to be transferred by the seller to the buyer.

CLOSING COSTS

The costs related to completion of the real estate transaction are called *closing costs* or *settlement costs*. These costs may be fees charged by attorneys, broker, or mortgage institutions, taxes, or the amount necessary to compensate the other party in the transaction. The contract should specify the costs to be paid by each party. Specific costs are usually borne by one party or another in accord with law or custom in the particular state, county, or municipality. In the following discussion, the costs are assigned by the most frequent method, but variations often exist among localities.

Buyer's Costs

At closing, the buyer is required to pay for fees, services, or other costs stipulated in the contract agreement. If a mortgage is involved, the lending institution usually provides the buyer with a good faith estimate of closing costs. This permits buyers to compare costs between lenders and also to make sure a buyer has sufficient money ready. The following possible fees or costs would apply where applicable, depending on the contract and the lending institution agreement.

1. *Appraisal fee.* Usually required by the mortgage-lending institution for a new mortgage.

2. **Points** *charged by lender.* This can be a loan origination fee or, as is more often the case, a one-time charge by the lender to increase the effective interest yield.

3. *Survey cost.* If required by lending institution or desired by buyer, the survey cost will be due unless the buyer has paid for it separately.

4. *Assumption fee.* Frequently required by the lending institution if the buyer is assuming the seller's mortgage.

5. *Title insurance premium.* If required and not paid by seller.

6. *Recording fee.* Paid by buyer to record deed and any mortgages.

7. *Legal fee.* Paid by buyer for attorney to examine title and render opinion on abstract. Sometimes the buyer will have his or her own attorney in addition to the institution's attorney.

8. *Attorney's fee.* Includes contract preparation or review and evaluation of title.

9. *Interest.* If the lending institution charges mortgage interest a month in advance, the purchaser would owe the interest on a new mortgage from the closing date to the next scheduled payment date.

10. *Impounds.* In addition to the principal and interest payment, most lending institutions require the mortgagor (buyer) to make monthly payments to be held by them and used to pay taxes and insurance when they next become due. These are called **impounds** and assure the lending institution that money will be available to make the payment when due. The lending institution must protect itself by assuring that

the fire insurance premium and taxes are paid when due, so that a tax lien will not assume precedence over the mortgage lien. Some institutions deduct the impounds as they are received each month from the loan balance, so that the home owner gains the benefit of the interest.

Seller's Costs

The contract or custom in the community may require that certain costs be paid by the seller. The costs may include any of these:

1. *Legal fees.*   Costs of title insurance, preparation of abstract, deed preparation, and fees charged by the seller's attorney.
2. *Pay-off of encumbrances.*   Any mortgages not assumed as well as any liens or other encumbrances must be paid and discharged before or at closing. This may include penalties, if applicable, to pay off loans in advance of final due date or fees for required releases.
3. *Transfer taxes* (sometimes called *transaction taxes*).   Taxes customarily based on selling price.
4. *FHA or VA fees.*   These fees would be paid, if due, by seller.

PRORATION

On the day of closing, the seller's ownership terminates and the buyer's ownership begins. It is, therefore, customary to apportion or prorate costs, interest, taxes, and rental income between the buyer and the seller so that both pay their prorated share for the period each owns the property.

The contract between the buyer and the seller usually states that the interest, taxes, insurance, rent, expenses, and utilities are to be prorated where applicable. In some cases, the seller has paid the cost in advance, covering some amount of time after the seller's ownership ends. In that case, the buyer would be obliged to reimburse the seller for that payment. In other cases, the seller may not have paid an expense accrued before the closing and, in that case, the seller would be obliged to credit the buyer's account so that the buyer can pay the bill when it later becomes due. Often there is a considerable amount of money involved, so it is important to allocate it properly and fairly. This necessitates a method of establishing the number of days each owns the property so that a proportionate share can be calculated. In most states or localities, it is customary that the day of closing be assigned to the seller for both costs and income for the purposes of proration.

Proration Methods

There are different methods of making the **proration** calculations, depending upon the contractual provisions and the customary procedures in the local area. The computations in this text carry division and multiplication to three decimal places. The final proration figure is then rounded off to two decimal places.

Statutory month method
(year = 12 months of 30 days each)
In this method, the yearly amount is divided by 12 to obtain the monthly amount. The monthly amount is then divided by 30 to determine the daily amount. Consider an example where yearly taxes are $600.

$$\text{Monthly amount} = \frac{\$600}{12} = \$50$$

$$\text{Daily amount} = \frac{\$50}{30} = \$1.667$$

If the closing date is August 20, the amount allocated to the first 20 days of August would be $20 \times 1.667 = \$33.340$. This assumes that the day of closing is assigned to the seller. This is usual practice; however, local tradition may be otherwise. The total taxes from January 1 to August 20 would be as follows:

$$
\begin{array}{lr}
7 \text{ months} \times \$50 = & \$350.00 \\
20 \text{ days} \times 1.667 = & \underline{33.34} \\
\text{Total} & \$383.34
\end{array}
$$

In this situation, the buyer would receive credit for $383.34 and would then pay the taxes when they later become due. If the month contained other than 30 days, the result would be the same.

The uniform method (actual days in month)
The uniform method calculates the monthly amount the same way as the statutory month method, by dividing the yearly rate by 12. The daily amount is calculated by dividing the monthly amount by the actual number of days in the month. If the yearly taxes were $600 and the closing date were August 20, the calculations would be as follows:

$$\text{Monthly rate} = \frac{\$600}{12} = \$50$$

$$\text{Daily rate} = \frac{\$50}{31} = \$1.613$$

Taxes from January 1 to August 20 would be calculated as follows:

$$
\begin{array}{lr}
7 \text{ months} \times \$50 = & \$350.00 \\
20 \text{ days} \times 1.613 = & \underline{32.26} \\
\text{Total} & \$382.26
\end{array}
$$

Actual days in the year method
The actual days in the year method has traditionally been used on all commercial sales, apartments, and transactions where the dollar amount is large. Prorations are carried out by dividing the yearly amount by the actual days in the year (365 or 366) to obtain the daily rate. The actual days owned by the party are then calculated for the year. If the closing is August 20, and the yearly interest is $6,000, the calculation is as follows:

$$Interest = \frac{\$6,000}{365} = \$16.438 \text{ per day}$$

January	31 days
February	28
March	31
April	30
May	31
June	30
July	31
August	20

January 1 to August 20 = 232 days

The interest through August 20 is 232 days × $16.438 = $3,813.62. This method will be used in this text for all problems dealing with commercial, industrial, or apartment properties.

Interest Proration

In closing transactions where the seller's mortgage is to be assumed by the purchaser, it will normally be necessary to prorate or apportion the interest between the buyer and the seller. If there is more than one mortgage to be assumed, interest on each mortgage will be prorated. Consider an example where the closing date was April 12 and the seller of the home had made the mortgage payment on April 1, which included payment of interest through April 30. The mortgage balance was $20,800 on April 1 and the interest is 8 percent per annum. The portion of interest due the seller is calculated as follows:

$$\text{One month's interest} = \frac{\$20,800 \times 0.08}{12} = \frac{1664}{12} = \$138.667$$

$$\text{The daily interest} = \frac{138.667}{30} = \$4.622$$

$$\text{Interest for 18 days} = 18 \times 4.622 = \$83.20$$

Figure 17–3 shows the schedule of interest with respect to ownership, including the eighteen days for which the buyer should reimburse the seller.

Tax Proration

All transactions involving real estate will require allocation of the taxes between the parties. The taxation laws of the particular state or other jurisdiction where the property is located determine whether the seller owes money to the buyer or vice versa. Some examples will illustrate how the taxes are prorated under various taxation laws.

Taxes required to be paid in current year

Assume that the taxes of $800 for 1981 are due May 1, 1981. The closing date of a real estate transaction is set for April 10, 1981. The schedule in

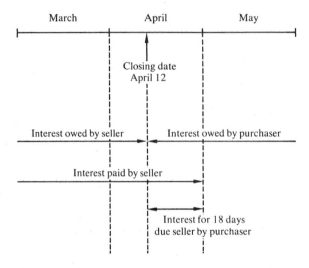

Figure 17–3
Schedule of interest with respect to ownership

Figure 17–4 shows the relationship of due date to closing date. The seller must pay to the purchaser the taxes for the period the property was owned by the seller from January 1 to April 10 because the buyer would be billed for the whole year's taxes on May 1, 1981.

$$\text{Monthly rate} = \frac{\$800}{12} = \$66.667$$

$$\text{Daily rate} = \frac{\$66.667}{30} = \$\ 2.222$$

Amount due purchaser

$$
\begin{aligned}
3 \text{ months} \times \$66.667 &= \$200.001 \\
10 \text{ days} \times \$2.222 &= \underline{22.220} \\
\text{Total} &= \$222.221 \text{ or } \$222.22 \text{ (rounded)}
\end{aligned}
$$

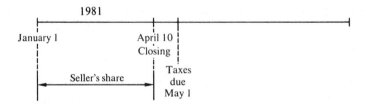

Figure 17–4
Relationship of tax due date to closing date

As another example, assume the closing date were September 18, 1981, and taxes were due May 1, 1981. The seller would have paid all of the 1981 taxes and would be due an amount from the purchaser to cover the rest of the year after September 19 as follows:

Sept. 19–Sept. 30 (12 days) 12 × $ 2.222 = $ 26.664
Oct.–Dec. 1981 (3 months)   3 × $66.667 = 200.001
Total = $226.665 or $226.67 (rounded)

In this example, the mortgage-lending institution may request the buyer to deposit additional money in an escrow account toward payment of the 1982 taxes due May 1, 1982. If the institution's policy is to deduct the impound from the mortgage balance until paid, the home owner benefits with respect to the interest charged.

Taxes paid in following year
Assume the taxes of $800 for 1979 are due on May 1, 1980. The closing date is April 10, 1980. Figure 17–5 shows the relationship between closing date and tax due date. In this situation, the buyer would be billed for the 1979

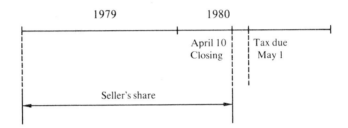

Figure 17–5
Schedule where taxes become due in the following year

taxes on May 1, 1980, and the following year he would be billed for the 1980 taxes on May 1, 1981. The seller owned the property during all of 1979 and part of 1980, so the seller owes the buyer as follows:

1979 taxes   = $ 800.000
3 months in 1980   3 × $66.667 =   200.001
10 days of April   10 × $ 2.222 =   22.220
Total = $1022.221 or $1022.22 (rounded)

The closing statement should then give the buyer credit for the full $1,022.22, and the same amount is debited to the seller.

Installment payment of taxes
Some states allow taxes to be paid in installments. Assume that one-half of the 1979 taxes are due on May 1, 1980 and the other half on September 1, 1980. The yearly taxes are $800 and the closing date is July 24, 1980. The May 1 payment was paid by the seller. The following shows the calculations to determine the credit due the buyer:

$$
\begin{aligned}
\text{Taxes 1979} & & = \ \ \$800 \\
\text{Half-payment made by seller} & & = -\underline{400} \\
\text{Balance} & & = \ \ \$400 \\
\text{Taxes 1980} \quad \text{6 months} \times \$66.667 & & = \ \ \$400.002 \\
\text{24 days} \times \$ \ 2.222 & & = \ \ \ \ \underline{53.328} \\
& & \$853.330
\end{aligned}
$$

The buyer should receive $853.33 from the seller so he can pay the $400 for 1979 on September 1, 1980, and the 1980 taxes when due in 1981.

Insurance Proration

An insurance proration is necessary when the purchaser is taking over the fire insurance policy or home owner's policy from the seller. Insurance policies are often written to provide coverage over a three- or five-year period. It is important to determine how much of the unexpired policy has been paid by the seller. Since insurance policies do not ordinarily run in calendar year periods, the calculation is performed differently from the tax and interest calculations. Assume the seller has a three-year paid up policy expiring July 21, 1983 for which the seller paid the $390 premium in full. The closing date for the property transaction is May 17, 1982. Calculations are made to determine the amount due to the seller from the buyer in order to compensate for the paid-up insurance coverage that the buyer is to receive from the seller. *Note:* Insurance prorations always use 30 days for a month.

$$
\text{Yearly amount} = \frac{\$390}{3} = \$130
$$

$$
\text{Monthly amount} = \frac{\$130}{12} = \$ \ 10.833
$$

$$
\text{Daily amount} = \frac{\$10.833}{30} = \$ \ \ 0.361
$$

Subtract the closing date from the expiration date to determine the policy period remaining as follows:

	Year	Month	Day
Expiration date	1983	7	21
Closing date	1982	5	17
Unexpired period	1	2	4

To subtract, start with the day column, and proceed just as with any subtraction problem. The total value of the unexpired portion of the policy is thus calculated as follows:

$$
\begin{aligned}
\text{1 year} \times \$130 & & = \$130.000 \\
\text{2 months} \times \$ \ 10.833 & & = \ \ \ 21.666 \\
\text{4 days} \times \$0.361 & & = \ \ \ \ \ \underline{1.444} \\
\text{Total due seller} & & = \$153.110
\end{aligned}
$$

In cases where the buyer wants to purchase her own insurance, it is not necessary to make any proration calculations. The seller would apply for a rebate from the insurance company for the unused portion of the policy, and the insurance would not be prorated.

To illustrate another situation, assume the same problem with the closing date now set at October 24, 1981. The calculations are as follows:

	Year	Month	Day
Expiration date	1983	7	21
Closing date	1981	10	24

In starting to perform subtraction, the 24 cannot be taken from the 21; therefore, it is necessary to borrow 30 days from the 7 in the month column to arrive at 51 in the day column. The subtraction in the day column can now take place.

	Year	Month	Day
Expiration date	1983	6	51
Closing date	1981	10	24
			27

Now the subtraction cannot take place in the month column; therefore, twelve months are borrowed from the 1983 in the year column to arrive at 18 months in the month column, as follows:

	Year	Month	Day
Expiration date	1982	18	51
Closing date	1981	10	24
Unexpired portion of policy	1	8	27

The amount due the seller is calculated as follows:

1 year × $130	= $130.000
8 months × $10.833 =	86.664
27 days × $0.361 =	9.747
Total due seller	= $226.411 (rounded to $226.41)

In this problem, if the seller had been paying on a yearly installment basis, he would have paid only through July 21, 1982. Thus the amount the buyer owes the seller would be $130 less than the $226.41, or $96.41. The $96.41 would then appear as a credit to the seller on the closing statement.

Rental Income and Wages

When the property involves rental income or wages for employees, an amount may be due to either the buyer or the seller, depending on the specific situation. Assume an apartment has two tenants and each pays $160 per month. The closing is May 12 and the seller has collected the rent for May in advance. It is necessary to calculate the amount due from the seller to the buyer. (Use actual days in the month for income and wages.)

$$\text{For one apartment, daily rent} = \frac{\$160}{31} = \$5.161$$

$$\text{Days remaining} = 31 - 12 = 19$$

For one apartment: 19 days × $5.161 = $ 98.059
For two apartments   × 2
Due purchaser on both apartments $196.118 (rounded to $196.12)

As mentioned before, the day of closing is considered a day of income and expense for the seller. In addition to rents paid or due, we must consider any damage deposits given to the landlord by a tenant. Any deposits that were received from tenants and are being held by the seller will be turned over to the buyer or credited to him at the closing.

Apartments often have a janitorial service. The wages or salaries must be prorated so that the buyer and seller pay the wages for the period each owns the property. Assume an apartment building had a janitor who was paid $250 per week for a seven-day work week. He was paid last on May 9 for the week ending May 9. Closing is May 12, so the janitor is owed three days' pay.

$$\text{Daily rate} = \frac{\$250}{7} = \$ 35.714$$

Days   × 3
Due purchaser $107.142 (rounded to $107.14)

The $107.14 would be credited to the buyer on the closing statement.

Utilities

Usually, the power company or the gas company will read the meter at the property location on the day of closing and bill each party separately for his portion. Sometimes, however, especially in the case of water, the meter is not read, and it is necessary to prorate the charges. Consider a case where the water and sewage fee of $30 is paid quarterly in advance and the closing is May 6. On April 1 the seller paid in advance for water in the months of April, May, and June, and therefore the purchaser owes the seller for more than one month's use. It is prorated in the same manner as rental income.

THE SETTLEMENT STATEMENT

The *settlement* (closing) *statement* itemizes and allocates all costs and monies between the various parties to the transaction. Its purpose is to allocate these funds clearly and accurately. It helps to calculate the figures far enough in advance to allow each party to make sure that she or he can arrange to have adequate funds available at the closing to complete the transaction. Although the preliminary copy of the closing statement may require minor adjustments later, it does serve as a basis for determining the approximate amount each party owes or will receive and also permits each party to check its accuracy before the settlement.

Property Address _1821 MASON_   Broker _HENDERSON REALTY_

Seller _KEVIN AND KATHY BECK_   Date of contract _JUNE 2, 1981_

Buyer _ALFRED AND AMY CROSS_

SETTLEMENT DATE: JULY 15, 1981	BUYER'S STATEMENT		SELLER'S STATEMENT	
	DEBIT	CREDIT	DEBIT	CREDIT
1. PURCHASE PRICE	57,500.00			57,500.00
2. EARNEST MONEY DEPOSIT		5,750.00		
3. MORTGAGE BALANCE		42,000.00	42,000.00	
4. PURCHASE MONEY MORTGAGE		8,000.00	8,000.00	
5. MORTGAGE INTEREST		160.89	160.89	
6. INSURANCE	413.34			413.34
7. GENERAL TAXES		378.23	378.23	
8. TRANSFER TAX			15.50	
9. TITLE INSURANCE	92.00		92.00	
10. ASSUMPTION FEE	100.00			
11. AGENT'S COMMISSION			3450.00	
12. LEGAL FEES			310.00	
13. SURVEY	85.00			
14. TERMITE INSPECTION			30.00	
15. OIL	66.00			66.00
DUE FROM BUYER TO CLOSE		1967.22		
DUE TO SELLER TO CLOSE			3542.72	
TOTALS:	58256.34	58256.34	57979.34	57979.34

Figure 17–6

Settlement statement

A typical settlement statement form is shown in Figure 17–6. This form is used by the Educational Testing Service (*ETS*) in real estate licensing examinations in over half of the states. Some forms have only two columns and may include a separate settlement portion for the broker to settle with the seller. Sometimes separate settlement statements are prepared for the buyer and seller.

The various entries are shown in Figure 17–6. The buyer's debit column is totaled first. The amount "Due from buyer to close" is entered in an amount that will cause the credit column and debit column to have equal totals. The seller's credit column is then totaled. Then the amount "Due to seller to close" is entered so that the seller's debit and credit columns have equal totals.

CLOSING PROBLEM EXAMPLE

The following example provides information for a real estate transaction. A closing statement is to be prepared from the information given.

Kevin and Kathy Beck of 1821 Mason Street in Foxboro have listed their house with Henderson Realty for $59,000. A 6 percent commission is to be paid on the actual sale price. The existing mortgage has a balance of $42,000 after the June 30, 1981, monthly payment was credited. No further payment was made. Monthly mortgage payments of $430 are due on the last day of each month and include the interest through and including that date. Interest on the mortgage balance is at 9.5 percent. On June 2, 1981, Alfred and Amy Cross signed a contract to purchase the house for $57,500. It was specified that they would assume the present mortgage. The Becks also agreed to take a purchase-money mortgage of $8,000.

The buyers gave the broker a 10 percent earnest money deposit, and the broker now holds this in his escrow account. The closing date is set for July 15, 1981. The agreement provided that the buyers and sellers would each pay half of the title insurance policy of $184. The real estate general tax for 1980 was $700 and was paid in full on June 1, 1981. The buyers have agreed to pay for the 120 gallons of oil in the tank at $0.55 per gallon. A four-year insurance policy on the house was paid in full by the Becks. It cost $800 and expires August 9, 1983. The buyers have agreed to take over this policy. The sellers will pay the transfer tax of $0.50 per $500 or fraction thereof. Prorations are based on the actual number of days in the month.

The buyers will pay an assumption fee of $100. The buyers are also to pay $85 for a survey. The sellers owe $30 for a termite inspection. The sellers' legal fees total $310.

Refer to Figure 17–6 as the settlement statement is completed.

Purchase Price

The purchase price of $57,500 is entered as a credit to the sellers and a debit to the buyers.

Earnest Money

The earnest money has already been paid by the buyers, and it appears as a credit of $5,720. It does not appear as a debit to the sellers unless they have already received the deposit from the broker.

Mortgage

Assumed mortgage: The $42,000 balance of the assumed mortgage is credited to the buyers since they assume this as a debt to be paid off in the future. It is entered as a debit to the sellers since this is deducted from their proceeds.

New mortgage: A new mortgage is always a credit to the buyers since they assume this obligation for future payment.

Purchase-money mortgage: The $8,000 purchase-money mortgage is credited to the buyers since they assume the obligation for future payment. It is also debited to the sellers since they do not receive it now.

Mortgage Interest

Assumed mortgage: Under an assumed mortgage the mortgage interest is prorated over the month of closing. The sellers pay up to and including the closing date, and the buyers pay for the rest of the month. If the sellers paid the month's interest in advance, the buyers will owe the seller money. If the interest is paid at the end of the month, the sellers will owe the buyers money.

$$\text{Yearly interest} = \$42,000 \times \$0.095 = \$3990.00$$

$$\text{Monthly interest} = \frac{3990}{12} = \$332.50$$

$$\text{Daily interest (July)} = \frac{332.50}{31} = \$10.726$$

$$\text{Interest (July 1–15)} = 10.726 \times 15 \text{ days} = \$160.89$$

The $160.89 is credited to the buyers and debited to the sellers since it is not paid until the end of the month.

New mortgage: At the closing, the buyers and the mortgagee will select a day of the month for future loan payments. If it is different from the settlement date, the buyers may have to pay interest in advance from the settlement date to the next loan payment date. This would appear as a debit to the buyers.

Second mortgage: Any second or other mortgages are handled the same as the first mortgage.

Taxes

If the taxes were paid in advance, the sellers are due a credit for the period the property is owned by the buyers. These taxes are then shown as a credit to the sellers. If the taxes have not been paid for a period of time over which the sellers owned the property, they are debited this amount. It is also credited to the buyers. The buyers will then pay taxes when due.

The 1980 tax was paid by the sellers on June 1, 1981. Since the 1981 tax is not known, it is customary to use the tax from the prior year, which is $700. The monthly and daily taxes are figured as follows:

$$\text{Monthly tax} = \frac{\$700}{12} = \$58.333$$

$$\text{Daily tax} = \frac{\$58.333}{31} = \$1.882 \text{ (for July)}$$

The sellers' share of the 1981 tax is from January 1 to July 15, or

$$6 \text{ months} \times \$58.333 = \$349.998$$
$$15 \text{ days} \times \$1.882 = \underline{28.230}$$
$$\$378.228 \text{ (rounded to \$378.23)}$$

This amount is credited to the buyers since they will have to pay the total 1981 tax on June 1, 1982.

In Figure 17–6 the taxes are debited to the sellers since they owe them. It is assumed that the purchasers will pay when due so they are given a credit.

Special Assessments

These assessments are owed by the owner as of January 1 each year and do not appear on the settlement sheets unless specified in the contract.

Insurance

New policy: The premium for a new policy is debited to the purchasers.

Assumed policy: Where an insurance policy is paid for by the sellers and taken over by the buyers, the buyers must pay the sellers for the remaining value of the policy. In our example, the sellers had paid the insurance policy premium in advance and, therefore, should be credited with the unused portion. The value of the policy from July 15, 1981, to the expiration date of August 9, 1983, is calculated as follows:

$$\text{Yearly cost} = \frac{\$800}{4} = \$200$$

$$\text{Monthly cost} = \frac{\$200}{12} = \$16.667$$

$$\text{Daily cost} = \frac{\$16.667}{30} = \$0.556$$

	Year	Month	Day
Expiration date =	1983	$\cancel{8}^{7}$	$\cancel{9}^{39}$
Closing date =	1981	7	15
	2	0	24

$$2 \text{ years} \times \$200 = \$400.00$$
$$0 \text{ months} \times \$16.667 = 0.00$$
$$24 \text{ days} \times \$0.556 = \underline{13.34}$$
$$\text{Unexpired value} = \$413.34$$

This amount is credited to the sellers and debited to the buyers.

Transfer Tax

The transfer tax is debited to the party responsible for paying it. The transfer tax on revenue stamps is computed at $0.50 per $500 or portion thereof. If there is no mortgage, the tax is based on the purchase price. Where there is a mortgage, the stamps are usually figured on the difference between the purchase price and the assumed mortgage, which in this case is

$$\$57,500 - \$42,000 = \$15,500$$

The revenue stamps would be $0.50 × 31 or $15.50 and debited to the sellers.

Title Insurance

The cost of title insurance is debited to the party responsible. In our problem, the title insurance cost is shared so that half is debited to the buyers and half to the sellers.

Loan Origination Fee (Points)

This fee is usually paid by the buyers and is computed as a percentage of the amount borrowed. For FHA loans it is paid by the sellers. There are no points in our example.

Assumption Fee

Where the mortgage is assumed, the buyers usually pay an assumption fee. In our example, $100 is debited to the buyers.

Agent's Commission

The real estate broker's commission to be paid by the sellers is figured as 6 percent of the purchase price of $57,500.

$$\text{Commission} = .06 \times \$57,500 = \$3,450$$

Legal Fees

The fees of an attorney are debited to the responsible party. In our example, the sellers pay $310.

Appraisal Fee

An appraisal fee is often required by the lender and is usually paid for by the buyer.

Survey

Sometimes a survey is required by a lender and paid for by the buyer unless the contract specifies otherwise. In our problem, $85 is paid by the buyers for a survey.

Termite Inspection

The cost of inspection plus any treatment necessary is paid for by the seller. In our problem, $30 is paid by the sellers for a termite inspection.

Water Bill

Usually, utility meters are read on the date of closing. If they are not, the cost is prorated based on the last paid bill.

Oil

It is normal practice to charge the buyer for oil left in the tank and credit this to the seller. In our example,

$$120 \text{ gal.} \times \$.55 = \$66.00$$

Impounds (Escrows)

If the seller has accumulated money in an escrow account kept by the mortgagee to pay taxes and insurance, it is credited to the seller.

Chattels (Personal Property)

If the buyer arranges to purchase personal property from the seller, this is handled by a bill of sale. It is a debit to the buyer and a credit to the seller.

Rents

For leased property, it may be necessary to prorate rents. Rent collected in advance is debited to the seller and credited to the buyer. Overdue rent is credited to the seller and debited to the buyer.

Salaries

Any salaries of persons (e.g., janitors who care for rental apartments) must be prorated as of the day of closing. If a salary is unpaid, the seller will be debited his share, and the buyer will receive a credit.

Penalties to Pay Off Loan

The mortgagee may charge a penalty to pay off a loan balance. This penalty is debited to the seller.

Lien Satisfaction

Any outstanding liens may be handled at the closing by a debit to the seller.

ACTIONS SUBSEQUENT TO CLOSING

After the closing is completed, the buyer or his attorney or agent should do the following:

1. Record deed obtained from the seller in recorder's office. The recorded deed then is retained by the new owner.
2. If the old mortgage was paid off, record the release of the mortgage, showing that the lending institution has no further legal interest in the property.

3. Have evidence of title brought down to closing date to show that no actions that could result in a lien or title defect took place between completion of title search and closing date.

4. Obtain home and liability insurance if not already purchased.

5. If persons are employed on the property, obtain workmen's compensation and Employer's Liability Insurance. Arrange for janitorial and any other services. Notify tenants to pay rent to the buyer.

The seller should make sure that the water, gas, and electric bills are transferred to the buyer's name. If there is a purchase money mortgage, the seller should have it recorded.

The lending institution should assure that its mortgage or deed of trust is recorded for its protection as discussed in Chapter 8 on liens and their priority.

SUMMARY

The closing (or settlement) is the procedure or event by which the property ownership transfers from the seller to the buyer. This can be handled at a meeting where the buyer and seller are present, or it may be handled by an escrow agent who looks after the interests of both parties and completes the transaction if and when each party's obligations are complied with.

At the closing, the monetary aspects of the transaction are completed such that the seller is paid the amount due him at the time the title is transferred to the buyer. Many of the items, such as mortgage interest, taxes, insurance, utilities, and income from rental property, may need to be apportioned so that each party pays or receives his proper share. This apportionment is called *proration.* All of these figures are calculated and entered in the closing (settlement) statement to show the amounts due to seller and buyer. The amounts due to the broker, the attorneys, the county recorder, and others can be handled on the same form or separately. A wide variety of forms are used in different localities.

TERMS AND CONCEPTS

You can check your understanding of these terms against the glossary or by review in this chapter.

Affidavit of title	Impounds
Certificate of occupancy	Points
Closing in escrow	Proration
Conveyance	Settlement
Escrow	Settlement statement
Escrow agent	Survey
ETS	

PROBLEMS

Prepare closing statements for each of the following transactions. (Consider the date of closing to belong to the seller, unless designated otherwise by your instructor.) You may reproduce copies of Figure 17–7 to record the results.

17–1. John and Sherry O'Hara listed their home at 1268 Marlon Avenue with the Henderson Real Estate Company. The selling price was $54,500, and possession was to be given two weeks following the signing of the contract. The listing agreement stated that the broker was to receive a commission of 6 percent of the selling price. On March 1, 1980, the balance on the mortgage was $43,700. The payments on the mortgage are $160 per month plus interest at the rate of 7 percent per annum on the unpaid balance. The O'Haras are willing to sell the property subject to the existing mortgage if the prospective purchasers can provide the necessary cash difference. They are not able to take a purchase-money mortgage.

On March 18, 1980, Henderson Real Estate Company submitted a contract offer to the O'Haras from Peg and Bill Miller. Mr. and Mrs. Miller offered $52,600 if they could take title subject to the existing mortgage. The O'Haras signed the acceptance on March 29, 1980. Closing was set for April 15, 1980, at the office of the Henderson Real Estate Company. A check for $4,000 was deposited with the broker as earnest money.

The sellers were to pay $220 for title service. They also owed the amount for revenue stamps at the rate of $.55 per $500 or fraction thereof and $14 for recording. There were two paid-up insurance policies for $20,000 and $30,000. The $20,000 policy cost $300 for three years and expires August 15, 1981. The five-year policy for $30,000 expires March 1, 1982 and has a premium of $450. General taxes for 1979 are due on June 1, 1980, in the amount of $840.

The seller paid the mortgage payment due April 1, 1980 covering interest through March 31. The contract stated that taxes, insurance, and interest are to be prorated, and the buyer is to pay a $150 assumption fee.

(a) Prepare the settlement statement using the statutory month method.

(b) Prepare the closing statement using the uniform method.

17–2. Mr. Ray Holt is selling his house at 584 Ridge Drive to a Mr. and Mrs. King. The contract is dated July 17, 1982, and has been signed by the buyer and the seller. The purchase price is $67,500. An earnest money deposit was paid to the Johnson Real Estate Company in the amount of $6,750. Johnson was employed by Mr. Holt.

Purchaser is to take title subject to the existing mortgage, which has an unpaid balance of $42,500. Payments are due quarterly on the last day of March, June, September, and December in the amount of $250 on the principal plus interest at 9 percent per annum on the amount of principal outstanding since the last quarterly payment. The last payment was made June 20, 1982.

Real estate taxes in the amount of $1,260 for 1981 were paid in full on June 1, 1982. The seller has a $60,000 fire insurance policy written for a three-year term that expires November 24, 1983, for which he paid a three-year premium of $480. The quarterly water bill in the amount of $96 was paid for the three months ending June 30, 1982. Closing is set for August 8, 1982.

Property Address _____   Broker _____

Seller _____   Date of contract _____

Buyer _____   _____

SETTLEMENT DATE:	BUYER'S STATEMENT		SELLER'S STATEMENT	
	DEBIT	CREDIT	DEBIT	CREDIT

Figure 17–7

Settlement statement worksheet

The seller paid the attorney $260 separately for the abstract. The seller owes the recording fees of $10 and the revenue stamps at $.55 per $500 or fraction thereof. The commission on the sale was 6 percent. The buyer will pay one point for the assumption fee.

Prepare the statement using the uniform method.

17–3.   Bob Jenkins and his wife Jane are selling their four-apartment structure to Alice Roll, an unmarried woman, of 520 Vine Street, Archdale, Nebraska. The property is at 1800 Main Street, Archdale, Nebraska. The lot is approximately 50 by 165 ft and is described as lot 9 in block 4 of Ipex subdivision in the SW quarter of Section 34, Township 2 North, Range 1 East of the sixth principal meridian.

The binder was drawn up on March 24, 1981, and a formal contract was executed April 1, 1981. The sale price was $139,000, and the buyer deposited $14,000 as earnest money with the Ficek Realty Company. Ficek was employed as a broker by the Jenkins. The title will be conveyed by warranty deed, and the sale will be closed on May 7, 1981. The purchaser is to assume the unpaid balance of the existing mortgage. The mortgage was originally for $102,000 and is payable at $400 per month for 255 months plus 8 percent interest on the outstanding balance at each payment. Payments are due on the first day of each month and include interest for the previous month. The May 1, 1981, payment has been made; the mortgage balance is $49,200 on May 1, 1981. The buyer will pay an assumption fee of $400.

The 1979 real estate tax was $2,200 and was paid on June 1, 1980. The 1980 tax is not yet known. The fire insurance policy for $120,000 expires September 3, 1983. The three-year premium of $1,220 was paid in full. There are 1000 gallons of oil in the tank priced at $0.71 per gallon.

The two-month water bill for the period ending May 15, 1981, of $48 is paid. The electric bill of $236 for the two-month period ending April 17, 1981, is paid. The following personal property is included in the sale price: lawn mower, storm doors and windows, TV antenna, and refrigerators and stoves in three apartments. Possession is to be given on the date of closing.

The three apartments are rented under leases expiring November 30, 1981. Monthly rent is $300, payable in advance on the first day of each month. The rent for May was paid May 1, 1981. Purchaser asked for and seller agreed to provide a survey (cost of $95) showing that the garage and building are within lot lines and that there are no encroachments.

The seller will owe $425 to the title company for title examination and will pay $90 for tax stamps. The exclusive listing defined the commission as 5 percent of the gross selling price. Prepare the closing statement using the actual days of the year method.

SUPPLEMENTARY READINGS

Bellavance, Russell C. *Real Estate Law.* St. Paul: West, 1978. Chapter 11.

Bergfield, Philip B. *Principles of Real Estate Law.* New York: McGraw-Hill, 1979. Chapter 13.

Ellis, John T. *Guide to Real Estate License Examinations.* Englewood Cliffs, N.J.: Prentice-Hall, 1974. Chapters 13 and 19.

Estes, Jack C., and Kokus, John, Jr. *Real Estate License Preparation Course for the Uniform Examinations*. New York: McGraw-Hill, 1976. Chapter 15.

French, William B.; Martin, Stephen J.; and Battle, Thomas E., III. *Guide to Real Estate Licensing Examinations*. Boston: Warren, Gorham, and Lamont, 1978. Chapter 16.

Galaty, Fillmore W.; Alloway, Wellington J.; and Kyle, Robert C. *Modern Real Estate Practice*. Chicago: Real Estate Education Corporation, 1978. Chapter 23.

Henderson, Thomas P.; Johnson, Ross H.; Kruse, Dennis; and Ficek, Edmund F. *Real Estate Examination Guide*. Columbus, Oh.: Charles E. Merrill, 1977. Chapter 17.

Ring, Alfred A., and Dasso, Jerome. *Real Estate Principles and Practices*. Englewood Cliffs, N.J.: Prentice-Hall, 1977. Chapter 12.

Siedel, George J., III. *Real Estate Law*. St. Paul: West, 1979. Chapter 10.

Property Development and Construction

The development of land and the construction of improvements is one of the most important single contributions to gross national product in the United States. Over three million persons are employed in the production of real estate improvements, and two million more are employed in manufacturing products going into homes and other new construction.

A large portion of this real estate product is the development of raw land into residential, industrial, or other usage. Cities and towns grow primarily through the process of developing unimproved parcels of land. When a tract of land is divided into smaller parts for development, the process is called *subdividing*. A *land developer* builds homes on the lots and sells them.

Subdivision and land development take time and involve a number of steps. The up-and-down cycles of the economy and the real estate business provide further risks to the *subdivider* or land developer. In view of these complexities, the care spent in planning a real estate project can determine its success or failure.

RESIDENTIAL SUBDIVISION AND DEVELOPMENT

The requirements and methods for developing raw land into residential or industrial subdivisions have changed considerably in the past thirty years. Residential development, in particular, has been subject to increasingly stringent standards and controls. These include federal and state regulations, as well as local standards.

Past Problems

In the recent past, many residential developments have been very successful, whereas others have been much less than successful. Some have not only been financial disasters for the developers, but they have also resulted in severe problems for the families who purchased sites or homes.

A few subdivision and land development projects have made developers wealthy at the expense of the people who invested in the real estate. Many of these problems can be traced to inadequate planning, inadequate financing, or a lack of concern by the developer for the long-term success of the property. Others were the result of unscrupulous developers, intent only upon their own interests, who "let the buyer beware." During the last thirty years, developers frequently were concerned only with a one-time development of a small parcel of land. Because of either their inexperience, ineptness, or lack of concern, they proceeded without adequate planning. The developers, financial backers, and land purchasers, as well as the community, all lose out if a development is unsuccessful.

The resulting problems have led to the following changes in the process and control of subdivision development.

1. There are now strict municipal regulations and controls over new subdivision developments. These include more stringent administration of zoning and building codes, as described in Chapter 10.
2. Many states have more stringent licensing requirements for those involved in real estate.
3. General urban area master plans have been prepared specifying use restrictions for urban land or land adjacent to the area.
4. Controls over existing utilities and their extension or the increase in demand for present capacity have been implemented.

Planning Steps

There are several steps followed in the planning and execution of a subdivision project. The following steps are typical:

1. Analyze the market to determine the desires and needs of potential customers in the area.
2. Identify alternative locations and select the best prospects for a successful development.
3. Draw a preliminary layout of the prospective areas. Investigate financing and the availability of utilities. Make a preliminary submission of a plat and plan to the municipal authorities.
4. Make a final decision on a location. Have a formal survey made and plat layout drawn including lots, streets, utilities, and land use restrictions.
5. Submit a formal plan to municipal authorities for approval.
6. Construct the necessary roads, provide grading and erosion control, and bring in utilities.

7. Sell sites to potential builders and begin construction of homes.

8. Complete roads, sidewalks, or other items under the responsibility of the developer. Provide for maintenance under developer's responsibility.

Market Evaluation

An evaluation of the market is comprised of a number of closely integrated investigations, analyses, and decisions. The objective is to end up with homes or home sites that customers will want within their price and location constraints.

Prior to purchase of land or initiation of any evaluation work, the developer should research overall market conditions. The general state of the economy is a first consideration. The local business picture is also important, as are local population trends. If a residential project is contemplated, the present availability of homes and apartment units should be analyzed. This availability is then compared to the findings of a market survey to determine who the potential buyers are and what they are looking for.

Information on potential buyers would include present living locations, work locations, earnings, family sizes, and other needs or desires. Next, the developer should investigate the competition. Which areas of need are the competitors aiming for? What can be done to provide better values than the competition has? One result will be a forecast of the number of homes needed on a year-by-year basis. From this evaluation, a line of residences can be chosen at prices, sizes, and styles that will have a good chance of selling.

The developer then must determine what land resources are available as well as the financial backing and the other resources needed and whether or not they are available. The human assets to accomplish the job are also significant. A marketing organization is needed to market the properties, whether it be the developer's own personnel or independent real estate brokers. Construction, site survey, planning, and legal services are also needed.

The search for a site will probably start with identifying a number of alternatives. Sometimes a prospective developer will start with a property that he owns; however, it is still wise to consider other alternatives. If the land under consideration does not have the attributes desired, it may be financially advantageous to abandon it and select a different site.

Planning Trade-Offs

The information from the market evaluation will help determine the attributes desired for the proposed subdivision. Municipality restrictions will, of course, have to be considered also. There is no standard list of attributes from which to make the final set of designs; however, the following choices should be carefully considered.

1. Privacy provided by large lots versus economy allowed by smaller lots.

2. Privacy and appearance provided by trees and vegetation versus economy of more efficient construction on bare or cleared land.

3. Privacy provided by distance from schools and commercial areas versus convenience in having schools and shopping areas close by.

4. Narrow winding roads to discourage traffic versus wider streets with curbs and sidewalks to accommodate pedestrian and automobile traffic.

5. Recreation areas versus economy of complete use of all land for home building.

6. Features such as family rooms and two baths versus economy.

Some developments are planned around a particular recreation site or facility such as a golf course, country club, waterfront area, lake, school, or shopping center. Other innovative developments center around a stable and riding track, as in Figure 18–1, or a private plane airstrip.

Once a general type of development has been determined, the developer should look for an equivalent development completed in the past few years.

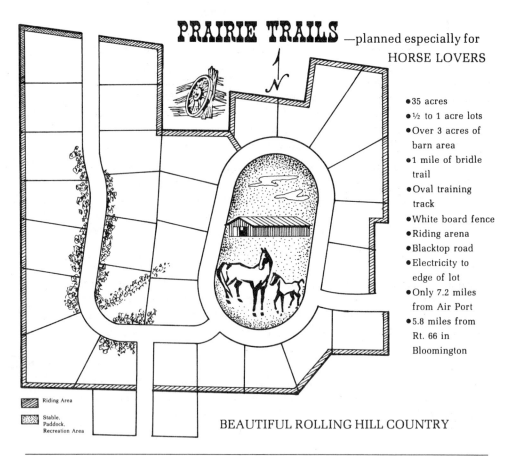

Source: Hal Riss Real Estate, Normal, Illinois.

Figure 18–1
Subdivision centered around stable and riding track

A drive through and a talk with some residents may reveal assets as well as problems. Also, the places from which the people moved would give an indication of the source of buyers. After the general objectives and constraints have been established, the developer can select the final location. In the Planned Unit Development (PUD), the developers obtain special zoning approval to integrate residential, commercial, and possibly certain industrial uses into a single unit (also see Chapter 10).

Steps Prior to Land Acquisition

At this stage in the planning process, one or more tracts are under consideration. The market evaluation has identified the important factors. The next step is to compare the alternative tracts of land, considering several factors.

Location

Is the tract in a location where natural growth or expansion of the urban area will proceed? Usually, the natural growth of an urban area will extend along important traffic routes that facilitate access. If a site is not in this natural expansion pattern, it could still be a satisfactory location; however, the costs of promotion will be greater and the rate of progress in selling the lots and homes and completing the project will be slower. Proximity to schools, shopping centers, and public transportation must also be considered.

Layout

Next, a rough layout is prepared of each area under consideration to determine how many lots could be expected. It would include proposed streets and a layout of the lots. An example of a layout is shown in Figure 18–2. Depending upon the terrain and other natural factors, a larger amount of acreage would not necessarily guarantee a greater number of lots. Some areas may not be usable because of the terrain.

Style

Along with the layout of each area, the style of homes or buildings proposed is considered, since it will have a significant impact upon the individual lot size. Of major importance in this decision is the style and price range of any existing properties in the area. The proximity and type of commercial and other properties must also be considered, since these factors affect marketability.

Soil

The nature of the soil on the site is important for several reasons. First, it must support structures and roadbeds. Erosion and drainage are important considerations. Factors such as rocky ground or high water level may preclude construction of basements. Filled land or underground mining operations can also affect the stability of the land. Another important factor is drainage. The ability to construct stable roadbeds and to have dry basements in the homes is important. The ability of the soil to drain or absorb water is also important where septic systems are planned.

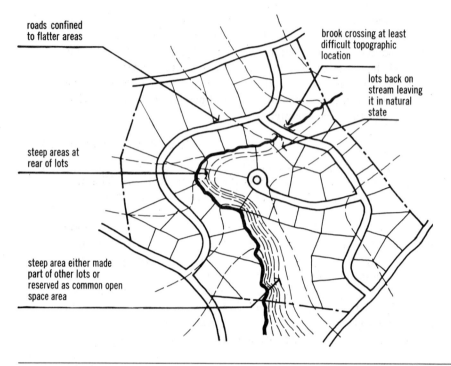

roads confined
to flatter areas

brook crossing at least
difficult topographic
location

lots back on
stream leaving
it in natural
state

steep areas at
rear of lots

steep area either made
part of other lots or
reserved as common open
space area

Source: State of New Hampshire, Office of State Planning. *Handbook of Subdivision Practice.* 1972.

Figure 18–2
Tentative layout of streets and lots

Utilities

Electricity, gas, water, and sewage are important considerations. Septic
systems can substitute for sewage systems, and wells substitute for city water.
The developer should determine the nearest location of each of these utilities,
the available capacity for expansion, and the cost of extending the lines or
pipes to the desired site. The mere existence of these facilities does not mean
that there is the necessary gas or water capacity or pressure or sewage
capacity. The size of the development will affect the amount that can be spent
to bring in these utilities. The cost should be computed on a per lot basis. This
method helps the developer understand how these costs will offset the sale
price of the lots, since all costs must be recovered through lot sale. A large
development will be able to support considerably more of these costs than
would a small development.

Access

A large part of the early improvement costs will be in providing roads. These
costs will have to be borne by the developer before receiving money from sale
of lots. Road costs include displacement costs for soil, leveling, providing
drainage and culverts or bridges, preparing a road base, paving, curbing, and

sometimes providing sidewalks. Sometimes the street construction must be closely integrated with the utility extension, as shown in the two alternatives of Figure 18–3.

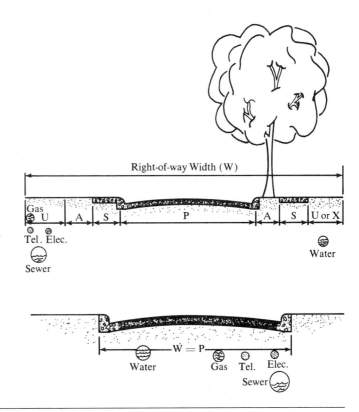

Source: National Association of Home Builders. *Land Development Manual.* Washington, D.C.: 1974.

Figure 18–3

Two methods of integrating utilities with street construction

Local zoning restrictions

In considering any site, the local zoning regulations must be considered. If the property is not presently zoned for the lot size and type of construction contemplated, the procedures to change the zoning must be investigated. The developer sometimes wants to place tighter restrictions on the development than those set by the municipality. This will help assure consistency in construction, protection of property values, and protection of values of unsold or undeveloped property.

Access to services

The developer should also consider access to fire protection, police protection, hospitals, schools, and churches. The tax rate of the municipality is also an important factor.

Government reports
Depending on the type of subdivision or development, it may be necessary to file an environmental impact statement or, for land sales, a federal or state property report. (These reports and when they apply were described in Chapter 12.)

Financing

Most land developers require some type of financing. Prior to selecting a site, the available financing in that location must be investigated. This financing would include FHA, VA, and other federal program funds, as well as conventional mortgage loans. An investigation of available financing is appropriate whether or not the developer needs funds to purchase and develop the land. Even if he has those funds, he needs to establish financing commitments so that prospective property buyers will be able to finance their houses.

Often, the developer will purchase the land himself or form a syndicate to make the purchase. A *syndicate* is a group of persons who combine their financial resources to undertake a venture which, in this case, is the development of the real estate. The formation of a syndicate has certain tax advantages to the participants and permits accumulation of the large amounts of money needed to carry out a real estate development project.

If the developer has funds to purchase the land, he can then obtain a mortgage on it to finance further development and construction. Usually, however, a bank or other lender will require that the subdivision be surveyed and other tests performed before furnishing financing to make sure the land is fully usable for the proposed construction.

In the loan agreement, the developers can arrange terms so that individual sites can be released from the total mortgage and sold to buyers. The buyers can then arrange to build their own homes with individual loans. A typical release provision might allow the sale of a site free and clear to the buyer, with a portion of the money from each lot sold going to the lender to repay the loan gradually. In any case, the developer would probably develop a smaller portion of the total tract and later expand the development as the lots are sold. This procedure would then give him the additional funds from the lot sales to proceed with extended development of the whole tract.

The use of an option to purchase provides another alternative to the developer who is short of funds to purchase the entire tract that he desires to develop. If the developer is offered 150 acres, he may purchase 50 acres outright and obtain options to purchase additional tracts at some time in the future. This gives him the opportunity to develop the first tract and, if successful, he will then be able to go ahead and expand the project. If the original tract is not successful, he would not take up the option to purchase the remainder.

Subdivision Planning

Once the parcel of land to develop has been selected and purchased, the extensive and detailed steps of layout and planning of the subdivision must follow. In some cases, a developer may take an option on a tract of land pending completion of the more detailed surveys and layouts required. The option would give him greater assurance that all factors would work out to his satisfaction before he actually made the land purchase.

The process of planning a subdivision requires a considerable initial outlay of money and time. However, careful planning can provide substantial monetary savings by allowing more efficient use of land as well as by identifying and avoiding potential problems. If unforeseen changes need to be made as a result of inadequate planning, the venture can become quite costly and the developer may go bankrupt. The plans prepared for the subdivision should describe the grading of roads, drainage, drainage dump, road paving, sidewalks, curbs, water mains, recreation areas, street signs, and municipal inspection fees. Some of the many preferred practices in the layout of a subdivision are shown in Figure 18–4. A *clustered layout,* for the same number of homes, can reduce street area and increase *open space* areas.

In addition to local constraints with which the developer must comply, if he plans to use FHA financing, there are standards for new subdivisions that must be met before FHA will approve loans. The development must contain the essential utilities, such as water, sewage and electricity, and these must comply with local regulations. Minimum size lots are specified based on the home size to be built, and a uniform setback from the road is required. To secure FHA and VA loans, the roads must be of approved width and surfacing. The homes must meet approved structural and appearance constraints and must be consistent with other improved property in the area. Other features such as recreational areas and barriers from industrial or commercial establishments must be present, along with adequate access to shopping areas and schools.

Covenants and Restrictions

The developer of a subdivision will usually prepare *covenants* and *restrictions* that become binding upon the property owners in the subdivision. These requirements are in addition to zoning and other local municipal restrictions. They are made a part of the contracts to purchase lots. Each purchaser thereby agrees to these provisions when purchasing a lot. Either the developer or another property owner can take legal action to enforce any covenant or restriction. The purpose is to protect the interests of the residents and to protect their property values. These covenants are particularly important if the subdivision is not under urban restrictions or is developed around a lake or other center of attraction where unauthorized persons may attempt to use the facilities. Here are some typical restrictions that appear in subdivision covenants:

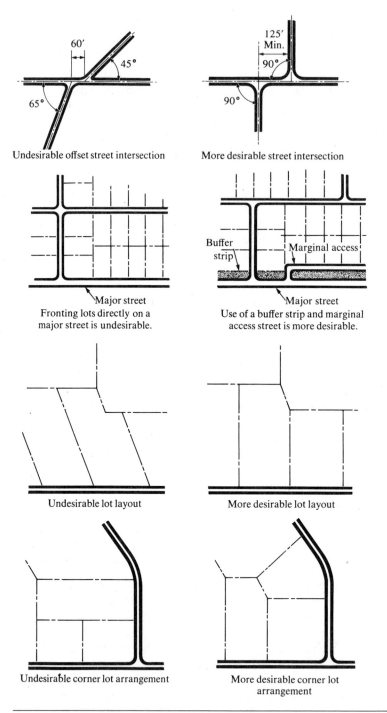

Undesirable offset street intersection

More desirable street intersection

Major street
Fronting lots directly on a
major street is undesirable.

Buffer strip

Marginal access

Major street
Use of a buffer strip and marginal
access street is more desirable.

Undesirable lot layout

More desirable lot layout

Undesirable corner lot arrangement

More desirable corner lot
arrangement

Source: State of New York, Office of Planning Services. *Control of Land Subdivision.* 1974.

Figure 18-4
Preferred practices in the layout of a subdivision

376

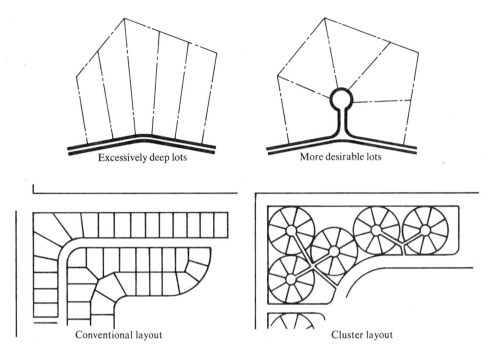

Excessively deep lots   More desirable lots

Conventional layout   Cluster layout

Figure 18–4
(Cont.)

1. Restriction to use of lots for residential construction only.

2. Approval of each home plan by the association or developer.

3. Prohibition of outbuildings and fences in certain areas.

4. Restrictions as to minimum house living area, minimum lot size, or setback of buildings.

5. Restriction of type of exterior construction materials.

6. Maintenance of lots in good order.

7. Restriction or design of septic systems and disposal of trash.

8. Prohibitions of signs, animals, parking on roadways, or temporary structures.

9. Easement rights.

10. Rules for use of recreational facilities, lake, or other special areas.

11. Membership in development association; power of association to levy fees and assessments; election of officers in association.

12. Right of first refusal to other property owners or the developer if an owner wants to sell.

Plat Approval

Most states and municipal governments have laws regulating the subdividing of land. Many of these laws have been passed because of past incompetence or fraudulent practices used by subdividers. Most municipalities have planning commissions that are authorized to review and approve plats of all proposed new subdivisions. The *plat* must be prepared by a licensed land surveyor at the expense of the developer and submitted to the commission. Sometimes the submission must be made in two or three steps. Figure 18–5 shows a preapplication sketch of a subdivision, with the planning board's comments added.

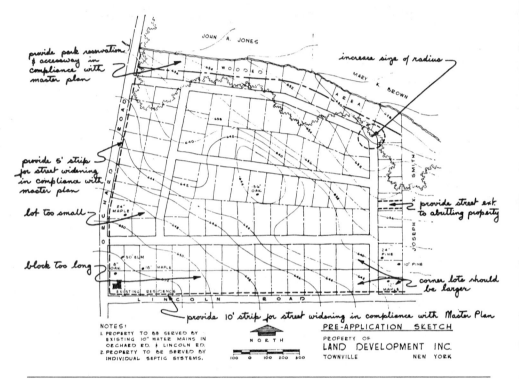

Source: State of New York, Office of Planning Services. *Control of Land Subdivision.* 1974, p. 25.

Figure 18–5
Preapplication sketch of a subdivision

Depending on the local regulations, various requirements must usually be met by the developer. Some common requirements include the following:

1. Road cuts to specified width.
2. Curbing.
3. Sidewalks.
4. Road paving, finishing, or oiling.
5. Locations for wells and cesspools.
6. National Building Codes.
7. Lot size restrictions.
8. Sufficient public areas (open space).

Normally, the developer must post a bond to assure that the actual construction is in accordance with the plat. The commissioner can then use the bond money to complete or reconstruct any work not in accordance with the approved plat.

Figure 18–6 shows a final subdivision plat. Table 18–1 shows a typical list of items that must be submitted with the plat. The table also shows a typical set of requirements that must be on the final plat. The final plat is then recorded. The act of recording becomes a public *dedication* of streets and designated open areas, such as a playground.

Figure 18–6
A subdivision plat

COMMERCIAL AND INDUSTRIAL DEVELOPMENTS

Commercial property includes income-producing property such as shopping centers, office buildings, gasoline stations, retail establishments, parking lots, and hotels and motels. Industrial properties are used for the manufacture and warehousing of industrial and consumer products and include factories,

Table 18-1
Typical items to be submitted with a plat

Submission Items

- ☐ Site survey map
- ☐ Site location map
- ☐ Soils map
- ☐ Percolation test data
- ☐ Soils test data
- ☐ Watershed outline and drainage computations
- ☐ Engineer's statement of suitability
- ☐ Statement of existing street work
- ☐ Cost estimates
- ☐ Deed restrictions
- ☐ Road profiles (final)
- ☐ Cross sections (final)
- ☐ Statement incorporating requirements of subdivision regulations
- ☐ Statement of responsibility and liability
- ☐ Sanitary sewerage computations
- ☐ Fish and Game Department approval
- ☐ Health and welfare: Division of Public Health approval
- ☐ Public works and highway approval
- ☐ WSPCC approval for subdivision
- ☐ Water Resources Board approval
- ☐ Fill and Dredge Special Board approval
- ☐ Municipal water supply approval
- ☐ Sewage disposal approval
- ☐ Other municipal approval
- ☐ Other state approval

Required on Final Plat

- ☐ Name of subdivision
- ☐ Name and address of owner
- ☐ North point
- ☐ Bar scale
- ☐ Date
- ☐ Area of site
- ☐ Parcel boundary
- ☐ Names and addresses of abutting owners
- ☐ Subdivisions and buildings 100' away
- ☐ Roads and drives 200' away
- ☐ Buildings to remain
- ☐ Existing and proposed street lines
- ☐ Existing and proposed street R.O.W. widths
- ☐ Street names
- ☐ Lot lines
- ☐ Setback lines
- ☐ Easements
- ☐ Watercourses
- ☐ Open space (acreage noted)
- ☐ Natural features
- ☐ Zoning district(s)
- ☐ Future subdivisions
- ☐ Topographic contour 5' interval
- ☐ Water mains and other utilities (final)
- ☐ Sanitary sewers (final)
- ☐ Drainage system (final)
- ☐ Name, address and seal of engineer
- ☐ Name, address and seal of surveyor
- ☐ Bearings and distances
- ☐ Lot dimensions
- ☐ Lot areas
- ☐ Lot numbering
- ☐ Stations
- ☐ Radii
- ☐ Curve data
- ☐ Pavement widths
- ☐ Monument locations

Source: State of New Hampshire, Office of State Planning. *Handbook of Subdivision Practice*, p. 31.

utilities, warehouses, and mining or lumbering operations. The development of these types of properties requires steps and considerations similar in some ways to that of residential properties, but different in other ways.

Development for Retail Establishments

Retail facilities can vary from the *freestanding store* to the small *neighborhood centers*, shopping centers developed on a nonplanned basis called *suburban shopping districts*, the larger *community shopping center* anchored by a department store or variety store, or the *regional shopping center* anchored by two or three larger stores or branches of stores.

Many land owners have successfully developed retail shopping centers. However, a considerable amount of planning is required to assure the success of this type of endeavor. The designer of a shopping center will try to start with a **generative business** (e.g., a branch of a major department store) which, through advertising, will generate business of its own efforts. The developer can then attempt to obtain the many smaller *shared businesses* that can thrive due to the pulling power of the larger stores. The shopping center would also include **suscipient businesses** (e.g., restaurants), which attract people for purposes other than shopping. The general theory is that the clustering of stores increases the overall sales volume of each one.

The market evaluation would include an analysis of the demand in the area, determination of the future potential in the trade area, and an evaluation of current and contemplated competition. This would include a consumer survey in the area. The planning phase would include a preliminary layout, an evaluation of the soil, utilities, road access, local restrictions, and financing, and an investigation of applicable government regulations. These and the plat approval would follow to some extent the guidelines given for residential developments; however, the many differences that vary by locality and type of establishment are discussed in the supplementary readings at the end of this chapter.

Land Use for Office Space

Office buildings can be placed in two categories. Those designed and built for a specific company's use fall into the group of **custom construction.** Other office buildings are constructed on a speculative basis for rental. Between 1950 and 1979, the proportion of white collar workers as a percentage of the total labor force expanded considerably. This factor, along with the growth of service industries during the same period, increased the demand for office space. One of the most significant trends over the past 25 years has been the shift of offices to the suburbs; however, the rehabilitation of downtown areas in large cities has also included new office construction.

Prior to acquiring land for office building construction on a speculative basis, a planner/developer should make a study of market demand. The developer needs initially to obtain one important figure, the current ratio of **net rented area** to **net rentable area** (in square feet) in the particular business community. A low ratio would indicate much unoccupied existing office space, and the contemplated project should probably be abandoned. If the ratio were high, the next phase of the study would be to forecast the needs in the area over the next five years. In this forecast, it is necessary to forecast new or increased business or government needs in the area and to convert the potential number of employees into office area needed. A figure of 260 to 280 square feet per employee is often used for the 1975–1985 period. Once the projected demand has been estimated, the developer will need to determine the types of uses contemplated. At that time, the type of building space to construct is selected, and the amount of potential space demand that the contemplated project could capture is estimated. Most other procedures in the planning and development for office space are similar to those for residential developments.

Industrial Sites

A company seeking a site for a plant has the choice of locating in an industrial park or on an individual site. Depending on the individual type of company, the following factors tend to be dominant in choosing a location:

1. Market-oriented companies tend to select locations near the consumers (users) of their products.
2. Labor-oriented companies tend to locate near sources of skilled labor to meet their needs.
3. Resource-oriented companies (such as steel) desire to locate near sources of raw materials. An aluminum company may choose to locate near sources of electric power.
4. A transportation-oriented firm would locate near the types of transport facilities that meet their needs.

Some industries tend to be independent of all of these factors and thus have greater freedom in selecting sites for new plants; however, a developer of an industrial park should consider how these factors would affect potential tenants for the particular industrial park. The development and use of industrial parks has increased, largely due to their ability to provide superior facilities (such as utilities and transportation) and enforced land use controls. They also provide an attractive appearance, police protection, and pleasant and safe working conditions. Frequently, the industrial park will target its promotional campaign toward a certain category of industry. In any case, an industrial development will need to plan sites or construction to suit the needs of particular industries that decide to locate in the park.

THE BUILDING INDUSTRY

The building industry is one of the largest elements of the national economy. Many manufacturers largely depend upon it as a market for their products, and industries in general depend on it to expand capacity. A large segment of the total labor force is engaged in building construction. All of these factors mean that the well-being of the construction industry has a heavy impact upon the national economic picture as a whole. The construction of individual residences makes up a large and important segment of the building industry. This aspect will be dealt with here in greater detail than the other segments.

A house is a rather complex product, since it is comprised of a large variety of elements and materials. Often, single elements such as windows or doors are special either in size, design, or color; this can cause problems because all the necessary materials must be gathered and used in a certain sequence. Building materials are normally distributed by manufacturers either through wholesalers or directly to retail lumberyards. Builders then procure their materials through lumberyards, wholesale plumbing supply houses, and many other sources. Many of these organizations do not sell directly to retail customers.

The bulky nature of most building products requires that those responsible for transporting and distributing them carefully control costs. Transportation, handling, and storage make up a considerable portion of the total costs of the delivered materials. Some products such as plywood and gypsum board break easily or are damaged by weather. These factors further complicate their transportation and storage. Some manufacturers furnish preassembled or prefabricated units of various sizes. Moving the assembled or prefabricated units is possible, but it is more difficult because of their extreme bulk. This higher transportation cost and greater risk of breakage or damage is often, however, counterbalanced by the greater efficiency and cheaper labor that can be provided in the manufacturing facilities compared with site construction.

The Home Builders

Some homes are constructed partially at a manufacturing plant and then transported to the building site, where the house is built from these prefabricated or partially assembled units. Most homes, however, are built by the contractor on the building site.

Construction at the building site is carried out by specialists under the overall direction and responsibility of the builder or contractor. The electrical work, plumbing, plastering, brickwork, excavation, and pouring of concrete are often subcontracted out, as are a few other skill areas—depending frequently on the skills of the builder and his labor force. Usually, the carpenters work directly for the builder on an hourly wage basis. All laborers who work on residential construction need some variety of skills and some knowledge of construction. Often, the same laborers who perform the rough carpentry will continue through the finished carpentry or woodwork, unless the contractor has a large operation and has several residences under way at the same time. The smaller operation still requires specialization, but workers with each type of skill, such as carpentry or masonry, will require a considerable amount of experience and background in order to adapt to the wide variety of types and stages of construction.

National Association of Home Builders (NAHB)

Persons in the business of building or rebuilding homes, apartments, or commercial or industrial structures can belong to the National Association of Home Builders (*NAHB*). It has over 600 local affiliates and over 75,000 members. The association prepares and distributes literature dealing with building construction and land development. NAHB also conducts research related to new concepts in design, construction, and land use. In addition, NAHB provides a focal point for working with the federal government to improve housing and housing programs. It presents the views of the building industry to Congress and to the pertinent agencies and departments in the executive branch of the government.

Building Trades

The building trades are well-organized in most cities. They tend to be organized along craft occupations, such as plumbers, carpenters, electricians, and bricklayers. Thus, the building contractor must work with several organizations. These trade organizations have been quite successful in establishing relatively high wage scales for their workers. The higher wages compensate, to some extent, for the seasonal work and weather constraints that result in many days each year without work. The high labor rates have brought about greater competition from nonunionized personnel.

Where organized trades prevail, the labor unions control many of the hiring practices and training methods of apprentices and prescribe other restrictions as to how work is to be performed. Building trade organizations also tend to be slow in their acceptance of new methods and materials; this factor can impede the use of potential economies in building that might otherwise be adopted more quickly. All these factors support high wage rates in the building trades.

RESIDENTIAL CONSTRUCTION

The construction of a new home can be closely integrated with the work of the developer, or it can involve only the owner of a single piece of property and the builder. Usually, the builder or a firm engaged in construction is involved in a particular project over a short period of time. However, the builder still faces a number of risks. Weather and labor strife always threaten delays and create uncertainties. During periods of inflation, costs of both labor and materials can increase quickly, or there may even be shortages of materials. All of these factors lead to a relatively high rate of business failures in the building industry.

The construction of a typical residence can be separated into the following systematic steps:

1. Planning and estimating;
2. Designing;

3. Selecting a builder;
4. Doing the construction work.

Construction of an entire development differs somewhat from individual unit construction; however, the processes are quite similar in most ways.

Planning and Estimating

The first planning step is to select the building site or lot. The lot selection must be integrated closely, however, with the design of the home. Usually, a subdivision or residential area is laid out to accommodate a certain size, price, or style of home, and this may be a starting constraint. Usually, there is also a price constraint to work with. The availability of mortgages and the percentage loan that can be obtained will also considerably influence the home size and price range.

The planning stage consists of the search for a number of alternative lots and some acceptable home designs and then the choice from among these alternatives and designs.

Design of the Home

A person planning to build a home can either hire an architect to design an individual home or select from an architect's existing designs. Many companies provide a number of home designs for which the drawings and specifications can be purchased. In some cases, these specifications may have to be modified to comply with local restrictions or constraints or the person's individual preferences. However, minor modifications can usually be made easily. In either case, the architect prepares the basic drawings of a home, which include the floor plans as well as the front, side, and rear views. A typical floor plan is shown in Figure 18–7, which also depicts the front elevation of the home. The *floor plan* shows the exact room sizes and their interrelationships, whereas the *front elevation* shows the finished house as it would more normally appear to someone viewing it at ground level.

In addition to the floor plan and external views, the architect prepares a specification and a bill of materials. The *specification* would describe requirements that might not be completely clear from the drawings. The type of framing, wood and nailing requirements, siding material, grade of concrete, and tests used to check the mixture are examples of items which might be in the specifications. Figure 18–9 shows some typical requirements.

The *bill of materials* would list the quantity of each item of material required to construct the house. If all of the items, such as studs, nails, and so on, are not specifically listed, the builder would have to determine this information by analysis of the drawings. Sometimes a bill of material is not furnished at all, and the prospective builder would need to figure quotations from the drawings to prepare a bid.

A final document needed would show the layout of the house on the lot, as in Figure 18–8.

The Concord "B" 2277 Square Feet, Plus Garage

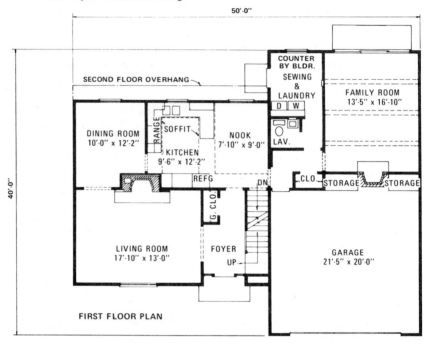

FIRST FLOOR PLAN

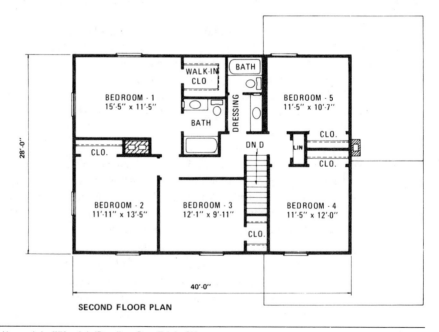

SECOND FLOOR PLAN

Source: Used by permission Widerschein/Strandberg Corp., Toledo, Ohio.

Figure 18–7

Typical single-family residence floor plans

Figure 18–7a
Front elevation of residence

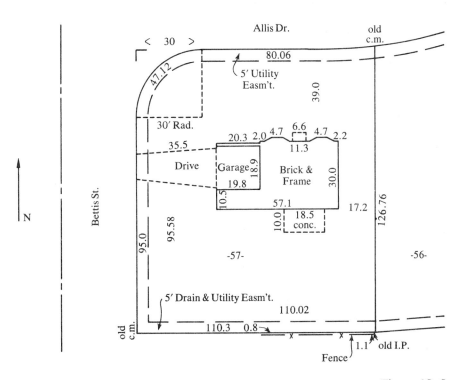

Figure 18–8
Survey—Layout of house on lot

SPECIFICATIONS FOR A HOME

The contractor shall provide all necessary labor and materials and perform all work of every nature whatsoever to be done in the erection of a residence for

Mr. and Mrs. John A. Halliburn

as owner, in accordance with these specifications and accompanying drawings. The location of the residence will be as follows:

421 Fourth Ave., Waynesboro, Va. 22980

General

The plans, elevations, sections, and detail drawings, together with these specifications, are to form the basis of the contract and are to be of equal force. The contractor shall comply with all health and building ordinances that are applicable.

Excavation and grading

The contractor shall do all necessary excavating and rough grading. The excavation shall be large enough to permit inspection of footings after the foundation has been completed. All excess dirt shall be hauled away by the contractor. Black surface loam shall be used in grading.

Concrete footings

Footings shall be of concrete having a minimum compressive strength of 2000#, 2500#, or 3000# per sq in at 28 days, whichever will be according to local code. Concrete shall be machine mixed with clean water to the proper consistency, and shall be placed immediately after mixing. Footings shall be thoroughly protected with hay or straw in freezing weather. All footings shall be set below the frost line and rest on firm soil, and shall be flat and level on the underside. Footings shall be of sizes shown on plan.

Basement walls and floor

Basement walls shall be constructed of 8 in concrete blocks of approved quality. Blocks shall be laid in a full bed of mortar, composed of one part of cement to three parts of sand. Mortar joints shall be filled thoroughly with cement mortar, neatly pointed on both sides. All walls shall have uniform bearing for framing, being straight, plumb, and level. Beam fill to be placed as shown on the plans. Basement walls shall be parged on exterior with 1/2 in cement mortar and waterproofed with 2 coats asphalt applied by brush. Basement floor shall be 4 in thick of concrete having minimum compressive strength of 2500# per sq in at 28 days and monolithically finished to a smooth hard surface and carefully pitched to drains.

Heating

Contractor shall and will provide all necessary labor and material and perform all heating work of every nature whatsoever to be done, including the installation of 135,000 BTU heating system of sufficient size to properly heat all parts of the house to 72°F at all times. If hot air system is to be used, it is to be installed according to the code of the National Society of Heating and Ventilating Engineers.

Figure 18–9

Typical requirements from a specification

Selecting a Builder

Selecting a builder to perform the actual construction work usually involves obtaining competitive bids. The drawings of the house, the specifications, and the bill of materials provide the information as to what the builder is required to do. These documents would be sent to each prospective builder to bid on the project. In some instances, the developer or the property owner could select a builder based on past experience or by reputation, but the best practice is to seek competitive bids. In the competitive bidding process, each prospective builder quotes a price on the identical drawings and specifications, so that the lowest bid could probably be accepted. The prospective owner should also consider the builder's reputation for meeting quality and scheduling requirements, in addition to the competitive prices. The builder's ability to provide a bond or other evidence of financial stability is also important. Otherwise, there may be delays or problems if the builder cannot obtain sufficient funds to complete the project. Sometimes, however, a bidder may take exception to a requirement or suggest an alternative method of construction or type of material. The property owner may accept the suggestion if it would improve the house or result in a lower cost. Since the total amount of money required to finance a home is substantial, most builders will require periodic payments as the work progresses. If so, the bids should clearly indicate the amounts and the point in construction where each is due.

Normally bids are requested for a *fixed price* for the entire building. The builder would estimate his costs for material and labor and add on a profit for himself. He would usually seek bids from subcontractors to install plumbing, electric wiring, concrete work, cabinets, or other portions that the builder does not plan to do himself. The builder would try to get fixed prices for these subcontracted tasks since he would want to make sure his subcontractors would not later raise their prices. The builder may also line up workers because, at times, good labor is difficult to find. Less competent laborers could cause delays and increased costs.

In order to avoid the risks related to a fixed price, some builders are willing to bid only on a *cost-plus-fixed-fee* basis. In this case, the property owner or developer would pay all the actual costs of labor and materials, and the builder would get a fixed fee for his effort. On a $40,000 house, the builder might get a typical fee of $4,000 above his costs. This type of contract places more risk with the property owner and less risk with the builder. In this case, the builder would not need to estimate the job so carefully. It would also leave the property owner greater freedom in making changes as the work progressed. At the same time, the total cost may vary considerably from what was originally planned or expected. Another agreement may provide for a cost-plus-percentage-of-cost basis. If the agreed figure were 10 percent, and the costs came to $43,000, the builder would receive the $43,000 cost plus a $4,300 fee. Since it is somewhat unwise to give the builder an incentive to end up with greater costs, this type of contract is not widely used and is not recommended.

Once the builder has been selected, a contract is signed between the builder and the property owner. The contract would contain all of the provisions outlined above and would refer to the plans and specifications. Usually, it is wise to specify a schedule for completion.

Payments

The contract should specify that the builder provide a performance bond. The payments to the contractor would be scheduled (e.g., one-third when shell is completed, one-third when plastered, and one-third upon issuance of occupancy permit). Prior to each payment, the contractor should be required to provide an affadavit or receipts showing that materials and subcontractors have been paid or, if not, he should provide lien waivers.

Construction Work

Once the contract has been negotiated and signed and a building permit has been issued by the designated public official, the builder can start construction. The nature of home construction requires that many tasks be performed in sequence. Some steps must be completed before others can start. The site preparation and completion of the foundation are necessary before the framing of the structure can begin. The next major steps are the framing, roof, and siding, since most of the later interior work must be performed under protection from the weather. Figure 18–10 and Appendix B show residential construction details, including the *joists* supporting the floor, the *studs* forming the basis for the walls, and the *rafters* supporting the roof. Numerous other parts of a typical home are also identified. The protection provided by the roof and walls will permit much of the interior work to be carried out regardless of the weather.

The remaining steps still require careful planning and coordination by the builder, so that the various specialists are scheduled to perform their tasks in the right sequence. For example, the heat ducts and electric wiring must be put in before the plaster. Then both the heating contractor and electrician must come back to finish the work that must be done after the plastering and interior painting. A delay at any stage can delay much of the other work. Much of the electrical, plumbing, and other work may need to be checked by the local inspector for conformance to building codes. The inspections must often take place before the work is covered up by later steps in the building sequence. If a builder is constructing a number of homes, he can initiate land clearance and digging at one time for several houses. Then, as each step on one house is completed, the specialists can go on to the next house, so as to result in more efficient use of time, labor, and delivery of materials.

Energy Efficient Homes

The salesperson or broker can help the potential home buyer evaluate the home from an energy efficiency standpoint, just as it would be evaluated for construction details and other assets or defects. The prudent home buyer of

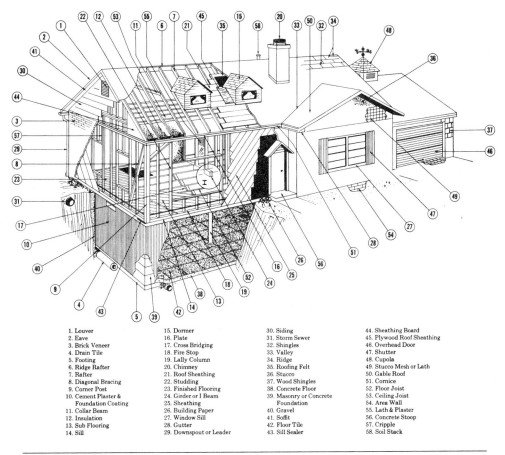

1. Louver	15. Dormer	30. Siding	44. Sheathing Board
2. Eave	16. Plate	31. Storm Sewer	45. Plywood Roof Sheathing
3. Brick Veneer	17. Cross Bridging	32. Shingles	46. Overhead Door
4. Drain Tile	18. Fire Stop	33. Valley	47. Shutter
5. Footing	19. Lally Column	34. Ridge	48. Cupola
6. Ridge Rafter	20. Chimney	35. Roofing Felt	49. Stucco Mesh or Lath
7. Rafter	21. Roof Sheathing	36. Stucco	50. Gable Roof
8. Diagonal Bracing	22. Studding	37. Wood Shingles	51. Cornice
9. Corner Post	23. Finished Flooring	38. Concrete Floor	52. Floor Joist
10. Cement Plaster &	24. Girder or I Beam	39. Masonry or Concrete	53. Ceiling Joist
Foundation Coating	25. Sheathing	Foundation	54. Area Wall
11. Collar Beam	26. Building Paper	40. Gravel	55. Lath & Plaster
12. Insulation	27. Window Sill	41. Soffit	56. Concrete Stoop
13. Sub Flooring	28. Gutter	42. Floor Tile	57. Cripple
14. Sill	29. Downspout or Leader	43. Sill Sealer	58. Soil Stack

Source: Dodge Building Cost Calculator and Valuation Guide. Copyright ©, 1975 McGraw-Hill Information Systems Company. 1221 Avenue of the Americas. New York, New York 10020.

Figure 18-10
Residential construction details

the 1980s looks at the energy saving features of the home as closely as the heating bill, tax bill, and interior and exterior condition.

Most older dwellings need considerable work to make them energy efficient. As a general rule, homes can be compared in a specific area by their fuel costs; however, since the living habits of the home owner can affect the heating cost significantly, several other items can also be checked.

The following checklist will provide an idea as to how energy-efficient an older home is (the numbering of the list refers to the numbers in Figure 18–11):

1. *Insulation* in ceiling, in walls, in attic floors, and in floors over garage and crawl space (refer to Figure 18–11a for R-values).
2. Vapor barrier wherever there is insulation.

Source: "Insulation for Thermal and Sound Control," p.1, Owens-Corning Fiberglas Corporation. Reprinted with permission.

Figure 18–11
An energy efficient home

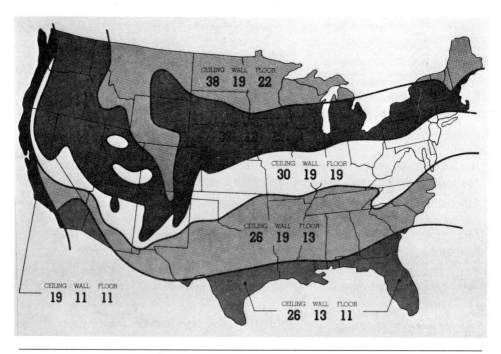

Source: Guide to Constructing an Energy Efficient Home, p. 17, Owens-Corning Fiberglas Corporation. Reprinted with permission.

Figure 18–11a
Recommended R-values for insulation

Table 18-2

Sequence activities and required times to finish a house

Job No.	Description	Immediate predecessors	Time (days)
a	Start		0
b	Excavate and pour footings	a	4
c	Pour concrete foundation	b	2
d	Erect wooden frame including rough roof	c	4
e	Lay brickwork	d	6
f	Install basement drains and plumbing	c	1
g	Pour basement floor	f	2
h	Install rough plumbing	f	3
i	Install rough wiring	d	2
j	Install heating and ventilating	d,g	4
k	Fasten plaster board and plaster (including drying)	i,j,h	10
l	Lay finishing flooring	k	3
m	Install kitchen fixtures	l	1
n	Install finish plumbing	l	2
o	Finish carpentry	l	3
p	Finish roofing and flashing	e	2
q	Fasten gutters and downspouts	p	1
r	Lay storm drains for rain water	c	1
s	Sand and varnish flooring	o,t	2
t	Paint	m,n	3
u	Finish electrical work	t	1
v	Finish grading	q,r	2
w	Pour walks and complete landscaping	v	5
x	Finish	s,u,w	0

Source: Elwood Buffa, Modern Production Management. New York: Wiley, 1973, p. 599.

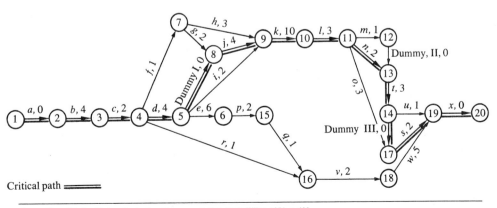

Critical path ═══

Source: Elwood Buffa, Modern Production Management. New York: Wiley, 1973, p. 602.

Figure 18-12

PERT network diagram for house construction

3.   Perimeter insulation along and under edges of foundation.

4.   Double-glazed windows or storm sash.

5.   Storm doors.

6.   Insulation on air handling ducts or hot water pipes.

7.   Windows and doors weather-stripped.

8.   Caulking and sealing to prevent air infiltration.

9.   Ventilation to exhaust attic air and moisture.

10.   Proper size of heating and cooling equipment.

An inspection by an insulation expert can be obtained easily if there is doubt as to the existing adequacy. Some utility companies offer free inspections to determine the energy efficiency of a home.

Scheduling

Scheduling aids are available for planning the sequence of building tasks. Table 18–2 shows a sequential list of tasks for building a house. Figure 18–12 shows a **PERT** (program evaluation review technique) network of those tasks, showing exactly which must be completed before others can start. Each line represents a task; the circles represent the end of a task or the start of another task. From this scheduling network diagram, the builder can determine factors such as these:

1.   The shortest possible completion time for the house if everything goes well; he can also determine the longest time if many problems occur.

2.   The mean completion time and the interval of time over which 90 percent of the homes such as the one being built would ordinarily be completed, considering the risks involved.

3.   The earliest and latest start times for each task under normal circumstances.

In addition, preparing the network forces the contractor to think through the building process carefully, perhaps turning up ideas for more efficient use of his time or personnel. This procedure is especially helpful if more than one building is under construction at one time and the tasks can be integrated.

Once the construction is done and the inspections completed by the architect, municipal authorities, and the owner, the project is finished.

SUMMARY

Real estate construction represents a large and important segment of our national economy. The development of subdivisions and the construction of homes make up a significant portion of this business. Other segments are the construction of commercial property, apartments, shopping centers, and industrial sites.

Experience has caused municipalities to place stringent restrictions and procedures on developers of subdivisions. These developments, whether they be residential, commercial, or industrial parks, require extensive planning and a considerable financial outlay. Most developers need to arrange for financing before they start any actual work, and they should carry out a market analysis and a variety of other investigations.

The construction of homes also requires experience and financial backing. The home builder faces risks due to uncertainties of weather, labor strife, and materials prices. Building a home requires planning and estimating, designing, selecting a builder, and doing the actual construction work. The sequential nature of the actual construction makes it a complex task requiring considerable planning and careful supervision and control.

TERMS AND CONCEPTS

You can check your understanding of these terms against the glossary or by review in this chapter.

Bill of materials	NAHB
Cluster layout	Open space
Cornice	PERT
Covenants	Plat
Custom construction	Rafter
Dedication	Restrictions
Dormer	Sill
Floor plans	Specification
Footings	Stud
Front elevation	Subdivider
Generative business	Subdivision
Insulation	Survey
Joist	Suscipient business
Land developer	Syndicate

What are the differences or relationships, if any, between the following?

Cluster and Grid subdivision layout	Net rented area and Net rentable area
Fixed price and Cost plus a fixed fee	Subdivider and Land developer
Joists and Rafters	

PROBLEMS

18–1. List the important steps in planning a residential subdivision.

18–2. List some of the covenants that might appear in deeds for a residential subdivision.

18–3. Assume that you are considering the purchase of a lot in a residential development. Prepare a checklist of items to ask about or investigate.

18–4. Sketch a floor plan of your home or apartment.

18–5. Make a sketch of your lot and the position of the house on the lot.

18–6. Use the energy checklist provided in this chapter to check your home or apartment for energy efficiency.

18–7. Discuss reasons why a payment schedule is important when contracting a home. Why are receipts important before payments are made?

18–8. Discuss reasons why a developer may impose more restrictions beyond the regular zoning restrictions.

SUPPLEMENTARY READINGS

Burchell, Robert W., and Hughes, James W. *Planned Unit Development.* New Brunswick, N.J.: Rutgers University Center for Urban Policy, 1972.

Control of Land Subdivision. Albany, N.Y.: New York State Office of Planning Services, 1974.

David, Philip. *Urban Land Development.* Homewood, Ill.: Irwin, 1972. Chapter 15.

Derven, Ronald, and Nichols, Carol. *How to Cut Your Energy Bill.* Farmington, Mich.: Structures Publishing Company, 1976.

Farley, John H. *Dodge Building Cost Calculator and Valuation Guide.* New York: McGraw-Hill, 1974.

Handbook for Subdivision Practice. Washington, D.C.: National Association of Home Builders, 1975.

Handbook of Subdivision Practice. Office of State Planning, State of New Hampshire, 1972.

Kinnard, William N.; Messner, Stephen D.; and Boyce, Byrl N. *Industrial Real Estate.* Washington, D.C.: Society of Industrial Realtors, 1979.

Land Development Manual. Washington, D.C.: National Association of Home Builders, 1975.

Land Use Controls. Urbana, Ill.: University of Illinois College of Agriculture Special Publication No. 7, 1963.

McKeever, J. Ross. *The Community Builders Handbook.* Washington, D.C.: Urban Land Institute, 1968.

McMahan, John. *Property Development.* New York: McGraw-Hill, 1976.

Nelson, Richard. *The Selection of Retail Locations.* New York: McGraw-Hill, 1958.

Real Estate Atlas. Miami: Real Estate Data, Inc. (Updated annually for certain areas)

Residential Construction Costs. Los Angeles: Marshall and Swift Publication Company, 1973.

Shenkel, William M. *Modern Real Estate Principles.* Dallas: Business Publications, 1977. Chapter 19.

Smith, Halpert C.; Tschappat, Carl J.; and Racster, Ronald L. *Real Estate and Urban Development.* Homewood, Ill.: Irwin, 1977. Chapter 12.

Smith, Wallace F. *Urban Development.* Berkeley: University of California Press. 1975.

Appraisal and Value

An appraisal gives an estimate or opinion of value. Appraisals are performed to solve a problem or answer a question concerning value. The question or problem may be very simple, such as what is the market value of the particular house? In fact, the vast majority of appraisal assignments involve the estimation of market value. On the other hand, the question or problem involving value may be very complex, such as what is the value of the sublessee's leasehold interest on a 30-year index lease that has 23 years remaining? The scope of the appraisal assignment will vary depending on the objective of the appraisal. This chapter will deal with some of the basic concepts.

Typical Appraisal Assignments

Why are appraisals performed? Who uses appraisals? Some answers to these questions follow:

- *Investors* often seek an expert opinion on value before making decisions on buying, selling, or exchanging real estate.
- *Property owners* of multifamily, commercial, or industrial buildings may request an opinion as to the economic feasibility of a proposed remodeling or rehabilitation program.
- *Buyers and sellers* of single-family homes may request an opinion of value before they consummate a purchase or sale.
- *Subdividers* frequently request the help of an appraiser in determining the feasibility of a proposed subdivision.

- *Developers* may desire a "highest and best use" analysis of a particular site or building.
- *Insurance agents or adjustors* may request an appraiser to estimate the insurable value of a client's property.
- *Lawyers* frequently request professional opinions on value for purposes of estate planning, property settlements, condemnation, estate liquidation, lawsuits, or lease negotiations.
- *Lending institutions* who make loans on real estate seek the appraiser's opinion of the market value of real estate that is to be pledged as security for the loan.
- *Local and state governments* seek the appraiser's assistance in determining market value when they exercise their power of eminent domain to acquire private property for public use.

Appraisal as a Profession

Real estate appraising is the most specialized area within the real estate industry. The need for professional appraisal service has long been recognized by banks, savings and loan institutions, government agencies, investors, endowed institutions, and others who make important and frequent decisions based on estimates of property value. Some state legislatures have either passed or are considering legislation requiring licensing of real estate appraisers.

The varied and technical nature of real estate appraising and the important decisions that stem from appraisals underscore the need for very specialized training and adherence to a strict professional code of ethics by the appraiser. Appraisers must not accept an assignment they are not qualified to carry out, nor should they let their biases or emotions jeopardize accurate objective findings of value. Two important professional appraisal organizations have contributed greatly to elevating appraisal to its current standing as a profession.

The American Institute of Real Estate Appraisers (AIREA) formed in 1932, an affiliate of the National Association of Realtors (NAR), is a leader in appraisal education, publications, and professional standards of practice in the industry. Their members subscribe to a strict code of ethics and must meet stringent educational and experience requirements before they are awarded either the *MAI* (member, appraisal institute) or the *RM* (residential member) designations.

The Society of Real Estate Appraisers (*SREA*) is the other major professional appraisal group responsible for elevating the art of real estate appraisal to a professional status. The society is also heavily involved in appraisal education, research, and publications. Their members also face lengthy educational and experience requirements before they earn their designations. The society's designations include the SRA (senior residential appraiser); SRPA (senior real property appraiser); and the SREA (senior real estate analyst).

Other appraisal organizations include the Association of Federal Appraisers and the American Society of Farm Managers and Rural Appraisers. In recent years, many universities have increased their course offerings in real estate appraisal. Professionally designated appraisers and others highly trained and experienced in forming accurate, unbiased estimates of value will continue to be in great demand in the future.

VALUE CONCEPTS

Value has been the subject of much writing by philosophers, economists, and lawmakers over the centuries. Many of today's concepts of value grew out of the ideas of such men as Aristotle, Adam Smith, John Stuart Mill, Karl Marx, Von Thünen, and others. Their writings on value theory form a fundamental basis for contemporary concepts.

Cost Concept of Value

The *cost concept of value* holds that value is equal to the total costs incurred in bringing a property into being.

Market Concept of Value

The *market concept of value* holds that value is equal to the open market price a willing buyer would pay and a willing seller would take for a parcel of property in a free market.

Economic Concept of Value

The *economic concept of value* holds that value is equal to the present worth of future benefits (income or annuities) that are expected to arise from ownership of property.

TYPES OF VALUE

An *appraisal* has been defined as an estimate or opinion of value. Many different kinds of value exist. The specific type of value to be estimated depends on the intended use of the appraisal. Some of the common uses of appraisals and the respective types of values estimated for those appraisals are listed below:

Use of Appraisal	Type of Value Estimated
To determine listing price	Market value
To determine the price to pay for a given investment	Investment value
To determine insurance needs	Insurable value
To establish rental values	Market value
To establish value of collateral to allocate value between land and building for depreciation	Market value

The three types of value most frequently estimated by the appraiser are market value, investment value, and insurable value.

Market Value

Most appraisal assignments involve the estimation of market value. Market value relates closely to the buying, selling, or exchanging of property. *Market value* is the price that a well-informed buyer would be willing to pay and at which a well-informed seller would be willing to sell, where neither the buyer nor the seller is under any undue pressure to act. The concept of market value also assumes the property is left on the market for a "reasonable" period of time. The determination of a "reasonable" period of time depends on the type of property and the existing market conditions. For instance, residential properties usually sell more quickly than commercial or industrial properties, and all properties tend to sell at a slower rate when the mortgage market is tight. Market value represents "value in exchange" and could be envisioned as the expected selling price of a property. Many other definitions of market value have been advanced by various courts, appraisal organizations, and scholars. Practicing appraisers must keep abreast of the accepted definitions of value.

Insurable Value

An appraiser may be asked to estimate the value of a building and its contents to determine the amount of insurance needed to fully indemnify or protect the insured in case of loss. Although the concept of *insurable value* is complex and beyond the scope of this book, it generally entails the following:

1. Estimation of replacement value of property.
2. Those portions of the property that are specifically exempt by the terms of the insurance contract are then subtracted. Examples are architectural fee, utility hookups, loan fee charges, and other construction costs that would not be incurred again in case of loss and reconstruction. These costs are deducted from the replacement value to arrive at *replacement cost, insurable.*
3. Depreciation for insurance purposes is subtracted next. Unlike depreciation as used in the general field of appraising (loss in value from any cause), *depreciation* for insurance purposes (loss in value from physical deterioration only) is subtracted from the replacement cost, insurable, to arrive at what appraisers call *insurable value, depreciated.* The insurance industry sometimes refers to insurable value, depreciated, as *actual cash value.* Appraisers feel this implies some relationship to market value, however, and since that is not the case, appraisers prefer to use the phrase *insurable value, depreciated.* Although there are different types of insurance policies as discussed in Chapter 11, this is the usual insurable value.

Investment Value

Clients will often request an appraisal when considering the property as an investment. They could be considering the investment as a potential source of income or in speculation for future sale. *Investment value* can be considered as the present worth of the property's future income stream and reversion to a specific investor.

The investment value to the individual is further influenced by the ability to obtain financing, the amount and terms of available financing, the investor's other income, how the acquisition of the property will affect the investor's tax bracket, and other specific objectives. Investment value represents "value in use" and is, therefore, a specific value to a particular or potential user. Considering this, a particular income-producing property may have a different investment value to each of several different potential investors. Investment value is used by clients making decisions whether or not to purchase a given property as an investment or by clients comparing alternative investment possibilities.

PREREQUISITES TO VALUE

Four basic elements are necessary for a property to have a market value. The degree to which each of these prerequisites is present determines the total value that can be assigned to the property.

Utility

Without utility or potential ability, there can be no market value. *Utility* is satisfaction derived from ownership of property, whether monetary return or psychological satisfaction. Although utility is essential before value can exist, utility alone does not create value. A common analogy clarifies this point. The air we breathe has considerable utility for all of us; however, there is no scarcity of air on the surface of the earth and, therefore, air has no market value. (Our society does incur certain indirect costs in order to provide *clean* air.)

Scarcity

Scarcity is a second prerequisite before market value can exist. Since ordinary air is not scarce, it has no market value. Air to a deep-sea diver is scarce, however, and certainly does have *utility*. However, if all deep-sea divers were without funds, they would be prevented from purchasing the air. Without this effective demand or purchasing power, no market value would be created.

Effective Demand

Effective demand is an economic term meaning that there is a need or desire for an item backed up by purchasing power. Purchasing power is normally created by, or results from, a person's income, existing assets, and/or the extension of credit. Without purchasing power, no effective demand would exist.

Transferability

Even though an item has three of the four prerequisites to value, if that item has no *transferability,* market value cannot be created. For example, a public highway has utility, relative scarcity, and a demand; however, it is not freely transferable and, therefore, has no market value. Only when the highway is closed and the necessary legal steps are performed to enable sale and transfer of the property will market value be created in the highway.

In summary, the interrelated prerequisites of utility, scarcity, effective demand, and transferability are all necessary to create market value. To the extent that all these prerequisites continue to exist, market value will be present. To the extent that these relationships change relative to one another, market value will change.

PRINCIPLES OF VALUE

Ten basic principles affect the value of real property.

Principle of Supply and Demand

As the supply of a particular type of property increases relative to demand, market value will decrease. As demand increases relative to supply, market value will increase. The interplay of supply and demand determine market value.

Principle of Change

The real estate market is dynamic and always changing. The forces of change affect specific properties, neighborhoods, cities, and nations. The wants and needs of buyers and sellers in the marketplace also change. Change affects supply and demand and, therefore, value.

Principle of Substitution

Properties that provide the same or similar utility are considered substitutes. Among available substitutes, consumers will generally choose the one with the lowest price.

Principle of Conformity

The highest values are realized in properties that show a reasonable degree of sociological, economic, and architectural similarity. For instance, the introduction of heavy industrial establishments into a residential area resulting in heavy truck traffic, air pollution, and noise pollution will adversely affect residential property values. Reasonable conformity is not meant to imply monotonous uniformity.

Principle of Highest and Best Use

Property is most profitable if used in a way to which it is best adapted and for which the demand is greatest. The *highest and best use* is that legal and probable use which is expected to produce the highest net return.

Principle of Balance

Maximum value is created and maintained when the following four agents of production are in balance: (a) labor (wages); (b) capital; (c) management; (d) land (rents). When these agents are out of balance, value is adversely affected. For example, when an apartment building has been overimproved, the market rents are insufficient to provide a satisfactory return for the capital invested.

Principle of Contribution
(Principle of Marginal Productivity)

The value of any one of the agents of production or any item of production is directly related to its contribution to the net income or present value of the property. The application of this principle is essential to any sound decision on remodeling or rehabilitating a building.

Principle of Increasing and Decreasing Returns

As mentioned earlier, real property value is affected by the contribution of the four agents of production, namely, labor, capital, management, and land (rents). Up to a point, incremental increases in capital invested (or any one of the other agents of production) will produce correspondingly greater increases in value (principle of increasing returns). Once maximum value is developed, any additional incremental increase in capital will produce a less than corresponding increase in value (principle of decreasing returns).

Principle of Competition

When a property generates a net income sufficient to satisfy the four agents of production, any excess is considered profit. In a competitive environment, uses of property that produce heavy profits attract competition. If this competition is excessive, it may result in a strongly competitive situation where few or none of the competitors make an adequate profit.

Principle of Anticipation

Value is created by the anticipated future benefits of ownership. Future benefits may be very different from those in the past. An accurate projection of future benefits is essential to a valid appraisal of value.

FORCES INFLUENCING VALUE

Value is dynamic. It is not inherent in property, but rather is a dynamic characteristic that changes with the changing wants and needs of the market.

Four major forces are constantly at work nationally, regionally, locally, and within the specific property itself to influence value. These are (a) governmental/political, (b) economic, (c) social/psychological, and (d) physical forces.

Figure 19–1 summarizes the four major forces influencing value and gives some examples of each. The summary shows forces with which the appraiser is confronted in collecting, organizing, and interpreting the necessary data to arrive at an estimate of value.

FORCES INFLUENCING VALUE

Governmental/Political Forces
    Zoning regulations
    Building codes
    Taxes
    Special assessments
    Police and fire protection
    Eminent domain
    Rent controls

Economic Forces
    Population growth
    Wages, salaries, and savings
    Availability and rates of mortgage money
    Employment growth and sources
    Labor availability and rates
    New construction rates
    Rental rates, vacancies, and existing supply of property
    Price range of existing homes

Social/Psychological Forces
    Demographic factors—Age, education, income, occupation, and number of children in family
    Social factors—Social participation, mobility, life styles, class, or subcultures
    Psychological factors—Self-concept, how risk is perceived, prestige

Physical Forces
    Location of neighborhood, degree built up, and general appeal
    Proximity to shopping, employment, recreation, schools, and churches
    Quality of schools and churches
    Street pattern, condition, sidewalks and curbs
    Utilities available
    Site size, shape, topography, subsoil, and landscaping
    Improvement, age, size, condition, exterior
    Interior, amenities, depreciation of buildings

Figure 19–1
The four forces influencing value

THE APPRAISAL PROCESS

To aid in planning and executing the appraisal assignment, the appraiser follows a systematic procedure called the appraisal process. This plan of action insures efficient and effective use of the appraiser's time and resources. Figure 19–2 depicts the steps as described in the text.

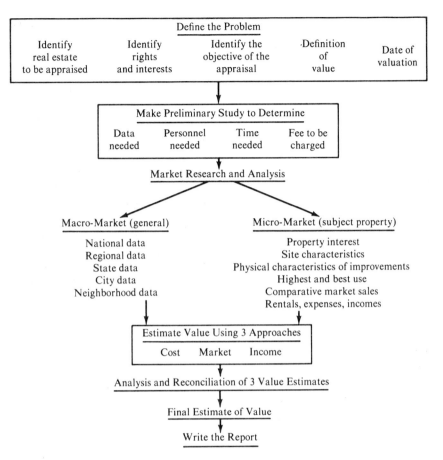

Figure 19–2
The appraisal process

Step 1—Define the Problem

The first step in the appraisal process consists of defining the problem:

a. *Identify the subject property by street address and legal description.*

b. *Identify the rights to be evaluated.*   Although most appraisals estimate the value of all the rights included in fee simple ownership, partial interests may also be considered and evaluated. Particular appraisals may require evaluation of leasehold interests, leased fee interests, sublessee's interests, mineral rights, air rights, or other partial interests.

c. *Identify the objective of the appraisal.*   Before taking on an appraisal assignment, the appraiser should clearly understand the client's objectives. Some appraisers and appraisal texts make a distinction between the function of an appraisal and its purpose. The function of the appraisal is concerned with the reason for the appraisal, that is, its use. The purpose of the appraisal refers to the type of value that is to be estimated. As mentioned earlier, most appraisal assignments involve the estimation of market value.

d. *State the date of the valuation.* It is essential that the date of the value estimate be specified. The principle of change is constantly at work influencing values daily. Therefore, any value estimate made is only valid at the time that it is formulated and can change from one day to the next. In most instances, appraisal assignments involve current value estimates; however, assignments involving value estimates as of some date in the past are not uncommon.

e. *Define the type of value to be estimated.* To avoid any misunderstanding later, the type of value estimated and reported should be clearly established before the appraisal process begins. This is important because the kinds of data collected depend to a large extent upon the type of value to be estimated. In addition, estimates of market value, investment value, insurable value, or salvage value all involve different methods and techniques in data analysis. The amount of weight or emphasis placed on all types of data varies, and there are differences in the methods and techniques used in interpreting the data to arrive at the desired value estimate.

Step 2—Preliminary Study

The second step consists of a study of the contemplated task. It includes the following considerations:

a. *Data needed.* The data to be gathered are determined by the type of property and the objective of the appraisal. The information gathered should include general market data as well as data about the specific property.

b. *Data sources.* All sources from which the primary and secondary data are to be obtained must be identified at this time.

c. *Personnel needed.* Identify the number and nature of any specialized help needed to carry out the appraisal. Such help may include cost estimators, engineers, or architects.

d. *Time needed.* The time required from start to completion of the assignment should be estimated. If the assignment is complex, a work schedule or flow chart should be developed.

e. *Determine fee.* Once the data, personnel, and time estimates have been established, a fee can be set. A description of the effort and the fee should be stated in writing and agreed to by both the client and the appraiser before further work takes place.

Step 3—Market Research and Analysis

The third step includes collecting and analyzing the data. The data may be broken down into the two main categories of external and internal data.

a. External or **macromarket data** relate to the governmental, economic, social, and physical forces affecting value. National, regional, city, and neighborhood data that influence value should be compiled and analyzed. Factors such as local population trends, employment outlook, mortgage terms available, rental rates, and taxes should be considered. The neighborhood factors that influence value include:

Zoning controls	Proximity to schools and churches
Availability of utilities	Recreation facilities
Transportation facilities	Percent built up in the immediate area
Street pattern and traffic	Types of construction in area
General appeal	Stage in life cycle of the neighborhood
Price range of area housing	Nuisances
Income and social status of neighborhood	

b.   Internal or *micromarket data* relate to the forces within the property itself that create or destroy value. These data include the specific site, its improvements, and any constraints on usage. Some factors influencing site value are the following:

Private deed restriction	Soil and subsoil
Lot or site frontage, size, and shape	Available utilities
	Sidewalks
Landscaping	Traffic
Topography	

Some factors influencing improvement value are the following:

Age of improvements	Plumbing
Size of improvements	Electricity
Interior condition	Quality of construction
Exterior condition	Amenities
Heating system	Number of bathrooms
Air conditioning	Number of bedrooms

Appraisers generally use a checklist during their inspection of the site and improvements to make sure they do not miss anything important. Figure 19–3 illustrates a FNMA/FHLMC appraisal form. In addition to collecting and analyzing the site and improvement data, appraisers must collect specific sales data, rental data, and income data on properties that are reasonably comparable to the property being appraised. This will be discussed at length later in this chapter under the market approach to value.

Step 4—Estimate Value Using the Three Approaches

Whenever possible, the fourth step should entail the use of all three approaches to value, namely, the cost approach, the market or comparative approach, and the income approach. The three different approaches serve as checks against one another.

COST APPROACH TO VALUE

The *cost approach to value,* or the *replacement cost approach* as it is sometimes called, is based on the idea that total property value is equal to the

RESIDENTIAL APPRAISAL REPORT

File No. _____

To be completed by Lender

Borrower	Census Tract _____ Map Reference _____
Property Address	
City	County _____ State _____ Zip Code _____
Legal Description	

Sale Price $ _____ Date of Sale _____ Loan Term _____ yrs Property Rights Appraised ☐ Fee ☐ Leasehold ☐ DeMinimis PUD

Actual Real Estate Taxes $ _____ (yr) Loan charges to be paid by seller $ _____ Other sales concessions _____

Lender/Client _____ Address _____

Occupant _____ Appraiser _____ Instructions to Appraiser _____

NEIGHBORHOOD

					Good	Avg.	Fair	Poor
Location	☐ Urban	☐ Suburban	☐ Rural					
Built Up	☐ Over 75%	☐ 25% to 75%	☐ Under 25%	Employment Stability	☐	☐	☐	☐
Growth Rate ☐ Fully Dev.	☐ Rapid	☐ Steady	☐ Slow	Convenience to Employment	☐	☐	☐	☐
Property Values	☐ Increasing	☐ Stable	☐ Declining	Convenience to Shopping	☐	☐	☐	☐
Demand/Supply	☐ Shortage	☐ In Balance	☐ Over Supply	Convenience to Schools	☐	☐	☐	☐
Marketing Time	☐ Under 3 Mos.	☐ 4–6 Mos.	☐ Over 6 Mos.	Adequacy of Public Transportation	☐	☐	☐	☐
Present Land Use ___% 1 Family ___% 2–4 Family ___% Apts. ___% Condo ___% Commercial				Recreational Facilities	☐	☐	☐	☐
___% Industrial ___% Vacant ___% ___				Adequacy of Utilities	☐	☐	☐	☐
Change in Present Land Use ☐ Not Likely	☐ Likely (*)	☐ Taking Place (*)		Property Compatibility	☐	☐	☐	☐
(*) From _____ To _____				Protection from Detrimental Conditions	☐	☐	☐	☐
Predominant Occupancy ☐ Owner	☐ Tenant	___% Vacant		Police and Fire Protection	☐	☐	☐	☐
Single Family Price Range $ _____ to $ _____ Predominant Value $ _____				General Appearance of Properties	☐	☐	☐	☐
Single Family Age _____ yrs to _____ yrs Predominant Age _____ yrs				Appeal to Market	☐	☐	☐	☐

Note: FHLMC/FNMA do not consider the racial composition of the neighborhood to be a relevant factor and it must not be considered in the appraisal.

Comments including those factors, favorable or unfavorable, affecting marketability (e.g. public parks, schools, view, noise) _____

SITE

Dimensions _____ - _____ Sq. Ft. or Acres _____ ☐ Corner Lot

Zoning classification _____

Highest and best use: ☐ Present use ☐ Other (specify) _____ Present improvements ☐ do ☐ do not conform to zoning regulations

	Public	Other (Describe)	OFF SITE IMPROVEMENTS	
Elec.	☐	_____	Street Access: ☐ Public ☐ Private	Topo _____
Gas	☐	_____	Surface _____	Size _____
Water	☐	_____	Maintenance: ☐ Public ☐ Private	Shape _____
San. Sewer	☐	_____	☐ Storm Sewer ☐ Curb/Gutter	View _____
	☐ Underground Elect. & Tel.	☐ Sidewalk ☐ Street Lights		Drainage _____

Is the property located in a HUD Identified Special Flood Hazard Area? ☐ No ☐ Yes

Comments (favorable or unfavorable including any apparent adverse easements, encroachments or other adverse conditions) _____

IMPROVEMENTS

☐ Existing ☐ Proposed ☐ Under Constr. No. Units _____ Type (det, duplex, semi/det, etc.) _____ Design (rambler, split level, etc.) _____ Exterior Walls _____

Yrs. Age: Actual _____ Effective _____ to _____ No. Stories _____

Roof Material _____ Gutters & Downspouts ☐ None Window (Type): _____ Insulation ☐ None ☐ Floor

☐ Storm Sash ☐ Screens ☐ Combination ☐ Ceiling ☐ Roof ☐ Walls

BSMT

☐ Manufactured Housing ___% Basement ☐ Floor Drain Finished Ceiling _____

Foundation Walls _____ ☐ Outside Entrance ☐ Sump Pump Finished Walls _____

☐ Concrete Floor ___% Finished Finished Floor _____

☐ Slab on Grade ☐ Crawl Space Evidence of: ☐ Dampness ☐ Termites ☐ Settlement

Comments _____

ROOM LIST

Room List	Foyer	Living	Dining	Kitchen	Den	Family Rm.	Rec. Rm.	Bedrooms	No. Baths	Laundry	Other
Basement											
1st Level											
2nd Level											

Finished area above grade contains a total of _____ rooms _____ bedrooms _____ baths. Gross Living Area _____ sq. ft. Bsmt Area _____ sq. ft.

INTERIOR FINISH & EQUIPMENT

Kitchen Equipment: ☐ Refrigerator ☐ Range/Oven ☐ Disposal ☐ Dishwasher ☐ Fan/Hood ☐ Compactor ☐ Washer ☐ Dryer

HEAT: Type _____ Fuel _____ Cond. _____ AIR COND: ☐ Central ☐ Other _____ ☐ Adequate ☐ Inadequate

					PROPERTY RATING	Good	Avg.	Fair	Poor
Floors	☐ Hardwood	☐ Carpet Over	☐		Quality of Construction (Materials & Finish)	☐	☐	☐	☐
Walls	☐ Drywall	☐ Plaster	☐		Condition of Improvements	☐	☐	☐	☐
Trim/Finish	☐ Good	☐ Average ☐ Fair ☐ Poor			Rooms size and layout	☐	☐	☐	☐
Bath Floor	☐ Ceramic	☐			Closets and Storage	☐	☐	☐	☐
Bath Wainscot	☐ Ceramic	☐			Insulation—adequacy	☐	☐	☐	☐
Special Features (including energy efficient items) _____					Plumbing—adequacy and condition	☐	☐	☐	☐
					Electrical—adequacy and condition	☐	☐	☐	☐
					Kitchen Cabinets—adequacy and condition	☐	☐	☐	☐
ATTIC: ☐ Yes ☐ No ☐ Stairway ☐ Drop-stair ☐ Scuttle ☐ Floored					Compatibility to Neighborhood	☐	☐	☐	☐
Finished (Describe) _____ ☐ Heated					Overall Livability	☐	☐	☐	☐
CAR STORAGE: ☐ Garage ☐ Built-in ☐ Attached ☐ Detached ☐ Car Port					Appeal and Marketability	☐	☐	☐	☐
No. Cars _____ ☐ Adequate ☐ Inadequate Condition _____					Yrs Est Remaining Economic Life _____ to _____ .Explain if less than Loan Term				

FIREPLACES, PATIOS, POOL, FENCES, etc. (describe) _____

COMMENTS (including functional or physical inadequacies, repairs needed, modernization, etc.) _____

FHLMC Form 70 Rev. 10/78 ATTACH DESCRIPTIVE PHOTOGRAPHS OF SUBJECT PROPERTY AND STREET SCENE FNMA Form 1004 Rev. 10/78

Figure 19–3
Appraisal form

VALUATION SECTION

Purpose of Appraisal is to estimate Market Value as defined in Certification & Statement of Limiting Conditions (FHLMC Form 439/FNMA Form 1004B). If submitted for FNMA, the appraiser must attach (1) sketch or map showing location of subject, street names, distance from nearest intersection, and any detrimental conditions and (2) exterior building sketch of improvements showing dimensions.

COST APPROACH

Measurements	No. Stories	Sq. Ft.
___ x ___	x ___	= ___
___ x ___	x ___	= ___
___ x ___	x ___	= ___
___ x ___	x ___	= ___
___ x ___	x ___	= ___
___ x ___	x ___	= ___

Total Gross Living Area (List in Market Data Analysis below) ___

Comment on functional and economic obsolescence: ___

ESTIMATED REPRODUCTION COST — NEW — OF IMPROVEMENTS:

Dwelling ___ Sq. Ft. @ $ ___ = $ ___
___ Sq. Ft. @ $ ___ = ___
Extras ___ = ___
___ = ___
Special Energy Efficient Items ___ = ___
Porches, Patios, etc. ___ = ___
Garage/Car Port ___ Sq. Ft. @ $ ___ = ___
Site Improvements (driveway, landscaping, etc.) ___ = ___
Total Estimated Cost New . . . . = $ ___

	Physical	Functional	Economic
Less			
Depreciation $ ___	$ ___	$ ___	= $ (___)

Depreciated value of improvements . . . . . . = $ ___
ESTIMATED LAND VALUE . . . . . . = $ ___
(If leasehold, show only leasehold value)

INDICATED VALUE BY COST APPROACH . . . $ ___

MARKET DATA ANALYSIS

The undersigned has recited three recent sales of properties most similar and proximate to subject and has considered these in the market analysis. The description includes a dollar adjustment, reflecting market reaction to those items of significant variation between the subject and comparable properties. If a significant item in the comparable property is superior to, or more favorable than, the subject property, a minus (-) adjustment is made, thus reducing the indicated value of subject; if a significant item in the comparable is inferior to, or less favorable than, the subject property, a plus (+) adjustment is made, thus increasing the indicated value of the subject.

ITEM	Subject Property	COMPARABLE NO. 1		COMPARABLE NO. 2		COMPARABLE NO. 3	
Address							
Proximity to Subj.							
Sales Price	$	$		$		$	
Price/Living area	$	$		$		$	
Data Source							
Date of Sale and Time Adjustment	DESCRIPTION	DESCRIPTION	+(-)$ Adjustment	DESCRIPTION	+(-)$ Adjustment	DESCRIPTION	+(-)$ Adjustment
Location							
Site/View							
Design and Appeal							
Quality of Const.							
Age							
Condition							
Living Area Room Count and Total	Total : B-rms : Baths	Total : B-rms : Baths		Total : B-rms : Baths		Total : B-rms : Baths	
Gross Living Area	Sq.Ft.	Sq.Ft.		Sq.Ft.		Sq.Ft.	
Basement & Bsmt. Finished Rooms							
Functional Utility							
Air Conditioning							
Garage/Car Port							
Porches, Patio, Pools, etc.							
Special Energy Efficient Items							
Other (e.g. fireplaces, kitchen equip., remodeling)							
Sales or Financing Concessions							
Net Adj. (Total)		☐ Plus; ☐ Minus $		☐ Plus; ☐ Minus $		☐ Plus; ☐ Minus $	
Indicated Value of Subject		$		$		$	

Comments on Market Data ___

INDICATED VALUE BY MARKET DATA APPROACH . . . . $ ___
INDICATED VALUE BY INCOME APPROACH (If applicable) Economic Market Rent $ ___ /Mo. x Gross Rent Multiplier ___ = $ ___

This appraisal is made ☐ "as is" ☐ subject to the repairs, alterations, or conditions listed below ☐ completion per plans and specifications.

Comments and Conditions of Appraisal: ___

Final Reconciliation: ___

Construction Warranty ☐ Yes ☐ No Name of Warranty Program ___ Warranty Coverage Expires ___

This appraisal is based upon the above requirements, the certification, contingent and limiting conditions, and Market Value definition that are stated in
☐ FHLMC Form 439 (Rev. 10/78)/FNMA Form 1004B (Rev. 10/78) filed with client ___ 19 ___ ☐ attached.

I ESTIMATE THE MARKET VALUE, AS DEFINED, OF SUBJECT PROPERTY AS OF ___ 19 ___ to be $ ___

Appraiser(s) ___ Review Appraiser (If applicable) ___
☐ Did ☐ Did Not Physically Inspect Property

FHLMC Form 70 Rev. 10/78

FNMA Form 1004 Rev. 10/78

Figure 19–3a

value of the land plus the current value of the improvement. The value is derived systematically in five steps:

1. Estimate the value of the land as if vacant (using the market approach).
2. Estimate the cost to replace the improvements at the present time.
3. Estimate property depreciation.
4. Deduct depreciation from replacement cost to arrive at the present depreciated value of improvements.
5. Add the land value to the depreciated value of improvements to arrive at the total estimate of value.

Land Value

Estimating land value as if vacant is done by using the market approach if sufficient data are available. This approach involves collecting data on recent sales of similar land. Similarities to and differences from the subject property are identified and weighed. We discuss the market approach more fully later in this chapter.

Current Replacement Cost

Replacement cost is estimated by one of four methods:

Square foot method
The **square foot method** is the most common and easiest to apply. The square foot replacement cost can be derived from local builders and contractors or from appraisal cost manuals. Some sources of these data are given in the supplementary readings at the end of this chapter. The replacement cost per square foot is multiplied by the number of square feet in the subject building; the result gives an estimate of the replacement cost. The square foot method of estimating replacement cost is prevalent in single-family home appraisals.

Cubic foot method
The **cubic foot method** is similar to the square foot method, except that the building volume is used as the basis for evaluation. The cubic foot costs are derived from contractor estimates or appraisal cost manuals. The cost per cubic foot is then multiplied by the number of cubic feet in the building being appraised to arrive at the replacement cost estimate.

Quantity survey method
The **quantity survey method** is the third and most detailed of the replacement cost procedures. It involves a detailed breakdown and pricing of all materials, labor, architectural and engineering services, insurance, and contractor's overhead and profit. This method is seldom used because of the time and costs involved. It may be necessary, however, to use this method for unusual structures or where other valid data are not available.

Units-in-place method

This fourth method involves the pricing of various "units-in-place," such as the roof, walls, or floors. It then considers the installed costs of each unit, such as plumbing, heating, electricity, and air conditioning. This method is also time-consuming and is, therefore, used infrequently. (See Figure 19–4.)

Depreciation

Depreciation, as it relates to appraising, is defined as loss in value from all causes. There are three basic types of depreciation: physical deterioration, functional obsolescence, and economic obsolescence. Each must be considered to determine its effect on the property value.

Physical deterioration

Physical deterioration is the loss in value due to exposure to rain, wind, and other elements, combined with lack of maintenance. This depreciation can be either curable or incurable. If the cost of curing the problem is less than the dollar increase in value afterwards, the deterioration is considered curable. Painting and new roofing are usually considered economically feasible, and hence, curable. Their deterioration is considered curable. Incurable physical deterioration includes factors such as sagging or structural deterioration. Physically curable deterioration is measured by estimating the "cost to cure" the deterioration. Physically incurable deterioration is measured by "capitalizing the rent loss" resulting from the incurable deterioration.

Example: Assume that the property being appraised is a large, older home with sagging floors and a faulty foundation. In the appraiser's opinion, this condition is "incurable" and results in a monthly rent loss of $100. To estimate the amount of physical, incurable deterioration, the appraiser multiplies the rent loss of $100 by the gross monthly rent multiplier (GMRM), which is derived from recent sales of rental properties. (See p. 418 for an illustration of the GMRM.)

Physical incurable deterioration = Monthly rent loss × GMRM

Functional obsolescence

Functional obsolescence refers to the loss in value due to loss of utility within a structure. It also can be further classified as either *curable* or *incurable*. If the cost to cure the obsolescence or inutility is less than the dollar increase in value of the property after the cure, the obsolescence is considered curable. Replacement of old bathroom fixtures with new ones and replacing old electrical wires with new wiring are examples of curable obsolescence. *Incurable obsolescence* occurs when the cost to cure the inutility is not economically feasible. A poor floor plan that creates traffic through one bedroom to get to another might be considered functional incurable obsolescence. Functional curable obsolescence is measured by the "cost to cure" the obsolescence. Functional incurable obsolescence can be measured by "capitalizing the rent loss" attributed to the obsolescence.

SEGREGATED COMPONENTS

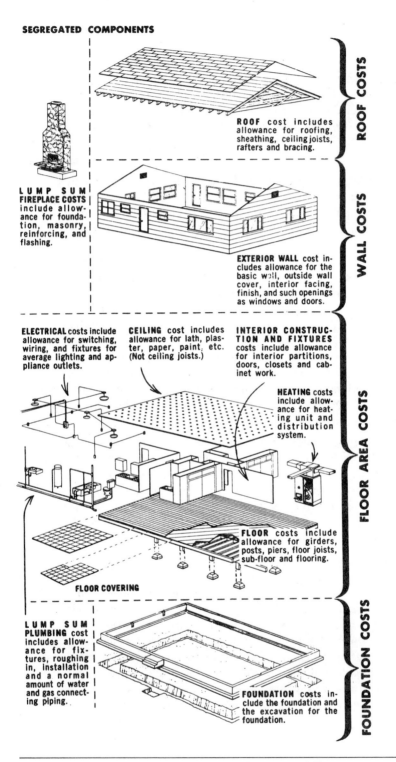

ROOF COSTS

ROOF cost includes allowance for roofing, sheathing, ceiling joists, rafters and bracing.

LUMP SUM FIREPLACE COSTS include allowance for foundation, masonry, reinforcing, and flashing.

WALL COSTS

EXTERIOR WALL cost includes allowance for the basic wall, outside wall cover, interior facing, finish, and such openings as windows and doors.

ELECTRICAL costs include allowance for switching, wiring, and fixtures for average lighting and appliance outlets.

CEILING cost includes allowance for lath, plaster, paper, paint, etc. (Not ceiling joists.)

INTERIOR CONSTRUCTION AND FIXTURES costs include allowance for interior partitions, doors, closets and cabinet work.

HEATING costs include allowance for heating unit and distribution system.

FLOOR AREA COSTS

FLOOR costs include allowance for girders, posts, piers, floor joists, sub-floor and flooring.

FLOOR COVERING

LUMP SUM PLUMBING cost includes allowance for fixtures, roughing in, installation and a normal amount of water and gas connecting piping.

FOUNDATION COSTS

FOUNDATION costs include the foundation and the excavation for the foundation.

Source: "Residential Cost Handbook," Marshall & Swift Publication Co., Los Angeles, Calif.

Figure 19–4
Units-in-place

412

Economic obsolescence

Economic obsolescence (or environmental obsolescence) refers to the loss in value due to adverse environmental factors external to the subject property. It is generally incurable because the property owner has little or no control over these factors and, therefore, cannot cure the problem whether the cure would be economically feasible or not. A property owner could not, for example, change the traffic pattern in a commercial area. A factory constructed across the street from a residential block or railroad tracks located in a residential area are other causes of economic or environmental obsolescence.

When the property being appraised is of a type that no rental market exists, it may be necessary to use "matched pairs" of sales to estimate economic obsolescence. In brief, this method involves finding several matched pairs of sales. Each pair must consist of one sale that was affected by the factor or factors causing economic obsolescence and another sale of a similar property that was not affected by that same economic obsolescence. After adjustments have been made between the two sales for all other differences, the remaining difference can be attributed to economic obsolescence. Economic obsolescence can also be measured by "capitalizing the rent loss" attributed to the obsolescence.

Example: Assume that the presence of a gas station across the street from a single-family rental property causes a monthly rent loss of $25. To calculate what effect this economic obsolescence has on the value of the property, we apply the gross monthly rent multiplier (GMRM) to the monthly rent loss as follows:

$$\$25 \times 125 \text{ (GMRM)} = \$3125 \text{ Value loss due to economic obsolescence}$$

Measuring Total Depreciation

Several methods of measuring each of the specific types of depreciation (physical, functional, and economic) have been mentioned. This discussion will be limited to one simple but widely used method of measuring total depreciation. Since it is difficult to measure depreciation by any scientific process, this method is substantially subjective. The estimate of depreciation and the method used are tempered by the knowledge, experience, and judgment of the appraiser.

The *effective age/economic life* concept of measuring total depreciation (physical, functional, and economic) uses a ratio of effective age to economic life. *Effective age* is estimated by observation, that is, estimating the age from appearance. It may be more than, equal to, or less than the actual age, depending on how well the property has been maintained.

Economic life means the total estimated time the property will be economically useful. The *remaining economic life* is the estimated number of useful years left in the property as of the date of the appraisal. This concept is illustrated by the following example:

Estimated replacement cost $47,082
    new (today) of buildings
Estimated effective age
    (by observation)   2 years
Estimated remaining
    economic life   38 years
Estimated total
    economic life   40 years

$$\frac{\text{Effective age}}{\text{Total economic life}} = \frac{2}{40} = .05 \text{ (or 5\%)}$$

Total depreciation = $47,082 \times .05 = \$2,354$

VALUATION SECTION

Purpose of Appraisal is to estimate Market Value as defined in Certification & Statement of Limiting Conditions (FHLMC Form 439/FNMA Form 1004B). If submitted for FNMA, the appraiser must attach (1) sketch or map showing location of subject, street names, distance from nearest intersection, and any detrimental conditions and (2) exterior building sketch of improvements showing dimensions.

Measurements	No. Stories	Sq. Ft.	ESTIMATED REPRODUCTION COST – NEW – OF IMPROVEMENTS:		
___ x ___	x	=	Dwelling ___1120___ Sq. Ft. @ $ ___34___	=	$ 38,080
___ x ___	x	=	___Basement 980___ Sq. Ft. @ $ 3	=	2,940
___ x ___	x	=	Extras ___RecRoom/Bsmt 140@$10___	=	1,400
___ x ___	x	=	___Chain Link Fence___	=	750
___ x ___	x	=	Special Energy Efficient Items ___	=	
___ x ___	x	=	Porches, Patios, etc. ___Deck___	=	500
Total Gross Living Area (List in Market Data Analysis below) ___			Garage/Car Port ___364___ Sq. Ft. @ $ 8	=	2,912
Comment on functional and economic obsolescence: ___			Site Improvements (driveway, landscaping, etc.)	=	500
___			Total Estimated Cost New	= $	47,082
___			Less Physical | Functional | Economic		
___			Depreciation $___ \|$___ |$___	= $(	2,354)
___			Depreciated value of improvements	= $	44,728
___			ESTIMATED LAND VALUE . . . . (If leasehold, show only leasehold value)	= $	8,000
___			INDICATED VALUE BY COST APPROACH . . .	$	52,728

Figure 19–5
The cost approach portion of the FHLMC/FNMA appraisal form

After the depreciation has been estimated, subtract it from the replacement cost of new buildings and other improvements; then add land value to arrive at the estimate of total property value. Figure 19–5 illustrates the cost approach.

The major weakness of the cost approach is the time and money involved in gathering information to estimate replacement costs and depreciation accurately. These weaknesses become more magnified in the appraisal of older buildings. Such appraisals should be supported, if possible, by the other two approaches. When churches or other special purpose buildings are appraised, the cost approach is given considerable weight. Often it is the only feasible approach because of a lack of market or income information.

MARKET APPROACH TO VALUE

The *market approach to value* entails comparing the property being appraised with similar properties that have sold recently. It is also referred to as the *comparative approach* or the *sales comparison approach*. Given a sufficient number of recent and comparable sales, the market approach provides a good measure for estimating value. In this approach, the appraiser must gather sales data for similar properties, compare the merits of each property in relation to the subject property, and adjust the price data for time, location, and physical characteristics, in arriving at an estimate of value.

Gathering Data

Sufficient sales data for comparable properties are gathered from such sources as the appraiser's own files, public records, attorneys, multiple listing services, brokers, banks, and lending institutions. The appraiser should collect data from as many comparable sales as possible, since some of them will have to be discarded for one reason or another.

Analyzing Data

Once a sufficient number of sales figures have been gathered, the data must be analyzed to determine comparability. A preliminary physical inspection of each property is recommended. These are some characteristics of good comparable sales:

1. The comparable sales should be recent. In residential appraising, no more than one year should have elapsed since the sale.
2. The comparable sales should be arm's length, that is, not between relatives or in situations where other factors may have influenced the selling price.
3. The comparable sales should have been handled with typical market financing. A sale involving a contract for deed is usually considered atypical and should not be used unless absolutely necessary, and then only after making the necessary adjustments.
4. The comparable sales should have been voluntary. Foreclosure sales would not represent valid comparisons.
5. The comparable sales should be in close proximity to the subject property and in similar environments.
6. The comparable sales should be physically similar to the subject property.

Comparing

In analyzing comparable sales, some will be rejected for not meeting one or more of the above characteristics. The appraiser should begin the comparison process with three to five good comparable sales. The ideal *comparable* (an appraiser's dream) is an exact replica of the subject property that sold today under typical market conditions. Unfortunately, such ideal comparables are seldom found. The appraiser must use the comparables available and make the necessary adjustments.

Adjusting

After selecting the comparable properties and making an analysis and comparison, it is necessary to adjust for differences in *time of sale, location,* and *physical characteristics.* If comparable sales with atypical financing must be used, adjustments should be made for terms of sale. Figure 19–6 illustrates the adjustment process.

The undersigned has recited three recent sales of properties most similar and proximate to subject and has considered these in the market analysis. The description includes a dollar adjustment, reflecting market reaction to those items of significant variation between the subject and comparable properties. If a significant item in the comparable property is superior to, or more favorable than, the subject property, a minus (-) adjustment is made, thus reducing the indicated value of subject; if a significant item in the comparable is inferior to, or less favorable than, the subject property, a plus (+) adjustment is made, thus increasing the indicated value of the subject.

ITEM	Subject Property	COMPARABLE NO. 1		COMPARABLE NO. 2		COMPARABLE NO. 3	
Address	300 E. Fifth Mackinaw, IL	106 Giles Mackinaw, IL		Lot 54 Heritage Lake RR, Mackinaw, IL		404 S. Eastern Ave. Minier, IL	
Proximity to Subj.							
Sales Price	$	$ 49,300		$ 50,900		$ 54,900	
Price/Living area	$	$		$		$	
Data Source	Inspection						
Date of Sale and Time Adjustment	DESCRIPTION —	DESCRIPTION Aug., 1978	Adjustment —	DESCRIPTION Aug., 1978	Adjustment —	DESCRIPTION April 1978	Adjustment —
Location	Good	Similar	—	Similar	—	Similar	—
Site/View	1/3 Acre/Good	84x120/Infer.	+ 500	107x275/Sim.	—	90x140/Infer.	+ 500
Design and Appeal	Good	Similar	—	Similar	—	Similar	—
Quality of Const.	Good	Similar	—	Similar	—	Similar	—
Age	3 years	Similar	—	Similar	—	Similar	—
Condition	Good	Similar	—	Similar	—	Similar	—
Living Area Room Count and Total	Total 6 B-rms 3 Baths 1	Total 6 B-rms 3 Baths 2	-1000	Total 6 B-rms 3 Baths 1-1/2	- 750	Total 6 B-rms 3 Baths 2	-1000
Gross Living Area	Sq.Ft.	Sq.Ft.		Sq.Ft.		Sq.Ft.	
Basement & Bsmt. Finished Rooms	Full Part. Finished	Similar	—	Full Unfinished	+ 500	None Inferior	+1500
Functional Utility	Good	Similar	—	Similar	—	Similar	—
Air Conditioning	Central	Similar	—	Inferior	+1000	Similar	—
Garage/Car Port	1-1/2 Attached	1 Car Attach.	+ 500	2 Car Attach.	- 500	2 Car Attach	- 500
Porches, Patio, Pools, etc.	Deck	Inferior	+ 500	Inferior	+ 500	Inferior	+ 500
Special Energy Efficient Items							
Other (e.g. fireplaces, kitchen equip., remodeling)	Back yard Chain Link Fence	Fireplace 10x12 Utility Shed	- 750 —	Inferior	+ 500	Inferior	+ 500
Sales or Financing Concessions							
Net Adj. (Total)		☐ Plus; ☒ Minus $ 250		☒ Plus; ☐ Minus $ 1,250		☒ Plus; ☐ Minus $ 1,500	
Indicated Value of Subject		$ 49,050		$ 52,150		$ 56,400	

Comments on Market Data	Comp #1	$49,050	x	.50 =	$24,525
	Comp #2	52,150	x	.40 =	20,860
	Comp #3	56,400	x	.10 =	5,640

INDICATED VALUE BY MARKET DATA APPROACH	. . . .	$ 51,025

Notes: + Comparable property is inferior to subject property
– Comparable property is superior to subject property

Figure 19–6
Market approach portion of FHLMC/FNMA appraisal form (revised 10/78)

As can be seen, the specific items or factors to be compared between the three comparable properties and the subject property are itemized in the left column. Moving from left to right on the table, the next column describes information on the subject property. The next three columns provide room for the same descriptive information for each of the three comparable sales. Each of these three columns has one space for the item description and another space to indicate the amount of adjustment to make (if any) for any differences in that item between the subject property being appraised and the comparable sale. The descriptive column was marked "similar" in the above example because the appraiser recognized no difference between the subject property and the comparable sale on that particular item and, consequently, made no adjustment.

Further, when comparing each item of the subject property that is being appraised to the comparable sales, the item of comparison was labeled either *similar, superior,* or *inferior* for each comparable sale. In all cases, the appraiser has compared and adjusted *from the comparable property to the subject property.* In other words, an item rated as "superior" indicates that the comparable property's item is superior to that same item of the subject property. Consequently, the selling price of the comparable property must be adjusted downward to reflect this difference so that, after all adjustments have been made, the adjusted selling prices of the comparable sales will accurately reflect what the subject property would sell for if it were on the market. This adjustment process is a difficult concept for many students to comprehend and can be made easier by following these guidelines:

1. Always compare and adjust from the comparable sale to the subject property.
2. When comparing the comparable property to the subject property, if the comparable property is *superior,* the comparable selling price should be adjusted downward.
3. If the comparable property is *inferior* to the subject property, the comparable selling price should be adjusted upward.

In making the adjustments, the appraiser must avoid the temptation of inserting personal opinions on how much and when to adjust. An appraisal is made to interpret the premiums or discounts that the *market* places on the elements and report them accordingly. The appraiser should neither influence nor determine value, but rather estimate it.

After all upward and downward adjustments have been made, their total provides a net adjustment (see bottom of Figure 19–6). This net adjustment is either added to or subtracted from the comparable property's selling price to arrive at the "indicated value" of the subject property (see last item of Figure 19–6). The last step in the market approach is to correlate and weight the three indications of value and arrive at a single estimate of value for the subject property using the market approach. In the example, Comparable No. 1 is weighted the heaviest (.50) and No. 3 the least (.10).

Usage

The market approach cannot be effectively used when there are few or no comparable sales available. It would carry little weight in determining the final estimate if there were only one or two comparable sales. When sufficient market data are available, however, the market approach is given considerable weight because it reflects value taken directly from the marketplace.

INCOME APPROACH TO VALUE—
RESIDENTIAL SINGLE-FAMILY UNITS

The third and last important approach to value, the *income approach* is based on the idea that value is the present worth of expected future benefits arising from property ownership. This approach has its greatest application in the appraisal of income-producing properties. The function of the appraiser is to determine the present value of the expected future income stream of the subject property.

In residential appraising, a gross monthly rent multiplier (*GMRM*) is used to estimate value. These steps are followed in applying the GMRM:

1. Locate and verify residential sales that are comparable to the subject property and that were renting at the time of sale.

2. Divide the selling price of each comparable sale by its monthly rental to obtain the GMRM.

3. Analyze and weigh the various multipliers obtained in step two and reconcile them into a single multiplier. The reconciliation process does not imply the simple averaging of the three GMRMs, but rather placing greater weight or emphasis on the GMRMs that best reflect the subject property.

4. Derive the market rent of the subject property from the marketplace by verifying rental data from similar rental properties and making necessary adjustments for any differences between the subject property and the rentals.

5. Multiply the weighted GMRM by the estimated economic rent of the subject property to arrive at the estimate of value for the subject property.

Example: The subject property's economic (market) rent has been derived from the market and estimated to be $250 per month. Recent sales of comparable rental property follow:

Sale #	Selling Price	÷	Rent	=	GMRM
1	$30,000	÷	$275	=	109
2	$28,000	÷	$250	=	112
3	$26,000	÷	$260	=	100

The indicated range of GMRM's is 100 to 112. Analysis of the GMRM's indicates that sales 1 and 2 should be given the most weight. Calculations of the weighting follow:

Weighted GMRM = $(109 \times .40) + (112 \times .40) + (100 \times .20) = 108$ (rounded)

The indicated value of subject property is, therefore,

$$
\begin{aligned}
\text{Value} &= \text{Rent} \times \text{GMRM} \\
&= \$250 \times 108 \\
&= \$27,000
\end{aligned}
$$

INCOME APPROACH TO VALUE—
INCOME-PRODUCING PROPERTIES

As we saw before, the concept behind the income approach is that value is the present worth of future income. The application of the income approach involves three steps.

1. Estimating the subject property's anticipated (future) net income.
2. Selecting an appropriate capitalization rate.
3. Translating the projected net income into an estimate of value by the process of capitalization.

Estimating Income

All *capitalization* methods start with the subject property's net income and work toward arriving at an estimate of value. If the appraiser works with an inflated estimate of income, the result is an inflated estimate of value. It is, therefore, imperative that the appraiser obtain accurate income and expense information for the property being evaluated. If possible, the appraiser should obtain a three-to-five-year operating history of the property that includes all income and expenses of the property.

Total income from the property being appraised should be identified. In an apartment building, this may include such items as rental income, income from coin-operated laundry facilities, and parking income. The expenses should be broken down into three categories: (a) fixed, (b) operating, and (c) reserve for replacement. *Fixed expenses* remain unchanged, regardless of the occupancy level of the building. Typical fixed expenses include taxes and insurance. *Operating expenses* vary with the occupancy level of the building and include, but are not limited to, the following: maintenance expense, management expense, utility expense, lawn care, snow removal, legal and accounting expense, and others. Finally, the *reserve for replacement* is an allowance in the annual operating statement to provide for the systematic replacement of items within a building (e.g., stoves, refrigerators, carpeting, water heaters, window air conditioning units) whose useful life is less than that of the building itself. The planned replacement of these items is necessary to sustain the anticipated net income.

The amount of allowance for each replacement item is usually calculated as the cost to replace the item divided by the item's remaining useful life. For example, if all the refrigerators in a four-unit apartment under appraisal are seven years old and the appraiser estimates a total useful life of ten years, a reserve must be set aside to replace the refrigerators in three years. Assuming each refrigerator costs $400, the total annual reserve for replacement for all refrigerators in the four units would be calculated as follows:

$$\text{Total annual reserve} = \frac{\$400 \times 4}{3} = \underline{\underline{\$533}} \text{ (rounded)}$$

The appraiser may increase or decrease the owner's reported income and expenses if market data justify such action. If the owner has included depreciation, debt service, and income taxes in the operating statements, the appraiser should eliminate them in the reconstructed operating statement because they represent owner expenses rather than property expenses. Such expenses would vary from owner to owner, depending on how each financed the purchase, the owner's tax bracket, and the depreciation technique used.

The analysis ends by preparing a reconstructed operating statement as illustrated in Figure 19–7. The appraiser then takes the projected net income from the operating statement and capitalizes, or converts it into an estimate of value using the appropriate capitalization method.

RECONSTRUCTED OPERATING STATEMENT

Potential Gross Income Estimate Assuming Economic Rent, 100% Occupancy			
Scheduled Rental Income		$24,000	
Other Income		0	
Total Potential Gross Income			$24,000
Less: Vacancy and Collection Losses			− 1,680
Effective Gross Income			22,320
Less Expenses:			
Fixed Expenses:			
Taxes	$2,700		
Insurance	1,000	3,700	
Operating Expenses:			
Management	1,440		
Maintenance	2,400		
Utilities	1,380		
Ground Maintenance	450		
Legal & Accounting	300		
Other		5,970	
Reserve for Replacement:			
Appliances	250		
Furnace	250	500	
Total Estimated Expenses			− 10,170
Net Income Before Recapture (NIBR)			$12,150

Figure 19–7
A format for reconstructing the operating statement

Capitalization Formulas

Capitalization formulas involve the three elements of income, rate, and value.

$$\text{Income} = \text{Rate times value}$$
$$\text{Rate} = \text{Income divided by value}$$
$$\text{Value} = \text{Income divided by rate}$$

If any two of the three components in the capitalization formulas are available or can be derived from the market data, the third component can be calculated. In economic theory, *rate* is a ratio between income and value expressed as a percentage:

$$\text{Rate} = \frac{\text{Income}}{\text{Value}}$$

This *rate of return on investment* or the *capitalization (interest) rate* applies to both the land and building. The greater the risk, the higher the rate; conversely, a safer investment will have a lower rate of return. The *rate of return of investment* or *recapture rate* applies to buildings only and allows for their future depreciation. It does not apply to land. The recapture rate for a building is the reciprocal of its remaining economic life.

$$\text{Recapture rate} = \frac{1}{\text{Remaining economic life in years}}$$

Example: If a given building has a remaining economic life of 25 years, the annual recapture rate necessary to recapture or recover the total building investment over its remaining economic life is $\frac{1}{25}$ or 4%. Thus, the recapture rate reflects the annual rate at which the building portion of the investment must be recaptured to recover it fully over the period of its economic life.

A $10,000 return on a $100,000 deposit in a savings and loan represents a 10% return on investment; however, this is not the case in a real estate investment since the real estate is composed, in part, of depreciable improvements. If we assume a $100,000 investment in an apartment building with a remaining economic life of 25 years, the investment must generate more than $10,000 to earn a 10% return. The difference lies in the recapture of the investment. The investor who invests $100,000 in a savings and loan is guaranteed the return of that $100,000, whereas the apartment owner has no such guarantee. The building portion of the investment is assumed to depreciate. Therefore, the property investment must generate $13,200 to provide for recapture or recovery of the investment. This amount is determined as follows:

Investment Composed of:	Requires: Return on	Return of	Total Rate	Return Dollars
Building value $80,000 (25-yr economic life)	.10	.04	.14	$11,200
Land value $20,000	.10	—	.10	2,000
Land and building				$13,200

Any rate used to capitalize or convert an estimated net income stream into value is called the *capitalization rate.* The term *building capitalization rate* means the sum of the capitalization (interest) rate plus the recapture rate. For example,

Capitalization (interest) rate	.10
Recapture rate	.04 (25-year life)
Building capitalization rate	.14

Determining the Capitalization (Interest) Rate

There are a number of ways to arrive at the appropriate capitalization (interest) rate. Three of the most common methods are (a) the built-up or summation method; (b) the band of investments method, and (c) extracting the interest rate from market sales.

Built-up, or summation method

The **built-up**, or **summation** method begins with a riskless or safe rate and then modifies it to reflect the nature of the investment. The following example illustrates the built-up method of deriving a basic capitalization rate.

The Built-Up Method

Riskless rate (Interest earned on riskless investment such as government bonds)	5%
Risk rate (Interest rate earned due to increased risk of this investment)	2%
Illiquidity (Interest rate earned due to nonliquid nature of this investment)	1%
Management (Interest rate earned due to management required for investment)	1%
Indicated basic capitalization rate	9%

This method is useful in understanding the composition of an interest or capitalization rate; however, it is of little practical value.

Band of investments method

The second method, called **band of investments,** is frequently used. This method recognizes that, in most real estate investments, several different firms and individuals supply the capital. Each supplier of capital is exposed to varying degrees of risk; therefore, each charges a different interest rate. The band of investments method is nothing more than a weighted average of the total cost of investment capital for a given investment under market conditions. The following illustrates how the band of investments method is used to derive a capitalization (interest) rate:

Suppliers of Capital in Band of Investments	Portion of Total Investment	Risk Rate	Weighted Rate
First mortgagee	.70	.08	.056
Second mortgagee	.20	.10	.020
Equity investor	.10	.12	.012
Indicated capitalization rate			.088

Extracting the Capitalization (Interest) Rate Directly from Market Sales

The appraiser can extract a capitalization (interest) rate directly from market sales if there have been a sufficient number of recent sales comparable in quality with similar anticipated declining income streams. The information needed includes the selling price, the net income, and the estimated remaining useful life of the improvements. The following example illustrates how to extract the capitalization rate from the market.

Deriving the Rate from the Market

Net income to land and building		$40,000
Sales price	$360,000	
Less land value (from the market)	−72,000	
Building value	$288,000	
Estimated remaining life		
of building (25 years)		
Indicated recapture rate is 4% ($\frac{1}{25}$)		
Less "return of" building value		
($288,000 × .04)		−11,520
"Return on" land and building		$28,480
Capitalization rate = ($28,480 ÷ $360,000) =		.079

Income Capitalization

Capitalization is a discounting process that converts a projected income stream into an estimate of present value. The essential variables in the capitalization formula are the projected net income and the proper rate at which the income stream should be discounted to arrive at the present value. Again, the discount, or interest rate used in the formula is called the *capitalization rate.*

Several capitalization methods are used to discount or convert net income into value. Each method has certain built-in assumptions about the nature of the income stream, the economic life of the improvements, and the division of value between land and improvements. Also, capitalization rates vary from period to period and from building to building, depending on the type of building, the age of the building, interest rates, and risks.

Capitalization in perpetuity

Capitalization in perpetuity is the basic capitalization method used when there is no time limit put on the receipt of the income stream and no provision for capital recapture. This method is used in valuing unimproved farm ground. It assumes that land does not depreciate and will be capable of generating an income indefinitely. Furthermore, upon resale, the proceeds will provide the seller with complete capital recovery. In essence, the income is being capitalized at a discount rate that will provide a *return on* the investment, but no *return of* investment. The basic capitalization formula is this:

$$\text{Present value of property} = \frac{\text{Net income}}{\text{Capitalization rate}}$$

The basic capitalization formula is sometimes presented as follows:

$$\frac{I}{R \mid V} \qquad \begin{aligned} I &= \text{Net income} \\ R &= \text{Capitalization rate} \\ V &= \text{Value} \end{aligned}$$

If any two of the three components in the capitalization formula are known or can be derived from the market data, the third component can be calculated.

For example, assume a property generates a net income of $12,000 and similar properties are selling at a capitalization rate of 9½ percent. By applying the basic capitalization formula, we can capitalize the $12,000 income stream into an estimate of value as follows:

$$V = \frac{I}{R} = \frac{\$12,000}{.095} = \$126,316 \text{ (rounded)}$$

Direct capitalization

In **direct capitalization,** an overall capitalization rate is extracted directly from market sales and applied to the net income of the subject property in the capitalization formula to arrive at the present value of the property.

The overall capitalization rate is composed of two rates:

1. Capitalization (interest) rate to provide a *return on* investment in both land and building.
2. Recapture (recovery) rate to provide a *return of* investment in the building portion of the investment.

There is a recapture provision inherent in the overall capitalization rate. Neither a specific time limit for recapture nor a remaining useful life of the building components is implied.

Derivation of Overall Capitalization Rate   The **overall capitalization rate** is derived from the market by analyzing the relationship between the net income and selling prices of recently sold comparable properties as follows:

Sale Number	Net Income	÷	Selling Price	=	Overall Cap. Rate
1	$12,000	÷	$126,000	=	.0952
2	14,000	÷	150,000	=	.0933
3	15,500	÷	158,000	=	.0981

As can be seen, similar properties are selling at an overall capitalization rate (or cap. rate, as it is sometimes called) of approximately 9½ percent. This rate merely shows the current market relationship between net income and selling price and expresses it as a percentage. The overall (cap.) rate is similar to the price/earnings ratio in the stock market. The logic behind this method of capitalization is merely that if, in the past, investors have been buying and selling similar properties at a cap. rate of 9½ percent, it is reasonable to assume that the net income of the subject property being appraised can be capitalized or converted into an estimate of value by using the same rate.

Application of the Overall Capitalization Rate   Once the range of the overall capitalization rates has been determined, the appraiser analyzes and weighs the various rates and reconciles them into a single cap. rate (R) to be applied to the net income of the subject property to arrive at an estimate of value as follows:

Subject property's net income $12,000
Overall rate (from the market)   9½%

$$\frac{I}{R|V}$$ Income ÷ Rate = Value
$12,000 ÷ .0950 = $126,300 (rounded)

This method is used when there are enough market transactions of comparable properties to derive an accurate overall rate. The comparable sales should be similar as to age, operating expense ratios, and land-to-building ratios. The primary difficulty with this method of capitalization is the inability to obtain accurate net income estimates from the comparable sales. In many cases, parties to the transaction consider such information as being confidential.

Straight line method—Land residual technique

The **land residual technique** assumes a declining income stream and implies a specific period of time over which the capital is to be recaptured in the building portion of the investment. This method of capitalization is appropriate under these conditions:

1. The improvements are new, or relatively new, and represent the highest and best use of the land.

2. The appraiser is confident of the building value.

3. The income stream is projected to decline.

For example, assume the subject property is a new apartment building with a remaining economic life of 50 years and that it generates a net income of $16,000. The structure cost $120,000 to build, and this represents current market value. Applying an 8 percent capitalization rate, we can capitalize the net income into value as follows:

Net income to land and building	$16,000
Less: Income attributable to the building	
Building Requirements are:	
"Return on" Investment .08 (interest rate)	
"Return of" Investment .02 (recapture rate)	
Building capitalization rate .10	

Apply the basic capitalization formula $\dfrac{I}{R|V}$ and the building capitalization rate to solve for I:

Income attributable to building ($120,000 × .10)	− 12,000
Residual or remaining income attributable to land	$ 4,000

Now apply the basic capitalization formula $\dfrac{I}{R|V}$ and the capitalization (interest) rate to solve for V:

Land value = ($4,000 ÷ .08) =	$ 50,000
Building value	120,000
Property value	$170,000

Straight line method—Building residual technique

The **building residual technique** also assumes a declining income stream and implies a specific period of time over which the capital is to be recaptured on the building portion of the investment. As with the land residual technique, this method of capitalization also provides a *return on* land and building investment as well as a *return of* the building portion of the investment. This method of capitalization is appropriate under these conditions:

1. The buildings are old.
2. Land value can readily be determined.

For example, assume the subject property is an older office building with a remaining economic life of ten years that generates a net income of $12,000. Recent land sales indicate the land value to be $15,000. Applying an 8 percent capitalization (interest) rate, we can convert the net income of the subject property into an estimate of value as follows:

Net income to land and building	$12,000
Less: Income attributed to land	
Calculated as follows:	
Land requirements are:	
"Return on" investment only (8% interest rate)	

Apply the basic capitalization formula $\dfrac{I}{R \mid V}$ to solve for I:

Income attributable to land = $15,000 × .08 =	−1,200
Residual or remaining income attributable to building	10,800

Now apply the same basic capitalization formula $\dfrac{I}{R \mid V}$ to solve for building value:

Building Value = $I \div R$	
= $10,800 ÷ .18 =	$60,000 Building value
Add back land value	15,000 Land value
Property value	$75,000 Property value

Note: The building cap. rate consists of

"Return on " investment	(Cap. or interest rate)	= .08
"Return of" investment	(Recapture rate)	= .10
Building cap. rate		.18

Annuity capitalization

All of the previously described methods of capitalization assume a declining income stream and use rates in the capitalization formula to convert the net income into an estimate of value. **Annuity capitalization** assumes a net, level income stream and uses present worth factors to discount a projected net income stream into an estimate of present value. The reader should be familiar with these three present value tables in order to understand annuity capitalization:

1. Compound amount of $1.00, column 1, Appendix D.
2. Present worth of $1.00 (reversionary table), column 4, Appendix D.
3. Present worth of $1.00/year (annuity table), column 5, Appendix D.

Compound Amount of $1.00   Table 19–1 represents the growth of one dollar at compound interest. Without the aid of the tables in the appendix, it is calculated as follows:

Table 19–1

Compound amount of $1.00

Year	Interest at 10%	Amount
0	0	$1
1	.10	1.10
2	.11	1.21
3	.121	1.331
4	.1331	1.4641
5	.14641	1.61051

Note that the addition of 10 percent interest every year is the same as multiplying the amount by 1.10. Hence, to calculate the value of $1.00 at the end of 5 years at 10 percent interest, the formula is $($1.10)^5$. As can be seen, the present value tables in Appendix D are based on end-of-year payments.

Present Worth of $1.00 (Reversionary Factors)   The present worth function is the reciprocal of the compound amount of $1.00 from Table 19–1. As can be seen from Table 19–1, $1.00 will grow to $1.10 in one year. It follows then that .909091 will grow to $1.00 in one year. The present worth of $1.00 to be received at the end of year one discounted at 10 percent is calculated by dividing the Table 19–1 amount of $1.10 into $1.00. The present worth of $1.00 to be received at the end of two years is calculated by dividing the Table 19–1 amount of $1.21 into $1.00. Five-year calculations follow:

Table 19–2

Present worth of $1.00 (reversionary factors)

Year	1/Amount of $1	Present Worth of $1
10% Interest (Discount) Rate		
1	1/1.10	.909091
2	1/1.21	.826446
3	1/1.331	.751315
4	1/1.4641	.683013
5	1/1.61051	.620921

Income to be received in the future is worth less than the same amount of money in hand today, since the money in hand now can earn interest. Therefore, future earnings must be discounted to arrive at their present value.

The present value of future income can be calculated by determining how much money would have to be invested today at a specific compound interest (discount) rate for today's investment to grow to the future payment in the given number of years. The amount of money that would have to be invested today is called the present value (PV) of the future payment or payments. *Present value,* or present worth is the current value of income to be received at some specified future time, discounted by a given rate of interest, using present worth of $1.00 factors.

Precomputed present worth of $1.00 (reversionary) factors for various rates of interest and periods of time are found in Appendix D, column 4. These factors are used to convert a single lump sum payment to be received at some time in the future into an estimate of present value. These tables are used to estimate the present worth of the property reversion.

Present Worth of $1.00 Per Year (Annuity Factors)   The present worth of a series of payments (annuity) is the total of the present values of all the payments. The present worth of $1.00 per year received for five years then is an accumulation of the present worth of $1.00 figures for years one through five as follows:

Table 19–3
Present worth of $1.00 per year (annuity factors)

	10% Interest (Discount) Rate	
Year	Present Worth of $1	Present Worth of $1/Year
1	.909091	.909091
2	.826446	1.735537
3	.751315	2.486852
4	.683013	3.169865
5	.620921	3.790786

Column 5 in Appendix D shows the precomputed present worth of $1.00/year annuity factors. The tables in Appendix D are used to convert an income stream into an estimate of present value. The *annuity factors* have a provision for capital recapture built into them, so there is no need to add a separate recapture rate.

Annuity capitalization is used when the projected income stream of the subject property has the characteristics of an annuity, that is, income expected at regular intervals in predictable amounts. This condition exists when the property being appraised is under long-term lease with a tenant of good credit standing.

Annuity capitalization method—
Property residual technique
Although the annuity capitalization method can be used in conjunction with all the residual techniques—land residual, building residual, and property residual—the *property residual technique* is the most popular method and is used when the subject property is under a long-term lease with readily

ascertainable rents. The leased fee value (lessor's interest) of leased property consists of two components:

1. *The present value of the income stream.* The income stream is discounted at an appropriate rate to reflect the risk involved.

2. *The present value of the property reversion to be received at the expiration of the lease.* The property reversion is discounted at a somewhat higher rate to reflect the additional risk involved in ownership of the property now that the lease has expired.

For example, assume the subject property is a new office building costing $400,000 to build on a $100,000 site and under a long-term 20-year net lease of $46,000 per year to a tenant with a triple A credit rating. The risk inherent in such an investment is small, and a discount rate of 9% is considered reasonable. The building has an estimated economic life of 40 years. The value of the property, as leased, is calculated as follows:

1. Present value of the 20-year income stream discounted at 9 percent:

     $46,000 × 8.0607* = $370,792

2. Present value of the property reversion in 20 years.

The property reversion consists of:

The land (value remains stable)	$100,000
The building	
$\dfrac{20 \text{ (years)}}{40 \text{ (years)}}$ × $400,000 =	$200,000
Total value	$300,000

Present value of property reversion = $300,000 × .1486** =	44,580
Present value of leased fee interest	$415,372

The leased fee value of $415,372 (usually rounded to $415,400) is considerably lower than the unleased value of $500,000. These figures indicate that the property is either being rented below economic (market) rent, thereby creating a positive leasehold interest in favor of the lessee, or that the building does not represent the highest and best use of the land.

CORRELATION AND FINAL ESTIMATE

At this point, the appraiser has applied the cost approach, the market approach, and the income approach and has derived three different estimates of value. Having developed a value range, she or he must now establish a final estimate of value by reviewing all of the three approaches for accuracy. The next step is to evaluate the applicability of each approach relative to the purpose of the appraisal and the type of property being appraised.

---

*From Appendix D, Column 5, annuity factor, 20 years, 9%.

**From Appendix D, Column 4, reversionary factor 20 years, 10% (higher discount rate used because of increased risk in unleased property).

If the property is being appraised for mortgage-lending puposes, its income-generating capacity takes precedence, and the income approach should be given greatest weight. If the property is being appraised for tax, condemnation, or sale purposes, the market approach should be given greater emphasis. If the appraisal is made for insurance purposes, the cost approach should be given greatest weight.

The type of property being appraised also determines which approach should be given the greatest weight. The cost approach should be emphasized on a special purpose property, such as a church or a factory, because of the lack of comparable sales and income data. The market approach should be given the greatest weight in appraising a home because the marketplace is filled with purchases and sales that constantly generate up-to-the-minute indications of market value. The market approach may be the only feasible approach on old, depreciated buildings with little or no dependable income data. Finally, when appraising income-producing properties, the appraiser should give greatest weight to the income approach because typical investors evaluate alternative investments similarly. The final estimate of value should be broken down between land and improvements.

If the appraiser carefully exercises skill, experience, and judgment in correlating the estimates, the results should indicate a valid final estimate of value. The results are then compiled and presented in a written report to the client.

SUMMARY

The purpose of an appraisal is to estimate value. Most appraisal assignments require an estimation of market value. However, the appraiser may be asked to estimate other types of value, depending on the client's needs. Other values commonly estimated include insurable value, investment value, going-concern value, and assessed value.

Major governmental, economic, social, and physical factors are constantly at work influencing value. The appraiser must observe, analyze, and interpret the effect of these factors on the value estimate.

Appraising is a systematic process. Prior to starting, the property must be clearly identified and the client's problem understood. Then the appraiser lays out a careful plan to determine how to conduct the appraisal. When the client and the appraiser agree on the plan, purpose, and fee, the appraiser proceeds to collect data and perform the analysis. The appraiser may apply the cost approach, market approach, or income approach; however, using a combination of all three usually gives the best results.

The cost approach to value is based on the estimated value of the land, plus the cost of replacing the improvements, minus any depreciation caused by physical deterioration, functional obsolescence, or economic obsolescence. The cost approach is best suited to special purpose properties, such as a church or factory, that lack income data or comparable sales. This approach is most reliable when the improvement is new or nearly new and the land is being utilized at its highest and best use. The cost approach is less reliable on older buildings.

The income approach takes the actual or estimated net income from the property and, through the process of capitalization, converts it into a property value. This approach is given the most weight for income-producing properties.

When applying the income approach to single-family homes and duplexes, a factor (GMRM) is derived from the market and applied to the estimated gross monthly rent of the appraised property to arrive at an estimate of value. This approach usually sets the lower limit of value in single-family residential appraising because it does not reflect many of the nonmonetary benefits of home ownership that accrue to the homeowner. Consequently, this approach is given little weight in most higher-priced single-family homes. However, if the home being appraised is in the lower value range and an active rental market exists for the property, the income approach is more reliable and should be given more weight.

The market approach compares the subject property being appraised to recent sales of similar properties. Differences between the subject property and the comparable properties are noted and dollar or percentage adjustments are made to the selling price of the comparable properties in arriving at a preliminary market value for the subject property. The market approach should be given considerable weight when sufficient market data are available.

TERMS AND CONCEPTS

You can check your understanding of these terms against the glossary or by review in this chapter.

Annuity capitalization	MAI
Annuity factor	Market value
Appraisal	Overall capitalization rate
Building capitalization rate	Present value
Building residual technique	Principle of contribution
Capitalization rate	Principle of increasing and
Comparable sale	decreasing returns
Depreciation	Principle of substitution
Economic life	Property residual technique
Effective age	Rate
Effective demand	Reserve for replacement
GMRM	RM
Highest and best use	Scarcity
Insurable value	SREA
Investment value	Transferability
Land residual technique	Utility

What are the differences or relationships, if any, between the following?

Built-up (summation) method and
  Band of investments method
Capitalization in perpetuity and
  Direct capitalization
Capitalization rate and Overall rate
Comparative approach to value and
  Market approach to value
Cost approach to value and Market
  approach to value
Cost concept of value, Market
  concept of value, and Economic
  concept of value
Fixed expenses and Operating
  expenses
Functional obsolescence and
  Economic obsolescence

Function of appraisal and
  Purpose of appraisal
Income approach to value
  and Capitalization
Macromarket data and Micromarket
  data
Physical deterioration and
  Physical depreciation
Recapture rate and Overall rate
Replacement cost, insurable and
  Insurable value, depreciated
Return on investment and Return
  of investment
Square foot method, Cubic foot
  method, and Quantity survey
  method

PROBLEMS

19–1. What are the three approaches to appraising? Explain and illustrate each approach.

19–2. Differentiate between market value and investment value.

19–3. Differentiate between effective age and actual age.

19–4. In appraising a residence, you find the following four comparative sales in the block:

Data	Subject Property	A	B	C	D
Price:	—	$40,000	$35,500	$38,000	$31,000
Date:	Now	this year	2 yr ago	1 yr ago	3 yr ago
Lot:	—	Equal	Equal	Equal	Double lot
Architecture:	—	Poorer	Better	Equal	Equal
Rooms:	7	6	7	6	7
Baths:	1½	1	1	1½	1
Condition:	—	Poorer	Better	Equal	Equal

Assuming that the double lot for *D* was responsible for $1,000 additional price, that each room is worth $500, and that the market increases 10 percent per year, and that other plus and minus adjustments average $500 apiece, what is the indicated value range for the subject property?

19–5. You have completed both the market and cost approach on a single-family house appraisal assignment. These two approaches develop value indications as follows:

Cost approach $36,600
Market approach $36,000

Sale	Sale Price	Monthly Rent
1	$37,500	$320
2	$36,000	$310
3	$35,500	$300
4	$35,900	$310
5	$34,800	$300

These sales are quite comparable to the subject property. Rental differences are due to the physical conditions of the homes. All sales are in the same neighborhood. Using the GMRM, find the income approach to value. The subject property's estimated rental is $300.

19–6. An apartment building produces an annual net operating income of $50,000. The interest rate for the property has been estimated at 10.25 percent, and the economic life of the improvement is estimated to be 25 years. Three highly similar and competitive apartment buildings within two blocks of the subject property, offering essentially the same service and improvements as the subject, have sold in the past month. Comparable sales data and net operating income are:

Comparable Sales	Selling Price	Net Operating Income
1	$400,000	$53,500
2	$450,000	$62,000
3	$325,000	$45,000

Using direct capitalization, capitalize or convert the subject property's net income into an estimate of value.

19–7. Use the information provided below for Comparables No. 1, No. 2, and No. 3 to arrive at an appraised value for a subject property in Rockingham County. Use the format of Figure 19–3a. The subject property was appraised in March, 1979.

Comparable No. 1 sold for $62,500 in May, 1978. Since the prices of homes have increased, use a time adjustment of $1,500. Comparable No. 2 sold for $62,500 in March, 1979, and no time adjustment is necessary. Comparable No. 3 sold for $53,600 in August, 1978, so a time adjustment of $1,000 is to be used. The locations of all four properties are equivalent.

The subject property and No. 1 each have 2.0 acres. No. 2 has ½ acre (adjustment + $2,000), and No. 3 has ⅓ acre (adjustment + $2,500). The appeal and quality of construction are good on all four properties.

The subject property is 27 years old, and older properties are considered of lower value. No. 1 is 6 years old (adjustment $2,000), and Nos. 2 and 3 are 13 years old (adjustment $1,000). All four properties are in good condition.

The subject property has the largest living area (1,982 square feet), which is valued greater than No. 1 (1,706 square feet) by $2,000, greater than No. 2 (1,463 square feet) by $3,500 and greater than No. 3 (1,528 square feet) by $2,800.

The subject property has a full basement. No. 3 is inferior as it has no basement. A $5,000 adjustment is required. The other two have full basements; however, No. 1 is better than the subject by $3,000, and No. 2 is better than the subject by $2,000. The functional utility of No. 1 is valued at $2,000 more than either of the other three properties. The garage for No. 3 is considered better than either of the others by $2,000.

Comparable No. 1 has a pool worth $6,000 more than subject property. No. 2 has a pool worth $2,000 more than the subject property. The subject property and No. 3 are equivalent.

The kitchens and fireplaces of the subject property and No. 1 are similar. No. 2 is poorer by $500, and No. 3 is poorer than the subject property by $2,500.

Weigh all comparable properties equally to arrive at an appraised value.

19–8.   If houses in one particular suburb have a GMRM of 116, what is the difference in value between a house on Foxbough that has gross rental income of $6,600 per year and a house on Woodvine Drive with a gross rental income of $5,240 per year?

19–9.   The property being appraised is a 25-year old apartment building producing a yearly net income of $60,000. Assuming a 20-year economic life for the building, determine the property value at a 9½ percent interest rate and an estimated land value of $100,000. Use the appropriate residual method of capitalization.

SUPPLEMENTARY READINGS

American Institute of Real Estate Appraisers. *The Appraisal of Real Estate,* 7th ed. Chicago: 1978.

Babcock, Henry A. *Appraisal Principles and Procedures.* Homewood, Ill.: Irwin, 1968.

Bloom, George F., and Harrison, Henry S. *Appraising the Single Family Residence.* Chicago: American Institute of Real Estate Appraisers, 1978.

Boeckh Building Valuation Manual, vol. 1, *Residential and Agricultural.* Milwaukee: American Appraisal Company, 1972.

Income Property Valuation: Principles and Techniques of Appraising Income-Producing Real Estate. Lexington, Mass.: Heath, 1971.

Kahn, Sanders A., and Case, Frederick E. *Real Estate Appraisal and Investment.* New York: Wiley, 1977.

Kinnard, William N., Jr. *An Introduction to Appraising Real Property.* Chicago: Society of Real Estate Appraisers, 1968.

Knowles, Jerome, Jr. *Single Family Residential Appraisal Manual.* Chicago: American Institute of Real Estate Appraisers, 1974.

Miles, Martin J. *Encyclopedia of Real Estate Formulas and Tables.* Englewood Cliffs, N.J.: Prentice-Hall, 1978. Chapters 7–10.

Murray, William G. *Farm Appraisal and Valuation.* Ames, Iowa: Iowa State University Press, 1969.

Ring, Alfred A. *Valuation of Real Estate,* 2nd ed. Englewood Cliffs, N.J.: Prentice-Hall, 1970.

Ring, Alfred A., and Dasso, Jerome. *Real Estate Principles and Practices,* 8th ed. Englewood Cliffs, N.J.: Prentice-Hall, 1977.

Shenkel, William M. *Modern Real Estate Appraisal.* New York: McGraw-Hill, 1978.

Smith, Halbert C. *Real Estate Appraisal.* Columbus, Ohio: Grid, 1976. Chapter 7.

Ventolo, William L., Jr., and Williams, Martha R. *Fundamentals of Real Estate Appraisal.* Chicago: Real Estate Education Company, 1977.

Wendt, Paul F. *Real Estate Appraisal.* Athens: University of Georgia Press, 1974. Chapters 1 and 9.

Property Management

A large number of the families and commercial enterprises in the United States are housed in large, multistoried buildings. These buildings represent the bulk of the total invested capital in the country, and their rental income is a substantial portion of the total national income. The large amount of money involved, the complexity of the task, the necessity for specialized knowledge, and the frequency of absentee ownership cause owners of buildings to employ professional property managers. Many property owners do have competence in this area, however, and manage their own property. Whether the owner or someone else manages the property, the concepts discussed in this chapter would apply.

Property management has become recognized as a special field of its own. Community colleges and universities offer courses as part of their real estate programs. In addition, many schools offer special courses in hotel management, country club management, and other specialized fields. The NATIONAL ASSOCIATION OF REALTORS® has established the Institute of Real Estate Management (*IREM*) for specialists in property management. Members of this institute can earn the professional designation of Certified Property Manager (*CPM*). The Building Owners and Managers Association (*BOMA*) offers the professional designation of Real Property Administrator (RPA). Professional property managers require a comprehensive understanding of property value based on income and its potential value in the future. They must be knowledgeable in marketing, consumer behavior, maintenance, accounting, and the legal aspects of property management.

SCOPE OF PROPERTY MANAGEMENT

Property management encompasses the management of all types of properties. Some multiple story buildings house only one large organization, whereas others house several tenants who lease smaller units of space. The full scope of the property manager's job is apparent in the management of large buildings. Even when there is only one tenant, someone has to supervise the service and maintenance tasks. These tasks comprise part of the property manager's job. Some important types of buildings and the related property management tasks are discussed below.

Office Buildings

Prior to 1950, the majority of the large office buildings were in the central business districts of the larger cities. The buildings were concentrated there near transportation and other commercial activities. Since the 1950s, office building construction has gradually expanded both in central areas and in outlying areas. This continued demand for office space has grown because of the expansion of service establishments involving office workers. In addition, those using office space have demanded improvements in the quality of their facilities.

Hotels and Motels

Hotel management, a specialized endeavor, has its own unique problems. The primary difference is that hotel clients are mostly transients. The resort hotel falls into this category but deals with vacationing transients who often stay for a longer period of time.

Industrial Buildings

Industrial buildings contain space that is suitable for manufacturing or warehousing. The buildings are usually not finished or carpeted inside. In the earlier part of this century, multiple story buildings were constructed primarily near central business areas or where rail transportation was available. Recently, the trend has been to locate one- or two-floor structures in industrial parks. In either case, the functions of managing industrial buildings include leasing space, maintenance, and providing the associated services.

Store Properties

Store properties take the form of department stores, shopping centers, or buildings housing retail establishments. Frequently, stores are located in the lower floor of buildings that have residential units or office space in the upper floors.

Residential Buildings

Several types of residential properties must be managed:

1. Apartment buildings. Large apartment buildings and complexes comprise a substantial portion of the nation's housing. These apartments may be (a) owned by private owners such as insurance companies who have invested their funds for income; (b) built as public housing and

operated with assistance from the federal government; or (c) owned by the residents either as a cooperative or as a condominium. Each category requires a full scope of property management services.

2. Single-family units.   Although the tendency is toward home ownership, a number of families still rent single-family dwellings. Homes that have been foreclosed by mortgage holders frequently end up as rental units, especially during slow sales periods in the market. The leasing of rental units makes up a substantial area of property management.

3. Duplexes.   A home designed for two families is called a *duplex.* These homes, and others designed for three or four families, make up a large part of the rental income market. This type of structure allows a greater return from the land investment than a single-family home. Duplexes are often managed by the owners, who often live in one of the units.

APPROACHES TO PROPERTY MANAGEMENT

Property management involves a wide variety of tasks and responsibilities. These responsibilities can be handled by one of three basic approaches:

1. A firm that deals exclusively in property management. This type of company will usually be headed by one or more Certified Property Managers. The sole function of the business is to manage property for others.

2. A real estate brokerage firm with a department set up to manage property. In this case, property management is only part of the firm's total business. Other functions may include buying and selling real estate, performing appraisals, or subdividing and developing. In this case, one person would probably act as head of the property management department. He or she would be responsible for all aspects of managing the properties.

3. A property manager who has responsibility for a specific building. Many apartment and office buildings have a property manager's office set up on the premises for the manager and other management personnel. The property manager may work directly for the owner and be responsible for only that property. If the management of one property is not a full-time job, the person may also manage other buildings.

THE PROPERTY MANAGER

Property managers must have a number of important qualifications. A broad knowledge of the technical aspects of real estate is, of course, basic. Understanding urban analysis and the economic forces affecting the properties is also mandatory. Business experience and education in business administration are also important. Since property managers hire and supervise other people, experience in handling people is another valuable asset.

As part of the task of keeping the rental space filled, property managers will need to make marketing analyses of the competition and of other external factors affecting the demand for and occupancy of the space. They must be able to establish rents and adjust them to economic and market conditions so that the operation will be profitable. Property managers must also know the many financial aspects of business and of real estate in particular. They should operate their properties so as to yield a satisfactory net income after all expenses and overhead have been paid.

Property managers should be familiar with the local area. Business contacts with banks, financial institutions, and professional associations provide important sources of clients. Knowledge of local economic forces help them formulate pricing and marketing strategies.

Recently there has been a trend toward specialization in property management. The skills of the apartment house manager can be somewhat different from those of the office building manager, the shopping center manager, or the industrial park manager. Farm management requires still other skills.

Certified Property Manager (CPM)

Members of the NATIONAL ASSOCIATION OF REALTORS® who specialize in property management are able to further their professional interests through membership in the Institute of Real Estate Management (IREM). The institute confers the title of Certified Property Manager (CPM) to each individual who meets the following requirements:

1. Is a member of the NATIONAL ASSOCIATION OF REALTORS® or a local real estate board.
2. Has been actively engaged in real estate management for at least three years.
3. Demonstrates the ability to manage real estate.
4. Meets minimum educational requirements.
5. Subscribes to the institute bylaws and pledge.
6. Provides evidence of honesty and integrity.
7. Passes written examinations administered by the IREM *or* waives an examination if proof is given of 15 years active property management experience.

The Management Contract

A management contract is an agreement between a property owner and the person hired as the property manager. The contract describes the rights and duties of the manager as well as the rights and obligations of the owner. Standard property management forms are available from IREM. The following items are important and should be clearly covered in the contract agreement:

1. Exact description of property to be managed.
2. The term during which the contract runs, showing the starting date and termination date.

3. The names of the owner and manager and a description of the duties of the manager. Usually, the manager is defined as the agent of the owner and can act in the owner's behalf.

4. Compensation of the manager. The compensation is usually based on a percentage of gross collections, with a typical range being 5–8 percent.

5. Responsibility of the property manager to collect rents, hire employees, and pay expenses. The agreement should explain how funds collected in excess of expenses are to be handled, as well as what happens if the collected funds are not sufficient to meet expenditures.

6. Reports to be furnished to owner and other persons.

7. The extent to which the manager can make repairs and alterations or spend funds without the owner's consent.

The initial effort to clarify the owner-manager relationship will help to alleviate problems in the future. The property management contract need not be on a particular form; however, the form published by the IREM provides a convenient basis for agreement. The term of the contract should depend upon the desires of both the owner and the manager. It need not necessarily be long-term. The continuance of a contract relationship should be based upon the owner's satisfaction with the work being performed as well as the manager's satisfaction with the relationship.

Functions of Property Managers

The overall function of property managers is to act for owners. In this capacity, they are responsible for all aspects of managing the property. They may be given this responsibility because some owners (a) do not want to be bothered with the effort, (b) live at a distance, or (c) are willing to pay for this service because a property manager can do a much better job of management. The functions of property managers can be divided into the following groups:

1. *Securing and keeping tenants for the property*
   a. Promotion and advertising
   b. Negotiating leases or rental contracts
   c. Modifying facilities to meet tenants' needs
   d. Acting as liaison with tenants and handling complaints

2. *Providing financial records and accounts*
   a. Management plans and reports
   b. Rent collection
   c. Public relations

3. *Providing upkeep and maintenance of property*
   a. Hiring employees
   b. Security, parking
   c. Cleaning

The extensive and varied functions of the property manager cannot be executed solely by one person. This is especially true for a large building or where several properties are handled. The manager should explain to the owners the workings of the management organization and the different responsibilities carried out by the subordinate personnel. Most owners understand that this delegation of tasks is necessary, as in any other business. A clear understanding initially will help to prevent future problems.

The manager should also discuss uncertainties of the business with the owner. Although the manager may put out a top-quality effort, local business conditions and economic cycles may result in periods of high vacancy rates causing decreased net income. It is important that the owner understand these uncertainties; it is just as important that the manager not make promises that may be impossible to meet.

ORGANIZATION FOR PROPERTY MANAGEMENT

As in any business, the form of the property management organization and the way in which responsibilities are delegated have much to do with the operation's success.

Consider a property management firm or a department in a brokerage firm. How should it be organized? The operation depends on demonstrated competence for its survival. Many of those who try to handle property management on a part-time basis end up in failure. Some brokers regard property management as a secondary function to supplement the brokerage business, and this concept can lead to failure. It is important that the persons involved understand their full responsibility and their need for commitment.

Two general approaches to organization can be applied to property management: *functional management* and *project management.* These approaches are consistent with general management theory and can be applied to any organization. Figure 20–1 shows a functional organization where people are delegated responsibility for one or more specialized functions. This chart may be more suitable for a larger property management firm. A smaller firm might have only four people (see *) with managerial responsibility. A very small organization may have only the property manager plus other specialists working directly for the manager to perform the many varied tasks.

The diagram in Figure 20–1 shows the various functions that must be performed. Almost any of these functions could be subcontracted to an outside agency. Independent agencies are available to handle accounts, advertising, maintenance, security, cleaning, or almost any of the needed services. An advantage to functional organization is that the functions are specialized and well-trained people can be hired to perform each special function.

Figure 20–2 shows a diagram of project organization. In the project organization, one person is delegated the complete responsibility for one or more buildings and is responsible for obtaining all personnel and services needed for buildings under his responsibility, whether the services be performed by hired personnel or subcontracted to others. The primary advantage of this organiza-

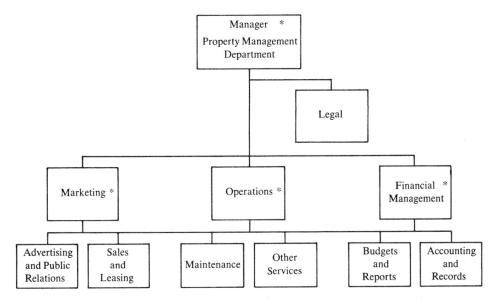

Figure 20–1
Functional organization

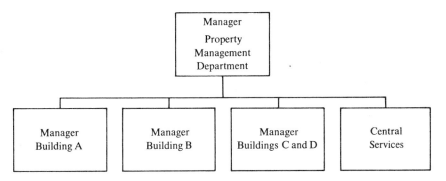

Figure 20–2
Project organization

tion is that one person can be held responsible for the operation and profitability of a particular building, development, or project.

The functional organization and the project organization each have their advantages. Figure 20–3 shows an organization chart that combines these two concepts. In this case, one person is responsible for each building or project, but most of the services are also centralized for efficiency. Each property manager can then draw upon the central group for the services he needs. This organization has some of the advantages of each of the others. The company executive can hold one person responsible for the profitable operation of a unit and, at the same time, can make more efficient use of specialists.

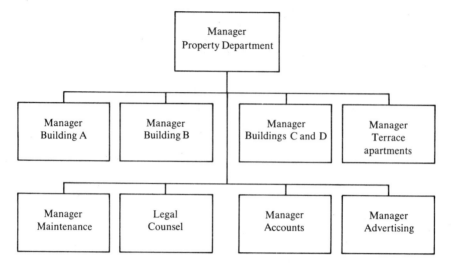

Figure 20–3
Combination functional and project organization

MARKETING OF INCOME PROPERTY

If the functions of a property manager are considered in the order in which they occur, the first element is to find qualified tenants to lease or rent the available units. This function is equivalent to marketing in any business. In this case, the product is building space. As with most products, marketing involves market research, product and space evaluation, formulation of a marketing strategy, advertising, and the ability to sell.

The marketing research function includes evaluating the particular property and comparing it to competitive properties. What are the specific advantages of this property? Who are its potential users? What price should be set to make it competitive? Analyzing the available competitive properties, their proximities, prices, numbers of existing vacancies, and other assets will provide information on the market situation and the current demand. In comparing it with other properties, it is necessary to consider their respective locations, ages, sizes of units, and the nature of existing users. Forms are available to use in describing a residential apartment unit. A good strategy is to inspect a sample of the competing properties and compare their attributes item-by-item with the subject property. This procedure will help determine if the price of the subject property is competitive. It can also be used as sales promotion data.

Having evaluated the property, the property manager must now identify its potential market. Consider a residential apartment unit. What do tenants look for when selecting apartments? Why do people select apartments instead of individual homes? Who are the potential tenants, and where are they now? Here are some possible answers to the last question: (a) They live in lower-priced units now and want to improve their living standard; (b) they are newly married or planning marriage; (c) they are single and highly mobile; (d) their family size has increased or decreased recently; or (e) they presently live in the property and may or may not renew their lease. This type of analysis is important since it will identify the potential renters. The next logical step is to decide what promotion or advertising media will be most successful in reaching that market segment. If most of the potential customers are expected to move in from outside the community, the advertising strategy would be much different than if the potential market consisted of local people who want to upgrade their living standards. The following are some possible advertising media or other approaches to reach the market:

- Newspapers
- Radio and television
- Direct mail advertising
- Billboards
- Company, community, church, or other bulletins
- Personal visits to prospects
- Displays in commercial establishments or motels
- Other real estate brokers
- Information included with rental billings

The final step is the sales promotion and selling, much of which is personal contact with present or potential clients. The data collected regarding the property, the competition, and the potential users will be useful in presenting an effective sales approach.

Commercial Property

The marketing of commercial property brings up a number of additional important factors. Location is very important to commercial establishments. Customer traffic is very important to retail businesses; however, the types of people who comprise the traffic should be considered as well as the traffic count. In promoting commercial real estate, data on the amount and types of pedestrian traffic are vital for the potential tenant. It is not always easy to collect valid data. Companies specializing in conducting traffic surveys can be hired. Usually, they obtain very reliable results. Pedestrian traffic, however, is of little significance to physicians, dentists, or lawyers who look to other factors such as parking facilities, public transportation, and appearance of the property.

Pricing commercial property usually differs from pricing residential space. Residential properties are usually priced on a per-unit basis, such as a one-bedroom apartment at $200 per month or a three-bedroom apartment at $360 per month. Commercial property is often rented on a percentage of gross sales basis, by the front footage on the street or mall, or by square footage of floor area. Consider the retail store in Figure 20–4 to compute rent by the three different methods:

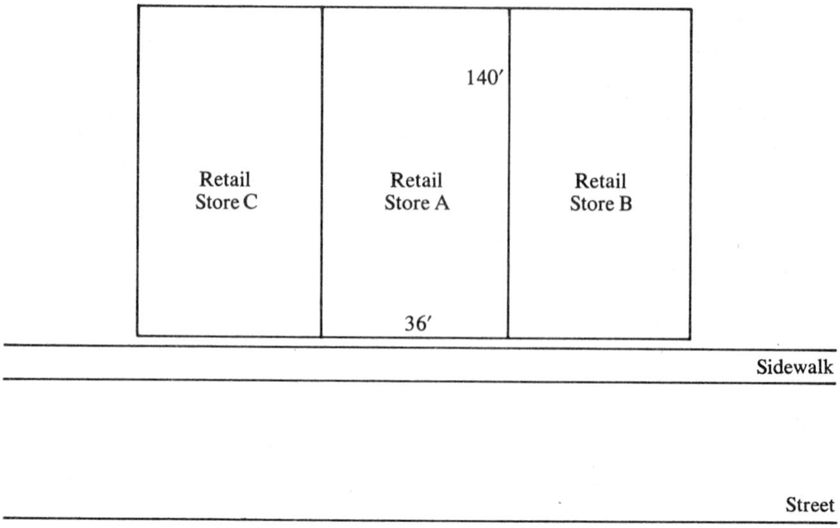

Figure 20–4
Retail store configuration

1. The rent is charged as two percent of gross sales. Consider the gross sales for the month of March as $37,500. With this method, the rent would be $0.02 \times \$37,500$, or $750 per month.

2. Consider the same property with the rent computed as $200 per front foot per year. Since the length along the street runs 36 feet, the rent would be

$$\$200 \times 36 \text{ ft} = \$7,200 \text{ per yr, or}$$

$$\frac{\$7,200}{12} = \$600 \text{ per mo}$$

3. On a square-foot basis, the area of the store is calculated as

$$140 \text{ ft} \times 36 \text{ ft} = 5,040 \text{ sq ft}$$

If the yearly rate is $1.50 per square foot, the rent would be:

$$\$1.50 \times 5,040 \text{ sq ft} = \$7,560 \text{ per yr, or}$$

$$\frac{\$7,560}{12} = \$630 \text{ per mo}$$

Leases may include combinations of these provisions and may, in addition, contain an escalator clause. A typical rent escalation clause could require the rent to increase with an increase in property taxes. An increase in the cost-of-living index or wage increases granted to employees resulting from a union contract might also call for a change in the rent under an escalation clause.

The property management business, as most other businesses, is competitive. Sometimes a manager will make concessions to a prospective tenant to get her to sign a lease. Typically, he might agree to remodel the space, pay a portion of the tenant's moving expenses, or provide free rent for the first month. The practice of giving a concession is more prevalent in times when vacancy rates are high. Concessions might also be used to induce tenants to move from their existing location into a new building.

OPERATIONS

The property manager is responsible for maintaining the structure, heating, grounds, trash disposal, operating equipment, and other items of common use by the tenants. Downs[1] separates the maintenance tasks into four basic categories:

1. Maintenance activities that protect the physical integrity of the building structure (e.g., repairs to foundations, roofs, exterior walls, stairways, driveways, and walks).

2. Maintenance associated with continued functional operation of a building and use by the occupants (e.g., heating, air conditioning, plumbing, electrical systems, elevators, laundry facilities, and swimming pools).

3. Standard housekeeping and cleaning operations.

4. Maintenance operations related to improving the appearance or otherwise improving the competitive appeal of the property (decorating, landscaping, carpeting, mowing lawns, and similar items).

Services

Services offered to the tenants affect the rental rates of units; however, these services can often be supplied by the landlord more efficiently for all tenants than if each tenant were to secure her or his own. The following services add to the expenses of property operation but are frequently provided:

Remodeling

Especially in the case of commercial properties, a tenant may require changes in layout or remodeling to suit particular business needs. It is often more efficient and economical for the manager to furnish this service. The cost could either be included in the rental rates or a separate charge levied. Property owners often maintain their own crew for this purpose or have subcontracts with outside agencies.

Cleaning

The manager is usually responsible for furnishing some cleaning services. In apartment buildings, cleaning services are generally restricted to the halls and other public areas. In office buildings, cleaning services are frequently provided for tenant-rented areas also. The cleaning crews can be employed directly, or the cleaning can be subcontracted to an outside agency.

---

[1]James C. Downs. *Principles of Real Estate Management*. Chicago: Institute of Real Estate Management, 1975. Chapter 28.

Security

Some residential and many commercial buildings furnish one or more security guards. Security can be handled by guards hired by the property manager or by a professional security agency.

Parking facilities

In suburban areas it is usually sufficient to provide unmonitored parking areas for tenant or customer parking. In areas where parking space is scarce, it is often necessary to provide either an attendant or automatic entrance control equipment to restrict parking facilities to authorized persons.

Managing Services

Providing services that meet the tenants' needs and desires is important to retain present tenants and secure new tenants. At the same time, the cost of the services must permit a satisfactory net income to the property owner.

When services are to be subcontracted, the manager should first seek a competitive bid for each service. Competitive bidding is also used in procuring maintenance supplies, especially when large amounts are involved. The first step in competitive bidding is to prepare a specification defining exactly what services or materials are required. Bidders can then quote their prices to furnish the specified services or materials. It is also usually desirable to allow bidders to submit auxiliary bids for performing the services in a way that differs from the specification. In some cases, suggestions of the bidders could provide adequate service, save money, and result in lower prices to the manager.

If contracts with service agencies can be made for long periods and the expenses budgeted in advance, cost control becomes easier. A contract to cover all maintenance and repairs to heating, electrical, and plumbing facilities removes the risk that unexpected breakdown will cause higher than planned expenses. This resembles an insurance policy in that the risks are transferred to the maintenance subcontractor. A maintenance subcontractor who has responsibility for all repairs at a fixed price may take more care in performing preventive maintenance.

If the management firm hires its own employees to do the maintenance, security, or cleaning, it will need experience in many aspects of personnel management. Wage scales must be formulated. Potential employees must be found and their qualifications evaluated. Careful initial selection of employees pays off in the long run. The selection process should be followed by a training program if the new employees do not have adequate experience.

Many aspects of personnel management should be outlined in written policies and procedures. Employee insurance, work schedules, sick leave, holidays, pay increases, and vacations should all be covered so that employees can understand the policies and management can administer them with consistency and fairness.

House Rules

The property manager should establish a pleasant living atmosphere and provide for the welfare of the tenants. House rules and regulations can help. The following factors should be covered by rules if they apply to the particular building:

1. Swimming pools—Who can use them; hours; safety regulations.
2. Maximum number of occupants per apartment.
3. Trash facilities—Where to put trash; collection schedules.
4. Use of playgrounds—Who is allowed; responsibility for injuries.
5. Activities permitted and prohibited in halls or front areas of the building and premises.
6. Moving in or out—How much advance notice is required; is moving restricted to weekdays or to particular daytime hours?
7. Radio and television aerials—Can they be installed?
8. Loud playing of radios and televisions after specified hours.
9. Pets.
10. Clothes washing and drying—Facilities available.
11. Parking rules and restrictions; identification stickers.
12. Night activities that may disturb other tenants and therefore are prohibited.
13. Use of electrical appliances in apartments.
14. Failure of electricity or landlord-maintained appliances—How to obtain maintenance service.
15. Car washing—Areas where it is permitted.
16. Fire regulations.
17. Storage facilities available—Their cost; accessibility.

FINANCIAL CONTROL

The primary objective in managing income property is to attain the highest net return. The long-term net profit must be considered along with the short-term goals. In addition, the management strategy must consider the risks involved. The risk from fire or other similar hazards can be alleviated by purchasing insurance. The manager must also deal with the risk that a larger than predicted number of units will remain vacant. This situation might result from changes in the general economy or from increased competition. High occupancy rates of office buildings in the 1960s encouraged excess construction of new office space. The result was aggravated by the economic situation and produced unfavorable vacancy rates in the 1970s. Another risk which must be considered is that operating expenses can increase during a one- or two-year period over which the lease specifies a fixed rent. These and other risks must be identified, evaluated, and controlled.

These factors and risks must be considered when establishing rental schedules. The income from rent less the costs of services and overhead should yield the desired net income. At the same time, the rental rates must compete with other rental rates in the local area, or the vacancy rate will be too high.

Income Management

Since rents are the primary source of income, the timely payment of rents is very important. This begins with procedures for selecting tenants and for writing valid lease contract terms. Each tenant's credit, business position, and other qualifications should be obtained from the local credit bureaus. Checking prior landlords or other references also helps to evaluate potential tenants and avoid future problems. If a business property is involved, the terms given to a tenant may reflect that tenant's business position. Sometimes rents are lower at first to accommodate a business just getting started.

Adherence to a firm rental collection policy is vital. The tenant should understand that rents are due on the specified date whether or not he receives a notice. Payment of rents in advance on the first day of the month is the policy recommended. Penalties for late payment should be clearly specified in the lease agreement. It is also important to enforce these terms so that tenants do not assume that the terms are unimportant. Although there may be a few extenuating circumstances, it does not pay to try to be nice to everyone who has a problem. If a property manager has not enforced rental payment terms in the past, it may lead to difficulty in enforcing them legally. Past practices provide implied consent that it is all right to disregard the terms. If tenants do not pay rents on time, the manager must pursue a rigid follow-up system of notices and legal action. At the time rents are paid, the tenants should be given receipts even if they pay by check; receipts provide accurate bookkeeping records.

Expense Control and Accountability

The property manager must account for all money received, as well as money due but not received. Rents provide the main source of incoming funds; however, security deposits must also be handled.

A record must be kept of all expenses related to the property. If there are employees, payroll records including payroll taxes and social security records must also be kept.

The property manager should provide periodic reports showing the financial status of the property. These should be prepared for the property owner whether he had demanded them or not. It is important that the owner be kept current on all matters and not be surprised at the end of the year. A typical report would include income, expenditures, and net income for the period and for the year to date. Each piece of property should be evaluated separately so as to identify profitable and unprofitable endeavors. Unprofitable properties should be carefully scrutinized for changes that could improve their profit status. These same records and reports should also be used to project future expenses, prepare next year's budget, and set rental schedules for new or renewed leases covering future periods.

Many forms and methods are available for keeping accounting records and for reporting to the owner. The supplementary readings at the end of the chapter go into detail on these (see especially Downs and Schwachter).

CONSULTING SERVICES

Property managers also provide consulting services to property owners or developers who often are considering conversion, rehabilitation, or modernization of an existing property. A person who wants to buy, sell, or develop a property also often needs an advisory service.

The property manager's function as a consultant is to make recommendations that will enhance the income-producing capability of the property through a variety of alternatives. The *rehabilitation* of a property involves restoring a structure for its current use. *Modernization* involves replacing equipment, painting, or other operations that would improve the property in its present use.

Property Conversions

The property consultant may recommend *conversion* of the property into a different use. For example, an old mansion might be converted into business offices. This often happens where areas change and are rezoned. The experienced property manager is often asked to recommend the best usage, layout, or suitable tenants for a property being evaluated. In this process of evaluation, a rental schedule would be drawn up to show the potential return on the investment. This schedule should include the property value, a market analysis, a neighborhood evaluation, and an income and expense analysis. In some cases, alternative plans would be considered. Consultants will often contract to manage the property in addition to making recommendations.

Conversions to Condominiums

Although we usually visualize a condominium as a newly constructed property, an owner often converts an existing property into a condominium. Conversion to a condominium may yield a high profit within a short period of time. However, since all properties are not easily converted, the property manager's advice is often sought. The success of a conversion to a condominium depends on the property's structure, location, the availability of financing at attractive interest rates, and the possible displacement of existing tenants.

SUMMARY

The task of managing apartments, office buildings, and other real estate involves many complexities. Thus, the need has evolved for professional property managers who work for a fee or salary. Generally, the terms and conditions of the manager's job are provided in a written contract between the manager and the owner. A manager might work as an independent, with a property management firm, or in a department of a brokerage firm.

The manager's job can be broken down into three main categories. The marketing function deals with securing and keeping tenants to occupy the space and provide income. Next, the manager must provide services such as security, maintenance, and cleaning. Third, the manager must maintain financial control over income and expenses and keep adequate accounts and records.

Property managers also serve as consultants to property owners or potential buyers of investment properties. In that capacity, they evaluate property for potential modernization, rehabilitation, or conversion into income-producing property or for condominiums. The property manager's advice is usually sought for securing the highest net income from a parcel of property.

TERMS AND CONCEPTS

You can check your understanding of these terms and concepts against the glossary or by review in this chapter.

BOMA	IREM
CPM	Modernization
Duplex	Project Management
Functional management	Rehabilitation

PROBLEMS

20–1. Assume that you are a broker who manages a real estate office of ten salespersons. You plan to start managing property. Write a position description defining the property manager's responsibilities and authority.

20–2. List the important elements that should be in a contract between an owner of an apartment building and a person hired by the owner to manage the apartment.

20–3. Assume you are the manager of an apartment building and want to subcontract lawn care and external and internal housekeeping of all areas except inside the apartments. Prepare a specification to be sent out for bids.

20–4. An investor paid $371,000 for an industrial building with 11,000 square feet. If the investor wants a 12 percent annual return on the investment, what should be the rent per square foot?

20–5. A merchant signs a lease that sets a monthly rental of $700 or six percent of gross sales, whichever is less. If gross sales in February were $11,000, what is the merchant's rent?

20–6. What are the significant differences in maintenance of office buildings as compared to residential properties?

20–7. A property management firm manages eight apartment buildings. List the functions that could be better centralized and those that would be best decentralized to each building.

20–8.   A commercial property containing 40,000 square feet is rented at $7.00 per square foot. If receipts last year were $172,000, what was the occupancy rate?

20–9.   Make a list of questions to be asked at a tenant exit interview for tenants who do not renew their lease.

SUPPLEMENTARY READINGS

Brauer, William; Sachar, Roger; Shepard, Reba; and Walters, William. *The Resident Manager*. Chicago: Institute of Real Estate Management, 1973.

Downs, James C. *Principles of Real Estate Management*. Chicago: Institute of Real Estate Management, 1975.

Hanford, Lloyd D., Sr. *The Property Management Process*. Chicago: Institute of Real Estate Management, 1972.

Kelley, Edward N. *Practical Apartment Management*. Chicago: Institute of Real Estate Management, 1976.

Kyle, Robert C., and Kennehan, Ann M. *Property Management*. Chicago: Real Estate Education Company, 1979.

The Property Manager's Guide to Forms and Letters. Chicago: Institute of Real Estate Management, 1971.

The Real Estate Management Department. Chicago: Institute of Real Estate Management, 1967.

Schwachter, Robert S. *How to Make Money Developing and Managing Income Producing Property*. Englewood Cliffs, N.J.: Executive Reports Corporation, 1973.

Shenkel, William M. *Modern Real Estate Principles*. Dallas: Business Publications, 1977. Chapter 19.

Wray, Albert M., ed. *Commercial and Industrial Real Estate*. Los Angeles: California Real Estate Association, 1973. Chapters 4–7.

Real Estate Investments

Real estate investments have several unique characteristics that make them very attractive for many people. The enduring quality and relative scarcity of real estate enhances its value, thereby making it good security for a loan.

Leverage

The investor may generally borrow up to 80 or 90 percent of the purchase price of real estate investments. This use of borrowed funds to purchase an investment is not unique to real estate; however, few other investments provide such high percentage financing. The use of other people's money (OPM) to finance an investment—*leverage*—may provide the investor a much greater return on her equity investment than she could realize in an unleveraged or low-leveraged investment.

Capital Appreciation

Historically, the increasing value of real estate investments has kept pace with or exceeded the general rate of inflation. This capital appreciation makes real estate investments an effective hedge against inflation.

Tax Benefits

The real estate investor is able to deduct the interest expense on his loan and the depreciation allowances on his investment from the operating income. These combined deductions usually result in a substantial sheltering of income from taxes. Finally, when the investment is sold, the profits may be taxed at the favorable capital gains rates.

The combined effects of financial leverage, tax advantages of depreciation deductions, interest expense deductions, and favorable capital gains treatment operate to make real estate investments one of the best routes to financial success for the investor who understands and applies these concepts. Each concept will be discussed in detail later in the chapter.

Cash Outlay

Real estate investments usually involve much larger initial outlays of cash than do other forms of investments. Whereas stocks and bonds can be purchased for as little as five or ten dollars, real estate investments, even with 90 percent financing, require initial cash outlays of hundreds, and more often, thousands of dollars.

Liquidity

Liquidity refers to the speed with which an investment can be converted to cash without substantial financial loss. Real estate investments generally involve a long-term commitment of investment funds. The principal reasons for most real estate investments being illiquid (not readily convertible to cash) are these:

1. The heterogeneous nature of the product. Since no two real estate investments are alike, one investment cannot readily be substituted for another. Consequently, the real estate market is more sluggish than the stock or bond market where the stocks or bonds of a specific company are homogeneous (similar) in nature and are therefore readily substitutable between and among various investors.

2. Unlike the stock market, no formal real estate market exists to expedite the buying, selling, or trading of real estate investments or investment information. The advent of the computer has begun to alleviate this problem somewhat by creating national referral and exchange networks. However, the localized nature of the real estate market itself and the unique nature of each real estate investment act to perpetuate the illiquid nature of most real estate investments.

Although the illiquidity of real estate investments is an obvious disadvantage, the real estate investor who would like to convert her investment to cash, without having to sell it first, may do so by refinancing. Although she does not take out all of her equity investment when refinancing, it may provide her with enough cash to satisfy her needs. Refinancing is illustrated later in the chapter.

Management

Unlike stocks and bonds, real estate investments must be managed. This function can be performed by the investor himself or by a professional real property management firm. In either case, the investor must recognize the added cost. Professional management firms normally charge a percentage of the gross income from the investment as a management fee. The fees charged range from five to ten percent of the gross income, depending on the type of building, age of building, type of tenants, location of the building, and the manager's duties and responsibilities stipulated in the property management agreement.

Risk

In *investment properties* (properties purchased primarily for capital appreciation with little or no cash flow during the investment holding period), *risk* refers to the chance of loss on the capital investment. The chance or possibility of a decrease or loss in property value is always present. As the probability of a decrease or loss in value increases, there is an increase in the risk of loss to the potential investor. The prudent investor will evaluate this increased risk and demand a higher return in that particular investment to compensate for the increased risk. The investor compensates for the increased risk by discounting or reducing the asking price for the investment.

On *income-producing properties* (properties purchased primarily for cash flow), investors must also examine the quantity, quality, and durability of the income stream as another measure of risk. The *quantity of the income stream* obviously refers to the amount; the *quality of the income stream* refers to the assuredness of its receipt. The investor would anticipate little or no risk in the collection of rent from a major, financially responsible tenant. Conversely, the investor may expect greater risk of collection from a tenant who is less financially secure. The *durability of the income stream* refers to the anticipated duration or length of time the investment will generate an income. A property having only three years remaining on its lease may not be as valuable as a similar property with ten years on the lease. *Durability* also refers to the remaining economic life of the property. Economic (useful) life is the period of time over which the property will be useful to a particular taxpayer in his business or in the production of income.

Risk Versus Return

A direct relationship exists between the *risk* an investor perceives in any given investment and the *return* anticipated for accepting the risk. The higher the perceived risk of an investment, the higher the anticipated return by the investor. The investor reflects her perceived risk in the marketplace by discounting the income stream or selling price of the investment in her negotiations with the seller.

The investment dollar is sought after by many different investment media throughout the world. Whenever one specific investment medium experiences a higher return than competing investments of similar risk, investment capital will be diverted to it. In time, with more and more investment funds being diverted to that higher yielding investment, the return from that investment will tend to decline. In essence, the economic principal of supply and demand operates in the capital market. In the long run, rates of return that are higher than normal probably result from the special analytical or management skills of the investor, the acceptance of an investment with a higher risk, or just plain luck.

INVESTMENT RETURNS

Investment returns generally come in one of two forms, a current return or a deferred return. Some investments experience a combination of both current return and deferred return.

Income that is generated by the investment periodically during the term of the investment holding period is called *current return* (sometimes referred to as *cash flow* or *cash on cash*). The current rate of return is usually expressed in one of two ways:

1. The relationship between the total investment value (purchase price) and the current return, that is,

$$\frac{\text{Current return}}{\text{Total investment value}} = \text{Rate of return on total investment}$$

2. The relationship between the equity investment (down payment) and the current return, that is,

$$\frac{\text{Current return}}{\text{Equity investment}} = \text{Rate of return on equity investment}$$

The rates of return may be used to reflect either "before tax" or "after tax" yields.

Examples of investments that usually generate current return are apartment buildings, office buildings, mobile home parks, and parking lots. These same *income-producing properties* may also realize some deferred return on resale.

Income not received until the investment property is sold is called *deferred return.* The deferred return is the realized profit on resale. This deferred gain is the result of property appreciation and/or mortgage amortization.

Most *investment properties* realize deferred returns only and receive no current returns during the period of investment ownership, called the *holding period.* The investor, meanwhile, may incur expenses of ownership, called *ripening expenses* (e.g., real estate taxes and maintenance costs) during the holding period. His return on investment is completely deferred until resale. In the meantime, he may experience a negative cash flow on his investment.

An example of an investment that usually shows a deferred return only is rolling timberland on the perimeter of a city. The investor anticipates that the property will ripen into prime land for future subdividing and developing.

FINANCIAL LEVERAGE

The use of borrowed funds to magnify the return on an equity investment is called *positive financial leverage.* Almost all real estate can be financed or leveraged up to 70 or 80 percent, and it is not uncommon to get 90 to 95 percent financing. Hence, a real estate investor may be able to buy and control $100,000 worth of real estate with no more than $5,000 or $10,000 of her own funds.

To illustrate, let us assume that investor A is considering the purchase of an investment with a selling price of $100,000. The investment generates a net income of $12,000 annually. The investor has the option of paying all cash for the investment or using borrowed funds at the rate of 10 percent interest to leverage the investment. Table 21–1 shows the effect of the use of borrowed funds on the equity return.

As can be seen, the use of borrowed funds has a very favorable effect on the investor's equity return. The use of 50 percent borrowed funds (Option 2) has increased the equity return from 12 to 14 percent. The use of 80 percent borrowed funds (Option 3) increases the equity return from 12 to 20 percent, a whopping 67 percent increase.

Although financial leverage is generally discussed in a positive sense, leverage sometimes works against the investor. Whenever the cost of borrowing is more than the free and clear return on an investment, the use of borrowed funds will magnify the loss to the equity investor. This is called *negative* (or reverse) *financial leverage.* In the previous example demonstrating the favorable effects of positive financial leverage, the cost of borrowing was 10 percent and the free-and-clear return was 12 percent. To demonstrate the adverse effects of negative financial leverage, let us assume the cost of borrowing increases to 14 percent. Examine Table 21–2 to see the effect.

As can be seen, when the cost of borrowing exceeds the free and clear return, the return on equity will be reduced. In this example, the use of financial leverage reduced the equity return from 12 to 10 percent (Option 2) and finally (Option 3), down to a dismal 4 percent return. You must remember that financial leverage is a double-edged sword. It magnifies both gains and losses.

Table 21–1
Positive financial leverage

	Option 1	Option 2	Option 3
		1:1 Leverage	*4:1 Leverage*
	All-Cash Purchase	*(50% borrowed/*	*(80% borrowed/*
	(100% equity)	*50% equity)*	*20% equity)*
Selling price	$100,000	$100,000	$100,000
Equity investment	100,000	50,000	20,000
Net income	12,000	12,000	12,000
Less: Cost of borrowing at 10% interest	0	−5,000	−8,000
Cash return	12,000	7,000	4,000
$\dfrac{\text{Cash return}}{\text{Equity investment}} =$	$\dfrac{12,000}{100,000} = 12\%$	$\dfrac{7,000}{50,000} = 14\%$	$\dfrac{4,000}{20,000} = 20\%$

Table 21–2
Negative financial leverage

	Option 1	Option 2	Option 3
		1:1 Leverage	*4:1 Leverage*
	All-Cash Purchase	*(50% borrowed/*	*(80% borrowed/*
	(100% equity)	*50% equity)*	*20% equity)*
Selling price	$100,000	$100,000	$100,000
Equity investment	100,000	50,000	20,000
Net income	12,000	12,000	12,000
Less: Cost of borrowing at 14% interest	0	−7,000	−11,200
Cash return	12,000	5,000	800
$\dfrac{\text{Equity investment}}{\text{Cash return}}$	$\dfrac{12,000}{100,000} = 12\%$	$\dfrac{5,000}{50,000} = 10\%$	$\dfrac{800}{20,000} = 4\%$

EQUITY GROWTH THROUGH FINANCIAL LEVERAGE

When an investor uses borrowed funds to purchase a real estate investment, any increase in property value (capital appreciation) accrues entirely to the equity investor, even though he may have an equity investment of only 5 or 10 percent of the total property value. As a result of this benefit, the investor's equity grows substantially even with just a modest increase in overall property value. An illustration will demonstrate this point.

Assume an investor is considering the alternatives of purchasing a $100,000 investment on either an all-cash basis or by using 90 percent financing. Assume further that the investor will hold the investment for 10 years and the investment is expected to increase at a modest 4 percent per year. Let us compare the equity growth from capital appreciation on an all-cash basis versus 90 percent financing.

	All-Cash Purchase	*90% Financing*
Purchase price	$100,000	$100,000
Equity investment	100,000	10,000

(4% appreciation/year)

10 Years Later

Investment value	$140,000	$140,000
Increase in equity (from appreciation)	40,000	40,000
Percentage increase in equity growth	$\dfrac{\text{Equity growth}}{\text{Original equity}} = 40\%$	$\dfrac{\text{Equity growth}}{\text{Original equity}} = 400\%$

DEPRECIATION ALLOWANCES

Depreciation allowance is a noncash flow, deductible expense used in calculating taxable income. This depreciation for taxes is an accounting concept and is not associated with the realities of the market value of the property. That is, even though an investment's market value actually appreciates, the depreciation expense for tax purposes is uneffected.

Rationale for Depreciation Allowances

The Internal Revenue Service (IRS) classifies the building portion of a real estate investment as a wasting asset. It is assumed that, given enough time, any building will eventually lose value. As such, any investor who invests capital in a wasting asset is allowed to recapture or recover her capital over its useful life.

Real estate that qualifies for the depreciation allowance must be used in the taxpayer's trade or business or for the production of income. Nonincome-producing property such as a single-family owner-occupied residence cannot be depreciated.

Steps in Calculating Depreciation Deductions

1. *Allocate purchase price between land and building.* When depreciating a real estate investment, the total investment value is allocated between the land and building since only the building portion of the investment can be depreciated. *Land does not depreciate.* There are four acceptable methods of making such an allocation. The investor should be cautioned, however, that regardless of the method used, if the allocation is not "reasonable," the IRS may contest it.

    a. Tax assessor's ratio—This method involves the use of a ratio derived from the tax assessor's assessment of the property. This same ratio is applied to the purchase price of the investment, thus giving an allocation between land and building for depreciation purposes. For example, assume a tax assessor has assessed property at $75,000, with $50,000 for the building and $25,000 for the land. This 2:1 building-to-land ratio is applied to the purchase price of $120,000, resulting in an $80,000 building value and a $40,000 land value.

    b. The value allocation may be stipulated in the sales contract between the buyer and seller.

    c. The value allocation may be made simply on the basis of a qualified appraiser's estimate.

    d. The investor may make the allocation herself.

2. *Determine useful life.* Once the value has been allocated between the land and building, next we determine the period of time over which the asset can be depreciated. This period is the building's "useful" (economic) life. Economic or useful life should not be confused with physical life. The fact that more buildings are torn down than fall down provides evidence that most improvements have a physical life that far outlasts their useful life. *Economic (useful) life* is the projected period over which the property will be useful to a particular taxpayer in his business or in the production of income. Since the annual depreciation allowance is tax deductible, the taxpayer's objective is to write off the investment as

quickly as possible, thereby providing a large deduction from taxable income. He is therefore tempted to use a very short useful life in computing his depreciation allowance. The Internal Revenue Service, however, has objectives of its own. It attempts to collect as much taxes as possible by closely examining tax returns with depreciation deductions to determine whether or not a "reasonable" useful life was used.

3. *Determine the method and technique of depreciation to be used.* There are three acceptable methods of estimating useful life. First, the investor may merely use his judgment, which is subject to IRS scrutiny. Second, there may be a mutual agreement between the IRS and the investor. The third method is an estimate based on guidelines of useful lives published by the U.S. Treasury Department.

METHODS OF CALCULATING DEPRECIATION

The recovery of the cost of the existing improvement can be accomplished by one of two methods. The first method, *composite depreciation,* treats the total depreciable asset as a single entity and assigns a single or composite useful life and value to it. *Component depreciation,* the second method, assigns separate useful lives to each of the various depreciable components of the asset.

Composite Method

Composite depreciation allowances may be computed by straight-line or accelerated techniques. The *straight-line technique* assumes that the property depreciates at the same rate throughout its useful life. *Accelerated techniques of depreciation* allow more rapid or stepped-up depreciation in the early years of the asset's useful life and smaller depreciation allowances in later years. Using the accelerated techniques, the larger depreciation allowances in the early years generate a higher cash flow than under the straight-line technique of depreciation. In later years, however, the depreciation allowances become smaller and smaller until they drop below straight-line allowances. Before that occurs, however, the investor may change from the accelerated technique to the straight-line technique in computing annual depreciation allowances.

Straight-line
The technique of *straight-line depreciation* can be employed on any depreciable property, new or used, regardless of its economic life. It is the *only* type that can be used on residential rental property with an economic life of less than 20 years. (See Figures 21–1 and 21–2.)

To calculate the annual straight-line depreciation allowances, the *depreciable basis* of the property, less salvage value, is divided by its economic life. The depreciable basis of an asset is its cost plus any capital improvement and minus any depreciation already taken. This annual depreciation allowance remains fixed throughout the building's economic life.

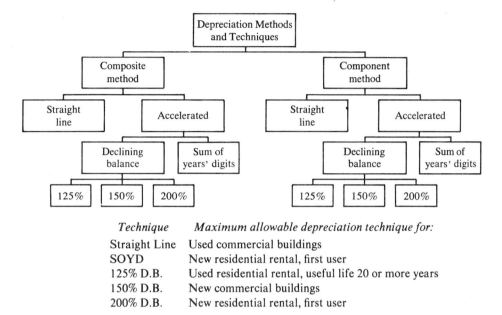

Technique	Maximum allowable depreciation technique for:
Straight Line	Used commercial buildings
SOYD	New residential rental, first user
125% D.B.	Used residential rental, useful life 20 or more years
150% D.B.	New commercial buildings
200% D.B.	New residential rental, first user

Figure 21–1
Comparison of depreciation techniques

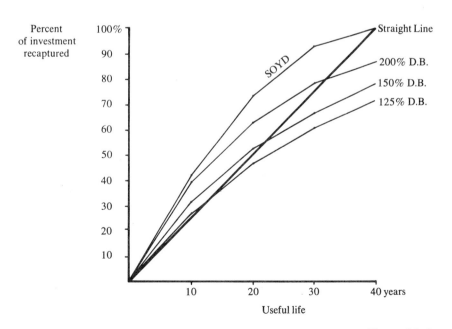

Figure 21–2
Graphic comparison of depreciation techniques

The amount of annual depreciation can also be calculated by dividing 100 percent by the economic life of the building to find the constant percentage by which the property depreciates. This percentage is then applied to the depreciable basis of the property, less salvage value, to determine the annual allowance.

Example: A building has an economic life of 10 years, depreciable basis of $30,000, and salvage value of $5,000. What is its annual depreciation allowance using the straight-line technique?

Solution:

$$\frac{\$30,000 - \$5,000}{10 \text{ yr}} = \frac{\$25,000}{10 \text{ yr}} = \$2,500 \text{ annual depreciation, or}$$

$$\frac{100\%}{10 \text{ yr}} \text{ (or } 10\%) \text{ of } \$25,000 = \$2,500 \text{ annual depreciation}$$

Accelerated Techniques

Double-declining balance

Double (or 200 percent) declining balance is a form of *accelerated depreciation* that can only be used on new residential rental property with a life of 20 years or more. The taxpayer must be the first user. Eighty percent of the total income must be from rents. Hotels and motels are not able to use this technique. It is called *double-declining balance* because the depreciation rate is twice that of straight-line. However, the amount of depreciation is *not* the same each year. It changes because the annual allowance is figured as a constant percentage of the ever-declining *book value* of the improvement. Under this technique, salvage value is ignored, since a residual value representing salvage value will always remain when the property is depreciated. The annual depreciation allowance using this technique may be determined in three steps:

1.   Determine the annual straight-line rate.
2.   Double the straight-line rate.
3.   Apply the rate derived in step 2 to the declining balance (or book value) of the improvement each year to arrive at the annual rate.

Example: A new apartment building has an economic life of 40 years. The building itself is valued at $200,000. What is its annual depreciation, using the double-declining balance technique?

Solution: The straight-line rate can be determined by dividing the useful life into 100 percent.

$$\frac{100\%}{40 \text{ yr}} = 2.5\%$$

Then double the straight-line rate (2.5% × 2 = 5%). By multiplying $200,000 by 5 percent, the first year's depreciation is found to be $10,000, leaving a balance of $190,000. The second year's depreciation is 5 percent of $190,000, or $9,500, leaving a balance of $180,500. The depreciation allowances for the first five years are as follows:

Year	Annual Depreciation	Remaining Book Value of Asset
1	$200,000 × .05 = $10,000	$190,000
2	$190,000 × .05 = $ 9,500	$180,500
3	$180,500 × .05 = $ 9,025	$171,475
4	$171,475 × .05 = $ 8,574	$162,901
5	$162,901 × .05 = $ 8,145	$154,756

150 percent declining balance

The 150 percent declining balance technique is the maximum fast write-off or depreciation allowable on new nonresidential property. It is figured at 1.5 times the rate of straight-line. For instance, if the straight-line rate were 5 percent, then the 150 percent declining balance rate would be 5 percent × 1.5, or 7.5 percent. As in the double-declining balance technique, salvage value is disregarded. The rate calculated is then applied to the declining balance of the property each year to arrive at the annual depreciation allowance.

Applying the 150 percent declining balance technique to a new commercial building valued at $100,000 with a 20-year useful life, the first five years' depreciation allowances are as follows:

Year	Annual Depreciation	Remaining Balance
1	$100,000 × .075 = $7,500	$92,500
2	$ 92,500 × .075 = $6,937	$85,562
3	$ 85,562 × .075 = $6,417	$79,145
4	$ 79,145 × .075 = $5,935	$73,209
5	$ 73,209 × .075 = $5,490	$66,718

125 percent declining balance

The 125 percent declining balance technique is the maximum fast write-off or depreciation allowable on used residential rental property with an economic life of 20 years or more. This rate is figured at 1.25 times the straight-line rate; and the annual depreciation rate is, again, a constant percentage of the declining balance. Again, salvage value is disregarded.

Example: A used apartment building has a value of $45,000 and an economic life of 25 years. Annual depreciation allowances for the first five years are as follows:

Year	Annual Depreciation	Remaining Balance
1	$45,000 × .05 = $2,250	$42,750
2	$42,750 × .05 = $2,137	$40,612
3	$40,612 × .05 = $2,030	$38,581
4	$38,581 × .05 = $1,929	$36,652
5	$36,652 × .05 = $1,832	$34,820

Sum-of-the-years' digits technique

The sum-of-the-years' digits technique of depreciation is commonly abbreviated *SOYD*. This accelerated technique is only available in those cases that can use the 200 percent declining balance technique, namely, on new residential rental property with a life of 20 years or more. The taxpayer must be the first user. Under this method, the *depreciable base* (adjusted basis reduced by the salvage value) is multiplied by a different fraction each year. The numerator of the fraction is the number of years of remaining economic life. The denominator is a constant, the total or sum of all the years' digits of the estimated economic life of the building. The denominator can also be determined by the following formula:

$$N\frac{(N + 1)}{2}, \text{where } N = \text{economic life in years}$$

Example: A new residential rental property has a building value of $110,000, estimated salvage value of $10,000, and an economic life of 25 years.

Solution: The denominator is the sum of all the years' digits of the estimated useful life: $1 + 2 + 3 + 4 + 5 \ldots + 25 = 325$, or, by application of the formula:

$$\frac{25(25 + 1)}{2} = 325$$

The numerator is the number of years of remaining useful life, 25 for the first year, 24 for the second year, and so forth. Year 1 depreciation is then found by multiplying $100,000 (depreciable basis less salvage value) by 25/325 and getting $7,692. Year 2 depreciation is $100,000 × 24/325, or $7,385.

Annual depreciation allowances for the first five years using the SOYD technique are as follows:

Year	Annual Depreciation (rounded)
1	$\frac{25}{325} \times 100,000 = \$7,692$
2	$\frac{24}{325} \times 100,000 = \$7,385$
3	$\frac{23}{325} \times 100,000 = \$7,077$
4	$\frac{22}{325} \times 100,000 = \$6,769$
5	$\frac{21}{325} \times 100,000 = \$6,462$

Component Method

The second basic method, known as *component depreciation,* assigns separate useful lives to each of the various component parts of the building—the foundation, heating system, electrical system, plumbing, roof, and elevator. Each is depreciated on a separate schedule. Up until 1973, component depreciation was used on new buildings only. As a result of a 1973 tax court ruling, it is now available on used buildings also. The difficulty in using component depreciation on new buildings is minimized if the cost figures on each of the component parts are available. However, determining the value of each component of an old building is extremely difficult and somewhat subjective. This, presumably, was the major reason the IRS allowed component depreciation on new buildings only until the tax court ruling of 1973. In many instances, taxpayers may be able to justify much higher depreciation allowances by using the component method instead of the composite method. Component depreciation may be used in combination with straight-line, 125 percent, 150 percent, 200 percent declining balance, or sum-of-the-years' digits techniques, as long as the building qualifies. (However, the excess recapture rule still applies to all component depreciation in excess of straight-line. Excess recapture will be treated later in this chapter.)

Example: A $100,000 building has a 40-year life and no salvage value. Using composite 200 percent declining balance depreciation, the first year's depreciation allowance would be $5,000. However, using component straight-line depreciation, we can arrive at a much larger first-year depreciation allowance without being penalized by the excess recapture rule on resale.

Item	Cost	Useful Life	Rate	1st Yr Depreciation
Shell of building	$ 40,000	40 yr	2½%	$1,000
Roof	$ 5,000	10 yr	10%	$ 500
Plumbing	$ 14,000	10 yr	10%	$1,400
Heating	$ 8,000	10 yr	10%	$ 800
Elevator	$ 10,000	10 yr	10%	$1,000
Air conditioning	$ 8,000	12.5 yr	8%	$ 960
Electrical	$ 15,000	10 yr	10%	$1,500
Total	$100,000			$7,160

Comparative Depreciation Techniques

Assume a new residential rental property with a building value of $100,000 and an economic life of 40 years. For illustration purposes, we will ignore salvage value. However, do not forget that salvage value must be considered in both the straight-line and SOYD techniques. Table 21–3 shows the annual depreciation allowances for various years using straight-line and accelerated techniques.

As can be seen from the table, the accelerated techniques provide larger depreciation deductions during the early years of the investment and much smaller deductions in the later years, whereas the straight-line technique provides a uniform depreciation deduction throughout the life of the invest- ment. Using the 200 percent declining balance technique, the annual deduc- tion allowance in the 15th year drops below the straight-line deduction

Table 21-3

Comparison of various depreciation techniques

Year	Straight-Line	200% D.B.	150% D.B.	125% D.B.	SOYD
1	$2,500	$5,000	$3,750	$3,125	$4,880
2	$2,500	$4,750	$3,610	$3,027	$4,750
3	$2,500	$4,510	$3,470	$2,932	$4,640
4	$2,500	$4,290	$3,340	$2,841	$4,510
5	$2,500	$4,070	$3,220	$2,752	$4,390
6	$2,500	$3,870	$3,100	$2,666	$4,260
7	$2,500	$3,680	$2,980	$2,588	$4,140
8	$2,500	$3,490	$2,870	$2,502	$4,020
9	$2,500	$3,320	$2,760	$2,424	$3,900
10	$2,500	$3,150	$2,660	$2,348	$3,780
⋮					
15	$2,500	$2,440	$2,200	$2,000	$3,180
⋮					
20	$2,500	$1,880	$1,810	$1,710	$2,560
⋮					
30	$2,500	$1,120	$1,240	$1,240	$1,340
⋮					
40	$2,500	$ 680	$ 850	$ 910	$ 120

allowance. Prior to the 15th year, however, the investor is allowed to switch from the 200 percent declining balance technique to the straight-line technique for the remaining useful life of the investment. This is the only instance where the IRS allows an investor to switch from one depreciation technique to another without seeking IRS approval.

Accelerated depreciation techniques have the advantage of providing larger tax deductions in the early years of an investment, thereby reducing taxable income. Thus, the investor reduces or eliminates tax payments and increases his cash flow in those early years. Recent tax legislation has limited the advantages of accelerated depreciation. Investors who use accelerated methods of depreciation may be subject to "excess recapture" upon resale.

Excess Recapture

Until the 1960s, an investor could use any of the accelerated techniques of depreciation on her depreciable real estate so that all of her operating income was sheltered. Together with her interest deductions, she could show a tax loss and use this loss to *shelter* other income. After four or five years, when depreciation and interest deductions began to decline, the investor could sell her property, and the gain, if any, was taxed as capital gain. Essentially, the investor was converting ordinary income into capital gain, thereby reducing tax liability upon sale through accelerated depreciation allowances.

In 1964 and again in 1969, the tax code was changed to greatly reduce this tax advantage. On any post-1969 purchases, depreciation recaptured in excess of the straight-line allowance is considered *excess recapture*. Upon the sale of the investment, it will be 100 percent recaptured as ordinary income to the extent of the gain.

Therefore, the taxpayer will have to compare the accelerated depreciation technique she used with the amount of depreciation allowed under the straight-line rate, taking into consideration the holding period of her investment, in determining her tax liability.

Example: Mr. Jansky bought a new apartment building with a 40-year life for $100,000. The apartment building was on leased ground. He used the 200 percent declining balance technique of depreciation. He sold it four years later for $200,000. Assume no salvage value. Compute his excess recapture:

	Annual Depreciation	
Year	*(200% D.B.)*	*Balance*
1	$ 5,000	$95,000
2	$ 4,750	$90,250
3	$ 4,512	$85,738
4	$ 4,287	$81,450
	$18,550	

$18,550	Accumulated accelerated depreciation
−$10,000	Accumulated straight-line depreciation (2,500 per year)
$ 8,500	Excess recapture treated as ordinary income

CAPITAL GAINS

Generally speaking, property held for investment is considered a capital asset. If it is held for over one year, it is given favorable capital gains treatment. Securities and vacant land are capital assets. Real estate used in a trade or business (i.e., office buildings, apartment buildings, and other commercial or industrial structures) are not considered capital assets and would create ordinary gain or loss instead of capital gain and loss if not for a special provision in the tax law. The IRS classifies these properties as *1231 assets.* These properties must be held for more than one year in order to qualify as 1231 assets. Section 1231 of the tax code allows the investor to claim long-term *capital gains* when, upon the sale of 1231 assets, the net gains exceed the net losses. This permits the investor to claim *ordinary* losses when losses exceed gains. The provision enables the taxpayer to have the best of two worlds—claim capital gains upon a gain or claim ordinary loss upon a loss. Timing the sale of 1231 assets can save the investor thousands of tax dollars.

Real estate held by a dealer as inventory for sale to customers in the ordinary course of his business is considered neither a capital asset nor a 1231 asset, and any gain upon sale is taxed as ordinary income.

A capital asset that is held for more than one year is classified as a *long-term capital gain* and qualifies for the preferred capital gains tax. A capital asset that is held for one year or less is classified as a *short-term capital gain* and does not qualify for the preferred capital gains tax.

Computing His Capital Gains:

$200,000	Selling price
$ 81,450	Adjusted basis (100,000 − 18,550)
$118,550	Total gain
−$ 8,550	Excess recapture taxed as ordinary income
$110,000	1231 gain[1] (see explanation below)

Computing Capital Gain (Individual Taxpayer)

The 1978 tax bill eliminated the alternative method of computing an individual's tax liability on any long-term capital gain. Today, 40 percent of the long-term gain is added to the taxpayer's ordinary income, and the income tax is calculated on the total amount. In essence, 60 percent of the long-term gain is excluded from the taxes.

Example: Assume a taxpayer with an adjusted gross income of $15,000 realizes an $800 net long-term capital gain. This $800 is reduced to $320 (40 percent of $800) and added to the $15,000 adjusted gross income. The taxpayer is taxed on an adjusted gross income of $15,320.

If an investor has transactions involving both gains and losses, she must net (offset) all long-term gains with long-term capital losses and then net (offset) short-term capital gains with short-term capital losses. This process will result in one of six tax situations. These situations, and the resultant tax consequences, are explained in the following sections.

Situation 1: **Net long-term capital gains exceed net short-term capital losses.**

In this situation, the net long-term gains are offset to the extent of the short-term losses and 40 percent of the balance is added to that year's ordinary income. The other 60 percent is excluded from tax.

Example:

Short-term capital gain	$2,000	
Short-term capital loss	($4,200)	
Net short-term capital loss		($2,200)
Long-term capital gain	$6,000	
Long-term capital loss	($3,000)	
Net long-term capital gain		$3,000
Balance of remaining long-term gain		$800
		×.40
Added to ordinary income		$320

---

[1] If 1231 gain exceeds 1231 losses, the excess is treated as a capital gain.

Situation 2:   **Net long-term capital losses exceed net short-term gains.**

In this situation, the two are offset to the extent of the short-term gain, and the balance of the long-term loss is applied to reduce up to $3,000 of ordinary income. However, each dollar of long-term capital loss will offset only 50 cents of ordinary income. Therefore, to take advantage of the total $3,000 deduction from ordinary income, the investor must experience a $6,000 long-term capital loss. Any remaining loss can be carried forward and used in later years.

Example:

Net long-term capital losses	($5,000)	
Net short-term capital gains	$3,000	
Balance of long-term losses		($2,000)

The short-term gains are offset against the long-term losses, and the balance of $2,000 in long-term losses is applied against ordinary income on a two dollar-for-one dollar basis, thereby reducing ordinary income by $1,000.

Situation 3:   **Net short-term capital losses exceed net long-term capital gains.**

In this situation, the long-term gains are completely offset against the short-term losses, and the balance of the short-term losses is applied to reduce ordinary income on a dollar-for-dollar basis up to $3,000. Any remaining short-term loss in excess of $3,000 is carried forward to the following year.

  Example: An investor experiences a $6,000 net long-term capital gain and a $9,000 net short-term capital loss during the year. The net long-term capital gain of $6,000 is offset against the net short-term loss of $9,000, and the balance of the short-term loss ($3,000) is used to reduce the investor's ordinary income by $3,000.

Situation 4:   **Net short-term capital gains exceed net short-term capital losses.**

In this situation, the two are offset against one another, and the balance of short-term gain is included in the investor's ordinary income for that year.

Example:

Net short-term gain	$6,000	
Net long-term loss	($4,000)	
Balance of short-term gain		$2,000

The $2,000 is added to the investor's ordinary income.

Situation 5:   **Net long-term capital gains and net short-term capital gains.**

In this situation, the investor includes *all* of the net short-term gains and 40 percent of the net long-term gains in his ordinary income for that year.

Situation 6:   **Net short-term losses and net long-term losses.**

In the situation where an investor experiences both short-term and long-term losses, a maximum of $3,000 of ordinary income can be offset in any one year.

Any remaining losses are carried forward and used to calculate net long-term and net short-term gains and losses in subsequent years. For individual taxpayers, there is no limit to the number of years that losses can be carried forward. However, the losses must be offset against ordinary income in any year where an offset is possible. The net short-term losses must be used to offset ordinary income first and on a dollar-for-dollar basis. If the investor experiences more than a $3,000 short-term loss in one year, the excess is carried forward to the next year along with the long-term losses.

Example: An investor experiences a $6,000 net short-term loss and a $2,000 net long-term loss. Of the $6,000 short-term loss, $3,000 is applied to reduce ordinary income by $3,000 (dollar-for-dollar basis). The remaining short-term loss and the entire $2,000 net long-term loss are carried forward to the next year and used to calculate the net short-term and net long-term gains and losses for that year.

After offsetting all net short-term losses against ordinary income, if the $3,000 maximum ordinary income offset has not been reached, then net long-term losses are used to offset ordinary income on a two dollar-for-one dollar basis until the $3,000 maximum has been reached. The remaining balance of the long-term losses is then carried forward.

Example: An investor experiences $1,500 of net short-term losses and $10,000 of net long-term losses in the same year. The $1,500 short-term loss offsets $1,500 of ordinary income (on a dollar-for-dollar basis). The net long-term loss of $10,000 is then applied to offset ordinary income on a two dollar-for-one dollar basis until ordinary income has been reduced to the maximum of $3,000. In this situation, $3,000 of the net long-term loss is applied to offset $1,500 more of ordinary income, bringing the ordinary income offset up to the $3,000 maximum. The remaining $7,000 of long-term capital loss is carried forward to the next year.

ANALYZING A REAL ESTATE INVESTMENT

In analyzing a real estate investment, the investor should conduct (a) a detailed analysis of the location, (b) a thorough inspection of the physical condition of the investment, and (c) a financial analysis. These steps are discussed in detail.

Location Analysis

It has been said many times that "the three most important factors influencing value are location, location, and location." The various factors and amenities that affect the neighborhood of the specific investment should be thoroughly analyzed. For instance, an investor who is considering the purchase of an apartment complex should consider location factors such as these:

1. Convenience to shopping, employment, recreation, schools, and public transportation.

2. Existing vacancy rates and turnover.
3. Proximity of competing apartment complexes.
4. Type of tenants in the neighborhood.
5. Existence of unimproved apartment sites.
6. Composition, age, and condition of neighborhood buildings.
7. Reputation of the neighborhood as a place to live.
8. Population growth.
9. Existence of sidewalks and street lights.
10. Condition of streets.
11. Availability of parking, snow removal, and trash collection.

The above list represents only a sampling of some of the factors that should be considered in evaluating the merits of a particular location. A wise investor will develop a checklist to ensure that he does not overlook any important factors.

Physical Analysis

The physical condition of the property will reflect the degree of care the present owners have exercised during their period of ownership. If the inspection reveals considerable needed maintenance, the new owners will soon be required to make considerable, and sometimes untimely, cash outlays.

In addition to deferring necessary maintenance, the seller may have delayed investing in needed capital improvements, such as repaving the parking lot or installing a new roof or furnace. The lack of needed capital improvements results in what appraisers call *physical and functional obsolescence,* a factor that may make the property difficult or impossible to rent. The prudent investor would be wise to consider the cost of the necessary expenditures and deduct it from the price he is willing to pay.

It should be clear that the physical condition of the building has a very definite influence on the quality, quantity, and durability of the subject investment's projected net income stream. Consequently, a detailed physical inspection of the building by a competent engineer is necessary to minimize the risk of purchasing an unwise investment.

Financial Analysis

Many of the concepts needed to analyze the property from a financial standpoint have been presented earlier in the chapter. These concepts, along with other relevant factors, are explained via the following step-by-step analysis of a hypothetical investment.

Case study

A middle-aged investor has asked you to analyze a property for him. The property is a one-year old brick four-unit apartment with an asking price of $125,000. The investment can be financed with an 80 percent, 25-year fully amortized mortgage at an interest rate of 9 percent with annual payments.

The building portion of the investment is considered as 80 percent of the total investment. Since the building is brick and only one year old, you feel the property must be depreciated over 40 years. You estimate that the investment will appreciate approximately 4 percent per year. You will use 125% declining balance depreciation. For ease in analysis, all income and expenses, including the mortgage payment, are annualized. The investor files a separate return and is in the 50 percent tax bracket. He wants to yield a 12 percent return on his equity investment. How much should he pay for the property?

Step 1:   Reconstruct an Operating Statement   Essentially, the investor in an income-producing property is purchasing an anticipated net income stream. The accuracy of any financial analysis begins with a realistic projection of the property's net income. The investor begins by obtaining the owner's existing income and expense records. He should be cautioned, however, that the records furnished by the owner should be examined with a jaundiced eye. The current owner's vested interest is sometimes sufficient motivation to distort, misrepresent, or conveniently forget vital information concerning the property's past income and expenses.

In addition, in verifying the past income and expense records, the potential investor should be aware of any pending increases in expenses and reflect them in the projected operating statement. Finally, the investor should compare the projected operating statement of the investment being analyzed to the income and expense records of similar investments in the area. Local property owner associations or professional property managers are excellent sources for such information. In addition, several organizations publish operating cost information. The Institute of Real Estate Management (IREM) publishes an analysis of income and expenses for apartment buildings, cooperatives, and condominiums. New York State College of Agriculture analyzes rental costs for variety stores and food chains. The Building Owners and Managers Association (BOMA) is also a valuable reference for office building expenses. The Urban Land Institute collects income and expense information on shopping centers. Most of these sources break the information down geographically and by size and age of buildings. Table 21–4 shows the reconstructed operating statement for the investment being analyzed. As can be seen, the investment generates a projected net income of $12,000. The remainder of our financial analysis proceeds as follows:

*Step 2:   Calculate **Taxable Income** (Loss)—Year One*

	Formula			*Calculations*
Net income			$12,000	(from operating statement)
Less: Interest expense	$9,000			(9% on $100,000 mortgage)
Depreciation deduction	3,125			(.025 × 1.25 × $100,000)
Total deductions			−12,125	
Taxable income (loss)			($125)	

As you can see, the investment will generate a tax loss of $125 in the first year using 125 percent declining balance, the maximum method available on used residential rental property with a useful life of 20 or more years.

Table 21–4
Projected (actual) operating statement

			Dollar Amount	Percentage of Gross Income
Gross income potential			$18,000	100.0%

Unit	Month Rent	Annual Rent
1	$375	$4,500
2	375	4,500
3	375	4,500
4	375	4,500

			Dollar Amount	Percentage of Gross Income
Less: Vacancy and collection loss			−900	.05
Effective gross rental income			$17,100	.95
Less expenses				
Fixed expenses:				
Taxes	$2,300			.127
Insurance	350			.019
Total fixed expenses		$2,650		
Operating expenses:				
Utilities (tenant)	0			
Maintenance	400			.022
Management	1,440			.08
Advertising	150			.008
Supplies	200			.011
Lawn care	150			.008
Accounting	110			.006
Total operating expenses		$2,450		.136
Total expenses			−$ 5,100	.283
Net operating income			$12,000	.663

Step 3: Calculate Before-Tax Cash Flow—Year One

Formula	Calculations
Net income	$12,000 (from reconstructed operating statement)
Less: Debt service	−10,180 (from amortization Table E–2a in Appendix E,
	Principal and interest payment on a $100,000
Before-tax cash flow	$ 1,820 loan for 25 years @ 9%, annual payment)

The investment generates a positive **before-tax cash flow** (sometimes called *gross spendable income*) of $1,820. In other words, before the investor pays any income taxes that might be due on the property, he has $1,820 in his pocket after paying all operating expenses and after making his mortgage payment. As our calculations showed us earlier, the investor pays no income taxes on the property the first year. Consequently, none of the before-tax cash flow is taxable. Further calculations follow.

Step 4: Calculate After-Tax Cash Flow Two of the most important criteria real estate investors use in evaluating a real estate investment are the amount of **after-tax cash flow** (sometimes called **net spendable income**) generated by the investment and the tax shelter the investment provides. The amount of after-tax cash flow is influenced by the type of financing available to the investor, the depreciation method, and the investor's tax bracket. After-tax cash flow is the amount of cash left over after the investor pays all operating expenses, pays the debt service (principal and interest) on his mortgage, and pays any income tax due on the property.

Formula	*Calculations*
Before-tax cash flow	$1,820 (from Step 3)
Less: Taxable income	0 (from Step 2)
After-tax cash flow	$1,820

As previously stated, all of the before-tax cash flow (sometimes called gross spendable income) is sheltered from taxes. In addition, the investor can use the $125 tax loss to shelter other income.

Calculation of the value of the tax loss:

Formula	*Calculations*
Tax loss	$125
× Investors tax bracket	×.50
Tax savings	$ 62.25

Table 21–5 shows a ten-year projected cash flow for the preceding investment. The columns are as follows:

1. Column D is net operating income (from the reconstructed operating statement)
2. Column E1 + E2 is debt service (principal and interest) ($10,180)
3. Column F is before-tax cash flow
4. Column G is annual depreciation (using the specified depreciation technique)
5. Column H is Column E1 + G (interest expense plus depreciation expense)
6. Column I is taxable income (Column D minus Column H, if positive)
7. Column J is tax loss (Column D minus Column H, if negative)
8. Column K is taxes payable (Column I times tax rate)
9. Column L is tax savings (Column J times tax rate)
10. Column M is after-tax cash flow plus the value of the tax loss (Column F – K or Column F + L)
11. Column N is Column M plus equity build-up (Column E2)

Note that for the first year the entire cash flow is tax sheltered and a $125 tax loss is available to offset other income. As deductible interest expense (Column E) and depreciation expense (Column G) decrease, a point is reached in the second year when total deductions (Column H) are less than net operating income (Column D). The investor must then begin to pay taxes on the investment. When the investor is faced with taxes, the after-tax cash flow (Column M) in year two will be less than the before-tax cash flow (Column F) by the amount of the taxes (Column K).

Table 21-5
Cash flow and tax benefits—125 percent declining balance method

CASH FLOW AND TAX BENEFITS
OF
INVESTMENT PROPERTY OWNERSHIP

PURCHASE PRICE		
LAND ALLOCATION	$ 25,000	
BUILDING ALLOCATION	$100,000	
TOTAL VALUE	$125,000	
FINANCED PCT.	.8000	
MORTGAGE AMOUNT	$100,000	
CASH EQUITY	$ 25,000	
NET OPERATING INCOME	$ 12,000	
TAX BRACKET	.5000	

MORTGAGE TERMS		
LENGTH OF LOAN	25	
INTEREST RATE	.0900	
ANNUAL PAYMENT (PRIN. INT.)	$10,180	
DEPRECIATION		
EST. ECONOMIC LIFE	40	
METHOD USED	125	DB

	(D)	(E1)	(E2)	(F)	(G)	(H)	(I)	(J)	(K)	(L)	(M)	(N)
YEAR	NET OPERATING INCOME	INTEREST	PRINCIPAL	(D-E1-E2) CASH FLOW	DEPRECIATION	DEDUCTS FOR TAX PURPOSES	(D-H) TAXABLE INCOME	TAXABLE LOSS	(IX TB.) TAX PAYABLE	(JX TB.) TAX SAVING	(F-K OR F+L) AFTER TAX CASH FLOW	TOTAL BENEFIT AFTER TAX
01	12,000	9,000	1,180	1,820	3,125	12,125		125		62	1,882	3,062
02	12,000	8,893	1,287	1,820	3,027	11,920	80		40		1,780	3,067
03	12,000	8,777	1,403	1,820	2,932	11,709	291		145		1,675	3,078
04	12,000	8,651	1,529	1,820	2,841	11,492	508		254		1,566	3,095
05	12,000	8,514	1,666	1,820	2,752	11,266	734		367		1,453	3,119
06	12,000	8,364	1,816	1,820	2,666	11,030	970		485		1,335	3,151
07	12,000	8,200	1,980	1,820	2,583	10,783	1,217		608		1,212	3,192
08	12,000	8,022	2,158	1,820	2,502	10,524	1,476		738		1,082	3,240
09	12,000	7,828	2,352	1,820	2,424	10,252	1,748		874		946	3,298
10	12,000	7,616	2,564	1,820	2,348	9,964	2,036		1,018		802	3,366
TOTAL	$120,000	$ 83,865	$ 17,935	$ 18,200	$ 27,200	$111,065	$ 9,060	125	$ 4,529	62	$ 13,733	$ 31,668

475

Tables 21–6 through 21–9 illustrate the cash flow of this same case study using the other available depreciation techniques.

Assume that our investor is in the 50 percent tax bracket and decides to invest $25,000 equity in the one-year old, brick apartment building. Having borrowed the funds to finance the balance, he will receive the following benefits in year one.

Current Return

Positive after-tax cash flow:	$1820.00
Tax savings:	+62.50
Total current return (after taxes)	$1882.50

Deferred Return

Equity growth from:		
Mortgage amortization	1180.00	
Capital appreciation (@ 4%/yr)	5000.00	
Total deferred return (before taxes)	$6180.00	
Total Return		$8062.50

Although the investor receives the current cash return (after-tax cash flow plus the value of the tax loss) in year one, he does not actually receive the deferred return until he either refinances or sells the property. If he sells the property, he will have long-term capital gain tax liability. Considering this, he may prefer to refinance rather than to sell.

Refinancing versus selling

Refinancing is a means whereby the investor can borrow on his own equity and obtain tax free use of funds without having to sell and lose control of his investment. Assume that the property appreciates 4 percent per year and the investor can refinance at 80 percent of market value. He would generate the following tax free funds:

Purchase price = $125,000 with a $100,000 original mortgage balance

|
10
years   4% appreciation/year
later

↓ Market Value in 10 years	$175,000
	.80
	$140,000 new 1st mortgage
	−82,740 (pay off old mortgage balance
Funds available for tax free use	$ 57,260 see Table F–2 in Appendix F)

The investor generally must pay a refinancing fee of from one to two percent of the amount borrowed. Also, the interest rate on the new mortgage will most likely increase. However, refinancing can sometimes be an attractive alternative to selling, especially when the owner wants to retain control of the building.

Table 21-6
Cash flow and tax benefits—Straight-line

CASH FLOW AND TAX BENEFITS
OF
INVESTMENT PROPERTY OWNERSHIP

PURCHASE PRICE $25,000
LAND ALLOCATION $100,000
BUILDING ALLOCATION $100,000
TOTAL VALUE $125,000

FINANCED PCT. .8000
MORTGAGE AMOUNT $100,000
CASH EQUITY $25,000

NET OPERATING INCOME $12,000
TAX BRACKET .5000

MORTGAGE TERMS
LENGTH OF LOAN 25
INTEREST RATE .0900
ANNUAL PAYMENT $10,180
(PRIN. INT.)

DEPRECIATION
EST. ECONOMIC LIFE 40

METHOD USED S. LINE

	(D) NET OPERATING INCOME	(E1) INTEREST	(E2) PRINCIPAL	(F) (D-E1-E2) CASH FLOW	(G) DEPRECIATION	(H) DEDUCTS FOR TAX PURPOSES	(I) (D-H) TAXABLE INCOME	(J) TAXABLE LOSS	(K) (IX TB.) TAX PAYABLE	(L) (JX TB.) TAX SAVING	(M) (F-K OR F+L) AFTER TAX CASH FLOW	(N) TOTAL BENEFIT AFTER TAX
YEAR												
01	12,000	9,000	1,180	1,820	2,500	11,500	500		250		1,570	2,750
02	12,000	8,893	1,287	1,820	2,500	11,393	607		303		1,517	2,804
03	12,000	8,777	1,403	1,820	2,500	11,277	723		361		1,459	2,862
04	12,000	8,651	1,529	1,820	2,500	11,151	849		424		1,396	2,925
05	12,000	8,514	1,666	1,820	2,500	11,014	986		493		1,327	2,993
06	12,000	8,364	1,816	1,820	2,500	10,864	1,136		568		1,252	3,068
07	12,000	8,200	1,980	1,820	2,500	10,700	1,300		650		1,170	3,150
08	12,000	8,022	2,158	1,820	2,500	10,522	1,478		739		1,081	3,239
09	12,000	7,828	2,352	1,820	2,500	10,328	1,672		836		984	3,336
10	12,000	7,616	2,564	1,820	2,500	10,116	1,884		942		878	3,442
TOTAL	$120,000	$83,865	$17,935	$18,200	$25,000	$108,865	$11,135		$5,560		$12,634	$30,569

477

Table 21-7
Cash flow and tax benefits—150 percent declining balance

CASH FLOW AND TAX BENEFITS
OF
INVESTMENT PROPERTY OWNERSHIP

PURCHASE PRICE			MORTGAGE TERMS	
LAND ALLOCATION	$25,000		LENGTH OF LOAN	25
BUILDING ALLOCATION	$100,000		INTEREST RATE	.0900
TOTAL VALUE	$125,000		ANNUAL PAYMENT	$10,180
			(PRIN. INT.)	
FINANCED PCT.	.8000			
MORTGAGE AMOUNT	$100,000		DEPRECIATION	
CASH EQUITY	$25,000		EST. ECONOMIC LIFE	40
NET OPERATING INCOME	$12,000		METHOD USED	150 DB
TAX BRACKET	.5000			

	(D) NET OPERATING INCOME	(E1) INTEREST	(E2) PRINCIPAL	(F) (D–E1–E2) CASH FLOW	(G) DEPRECIATION	(H) DEDUCTS FOR TAX PURPOSES	(I) (D–H) TAXABLE INCOME	(J) TAXABLE LOSS	(K) (IX TB.) TAX PAYABLE	(L) (JX TB.) TAX SAVING	(M) AFTER TAX CASH FLOW	(N) TOTAL BENEFIT AFTER TAX
YEAR												
01	12,000	9,000	1,180	1,820	3,750	12,750		750		375	2,195	3,375
02	12,000	8,893	1,287	1,820	3,609	12,502		502		251	2,071	3,358
03	12,000	8,777	1,403	1,820	3,474	12,251		251		125	1,945	3,348
04	12,000	8,651	1,529	1,820	3,343	11,994	6		3		1,817	3,346
05	12,000	8,514	1,666	1,820	3,218	11,732	268		134		1,686	3,352
06	12,000	8,364	1,816	1,820	3,097	11,461	539		269		1,551	3,367
07	12,000	8,200	1,980	1,820	2,981	11,181	819		409		1,411	3,391
08	12,000	8,022	2,158	1,820	2,869	10,891	1,109		554		1,266	3,424
09	12,000	7,828	2,352	1,820	2,762	10,590	1,410		705		1,115	3,467
10	12,000	7,616	2,564	1,820	2,658	10,274	1,726		863		957	3,521
TOTAL	$120,000	$83,865	$17,935	$18,200	$31,761	$115,626	$5,877	1,503	$2,937	751	$16,014	$33,949

Table 21-8
Cash flow and tax benefits—Double-declining balance

CASH FLOW AND TAX BENEFITS
OF
INVESTMENT PROPERTY OWNERSHIP

PURCHASE PRICE	$ 25,000	
LAND ALLOCATION	$100,000	
BUILDING ALLOCATION	$125,000	
TOTAL VALUE		
FINANCED PLT.	.8000	
MORTGAGE AMOUNT	$100,000	
CASH EQUITY	$ 25,000	
NET OPERATING INCOME	$ 12,000	
TAX BRACKET	.5000	

MORTGAGE TERMS		
LENGTH OF LOAN	25	
INTEREST RATE	.0900	
ANNUAL PAYMENT (PRIN. INT.)	$10,180	
DEPRECIATION		
EST. ECONOMIC LIFE	40	
METHOD USED	200 DB	

	(D)	(E1)	(E2)	(F)	(G)	(H)	(I)	(J)	(K)	(L)	(M)	(N)
YEAR	NET OPERATING INCOME	INTEREST	PRINCIPAL	(D-E1-E2) CASH FLOW	DEPRECIATION	DEDUCTS FOR TAX PURPOSES	(D-H) TAXABLE INCOME	TAXABLE LOSS	(I X TB.) TAX PAYABLE	(J X TB.) TAX SAVING	(F-K OR F+L) AFTER TAX CASH FLOW	TOTAL BENEFIT AFTER TAX
01	12,000	9,000	1,180	1,820	5,000	14,000		2,000		1,000	2,820	4,000
02	12,000	8,893	1,287	1,820	4,750	13,643		1,643		821	2,641	3,928
03	12,000	8,777	1,403	1,820	4,512	13,289		1,289		644	2,464	3,867
04	12,000	8,651	1,529	1,820	4,286	12,937		937		468	2,288	3,817
05	12,000	8,514	1,666	1,820	4,072	12,586		586		293	2,113	3,779
06	12,000	8,364	1,816	1,820	3,869	12,233		233		116	1,936	3,752
07	12,000	8,200	1,980	1,820	3,675	11,875	125		62		1,758	3,738
08	12,000	8,022	2,158	1,820	3,491	11,513	487		243		1,577	3,735
09	12,000	7,828	2,352	1,820	3,317	11,145	855		427		1,393	3,745
10	12,000	7,616	2,564	1,820	3,151	10,767	1,233		616		1,204	3,768
TOTAL	$120,000	$ 83,865	$ 17,935	$ 18,200	$ 40,123	$123,988	$ 2,700	$ 6,688	$ 1,348	$ 3,342	$ 20,194	$ 38,129

479

Table 21-9
Cash flow and tax benefits—Sum-of-the-years' digits

CASH FLOW AND TAX BENEFITS
OF
INVESTMENT PROPERTY OWNERSHIP

PURCHASE PRICE
LAND ALLOCATION $ 25,000
BUILDING ALLOCATION $100,000
  TOTAL VALUE $125,000

FINANCED PCT.   .8000
MORTGAGE AMOUNT $100,000
CASH EQUITY $ 25,000

NET OPERATING INCOME $ 12,000
TAX BRACKET   .5000

MORTGAGE TERMS
LENGTH OF LOAN   25
INTEREST RATE   .0900
ANNUAL PAYMENT $10,180
  (PRIN. INT.)

DEPRECIATION
EST. ECONOMIC LIFE   40

METHOD USED   SUM OF YEARS

	(D)	(E1)	(E2)	(F)	(G)	(H)	(I) (D-H)	(J)	(K) (IX TB.)	(L) (JX TB.)	(M) (F-K OR F+L)	(N) TOTAL
YEAR	NET OPERATING INCOME	INTEREST	PRINCIPAL	(D-E1-E2) CASH FLOW	DEPRECIATION	DEDUCTS FOR TAX PURPOSES	TAXABLE INCOME	TAXABLE LOSS	TAX PAYABLE	TAX SAVING	AFTER TAX CASH FLOW	BENEFIT AFTER TAX
01	12,000	9,000	1,180	1,820	4,870	13,870		1,870		935	2,755	3,935
02	12,000	8,893	1,287	1,820	4,750	13,643		1,643		821	2,641	3,928
03	12,000	8,777	1,403	1,820	4,630	13,407		1,407		703	2,523	3,926
04	12,000	8,651	1,529	1,820	4,510	13,161		1,161		580	2,400	3,929
05	12,000	8,514	1,666	1,820	4,390	12,904		904		452	2,272	3,938
06	12,000	8,364	1,816	1,820	4,260	12,624		624		312	2,132	3,948
07	12,000	8,200	1,980	1,820	4,140	12,340		340		170	1,990	3,973
08	12,000	8,022	2,158	1,820	4,020	12,042		42		21	1,841	3,999
09	12,000	7,828	2,352	1,820	3,900	11,728	272		136		1,684	4,036
10	12,000	7,616	2,564	1,820	3,780	11,396	604		302		1,518	4,082
TOTAL	$120,000	$ 83,865	$ 17,935	$ 18,200	$ 43,250	$127,115	$ 876	$ 7,991	$ 438	$ 3,994	$ 21,756	$ 39,691

480

Calculating Net Proceeds on Sale   If the investor decides to sell rather than refinance, he is faced with several expenses that must be paid out of the sale proceeds. The typical expenses involved in the sale of an investment property include the sales commission expense, attorney fees, the tax liability, and the payment of any remaining mortgage balance. Table 21–10 demonstrates the procedure in arriving at the net proceeds on the sale of the case study investment.

Calculation of Investment Value   The total investment value of the property to the investor is the summation of

1. The present value of the after-tax cash flow; and
2. The present value of the after-tax equity reversion (sometimes called *net proceeds on sale*); and
3. The value of obtainable mortgage.

1.   The annual after-tax cash flows for the 10-year holding period are shown in Column M of Tables 21–5 thru 21–9. These projected after-tax cash flows can be discounted at any desired equity yield rate to obtain the present value for that rate. The higher the desired equity yield rate, the lower the present value. Our investor desires an equity yield of 12 percent. Discounting the after-tax cash flow from Table 21–5 at 12 percent, we have:

Year	After-Tax Cash Flow	Present Value Factor at 12% (see Appendix D, Table D–5)	After-Tax Cash Flow Discounted to Present Value at a 12% Rate
1	$1882	× .892857 =	$1680.35
2	1780	× .797194 =	1419.00
3	1675	× .711780 =	1192.23
4	1566	× .635518 =	995.22
5	1453	× .567427 =	824.47
6	1335	× .506631 =	676.35
7	1212	× .452349 =	548.24
8	1082	× .403883 =	437.00
9	946	× .360610 =	341.13
10	802	× .321973 =	258.22
Present value of all annual cash flows			$8372.21

2.   *Add:*   Present value of equity reversion in 10 years

After tax equity reversion to be received in 10 years from Table 21–10, net proceeds on sale (equity reversion)	×	Reversionary factor at 12% from Table D–5, Appendix D	=	Present value of equity reversion
$64,576	×	.321973	=	$20,791.73
Total present value of equity position				$29,163.94

3.   *Add:*   Original mortgage value $100,000.00
Total investment value $129,163.94

                              Rounded to $129,000.00

Table 21–10
Calculations of net proceeds on sale—Equity reversion

	Adjusted Basis		
	Original basis	$125,000	
Plus	Capital improvements	0	
Plus	Cost of sale (7%)	12,250	
Equals	Subtotal	$137,250	
Minus	Depreciation	27,200	
Minus	Partial sales	0	
Equals	Adjusted basis at sale	$110,050	
	Excess Depreciation		
	Total depreciation	27,200	
Minus	Straight-line depreciation	25,000	
Equals	Excess depreciation	$ 2,200	
	Gain		
	Sale price	$175,000	
Minus	Adjusted basis	110,050	
Equals	Total gain	64,950	
Minus	Excess recapture	2,200	
Equals	Capital gain (long-term)	$ 62,750	
	Tax Consequence of Investment		
	Investor's original taxable income	$ 34,000	
	*Tax liability without investment		12,430
Plus	Excess recapture	2,200	
Plus	Taxable long-term gain		
	($62,750 × .40 = $25,100)		
	(60% of the gain is excluded)	25,100	
Equals	Investor's new taxable income	$ 61,300	
	*Tax liability with investment		28,604
Equals	Tax consequence of investment		16,174
	Net Sale Proceeds—Equity Reversion		
	Sale price	$175,000	
Minus	Sale cost (7%)	12,250	
Minus	Mortgage balance	82,000	
Equals	Proceeds before taxes	80,750	
Minus	Tax liability as a consequence of the investment	16,174	
Equals	After tax equity reversion or net proceeds on sale	$ 64,576	

Note: *Effective for years beginning in 1979, there is a new, alternative minimum tax. It did not apply in this example, but it may apply in other similar situations.
*1978 tax tables used, married, filing separately.

Based on the assumptions and conditions stated, if our hypothetical investor wants an after-tax equity yield of 12 percent, he can afford to pay $129,000 for the property.

Tax-deferred exchange

Our investor could, through proper planning, preserve almost 50 percent of his equity by using an exchange rather than paying the $39,232 tax liability due on sale. A thumbnail sketch of *tax-deferred exchanges* follows.

General Requirements   Under Section 1031 of the Internal Revenue Code, no gain or loss is recognized "if property held for productive use in trade or business or for investment is exchanged solely for property of 'like kind' which is to be held either for productive use in trade or business or for investment." Inventory held primarily for sale does not qualify for a nontaxable exchange. Although the IRS does not publish specific guidelines concerning the necessary holding period to qualify for a nontaxable exchange, clearly a home built by a contractor does not qualify. Another classification that does not qualify is the primary residence (Chapter 9 discussed other techniques to defer the gain on primary residences). The requirement that the property be of *like kind* refers to the distinction between personal property and real property. In essence, personal property may be exchanged for personal property, and real property may be exchanged for real property. Real property may not be exchanged for personal property.

Boot   Very few exchanges are made that do not involve a tax liability to one of the participants. This occurs because of the value differences between properties exchanged and the resultant need for one of the parties to pay some "boot." *Boot* is considered any "unlike kind property" received and may include any of these:

● Relief from indebtedness
● Personal property for real estate
● Money
● Note, mortgage, and so forth

In order for our investor to structure a completely tax-deferred exchange on a property that shows a gain, he must receive property with an equal or greater equity and a higher market value than the property he transferred. In other words, our investor must pay boot and assume a larger loan. Figure 21–3 shows how an exchange might look to our investor.

The possibilities for a tax-deferred exchange are almost endless and should be given careful consideration as a means of preserving equity, increasing financial leverage, pyramiding investments, maximizing depreciation deductions, increasing cash flow, and dozens of other investment objectives. The prudent investor should spend time researching the intricacies of tax-deferred exchanges and dispel the theory that such techniques are too complicated to understand and apply.

Figure 21–3

Case study—Exchange

After ten years, our investor's four-unit apartment is worth $175,000 and has a loan balance of $82,000. His basis is $110,050. He may exchange for an office complex valued at $250,000 with a first mortgage of $125,000 and a basis of $100,000. This exchange would be completely tax-free for him, thereby preserving nearly 50 percent of the equity he would otherwise have to pay out in taxes if he were to sell. The three steps used to calculate his recognized gain follow.

Step 1:   Balancing Equities

	Investor's 4-Unit	Office Complex
Market value	$175,000	$250,000
Loans	−82,000	−125,000
Equity	$ 93,000	$125,000
Boot paid	+ 32,000	–0–
Balance	$125,000	$125,000

Our investor must pay an additional $32,000 in boot to balance the equities of the properties.

Step 2:   Computing Realized Gain

	Investor's 4-Unit	Office Complex
Real estate received	$250,000	$175,000
Boot received	–0–	32,000
Loans on property transferred	+ 82,000	+125,000
Total consideration	332,000	332,000
Less: Adjusted basis of property transferred	−110,050	−100,000
Less: Loans on property received	−125,000	− 82,000
Realized gain	$ 96,950	$150,000

Step 3:   Computing Recognized Gain

	Investor's 4-Unit	Office Complex
Loans on property transferred	82,000	125,000
Less: Loans on property received	−125,000	− 82,000
Equals mortgage boot	–0–	33,000
Plus cash boot	–0–	+ 32,000
Equity total boot received	–0–	65,000
*Recognized gain	–0–	65,000

*Recognized gain is the lesser of either (a) realized gain or (b) boot received. As can be seen, our four-unit investor has realized a gain of $96,950. However, none of this gain is recognized (taxable) in the year of sale. The entire gain of $96,950 is deferred. The second party to the exchange has a realized gain of $150,000 and a $65,000 recognized (taxable) gain in the year of the sale. He defers $85,000 of his gain. The deferred gain is subtracted from the basis of the newly acquired investments for both parties to the exchange, thereby resulting in an adjusted basis for the new investment.

ALTERNATIVE INVESTMENT MEDIA

Although this chapter focused primarily on an apartment building investment in its discussion of various principles and concepts, many other types of real estate investments offer the same benefits and share the same or similar risks. Table 21–11 provides a ready comparison of some of these real estate investments and their important characteristics.

Over the last ten years, the number of new real estate investment media available to the investor has increased considerably. With the advent of joint ventures, syndications, and limited partnerships, the investor may participate jointly in ski resorts, motel condominiums, medicos or medical condominiums, recreational land development, miniwarehouses, camping resorts, office buildings, subdivisions, indoor tennis clubs, long-term leases, and hundreds of other investments. The Real Estate Investment Trust (*REIT*), sometimes called "the mutual funds of real estate," is also available to the small investor who could not otherwise invest in real estate. Real estate investment trust certificates are sold in small denominations through the organized stock exchanges. They are not subject to corporate, federal income tax so long as 90 percent of the profits are distributed to the investors. The REIT, in turn, reinvests the money in construction and development loans, other long-term mortgages, and real property investments.

SUMMARY

The interplay of depreciation and interest expense deductions, financial leverage, and property value appreciation are the three key elements that make real estate investments so popular. Two of the most commonly used criteria in evaluating real estate investments are *cash flow* and *tax shelter*. The real estate investor's ability to deduct interest expense and depreciation deductions from operating income creates, in many instances, a positive cash flow, and yet a tax loss that may be used to shelter other income. The investor has several depreciation methods and techniques available. The methods and techniques used vary depending on the type of property, the useful life of the property, the investor's objectives, and lastly, current tax legislation and rulings. Upon the sale of real estate, favorable capital gain treatment minimizes tax liability. In many instances, refinancing is an attractive alternative to selling when the investor's primary objective is to free up some capital. Over the last few years, property exchanges have become increasingly popular as a means of deferring capital gains tax.

Even though legislation over the years has whittled away at many of the tax advantages of investing in real estate, it remains as one of the most effective hedges against inflation and will likely continue as a worthy investment medium in the future.

Table 21-11
Characteristics of property types

	Agricultural and Undeveloped Land	Predeveloped Land	New Apartments	Existing Apartments	Hotel and Motel
Function	Agricultural, forest, and mineral production; recreation	Held for investment and speculation on successful development	Shelter, housing, amenities, and living environment	Shelter, housing, amenities, and living environment	Protection for travelers, home away from home for travelers, a communications related property
Investment characteristics:					
Cash flow	Low (or negative)	Negative	Low to medium	Reasonable	Possibly high
Tax shelter	Low	Low	High	Low to medium	Medium to high
Inflation hedge	Good	Good	Good	Good	Good
Operating risk	High	High	High	Average	High
Liquidity	Relatively illiquid	Generally hard to sell	Generally good for smaller units	Generally good for smaller units	Harder to sell because of operating risks
Mortgage financing	Financing primarily by sellers and specialized government programs	Financing almost exclusively available from seller; favorable financing terms reflected in higher selling price	70 to 80% conventional financing, with land lease possible for developer to "mortgage out"	70 to 80% financing available from conventional sources; seller often carries back secondary financing	Financing dependent upon previous operating record and strength of management
Ownership characteristics:					
Owner's equity	Generally owned by user with increasing tendency to investment by institutional investors and partnerships	Owned primarily by individuals, partnerships, and large corporations	All types of owners, including many individuals and partnerships	All types of owners, including many individuals and partnerships	By operating companies or when owned by individuals or partnerships, generally leased to an operating company
Size	Can be bought in all sizes, but meaningful operating economies require substantial holdings	Can be of any size	All sizes; tend to be somewhat larger than existing apartments	All sizes; tend to be many small units available	Range from "Mom and Pop" operations to very large units
Management time required	Heavy; constant supervision required if in use	Low, although it is essential that important developments be monitored, but when disposition occurs, substantial management time could be required	Extensive for initial rent-up; average to heavy for ongoing operations	Average, except that "problems" can make excessive time demands	Excessive; a 24-hour operation requiring constant attention

Management expertise required	Very high; timing of paramount importance	Moderate, although ability to interpret—and influence—political and economic trends is important	Average	Average	High; the constant client contact and continual turnover, combined with diverse array of services provided, require broad knowledge
Economies of size	With the trend to use of more advanced technology and larger capital-intensive equipment, large land holdings advantageous	Large acreage can represent substantial economies of scale	Substantial economies realized with larger units	Substantial economies realized with larger units	Trend to larger units is more efficient for operations
Economic characteristics:					
Users	Farmers, ranchers, individuals, corporations	Large corporations, individual speculators	Families and individuals of moderate means or those who choose not to own a home (usually rents for more than an existing unit)	Families and individuals of moderate means or those who choose not to own a home	Individuals, families, travelers, business
Term of use	Lifetime down to yearly leases	1 to 5 years	Year leases, condominiums, and cooperatives to lifetime	Month to month, some year leases, condominiums and cooperatives	Overnight, weekly
Demand influences	Population levels, food and other consumption levels, technology, transportation systems	Population trends, general economic conditions, land-use controls, transportation systems, availability of money for development, government programs (new communities financing)	Population increases, family formation rates, social and economic changes, life-style modes, amenity packages offered	Population increases, family formation rates, social and economic changes	General economic conditions, recreation and leisure trends, transportation availability and pricing, special events (conventions, conferences, expositions)
Supply influences	Water availability, transportation access, removals due to development activity, fertility and soil conditions, scenic or other recreational possibilities	Land-use regulations, conversion to developed status, establishment of parks and natural preserves, regional growth patterns, density and sprawl trends, volume of land promotion activity	Removals from housing stock by demolition or condemnation, availability of money for new financing, land-use approval process, political environment, special government programs (FHA subsidized housing, housing allowances)	Removals from housing stock by demoliton or condemnation, political environment, conversions to other use (condominiums), conversions from other uses (e.g., hotels), supply of new units	Removal of space of existing units from market; conversion of existing units to alternative uses; perceived demand; financing availability; land-use regulations; conference, convention, and exposition demand
Government controls	Crop subsidy programs, formal financing programs, land-use controls	Land-use controls, restrictions on marketing practices	Restrictions on condominiums, property tax assessment policies, financing availability (specialized government programs), land-use regulations	Restrictions on convertibility to condominiums, property tax assessment policies, financing availability (specialized government programs)	Restrictions on convertibility to condominiums, property tax assessment policies, financing availability (specialized government programs), land-use regulations

Table 21–11

Characteristics of property types, continued

	Individual, Strip, Commercial, and Small Office Properties	Shopping Centers	Office Buildings	Industrial Property
Function	Exchange goods; distribution centers; personal services; administration and management	Exchange goods; distribution centers; opportunity for concentrated shopping experience	Personal services, administration and management of economic and social systems	Conversion of raw materials, production of manufactured goods, labor, land and capital meet here
Investment characteristics:				
Cash flow	Average to good	Average to good	Average	Average to high
Tax shelter	Low to medium	Low to medium	Low	Low
Inflation hedge	Low	Average	Average	Poor
Operating risk	Average to high	Low	Average	High
Liquidity	Low to average	Relatively good if leases are strong	Relatively good if leases are strong	Very hard to sell unless there is strong long-term lease
Mortgage financing	70 to 80% conventional sources; seller may often provide secondary financing	Financing dependent upon major department store as anchor tenant as well as designated percentage of leases signed	Financed often on a floor-ceiling arrangement whereby additional increments of financing depend on threshold levels of leasing being achieved	Financing depends on credit rating, often owned by occupant; if not, financing will depend on credit rating of lessee
Ownership characteristics:				
Owner's equity	Smaller investors, individuals, small groups	Tend more to be owned by larger investors including corporations, REITs, and insurance companies	Tend more to be owned by larger investors including corporations, REITs, and insurance companies	Often owned by users; otherwise, REITs and other institutional investors
Size	Moderate	Some smaller investment properties available, but tend to become larger	Come in all sizes, but a number are very large and require substantial capital	Tend to be medium-sized to larger units
Management time required	Average to high, particularly where leases are of shorter term	High; requires constant promotion and attention to maintenance and tenant satisfaction	Average to low	Relatively low, although negotiating leases can be very time-consuming
Management expertise required	Average	High, particularly in negotiating leases and conducting promotions	Average, though lease negotiation requires high level of sophistication and expertise	Average to high; lease negotiation can be particularly complex

488

Economies of size	Low, unless multiple properties owned	Substantial management economies with larger centers; can enjoy joint promotion activities	Size tends to be of less concern, although it can effect certain savings	Manufacturing trend to larger facilities, although many businesses require modest amount of space
Economic characteristics:				
Users	Households, small businesses, chain stores, white-collar workers	All households (particularly heavy usage in suburbs); small businesses and chain stores	White-collar workers, administrators and managers, large and small businesses	Blue-collar workers, managers, large and small corporations
Term of use	1-year to long-term leases	1 to 50-year leases	1- to 10-year or longer leases	Lifetime down to short-term
Demand influences	Population levels, transportation access and technology, parking, competition	Population, density, general economic conditions, spending patterns, presence of demand "magnet" (special attraction to bring people to center)	Economy, politics, social modes, communications technology, size of work force, work technologies (space per worker, equipment per worker)	Economic conditions, business cycles in specific industry, foreign trade and tariffs, raw-material availability, technological developments, land-use laws
Supply influences	Land or lot availability, existence of commercial "strip," local government attitude toward transportation and strip development	Capital availability, competitors' perceptions of demand potential, department-store location decisions, new housing development, economic conditions, government regulations	Corporate location decisions, financing availability, government decision (i.e., locating new facilities), corporate "image" decision, space utilization patterns, business climate, removal of space from market, movement in direction of "urban" downtown	Land-use controls, pollution regulations, technological obsolescence, changing manufacturing or service orientation of economy, conversion of space to alternative uses, removal of industrial space from market
Government controls	Zoning, building codes, willingness to supply services, traffic control	Property tax assessment policies, financing availability (specialized government programs), land-use regulations	Restrictions on convertibility to condominiums, property tax assessment policies, financing availability (specialized government programs)	Property tax assessment policies, financing availability (specialized government programs), land-use regulations, pollution emission standards

From *Real Estate Investment and Finance* by Sherman J. Maisel and Stephen E. Roulac. New York: McGraw-Hill Book Company, 1976.

TERMS AND CONCEPTS

You can check your understanding of these terms against the glossary or by review in this chapter.

Accelerated depreciation	Economic (useful) life
After-tax cash flow (Net spendable income)	Excess recapture
	Holding period
1231 Assets	Leverage
Before-tax cash flow (Gross spendable income)	"Like kind" property
	Liquidity
Boot	Refinancing
Capital gain or loss	REIT
Cash flow	Ripening expenses
Component depreciation	SOYD
Composite depreciation	Straight-line depreciation
Depreciable base	Taxable income
Depreciable basis	Tax-deferred exchange
Depreciation	Tax shelter
Double-declining balance depreciation	

What are the differences or relationship, if any, between the following:

1231 Assets and Capital assets	Investment property and Income-producing property
Before-tax cash flow and After-tax cash flow	Positive financial leverage and Negative financial leverage
Composite and Component depreciation	Risk and Return
Current return and Deferred return	Short-term capital gain and Long-term capital gain
Excess recapture and Ordinary income	SOYD and Double-declining balance

PROBLEMS

21–1.   A building has an economic life of 40 years. The value of the building has been determined to be $120,000. Determine the amount of annual depreciation using straight-line depreciation. Assume no salvage value.

Use the double-declining balance method in the three following questions.

21–2.   Find the first three years' depreciation of a new apartment building having an economic life of 25 years and a value of $120,000.

21–3.   Determine the balance after three years of depreciating a new apartment building worth $80,000 and having an economic life of 40 years.

21–4.   What is the third year's depreciation if a building has an economic life of 40 years and is valued at $250,000?

21–5.   Find the first three years' depreciation using the SOYD method for a new apartment having a value of $120,000 and an economic life of 30 years. Assume no salvage value.

21–6.   A building has been valued at $100,000 and has a useful life of 40 years. What is the depreciation for the fifth and sixth years? Assume no salvage value. Use sum-of-the-years' digits depreciation.

21–7. Compute the after-tax cash flow on the following investment. Ms. Sirocco purchased a used residential rental property with a useful life of 20 years for $200,000. The building value was $160,000. She obtained a 75 percent, 20-year, 10 percent interest, completely amortized loan with annual payments (principal and interest) of $17,619. The net operating income from the property was $25,000. Assume a 50 percent tax bracket. She used the highest legal composite method of depreciation.

21–8. Compute the amount of excess recapture that will be taxed as ordinary income in the following investment. In 1980, Mr. Buntz purchased a new apartment building with a 40-year life for $100,000. The apartment was on *leased ground*. He used the 200 percent declining balance composite depreciation technique. Two years later, he sold his investment for $125,000. He is in the 50 percent tax bracket.

21-9. Assume an investor experiences $4,000 in net long-term capital losses and $2,000 in net short-term capital gains in the same year. What are the tax consequences?

21-10. Explain the significant differences in tax treatment between 1231 assets and capital gains.

SUPPLEMENTARY READINGS

Anderson, Paul E. *Tax Factors in Real Estate Operations.* Englewood Cliffs, N.J.: Prentice-Hall, 1976.

Beaton, William R. *Real Estate Investment.* Englewood Cliffs, N.J.: Prentice-Hall, 1971. Chapters 1–3.

Casey, William J. *Real Estate Investment Planning.* New York: Institute for Business Planning.

Greer, Gaylon E. *The Real Estate Investor and the Federal Income Tax.* New York: John Wiley and Sons, 1978.

Maisel, Sherman J., and Roulac, Stephen E. *Real Estate Investment and Finance.* New York: McGraw-Hill, 1976.

Messner, Stephen D.; Schreiber, Irvin; and Lyon, Victor L. *Marketing Investment Real Estate.* Chicago: Realtors National Marketing Institute, 1975.

Ring, Alfred A., and Dasso, Jerome. *Real Estate Principles and Practices.* Englewood Cliffs, N.J.: Prentice-Hall, 7th ed., 1978. Chapter 14.

Schraub, Edgar W. *What You Must Know Before You Invest.* Englewood Cliffs, N.J.: Prentice-Hall, 1968. Chapters 1–4.

Tappan, William T., Jr. *Real Estate Exchange and Acquisition Techniques.* Englewood Cliffs, N.J.: Prentice-Hall, 1978.

Wendt, Paul F., and Cerf, Alan R. *Real Estate Investment Analysis and Taxation.* New York: McGraw-Hill, 1969. Chapters 1, 3, and 10.

APPENDICES

Glossary

Abatement. The termination of an offensive activity, as the *abatement* of a nuisance.

Abstract of title. A summary, arranged in chronological order, of the essential provisions of every recorded document pertaining to a particular parcel of land.

Abut. To be next to or touch another property or body of water.

Acceleration clause. A provision in a note such that, if payments are in default, the owner of the note can declare the entire balance due and payable earlier than the stated due date.

Acceptance. An expression by one to whom an offer is made (the offeree) of his assent to the terms set forth in the offer, which is communicated to the one who makes the offer (the offeror).

Access. The right of a property owner to have a means of entry and exit from her property to a public street.

Accretion. The process by which the area of a parcel of land bounded by a river, lake, or waters is gradually increased by the deposit of soil due to the natural action of water.

Accrued depreciation. The actual depreciation in a property that has already accrued as of a given date; past depreciation.

Acknowledgment. A certification by a notary public or other public officer of a statement by a person that he executed a particular document as a free and voluntary act.

Acre. A measure of land area equal to 43,560 sq. ft.

Action. A court process to enforce a right.

Actual age. The number of years a building has been in existence; chronological age.

Actual notice. Knowledge of a fact acquired by a person who is expressly told of the fact, or who personally observes the fact.

Administrator. A person appointed by a probate court to handle the estate of a deceased person who left no will.

Ad valorem. According to value.

Ad valorem tax. A real property tax based on the value of the property.

Adverse possession. Title to real property is acquired by adverse possession when it is possessed for a statutorily prescribed period of time in such a manner that the owner's title is lost and that title is vested in the possessor.

Adverse user. The term is used in connection with easements by prescription. An adverse user is one who, as a trespasser, enters upon and uses the land of another and, by continuing her wrongful use of the property for a period of time specified by statute, acquires a right to use the property.

After acquired title. A doctrine under which a prior grantee automatically obtains title to real estate acquired by a grantor who previously attempted to convey title which he did not in fact own.

Agency. The relationship between a principal and agent whereby the agent represents the principal in dealing with third parties.

Agent. A person who has authority to act for another.

Agreement for deed. *See* installment sale contract.

Air rights. A landowner's right to the use and enjoyment of the space above her land to the extent that she can effectively occupy it.

Alienate. To transfer an interest or interests in real property.

Alluvion. Soil that is deposited on land bounded by a river, lake, or tidal waters as a result of current, wave, or tidal action.

ALTA. American Land Title Association.

ALTA title insurance policy. A broad form of title insurance policy that includes unusual risks such as factors that could be disclosed by inspection of the land or by a survey.

Amenities. Those qualities that are pleasing and agreeable; intangible benefits of property ownership such as pride of ownership or scenic beauty.

Amortization. The payment of a debt in periodic installments over a prescribed term.

Annexation. The act of attaching or adding personal property to land so that it becomes a part of the real property.

Appraisal. An estimate of value of a parcel of property.

Appraisement. See appraisal.

Appraiser. A person qualified by experience and education to make value estimates or appraisals of real property.

Appreciation. An increase in property value.

Appurtenance. As it pertains to real estate, anything part of the land or transferred with it when the land is conveyed.

Assess. Estimate property value as a basis for taxation.

Assessed value. See assessment.

Assessment. A valuation placed on real property as a basis to set the amount of tax to be levied. (*See also* special assessment.)

Assessor. A person who has the official responsibility to make property assessments.

Assignee. The person to whom an assignment is made.

Assignment. As usually used, the word refers to the transfer of a right.

Assignor. The person who assigns or transfers a right or legal interest to another.

Assumption. An agreement whereby one person assumes the obligation of another, such as the assumption of a mortgage.

Attachment. Same as lien.

Attestation. The act of a witness signing his name to an instrument, deed, or other document as a means of establishing its validity.

Avigation easement. The right to control use of space at a set height and distance from airport runways.

Balloon payment. The unpaid balance of a long-term loan that is paid off in a lump sum at the end of the loan term.

Baseline. A reference line running east and west in the government survey system.

Bench mark. A permanent marker used by surveyors.

Bequest. A gift of personal property by will.

Bilateral contract. A contract consisting of mutual exchange of promises by the parties.

Bill of sale. An instrument in writing that transfers ownership of tangible personal property, such as furniture.

Bill to quiet title. A legal proceeding to determine the condition of title to real estate.

Binder. Same as offer and acceptance.

Blanket mortgage. A single mortgage covering more than one piece of real estate.

Bona fide. In good faith.

Bona fide purchaser. One who purchases something in good faith and for value without knowledge of any adverse rights or claims of persons other than the seller.

Breach of contract. The unjustified or unexcused failure of a party to a contract to perform her obligations at all, or her performance of such obligations is not in conformance with the terms of the contract.

Broker. A real estate broker is a person who acts as the agent of another in the process of buying or selling real property.

Building codes. Regulations concerning the quality of building materials and methods having the objective of preventing fire, injury, or spread of disease.

Bundle of rights. The group of interests and rights of a person who owns real property.

Capacity. See competency.

Capitalization. An approach to property appraisal using net income and return on investment to estimate value.

Caveat emptor. Let the buyer beware.

Chain. A unit of measure equal to 66 ft.

Chain of title. The recorded history of all transactions involving title to a given parcel of land beginning with the patent or deed from the government or other original owner to the present time.

Chattel. Personal property.

Chattel mortgage. A mortgage on personal property.

Civil action. A court action involving civil laws (rather than criminal law).

Claim of title. Also known as a claim of right. A term used in connection with adverse possession to mean that an adverse possessor, without any actual right or title, enters upon and occupies another person's real estate with the intent to make it his own.

Closing statement. A statement prepared for the settlement of a sale of real property that includes the computations and adjustments of money for buyer, seller, and sometimes the broker.

Cloud on title. An adverse claim against title to a parcel of land that appears from the public records to be valid but which in fact is invalid or barred for reasons that must be proved by evidence outside the public records.

Codicil. An amendment or addition to an existing will.

Collateral heirs. Persons not lineally related to a decedent (e.g., an uncle, niece, or nephew).

Color of title. A term used to indicate that an occupant who wrongfully possesses another person's real property does so on the basis of an instrument or judicial decree that appears to give her title to the property but which in fact does not do so.

Commercial. Relating to buying and selling activities on a regular basis.

Commingle. To mix funds of a client with the funds of the broker or agent.

Commission. The payment the broker receives for rendering a service, usually expressed as a percentage of the property sale price.

Commitment. When used by a mortgage institution, a promise to give a loan to the applicant.

Common elements. Those areas within a condominium that each owner of a condominium unit has the right to use in common with each other owner.

Common law. The body of law based on custom and usage and created by the courts.

Community property. A type of co-ownership of property between husband and wife in which each spouse owns half of all property acquired during marriage by their joint efforts.

Competency. The ability of a person to acquire rights and incur liabilities and thereby alter his or her legal status.

Concurrent ownership. Ownership where two or more persons possess simultaneous estates in the same property.

Condemnation. The legal proceedings by means of which the right of eminent domain is exercised and private property is taken for a public use.

Condition. In contract law, a condition is an act or event the happening of which either creates (condition precedent) or extinguishes (condition subsequent) a duty on the part of a promisor.

Condition precedent. An act or event that must occur before a promisor's duty to perform arises.

Condition subsequent. An act or event the occurrence of which extinguishes a duty owed by a promisor.

Conditional acceptance. An acceptance by the terms of which an offeree indicates her agreement to an offer providing or on the condition that the offeror do something more or different that he promised to do in the offer. (See also counteroffer.)

Condominium. A form of ownership of real property in which each unit in a multi-unit building is individually owned in fee simple and all common areas (land, halls, exterior walls, recreational facilities, etc.) are co-owned by the unit owners in tenancy in common.

Conservator. A person appointed by a court to take legal charge of the person and property of a person incapable of managing his affairs.

Consideration. In contract law, consideration is something that a promisor bargains for and receives in exchange for her promise and which results in a legal benefit to the promisor or a legal detriment to the promisee.

Constructive eviction. Occurs when wrongful acts on the part of a landlord, or someone acting under her authority, deprive a tenant of his beneficial use and enjoyment of leased premises.

Constructive notice (public notice). Knowledge of a fact that is attributed to an individual by operation of law even though she has no actual knowledge of the fact.

Consummate dower. After the death of a husband, the dower interest which the wife had in her husband's estate.

Contiguous. Next to and in actual contact.

Contingent. Dependent upon a future event that is uncertain.

Contingent remainder. An estate in land, the possession and enjoyment of which is delayed until the termination of a preceding estate and the occurrence of a condition.

Contour. Surface shape of land.

Contract. An agreement that the law will enforce. For an agreement to be a contract, the following elements must be present: (a) mutual assent, (b) consideration, (c) reality of consent, (d) competent parties, (e) legality of subject matter, and (f) be in writing when required by statute.

Contract for deed. *See* installment sale contract.

Contract of sale. A binding agreement between a buyer and a seller of real estate.

Conventional mortgage. A mortgage other than one guaranteed by FHA or VA.

Convey. To transfer a legal interest or interests in real property.

Conveyance. The transfer of a legal interest or interests in real property.

Cooperative. An apartment or multifamily building owned by several persons through a corporation, such that each owner is a stockholder and also leases a portion of the building.

Co-owner. Also known as a cotenant. Any one of two or more owners of simultaneous interests in the same property.

Co-ownership. Also known as cotenancy. Ownership of a legal interest in property by two or more persons at the same time.

Corporation. An artificial entity created by and under the authority of a state or other government for private or public purposes.

Cost approach. A property appraisal process in which the appraiser estimates building value as replacement cost minus depreciation and then adds land value.

Cotenancy. *See* co-ownership.

Cotenant. *See* co-owner.

Counteroffer. A counter proposal by an offeree to an offeror that impliedly manifests the offeree's unwillingness to assent to the terms of the original offer. (*See also* conditional acceptance.)

Covenant (warranty). A covenant in a deed is a promise by the grantor that certain conditions exist and that something is true. Covenants in deeds and leases may also restrict the use that may be made of property, and they are commonly known as "restrictive covenants."

Covenant of seizin (covenant of title). A promise or assurance by a grantor in a deed that he owns the estate or interest that he purports to convey by the deed.

Covenant of title. A promise or assurance by a grantor in a deed that she is the owner of the property being transferred, that she has the right to convey it, and that it is free of encumbrances or claims of other persons.

Covenant running with the land. A covenant is said to "run with the land" when both the benefit and the burden created by the covenant attach to or become appurtenant to the lands of the covenantor (promisor) and the covenantee (promisee).

CPM.   Certified Property Manager.

Cul de sac.   A circular turn-around street in a property development.

Curtesy.   At common law, the rights acquired by a husband at the time of marriage in real property owned by his wife.

Damages.   Indemnity or compensation for loss or injury to a person or property resulting from a breach of contract or other wrongful act.

Datum.   A plan of elevation from which heights and depths are measured.

Decedent.   A deceased person.

Declaration of restrictions.   An instrument other than a deed containing restrictive covenants that is incorporated by reference and made part of a deed.

Decree.   A court order as a result of a judicial proceeding.

Dedication.   The gift of an interest in real property to a government for public use.

Deed.   A written instrument that, when legally delivered and accepted, transfers title to real property from one person to another.

Deed of trust.   Also known as a trust deed. A written instrument by means of which a debtor (trustor) transfers title to real estate to a trustee who holds it in trust for a creditor (beneficiary) to secure performance of an obligation owed by the debtor to the creditor.

Default.   The failure of a person to fulfill a duty.

Defeasance clause.   The clause in a mortgage note that allows the mortgagor to redeem his property after all payments due the mortgagee are paid.

Deficiency judgment.   A personal judgment against a mortgagor-debtor for an amount by which the net proceeds of a foreclosure sale of mortgaged property fail to satisfy the defaulted debt.

Delivery of a deed.   Also known as legal delivery. Legal delivery of a properly execu-

ted deed is essential to the transfer of title to real property. Legal delivery is not a formal act, but is entirely a matter of the grantor's intent to make a deed operative. The intent is determined from the grantor's words and conduct and all circumstances surrounding the transaction.

Demise.   The transfer of land by the owner to another person.

Deposit receipt.   A printed form offer that constitutes a receipt for a deposit made by a prospective purchaser of real estate; it becomes a contract when properly signed by the purchaser and accepted and signed by the seller.

Depreciation.   A loss of real property value due to physical deterioration, functional obsolescence, and/or economic obsolescence. Also, a tax-deductible, noncash flow expense.

Deterioration.   Loss of utility due to wear and tear, usage, action of the elements, or disintegration.

Devise.   The transfer of real property by will.

Devisee.   A person to whom real property is transferred by will.

Divided interest.   Ownership of a portion of a larger parcel of property.

Domicile.   The legal residence of a person.

Dominant estate.   The parcel of land that benefits from an easement appurtenant.

Donee.   One who receives a gift.

Donor.   One who makes a gift.

Dower.   At common law, the rights acquired by a wife at the time of marriage in real property owned by her husband.

Due process of law.   A constitutional guarantee that provides protection for rights of individuals in two ways: (a) Procedural due process requires that a person be given notice of the intention to deprive him of his life, liberty, or property and that he be afforded a hearing in which to defend himself. (b) Substantive due process guarantees an individual that she shall not be unreasonably or arbitrarily deprived of life, liberty, or property.

Duress.   Consists of a threat to do, or the actual doing of, a wrongful act that compels another person to enter into a contract through fear.

Earnest money. Money given by a purchaser to show good faith intention to perform the terms of a contract.

Easement. A legal interest that one person has in land belonging to or in the possession of another person that entitles the owner of the easement to use of the other person's land.

Easement appurtenant. An easement that burdens one parcel of land (the servient estate) for the benefit of another parcel (the dominant estate).

Easement by necessity. An easement that is created by operation of law when a grantor conveys a portion of a larger parcel of land and in doing so "landlocks" either the portion that is transferred or the part that is retained.

Easement by prescription. An easement that is acquired by adverse use for a statutory period of time.

Easement in gross. An easement that is not attached to any parcel of land but is merely a personal right to use the land of another.

Economic life. The period of time over which the property is estimated to be profitably utilized.

Economic obsolescence. Loss in property value caused by conditions external to the property.

Economic rent. The rent that a property could generate if it were available today; market rent.

Effective age. The apparent age of a property based on its appearance; may be more than, the same as, or less than the actual or chronological age.

Egress. A means of exit from a parcel of land.

Eminent domain. The power by which government can take private property for public use upon payment of an equitable compensation.

Encroachment. The projection of a building or structure on the land of one owner beyond the common boundary line onto the land or into the airspace of an adjoining owner.

Encumber. To burden a parcel of land with an adverse legal interest.

Encumbrance. Anything that imposes a legal burden on title to land such as liens for security purposes, easements, and restrictive covenants.

Environment. Consists of the totality of human surroundings—the natural and artificial physical, biological, and cultural factors that affect health, senses, and intellect.

Equity. The value of a property owner's interest above the amount of the outstanding mortgage debt.

Equity of redemption. The right of a mortgagor-debtor who is in default on his debt to prevent foreclosure and have the encumbrance of the mortgage removed from his title by paying the full amount of the outstanding debt plus interest and any expenses incurred by the mortgagee-creditor.

Erosion. The loss of land by wearing action of water or wind.

Escalator clause. A contract clause that provides for an upward or downward adjustment in interest, rent, or other factors to cover specified contingencies.

Escheat. The passing of title to property to the state, or a county of a state, when a property owner dies without leaving a will and without heirs.

Escrow. The term refers to a legal arrangement for closing or completing a real estate transaction. In its narrower meaning, an escrow is a written instrument or item of value deposited with an escrow agent to be delivered by her to another person upon the fulfillment of a condition.

Escrow account. Same as impound.

Escrow agent (escrowee). A person or corporation employed by parties to a real estate transaction to receive documents and money and deliver them in accordance with instructions given by the parties.

Escrow agreement (escrow instructions). A contract between the parties to a real estate transaction to effect a settlement of the transaction in escrow.

Escrow instructions (escrow agreement). Instructions given by parties to a real estate transaction to an escrow agent concerning things to be done by him to complete the transaction.

Estate. The nature, quantity, and quality of an ownership interest in real estate that is presently possessory or may become possessory in the future.

Estate at sufferance (tenancy at sufferance). An interest in real property that exists when a tenant (lessee) or mortgagor remains in possession of leased premises or "holds over" after her right to possession has ended.

Estate at will (tenancy at will). An interest in real property that has no fixed period of duration and is terminable at the desire of the owner of the real estate or the tenant.

Estate for life. *See* life estate.

Estate for years (for a term). A legal interest in real property the duration of which is measured by a fixed or definite period of time.

Estate from year-to-year (from period-to-period). A legal interest in real property that continues from week-to-week, month-to-month, or year-to-year.

Estate of inheritance. An estate that may descend to heirs by will or intestate succession.

Estoppel. A doctrine of law that prevents a person from asserting rights that are not consistent with his prior words or conduct.

Ethics. Duties of a member of a profession toward clients, the public, or others in the profession.

Eviction. The physical dispossession by a landlord of a tenant from leased premises.

Exception. A right or portion of property reserved in the grantor in a conveyance by deed.

Exclusive agency listing. A listing agreement between a seller and a broker by which either has a right to sell the property; if sold by the broker, a commission will be due.

Exclusive right to sell. A listing agreement between a seller and a broker whereby the broker receives a commission, regardless of who sells the property.

Exculpatory clause. A clause in an agreement that attempts to absolve one party from liability for personal injury or property damage resulting from her own negligent conduct.

Execute. To sign and deliver an instrument, such as a deed.

Executor. A person specified in a will to carry out the provisions of the will.

Express easement. An easement that comes into being by means of written language that reflects an intent to create it.

Express contract. A contract in which the promises of the parties are revealed in words, either orally or in writing.

Fee simple absolute. The largest estate in real property an owner can own. Estate of inheritance, of indefinite duration, with no restrictions.

Fee simple determinable. An estate in fee simple that terminates automatically upon the happening of a condition.

Fee subject to a condition subsequent. An estate in fee simple that may be terminated by the holder of a right of entry upon the happening of a condition.

FHA. Federal Housing Administration; a federal agency that insures home mortgages.

Fiduciary. A relationship of trust and confidence between a principal and agent.

Financing statement. An instrument filed with the recorder or register of deeds indicating that personal property is encumbered.

Fixture. Anything that originally was personal property but which has been attached to real property in such a manner as to be regarded in law as part of the real property.

Flashing. Sheet metal or other material used around chimneys or other places to prevent water seepage.

Footing. The base on which a home foundation stands.

Forbearance. The giving up of a right to which a person is entitled.

Foreclosure. A legal process by which property serving as security for an obligation is sold when a default occurs.

Forfeiture. The loss of money or right due to default or failure to perform in accord with a contract.

Foundation. The portion of a structure that supports the first floor and construction above it.

Fraud. A false representation or concealment of a material fact, made with knowledge of its falsity and with the intent to mislead, that is justifiably relied on by the one to whom it is made and which results in injury to that person.

Freehold estate. An ownership interest in real property that lasts for an uncertain period of time.

Front foot. A measure of property by which the distance is measured along the street, highway, stream, or other body of water.

Functional obsolescence. Outdated design, fixtures, and other factors within the structure itself that detract from a building value.

Future interest. A legal interest in real property that postpones an owner's right of possession and enjoyment of the property.

General lien. A lien effective against all of a person's property, both real and personal.

Grade. The level of the ground at the structure foundation.

Graduated lease. A lease providing for a variable rate of rent depending upon some future event.

Grant. To transfer or convey a legal interest in property.

Grantee. The person to whom title to real estate is transferred by a deed.

Grantor. The person who transfers title to real estate by a deed.

Gross lease. A lease agreement whereby the property owner pays taxes, insurance, repairs, and other costs.

Ground lease. An agreement for rental of land only.

Ground rent. The portion of property income attributed to the ground value itself; used in a few states whereby a person can own a structure and rent the ground.

Guardian. A person granted power by a court to take care of and manage the property of another person who has been declared legally incapable of administering his own affairs.

Habendum. A provision in a deed that defines the extent of the ownership to be granted to and enjoyed by the grantee.

Heirs. The persons designated by statute to receive an estate where there is no will.

Hereditaments. Any property that can be inherited.

Highest and best use. The use of a property that will yield the greatest return on the property.

Homestead. Any real estate where the owner resides and which is exempt from creditor's claims to an amount specified by state law.

HUD. Federal Department of Housing and Urban Development.

Hypothecate. To give something as security without giving up its possession.

Implied contract. A contract in which no promises are expressly stated (orally or in writing) by the parties, but the existence of the contract and its terms are manifested by the conduct of the parties.

Impound. Account where funds are set aside to pay taxes, insurance, and so forth when due.

Improvements. Structures on real property.

Incapacity. See incompetency.

Inchoate. Not complete, such as a wife's dower interest while the husband is living.

Income approach. A valuation method that capitalizes or converts the net income stream of the property into an estimate of value.

Incompetent. A person who is not legally able to enter into binding contracts due to insanity, senility, insufficient age, mental infirmity, or other reason.

Incorporeal. Rights, such as an easement, that are intangible and without physical existence.

Infant (minor). A person who lacks the legal capacity or competency to alter his legal status by incurring liabilities or acquiring rights because of youthfulness. Depending upon the statutory provisions in a particular state, a person is a minor if he or she is under 18 or 21 years of age.

Ingress. A means of entry to a property.

Inheritance tax. A tax on the right to receive property from a decedent either by will or by intestate succession.

Injunction. An order by a court instructing a person to do or not to do something.

Installment sale contract (land contract, installment contract, and contract for deed). A contract in which an owner-seller of real estate promises to deliver a deed to the buyer at sometime in the future after the buyer will have, in an agreed number of payments of principal and interest, paid the purchase price in full.

Instrument. A written legal document.

Insurable interest. A person's interest in property such that an occurrence of a peril would cause financial loss to that person.

Insurance. A contractual agreement where the insurer agrees to reimburse the insured for financial loss.

Interest. A share or right in property ownership.

Intestate. Dies leaving no will.

Intestate succession. The distribution of the assets of one who dies leaving no will among heirs in accordance with the provisions of a state statute.

Involuntary lien. A lien such as taxes or mechanic's lien imposed without consent of the property owner.

Joint tenancy. Co-ownership of property by two or more persons (joint tenants) in equal shares. Upon the death of a co-owner, his interest in the property passes to the surviving co-owners.

Joint tenant. One who co-owns property in joint tenancy with another person or persons.

Joists. Wood beams in a house to which the floor is nailed and the ceiling lath of the floor below is nailed.

Judgment. A court determination of a legal dispute.

Judgment lien. A lien on real property created by the recording of a court judgment.

Just compensation. A term used in connection with the taking of property by eminent domain that refers to the damages to be awarded to an owner whose property is taken. The damages are measured by the value of the property.

Land. In the narrow use of the word, land consists of the surface of the earth, the airspace above the surface, and the subsurface below it. In its broader use, the word *land* is synonymous with real estate and real property.

Land contract. *See* installment sale contract.

Landlocked. Surrounded by adjacent land with no means of access.

Landlord. A property owner who leases to another person.

Land trust. Trust in which a trustee receives record title to real estate restricted by an ancillary agreement whereby the beneficiary of the trust retains full control and management over the trust real estate.

Latent defect. Concealed defects not easily determined from an inspection of the property.

Lease. A contract between the property owner and another person to use or occupy the land for a set period of time.

Leased fee. The landlord's interest.

Leasehold. A possessory legal interest in real property acquired by a tenant (lessee) when she enters into a rental agreement with the owner of the property (landlord or lessor).

Leasehold estate. The interest of a tenant.

Legal capacity. The legal ability to enter into contracts or to convey title to property.

Legal description. A property description sufficient for use in a deed or other instrument.

Legatee. A person who receives personal property in a will.

Lessee. The tenant in a lease agreement.

Lessor. The landlord in a lease agreement.

Levy. To place a tax on a person or property.

License. A permission granted to use the land of another; also a right granted by the state to engage in a business.

Lien. An encumbrance in which the land serves as security for the payment of a debt or discharge of an obligation.

Life estate. An ownership interest in real property the duration of which is measured by the life or lives of one or more persons.

Life estate pur autre vie. A life estate the duration of which is measured by a lifetime of someone other than the owner of the life estate.

Life tenant. The owner of a life estate.

Lineal heirs. Direct line descendants (i.e., children and grandchildren).

Liquidated damages. A specified sum of money agreed upon by contracting parties that will be received by one of them if the other commits a breach of the contract.

Lis pendens. A notice recorded to indicate that a lawsuit is pending.

Listing (agreement). A contract of employment between an owner (seller) of real estate and a real estate broker that authorizes the latter, as an agent, to find a buyer who is ready, willing, and able to purchase the owner's property.

Lot. A plot of ground.

MAI. A professional designation earned by a member of the American Institute of Real Estate Appraisers qualified to specified requirements.

Marginal land. Land in use that barely pays the cost of working it.

Marketable title (merchantable title). A title to real estate that is so free from defects and encumbrances that there can be no doubt as to its validity nor any reasonable apprehension of danger of litigation with respect to it.

Market approach. The process of property appraisal by comparing it to equivalent properties sold recently.

Market value. The price that property would be expected to bring in the open market under normal conditions.

Meandered. Area such as a lake on which taxes are not paid.

Meander line. The approximate border of a natural body of water.

Mechanic's lien. A lien that can be filed by mechanics or material suppliers; it is against real property created by statute for the purpose of securing payment for services performed or materials furnished in the construction or repair of buildings or making other improvements to land.

Meridian. Map lines running north and south to locate land under the governmental survey system.

Metes and bounds. A method of legal description by use of measurements, boundaries, and directions.

Mineral rights. A legal interest in land that includes the right to remove minerals from land.

Minor. A person not of legal age. (*See* infant.)

Modernization. Replacement of outmoded fixtures, equipment, and other features of an improvement with modern features.

Monument. A fixed object, either natural or artificial.

Mortgage. A written instrument in which real estate is used as security for repayment of a debt or obligation.

Mortgagee. The party who lends money for a mortgage.

Mortgagor. The party who borrows money with property as security.

Multiple listing. A service whereby other brokers in an organization are allowed to sell a listed property.

Mutual assent. An offer to contract made by one party (offeror) and an acceptance given by the party to whom it is made (offeree).

Mutual mistake. In contract law, a mistake is mutual when both parties enter into an agreement under a mistaken assumption concerning a material fact.

Navigable water. A waterway capable of passage by watercraft; navigable if so designated on a U.S. or state map.

Negligence. The failure to exercise reasonable care under the circumstances.

Net lease. A lease agreement in which the tenant pays rent plus all taxes, insurance, repairs, and other costs.

Net listing. A listing agreement whereby the owner receives a set amount if the property is sold and the broker receives all above that amount.

Nominal consideration. Consideration having no relationship to the actual value of the contract or property conveyed.

Nonconforming use. A use of land that lawfully existed before a zoning ordinance was enacted and that is legally continued after the effective date of the ordinance, even though the use no longer conforms to the new zoning regulations.

Nonfreehold estate. Any estate in land other than a fee simple and a life estate.

Notice. To have notice of something is to have knowledge of it. Notice may be either actual or constructive (public).

Nuisance. The wrongful interference by one person with the use and enjoyment of real estate owned by another.

Obsolescence. Loss in value due to obsolete or out-of-date design or construction.

Offer. A promise made by one person (the offeror) to another person (the offeree) which by its terms invites the formation of a contract.

Open end mortgage. A mortgage agreement such that the mortgagor can borrow additional funds in the future without rewriting the mortgage.

Open listing. A listing agreement whereby either the owner or the broker can sell the property; if the broker is the procuring cause, a commission is due.

Option. A contract by the terms of which one party obligates herself to hold an offer open for a stated period of time.

Optionee. A person who holds an option.

Optionor. An owner who gives an option to another person.

Ordinance. A law passed by the legislative body.

Overhang. The portion of a roof extending beyond the walls.

Package mortgage. A mortgage that includes personal property as part of the security.

Partition. An action seeking to have property owned by two or more persons sold and the proceeds divided between the parties, or to have the property divided into two or more portions.

Partnership. An association of two or more persons to carry on a business for profit as co-owners.

Party wall. A wall erected on the line between two adjacent properties for the use of both parties.

Patent. A grant of title to land by a government or sovereign of a country to one or more individuals.

Percentage lease. A lease whereby the fee paid is a percentage of the income from business done on the premises.

Personal property. Same as chattel. All things, tangible and intangible, capable of being owned, that are not real property.

Physical depreciation. Physical deterioration and concurrent loss in property value caused by wear, tear, and decay of the property.

Plat. A map showing how a property is subdivided into lots.

Plottage. The process of combining two or more plots of ground together, resulting in greater utility and value than when held separately.

Point of beginning. The starting point in a metes and bounds legal description.

Police power. The inherent power of the state to enact legislation to promote the health, safety, morals, and general welfare of society by reasonable regulation of individual rights.

Possession. Actual control or the right to control.

Possibility of reverter. A legal interest in real property that causes title to automatically vest in the owner of the interest when a fee simple determinable comes to an end because of the occurrence of a condition.

Power of attorney. A written instrument in which one person authorizes another to act in his or her behalf.

Prefabricated home. Home built or partially assembled prior to delivery to the building site.

Prepayment penalty. A penalty for payment of a mortgage balance before it is due.

Prescription. Acquiring a right in property by means of adverse use of the property that is continuous for the period established by statute.

Prescriptive easement. An easement obtained by adverse use.

Principal. The person who employs an agent. Also, the amount of a loan.

Principal meridian. One of the north and south survey lines established to locate property.

Probate. In its narrower sense, to establish the authenticity of a will in an appropriate court. In its broader sense, probate refers to all matters pertaining to the estates of deceased persons over which probate courts have jurisdiction.

Procuring cause. The broker or other person who was the prime factor in bringing about the sale of a property.

Profit. Also known as *profit à prendre.* The right of a person to enter upon the land of another person and remove something from it.

Promise. An assurance by a person (promisor) that he will conduct himself in a certain way or bring about a specified result in the future, which is communicated to another person (promisee).

Promissory note. A written promise of a person (maker) to pay a specified sum of money to another person (payee) in accordance with terms and conditions agreed upon by the parties.

Property. The term is used in two senses: (a) to refer to rights that a person has in something that is owned; and (b) to refer to the object itself in which such rights exist.

Proration. A division of taxes, interest, insurance, and so forth, so that the seller and the buyer each pays the portion covering her or his period of ownership.

Publication. A formal declaration made by a testator at the time of signing a will that it is his or her last will and testament.

Purchase money mortgage. A mortgage taken by the seller as part of the purchase price.

Quasi. Similar to but not actually.

Quiet enjoyment. Right of property owner to use his property without adverse claims of another to title or interest.

Quitclaim deed. A deed that conveys title or interest, if any, which the grantor has in the property.

Rafter. A board that supports the roof of a house.

Raw land. Land with no improvements.

Real estate. Real property; land and improvements to the land.

Real property. Real estate.

REALTOR®. A registered trademark for use of active members of the NATIONAL ASSOCIATION OF REALTORS®.

Recordation. The process by which instruments relating to legal interests in real estate are reproduced in official records and are available to the public.

Recovery fund. A fund established in some states by fees from licensed brokers and salespeople to reimburse individuals for actual unrecoverable losses due to wrongful acts of licensees.

Rectangular survey system. A system for legal description of property based on principal meridians, baselines, and a grid system.

Redemption. Buying back one's property subsequent to a court sale.

Rehabilitation. Restoration of existing structure without changing its floor plan or style.

Release. The act of relinquishment, concession, or giving up of a right, claim, or privilege by the person in whom it exists or to whom it accrues to the person against whom it might have been demanded or enforced.

Remainder. An estate in land where the right of possession and enjoyment of the property is postponed until after the termination of a life estate.

Remainderman. The person designated as being entitled to own an estate after a life estate has terminated.

Remedy. Legal relief available through court action to redress a wrong.

Rent. Consideration paid for use of property.

Replacement cost. The cost incurred in replacing one property with another of similar utility, using modernized equipment, materials, and techniques.

Reproduction cost. The cost of reproducing an exact replica property based on current prices.

Rescind. To avoid a contract and restore the contracting parties to the legal and monetary positions they enjoyed prior to the contract.

Reservation. A right kept by a grantor when conveying property.

RESPA. Real Estate Settlement Procedures Act.

Restriction. An encumbrance created by deed or special agreement that limits use of the property.

Reversion. The portion of an estate remaining with the original grantor after the termination of a leasehold or life estate.

Revocation. The withdrawal of an offer by the offeror before it has been accepted by the offeree.

Right. A legal interest protected by the law.

Right of entry. The right to bring legal action to terminate a fee subject to a condition subsequent upon the happening of a prohibited condition.

Right of redemption. A person's right by law to buy back property taken by forced sale for a period of time stated by law.

Right of severance. The right of a joint tenant to terminate or "sever" his co-ownership interest in property by transferring that interest to another person with or without the consent of the other joint tenants.

Right of survivorship. An incident of co-ownership by means of which a deceased co-owner's interest in property passes to the surviving co-owner rather than to the descendent's estate.

Right of way. The right to cross over or under another person's property for ingress, egress, utility lines, sewers, and so forth.

Riparian rights. Rights of an owner of property abutting water to use the water and have uninterrupted flow.

Rod. A measure of length equal to 16½ ft.

Run with the land. Easements or restrictions are said to run with the land when they do not expire when ownership is transferred.

Rural. Pertaining to the country, rather than urban.

Satisfaction. Discharge of lien upon payment of debt.

Seal. An impression made to attest to the execution of a written instrument; also the word "seal" typed in to form a sealed document.

Section. A unit of land measure one mile square containing 640 acres.

Seizin. The possession of land under a claim of freehold estate.

Separate property. In states recognizing community property, separate property is any property owned by either spouse before marriage or property acquired by either spouse by gift or inheritance.

Septic tank. An underground tank used for sewage treatment where city sewage is not available.

Servient estate. Land that carries the burden of an easement.

Servient owner. The owner of a parcel of land (servient estate) that is burdened by an easement.

Setback. A distance from the curb to the building. Often a minimum setback is specified by ordinance.

Settlement. The process of completing the sale of real property. Same as closing.

Severalty. Sole ownership; by one person.

Severance. Take from the land, such as minerals or timber.

Sheriff's deed. A deed given as a result of a court order to sell property in satisfaction of a judgment.

Signature. The act of writing a person's name or making a mark or symbol with the intent that it attest the validity of a written instrument.

Site. A plot of ground upon which anything is, has been, or will be located.

Situs. Location.

Special assessment. An assessment against real estate to pay for improvements such as sidewalks, curbs, street lights, or other items which benefit certain property owners.

Special warranty deed. A form of deed whereby the grantor warrants the title only against claims generated while the grantor owned the property.

Specification. A document describing requirements for a house, subdivision, or other project.

Specific lien. A lien that affects only a single parcel of property.

Specific performance. A legal action to compel the performance of the terms of an agreement, such as the sale of a home.

Spot zoning. Zoning that sets aside certain areas for purposes different from the general area requirements.

Statement of record. A statement that must be filed with HUD for lot sales subject to the Interstate Land Sales Full Disclosure Act.

Statute. State or federal legislative law.

Statute of Frauds. The state law which requires that certain contracts, including those for the sale of real property, must be in writing.

Statutory right of redemption. A right given to a mortgagor-debtor by statute in some states that enables her to buy back her property from the bidder who purchased it at a foreclosure sale.

Strawman. One who purchases property for another in order to conceal the identity of the real purchaser.

Strict foreclosure. A court decree vesting title to mortgaged property in the mortgagee upon the default of the mortgagor without any sale of the property.

Stud. Vertical timbers in a house wall.

Subdivision. A tract of land divided into lots suitable for residential purposes.

Subject to. The purchase of real property subject to a mortgage, whereby the original holder remains personally liable for the mortgage.

Sublease. A transfer to another person by a tenant of a legal interest in leased premises that is less than the tenant's leasehold interest.

Subordinate. To make a mortgage subservient to another mortgage.

Subsequent purchaser for value. A purchaser for value in good faith and without notice of any adverse interest in the property purchased.

Survey. The process that determines the shape, area, and position of a parcel of land by locating its boundaries.

Syndicate. A group of persons joining together to deal in real property for profit.

Tangible. Existing physically; that which can be touched.

Tax. A levy for governmental purposes.

Tax deed. A deed to real estate executed and delivered by a county officer to the successful purchaser at a tax foreclosure sale.

Tax lien. A charge against property that makes it security for unpaid taxes.

Tax sale. Sale of property as a result of nonpayment of taxes.

Tenancy at sufferance (estate at sufferance). An interest in real property that exists when a tenant (lessee) or mortgagor remains in possession of leased premises or "holds over" after his right to possession has ended.

Tenancy at will. An interest in real property that has no fixed period of duration and is terminable at the desire of the landlord or the tenant.

Tenancy by the entirety. A form of co-ownership of property between husband and wife, each having an equal undivided interest and the right of survivorship.

Tenancy for a term (estate for years). An ownership interest in real property created by a lease, the duration of which is measured by a fixed or definite period of time.

Tenancy from period-to-period. See estate from year-to-year.

Tenancy in common. Co-ownership of property by two or more persons whose shares may be unequal and among whom there is no right of survivorship.

Tenements. Rights in real property that pass with conveyance of the property.

Termites. Antlike insects that eat wood and cause destruction.

Testamentary disposition. A transfer of property by will at death.

Testate. Having a will.

Testator. One who makes a will.

Tideland. Land that is covered by water at high tide and uncovered at low tide.

Time is of the essence. A contract clause that makes it essential that the provisions be carried out at the specified time.

Title. The term is used in two ways: (a) ownership (all the rights an owner may have with respect to land); (b) the evidence upon which ownership is based.

Title defect. An adverse right of one person to an interest in another person's title.

Title insurance. A policy of title insurance is a contract according to the terms of which a title insurance company obligates itself to indemnify a buyer or a lender against losses resulting from defects in the title to a specified parcel of land.

Title of record. Title as revealed in public records.

Title search. An examination of public records pertaining to a parcel of land to determine the status of ownership of the property.

Topography. The nature of the surface of land, such as level, rolling, and so forth.

Torrens system. A system of land title registration that makes the status of title to land ascertainable from a certificate issued by a public official.

Tort. A civil wrong against a person or his property.

Tort liability. The responsibility of one who commits a tort to pay damages to one who sustains injury or property damage as a result of her wrongful conduct.

Township. A unit in the governmental survey system six miles square.

Tract. An area of land.

Trade fixture. An item of personal property attached to leased premises by a tenant for purposes of use in her trade or business.

Transaction. A business deal.

Trespass. The unlawful entry upon another's land or interference with an occupant's right of possession of it.

Trust. Title to property, real or personal, held by a trustee for the benefit of a beneficiary.

Trust deed. See deed of trust.

Trustee. A person who receives property or title to property under an agreement to hold it for the benefit of another (beneficiary).

Trustee's deed. A deed by a trustee to convey land held in trust.

Undue influence. A circumstance in which one person who is under the domination of another is induced to do something he would not otherwise have done had it not been for the unfair persuasion by the dominant party.

Unenforceable contract. An otherwise valid contract that fails to meet the requirements of some particular statute or rule of law and thus is not entitled to a legal remedy when it is breached.

Unilateral contract. A contract in which one of the parties has made a promise in exchange for an act or forbearance.

Unilateral mistake. A mistake is unilateral when only one party enters the agreement under an erroneous assumption concerning a material fact.

Urban. Property in a city or heavily settled area.

Usury.   Interest on a loan at a rate higher than allowed by law.

VA.   Veterans Administration.

Valuable consideration.   A right, interest, profit, or benefit accruing to one party or some forbearance, detriment, loss, or responsibility given or suffered by a party to a deed or contract.

Value.   The dollar amount that property will bring in the open market.

Variance.   The right to deviate from the use of land prescribed by an existing zoning ordinance.

Vendee.   The buyer.

Vendor.   The seller.

Vest.   To give an interest in property.

Vested remainder.   An estate in land, the possession and enjoyment of which is delayed only until the termination of a preceding estate.

Void.   Having no legal or binding effect.

Voidable.   Subject to being rescinded.

Voidable contract.   An agreement that is binding on its parties until one of them exercising her rights elects to rescind the agreement.

Voidable deed.   A voidable deed transfers voidable title until the grantor or his legal respresentative has the transfer rescinded or avoided because of fraud, undue influence, infancy, duress, mental infirmity, or other legal reason.

Voluntary lien.   A lien created by an agreement, such as a mortgage, that results in a debt.

Ward.   An infant or other legally incompetent person placed by court under the care of a guardian or conservator.

Warranty.   *See* covenant.

Warranty deed.   A deed that includes covenants of (a) seizin, (b) right to quiet enjoyment, (c) freedom from encumbrances, (d) further assurance, and (e) warranty forever.

Waste.   The neglect, misuse, alteration, or destruction of land by a person rightfully in possession that causes a substantial and permanent decrease of its value to the estate or legal interest owned by another person.

Water rights.   Rights associated with the use of water adjacent to, in, or underneath property.

Will.   An oral or written declaration by an owner by means of which he makes a disposition of his property to take effect upon his death.

Witnessed will (formal will).   A written will that is signed by the maker (testator) whose signature is witnessed or attested to by witnesses whose signatures must also appear on the will.

Wraparound mortgage.   A second mortgage that includes an existing mortgage.

Zoning.   The term denotes the division of an area or community by a government into districts or zones with regulations as to the use of land varying from one zone to another.

Residential Construction Nomenclature

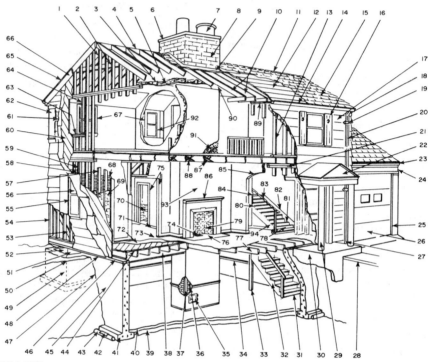

1 GABLE STUD	31 BASEMENT STAIR RISER	63 ROUGH HEADER
2 COLLAR BEAM	32 STAIR STRINGER	64 WINDOW STUD
3 CEILING JOIST	33 GIRDER POST	65 CORNICE MOULDING
4 RIDGE BOARD	34 CHAIR RAIL	66 FRIEZE OR BARGE BOARD
5 INSULATION	35 CLEANOUT DOOR	67 WINDOW CASING
6 CHIMNEY CAP	36 FURRING STRIPS	68 LATH
7 CHIMNEY POTS	37 CORNER STUD	69 INSULATION
8 CHIMNEY	38 GIRDER	70 WAINSCOTING
9 CHIMNEY FLASHING	39 CINDER OR GRAVEL FILL	71 BASEBOARD
10 RAFTERS	40 CONCRETE BASEMENT FLOOR	72 BUILDING PAPER
11 RIDGE	41 FOOTING FOR FOUNDATION WALL	73 FINISH FLOOR
12 ROOF BOARDS	42 PAPER STRIP	74 ASH DUMP
13 STUD	43 FOUNDATION DRAIN TILE	75 DOOR TRIM
14 EAVE TROUGH OR GUTTER	44 DIAGONAL SUBFLOORING	76 FIREPLACE HEARTH
15 ROOFING	45 FOUNDATION WALL	77 FLOOR JOISTS
16 BLIND OR SHUTTER	46 SILL	78 STAIR RISER
17 BEVEL SIDING	47 BACKFILL	79 FIRE BRICK
18 DOWNSPOUT OR LEADER GOOSENECK	48 TERMITE SHIELD	80 NEWEL CAP
19 DOWNSPOUT OR LEADER STRAP	49 AREAWAY WALL	81 STAIR TREAD
20 DOWNSPOUT OR LEADER CONDUCTOR	50 GRADE LINE	82 FINISH STRINGER
21 DOUBLE PLATE	51 BASEMENT SASH	83 STAIR RAIL
22 ENTRANCE CANOPY	52 AREAWAY	84 BALUSTERS
23 GARAGE CORNICE	53 CORNER BRACE	85 PLASTER ARCH
24 FRIEZE	54 CORNER STUDS	86 MANTEL
25 DOOR JAMB	55 WINDOW FRAME	87 FLOOR PLATE
26 GARAGE DOOR	56 WINDOW LIGHT	88 BRIDGING
27 DOWNSPOUT OR LEADER SHOE	57 WALL STUDS	89 LOOKOUT
28 SIDEWALK	58 HEADER	90 ATTIC SPACE
29 ENTRANCE POST	59 WINDOW CRIPPLE	91 METAL LATH
30 ENTRANCE PLATFORM	60 WALL SHEATHING	92 WINDOW SASH
	61 BUILDING PAPER	93 CHIMNEY BREAST
	62 PILASTER	94 NEWEL

Source: Marshall & Swift Publication Co., Los Angeles, Calif.

State Commissions and Their Publications

Alabama

Alabama Real Estate Commission
750 Washington St.
Montgomery 36130
*Alabama Real Estate Law
Update* (Newsletter)

Alaska

Department of Commerce and Economic Development
Real Estate Division
Pouch "D"
Juneau 99811
Real Estate Brokers and Salesmen

Arizona

Department of Real Estate
1645 W. Jefferson
Phoenix 85007
Instructions to License Applicants

Arkansas

Authority of Arkansas Real Estate Commission
P.O. Box 3173, 101 Main St.
Little Rock 72203
*Real Estate License Law and Regulations
Arkansas Real Estate Examinations*

California

California Department of Real Estate
714 P St.
Sacramento 95814
*Instructions to License Applicants
Real Estate Law
Real Estate Education in California*
(several others)

Colorado

Colorado Real Estate Commission
1525 Sherman St.
Denver 80203
*Colorado Real Estate Commission
Real Estate Manual*

Connecticut

> Real Estate Commission
> 90 West Washington St.
> Hartford 06115
>> *Real Estate Licensing, Law and Regulations Concerning the Conduct of Real Estate Brokers and Salesmen*

Delaware

> Delaware Real Estate Commission
> Department of Administrative Services, Division of Business and Occupational Regulation
> State House Annex
> Dover 19901
>> *Real Estate License Act and Primer*
>> *Newsletter*

District of Columbia

> Real Estate Commission
> 614 H Street N.W.
> Washington 20001

Florida

> Florida Real Estate Commission
> State Office Building
> 400 W. Robinson St., P.O. Box 1900
> Orlando 32802
>> *Florida Real Estate License Law*
>> *Florida Real Estate Commission Handbook*
>> *Broker's Course Textbook*

Georgia

> Real Estate Commission
> 40 Pryor St. S.W.
> Atlanta 30303
>> *Georgia Real Estate Manual*

Hawaii

> Real Estate Commission
> P.O. Box 3469
> Honolulu 96801
>> *Hawaii Real Estate License Law*

Idaho

> Real Estate Commission
> 633 North 4th Street
> Boise 83702
>> *Idaho Real Estate Brokers Law*
>> *Certification of Real Estate Schools*
>> *Real Estate Education in Idaho*
>> *The Real Estatement* (quarterly)

Illinois

Department of Registration and Education
628 E. Adams
Springfield 62786
Real Estate Brokers and Salesman License Act
Rules and Regulations

Indiana

Indiana Real Estate Commission
State Office Building, Room 1022
100 N. Senate Ave.
Indianapolis 46204
Real Estate License Laws
Indiana Real Estate Law and Practice Manual

Iowa

Iowa Real Estate Commission
1223 East Court Ave.
Des Moines 50319
Real Estate License Law
Real Estate Rules and Regulations

Kansas

Kansas Real Estate Commission
535 Kansas Ave., Room 1212
Topeka 66603
Kansas Real Estate Broker's License Law
Kansas Real Estate Recovery Fund Act

Kentucky

Kentucky State Real Estate Commission
100 E. Liberty St., Suite 204
Louisville 40202
Law Governing Real Estate Brokers and Salespersons

Louisiana

Real Estate Commission
P.O. Box 14785
Baton Rouge 70808
Louisiana Real Estate License Law
Louisiana Real Estate Commission Rules and Regulations
Louisiana Real Estate Manual
Louisiana Real Estate Newsletter

Maine

Maine Real Estate Commission
State Office Building
Augusta 04333
License Law, Rules and Regulations
Real Estate Transaction Handbook

Maryland

> Maryland Real Estate Commission
> 1 South Calvert St.
> Baltimore 21202
> > *Real Estate Law*

Massachusetts

> Board of Registration of Real Estate Brokers and Salesmen
> Leverett Saltonstall Building
> 100 Cambridge St.
> Boston 02202
> > *Division of Registration, Rules and Regulations*

Michigan

> Department of Licensing and Regulation
> P.O. Box 30018
> Lansing 48909
> > *Real Estate Red Book, Real Estate License Laws and Rules*

Minnesota

> Department of Administration
> St. Paul 55155
> > *Minnesota Law, Real Estate Regulations*

Mississippi

> Mississippi Real Estate Commission
> P.O. Box 2454
> Jackson 39205
> > *Real Estate Brokers License Act*
> > *Rules and Regulations, Code of Ethics*

Missouri

> Missouri Real Estate Commission
> 3523 North Ten Mile Drive, P.O. Box 1339
> Jefferson City 65102
> > *Missouri Real Estate Commission, Rules and Regulations*

Montana

> Board of Real Estate
> 42½ North Main
> Helena 59601
> > *Real Estate Act*

Nebraska

> Nebraska Real Estate Commission
> 301 Centennial Mall South, P.O. Box 94667
> Lincoln 68509
> > *Nebraska Real Estate License Laws and Rules and Regulations*
> > *Nebraska Real Estate Appraiser License Act*
> > *Commission Comments* (quarterly)
> > *Nebraska Real Estate Manual*
> > *Directory of Licensed Brokers and Salespersons*
> > *Directory of Licensed Appraisers*

Nevada

Real Estate Division, Department of Commerce
201 South Fall St.
Carson City 89710
Nevada Handbook for Real Estate Licensees

New Hampshire

Real Estate Commission
3 Capital St.
Concord 03301
Real Estate Law
Rules and Regulations

New Jersey

Division of the New Jersey Real Estate Commission
201 East State St., P.O. Box 1510
Trenton 08625
The New Jersey Real Estate License Act and Rules and Regulations

New Mexico

The New Mexico Real Estate Commission
600 Second Ave. N.W., Suite 608
Albuquerque 87102
State of New Mexico Real Estate Law and Rules and Regulations
Real Estate Education Program Handbook

New York

Department of State, Division of Licensing Services
162 Washington Ave.
Albany 12231
Real Estate Salespersons
License Law for Brokers

North Carolina

North Carolina Real Estate Licensing Board
P.O. Box 27447
Raleigh 27611
North Carolina Real Estate Licensing Law
North Carolina Real Estate Licensing Board

North Dakota

North Dakota Real Estate Commission
P.O. Box 727
Bismarck 58501
Real Estate License Law and Commission Rules and Regulations
Real Estate News and Views (quarterly)

Ohio

Ohio Division of Real Estate and Ohio Real Estate Commission
180 E. Broad St.
Columbus 43215
Real Estate License Law and Commerce Rules

Oklahoma

The Oklahoma Real Estate Institute
4040 Lincoln Blvd., Suite 100
Oklahoma City 73105
Oklahoma Real Estate License Code and Rules and Regulations

Oregon

Department of Commerce, Real Estate Division
158 12th St. N.E.
Salem 97310
Oregon Real Estate Manual
Directory of Real Estate Salespersons and Brokers
Oregon Real Estate News Journal

Pennsylvania

Commissioner of Professional and Occupational Affairs
State Real Estate Commission
P.O. Box 2649
Harrisburg 17120
Rules and Regulations of the State Real Estate Commission
Real Estate Brokers License Act

Rhode Island

Rhode Island Real Estate Division
Department of Business Regulation
100 North Main St.
Providence 02903
Real Estate Licensing Laws and Rules and Regulations

South Carolina

South Carolina Real Estate Commission
2221 Devine St.
Columbia 29205
License Laws and Regulations

South Dakota

South Dakota State Real Estate Commission
P.O. Box 490
Pierre 57501
South Dakota Real Estate License Laws and Rules and Regulations

Tennessee

The Tennessee Real Estate Commission
556 Capitol Hill Building
Nashville 37219
Real Estate Manual

Texas

Texas Real Estate Commission
P.O. Box 12188, Capitol Station
Austin 78711
The Real Estate License Act
Rules of the Texas Real Estate Commission
Study Material for Applicants

Utah

Department of Business Regulation, Real Estate Division
330 E. Fourth St.
Salt Lake City 84111
Real Estate License Law
Utah Uniform Land Sales Practices Act
Real Estate Recovery Fund Act
Utah Real Estate News (quarterly)

Vermont

Vermont Real Estate Commission
Montpelier 05602
Vermont Statutes Annotated, Chapter 41 Real Estate Brokers and Salesmen
Rules of the Vermont Real Estate Commission
Roster of Licensed Real Estate Brokers and Salesmen

Virginia

Virginia Real Estate Commission
P.O. Box 1–X
Richmond 23202
Virginia Real Estate Commission Manual
Educational Requirements for Real Estate Applicants

Washington

Department of Licensing, Real Estate Division
P.O. Box 247
Olympia 98504
Law Governing Licensing of Real Estate Brokers and Salesmen
Law—Escrow Agent Registration Act
Real Estate News

West Virginia

West Virginia Real Estate Commission
1033 Quarrier St., Suite 400
Charleston 25301
West Virginia Real Estate License Law and Administrative Regulations

Wisconsin

Real Estate Examining Board
1400 East Washington Ave.
Madison 53702
Wisconsin Real Estate Law

Wyoming

Wyoming Real Estate Commission
Supreme Court Building
Cheyenne 82002
Wyoming Real Estate Laws and Regulations
Wyoming Real Estate Manual

Present Value Tables

Annual compound interest (8%)—Effective rate = 8%; Base = 1.08

	1 AMOUNT OF I AT COMPOUND INTEREST $S^n = (1+i)^n$	2 ACCUMULATION OF I PER PERIOD $S_{\overline{n}|} = \dfrac{S^n - 1}{i}$	3 SINKING FUND FACTOR $1\,S_{\overline{n}|} = \dfrac{i}{S^n - 1}$	4 PRES. VALUE REVERSION OF I $V^n = \dfrac{1}{S^n}$	5 PRESENT VALUE ORD. ANNUITY I PER PERIOD $a_{\overline{n}|} = \dfrac{1 - V^n}{i}$	6 INSTALMENT TO AMORTIZE I $1\,a_{\overline{n}|} = \dfrac{i}{1 - V^n}$	n YEARS
1	1.080000	1.000000	1.000000	.925926	.925926	1.080000	1
2	1.166400	2.080000	.480769	.857339	1.783265	.560769	2
3	1.259712	3.246400	.308034	.793832	2.577097	.388034	3
4	1.360489	4.506112	.221921	.735030	3.312127	.301921	4
5	1.469328	5.866601	.170456	.680583	3.992710	.250456	5
6	1.586874	7.335929	.136315	.630170	4.622880	.216315	6
7	1.713824	8.922803	.112072	.583490	5.206370	.192072	7
8	1.850930	10.636628	.094015	.540269	5.746639	.174015	8
9	1.999005	12.487558	.080080	.500249	6.246888	.160080	9
10	2.158925	14.486562	.069029	.463193	6.710081	.149029	10
11	2.331639	16.645487	.060076	.428883	7.138964	.140076	11
12	2.518170	18.977126	.052695	.397114	7.536078	.132695	12
13	2.719624	21.495297	.046522	.367698	7.903776	.126522	13
14	2.937194	24.214920	.041297	.340461	8.244237	.121297	14
15	3.172169	27.152114	.036830	.315242	8.559479	.116830	15
16	3.425943	30.324283	.032977	.291890	8.851369	.112977	16
17	3.700018	33.750226	.029629	.270269	9.121638	.109629	17
18	3.996019	37.450244	.026702	.250249	9.371887	.106702	18
19	4.315701	41.446263	.024128	.231712	9.603599	.104128	19
20	4.660957	45.761964	.021852	.214548	9.818147	.101852	20
21	5.033834	50.422921	.019832	.198656	10.016803	.099832	21
22	5.436540	55.456755	.018032	.183941	10.200744	.098032	22
23	5.871464	60.893296	.016422	.170315	10.371059	.096422	23
24	6.341181	66.764759	.014978	.157699	10.528758	.094978	24
25	6.848475	73.105940	.013679	.146018	10.674776	.093679	25
26	7.396353	79.954415	.012507	.135202	10.809978	.092507	26
27	7.988061	87.350768	.011448	.125187	10.935165	.091448	27
28	8.627106	95.338830	.010489	.115914	11.051078	.090489	28
29	9.317275	103.965936	.009619	.107328	11.158406	.089619	29
30	10.062657	113.283211	.008827	.099377	11.257783	.088827	30
31	10.867669	123.345868	.008107	.092016	11.349799	.088107	31
32	11.737083	134.213537	.007451	.085200	11.434999	.087451	32
33	12.676050	145.950620	.006852	.078889	11.513888	.086852	33
34	13.690134	158.626670	.006304	.073045	11.586934	.086304	34
35	14.785344	172.316804	.005803	.067635	11.654568	.085803	35
36	15.968172	187.102148	.005345	.062625	11.717193	.085345	36
37	17.245626	203.070320	.004924	.057986	11.775179	.084924	37
38	18.625276	220.315945	.004539	.053690	11.828869	.084539	38
39	20.115298	238.941221	.004185	.049713	11.878582	.084185	39
40	21.724521	259.056519	.003860	.046031	11.924613	.083860	40
41	23.462483	280.781040	.003561	.042621	11.967235	.083561	41
42	25.339482	304.243523	.003287	.039464	12.006699	.083287	42
43	27.366640	329.583005	.003034	.036541	12.043240	.083034	43
44	29.555972	356.949646	.002802	.033834	12.077074	.082802	44
45	31.920449	386.505617	.002587	.031328	12.108401	.082587	45
46	34.474085	418.426067	.002390	.029007	12.137409	.082390	46
47	37.232012	452.900152	.002208	.026859	12.164267	.082208	47
48	40.210573	490.132164	.002040	.024869	12.189136	.082040	48
49	43.427419	530.342737	.001886	.023027	12.212163	.081886	49
50	46.901613	573.770156	.001743	.021321	12.233485	.081743	50
51	50.653742	620.671769	.001611	.019742	12.253227	.081611	51
52	54.706041	671.325510	.001490	.018280	12.271506	.081490	52
53	59.082524	726.031551	.001377	.016925	12.288432	.081377	53
54	63.809126	785.114075	.001274	.015672	12.304103	.081274	54
55	68.913856	848.923201	.001178	.014511	12.318614	.081178	55
56	74.426965	917.837058	.001090	.013436	12.332050	.081090	56
57	80.381122	992.264022	.001008	.012441	12.344491	.081008	57
58	86.811612	1072.645144	.000932	.011519	12.356010	.080932	58
59	93.756540	1159.456755	.000862	.010666	12.366676	.080862	59
60	101.257064	1253.213296	.000798	.009876	12.376552	.080798	60

Table D–2
Annual compound interest (9%)—Effective rate = 9%; Base = 1.09

YEARS	1 AMOUNT OF I AT COMPOUND INTEREST $s^n = (1+i)^n$	2 ACCUMULATION OF I PER PERIOD $S_{\overline{n}|} = \frac{s^n-1}{i}$	3 SINKING FUND FACTOR $1.S_{\overline{n}|} = \frac{i}{s^n-1}$	4 PRES. VALUE REVERSION OF I $v^n = \frac{1}{s^n}$	5 PRESENT VALUE ORD. ANNUITY 1 PER PERIOD $a_{\overline{n}|} = \frac{1-v^n}{i}$	6 INSTALMENT TO AMORTIZE I $1/a_{\overline{n}|} = \frac{i}{1-v^n}$	n YEARS
1	1.090000	1.000000	1.000000	.917431	.917431	1.090000	1
2	1.188100	2.090000	.478469	.841680	1.759111	.568469	2
3	1.295029	3.278100	.305055	.772183	2.531295	.395055	3
4	1.411582	4.573129	.218669	.708425	3.239720	.308669	4
5	1.538624	5.984711	.167092	.649931	3.889651	.257092	5
6	1.667100	7.523335	.132920	.596267	4.485919	.222920	6
7	1.828039	9.200435	.108691	.547034	5.032953	.198691	7
8	1.992563	11.028474	.090674	.501866	5.534819	.180674	8
9	2.171893	13.021036	.076799	.460428	5.995247	.166799	9
10	2.367364	15.192930	.065820	.422411	6.417658	.155820	10
11	2.580426	17.560293	.056947	.387533	6.805191	.146947	11
12	2.812665	20.140720	.049651	.355535	7.160725	.139651	12
13	3.065805	22.953385	.043567	.326179	7.486904	.133567	13
14	3.341727	26.019189	.038433	.299246	7.786150	.128433	14
15	3.642482	29.360916	.034059	.274538	8.060688	.124059	15
16	3.970306	33.003399	.030300	.251870	8.312558	.120300	16
17	4.327633	36.973705	.027046	.231073	8.543631	.117046	17
18	4.717120	41.301338	.024212	.211994	8.755625	.114212	18
19	5.141661	46.018458	.021730	.194490	8.950115	.111730	19
20	5.604411	51.160120	.019546	.178431	9.128546	.109546	20
21	6.108808	56.764530	.017617	.163698	9.292244	.107617	21
22	6.658600	62.873338	.015905	.150182	9.442425	.105905	22
23	7.257874	69.531939	.014382	.137781	9.580207	.104382	23
24	7.911083	76.789813	.013023	.126405	9.706612	.103023	24
25	8.623081	84.700896	.011806	.115968	9.822580	.101806	25
26	9.399158	93.323977	.010715	.106393	9.928972	.100715	26
27	10.245082	102.723135	.009735	.097608	10.026580	.099735	27
28	11.167140	112.968217	.008852	.089548	10.116128	.098852	28
29	12.172182	124.135356	.008056	.082155	10.198283	.098056	29
30	13.267678	136.307539	.007336	.075371	10.273654	.097336	30
31	14.461770	149.575217	.006686	.069148	10.342802	.096686	31
32	15.763329	164.036987	.006096	.063438	10.406240	.096096	32
33	17.182028	179.800315	.005562	.058200	10.464441	.095562	33
34	18.728411	196.982344	.005077	.053395	10.517835	.095077	34
35	20.413968	215.710755	.004636	.048986	10.566821	.094636	35
36	22.251225	236.124723	.004235	.044941	10.611763	.094235	36
37	24.253835	258.375948	.003870	.041231	10.652993	.093870	37
38	26.436680	282.629783	.003538	.037826	10.690820	.093538	38
39	28.815982	309.066463	.003236	.034703	10.725523	.093236	39
40	31.409420	337.882445	.002960	.031838	10.757360	.092960	40
41	34.236268	369.291865	.002708	.029209	10.786569	.092708	41
42	37.317532	403.528133	.002478	.026797	10.813366	.092478	42
43	40.676110	440.845665	.002268	.024584	10.837951	.092268	43
44	44.336960	481.521775	.002077	.022555	10.860505	.092077	44
45	48.327286	525.858735	.001902	.020692	10.881197	.091902	45
46	52.676742	574.186021	.001742	.018984	10.900181	.091742	46
47	57.417649	626.862762	.001595	.017416	10.917597	.091595	47
48	62.585237	684.280411	.001461	.015978	10.933575	.091461	48
49	68.217908	746.865648	.001339	.014659	10.948234	.091339	49
50	74.357520	815.083556	.001227	.013449	10.961683	.091227	50
51	81.049697	889.441077	.001124	.012338	10.974021	.091124	51
52	88.344170	970.490773	.001030	.011319	10.985340	.091030	52
53	96.295145	1058.834943	.000944	.010385	10.995725	.090944	53
54	104.961708	1155.130088	.000866	.009527	11.005252	.090866	54
55	114.408262	1260.091796	.000794	.008741	11.013993	.090794	55
56	124.705005	1374.500057	.000728	.008019	11.022012	.090728	56
57	135.928456	1499.205063	.000667	.007357	11.029369	.090667	57
58	148.162017	1635.133518	.000612	.006749	11.036118	.090612	58
59	161.496598	1783.295535	.000561	.006192	11.042310	.090561	59
60	176.031292	1944.792133	.000514	.005681	11.047991	.090514	60

Annual compound interest (10%)—Effective rate = 10%; Base = 1.10

YEARS	1 AMOUNT OF I AT COMPOUND INTEREST $S^n = (1+i)^n$	2 ACCUMULATION OF I PER PERIOD $S_{\overline{n}} = \frac{S^n-1}{i}$	3 SINKING FUND FACTOR $1\,S_{\overline{n}} = \frac{i}{S^n-1}$	4 PRES. VALUE REVERSION OF I $v^n = \frac{1}{S^n}$	5 PRESENT VALUE ORD. ANNUITY 1 PER PERIOD $a_{\overline{n}} = \frac{1-v^n}{i}$	6 INSTALMENT TO AMORTIZE I $1/a_{\overline{n}} = \frac{i}{1-v^n}$	n YEARS
1	1.100000	1.000000	1.000000	.909091	.909091	1.100000	1
2	1.210000	2.100000	.476190	.826446	1.735537	.576190	2
3	1.331000	3.310000	.302115	.751315	2.486852	.402115	3
4	1.464100	4.641000	.215471	.683013	3.169865	.315471	4
5	1.610510	6.105100	.163797	.620921	3.790787	.263797	5
6	1.771561	7.715610	.129607	.564474	4.355261	.229607	6
7	1.948717	9.487171	.105405	.513158	4.868419	.205405	7
8	2.143589	11.435888	.087444	.466507	5.334926	.187444	8
9	2.357948	13.579477	.073641	.424098	5.759024	.173641	9
10	2.593742	15.937425	.062745	.385543	6.144567	.162745	10
11	2.853117	18.531167	.053963	.350494	6.495061	.153963	11
12	3.138428	21.384284	.046763	.318631	6.813692	.146763	12
13	3.452271	24.522712	.040779	.289664	7.103356	.140779	13
14	3.797498	27.974983	.035746	.263331	7.366687	.135746	14
15	4.177248	31.772482	.031474	.239392	7.606080	.131474	15
16	4.594973	35.949730	.027817	.217629	7.823709	.127817	16
17	5.054470	40.544703	.024664	.197845	8.021553	.124664	17
18	5.559917	45.599173	.021930	.179859	8.201412	.121930	18
19	6.115909	51.159090	.019547	.163508	8.364920	.119547	19
20	6.727500	57.274999	.017460	.148644	8.513564	.117460	20
21	7.400250	64.002499	.015624	.135131	8.648694	.115624	21
22	8.140275	71.402749	.014005	.122846	8.771540	.114005	22
23	8.954302	79.543024	.012572	.111678	8.883218	.112572	23
24	9.849733	88.497327	.011300	.101526	8.984744	.111300	24
25	10.834706	98.347059	.010168	.092296	9.077040	.110168	25
26	11.918177	109.181765	.009159	.083905	9.160945	.109159	26
27	13.109994	121.099942	.008258	.076278	9.237223	.108258	27
28	14.420994	134.209936	.007451	.069343	9.306567	.107451	28
29	15.863094	148.630930	.006728	.063039	9.369606	.106728	29
30	17.449402	164.494023	.006079	.057309	9.426914	.106079	30
31	19.194342	181.943425	.005496	.052099	9.479013	.105496	31
32	21.113777	201.137767	.004972	.047362	9.526376	.104972	32
33	23.225154	222.251544	.004499	.043057	9.569432	.104499	33
34	25.547670	245.476699	.004074	.039143	9.608575	.104074	34
35	28.102437	271.024368	.003690	.035584	9.644159	.103690	35
36	30.912681	299.126805	.003343	.032349	9.676508	.103343	36
37	34.003949	330.039486	.003030	.029408	9.705917	.103030	37
38	37.404343	364.043434	.002747	.026735	9.732651	.102747	38
39	41.144778	401.447778	.002491	.024304	9.756956	.102491	39
40	45.259256	442.592556	.002259	.022095	9.779051	.102259	40
41	49.785181	487.851811	.002050	.020086	9.799137	.102050	41
42	54.763699	537.636992	.001860	.018260	9.817397	.101860	42
43	60.240069	592.400692	.001688	.016600	9.833998	.101688	43
44	66.264076	652.640761	.001532	.015091	9.849089	.101532	44
45	72.890484	718.904837	.001391	.013719	9.862808	.101391	45
46	80.179532	791.795321	.001263	.012472	9.875280	.101263	46
47	88.197485	871.974853	.001147	.011338	9.886618	.101147	47
48	97.017234	960.172338	.001041	.010307	9.896926	.101041	48
49	106.718957	1057.189572	.000946	.009370	9.906296	.100946	49
50	117.390853	1163.908529	.000859	.008519	9.914814	.100859	50
51	129.129938	1281.299382	.000780	.007744	9.922559	.100780	51
52	142.042932	1410.429320	.000709	.007040	9.929599	.100709	52
53	156.247225	1552.472252	.000644	.006400	9.935999	.100644	53
54	171.871948	1708.719477	.000585	.005818	9.941817	.100585	54
55	189.059142	1880.591425	.000532	.005289	9.947106	.100532	55
56	207.965057	2069.650567	.000483	.004809	9.951915	.100483	56
57	228.761562	2277.615624	.000439	.004371	9.956286	.100439	57
58	251.637719	2506.377186	.000399	.003974	9.960260	.100399	58
59	276.801490	2758.014905	.000363	.003613	9.963873	.100363	59
60	304.481640	3034.816395	.000330	.003284	9.967157	.100330	60

Table D-4

Annual compound interest (11%)—Effective rate = 11%; Base = 1.11

	1 AMOUNT OF 1 AT COMPOUND INTEREST $S^n = (1 + i)^n$	2 ACCUMULATION OF 1 PER PERIOD $S_{\overline{n}|} = \frac{S^n - 1}{i}$	3 SINKING FUND FACTOR $1/S_{\overline{n}|} = \frac{i}{S^n - 1}$	4 PRES. VALUE REVERSION OF 1 $V^n = \frac{1}{S^n}$	5 PRESENT VALUE ORD.ANNUITY 1 PER PERIOD $a_{\overline{n}|} = \frac{1 - V^n}{i}$	6 INSTALMENT TO AMORTIZE 1 $1/a_{\overline{n}|} = \frac{i}{1 - V^n}$	n
YEARS							YEARS
1	1.110000	1.000000	1.000000	.900901	.900901	1.110000	1
2	1.232100	2.110000	.473934	.811622	1.712523	.583934	2
3	1.367631	3.342100	.299213	.731191	2.443715	.409213	3
4	1.518070	4.709731	.212326	.658731	3.102446	.322326	4
5	1.685058	6.227801	.160570	.593451	3.695897	.270570	5
6	1.870415	7.912860	.126377	.534641	4.230538	.236377	6
7	2.076160	9.783274	.102215	.481658	4.712196	.212215	7
8	2.304538	11.859434	.084321	.433926	5.146123	.194321	8
9	2.558037	14.163972	.070602	.390925	5.537048	.180602	9
10	2.839421	16.722009	.059801	.352184	5.889232	.169801	10
11	3.151757	19.561430	.051121	.317283	6.206515	.161121	11
12	3.498451	22.713187	.044027	.285841	6.492356	.154027	12
13	3.883280	26.211638	.038151	.257514	6.749870	.148151	13
14	4.310441	30.094918	.033228	.231995	6.981865	.143228	14
15	4.784589	34.405359	.029065	.209004	7.190870	.139065	15
16	5.310894	39.189948	.025517	.188292	7.379162	.135517	16
17	5.895093	44.500843	.022471	.169633	7.548794	.132471	17
18	6.543553	50.395936	.019843	.152822	7.701617	.129843	18
19	7.263344	56.939488	.017563	.137678	7.839294	.127563	19
20	8.062312	64.202832	.015576	.124034	7.963328	.125576	20
21	8.949166	72.265144	.013838	.111742	8.075070	.123838	21
22	9.933574	81.214310	.012313	.100669	8.175739	.122313	22
23	11.026267	91.147884	.010971	.090693	8.266432	.120971	23
24	12.239157	102.174151	.009787	.081705	8.348137	.119787	24
25	13.585464	114.413307	.008740	.073608	8.421745	.118740	25
26	15.079865	127.998771	.007813	.066314	8.488058	.117813	26
27	16.738650	143.078636	.006989	.059742	8.547800	.116989	27
28	18.579901	159.817286	.006257	.053822	8.601622	.116257	28
29	20.623691	178.397187	.005605	.048488	8.650110	.115605	29
30	22.892297	199.020878	.005025	.043683	8.693793	.115025	30
31	25.410449	221.913175	.004506	.039354	8.733146	.114506	31
32	28.205599	247.323624	.004043	.035454	8.768600	.114043	32
33	31.308214	275.529222	.003629	.031940	8.800541	.113629	33
34	34.752118	306.837437	.003259	.028775	8.829316	.113259	34
35	38.574851	341.589555	.002927	.025924	8.855240	.112927	35
36	42.818085	380.164406	.002630	.023355	8.878594	.112630	36
37	47.528074	422.982490	.002364	.021040	8.899635	.112364	37
38	52.756162	470.510564	.002125	.018955	8.918590	.112125	38
39	58.559340	523.266726	.001911	.017077	8.935666	.111911	39
40	65.000867	581.826066	.001719	.015384	8.951051	.111719	40
41	72.150963	646.826934	.001546	.013860	8.964911	.111546	41
42	80.087569	718.977896	.001391	.012486	8.977397	.111391	42
43	88.897201	799.065465	.001251	.011249	8.988646	.111251	43
44	98.675893	887.962666	.001126	.010134	8.998780	.111126	44
45	109.530242	986.638559	.001014	.009130	9.007910	.111014	45
46	121.578568	1096.168801	.000912	.008225	9.016135	.110912	46
47	134.952211	1217.747369	.000821	.007410	9.023545	.110821	47
48	149.796954	1352.699580	.000739	.006676	9.030221	.110739	48
49	166.274619	1502.496534	.000666	.006014	9.036235	.110666	49
50	184.564827	1668.771153	.000599	.005418	9.041653	.110599	50
51	204.866958	1853.335979	.000540	.004881	9.046534	.110540	51
52	227.402323	2058.202936	.000486	.004397	9.050932	.110486	52
53	252.416579	2285.605259	.000438	.003962	9.054894	.110438	53
54	280.182402	2538.021837	.000394	.003569	9.058463	.110394	54
55	311.002466	2818.204239	.000355	.003215	9.061678	.110355	55
56	345.212738	3129.206705	.000320	.002897	9.064575	.110320	56
57	383.186139	3474.419443	.000288	.002610	9.067185	.110288	57
58	425.336614	3857.605581	.000259	.002351	9.069536	.110259	58
59	472.123641	4282.942195	.000233	.002118	9.071654	.110233	59
60	524.057242	4755.065835	.000210	.001908	9.073562	.110210	60

From ELLWOOD TABLES FOR REAL ESTATE APPRAISING AND FINANCING, Fourth edition, Copyright 1977, American Institute of Real Estate Appraisers. Reprinted with permission from Ballinger Publishing Company.

Table D–5

Annual compound interest (12%)—Effective rate = 12%; Base = 1.1200

	1 AMOUNT OF 1 AT COMPOUND INTEREST $S^n = (1+i)^n$	2 ACCUMULATION OF 1 PER PERIOD $S_{\overline{n}} = \frac{S^n-1}{i}$	3 SINKING FUND FACTOR $1/S_{\overline{n}} = \frac{i}{S^n-1}$	4 PRES. VALUE REVERSION OF 1 $V^n = \frac{1}{S^n}$	5 PRESENT VALUE ORD.ANNUITY 1 PER PERIOD $a_{\overline{n}} = \frac{1-V^n}{i}$	6 INSTALMENT TO AMORTIZE 1 $1/a_{\overline{n}} = \frac{i}{1-V^n}$	n
YEARS							YEARS
1	1.120000	1.000000	1.000000	.892857	.892857	1.120000	1
2	1.254400	2.120000	.471698	.797194	1.690051	.591698	2
3	1.404928	3.374400	.296349	.711780	2.401831	.416349	3
4	1.573519	4.779328	.209234	.635518	3.037349	.329234	4
5	1.762342	6.352847	.157410	.567427	3.604776	.277410	5
6	1.973823	8.115189	.123226	.506631	4.111407	.243226	6
7	2.210681	10.089012	.099118	.452349	4.563757	.219118	7
8	2.475963	12.299693	.081303	.403883	4.967640	.201303	8
9	2.773079	14.775656	.067679	.360610	5.328250	.187679	9
10	3.105848	17.548735	.056984	.321973	5.650223	.176984	10
11	3.478550	20.654583	.048415	.287476	5.937699	.168415	11
12	3.895976	24.133133	.041437	.256675	6.194374	.161437	12
13	4.363493	28.029109	.035677	.229174	6.423548	.155677	13
14	4.887112	32.392602	.030871	.204620	6.628168	.150871	14
15	5.473566	37.279715	.026824	.182696	6.810864	.146824	15
16	6.130394	42.753280	.023390	.163122	6.973986	.143390	16
17	6.866041	48.883674	.020457	.145644	7.119630	.140457	17
18	7.689966	55.749715	.017937	.130040	7.249670	.137937	18
19	8.612762	63.439681	.015763	.116107	7.365777	.135763	19
20	9.646293	72.052442	.013879	.103667	7.469444	.133879	20
21	10.803848	81.698736	.012240	.092560	7.562003	.132240	21
22	12.100310	92.502584	.010811	.082643	7.644646	.130811	22
23	13.552347	104.602894	.009560	.073788	7.718434	.129560	23
24	15.178629	118.155241	.008463	.065882	7.784316	.128463	24
25	17.000064	133.333870	.007500	.058823	7.843139	.127500	25
26	19.040072	150.333934	.006652	.052521	7.895660	.126652	26
27	21.324881	169.374007	.005904	.046894	7.942554	.125904	27
28	23.883866	190.698887	.005244	.041869	7.984423	.125244	28
29	26.749930	214.582754	.004660	.037383	8.021806	.124660	29
30	29.959922	241.332684	.004144	.033378	8.055184	.124144	30
31	33.555113	271.292606	.003686	.029802	8.084986	.123686	31
32	37.581726	304.847719	.003280	.026609	8.111594	.123280	32
33	42.091533	342.429445	.002920	.023758	8.135352	.122920	33
34	47.142517	384.520979	.002601	.021212	8.156564	.122601	34
35	52.799620	431.663496	.002317	.018940	8.175504	.122317	35
36	59.135574	484.463116	.002064	.016910	8.192414	.122064	36
37	66.231843	543.598690	.001840	.015098	8.207513	.121840	37
38	74.179664	609.830532	.001640	.013481	8.220993	.121640	38
39	83.081224	684.010196	.001462	.012036	8.233030	.121462	39
40	93.050970	767.091420	.001304	.010747	8.243777	.121304	40
41	104.217087	860.142390	.001163	.009595	8.253372	.121163	41
42	116.723137	964.359477	.001037	.008567	8.261939	.121037	42
43	130.729914	1081.082614	.000925	.007649	8.269589	.120925	43
44	146.417503	1211.812527	.000825	.006830	8.276418	.120825	44
45	163.987604	1358.230031	.000736	.006098	8.282516	.120736	45
46	183.666116	1522.217634	.000657	.005445	8.287961	.120657	46
47	205.706050	1705.883750	.000586	.004861	8.292822	.120586	47
48	230.390776	1911.589800	.000523	.004340	8.297163	.120523	48
49	258.037669	2141.980576	.000467	.003875	8.301038	.120467	49
50	289.002189	2400.018245	.000417	.003460	8.304498	.120417	50
51	323.682452	2689.020434	.000372	.003089	8.307588	.120372	51
52	362.524346	3012.702886	.000332	.002758	8.310346	.120332	52
53	406.027268	3375.227233	.000296	.002463	8.312809	.120296	53
54	454.750540	3781.254500	.000264	.002199	8.315008	.120264	54
55	509.320605	4236.005040	.000236	.001963	8.316972	.120236	55
56	570.439077	4745.325645	.000211	.001753	8.318725	.120211	56
57	638.891767	5315.764723	.000188	.001565	8.320290	.120188	57
58	715.558779	5954.656489	.000168	.001398	8.321687	.120168	58
59	801.425832	6670.215267	.000150	.001248	8.322935	.120150	59
60	897.596932	7471.641099	.000134	.001114	8.324049	.120134	60

Amortization Tables: Monthly and Annually

MONTHLY

Table E-1a
Monthly payment to amortize a $1000.00 loan (8%-10.75%)

INTEREST	8.00%	8.25%	8.50%	8.75%	9.00%	9.25%	9.50%	9.75%	10.00%	10.25%	10.50%	10.75%
YEARS												
.5	170.58	170.70	170.83	170.95	171.07	171.20	171.32	171.44	171.57	171.69	171.81	171.94
1.0	86.99	87.11	87.22	87.34	87.46	87.57	87.69	87.80	87.92	88.04	88.15	88.27
1.5	59.15	59.26	59.37	59.49	59.60	59.72	59.83	59.95	60.06	60.18	60.29	60.41
2.0	45.23	45.35	45.46	45.58	45.69	45.80	45.92	46.03	46.15	46.27	46.38	46.50
2.5	36.89	37.01	37.12	37.24	37.35	37.47	37.58	37.70	37.82	37.93	38.05	38.17
3.0	31.34	31.46	31.57	31.69	31.80	31.92	32.04	32.15	32.27	32.39	32.51	32.63
3.5	27.38	27.50	27.62	27.73	27.85	27.97	28.09	28.20	28.32	28.44	28.56	28.68
4.0	24.42	24.54	24.65	24.77	24.89	25.01	25.13	25.25	25.37	25.49	25.61	25.73
4.5	22.12	22.24	22.36	22.47	22.59	22.71	22.84	22.96	23.08	23.20	23.32	23.44
5.0	20.28	20.40	20.52	20.64	20.76	20.88	21.01	21.13	21.25	21.38	21.50	21.62
5.5	18.78	18.90	19.03	19.15	19.27	19.39	19.52	19.64	19.76	19.89	20.01	20.14
6.0	17.54	17.66	17.78	17.91	18.03	18.15	18.28	18.41	18.53	18.66	18.78	18.91
6.5	16.49	16.61	16.74	16.86	16.99	17.11	17.24	17.36	17.49	17.62	17.75	17.88
7.0	15.59	15.72	15.84	15.97	16.09	16.22	16.35	16.48	16.61	16.74	16.87	17.00
7.5	14.82	14.94	15.07	15.20	15.32	15.45	15.58	15.71	15.84	15.97	16.11	16.24
8.0	14.14	14.27	14.40	14.53	14.66	14.79	14.92	15.05	15.18	15.31	15.45	15.58
8.5	13.55	13.68	13.81	13.94	14.07	14.20	14.33	14.46	14.60	14.73	14.87	15.00
9.0	13.02	13.15	13.28	13.42	13.55	13.68	13.81	13.95	14.08	14.22	14.36	14.49
9.5	12.56	12.69	12.82	12.95	13.09	13.22	13.36	13.49	13.63	13.76	13.90	14.04
10.0	12.14	12.27	12.40	12.54	12.67	12.81	12.94	13.08	13.22	13.36	13.50	13.64
10.5	11.76	11.89	12.03	12.16	12.30	12.44	12.58	12.71	12.85	12.99	13.14	13.28
11.0	11.42	11.56	11.69	11.83	11.97	12.10	12.24	12.38	12.52	12.67	12.81	12.95
11.5	11.11	11.25	11.38	11.52	11.66	11.80	11.94	12.08	12.23	12.37	12.51	12.66
12.0	10.83	10.97	11.11	11.24	11.39	11.53	11.67	11.81	11.96	12.10	12.25	12.39
12.5	10.57	10.71	10.85	10.99	11.13	11.28	11.42	11.56	11.71	11.86	12.00	12.15
13.0	10.34	10.48	10.62	10.76	10.90	11.05	11.19	11.34	11.48	11.63	11.78	11.93
13.5	10.12	10.26	10.40	10.55	10.69	10.83	10.98	11.13	11.28	11.43	11.58	11.73
14.0	9.92	10.06	10.20	10.35	10.49	10.64	10.79	10.94	11.09	11.24	11.39	11.54
14.5	9.73	9.88	10.02	10.17	10.31	10.46	10.61	10.76	10.91	11.06	11.22	11.37
15.0	9.56	9.71	9.85	10.00	10.15	10.30	10.45	10.60	10.75	10.90	11.06	11.21
15.5	9.40	9.55	9.70	9.84	9.99	10.14	10.30	10.45	10.60	10.76	10.91	11.07
16.0	9.25	9.40	9.55	9.70	9.85	10.00	10.15	10.31	10.46	10.62	10.78	10.94
16.5	9.12	9.26	9.41	9.57	9.72	9.87	10.02	10.18	10.34	10.49	10.65	10.81
17.0	8.99	9.14	9.29	9.44	9.59	9.75	9.90	10.06	10.22	10.38	10.54	10.70
17.5	8.87	9.02	9.17	9.32	9.48	9.63	9.79	9.95	10.11	10.27	10.43	10.59
18.0	8.75	8.91	9.06	9.21	9.37	9.53	9.68	9.84	10.00	10.16	10.33	10.49
18.5	8.65	8.80	8.96	9.11	9.27	9.43	9.59	9.75	9.91	10.07	10.23	10.40
19.0	8.55	8.70	8.86	9.02	9.17	9.33	9.49	9.65	9.82	9.98	10.15	10.31
19.5	8.46	8.61	8.77	8.93	9.09	9.25	9.41	9.57	9.73	9.90	10.06	10.23
20.0	8.37	8.53	8.68	8.84	9.00	9.16	9.33	9.49	9.66	9.82	9.99	10.16
20.5	8.29	8.44	8.60	8.76	8.92	9.09	9.25	9.42	9.58	9.75	9.92	10.09
21.0	8.21	8.37	8.53	8.69	8.85	9.01	9.18	9.35	9.51	9.68	9.85	10.02
21.5	8.14	8.30	8.46	8.62	8.78	8.95	9.11	9.28	9.45	9.62	9.79	9.96
22.0	8.07	8.23	8.39	8.55	8.72	8.88	9.05	9.22	9.39	9.56	9.73	9.90
22.5	8.00	8.16	8.33	8.49	8.66	8.82	8.99	9.16	9.33	9.50	9.68	9.85
23.0	7.94	8.10	8.27	8.43	8.60	8.77	8.93	9.11	9.28	9.45	9.62	9.80
23.5	7.88	8.04	8.21	8.38	8.54	8.71	8.88	9.05	9.23	9.40	9.58	9.75
24.0	7.83	7.99	8.16	8.32	8.49	8.66	8.83	9.01	9.18	9.35	9.53	9.71
24.5	7.77	7.94	8.11	8.27	8.44	8.61	8.79	8.96	9.13	9.31	9.49	9.67
25.0	7.72	7.89	8.06	8.23	8.40	8.57	8.74	8.92	9.09	9.27	9.45	9.63
25.5	7.68	7.84	8.01	8.18	8.35	8.53	8.70	8.88	9.05	9.23	9.41	9.59
26.0	7.63	7.80	7.97	8.14	8.31	8.49	8.66	8.84	9.01	9.19	9.37	9.55
26.5	7.59	7.76	7.93	8.10	8.27	8.45	8.62	8.80	8.98	9.16	9.34	9.52
27.0	7.55	7.72	7.89	8.06	8.24	8.41	8.59	8.77	8.95	9.13	9.31	9.49
27.5	7.51	7.68	7.85	8.03	8.20	8.38	8.56	8.73	8.91	9.10	9.28	9.46
28.0	7.47	7.64	7.82	7.99	8.17	8.35	8.52	8.70	8.88	9.07	9.25	9.43
28.5	7.44	7.61	7.78	7.96	8.14	8.31	8.49	8.67	8.86	9.04	9.22	9.41
29.0	7.40	7.58	7.75	7.93	8.11	8.29	8.47	8.65	8.83	9.01	9.20	9.38
29.5	7.37	7.55	7.72	7.90	8.08	8.26	8.44	8.62	8.80	8.99	9.17	9.36
30.0	7.34	7.52	7.69	7.87	8.05	8.23	8.41	8.60	8.78	8.97	9.15	9.34
35	7.11	7.29	7.47	7.66	7.84	8.03	8.22	8.41	8.60	8.79	8.99	9.18
40	6.96	7.15	7.34	7.53	7.72	7.91	8.11	8.30	8.50	8.69	8.89	9.09

From *Interest Amortization Tables* by Jack C. Estes. New York: McGraw-Hill Book Company, 1976.

MONTHLY

Table E-1b
Monthly payment to amortize a $1000.00 loan (11-13.75%)

INTEREST YEARS	11.00%	11.25%	11.50%	11.75%	12.00%	12.25%	12.50%	12.75%	13.00%	13.25%	13.50%	13.75%
.5	172.06	172.18	172.31	172.43	172.55	172.68	172.80	172.92	173.05	173.17	173.30	173.42
1.0	88.39	88.50	88.62	88.74	88.85	88.97	89.09	89.21	89.32	89.44	89.56	89.67
1.5	60.52	60.64	60.76	60.87	60.99	61.10	61.22	61.34	61.45	61.57	61.69	61.80
2.0	46.61	46.73	46.85	46.96	47.08	47.20	47.31	47.43	47.55	47.66	47.78	47.90
2.5	38.28	38.40	38.52	38.64	38.75	38.87	38.99	39.11	39.23	39.35	39.46	39.58
3.0	32.74	32.86	32.98	33.10	33.22	33.34	33.46	33.58	33.70	33.82	33.94	34.06
3.5	28.80	28.92	29.04	29.16	29.28	29.40	29.52	29.65	29.77	29.89	30.01	30.14
4.0	25.85	25.97	26.09	26.22	26.34	26.46	26.58	26.71	26.83	26.96	27.08	27.21
4.5	23.57	23.69	23.81	23.94	24.06	24.19	24.31	24.44	24.56	24.69	24.82	24.94
5.0	21.75	21.87	22.00	22.12	22.25	22.38	22.50	22.63	22.76	22.89	23.01	23.14
5.5	20.27	20.39	20.52	20.65	20.78	20.90	21.03	21.16	21.29	21.42	21.55	21.68
6.0	19.04	19.17	19.30	19.43	19.56	19.69	19.82	19.95	20.08	20.21	20.34	20.48
6.5	18.01	18.14	18.27	18.40	18.53	18.66	18.79	18.93	19.06	19.20	19.33	19.47
7.0	17.13	17.26	17.39	17.52	17.66	17.79	17.93	18.06	18.20	18.33	18.47	18.61
7.5	16.37	16.50	16.64	16.77	16.91	17.04	17.18	17.32	17.45	17.59	17.73	17.87
8.0	15.71	15.85	15.98	16.12	16.26	16.40	16.53	16.67	16.81	16.95	17.09	17.23
8.5	15.14	15.27	15.41	15.55	15.69	15.83	15.97	16.11	16.25	16.39	16.54	16.68
9.0	14.63	14.77	14.91	15.05	15.19	15.33	15.47	15.62	15.76	15.90	16.05	16.19
9.5	14.18	14.32	14.46	14.60	14.75	14.89	15.03	15.18	15.32	15.47	15.62	15.76
10.0	13.78	13.92	14.06	14.21	14.35	14.50	14.64	14.79	14.94	15.08	15.23	15.38
10.5	13.42	13.56	13.71	13.85	14.00	14.15	14.29	14.44	14.59	14.74	14.89	15.04
11.0	13.10	13.24	13.39	13.54	13.68	13.83	13.98	14.13	14.28	14.43	14.58	14.74
11.5	12.81	12.95	13.10	13.25	13.40	13.55	13.70	13.85	14.00	14.16	14.31	14.46
12.0	12.54	12.69	12.84	12.99	13.14	13.29	13.44	13.60	13.75	13.91	14.06	14.22
12.5	12.30	12.45	12.60	12.75	12.90	13.06	13.21	13.37	13.52	13.68	13.84	14.00
13.0	12.08	12.23	12.38	12.54	12.69	12.85	13.00	13.16	13.32	13.48	13.63	13.80
13.5	11.88	12.03	12.19	12.34	12.50	12.65	12.81	12.97	13.13	13.29	13.45	13.61
14.0	11.70	11.85	12.01	12.16	12.32	12.48	12.64	12.80	12.96	13.12	13.28	13.45
14.5	11.53	11.68	11.84	12.00	12.16	12.32	12.48	12.64	12.80	12.96	13.13	13.29
15.0	11.37	11.53	11.69	11.85	12.01	12.17	12.33	12.49	12.66	12.82	12.99	13.15
15.5	11.23	11.39	11.55	11.71	11.87	12.03	12.20	12.36	12.53	12.69	12.86	13.03
16.0	11.10	11.26	11.42	11.58	11.74	11.91	12.07	12.24	12.40	12.57	12.74	12.91
16.5	10.97	11.13	11.30	11.46	11.63	11.79	11.96	12.13	12.29	12.46	12.63	12.80
17.0	10.86	11.02	11.19	11.35	11.52	11.68	11.85	12.02	12.19	12.36	12.53	12.71
17.5	10.75	10.92	11.08	11.25	11.42	11.59	11.75	11.93	12.10	12.27	12.44	12.62
18.0	10.66	10.82	10.99	11.16	11.32	11.49	11.67	11.84	12.01	12.18	12.36	12.53
18.5	10.56	10.73	10.90	11.07	11.24	11.41	11.58	11.75	11.93	12.10	12.28	12.46
19.0	10.48	10.65	10.82	10.99	11.16	11.33	11.50	11.68	11.85	12.03	12.21	12.39
19.5	10.40	10.57	10.74	10.91	11.08	11.26	11.43	11.61	11.78	11.96	12.14	12.32
20.0	10.33	10.50	10.67	10.84	11.02	11.19	11.37	11.54	11.72	11.90	12.08	12.26
20.5	10.26	10.43	10.60	10.78	10.95	11.13	11.30	11.48	11.66	11.84	12.02	12.20
21.0	10.19	10.37	10.54	10.72	10.89	11.07	11.25	11.43	11.61	11.79	11.97	12.15
21.5	10.13	10.31	10.48	10.66	10.84	11.01	11.19	11.37	11.55	11.74	11.92	12.10
22.0	10.08	10.25	10.43	10.61	10.78	10.96	11.14	11.33	11.51	11.69	11.87	12.06
22.5	10.02	10.20	10.38	10.56	10.74	10.92	11.10	11.28	11.46	11.65	11.83	12.02
23.0	9.98	10.15	10.33	10.51	10.69	10.87	11.05	11.24	11.42	11.61	11.79	11.98
23.5	9.93	10.11	10.29	10.47	10.65	10.83	11.01	11.20	11.38	11.57	11.76	11.94
24.0	9.89	10.06	10.25	10.43	10.61	10.79	10.98	11.16	11.35	11.53	11.72	11.91
24.5	9.84	10.02	10.21	10.39	10.57	10.76	10.94	11.13	11.31	11.50	11.69	11.88
25.0	9.81	9.99	10.17	10.35	10.54	10.72	10.91	11.10	11.28	11.47	11.66	11.85
25.5	9.77	9.95	10.14	10.32	10.50	10.69	10.88	11.07	11.25	11.44	11.63	11.83
26.0	9.74	9.92	10.10	10.29	10.47	10.66	10.85	11.04	11.23	11.42	11.61	11.80
26.5	9.70	9.89	10.07	10.26	10.45	10.63	10.82	11.01	11.20	11.39	11.59	11.78
27.0	9.67	9.86	10.05	10.23	10.42	10.61	10.80	10.99	11.18	11.37	11.56	11.76
27.5	9.65	9.83	10.02	10.21	10.39	10.58	10.77	10.97	11.16	11.35	11.54	11.74
28.0	9.62	9.81	9.99	10.18	10.37	10.56	10.75	10.94	11.14	11.33	11.52	11.72
28.5	9.59	9.78	9.97	10.16	10.35	10.54	10.73	10.92	11.12	11.31	11.51	11.70
29.0	9.57	9.76	9.95	10.14	10.33	10.52	10.71	10.91	11.10	11.29	11.49	11.68
29.5	9.55	9.74	9.93	10.12	10.31	10.50	10.69	10.89	11.08	11.28	11.47	11.67
30.0	9.53	9.72	9.91	10.10	10.29	10.48	10.68	10.87	11.07	11.26	11.46	11.66
35	9.37	9.57	9.77	9.96	10.16	10.36	10.56	10.76	10.96	11.16	11.36	11.56
40	9.29	9.49	9.69	9.89	10.09	10.29	10.49	10.70	10.90	11.10	11.31	11.51

From *Interest Amortization Tables* by Jack C. Estes. New York: McGraw-Hill Book Company, 1976.

ANNUALLY

Table E-2a
Annual payment to amortize a $1000.00 loan (8-10.75%)

INTEREST YEARS	8.00%	8.25%	8.50%	8.75%	9.00%	9.25%	9.50%	9.75%	10.00%	10.25%	10.50%	10.75%
1.0	1080.00	1082.50	1085.00	1087.50	1090.00	1092.50	1095.00	1097.50	1100.00	1102.50	1105.00	1107.50
2.0	560.77	562.70	564.62	566.55	568.47	570.40	572.33	574.26	576.20	578.13	580.06	582.00
3.0	388.04	389.79	391.54	393.30	395.06	396.82	398.58	400.35	402.12	403.89	405.66	407.44
4.0	301.93	303.61	305.29	306.98	308.67	310.37	312.07	313.77	315.48	317.18	318.90	320.61
5.0	250.46	252.11	253.77	255.43	257.10	258.77	260.44	262.12	263.80	265.49	267.18	268.88
6.0	216.32	217.96	219.61	221.27	222.92	224.59	226.26	227.93	229.61	231.30	232.99	234.68
7.0	192.08	193.72	195.37	197.03	198.70	200.37	202.04	203.72	205.41	207.10	208.80	210.51
8.0	174.02	175.67	177.34	179.00	180.68	182.36	184.05	185.75	187.45	189.16	190.87	192.60
9.0	160.08	161.75	163.43	165.11	166.80	168.50	170.21	171.92	173.65	175.37	177.11	178.86
10.0	149.03	150.72	152.41	154.11	155.83	157.54	159.27	161.01	162.75	164.50	166.26	168.03
11.0	140.08	141.78	143.50	145.22	146.95	148.69	150.44	152.20	153.97	155.74	157.53	159.32
12.0	132.70	134.42	136.16	137.90	139.66	141.42	143.19	144.98	146.77	148.57	150.38	152.20
13.0	126.53	128.27	130.03	131.79	133.57	135.36	137.16	138.97	140.78	142.61	144.45	146.30
14.0	121.30	123.07	124.85	126.64	128.44	130.25	132.07	133.91	135.75	137.61	139.47	141.35
15.0	116.83	118.62	120.43	122.24	124.06	125.90	127.75	129.61	131.48	133.36	135.25	137.16
16.0	112.98	114.79	116.62	118.46	120.30	122.17	124.04	125.92	127.82	129.73	131.65	133.58
17.0	109.63	111.47	113.32	115.18	117.05	118.94	120.84	122.75	124.67	126.60	128.55	130.51
18.0	106.71	108.56	110.44	112.32	114.22	116.13	118.05	119.99	121.94	123.90	125.87	127.85
19.0	104.13	106.01	107.91	109.81	111.74	113.67	115.62	117.58	119.55	121.54	123.54	125.55
20.0	101.86	103.76	105.68	107.61	109.55	111.51	113.48	115.47	117.46	119.48	121.50	123.53
21.0	99.84	101.76	103.70	105.65	107.62	109.60	111.60	113.61	115.63	117.66	119.71	121.77
22.0	98.04	99.98	101.94	103.92	105.91	107.91	109.93	111.96	114.01	116.07	118.14	120.22
23.0	96.43	98.39	100.38	102.37	104.39	106.41	108.45	110.51	112.58	114.66	116.75	118.86
24.0	94.98	96.97	98.97	100.99	103.03	105.08	107.14	109.21	111.30	113.41	115.52	117.65
25.0	93.68	95.69	97.72	99.76	101.81	103.88	105.96	108.06	110.17	112.30	114.43	116.58
26.0	92.51	94.54	96.59	98.65	100.72	102.81	104.91	107.03	109.16	111.31	113.47	115.64
27.0	91.45	93.50	95.57	97.64	99.74	101.85	103.97	106.11	108.26	110.43	112.60	114.79
28.0	90.49	92.56	94.64	96.74	98.86	100.99	103.13	105.29	107.46	109.64	111.83	114.04
29.0	89.62	91.71	93.81	95.93	98.06	100.21	102.37	104.54	106.73	108.93	111.15	113.37
30.0	88.83	90.94	93.06	95.19	97.34	99.51	101.69	103.88	106.08	108.30	110.53	112.78
31.0	88.11	90.23	92.37	94.52	96.69	98.87	101.07	103.28	105.50	107.74	109.98	112.24
32.0	87.46	89.59	91.75	93.92	96.10	98.30	100.51	102.74	104.98	107.23	109.49	111.76
33.0	86.86	89.01	91.18	93.37	95.57	97.78	100.01	102.25	104.50	106.77	109.05	111.34
34.0	86.31	88.48	90.66	92.87	95.08	97.31	99.55	101.81	104.08	106.36	108.65	110.95
35.0	85.81	87.99	90.19	92.41	94.64	96.89	99.14	101.41	103.69	105.99	108.29	110.61
36.0	85.35	87.55	89.77	92.00	94.24	96.50	98.77	101.05	103.35	105.65	107.97	110.30
37.0	84.93	87.14	89.37	91.62	93.88	96.15	98.43	100.73	103.03	105.35	107.68	110.02
38.0	84.54	86.77	89.01	91.27	93.54	95.83	98.12	100.43	102.75	105.08	107.42	109.77
39.0	84.19	86.43	88.69	90.96	93.24	95.54	97.85	100.17	102.50	104.84	107.19	109.55
40.0	83.87	86.12	88.39	90.67	92.96	95.27	97.59	99.92	102.26	104.62	106.98	109.35
41.0	83.57	85.83	88.11	90.41	92.71	95.03	97.36	99.70	102.05	104.42	106.79	109.16
42.0	83.29	85.57	87.86	90.17	92.48	94.81	97.15	99.50	101.86	104.24	106.61	109.00
43.0	83.04	85.33	87.63	89.95	92.27	94.61	96.96	99.32	101.69	104.07	106.46	108.85
44.0	82.81	85.11	87.42	89.74	92.08	94.43	96.79	99.16	101.54	103.92	106.32	108.72
45.0	82.59	84.90	87.22	89.56	91.91	94.26	96.63	99.01	101.40	103.79	106.19	108.60
46.0	82.39	84.71	87.05	89.39	91.75	94.11	96.49	98.87	101.27	103.67	106.08	108.49
47.0	82.21	84.54	86.88	89.24	91.60	93.97	96.36	98.75	101.15	103.56	105.98	108.40
48.0	82.05	84.38	86.73	89.09	91.47	93.85	96.24	98.64	101.05	103.46	105.88	108.31
49.0	81.89	84.24	86.60	88.96	91.34	93.73	96.13	98.54	100.95	103.37	105.80	108.23
50.0	81.75	84.10	86.47	88.85	91.23	93.63	96.03	98.44	100.86	103.29	105.72	108.16

From *Interest Amortization Tables* by Jack C. Estes. New York: McGraw-Hill Book Company, 1976.

ANNUALLY

Table E–2b

Annual payment to amortize a $1000.00 loan (11–13.75%)

INTEREST YEARS	11.00%	11.25%	11.50%	11.75%	12.00%	12.25%	12.50%	12.75%	13.00%	13.25%	13.50%	13.75%
1.0	1110.00	1112.50	1115.00	1117.50	1120.00	1122.50	1125.00	1127.50	1130.00	1132.50	1135.00	1137.50
2.0	583.94	585.88	587.82	589.76	591.70	593.65	595.59	597.54	599.49	601.44	603.39	605.34
3.0	409.22	411.00	412.78	414.57	416.35	418.14	419.94	421.73	423.53	425.33	427.13	428.93
4.0	322.33	324.05	325.78	327.51	329.24	330.97	332.71	334.45	336.20	337.95	339.70	341.45
5.0	270.58	272.28	273.99	275.70	277.41	279.13	280.86	282.59	284.32	286.06	287.80	289.54
6.0	236.38	238.09	239.80	241.51	243.23	244.96	246.68	248.42	250.16	251.90	253.65	255.40
7.0	212.22	213.94	215.66	217.39	219.12	220.86	222.61	224.36	226.12	227.88	229.65	231.42
8.0	194.33	196.06	197.80	199.55	201.31	203.07	204.84	206.61	208.39	210.18	211.97	213.77
9.0	180.61	182.37	184.13	185.90	187.68	189.47	191.27	193.07	194.87	196.69	198.51	200.34
10.0	169.81	171.59	173.38	175.18	176.99	178.80	180.63	182.46	184.29	186.14	187.99	189.85
11.0	161.13	162.94	164.76	166.58	168.42	170.26	172.12	173.98	175.85	177.72	179.61	181.50
12.0	154.03	155.87	157.72	159.58	161.44	163.32	165.20	167.09	168.99	170.90	172.82	174.74
13.0	148.16	150.02	151.90	153.79	155.68	157.59	159.50	161.42	163.36	165.30	167.24	169.20
14.0	143.23	145.13	147.04	148.95	150.88	152.81	154.76	156.71	158.67	160.64	162.63	164.62
15.0	139.07	140.99	142.93	144.87	146.83	148.79	150.77	152.75	154.75	156.75	158.76	160.78
16.0	135.52	137.47	139.44	141.41	143.40	145.39	147.39	149.41	151.43	153.46	155.51	157.56
17.0	132.48	134.46	136.45	138.45	140.46	142.48	144.52	146.56	148.61	150.68	152.75	154.83
18.0	129.85	131.85	133.87	135.90	137.94	139.99	142.05	144.12	146.21	148.30	150.40	152.51
19.0	127.57	129.60	131.65	133.70	135.77	137.85	139.93	142.03	144.14	146.26	148.38	150.52
20.0	125.58	127.64	129.71	131.79	133.88	135.99	138.10	140.22	142.36	144.50	146.66	148.82
21.0	123.84	125.93	128.02	130.13	132.25	134.37	136.51	138.66	140.82	142.99	145.17	147.35
22.0	122.32	124.43	126.54	128.67	130.82	132.97	135.13	137.30	139.48	141.68	143.88	146.09
23.0	120.98	123.11	125.25	127.40	129.56	131.74	133.92	136.12	138.32	140.54	142.76	144.99
24.0	119.79	121.94	124.11	126.28	128.47	130.66	132.87	135.09	137.31	139.55	141.79	144.05
25.0	118.75	120.92	123.10	125.30	127.50	129.72	131.95	134.18	136.43	138.69	140.95	143.22
26.0	117.82	120.01	122.22	124.43	126.66	128.89	131.14	133.39	135.66	137.93	140.22	142.51
27.0	116.99	119.21	121.43	123.66	125.91	128.16	130.43	132.70	134.98	137.28	139.57	141.88
28.0	116.26	118.49	120.73	122.99	125.25	127.52	129.80	132.09	134.39	136.70	139.02	141.34
29.0	115.61	117.86	120.12	122.39	124.67	126.95	129.25	131.56	133.87	136.20	138.53	140.86
30.0	115.03	117.29	119.57	121.85	124.15	126.45	128.77	131.09	133.42	135.75	138.10	140.45
31.0	114.51	116.79	119.08	121.38	123.69	126.01	128.34	130.67	133.01	135.36	137.72	140.09
32.0	114.05	116.34	118.65	120.96	123.29	125.62	127.96	130.31	132.66	135.02	137.39	139.77
33.0	113.63	115.94	118.26	120.59	122.93	125.27	127.62	129.98	132.35	134.72	137.10	139.49
34.0	113.26	115.59	117.92	120.26	122.61	124.96	127.33	129.70	132.08	134.46	136.85	139.25
35.0	112.93	115.27	117.61	119.96	122.32	124.69	127.06	129.45	131.83	134.23	136.63	139.04
36.0	112.64	114.98	117.34	119.70	122.07	124.45	126.83	129.22	131.62	134.02	136.43	138.85
37.0	112.37	114.73	117.09	119.46	121.84	124.23	126.63	129.03	131.43	133.85	136.26	138.68
38.0	112.13	114.50	116.87	119.26	121.64	124.04	126.44	128.85	131.27	133.69	136.11	138.54
39.0	111.92	114.29	116.68	119.07	121.47	123.87	126.28	128.70	131.12	133.55	135.98	138.42
40.0	111.72	114.11	116.50	118.90	121.31	123.72	126.14	128.56	130.99	133.42	135.86	138.30
41.0	111.55	113.95	116.35	118.75	121.17	123.59	126.01	128.44	130.88	133.32	135.76	138.21
42.0	111.40	113.80	116.21	118.62	121.04	123.47	125.90	128.34	130.78	133.22	135.67	138.12
43.0	111.26	113.67	116.08	118.50	120.93	123.36	125.80	128.24	130.69	133.14	135.59	138.05
44.0	111.13	113.55	115.97	118.40	120.83	123.27	125.71	128.16	130.61	133.06	135.52	137.98
45.0	111.02	113.44	115.87	118.30	120.74	123.18	125.63	128.08	130.54	133.00	135.46	137.92
46.0	110.92	113.35	115.78	118.22	120.66	123.11	125.56	128.02	130.48	132.94	135.40	137.87
47.0	110.83	113.26	115.70	118.14	120.59	123.04	125.50	127.96	130.42	132.89	135.36	137.83
48.0	110.74	113.18	115.63	118.08	120.53	122.98	125.44	127.91	130.37	132.84	135.32	137.79
49.0	110.67	113.11	115.56	118.02	120.47	122.93	125.40	127.86	130.33	132.80	135.28	137.75
50.0	110.60	113.05	115.50	117.96	120.42	122.89	125.35	127.82	130.29	132.77	135.25	137.72

From *Interest Amortization Tables* by Jack C. Estes. New York: McGraw-Hill Book Company, 1976.

Remaining Mortgage Balance Tables

Table F–1

Remaining balance tables (8.5, 8.75%)

ORIGINAL TERM IN YEARS

8.50%

AGE OF LOAN	1	2	3	4	5	6	7	8	9	10	15	20	25	30	35	40
1	0.	52.12	69.45	78.08	83.24	86.65	89.08	90.88	92.27	93.37	96.55	98.01	98.79	99.24	99.52	99.69
2		0.	36.19	54.22	64.99	72.13	77.19	80.95	83.85	86.15	92.80	95.84	97.47	98.42	99.00	99.35
3			0.	28.26	45.14	56.32	64.25	70.15	74.69	78.29	88.71	93.49	96.04	97.53	98.43	98.99
4				0.	23.52	39.11	50.17	58.39	64.73	69.74	84.26	90.92	94.48	96.55	97.81	98.59
5					0.	20.38	34.84	45.59	53.88	60.43	79.42	88.13	92.79	95.49	97.13	98.16
6						0.	18.16	31.66	42.07	50.30	74.16	85.09	90.94	94.34	96.40	97.68
7							0.	16.50	29.21	39.28	68.42	81.78	88.93	93.08	95.60	97.17
8								0.	15.23	27.28	62.18	78.18	86.74	91.71	94.73	96.61
9									0.	14.22	55.39	74.26	84.36	90.22	93.78	96.00
10										0.	48.00	69.99	81.77	88.60	92.75	95.34
11										0.	39.95	65.35	78.95	86.84	91.63	94.62
12										0.	31.19	60.30	75.88	84.92	90.41	93.84
13										0.	21.66	54.80	72.54	82.83	89.08	92.98
14										0.	11.29	48.81	68.90	80.56	87.64	92.05
15											0.	42.30	64.95	78.08	86.06	91.04
16											0.	35.21	60.64	75.39	84.35	89.94
17											0.	27.49	55.95	72.46	82.48	88.74
18											0.	19.09	50.85	69.27	80.46	87.44
19											0.	9.95	45.29	65.80	78.25	86.02
20												0.	39.25	62.02	75.84	84.48
21												0.	32.67	57.90	73.23	82.79
22												0.	25.51	53.43	70.38	80.96
23												0.	17.71	48.55	67.28	78.97
24												0.	9.23	43.25	63.91	76.80
25													0.	37.48	60.24	74.45
26													0.	31.20	56.24	71.88
27													0.	24.36	51.89	69.08
28													0.	16.92	47.16	66.04
29													0.	8.82	42.01	62.73
30														0.	36.40	59.13
35															0.	35.73
40																0.

8.75%

AGE OF LOAN	1	2	3	4	5	6	7	8	9	10	15	20	25	30	35	40
1	0.	52.18	69.53	78.17	83.33	86.74	89.17	90.97	92.36	93.45	96.62	98.07	98.84	99.28	99.55	99.71
2		0.	36.28	54.35	65.14	72.28	77.35	81.11	84.01	86.31	92.94	95.96	97.57	98.50	99.05	99.40
3			0.	28.36	45.29	56.50	64.45	70.36	74.91	78.51	88.92	93.66	96.19	97.64	98.52	99.06
4				0.	23.63	39.28	50.38	58.63	64.98	70.01	84.53	91.16	94.68	96.71	97.93	98.68
5					0.	20.50	35.03	45.83	54.15	60.73	79.75	88.42	93.03	95.69	97.29	98.28
6						0.	18.28	31.86	42.33	50.60	74.53	85.43	91.24	94.58	96.59	97.83
7							0.	16.63	29.43	39.56	68.83	82.18	89.28	93.36	95.83	97.35
8								0.	15.36	27.50	62.61	78.62	87.14	92.04	94.99	96.82
9									0.	14.35	55.83	74.74	84.81	90.60	94.08	96.24
10										0.	48.43	70.51	82.26	89.02	93.09	95.61
11										0.	40.35	65.90	79.48	87.30	92.01	94.92
12										0.	31.54	60.86	76.45	85.43	90.83	94.17
13										0.	21.93	55.36	73.14	83.38	89.55	93.36
14										0.	11.44	49.36	69.54	81.15	88.14	92.46
15											0.	42.82	65.60	78.71	86.61	91.49
16											0.	35.68	61.30	76.06	84.94	90.43
17											0.	27.89	56.62	73.16	83.11	89.27
18											0.	19.39	51.50	69.99	81.12	88.00
19											0.	10.12	45.93	66.54	78.95	86.62
20												0.	39.84	62.77	76.58	85.12
21												0.	33.20	58.66	73.99	83.47
22												0.	25.95	54.18	71.17	81.68
23												0.	18.04	49.28	68.09	79.72
24												0.	9.41	43.95	64.73	77.59
25													0.	38.12	61.07	75.26
26													0.	31.76	57.07	72.72
27													0.	24.83	52.71	69.94
28													0.	17.26	47.95	66.92
29													0.	9.01	42.75	63.62
30														0.	37.09	60.02
35															0.	36.45
40																0.

From *Interest Amortization Tables* by Jack C. Estes. New York: McGraw-Hill Book Company, 1976.

Table F-2
Remaining balance tables (9, 9.25%)

ORIGINAL TERM IN YEARS

9.00%

AGE OF LOAN

Age	1	2	3	4	5	6	7	8	9	10	15	20	25	30	35	40
1	0.	52.24	69.61	78.26	83.42	86.84	89.26	91.06	92.44	93.54	96.69	98.13	98.88	99.32	99.57	99.73
2		0.	36.36	54.47	65.28	72.44	77.51	81.27	84.17	86.47	93.08	96.08	97.66	98.57	99.11	99.44
3			0.	28.46	45.44	56.68	64.65	70.57	75.13	78.73	89.12	93.84	96.33	97.75	98.60	99.12
4				0.	23.74	39.46	50.60	58.87	65.24	70.28	84.80	91.39	94.87	96.86	98.04	98.77
5					0	20.61	35.22	46.07	54.42	61.02	80.07	88.71	93.27	95.88	97.44	98.39
6						0.	18.40	32.07	42.59	50.90	74.89	85.77	91.53	94.81	96.77	97.97
7							0.	16.75	29.64	39.84	69.23	82.57	89.62	93.71	96.04	97.51
8								0.	15.49	27.73	63.04	79.06	87.53	92.36	95.25	97.01
9									0.	14.49	56.27	75.22	85.24	90.96	94.37	96.47
10										0.	48.86	71.03	82.74	89.43	93.42	95.87
11										0.	40.76	66.44	80.00	87.75	92.38	95.21
12										0.	31.90	61.41	77.01	85.92	91.24	94.49
13										0.	22.20	55.92	73.74	83.92	89.99	93.71
14										0.	11.60	49.91	70.16	81.73	88.63	92.85
15											0.	43.34	66.25	79.33	87.14	91.92
16											0.	36.16	61.97	76.71	85.51	90.89
17											0.	28.29	57.28	73.84	83.72	89.77
18											0.	19.69	52.16	70.70	81.77	88.54
19											0.	10.29	46.56	67.27	79.63	87.20
20												0.	40.43	63.52	77.30	85.73
21												0.	33.72	59.41	74.74	84.13
22												0.	26.39	54.92	71.95	82.37
23												0.	18.37	50.01	68.89	80.45
24												0.	9.60	44.64	65.55	78.35
25													0.	38.76	61.89	76.05
26													0.	32.33	57.89	73.54
27													0.	25.30	53.51	70.79
28													0.	17.61	48.73	67.78
29													0.	9.20	43.49	64.49
30														0.	37.77	60.89
35															0.	37.16
40																0.

9.25%

Age	1	2	3	4	5	6	7	8	9	10	15	20	25	30	35	40
1	0.	52.30	69.69	78.34	83.51	86.93	89.35	91.14	92.53	93.62	96.76	98.18	98.93	99.35	99.60	99.75
2		0.	36.45	54.59	65.42	72.59	77.66	81.43	84.33	86.62	93.22	96.19	97.75	98.64	99.16	99.48
3			0.	28.55	45.59	56.87	64.85	70.79	75.35	78.95	89.33	94.01	96.47	97.86	98.68	99.18
4				0.	23.84	39.63	50.81	59.11	65.50	70.54	85.06	91.61	95.05	97.00	98.15	98.85
5					0.	20.73	35.41	46.31	54.69	61.32	80.39	88.99	93.51	96.06	97.58	98.49
6						0.	18.52	32.07	42.85	51.21	75.26	86.11	91.81	95.04	96.94	98.10
7							0.	16.88	29.86	40.12	69.63	82.95	89.94	93.91	96.25	97.67
8								0.	15.62	27.96	63.47	79.49	87.90	92.67	95.49	97.20
9									0.	14.62	56.71	75.70	85.66	91.31	94.65	96.68
10										0.	49.29	71.53	83.21	89.82	93.74	96.11
11										0.	41.16	66.97	80.52	88.19	92.73	95.48
12										0.	32.25	61.97	77.57	86.40	91.63	94.80
13										0.	22.47	56.48	74.33	84.44	90.42	94.05
14										0.	11.75	50.46	70.78	82.29	89.10	93.23
15											0.	43.86	66.89	79.93	87.65	92.33
16											0.	36.63	62.62	77.35	86.06	91.34
17											0.	28.70	57.94	74.51	84.31	90.25
18											0.	20.00	52.81	71.40	82.40	89.06
19											0.	10.46	47.18	67.99	80.30	87.76
20												0.	41.01	64.26	78.00	86.33
21												0.	34.25	60.16	75.47	84.76
22												0.	26.83	55.66	72.71	83.04
23												0.	18.70	50.73	69.67	81.16
24												0.	9.78	45.33	66.35	79.09
25													0.	39.40	62.70	76.82
26													0.	32.90	58.70	74.34
27													0.	25.78	54.31	71.61
28													0.	17.96	49.50	68.62
29													0.	9.39	44.23	65.35
30														0.	38.45	61.75
35															0.	37.87
40																0.

From *Interest Amortization Tables* by Jack C. Estes. New York: McGraw-Hill Book Company, 1976.

Table F-3

Remaining balance tables (9.5, 9.75%)

ORIGINAL TERM IN YEARS

9.50%

AGE OF LOAN	1	2	3	4	5	6	7	8	9	10	15	20	25	30	35	40
1	0.	52.36	69.77	78.43	83.60	87.01	89.44	91.23	92.61	93.70	96.83	98.24	98.97	99.38	99.62	99.77
2		0.	36.53	54.72	65.56	72.74	77.82	81.59	84.49	86.78	93.35	96.30	97.84	98.71	99.21	99.52
3			0.	28.65	45.74	57.05	65.06	71.00	75.57	79.17	89.53	94.18	96.60	97.96	98.76	99.24
4				0.	23.95	39.80	51.02	59.35	65.75	70.81	85.32	91.84	95.23	97.14	98.26	98.93
5					0.	20.84	35.60	46.55	54.97	61.61	80.70	89.27	93.73	96.24	97.71	98.59
6						0.	18.64	32.48	43.11	51.51	75.62	86.44	92.08	95.25	97.11	98.22
7							0.	17.01	30.08	40.40	70.03	83.33	90.27	94.16	96.45	97.82
8								0.	15.75	28.18	63.89	79.92	88.27	92.97	95.72	97.37
9									0.	14.76	57.14	76.16	86.08	91.65	94.92	96.88
10										0.	49.72	72.04	83.67	90.21	94.04	96.34
11										0.	41.56	67.50	81.02	88.62	93.07	95.74
12										0.	32.60	62.51	78.11	86.87	92.01	95.09
13										0.	22.74	57.03	74.91	84.95	90.84	94.37
14										0.	11.91	51.01	71.39	82.84	89.56	93.58
15											0.	44.38	67.52	80.52	88.14	92.72
16											0.	37.10	63.27	77.97	86.59	91.76
17											0.	29.10	58.59	75.17	84.88	90.71
18											0.	20.30	53.46	72.09	83.01	89.56
19											0.	10.63	47.81	68.70	80.95	88.30
20												0.	41.60	64.98	78.68	86.90
21												0.	34.78	60.89	76.19	85.37
22												0.	27.27	56.39	73.45	83.69
23												0.	19.03	51.45	70.44	81.84
24												0.	9.96	46.01	67.13	79.81
25													0.	40.04	63.50	77.58
26													0.	33.47	59.50	75.12
27													0.	26.25	55.10	72.42
28													0.	18.31	50.27	69.45
29													0.	9.59	44.96	66.19
30														0.	39.12	62.60
35															0.	38.57
40																0.

9.75%

AGE OF LOAN	1	2	3	4	5	6	7	8	9	10	15	20	25	30	35	40
1	0.	52.43	69.85	78.52	83.68	87.10	89.52	91.32	92.70	93.78	96.90	98.29	99.01	99.41	99.65	99.79
2		0.	36.62	54.84	65.71	72.89	77.98	81.75	84.65	86.94	93.49	96.41	97.93	98.77	99.26	99.55
3			0.	28.75	45.89	57.23	65.26	71.21	75.78	79.39	89.72	94.34	96.73	98.06	98.83	99.29
4				0.	24.06	39.97	51.24	59.59	66.01	71.07	85.58	92.05	95.41	97.27	98.36	99.00
5					0.	20.96	35.79	46.79	55.24	61.91	81.01	89.54	93.95	96.41	97.84	98.69
6						0.	18.76	32.68	43.37	51.81	75.97	86.76	92.35	95.46	97.27	98.34
7							0.	17.13	30.29	40.68	70.43	83.71	90.58	94.41	96.63	97.96
8								0.	15.88	28.41	64.31	80.34	88.65	93.26	95.94	97.53
9									0.	14.89	57.57	76.62	86.49	91.98	95.17	97.07
10										0.	50.15	72.53	84.12	90.58	94.33	96.56
11										0.	41.97	68.02	81.51	89.03	93.40	95.99
12										0.	32.95	63.06	78.64	87.33	92.37	95.37
13										0.	23.01	57.58	75.48	85.45	91.24	94.68
14										0.	12.07	51.55	71.99	83.38	89.99	93.92
15											0.	44.90	68.15	81.10	88.62	93.09
16											0.	37.58	63.91	78.59	87.11	92.17
17											0.	29.50	59.24	75.82	85.44	91.16
18											0.	20.61	54.10	72.77	83.60	90.04
19											0.	10.80	48.43	69.41	81.58	88.81
20												0.	42.19	65.70	79.35	87.46
21												0.	35.30	61.62	76.89	85.97
22												0.	27.72	57.12	74.18	84.32
23												0.	19.36	52.16	71.20	82.51
24												0.	10.15	46.69	67.91	80.51
25													0.	40.67	64.28	78.31
26													0.	34.04	60.28	75.88
27													0.	26.72	55.88	73.21
28													0.	18.67	51.03	70.26
29													0.	9.79	45.68	67.01
30														0.	39.79	63.44
35															0.	39.27
40																0.

From *Interest Amortization Tables* by Jack C. Estes. New York: McGraw-Hill Book Company, 1976.

Table F-4

Remaining balance tables (10, 10.25%)

ORIGINAL TERM IN YEARS

10.00%

AGE OF LOAN	1	2	3	4	5	6	7	8	9	10	15	20	25	30	35	40
1	0.	52.49	69.93	78.60	83.77	87.19	89.61	91.40	92.78	93.87	96.97	98.35	99.05	99.44	99.67	99.80
2		0.	36.70	54.96	65.85	73.04	78.13	81.91	84.81	87.09	93.62	96.52	98.01	98.83	99.30	99.58
3			0.	28.85	46.04	57.41	65.46	71.42	75.99	79.60	89.92	94.50	96.85	98.15	98.90	99.34
4				0.	24.17	40.15	51.45	59.83	66.26	71.33	85.83	92.27	95.57	97.40	98.45	99.07
5					0.	21.07	35.98	47.03	55.51	62.20	81.32	89.80	94.16	96.57	97.96	98.78
6						0.	18.88	32.88	43.63	52.10	76.33	87.08	92.61	95.66	97.42	98.45
7							0.	17.26	30.51	40.96	70.82	84.07	90.88	94.65	96.81	98.09
8								0.	16.01	28.64	64.73	80.75	88.98	93.53	96.15	97.69
9									0.	15.03	58.01	77.08	86.88	92.30	95.42	97.25
10										0.	50.58	73.02	84.56	90.94	94.60	96.76
11										0.	42.37	68.54	82.00	89.43	93.71	96.22
12										0.	33.30	63.60	79.17	87.77	92.72	95.63
13										0.	23.29	58.13	76.04	85.93	91.63	94.97
14										0.	12.22	52.09	72.58	83.91	90.42	94.25
15											0.	45.42	68.76	81.66	89.08	93.45
16											0.	38.05	64.54	79.19	87.61	92.56
17											0.	29.91	59.88	76.45	85.98	91.58
18											0.	20.91	54.74	73.43	84.18	90.50
19											0.	10.98	49.05	70.09	82.19	89.31
20												0.	42.77	66.41	80.00	87.99
21												0.	35.83	62.33	77.57	86.54
22												0.	28.16	57.83	74.89	84.93
23												0.	19.69	52.86	71.93	83.15
24												0.	10.34	47.37	68.66	81.19
25													0.	41.30	65.05	79.02
26													0.	34.60	61.06	76.62
27													0.	27.20	56.65	73.98
28													0.	19.02	51.78	71.05
29													0.	9.98	46.40	67.82
30														0.	40.46	64.26
35															0.	39.97
40																0.

10.25%

AGE OF LOAN	1	2	3	4	5	6	7	8	9	10	15	20	25	30	35	40
1	0.	52.55	70.01	78.69	83.86	87.28	89.70	91.49	92.86	93.95	97.03	98.40	99.09	99.47	99.69	99.82
2		0.	36.79	55.09	65.99	73.20	78.29	82.06	84.96	87.24	93.75	96.62	98.09	98.89	99.35	99.61
3			0.	28.95	46.20	57.60	65.65	71.63	76.21	79.82	90.11	94.65	96.97	98.24	98.96	99.39
4				0.	24.28	40.32	51.66	60.07	66.51	71.59	86.08	92.48	95.74	97.52	98.54	99.14
5					0.	21.19	36.17	47.27	55.78	62.49	81.62	90.06	94.37	96.73	98.08	98.86
6						0.	19.01	33.09	43.89	52.40	76.68	87.39	92.86	95.85	97.56	98.55
7							0.	17.39	30.73	41.24	71.21	84.43	91.18	94.88	96.99	98.21
8								0.	16.15	28.87	65.15	81.16	89.33	93.80	96.35	97.83
9									0.	15.17	58.44	77.53	87.27	92.61	95.65	97.42
10										0.	51.00	73.51	84.99	91.29	94.87	96.96
11										0.	42.77	69.06	82.47	89.82	94.01	96.44
12										0.	33.66	64.13	79.68	88.20	93.05	95.88
13										0.	23.56	58.67	76.59	86.41	92.00	95.25
14										0.	12.38	52.63	73.16	84.42	90.83	94.56
15											0.	45.94	69.37	82.21	89.53	93.79
16											0.	38.52	65.17	79.78	88.09	92.93
17											0.	30.31	60.52	77.08	86.50	91.99
18											0.	21.22	55.37	74.08	84.74	90.95
19											0.	11.15	49.67	70.77	82.79	89.79
20												0.	43.35	67.10	80.63	88.51
21												0.	36.35	63.04	78.24	87.09
22												0.	28.61	58.54	75.59	85.52
23												0.	20.03	53.56	72.66	83.77
24												0.	10.52	48.04	69.41	81.85
25													0.	41.93	65.81	79.71
26													0.	35.16	61.83	77.35
27													0.	27.67	57.42	74.73
28													0.	19.37	52.53	71.83
29													0.	10.18	47.12	68.62
30														0.	41.13	65.06
35															0.	40.66
40																0.

From *Interest Amortization Tables* by Jack C. Estes. New York: McGraw-Hill Book Company, 1976.

Table F–5

Remaining balance tables (10.5, 10.75%)

ORIGINAL TERM IN YEARS

10.50%

AGE OF LOAN	1	2	3	4	5	6	7	8	9	10	15	20	25	30	35	40
1	0.	52.61	70.08	78.77	83.95	87.37	89.78	91.57	92.95	94.03	97.10	98.45	99.13	99.50	99.71	99.83
2		0.	36.87	55.21	66.13	73.35	78.44	82.22	85.11	87.39	93.88	96.72	98.16	98.94	99.39	99.64
3			0.	29.05	46.35	57.78	65.85	71.83	76.42	80.03	90.30	94.81	97.09	98.33	99.03	99.43
4				0.	24.38	40.49	51.88	60.30	66.77	71.85	86.33	92.68	95.90	97.64	98.63	99.19
5					0.	21.30	36.36	47.50	56.05	62.78	81.92	90.32	94.57	96.88	98.18	98.94
6						0.	19.13	33.29	44.15	52.70	77.03	87.70	93.10	96.04	97.69	98.65
7							0.	17.52	30.94	41.52	71.59	84.79	91.47	95.10	97.15	98.33
8								0.	16.28	29.10	65.56	81.56	89.66	94.06	96.54	97.97
9									0.	15.31	58.86	77.97	87.65	92.90	95.87	97.58
10										0.	51.43	73.99	85.42	91.62	95.12	97.14
11										0.	43.17	69.57	82.94	90.20	94.29	96.65
12										0.	34.01	64.66	80.19	88.62	93.37	96.11
13										0.	23.84	59.21	77.13	86.86	92.35	95.51
14										0.	12.54	53.16	73.74	84.91	91.22	94.85
15											0.	46.45	69.97	82.75	89.96	94.11
16											0.	38.99	65.79	80.35	88.56	93.29
17											0.	30.72	61.15	77.68	87.01	92.38
18											0.	21.53	56.00	74.73	85.29	91.37
19											0.	11.33	50.28	71.44	83.37	90.25
20												0.	43.93	67.79	81.25	89.00
21												0.	36.88	63.74	78.89	87.62
22												0.	29.05	59.24	76.27	86.08
23												0.	20.36	54.25	73.37	84.38
24												0.	10.71	48.71	70.14	82.49
25													0.	42.56	66.56	80.38
26													0.	35.73	62.58	78.05
27													0.	28.14	58.17	75.46
28													0.	19.72	53.27	72.59
29													0.	10.38	47.83	69.40
30														0.	41.79	65.85
35															0.	41.34
40																0.

10.75%

AGE OF LOAN	1	2	3	4	5	6	7	8	9	10	15	20	25	30	35	40
1	0.	52.67	70.16	78.86	84.04	87.46	89.87	91.66	93.03	94.10	97.16	98.49	99.16	99.53	99.73	99.84
2		0.	36.96	55.33	66.27	73.50	78.60	82.37	85.27	87.54	94.00	96.82	98.23	99.00	99.42	99.67
3			0.	29.14	46.50	57.96	66.05	72.04	76.63	80.24	90.49	94.95	97.20	98.41	99.08	99.47
4				0.	24.49	40.67	52.09	60.54	67.02	72.11	86.57	92.88	96.05	97.75	98.71	99.25
5					0.	21.42	36.55	47.74	56.32	63.07	82.22	90.57	94.77	97.03	98.29	99.01
6						0.	19.25	33.50	44.41	53.00	77.37	88.0C	93.34	96.22	97.82	98.74
7							0.	17.64	31.16	41.80	71.98	85.14	91.75	95.31	97.30	98.44
8								0.	16.41	29.33	65.97	81.95	89.98	94.31	96.72	98.10
9									0.	15.45	59.29	78.41	88.02	93.19	96.08	97.73
10										0.	51.85	74.46	85.83	91.95	95.37	97.31
11										0.	43.58	70.07	83.39	90.56	94.57	96.85
12										0.	34.36	65.19	80.68	89.02	93.68	96.34
13										0.	24.11	59.75	77.66	87.31	92.69	95.76
14										0.	12.70	53.7C	74.30	85.40	91.60	95.13
15											0.	46.96	70.57	83.28	90.37	94.42
16											0.	39.47	66.41	80.91	89.01	93.63
17											0.	31.12	61.78	78.28	87.50	92.75
18											0.	21.84	56.62	75.35	85.81	91.77
19											0.	11.50	50.89	72.09	83.94	90.69
20												0.	44.50	68.47	81.85	89.48
21												0.	37.40	64.43	79.53	88.13
22												0.	29.49	59.94	76.94	86.63
23												0.	20.69	54.94	74.06	84.96
24												0.	10.90	49.37	70.86	83.11
25													0.	43.18	67.30	81.04
26													0.	36.29	63.33	78.74
27													0.	28.62	58.91	76.18
28													0.	20.08	54.00	73.33
29													0.	10.58	48.53	7C.16
30														0.	42.44	66.63
35															0.	42.02
40																0.

From *Interest Amortization Tables* by Jack C. Estes. New York: McGraw-Hill Book Company, 1976.

Table F–6

Remaining balance tables (11, 11.25%)

ORIGINAL TERM IN YEARS

11.00%

AGE OF LOAN	1	2	3	4	5	6	7	8	9	10	15	20	25	30	35	40
1	0.	52.73	70.24	78.94	84.12	87.54	89.96	91.74	93.11	94.18	97.22	98.54	99.20	99.55	99.74	99.85
2		0.	37.04	55.45	66.41	73.65	78.75	82.53	85.42	87.69	94.13	96.91	98.31	99.05	99.46	99.69
3			0.	29.24	46.65	58.14	66.25	72.25	76.84	80.45	90.67	95.10	97.31	98.49	99.14	99.51
4				0.	24.60	40.84	52.30	60.78	67.27	72.37	86.81	93.07	96.20	97.86	98.78	99.30
5					0.	21.54	36.74	47.98	56.59	63.36	82.51	90.81	94.95	97.16	98.39	99.08
6						0.	19.37	33.70	44.67	53.30	77.71	88.29	93.57	96.39	97.94	98.82
7							0.	17.77	31.38	42.08	72.36	85.48	92.03	95.52	97.45	98.54
8								0.	16.55	29.56	66.38	82.34	90.30	94.55	96.90	98.22
9									0.	15.59	59.71	78.84	88.38	93.47	96.28	97.87
10										0.	52.28	74.93	86.23	92.26	95.60	97.48
11										0.	43.98	70.57	83.84	90.92	94.83	97.04
12										0.	34.72	65.71	81.17	89.42	93.98	96.55
13										0.	24.39	60.28	78.19	87.74	93.02	96.00
14										0.	12.86	54.23	74.86	85.87	91.96	95.39
15											0.	47.47	71.15	83.79	90.77	94.71
16											0.	39.94	67.01	81.46	89.45	93.95
17											0.	31.53	62.39	78.87	87.97	93.11
18											0.	22.15	57.24	75.97	86.33	92.16
19											0.	11.68	51.49	72.74	84.49	91.11
20												0.	45.08	69.13	82.44	89.93
21												0.	37.92	65.11	80.15	88.62
22												0.	29.94	60.63	77.59	87.16
23												0.	21.03	55.62	74.74	85.53
24												0.	11.09	50.03	71.57	83.71
25													0.	43.80	68.02	81.67
26													0.	36.85	64.06	79.41
27													0.	29.09	59.65	76.88
28													0.	20.43	54.72	74.05
29													0.	10.78	49.23	70.90
30														0.	43.09	67.39
35															0.	42.70
40																0.

11.25%

AGE OF LOAN	1	2	3	4	5	6	7	8	9	10	15	20	25	30	35	40
1	0.	52.80	70.32	79.03	84.21	87.63	90.04	91.82	93.19	94.26	97.28	98.59	99.23	99.57	99.76	99.86
2		0.	37.13	55.58	66.55	73.79	78.90	82.68	85.57	87.84	94.25	97.01	98.37	99.10	99.49	99.71
3			0.	29.34	46.80	58.32	66.45	72.45	77.05	80.66	90.85	95.24	97.41	98.56	99.19	99.54
4				0.	24.71	41.01	52.51	61.01	67.52	72.63	87.05	93.26	96.34	97.97	98.86	99.35
5					0.	21.65	36.93	48.22	56.86	63.64	82.80	91.05	95.14	97.30	98.48	99.14
6						0.	19.50	33.91	44.94	53.59	78.05	88.58	93.79	96.55	98.06	98.90
7							0.	17.90	31.60	42.36	72.73	85.82	92.29	95.72	97.59	98.63
8								0.	16.68	29.79	66.79	82.72	90.61	94.78	97.06	98.34
9									0.	15.73	60.14	79.26	88.73	93.74	96.48	98.00
10										0.	52.70	75.39	86.63	92.57	95.82	97.63
11										0.	44.38	71.07	84.27	91.26	95.08	97.21
12										0.	35.07	66.23	81.64	89.80	94.26	96.75
13										0.	24.66	60.81	78.70	88.16	93.34	96.23
14										0.	13.02	54.76	75.41	86.33	92.31	95.64
15											0.	47.98	71.73	84.29	91.16	94.99
16											0.	40.41	67.61	82.00	89.87	94.26
17											0.	31.93	63.01	79.44	88.43	93.45
18											0.	22.46	57.85	76.57	86.82	92.54
19											0.	11.86	52.09	73.37	85.02	91.52
20												0.	45.65	69.79	83.00	90.37
21												0.	38.44	65.78	80.75	89.10
22												0.	30.38	61.30	78.23	87.67
23												0.	21.36	56.29	75.41	86.07
24												0.	11.28	50.69	72.26	84.29
25													0.	44.42	68.73	82.29
26													0.	37.40	64.78	80.05
27													0.	29.56	60.37	77.56
28													0.	20.79	55.44	74.76
29													0.	10.97	49.92	71.63
30														0.	43.74	68.14
35															0.	43.36
40																0.

From *Interest Amortization Tables* by Jack C. Estes. New York: McGraw-Hill Book Company, 1976.

Professional, Trade, and Other Real Estate Associations

American Chapter, International Real Estate Federation (AC/IREF)

430 N. Michigan Ave.
Chicago, IL 60611
312-664-9700

American Conference of Real Estate Investment Trusts

608 13th St., N.W.
Washington, D.C. 20005
202-347-9464

American Institute of Real Estate Appraisers (AIREA)

430 N. Michigan
Chicago, IL 60611

This group formulates and enforces standards of professional conduct for its members, promotes research, and publishes materials related to appraisal of real property. The institute confers the MAI (Member, Appraisal Institute) designation upon persons who meet requirements for experience, education, and examinations. It also awards the RM (Residential Member) to REALTORS® who specialize in residential property appraisal. They pass requirements less strenuous than those for the MAI.

American Land Title Association (ALTA)

1828 L St. N.W. Suite 303
Washington, D.C. 20036
209-296-3671

Abstractors, title insurance companies, and attorneys belong to this organization. It provides information and services to its members and the public.

American Society of Real Estate Counselors (ASREC)

430 N. Michigan Ave.
Chicago, IL 60611
312-440-8091

This branch of the NATIONAL ASSOCIATION OF REALTORS® includes members who counsel and advise on real estate problems on a professional basis. The designation CRE (Counselor of Real Estate) is awarded to those engaged in professional consulting on real estate who meet other qualifications.

Farm and Land Institute

430 N. Michigan Ave.
Chicago, IL 60611
312-664-9700

This group is composed of REALTORS® who specialize not only in rural property, but in subdivisions, shopping centers, and recreational facilities as well. The institute awards the AFB (Accredited Farm Broker) designation to those with sufficient experience who pass an examination.

Institute of Real Estate Management (IREM)

430 N. Michigan Ave.
Chicago, IL 60611

This group was organized to recognize persons who have demonstrated qualifications in real property management. The CPM (Certified Property Manager) designation is awarded to persons with experience, courses, and qualifications in property management. The institute also awards the AMO (Accredited Management Organization) to firms that specialize in property management, provided the firm is under the responsibility of a CPM and has all employees bonded.

National Association of Home Builders of the United States (NAHB)

1625 L St. N.W.
Washington, D.C. 20036

The association is concerned with adequate housing in the U.S., improvement of home building materials and techniques, and holding to high professional standards and ethics. It was formerly associated with NAREB as the Home Builders Institute.

National Association of Housing Cooperatives (NAHC)

1828 L St. N.W.
Washington, D.C. 20036
202-872-0550

The goal of NAHC is to promote the interests of cooperative housing communities.

National Association of Real Estate Appraisers

853 Broadway
New York, NY 10003
212-673-2300

National Association of Real Estate Brokers

1025 Vermont Ave., N.W.
Suite 1111
Washington, D.C. 20005
202-638-1280

National Association of Real Estate Investment Trusts (NAREIT)

1101 17th St. N.W.
Suite 700
Washington, D.C. 20036
202-785-8717

National Association of Real Estate License Law Officials (NARELLO)

430 N. Michigan Ave.
Chicago, IL 60611

The memberships include officials involved with the administration and enforcement of real estate sales and brokerage license laws in the various states. The objective of the organization is to raise standards of competency and provide uniformity in licensing for the protection of the public and the betterment of the real estate profession.

NATIONAL ASSOCIATION OF REALTORS® (NAR)

430 N. Michigan Ave.
Chicago, IL 60611
(see Chapter 13)

REALTORS® National Marketing Institute

430 N. Michigan Ave.
Chicago, IL 60611
312-440-8510

This institute serves specialists in commercial investment brokerage, residential sales, and real estate office administration. It awards the designation CRB (Certified Residential Broker) to a REALTOR® who has practiced for five years, is certified as a GRI, and who has completed adequate course work.

Society of Industrial Realtors (SIR)

925 15th St. N.W.
Washington, D.C. 20005

Real estate brokers who are involved in industrial property transactions or public utilities or who work in financial institutions belong to this organization. The SIR designations of Salesman Affiliate or Firm Affiliate are granted to qualified members.

Society of Real Estate Appraisers (SREA)

7 South Dearborn St.
Chicago, IL 60603
312-346-7422

The society provides courses and conferences related to real property appraisal. Prior to 1963, the name was Society of Residential Appraisers. The award SREA (Senior Real Estate Appraiser) is given to those completing specified requirements.

Urban Land Institute (ULI)

1200 18th St. N.W.
Washington, D.C. 20036
202-331-8500

The membership is comprised of individuals, firms, corporations, and associations to promote better planning and development of urban areas. The institute performs studies and prepares reports on trends that affect the development and use of land. ULI is an independent, nonprofit, research and educational organization incorporated in 1936 to improve the quality and standards of land use and development. The institute conducts practical research in various fields of real estate knowledge;

identifies and interprets land use trends in relation to changing economic, social, and civic needs; and disseminates pertinent information leading to orderly and more efficient use and development of land.

Women's Council of REALTORS®

430 N. Michigan Ave.
Chicago, IL 60611
312-440-8082

This group was formed to cater to the needs of women in the real estate field. It offers specialized programs, training, and publications.

Section of Land Showing Acreage and Distances

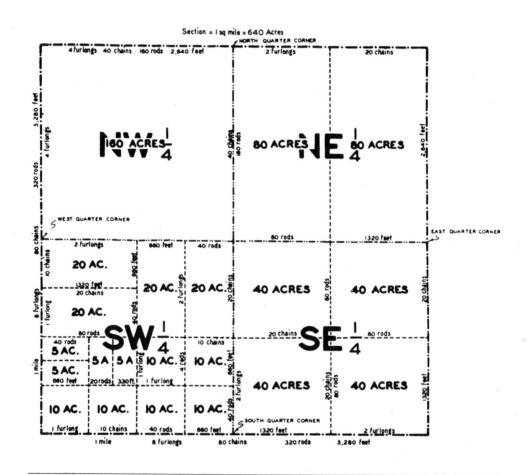

From John S. Hoag, *Fundamentals of Land Measurement*, Chicago Title and Trust Co.

1 Link = 7.92 in
1 Rod = 16½ ft
1 Chain = 4 rods = 66 ft
4 Rods = 100 links
1 Furlong = 660 ft = 40 rods
1 Mile = 8 furlongs = 320 rods = 80 chains = 5280 ft
1 Acre = 43,560 sq ft
1 Section = 640 acres = 1 sq mi

INDEX

(Also see Glossary on page 494 for other definitions)

Abstract of title, 105
Acceleration clause, 154
Accretion, 107
Administrator, 109
Adverse possession, 106
Advertising, 285, 295
  classes of, 296
  ethics in, 312
  institutional, 296
  interest rates, 257
  media, 296
  name, 296
  objectives of, 296
  specific, 296
Affidavit of title, 344
After-tax cash flow, 456
Agency, 268
  brokerage and, 268
  coupled with an interest, 269
  duration, 272
  duties, 270
  functions of, 268
  termination of, 272–73
  types of, 269
Agents, 269
Air rights, 37, 44
Alien ownership, 261
American Institute of Real Estate Appraisers, 398
American Land Title Association, 536
American Society of Real Estate Counselors, 536
Amortization
  nonconforming use, 233
Annexation, 44
Annuity capitalization method
  property residual, 426
Apartments, 3
Appraisal, 397–431
  function, 397
  process, 404–7
  purpose, 397
Appraisal cost manuals, 434
Appraising
  definition, 397
  process of, 404–7
Appurtenances, 36

Assessments
  appeal, 183
  roll, 183, 186
  tax, 182
  special, 186
Assignment
  of leases, 133, 140
  of real estate contracts, 96
Assumption, 166

Banks
  commercial, 172
  mutual savings, 172
Bargain-and-sale deed, 117
Baseline, 23
Bearings, 32
Before-tax cash flow, 456
Being clause, 34
Bellwood ruling, 257
Bill of sale, 345
Bona fide purchaser, 121
Brokerage, 8, 267–83
  agency and, 268
  as agent of the principal, 268
  commissions, 275, 281
  employee compensation, 281
  employees, 280
  franchised, 278
  more than one, 274
  operating guidelines, 277
  organization, 277–78
  staffing, 279
  termination of agency, 272
Broker, 8, 267
  as agent of principal, 268
  authority, 269
  commissions, 275
  duty of principal to, 270
  duty to principal, 270
  functions of, 269
Builders, 389
Building codes, 227
Building industry, 382
Building moratoriums, 225
Building trades, 384

Buyers
  analysis of, 298
  motivations, 297
  sources of, 298

Capital
  asset, 467
  short-term asset, 467
Capital gains
  1231 assets, 467
  computation, 468
  regular method, 468
  alternative method, 468
Capital gain taxes, 205
Capitalization, 421
  Building capitalization rate, 421
  direct, 422
  methods, 422–29
  rate, 423
Careers (real estate), 7
Cash flow, 456
Certificate of occupancy, 345
Certified Property Manager (CPM), 435
Chain of title, 105, 121
Check, 26
Closing, 341–61
  actions subsequent to, 360
  costs, 346–54
  documents needed, 344
Cobrokerage, 274
Coinsurance, 247
Commercial banks, 173
Commercial property, 5
Commissions, 275
Community property, 57, 107
Comparable sales, 414
Concurrent ownership, 55
Condemnation, 106, 142
Conditional use permit, 233
Condominiums, 4, 58–59, 214–15, 449
Confession of judgment, 141
Consent statutes, 188
Consideration
  in contracts, 76–77
  in deeds, 114
Consumer Credit Protection Act, 257
Consumer protection, 256
Construction
  bids, 389
  loans, 162
  residential, 383–92
  scheduling, 394
  selection of a builder, 389
  specifications, 388
Contingencies, 326
Contingent remainder, 51
Contracts, 71–101, 321–24
  assignment of, 96
  consideration, 76–77
  contingencies, 322, 326
  for deed, 209

  default, 97
  description of property, 90
  earnest money, 88
  elements of, 72–83
  escrow, 94, 96, 98
  for exchange of real estate, 97
  failure to perform, 97
  for deed, 209
  form of deed, 90–91
  forms, 324
  installment, 209
  land, 209
  listing agreement, 86–87
  loss in case of fire, 94
  nonperformance of, 97
  offer and acceptance, 72–75
  options, 97
  parties to, 73, 89
  possession, 94, 96
  price, 73, 90, 95
  property management, 439
  prorating, 92–93
  real estate, 85–100
  reality of assent, 77
  remedies upon breach, 83–84, 97
  title exceptions, 91
  void, 72
  voidable, 72
Conveyancing, 341–61
Cooperatives, 4, 215–16
Corrections in survey, 25, 28
Correlative rights, 38
Cost
  approach to appraising, 404
  approach to value, 407–14
  replacement, 410
  reproduction, 407
  settlement, 346–54
Cotenants, 56
Counteroffer, 74
Covenants
  restrictive, 375
  subdivision, 375
Cubic foot method, 407

Datum, 37
Decedent
  debts, 192
  estate, 109
Dedication, 32, 379
Deeds, 110–19
  acknowledgment, 114
  administrator's, 118
  cession, 118
  at closing, 344
  of confirmation, 119
  consideration in, 114
  contracts for, 166
  covenants, 115–16
  defined, 110
  delivery, 113

executor's, 118
in foreclosure, 119
full covenant and warranty, 115–17
general warranty, 116
of gift, 118
grant, 117
guardian's, 118
habendum clause, 115
in partition, 118
quitclaim, 116
of release, 119
reservations, 114
seals, 114
of surrender, 118
in trust, 117
of trust, 117, 149
trustee's, 118
warranty, 115–17
Default, 168
Defeasance clause, 152
Deferred gain, 456
Density controls, 225
Deposit receipts, 87
Deposits, 273
Depreciation
accelerated techniques, 462–64
component, 464
composite, 460
deductions, 204, 459
defined, 204, 411, 458
excess, 482
primary residence, 459
straight-line, 460–62
Descent, title by, 108
Destruction of property, 142
Development, 367
Devise, 107
Devisee, 107
Diminution by loss, 248
Discount points, 164
Distress for rent due, 141
Duress, 77

Earnest money, 88, 92, 273
Easements, 51–55
appurtenant, 51
creation of, 52–53
in gross, 51
termination, 54–55
Economic life, 413
Eminent domain, 46, 62
Employee records, 345
Encroachments, 92
Energy efficient homes, 390–91
Environmental
controls, 259
protection laws, 260
Equalization, 184
Equity build-up, 458
Escalation, 154
Escheat, 46, 107

Escrow, 94, 96, 98, 327–28
agent, 98, 343
closing, 327–38, 342–43
delivery in, 98
Estates, 46–51
for a stated term, 130
freehold, 47–49
from period to period, 130
leasehold, 129
life, 48
nonfreehold, 47, 49–50
possessory, 46
by sufferance, 131
at will, 131
Ethics, 303–13
Eviction, 143
Exclusion, 208
Excess recapture, 466
Exclusive agency listing, 291
Exclusive right to sell, 291
Executor, 109

FHA, 163
Fair Housing Act of 1968, 254–55
Federal Home Loan Bank System, 177
Federal Home Mortgage Corporation, 177
Federal Housing Act of 1934, 163
Federal Housing Administration, 163
Federal National Mortgage Association
(FNMA), 176
Federal regulations, 253
Fee simple, 47
Fee simple absolute, 47
Fee simple on a condition subsequent, 49
Fee simple determinable, 49
Fences, 34
Fiduciary, 269
Financing, 10, 149
developments, 374
syndicate ownership, 374
Fixity, 22
Fixtures, 44
trade, 44
Foreclosure, 151, 168–70
deed in, 119
judicial, 169
of leased fee interest, 144
sales, 106
steps in, 169
strict, 168
Franchise, 278
Fraud, 77, 310
Frauds, Statute of, 80
Freehold estates, 47–49
Future interest, 47, 50

Gain
deferred, 206
realized, 206–8
recognized, 206–8
Gift, 110

Government
  lots, 29
  surplus lands, 7
  survey system, 23–30
Government National Mortgage Association (GNMA), 176
Granting clause, 112
Grantor-grantee index, 120
Ground lease, 226

Home ownership, 197–216
  advantages, 201–4
  capital gains, 205–9
  costs of, 210
  depreciation, 204
  disadvantages, 210–11
  exclusions from capital gain, 208
  interest expense, 204
  renting versus buying, 211
  tax benefits, 204–9
  trends in, 197–99
Homes
  single-family, 198–201, 383
Homestead exemption, 204
House-hunting checklist, 212
Housing codes, 227
HOW, 240, 258

Immobility of land, 19–20
Improvements, 22, 44, 134
Income
  approach to appraising, 418
  approach to value, 418
Indemnity
  principle of, 241
Indestructibility, 19
Industrial property, 6
Innocent misrepresentation, 66
Installment Land Contract, 166, 209
Institute of Real Estate Management, 534
Insurance, 237–49
  actual cash value clause, 248
  assumption of, 344
  business, 246
  cancellation, 244
  claims, 249
  co-insurance, 241, 247
  crime, 239
  deductible, 244
  endorsements, 237, 239
  extended coverage, 245
  fire, 239, 245
  flood, 239
  homeowners' (package) policy, 245
  leasehold, 246
  liability, 239
  loss payable clause, 248
  named on policy clause, 248
  need for, 237
  premium, 237
  pro rata, 247
  public liability, 239
  rates, 241
  rent, 246
  rental, 246
  structural defects, 240
  subrogation of, 248
  title, 240
Interest, insurable, 248
Interest proration, 349
Intermediation, 172
Interstate land sales, 258
Intestate, 108
Investment
  after-tax cash flow, 473
  analysis of, 470
  before-tax cash flow, 473
  capital gains, 468–70
  fixed, 22
  income tax shelters, 474
  land, 22
  real estate, 453
  recapture, 466
  returns, 456
  risk, 455

Joint and several liability, 132
Joint tenancy, 56
Judgments, 191

Lakes, 38
Land, 43
  characteristics, 19–22
  contracts, 166
  descriptions, 22–37
  development, 367
  economic characteristics, 20–22
  as immobile, 19
  improvements, 22
  location, 22
  physical, 19
  reutilization authorities, 225
  scarcity, 20
  situs, 22
  use, 219–27
Land use districts, 229
Landlord-tenant relationship, 129, 144
Leasehold, 49, 129
Leases, 49, 98, 129–45
  agricultural, 137
  assign, 133, 140
  assignee, 140
  at closing, 345
  cash rental, 138
  confession of judgment, 141
  crop share, 138
  distress for rent due, 141
  escalation clauses, 133
  eviction, 141, 143
  fixed rental, 136
  gross, 136
  improvements, 134
  index, 137
  landlord and tenant, 49

leased fee interest, 129
leasehold interest, 129
maintenance, 134
net, 135, 137
option to, 135
parties to, 131–32
percentage, 137
possession, 133
reappraisal, 137
rent, 133
repairs, 134
requirements of, 131
sale-leaseback, 138
subletting, 140
sue for rent due, 141
termination of, 141–44
types of, 136–39
use of premises, 133
Legal descriptions, 22–36
rectangular survey, 23–30
metes and bounds, 23, 30–32
subdivision and lots, 23, 32
Lessee, 50
Lessor, 49
Leverage, 453, 456, 458
Liability
joint and several, 132
License, 55
Licensing, 262
Life estate, 48
Liens, 187–93
bail bond, 191
of decedent's debts, 192
defined, 187
discharges, 344
enforcement, 189
equitable, 187
general, 191–92
judgments, 191
mechanic's, 187–89
discharge of, 189
mortgage, 190
priority of, 192
specific, 187-91
statutory, 187
tax, 184, 190
vendee's, 190
vendor's, 190
voluntary, 187
Life insurance companies, 174
Listing agreements (*See* listings)
Listings, 86–87, 286
exclusive agency, 291
exclusive right to sell, 291
multiple, 292
net, 291
open, 289
types, 289
Littoral rights, 38
Location, 12, 22

Magnuson-Moss Act, 258
Market
approach to appraising, 399
approach to value, 399
characteristics, 13
demand, 14
measures of conditions, 15
Member Appraisal Institute (MAI), 398
Merger, 143
Meridians, 23–24
Metes and bounds, 30
Minerals, 36
Minors, 78
Misrepresentation, 77, 308–10
Mobile homes, 4
Monuments, 33
"More or less" term, 30
Moratoriums, 225
Mortgage
market, 174–75
money, 171–78
Mortgagee, 150
Mortgages, 149–78
amortized, 157
assumption, 166, 357
blanket, 160
budget, 160
chattel, 151
clauses
acceleration, 154
alienation, 156
default in prior mortgage, 156
defeasance, 152
escalation, 154
owner's rent, 155
prepayment, 154
receiver, 155
subordination, 155
conventional, 165
covenants, 153
default, 168
FHA, 163
foreclosure, 168
graduated payment, 157
junior, 163
by municipal bonds, 167
open-end, 161
package, 151
prepayment, 154
purchase money, 156, 161
refinancing, 167
reverse annuity, 159
senior, 163
straight-term, 156
strict foreclosure, 168
trust deed, 117, 149
VA guaranteed, 165
variable rate, 159
wrap-around, 161
Motivation, buyer, 297
Multiple-listing service, 292–94
Mutual savings banks, 172

National Association of Home Builders, 534
NATIONAL ASSOCIATION OF REAL-
  TORS® (NAR), 314–16, 538
National Association of Real Estate License Law
  Officials (NARELLO), 538
Navigable waterways, 35
Noise control, 261
Nonconforming use, 231
Nondisclosure, 310
Nonhomogeneity, 19–20
Note, 150
Nuisance, 64

Obsolescence
  economic, 413
  environmental, 413
  functional, 411
Offer and acceptance, 72-75
Offer to purchase, 87
Office buildings, 436
Open space, 379
Option, 97
Organizations
  professional, 536
Ownership, 46
  alien, 261
  concept of ,46
  concurrent, 46
  condominium, 58
  cooperative, 59
  interval, 59
  personalty, 44–45
  private restrictions, 46
  syndicate, 59, 374
  time share, 58

Parallel, 25
Partition sale, 106
Partnership, 277
Patent, 107
Personalty (personal property), 44–45
Planned unit devlopment, 223
Plat map, 23, 32, 377
Point of beginning, 30
Points, 359
Police power, 46, 62
Present value of reversion, 427
Price
  selling, 287
Prior appropriation, 38
  meridians, 23–24
Procuring cause, 274
Professional associations, 313
Profit à prendre, 55
Promotion, 295
Property
  assessed value, 182
  commercial, 5, 381
  community, 57, 107
  conversion, 449
  descriptions, 22–36

destruction, 142
development, 367–94
exchanges, 483
farm, 6
industrial, 6, 382
personalty, 44–45
recreational, 6
report, 259
residential, 3, 436
restrictions, 46, 373
rural, 6
Property management, 435–50
  approaches, 437
  commercial, 443
  contracts, 438–39
  financial control, 447–48
  functions of, 439–40
  manager, 437–40
  marketing of, 442
  operations, 445
  organization for, 440
  residential, 436
  services, 446
Proration, 347–60
  actual days method, 348
  insurance, 352
  interest, 349
  rent, 353
  statutory month method, 348
  tax, 349
  uniform method, 347
  wages, 353
Public Housing Administration, 253
Purchase money mortgage, 156

Range lines, 25
Real estate
  characteristics, 12, 19–22
  definition, 1, 43
  investments, 453–90
  market, 11
Real Estate Settlement Procedures Act, 258, 332
Real property, 43
Recapture, 466
Recordation, 119–23
Recording systems, 120
Rectangular (government) survey method, 23–30
  corrections, 25, 28
Redemption
  right of, 151, 184
Refinancing, 168, 476
Regulation Z, 256
Remainder, 49–51
Remedies of lenders, 168
Rent, 141
Rental market, 14
Replacement cost, 410
Residential property, 3
Restrictions
  on private ownership, 46
  subdivision, 373, 375

Return of investment, 424
Return on investment, 424
Reversion, 49–50
Right of entry, 49–50
Rights, 40–41
   air, 37
   correlative, 38
   governmental, 52–54
   prescriptive, 38
   riparian, 38
   water, 38–39
Riparian rights, 38
Risk of investment, 455
Roads, 34

Sale
   bill of , 345
   contract, 85–100
   partition, 106
Salesperson, 8, 299
Savings and loan associations, 172
Scarcity
   of land, 20
Section, 27
Settlement (*See* closing)
Settlement Procedures Act, 258, 332
Situs, 22
Society of Industrial Realtors, 538
Society of Real Estate Appraisers, 538
Special assessments, 186
Specific performance, 20
State licensing, 262
State plane coordinate system, 35
Statute of Frauds, 80
Statutory right of redemption, 151, 184
Streams, 35
Street and number, 34
Subdivision
   development, 367
   financing, 374
   and lots, 23, 32
   marketing, 369
   planning, 368, 375
   plat, 377
   restrictions, 373, 375
Subordination clause, 136, 155
Subrogation, 248
Sum-of-years'-digit method, 464
Survey, 331, 345
Syndicate, 59, 374

Tax benefits of home ownership, 204–9
Tax levy, 182
Taxes, 181–86
   ad valorem, 182
   assessment, 182
   calculations, 183
   collection, 184
   enforcement, 184
   equalization, 184
   exemption, 185

   general, 182
   property, 181–86
   proration, 181
   rate, 183
   special assessments, 181–82, 186
   transfer, 359
TDR, 226
Tenancies
   in common, 56–57
   by entirety, 57
   joint, 56
   kinds of, 55
   in partnership, 57
Tenant, 140
Termite certificate, 345
Testate, 107
Testator, 107
Time sharing, 215
Time is of essence, 332
Title
   abstract of, 105
   chain of, 105
   defined, 105
   equitable, 74
   insurance, 240
   theory, 152
   transfer of, 105
      by accretion, 107
      adverse possession, 106
      by condemnation, 106
      by descent, 108
      by escheat, 107
      by foreclosure sale, 106
      by gift, 110
      involuntary, 105–7
      partition sale, 106
      registration, 122
      Torrens system, 122–23
      voluntary, 107–19
      by will, 107–9
Torrens system, 122–23
Tort, 66
Townships, 25–27
Tract index, 120
Tracts, 34
Trade fixture, 44
Transaction, 319–37
Transfer development rights, 226
Transfer tax, 359
Trust deed, 149
Truth-in-lending law, 256–57

Unit-in-place method, 411
Urban Land Institute, 538
Urban planning, 219
   levels, 220
   procedures, 221
   renewal, 223
   transportation, 223

Value
    cost approach to, 407–10
    cost concepts, 399
    economic concept of, 397, 399
    forces influencing, 403
    income approach to, 418–29
    insurable, 400
    investment, 400
    land, 410
    market, 399, 400
    market approach to, 414–18
    market concept of, 399
    principles of, 402
    prerequisites to, 401
    replacement cost approach, 410
Variance, 233
Vested remainder, 51
Violations
    of license laws, 264

Waste, 48, 64, 135

Water
    quality, 260
    rights, 38
Will, 107

Zoning, 227–32
    aesthetic, 228
    bulk, 228
    categories, 228–29
    changes in, 231
    cumulative, 229
    directive, 228
    enforcement, 229
    exclusionary, 230
    incentive, 228
    inclusionary, 230
    interim, 228
    nonconforming use, 231
    protective, 228
    purpose, 227
    spot, 230
    variance, 233

81
83
85
88